The
PRESIDENTIAL
RECORDINGS

——LYNDON B. JOHNSON——

The

PRESIDENTIAL
RECORDINGS

LYNDON B. JOHNSON

*Mississippi Burning and
the Passage of the Civil Rights Act
Volume Seven*

+>+>+JUNE 1, 1964–JUNE 22, 1964+<+<+

Guian A. McKee
Editor

Ashley Havard High
Associate Editor

Patricia Dunn
Assistant Editor

Timothy Naftali
General Editor

W. W. NORTON & COMPANY • NEW YORK • LONDON

The Presidential Recordings Program is supported in part by grants from
the National Historical Publications and Records Commission.

For information about permission to reproduce selections from this book,
write to Permissions, W. W. Norton & Company, Inc.,
500 Fifth Avenue, New York, NY 10110

For information about special discounts for bulk purchases, please contact
W. W. Norton Special Sales at specialsales@wwnorton.com or 800-233-4830

Manufacturing by RR Donnelley Harrisonburg
Book design by Dana Sloan
Production manager: Julia Druskin

The Library of Congress has cataloged earlier volumes as follows:

Lyndon B. Johnson, the Kennedy assassination, and the transfer of power,
November 1963–January 1964 / Max Holland, editor..
p. cm. — (The presidential recordings)
Includes bibliographic references and indexes.
Contents: v. 1. November 22–30, 1963 / edited by Max Holland—v. 2. December
1963 / edited by Robert David Johnson and David Shreve—v. 3. January
1964 / edited by Kent B. Germany and Robert David Johnson.
ISBN 0-393-06001-2 (set)
1. United States—Politics and government—1963–1969—Sources.
2. United States—Politics and government—1961–1963—Sources.
3. Johnson, Lyndon B. (Lyndon Baines), 1908–1973—Archives.
4. Presidents—United States—Archives. 5. Kennedy, John F. (John Fitzgerald), 1917–1963—
Assassination—Sources. I. Holland, Max. II. Johnson, Robert David,
1967– III. Shreve, David, 1961– IV. Germany, Kent B., 1971– V. Series.
E846.L945 2005
973.923—dc22

2004066167

ISBN 978-0-393-08118-3 (for the set of two volumes)

W. W. Norton & Company, Inc.
500 Fifth Avenue, New York, N.Y. 10110
www.wwnorton.com

W. W. Norton & Company Ltd.
Castle House, 75/76 Wells Street, London W1T 3QT

1 2 3 4 5 6 7 8 9 0

In memory of Ernest R. May, 1928–2009

Contents

The Presidential Recordings Program

B etween 1940 and 1973, presidents of the United States secretly recorded thousands of their meetings and conversations in the White House. Though some recorded a lot and others just a little, they all created a unique and irreplaceable source for understanding not only their presidencies and times but, indeed, the essential process of high-level decision making. These recordings by no means displace more traditional sources of historical knowledge such as official documents, private diaries and letters, memoirs, and contemporaneous journalism. Rather, they augment these sources much as photographs, films, and recordings augment printed records of presidents' public appearances. But they also do much more than that.

Because the recordings capture a series of formal meetings, informal office conversations, and telephone calls, and not just highlights recorded by a note taker or recalled afterward in a memorandum or memoir, they pierce the presidential veil created by staffers and image-makers. Presidents are human beings, with emotions, prejudices, and preferences, and the tapes are remarkable in the extent to which they convey that humanity, flaws and all. Left out of presidential statements and even many internal records are signs of indecision, uncertainty, anger, or alarm. And leaders are often not as decisive, implacable, and sure of their next step as they would like to be. Nor are they as in control of events as they would wish. The tapes offer a dynamic picture of how the various responsibilities of a president are constantly converging to test them—how a president could be simultaneously, not consecutively, a commander in chief worrying about war, a policymaker conscious that his missteps in economic policy could bring on a market collapse, a chief mediator among interest groups, a chief administrator for a myriad of public programs, a spokesperson for the interests and aspirations of the nation, a head of a sprawling political party.

The secret tapes also reveal how decisions and policies actually emerge. Presidential advisers can be heard debating with one another, adapting to the perspectives of others, and changing their minds. The president's own views are often reshaped as well, sometimes by a subtle but profound shift in the definition of an issue or the stakes involved. While participants rarely have a clear memory of such changes, the tapes record them word for word.

Finally, they provide audio snapshots of a dramatic era, both inside and outside of government. The White House does not exist in a vacuum. During the era that presidents were secretly taping, events in Congress and the Supreme Court were shaping the American story. So, too, were actions in the streets, at home or abroad, constantly challenging, worrying, or inspiring the occupants of those bugged rooms. Appearing on the tapes are some of the most influential individuals of the period—for example, A. Philip Randolph, Martin Luther King Jr., Jean Monnet, Golda Meir, Douglas MacArthur, Reverend Billy Graham—who also shaped the use of U.S. presidential power and authority.

Though Franklin D. Roosevelt, Harry S. Truman, and Dwight D. Eisenhower all made a few secret recordings, John F. Kennedy was the first president to install an elaborate taping system and to make extensive use of it. His family and aides removed the system almost immediately after his murder in 1963. Lyndon B. Johnson then installed a different system, of which he too made frequent use. Richard Nixon, after two years without using any recording devices, installed a voice-activated system that captured every conversation in a room containing a microphone.

The existence of Kennedy's taping system was known at the time only to the President himself, his private secretary (Evelyn Lincoln), and the two Secret Service agents who installed and maintained it. President Kennedy's brother Robert learned of the system at some point, and the circle probably eventually extended to include the President's close aide, Kenneth O'Donnell. Other senior White House officials like special counsel Theodore Sorensen or national security assistant McGeorge Bundy knew nothing about it. President Kennedy had to activate the system with a buzzer press, and he tended to use it as a kind of electronic diary to record meetings he considered important, probably with a view to memoirs that he never had the chance to write. He and his brother had the tapes from the Cuban missile crisis period transcribed in the summer of 1963. No records have turned up to explain why; perhaps the transcripts were made with an eye to their being compiled for the 1964 campaign. In general, however, President Kennedy paid little attention to the tapes while he was President, leaving them to Mrs. Lincoln to store away for later.

During the period covered by these volumes, President Johnson only recorded telephone conversations and the occasional office conversation caught while the speakerphone was activated. Johnson employed a system that used Dictaphone equipment. Originally produced as a Gramophone from patents by Thomas A. Edison, early Dictaphone recorders recorded sound by stylus cutting on wax-coated cylinders. During and after World War II, the Dictaphone Corporation developed electronic recording devices and in 1947 began to distribute Time-Master machines with reusable plastic dictabelts. These went into common use for dictation to be transcribed by stenographers. President Kennedy had used such a device to supplement his secret reel-to-reel taping system. President Johnson first taped telephone calls when he was majority leader in the Senate and then as Vice President, and he began to do so in the White House as soon as he became President. Later—though not in the period covered by these volumes—Johnson would install a system of his own for making secret recordings of meetings.

Richard Nixon created by far the largest collection of secret recordings. Between February 16, 1971, and July 12, 1973, Nixon taped over 3,700 hours of his meetings and telephone conversations. Eventually, the U.S. Secret Service installed microphones in five locations ranging from the Oval Office and Nixon's hideaway office in what is now the Eisenhower Executive Office Building to Camp David. An avid reader of history, Nixon had kept a recorded diary when he was Vice President. As President, he intended to make use of meeting and telephone tapes to write his memoirs.

On the premise that these and the other secretly made presidential recordings will remain important historical sources for years to come, the University of Virginia's Miller Center of Public Affairs is producing transcripts and annotations for these presidential recordings. This work is organized in the Center's Presidential Recordings Program (PRP), directed by David Coleman. For the Kennedy and Johnson presidencies, the recordings are arranged in reference volumes organized chronologically. In 2001 the first three volumes in the John F. Kennedy series appeared, covering all taped meetings and conversations between July 30, 1962, and October 28, 1962. This was followed in 2005 by the first three volumes of the Lyndon B. Johnson series, which included all taped meetings and conversations between November 22, 1963, and January 31, 1964. A second set of three Johnson volumes, covering February through May 1964, was published in 2007. The PRP also produces policy or thematic volumes in which scholars present a selection of transcripts to tell a particular story. Two of these books have appeared so far: *The Kennedy Tapes: Inside the White House*

During the Cuban Missile Crisis (the Concise Edition) by Ernest May and Philip Zelikow (2002) and *Kennedy, Johnson, and the Quest for Justice: The Civil Rights Tapes* by Jonathan Rosenberg and Zachary Karabell (2003). Finally, since 2006, the PRP has been working with the University of Virginia Press on producing digital thematic editions for publication in the Press's groundbreaking Rotunda digital imprint.

When the PRP began its work in 1998, it sought to build upon the methods and style developed by May and Zelikow to produce the original edition of *The Kennedy Tapes*, the first scholarly compilation of Cuban missile crisis transcripts. May and Zelikow had initially used court reporters and then settled on producing the transcripts themselves by listening to analog or cassette recordings without any amplification. Timothy Naftali, who led the PRP from 1998 to 2006, worked with George Eliades, then a scholar at the Center, to find better hardware and to develop a rigorous team method to produce transcripts. With principal editorial guidance from May and Zelikow, and the help of an editorial advisory board, PRP scholars subsequently developed a number of methodological guidelines for the preparation of the presidential recordings volumes:

First, the work is done by trained professional historians who are specialists on the period covered by the tapes and on some of the central themes of the meetings and conversations. Without such expertise, transcribing and interpreting presidential tapes can be a bit like trying to assemble a jigsaw puzzle without being able to see the picture on the puzzle box. Each volume has one or two lead editors, who write the daily introductions, conversation introductions, policy descriptions, and footnotes and are responsible for the final versions of the transcripts. The volume editors are listed on the cover. Assisting these editors are associate editors who also draft and critique transcripts and help with the research. The complete list of editors for each reference volume appears on the title page. These historians not only delve into documentary sources but sometimes interview living participants who can help us comprehend the taped discussions. Our voice identifications are based on samples we have compiled and on our research. We list only the names of the participants we can identify.

Second, the transcription process is built on the foundation of a team method. By having each transcript corrected and edited by several scholars, it maximizes the pool of expertise while at the same time minimizing some of the physical and psychological factors that complicate any transcribing effort (e.g., different people often hear slightly different things). By the time a transcript has passed through the process, it has been subjected to possibly hundreds of hours of listening and research by different scholars. The process is adaptable according to the degree of difficulty of the original recording, but every transcript has benefited from at least four listeners. The first stage is to generate raw, rough transcripts from the audio recordings. The PRP draws on the talents and enthusiasm of a team of carefully trained undergraduate and graduate student interns to construct a first draft. For office recordings, which are the most difficult to transcribe, usually one or two scholars painstakingly produce a primary draft (referred to as an A-version). Two or more scholars then carefully go over the transcript, individually or sometimes with two listening at the same time. They edit, correct, annotate, and update the transcript as they go (creating B- and C-versions). For telephone recordings, which are more audible and easier to understand because they typically involve only two participants, the A- and B-versions may be produced by student interns and then returned to Miller Center scholars for the C-, or third, review. In all cases, the transcript is then returned to the original scholar, who has the responsibility for pursuing any remaining annotation or research issues (creating a D-version). The reference volume editors remain accountable for checking the quality and accuracy of all the work in their set of transcripts, knitting them together with the annotations. We, as the general editors, then review this work. This method is by no means perfect, but it is the best we have been able to devise so far given available time and resources.

Third, the Program uses the best technology that the project can afford. As of 2006, the Program uses high-quality CDs made available by the National Archives and Records Administration. Using computer software and studio-quality headphones and amplification equipment, transcribers are able to examine each audio recording in minute detail and enhance the audio signal when necessary. The PRP made great strides in 2001 after the program-wide adoption of digital audio software, which had been introduced by Coleman, who had joined the PRP in 1999.

Fourth, we strive to make the transcripts accessible to and readable by anyone interested in history, including students. This requires a considerable amount of subjective editorial work. Since people often do not speak in complete and grammatically correct sentences, the transcriber has to infer and create sentence and paragraph structure, placing commas, semicolons, and periods. We omit the verbal stutters or tics such as the *uhs* that dot almost anyone's speech if they do not convey any information. This approach reflects the fact that listeners unconsciously filter out such debris in interpreting what someone is saying. But there are gray areas. If someone says, for example, "sixteen . . . uh, sixty . . . ," the editors have to decide whether this slip conveys anything about what the speaker was trying to say. These judgment calls are usually no more difficult than those involved in deciding whether to insert punctuation or paragraphing. In the effort to be exhaustive, sometimes there is the temptation to overtranscribe, catching every verbal fragment, however indistinct. Such attempts can add too much intrusive static, making the substance less understandable to readers now than it was to the hearers then. The goal is to give the reader the truest possible sense of the actual dialogue as the participants themselves understood it.

The tape quality varies and the scholars are occasionally unable to make out a word or a passage. In those instances, the editors have placed "[*unclear*]" in the text. The transcribers and editors aim for completeness. Rather than guess at an indistinct passage, however, it is their preference to indicate to the reader this lack of certainty. Over time, others using the transcripts and listening to the tapes or with access to better technology may be able to fill in passages marked as "unclear." Although the Miller Center volumes are intended to be reliable reference works, the transcripts will always be subject to amendments. The PRP welcomes suggestions and corrections and has in the past placed transcript updates on its website, whitehousetapes.net.

Fifth, the scholars seek to embed the transcripts in the political, international, cultural, and social context of the period. Each reference volume includes explanations and annotations intended to enable readers to understand the background and circumstances of a particular conversation or meeting. With rare exceptions, we do not add information that participants would not have known, and we comment on the significance of items of information only when necessary to make a conversation fully comprehensible. As with all historical sources, interpretations will have to accumulate over time.

For additional information on the Presidential Recordings Program and access to tapes and transcripts, see whitehousetapes.net.

The general editor wishes to make special mention of the work of Pat Dunn, who developed the style guide for the series and passes a keen eye over each volume.

Finally, a very sad note: Professor Ernest R. May died during the preparation of Volumes 7 and 8 of the Johnson series. In addition to inspiring the Miller Center's presidential tapes research effort with Philip Zelikow, Professor May served as a general editor for all previous PRP publications. The standards of academic rigor, accessibility, and good sense aspired to by all members of the PRP are a testament to Professor May's enduring legacy as a scholar, teacher, and editor. The PRP dedicates these new volumes to his memory.

Editor's Acknowledgments

The production of this volume in the Presidential Recordings series drew on the talents of many people and the resources of several institutions. In particular, this book reflects the long-term commitment of both the Lyndon B. Johnson Library and the University of Virginia's Miller Center of Public Affairs. In both preserving historical records and providing access to researchers, the LBJ Library is a model institution. Without its efforts to make the Johnson recordings available to scholars and the general public, this series would not have been possible. The library is a core resource in any effort to understand the history of the 1960s.

The Miller Center of Public Affairs provided an institutional home for this project as well as critical support and funding. The editor specifically wishes to thank Timothy Naftali, general editor and former director of the Presidential Recordings Program. Tim read every line of this volume and offered crucial advice that improved its substance and structure. The current chair of the PRP, David Coleman, has provided an exceptional level of administrative and technical support that has allowed the editor to focus on the scholarship necessary to complete this and other projects. Professor Coleman's extensive efforts in improving the program's technological capacity, information management, and online presence are especially appreciated. Other scholars affiliated with the Miller Center during the period of this volume's creation have also greatly improved this work. In particular, I would like to thank Kent Germany, David Shreve, and Marc Selverstone, as well as Philip Zelikow, Taylor Fain, Ken Hughes, and Erin Mahan. Several other scholars contributed to this volume through discussing Johnson's career with the editor. These include Gareth Davies, Tom Jackson, David Carter, Taylor Branch, Bill Miller, Sidney Milkis, and Brian Balogh. Ashley Havard High listened to every second of the tapes covered in the volume and went above and beyond the call of duty in suggesting annotations and raising questions about the material. The indefatigable Patricia Dunn is the kind of editor that all authors want. She copyedited every manuscript page and was unyielding in her commitment to the highest standards. The quality of this and every other volume in the series reflects Pat's dedication. Several University of Virginia students also assisted with the project. They included in particular John Monahan, Noah Peters, Daniel Lipton, and Blair Hawkins, as well as others in our team of talented interns who worked on various aspects of research and support. Finally, Gerald Baliles and Taylor Reveley, director and associate director of the Miller Center, provided invaluable support for the project. The late Mike Mullen also provided essential advice and support during production of this volume.

At Norton, Drake McFeely and Jeff Shreve played a crucial role in moving the manuscript through publication. The National Historical Publications and Records Commission provided funding that made this volume possible. Their distribution of funding keeps critical parts of U.S. history alive and encourages deeper exploration of the nation's complicated past. It also represents a critical public commitment to the support of historical research and documentary editing.

Family and friends too numerous to name have provided key support. A special note of thanks and appreciation to my mother, Linda Jones McKee, and to Richard Carey; to my father, Michael McKee; and to my brother and sister-in-law, Colin McKee and Lucinda Fleurant. Above all, I must thank my wife, Joanna Vondrasek, and my sons, Reece and Nathaniel, for their patience as I completed this project.

Finally, this volume is dedicated to the memory of Professor Ernest May, one of the founders of the recordings program. Without his vision and dedication, this and the other volumes in the series simply would not exist.

A Note on Sources

Several general references sources were used in this volume to verify details regarding dates, people, positions, and other matters. They include the Office of the Federal Register, National Archives and Records Service, *U.S. Government Organization Manual* (Washington, DC: GPO, 1963–1965); Joint Committee on Printing, *Official Congressional Directory for the Use of the United States Congress* (Washington, DC: GPO, 1964–1965); Charles B. Brownson, ed., *Congressional Staff Directory*, volumes 1963 and 1964 (Washington, DC: The Congressional Staff Directory, 1963–1964); Congressional Quarterly Service, *Congressional Quarterly Almanac*, volumes 19 and 20 (Washington, DC: Congressional Quarterly, Inc., 1964–1965); Congressional Quarterly Service, *Congress and the Nation, 1945–1964: A Review of Government and Politics in the Postwar Years* (Washington, DC: Congressional Quarterly, Inc., 1965); *Biographical Directory of the United States Congress, 1774–Present*; http://bioguide.congress.gov/biosearch/biosearch.asp; U.S. Department of State, Office of the Historian, www.state.gov/r/pa/ho; Federal Judicial Center, www.fjc.gov; and the LBJ Daily Diary compiled by the White House staff and preserved by the LBJ Library.

Conversation Participants
and Major Figures

Agger, Carol: Attorney in Washington, D.C., and wife of Abe Fortas

Albert, Carl B.: U.S. Representative, Democrat, from Oklahoma, 1947–1977, House Majority Leader, 1963–1970

Anderson, Robert: Texas businessman, active in oil and banking; part owner, Texas Broadcasting Company, 1939–1943

Ball, George: Under Secretary of State, 1961–1966

Bell, David: Administrator, Agency for International Development, since 1962

Boggs, Thomas Hale: U.S. Representative, Democrat, from Louisiana, 1941–1943, 1947–1973; House Majority Whip, 1961–1970

Boring, Floyd: U.S. Secret Service Agent in service to President Johnson

Brown, Edmund G. "Pat": Democratic Governor of California since 1959

Bundy, McGeorge: Special Assistant to the President for National Security Affairs, 1961–1966

Burns, John: Governor of Hawaii, 1962–1974

Bustamante, William: First Prime Minister of Jamaica, 1962–1967

Carter, Cliff: Longtime friend and administrative assistant to Lyndon Johnson, 1937–1966

Cater, Douglass: Special Assistant to the President, 1964–1968; special emphasis on health, education and welfare

Clements, Earle: Lobbyist and president of the Tobacco Institute, 1964–1976; worked on Johnson's vice presidential campaign

Connally, John: Governor of Texas and one of Lyndon Johnson's closest advisers; joined Johnson's congressional staff in 1938 and managed Johnson's campaign for the 1960 Democratic nomination; seriously injured during the assassination of President Kennedy

Corriden, Thomas: Senior surgeon at Cooley-Dickinson Hospital in Northampton, Massachusetts, where Senator Edward Kennedy was treated following a 1964 plane crash

Deschler, Lew: Parliamentarian, U.S. House of Representatives, 1928–1974

Dirksen, Everett M.: U.S. Senator, Republican, from Illinois, 1951–1969; Senate Minority Leader, 1959–1969

Fehmer, Marie: Personal secretary to Lyndon Johnson

Feldman, Myer: Deputy Special Counsel to the President, 1961–1964; Counsel to the President, 1964–1965

Forrestal, Mike: Member, National Security Council staff

Fortas, Abe: Prominent Washington attorney and confidant of President Johnson

Freeman, Orville: Secretary of Agriculture, 1961–1969

Gonella , Ashton: Member of Johnson's White House staff

Goodwin, Richard: Special Assistant to the President, 1964–1965

Halleck, Charles: U.S. Representative, Republican, from Indiana, 1935–1969; House Minority Leader, 1959–1964; House Majority Leader, 1947–1948, 1953–1954

Harte, Houston: Publisher and cofounder of the Texas-based Harte-Hanks newspaper publishing chain

Heller, Walter W.: Chairman, President's Council of Economic Advisers, 1961–1964; Special Consultant to the President, 1964–1969

Hodges, Luther H.: Secretary of Commerce, 1961–1965

Humphrey, Hubert: U.S. Senator, Democrat, from Minnesota, 1949–1964, 1971–1978; Democratic Whip, 1961–1964; Vice President of the United States, 1965–1969

Jenkins, Walter: Johnson's office manager, personnel chief, and administrative assistant, 1939–1963; Special Assistant to the President, 1963–1964

Johnson, Lady Bird (née Claudia Alta Taylor): Wife of Lyndon Johnson since 1934

Johnston, Olin: U.S. Senator, Democrat, from South Carolina, 1945–1965; Chairman, Committee on Post Office and Civil Service

Kennedy, Jacqueline Bouvier: Widow of President John F. Kennedy

Kennedy, Robert: Younger brother of President Kennedy; campaign manager in 1960; Attorney General of the United States since 1961

Leahy, Jane: Secretary to Attorney General Robert Kennedy

Loney, Kathryn: Johnson's first schoolteacher at Junction Elementary School

Mahon, George: U.S. Representative, Democrat, from Texas, 1935–1979; Chairman, House Appropriations Committee, 1964–1978

Mann, Thomas: U.S. Ambassador to Mexico, 1961–1963; Special Assistant to the President and Coordinator of the Alliance for Progress, 1964–1965; Under Secretary of State for Economic Affairs, 1965–1966

Manning, Bob: Journalist who served as Assistant Secretary of State for Public Affairs, 1962–1964; executive editor of *The Atlantic Monthly* from 1964

Mansfield, Mike: U.S. Senator, Democrat, from Montana, 1953–1977; Senate Majority Leader, 1961–1977

McCammon, Vicki: Secretary to President Johnson

McClellan, John: U.S. Senator, Democrat, from Arkansas, 1943–1977

McCormack, John W.: U.S. Representative, Democrat, from Massachusetts, 1928–1971; Speaker, U.S. House of Representatives, 1961–1971

McDonald, David J.: President, United Steelworkers of America, 1953–1965

McGill, Ralph: Nationally syndicated columnist for the *Atlanta Constitution*; recipient of Pulitzer Prize, 1959, and Presidential Medal of Freedom, 1964

McNamara, Robert S.: Secretary of Defense, 1961–1968

Mills, Wilbur: U.S. Representative, Democrat, from Arkansas, 1939–1977; Chairman, House Ways and Means Committee, 1958–1975

Moyers, Bill D.: Deputy Director, Peace Corps, 1961–1964; Special Assistant to the President, 1963–1967

Mundt, Karl E.: U.S. Senator, Republican, from South Dakota, 1948–1973

Nelson, Richard: White House aide

Nichols, Dorothy: Secretary to Horace Busby, Special Assistant to the President; former secretary to Johnson while he served in Congress

O'Brien, Larry: Special Assistant to the President for Congressional Affairs, 1961–1965

Powell, Adam Clayton, Jr.: U.S. Representative, Democrat, from New York, 1945–1967, 1969–1971; Chairman, House Education and Labor Committee, 1961–1966

Reedy, George E.: White House Press Secretary, 1964–1965

Reston, James "Scotty": Washington, D.C., bureau chief and columnist, *New York Times*, 1953–1964; associate editor, *New York Times*, 1964–1968; executive editor, *New York Times*, 1968–1969; vice president, *New York Times*, 1969–1974; recipient of the Pulitzer Prize for National Reporting in 1945 and 1957

Reuther, Walter P.: President, United Automobile Workers (UAW), 1946–1970; Vice President, Congress of Industrial Organizations (CIO), 1946–1952; President, CIO, 1952–1955; Vice President, American

Federation of Labor–Congress of Industrial Organizations (AFL-CIO), 1955–1969; President, Alliance for Labor Action, 1969–1972

Roberts, Juanita: Longtime personal secretary to Lyndon Johnson

Rusk, Dean: Secretary of State, 1961–1969

Russell, Richard: U.S. Senator, Democrat, from Georgia, 1933–1971; Chairman, Senate Armed Services Committee, 1951–1953, 1955–1969

Sidey, Hugh: Reporter, *Time* magazine

Sisk, Bernie: U.S. Representative, Democrat, from California, 1955–1978

Smathers, George: U.S. Senator, Democrat, from Florida, 1951–1969; member of the Finance Committee

Smith, Stephen: Husband of Jean Ann Kennedy and fund-raiser for the John F. Kennedy Presidential Library

Sparkman, John J.: U.S. Senator, Democrat, from Alabama, 1946–1979

Staats, Elmer B.: Deputy Director, U.S. Bureau of the Budget, 1959–1966; Comptroller General of the United States, 1966–1981

Taylor, George: Professor of Finance, Wharton School of Business, University of Pennsylvania; Chairman, War Labor Board, 1945; Chairman, Wage Stabilization Board, 1950; federal mediator in negotiations between railroads and labor unions, 1964

Unruh, Jesse: Speaker of the California State Assembly, 1961–1969

Valenti, Jack: Special Assistant to the President, 1963–1966

White, Lee C.: Associate Counsel to the President, 1963–1965

Wilkins, Roy: Executive Secretary, National Association for the Advancement of Colored People (NAACP), 1955–1964; Executive Director, NAACP, 1965–1977

Wirtz, Williard: Secretary of Labor, 1962–1969

Young, Whitney M., Jr.: Executive Director, National Urban League, 1961–1971

The
PRESIDENTIAL
RECORDINGS

—— LYNDON B. JOHNSON ——

Monday, June 1, 1964

I think a bill will pass. I hope that these—Mike [Mansfield] announced today he was filing a petition for cloture on Saturday and he would try to vote on Monday. Now, I hope that he's done his counting and has got the votes.

—George Smathers to President Johnson

On the first day of June 1964, Senate Majority Leader Mike Mansfield announced that he would file a petition for cloture of debate on the civil rights bill the following Saturday. Under the rules of the Senate, a cloture vote would be required during the first hour of Senate business on the second business day after the petition had been filed. This meant that a vote would take place on Tuesday, June 9, potentially bringing a nearly 11-week filibuster by southern senators to a close. This action represented a key part of the bipartisan Senate leadership's drive to build a coalition that would support the bill. Although Mansfield stated that he was not sure if he had the votes necessary to attain cloture, the motion would pass on June 10.[1]

This progress on the civil rights bill marked a significant step toward what would be one of the Johnson administration's most significant and lasting achievements. Halfway around the globe, however, the administration's foreign policy elite was simultaneously plotting a course that would ultimately undermine Lyndon Johnson's presidency. At the U.S. Pacific Command Headquarters on the Aiea Heights above Hawaii's Pearl Harbor, 55 leading U.S. national security officials began

---

1. E. W. Kenworthy, "Rights Closure Vote Set for Next Week," *New York Times*, 2 June 1964; Susanna McBee, "Petition to End Debate Will Come Saturday," *Washington Post*, 2 June 1964.

two days of face-to-face meetings to discuss the status and future direction of U.S. policy in Southeast Asia. The first day of meetings exposed distinctly different perspectives on the progress of the U.S effort to stabilize South Vietnam against a Communist insurgency aided by North Vietnam. General William Westmoreland, the Deputy Commander of the Military Assistance Command, Vietnam, summarized the position of the South Vietnamese government and military as "tenuous, but far from hopeless."[2] Secretary of Defense Robert McNamara disagreed, arguing that "we should consider the military situation as worse than tenuous. It was approaching the hopeless category." McNamara cited high desertion and low recruitment rates in the South Vietnamese army and the overall low morale of the government forces. He also pointed out that a "pacification" program had largely failed in its goal of removing Vietcong guerrillas from rural areas in South Vietnam. Not all of the officials were this pessimistic. Secretary of State Dean Rusk argued that while the government in South Vietnam might still be deteriorating, it was not doing so as rapidly as it had been a year earlier.[3]

Back in Washington, President Johnson began his workweek with unrecorded calls from the White House Mansion to Mary Margaret Valenti at 8:35 A.M., and after learning that Mary Margaret's husband had already left, to Special Assistant Jack Valenti at 8:55 and to Special Assistant Walter Jenkins at 9:25.

10:30 A.M.: President Johnson arrived at the Oval Office.

10:35 A.M.: Unrecorded call to Jack Valenti.

10:40 A.M.: Meeting with National Security Adviser McGeorge Bundy and National Security Council staff member Robert Komer.

10:53 A.M.: Special Counsel Myer Feldman joined the meeting.

11:10 A.M.: Welcomed Israeli Prime Minister Levi Eshkol to the White House.

Eshkol's arrival marked the first state visit of an Israeli prime minister to Washington, and thus was an important step in the development of Israeli-American relations. A May 28 briefing memo for the President pointed out that one risk of

---

2. On 19 June, Westmoreland would replace General Paul Harkins as commander of the U.S. Military Assistance Command, Vietnam.

3. "Summary Record of a Meeting, Honolulu," 1 June 1964, 8:30 A.M.–12:30 P.M., and "Summary Record of a Meeting, Honolulu," 1 June 1964, 2:15–6:15 P.M., U.S. Department of State, *Foreign Relations of the United States (FRUS), 1964–1968: Vietnam 1964*, ed. Edward C. Keefer and Charles S. Sampson (Washington, DC: U.S. Government Printing Office [hereafter GPO], 1992), 1:412–28.

the visit, particularly in the aftermath of Soviet Premier Nikita Khruschev's recent visit to Cairo, was the possible appearance to the Arab states that the United States had abandoned its formal policy of neutrality between Israeli and Arab interests in favor of an explicit alliance with Israel.[4]

11:30 A.M.–11:45 A.M.: Following welcoming remarks, met privately with Eshkol in the Oval Office, afterward joined by Feldman and Israeli Ambassador to the United States Avraham Harman.

12:02 P.M.: Unrecorded call to Valenti.

12:02 P.M.: The meeting expanded to include Robert Komer, Under Secretary of State for Political Affairs W. Averell Harriman, U.S. Ambassador to Israel Walworth Barbour, Assistant Secretary of State for Near Eastern and South Asian Affairs Phillips Talbot, and Israeli Deputy Defense Minister Shimon Peres.

Feldman prepared a memorandum summarizing the meeting from the time at which he entered.[5] Key issues of discussion included a U.S. plan to secretly provide tanks to Israel by way of West Germany and the United Kingdom to partially counter the threat to Israel posed by Egypt's rapid military buildup.[6] Eshkol recognized the strategic necessity of keeping the sale secret, but emphasized the critical importance to Israel of receiving the modern M48 tanks instead of the outdated Centurion tank and added that they had an option to obtain the M48s from Italy if the German and British sources could not provide them. Johnson assured Eshkol of the U.S. commitment to Israel's security and noted that while the Centurion "was a good tank," the United States would attempt to provide the M48s that Israel preferred. The President warned, however, that the United States opposed the development of nuclear weapons or long-range missile capabilities by either

4. "Memorandum From Robert W. Komer of the National Security Council Staff to President Johnson," 28 May 1964, *FRUS, 1964–1968: Arab-Israeli Dispute, 1964–1967*, ed. Harriet Dashiell Schwar (Washington, DC: GPO, 2000), 18:147–51.
5. No record exists of the private meeting between Johnson and Eshkol, and a day later, Komer suggested to Under Secretary of State George Ball that such closed meetings between the President and foreign leaders could create serious problems when top advisers were not privy to the discussions. "Memorandum of Telephone Conversation Between Robert W. Komer of the National Security Council Staff and the Under Secretary of State (Ball)," 2 June 1964, *FRUS, 1964–1968*, 18:159–60.
6. See McGeorge Bundy to Johnson, 3:35 P.M., 13 May 1964, in Guian A. McKee, ed., *The Presidential Recordings, Lyndon B. Johnson: Toward the Great Society, February 1, 1964–May 31, 1964*, vol. 6, *April 14, 1964–May 31, 1964* (New York: Norton, 2007), pp. 632–34.

Israel or Egypt. Johnson urged the Prime Minister to accept international controls on its nuclear energy programs and to allow the United States to inform Nasser that Israel's Dimona nuclear reactor would be used only for peaceful purposes. Eshkol indicated that while he appreciated the U.S. commitment to Israel, the development of an independent capacity for self-defense lay at the core of Israeli policy and that he would reject the President's advice unless the United States could convince Nasser to halt his arms buildup. On June 3, however, the Israelis changed their position on the Dimona issue.[7]

12:46 P.M.: Posed for photographs with the U.S. ambassadors to Chad and to Ethiopia and the U.S. minister to Romania.

1:01 P.M.: Meeting with Special Assistant Kenneth O'Donnell.

1:04 P.M.

From McGeorge Bundy[8]

National Security Adviser Bundy reported on a recent meeting between New York attorney, former Treasury Secretary, and sometimes Johnson adviser Robert Anderson and French President Charles de Gaulle.[9] Johnson had as strained a relationship with the French leader as President Kennedy did before him. De Gaulle had recently recognized China and, more important, had emerged as a leading international critic of U.S. policy in Southeast Asia with his advocacy of an international conference to prepare a neutralization plan for Vietnam. While in Europe two days earlier, Anderson had unexpectedly been summoned to meet the French President. De Gaulle informed Anderson of his interest in improving communication with his U.S. counterpart. Just before leaving Paris, Anderson had received a follow-up message with de Gaulle's phone number. In this conversation, Johnson and Bundy discussed how to respond to the French overture.[10]

---

7. Feldman's summary can be found as "Memorandum of Conversation," 1 June 1964, *FRUS, 1964–1968*, 18:152–59.
8. Tape WH6406.01, Citation #3601, Recordings of Telephone Conversations—White House Series, Recordings and Transcripts of Conversations and Meetings, Lyndon B. Johnson Library.
9. Anderson had served as secretary of the Treasury under President Eisenhower.
10. "Memorandum from the President's Special Assistant for National Security Affairs (Bundy) to President Johnson," 1 June 1964, *FRUS, 1964–1968, Western Europe*, ed. James E. Miller (Washington, DC: GPO, 2001), 12:53–54.

President Johnson: . . . what you've said. Now, what's his [Robert Anderson's] theory?

McGeorge Bundy: His theory is the general [Charles de Gaulle] sent for him and talked to him for an hour on Saturday and expressed his great desire to reestablish communication in an effective way with the U.S. government, and the . . . he said that he hadn't got along well with Kennedy, but that he would like to try again, that he had been greatly impressed by the short meeting in November, and did you value letters or telephone communication. And Anderson said he didn't know any reason why not, but of course he wasn't empowered to speak.

They did not talk substance because de Gaulle said he wasn't just that much caught up after his illness, and the only thing you'd really have to say to him if you did call him up is "I'm glad you received my man, and I have his message, and I'm glad you're getting better, and I hope we'll be in touch."[11] Then you might add [that] we have asked that George Ball get an interview with him on his way to Europe this week so that we not seem to be bypassing the French. And you could say that George is coming in.

Now, I don't think it's crucial to do it by telephone, and of course there is a language problem, which means there would have to be an interpreter. We can send a message to this effect through Ball when he goes, if you'd rather do it that way. But Bob made such a point of your making a phone call that he asked me to check with you right away. He said he referred two or three times *to* the telephone and that he thought this would be fairly easy money.

President Johnson: It doesn't appeal to me, Mac. I don't know—

Bundy: Well, Mr. President, your own personal sense of this may be the best. The—I don't want to press it. You don't want to feel as if you're going to him at a time when he's making us all this much trouble, or is there some other reason?

President Johnson: Well, first, I think the language difficulty, and without any real reason . . .

Bundy: Yeah, there is language difficulties.

President Johnson: . . . without any real . . . single thing to call up. I thought if we could save—

Bundy: Suppose we just send another letter by George Ball.

President Johnson: —the world, why, we could do it. But I don't— I'm not . . . I'm not arbitrary about it, I just—it's [*unclear*] harsh.

Bundy: Well, frankly, he only had one phone call with Kennedy, and it

---

11. In mid-April, de Gaulle had undergone prostate surgery. Drew Middleton, "De Gaulle Gaining After Operation; Pompidou at Helm," *New York Times,* 18 April 1964.

didn't work very well. We asked him for something, and he wouldn't give it to us. I think he may have mentioned the phone myself because he may have read in the papers that that's the only way you do business, which is, of course, nonsense.

President Johnson: Mm-hmm.

Bundy: But Anderson is a shrewd man, and his own judgment was that this fellow is feeling out for communication. The other side of the notion is simply that he's trying to take you in camp, but that isn't going to happen, and I'm not a bit frightened about that.

President Johnson: Well, what I would do, let's just let it go . . .

Bundy: Right.

President Johnson: And—

Bundy: Why don't we write another friendly little note for George Ball to take if he gets his appointment?

President Johnson: All right. All right.

Fifteen seconds excised as classified information.

President Johnson: Well, I don't want to . . . I'm willing to meet anybody halfway.

Bundy: One of the things that's on my mind, Mr. President, is that we should be awful clear that we've gone more than halfway. This is one reason for having George go. If we have to get into a row with our friends like [Walter] Lippmann and [Mike] Mansfield, we don't want them to have the easy score that we didn't even try to talk to the French, you know.[12]

President Johnson: Mm-hmm.

Bundy: And I think Anderson has something to say about [Charles] Bohlen, which he wouldn't tell me on the phone, but I imagine it will be similar to what Lippmann said because he will have heard from French sources that we have an unfriendly ambassador and that kind of thing.[13]

President Johnson: Mm-hmm.

Bundy: Well, we can do this by a note, which is just as good in my point of view, but I had an obligation to Bob to check it with you.

President Johnson: Thank you.

Bundy: Right.

---

12. Syndicated columnist Walter Lippmann and Senate Majority Leader Mike Mansfield had recently endorsed the neutralization policy that de Gaulle favored for Southeast Asia.

13. Charles E. Bohlen served as U.S. ambassador to France. Although Lippmann had written frequently about de Gaulle in the winter and spring of 1964, none of his recent columns had mentioned Bohlen. Bundy may have been referring to opinions expressed by the journalist during a 27 May meeting at the White House. See McKee, *The Presidential Recordings, Johnson*, vol. 6, *April 14, 1964–May 31, 1964*, pp. 905–6.

1:12 P.M.: Unrecorded call to Press Secretary George Reedy.

1:15 P.M.: Unrecorded call to McGeorge Bundy.

1:20 P.M.–1:29 P.M.: Off-the-record meeting with Senator Clinton P. Anderson of New Mexico.

1:29 P.M.–2:40 P.M.: Meeting with special assistants Jack Valenti, Horace Busby, Douglass Cater, Bill Moyers, and Richard Goodwin to examine procedures for preparing presidential speeches. After the others left, Valenti remained and discussed the President's upcoming appointments.

2:45 P.M.: Unrecorded call to Walter Jenkins.

2:48 P.M.

To George Smathers[14]

This call to Senator Smathers demonstrated President Johnson's capacity to obtain information and exert influence through the network of acquaintances that he had built up during his years in the Senate, especially conservative southern Democrats. The conversation touched on a wide range of subjects, including the status of Senate efforts to obtain cloture on the civil rights bill, episodes of violence against Martin Luther King Jr.'s newly launched campaign for racial integration in St. Augustine, Florida, and Smathers's role in heading off adjustments to the federal excise tax that would undermine the revenue side of Johnson's carefully calibrated federal budget. Smathers eventually shifted the conversation to Vietnam, on which his views revealed the extent of the domestic political challenge already confronting Johnson. The senator indicated that while he understood the argument for supporting the South Vietnamese government, he actually favored a de facto policy of neutralization, albeit one couched in the language of transferring responsibility for the region to "some international agency." Johnson responded with a classic statement of the domino theory rationale for stopping the advance of Communism. Although Smathers promised continued support of the President regardless of what policy he pursued in Vietnam, the idea of neutralization remained anathema to Johnson and his advisers—even as it was becoming the preference of a growing contingent of Democratic senators.

---

14. Tape WH6406.01, Citations #3602, #3603, and #3604, Recordings of Telephone Conversations—White House Series, Recordings and Transcripts of Conversations and Meetings, Lyndon B. Johnson Library.

An office conversation with Jack Valenti precedes the call.

Jack Valenti: I thought you ought to know what he said to me. I don't want him to think that I'm coming in here telling tales to you, but he thinks that he doesn't get his [*unclear*] like he ought to. [*Pauses.*] So I told him to call me anytime—call me direct. [*Long pause.*] Want me to ring him for you?[15]

President Johnson: No. I'll get him. [*Pauses.*]

Tell Walter [Jenkins] to see that [Olin] Teague is offered that job, to go over there and then talk to him on this . . . beforehand—Wait a minute.[16]

Valenti: [*Unclear.*] [*Long pause.*] See that Teague is offered the job . . .

President Johnson: To D-day.

Valenti: Oh, yes, sir, that's already been—Walter—

President Johnson: Well, once he gets it and makes him feel good about that, then tell him to call him back on this and see what he can do on this. [*Pauses.*]

[*whispering*] Tell her to . . . tell her to—

The office conversation is interrupted by a brief operator conversation regarding the Smathers call. The operator then informs the President that Smathers is on the floor of the Senate and that they are attempting to reach him. Scattered office conversation continues as the President holds for Smathers.

President Johnson: I don't think I got [*unclear*] because . . . And talk to [McGeorge] Bundy and say, "We sure want you-all to—you and State—to watch these requests because he's not having enough time to get his reading. He can't see his stuff because they're just—they're flagging these people in to us." [*Valenti's response is inaudible.*] [*Long pause.*] Talk to Lee and tell him to see if he can't avoid us.[17] If we have to, why, we just have to, but I don't want to. [*Pauses.*] Tell him that I can't go and that I'm going to be in Cleveland. I don't—this son of a bitch is no good anyway.

Valenti: Yes, sir. I just wanted you to see it. I [*unclear*] to say no to it. Just see it. [*Pause.*]

President Johnson: Just tell him that since I'll be out of town [*the operator reports that Smathers is coming on the line*], I'm designating Mr. Ralph Dungan to receive it, or somebody.[18] [*Long pause.*] Turn it over to Kermit Gordon and tell him to get back to [*unclear*].[19]

---

15. This passage is probably referring to Senator Smathers.
16. Olin E. "Tiger" Teague was a Democratic representative from Texas and the chairman of the House Veterans Affairs Committee.
17. Johnson may have been referring to Associate Counsel to the President Lee C. White.
18. Ralph A. Dungan served as special assistant to the President.
19. Kermit Gordon served as director of the Bureau of the Budget.

[*on phone*] Hello, George.

George Smathers: Mr. President, how are you?

President Johnson: Fine, George. Jack Valenti says you've been trying to get to see me, and . . .

Smathers: Well, I told him today that I knew you were busy, and actually—

President Johnson: We can't find out who in the hell you talked to. We've tried everybody around here. I called Walter, and he said nobody had called him, said that Juanita [Roberts] had called Friday afternoon, talked to a stenographer in his office . . .[20]

Smathers: That was a week ago Friday.

President Johnson: Yeah.

Smathers: That's all right, and I told you I'd [*unclear*]—

President Johnson: Well, but . . . if I call one of your county chairmen down there in Florida—This girl's got nothing to do with it; she just types letters that Juanita called.

Smathers: Yeah.

President Johnson: I got an appointment secretary, Jack Valenti, and anytime you got something that you think you want to see me about, call him and he'll set it up.

Smathers: Fine.

President Johnson: What have you got on your mind?

Smathers: Now . . .

President Johnson: See, this girl Mildred Stegall, I never heard of it.[21] She didn't know one thing about it. Just like my calling over to [Spessard] Holland's secretary and saying, "How's Smathers doing?"[22]

Smathers: Yeah.

President Johnson: Because she didn't know anything about it.

Smathers: Yeah, all right. Now, let me just—two things: First . . . if you can manage in your conversations with the Prime Minister of Israel, [Levi] Eshkol, to just mention those schools. You will recall that we had all those Jews over there that day and put on those beanies and had the little prayer. That is an orthodox Jewish group. And they want a school in Israel, and the schools are actually being planned for and programmed and going ahead. But they have asked me to see if I could get you just to mention how pleased you were that Eshkol was doing this. That that would help them go forward with the schools there. As you know, there are three Jewish groups: reform, which is the liberal group;

---

20. Juanita Roberts was Johnson's longtime personal secretary.

21. A longtime Johnson employee, Mildred F. Stegall served on the White House staff.

22. Spessard L. Holland was Florida's senior senator.

and the conservative, which is sort of the middle group; and the ortho-dox, which are the very old-fashioned Jewish type. Now, the reform and the . . . conservative groups, they have—they already have a school, so now the orthodox are trying to get theirs.

President Johnson: All right.

Smathers: So, that's one thing.

President Johnson: Wonderful. OK, I'll try to do that tonight.

Smathers: Second thing . . . some of your friends whom you know are talking about . . . prospective good appointee for this Internal Revenue [Service] commissioner when [Mortimer] Caplin retires.[23] I—

President Johnson: I think I've got a man for it. I think—

Smathers: Well, that's good. They just—

President Johnson: —before he resigned. We pretty well set our minds on one.

Smathers: Well, that's good. That's fine. Just [unclear]—I'll just—This fellow was Drew O'Keefe, whom I understand Tom Clark is very high on.[24] He comes from Pennsylvania, is U.S. attorney up in that area.

President Johnson: Mm-hmm.

Smathers: So I don't know the man myself at all, but I understood that they said that *you* knew him and that Tom Clark knew him *very* highly and we recommended him for another job, but that they thought he might be good even at this one in order to try to qualify himself later on for a federal judicial position. So I was asked *by* them to just mention it to you if I had the chance to do so.

President Johnson: Good. What else you know?

Smathers: Well, we . . . Everything else is all right. We took a poll in our state, which . . . we've had three now, and unfortunately . . . your popularity is still, of course, strong, but while the civil rights thing is going on, it will drop. It's come down eight points since we took the first one, which is just about now two months ago. But I'm not at all worried about it, and I don't think anybody else is. I think when we get through with the damn civil rights bill—

President Johnson: What's going to happen to civil rights?

---

23. Internal Revenue Service Commissioner Mortimer M. Caplin had announced his resigna-tion on 22 May; in July, Deputy Commissioner Bertrand M. Harding would be named to the post of acting commissioner, and in December, IRS Chief Counsel Sheldon Cohen would be named as Caplin's permanent replacement. "Harding Is Promoted by President to Acting Chief of Internal Revenue," *Washington Post*, 11 July 1964; "Johnson Picks S. Cohen as Chief of IRS," *Wall Street Journal*, 29 December 1964.

24. Tom C. Clark was an associate justice of the Supreme Court. Drew J. T. O'Keefe served as U.S. attorney for the eastern district of Pennsylvania.

Smathers: Well, I think that . . . I think a bill will pass. I hope that these—Mike [Mansfield] announced today he was filing a petition for cloture on Saturday and he would try to vote on Monday. Now, I hope that he's done his counting and has got the votes.[25]

President Johnson: Do you think he has?

Smathers: I don't know. Now, [Bourke] Hickenlooper, just between us, told me that at this stage of the proceedings unless some other amendments were adopted, he had a little group that ranged between, he figured, between six and ten who would not vote for this present bill unless it was further amended.[26]

President Johnson: Mm-hmm.

Smathers: Now, I don't know. This is—then I said, "Well, Bourke, are you going to offer additional amendments yourself?" And he said that he *was*. Now, I don't know how they're counting him, but he told me this, this past Friday. So . . . I presume that Mike and Hubert [Humphrey] know what they're doing.[27]

President Johnson: I would doubt it; I would doubt it; I would doubt it. It's mighty hard to figure out these things, and . . .

Smathers: Well . . . it may be the strategy is they want to lose the first cloture vote to establish the fact that they have to give more. Now, that may be their strategy. I don't know. If it is, why, then I would think if—if by—in that case I'd file the damn cloture petition on Wednesday, and get the vote on Friday, and move it along.

---

25. Senate rules required a cloture vote on the second *business* day after the petition had been filed. Because Sunday was not a business day, the vote could not take place until the following Tuesday, 9 June. Although this was what Mansfield had actually announced, the vote would be delayed an additional day due to a final round of amendments, but the cloture motion would pass on 10 June. E. W. Kenworthy, "Rights Closure Vote Set for Next Week," *New York Times*, 2 June 1964.

26. Republican Senator Bourke Hickenlooper of Iowa chaired the Senate Republican Policy Committee. By the end of May 1964, he had emerged as a key Republican swing vote on the civil rights bill because he was believed to control the vote of as many as 20 other conservative Republican senators. During a 31 May appearance on the ABC News show *Issues and Answers*, Hickenlooper stated that he would not vote for cloture without further amendments to the civil rights bill. On 6 June, Senate leaders agreed to the consideration of three additional Republican amendments, one of which—permitting jury trials in criminal contempt cases that did not involve voting rights—passed. Hickenlooper then voted for cloture on 10 June. For an earlier conversation about Hickenlooper's position, see Johnson to Mike Manatos, 6:11 P.M., 20 May 1964, in McKee, *The Presidential Recordings, Johnson*, vol. 6, *April 14, 1964–May 31, 1964*, pp. 776–78; "Hickenlooper Opposes Closure Till Rights Bill Is Modified More," *New York Times*, 1 June 1964; Robert E. Baker, "Rights Bill Trial Section Altered on Eve of Test," *Washington Post*, 10 June 1964; *Congressional Quarterly Almanac*, 88th Cong., 2nd Sess., 1964, vol. 20 (Washington, DC: Congressional Quarterly Service, 1965), pp. 365–69.

27. Not yet President Johnson's running mate for the 1964 election, Senator Humphrey of Minnesota served as the Democratic whip in the Senate.

President Johnson: Mm-hmm.

Smathers: And then they could give some more and file the next one a week from Wednesday and maybe get the thing voted on the following weekend, and they'd really finish the thing up in about three weeks. But I think they've got to start taking some actions.

President Johnson: What about St. Augustine? They're giving me unshirted hell on that, and we've called down and talked to the governor [Farris Bryant], and he says that he's watching it very carefully, but they say they're shooting into [Martin Luther] King's white man's house down there—this assistant to King—and a lot of trouble like that.[28] He's demanding we go in. We've talked to the governor; he thinks he's got it, and he's watching it and pretty alert to it.

Smathers: Well, I think that . . . I don't—

President Johnson: They're in this morning wanting me to call on Henry Ford and his committee—some commission appointed, or something down there—to see if they can't do something about it.[29]

Smathers: Well, this is the commission for which you went down and made a speech earlier, see.

President Johnson: Yeah . . . yeah.

Smathers: That's what they're talking about.

President Johnson: Yeah.

Smathers: Now, King rented a house. Frankly, I think it's—my own judgment is—and I hope I'm still maintaining some of my objectivity—but that King . . . This is a damn plant. I don't believe they fired through

---

28. Democrat Farris Bryant served as Florida's governor from 1961 to 1965. The shooting incident took place early on the morning of 29 May at a home rented to an assistant of Martin Luther King in the unincorporated beach community of Anastasia, just outside of St. Augustine. In a second incident, King's white special assistant Harry Boyte and his son had just returned to their motel when their car windows were shattered by buckshot. Neither of the Boytes were injured in the attack. In response, King sent a telegram to Johnson that called for federal protection for blacks in the city. The incidents followed a violent attack by segregationists on civil rights marchers and reporters during the evening of 28 May. "Nightriders Fire on Dr. King's Aide," *New York Times*, 30 May 1964; "Shots Fired at Cottage of Dr. King," *Washington Post*, 30 May 1964; Taylor Branch, *Pillar of Fire: America in the King Years 1963–65* (New York: Touchstone, 1998), pp. 324–27.

29. In November 1962, President Kennedy had appointed a St. Augustine Quadricentennial Commission to plan events marking the 400th anniversary of the founding of St. Augustine, Florida. Henry Ford II of the Ford Motor Company served as one of the commission's members. As vice president, Johnson had sworn in the commission during a March 1963 visit to the city; his pledge to the local NAACP not to attend segregated events during the visits had helped to initiate the conflict over civil rights in the city. "Florida Milestone," *New York Times*, 18 November 1962; "Oldest City to Initiate Restoration," *Washington Post*, 11 March 1963; Branch, *Pillar of Fire*, pp. 33–40.

that house, because the facts show that for three straight nights when he was there, there was nothing was at all shot at. And the night that he announced publicly he was going to leave, it was then shot into, and the next night he was back there and nobody has bothered him at all.[30] Now, it is going to be—he's going to, you know, make that his focal point of his efforts currently here for a little while. Of course, he—

President Johnson: Is St. Augustine a pretty bad place?

Smathers: No. No, St. Augustine, it's a typically rural place. But what they're doing is, they're trying to squeeze St. Augustine on the basis that they're having this quadracentennial celebration starting this fall, their 400th anniversary, and they know damn well that while they don't have much integration—in fact I don't think they have any. It's a typical, sort of a small Florida community. So . . . but it's going to get a good deal of attention because it's the 400th anniversary, and they're going to screw it up! And to try to break in there.

Now, we've done—I made two commencement speeches over this weekend, and both junior college commencements where I spoke were integrated, first time in the history that they had been. Of course, one of them is first commencement. But anyway . . . but a lot of progress being made.

But King is . . . naturally, he loves a headline, and I think frankly that it would be very bad if the federal government did anything more than confer with Bryant, who has frankly handled the matter very well up to this point. And Bryant's a reasonable fellow, a graduate of Harvard, damn smart fellow, and I think you just—if you just say that you've conferred, he assures you that everything's in good shape, and that actually, FBI agents could go down to try to find out who was doing the shooting. That may be justified, but anything beyond that I think would be very bad.

President Johnson: Good. OK. That's what we'll do.

Martin Anderson's been writing me and talking to me from time to time—writing, communicating, sending me stuff on the cattle prices.[31]

Smathers: Right.

President Johnson: And I know how he feels because I understand it. Our . . . we don't know what the hell we can do about it. The cattle-men . . . got up 106 million head from about 92 million, and they're just running out of their ears, and there's more surplus than you ever saw. It's

---

30. King had been in California on the night of the shooting.
31. Martin Anderson was the publisher of the *Orlando Sentinel*. After supporting the Republican nominee in the three previous elections, the paper would endorse Johnson in 1964. "Humphrey Urges Clean Contest," *Washington Post*, 2 September 1964.

down now to where meats sell pretty cheap because it's got such a hell of a surplus. The imports have got practically nothing to do with it. We've gone in and bought up enough stuff and reduced them enough to give them the five-year average that they were arguing for, and we're below the five-year average now in imports.[32] But the imports don't run 6, 7 percent of the total amount; 93 percent that's bothering us is this damn overproduction. But they've got it, and they're all holding back, of course. [*Chuckles.*] They don't want to sell cheap prices, and we've got to get rid of it someway, and everybody—every doctor and every oilman and everybody else [who] wanted to get some tax haven went out and got in cattle, and they're there, and I've got them running out of my ears.

So I'm just buying all of it I can for school lunch [programs] and all of it we can to ship overseas to our soldiers.[33] We used to buy it over there, but I'm shipping our stuff over there now, and I'm encouraging them to have barbecues and cookouts and everything else to . . . We've increased the consumption about 35 percent through the chain stores, but we still— the fact is, we've got 106 million head and we need 92. And everybody's got the surplus. I don't know what else to do about it. And if we barred all imports, it wouldn't make one-tenth of a cent difference.

Smathers: I have often thought that it might be someday—

President Johnson: And what we're trying to do—I've sent a mission over there, and there's a shortage in France and there's a shortage in England and there's shortage in Germany, and we're trying to . . . instead of raise hell about imports and letting them raise hell about our imports, we're trying to import a lot of stuff into their countries.

Smathers: Right.

President Johnson: And they think we're going to be able to do it. They're not positive, but . . . Our stuff's all marble stuff, all fat stuff, and most people don't like that fat. They can't eat it. They just want lean meat.

Smathers: Yeah.

President Johnson: And our people have been sending them to Nebraska and having them fed up, you know, and put all that marble on them and all that fat. And it does give them a little better flavor.

---

32. For a summary of the administration's efforts to raise beef prices, see Johnson to Charles Murphy and Orville Freeman to Johnson, 10:40 A.M. and 6:05 P.M., respectively, 5 May 1964, in McKee, *The Presidential Recordings, Johnson*, vol. 6, *April 14, 1964–May 31, 1964*, pp 456–59, 466–68.

33. For beef purchases by the Department of Defense, see Robert McNamara to Johnson, 6:10 P.M., 5 May 1964, in McKee, *The Presidential Recordings, Johnson*, vol. 6, *April 14, 1964–May 31, 1964*, pp. 468–69.

Smathers: Yeah.

President Johnson: But when you sit down, they say they'll give you that for a dollar and a half a pound. Well, then you cut that marble off, it sells for $3 a pound, you see.

Smathers: Right. Well, someday we're going to have to look at the tax bill. . . . It really should not be a tax haven. I think it's just enough— these doctors and rich people raising these cattle is just enough to make the oversupply and just enough to make it really tough for the genuine cattle raiser.

President Johnson: I think that that's the basic weakness. I don't know what tax benefits it has. I never have felt any myself, but I guess to a fellow that's got a big registered herd or something, there's some real benefits.

Smathers: Right.

President Johnson: And we ought to watch it, and I hope that next year when we get this election behind us—My God, George, I hope you-all don't really do anything to these excise taxes.[34]

Smathers: Well . . .

President Johnson: Don't mess with that now. I've just got a big 12 billion.

Smathers: We're not. I put in a bill on the telephone [service tax] to head [Frank] Carlson and them off, see.[35] Carlson—

President Johnson: [*with Smathers acknowledging*] Well, you head them off because if I get on that—Now, the Republicans are starting a movement to really make us fiscally irresponsible. I've got them in a hole on this, and I can screw them to death because I'm going to stay within my budget, and I'm just fighting like hell to do it. But I'm going to do it, and I'm a billion dollar[s] under them, but if they can cause me to lose a lot of taxes . . . Now, they caused that committee to delay for two months, you know—the Senate committee—and as a result of that delay I missed my guess on revenues because . . . I thought the bill would go into effect quicker than it did. But now they're going to try to mess us up on this

---

34. Smathers served on the Senate Finance Committee, which in June would begin consideration of the 1964 excise tax extension bill. Johnson wanted no cuts in the existing excise tax structure because the resulting decrease in federal revenues would undermine his budget projections. Although the committee did accept a number of cuts, they were eliminated in a House-Senate conference committee. Smathers favored the excise tax cuts approved by the Senate. *Congressional Quarterly Almanac*, 1964, vol. 20, pp. 540–43.

35. Senator Frank Carlson was a Republican from Kansas who served on the Senate Finance Committee.

extension, and I just hope that you'll watch them and not let them do it.[36]

Smathers: Yeah. Now, let me just say this: I put a bill in to . . . take off the telephone tax over a period of five years.[37] They'll gradually reduce it. Now, the reason I did that is because Carlson and these Republicans had been pushing this for quite a long time, and when we took up the tax bill, everybody brought up the need for removing the excise taxes, and we fought them off on the ground that, well, we were later going to consider all that.

President Johnson: Well, consider it after the election.

Smathers: That's right. Now then . . . now, if we can . . . well, of course, we got to extend it for the 31st.[38]

President Johnson: Yeah . . . that's right.

Smathers: We got to figure out some way, and I think they will—

President Johnson: But Wilbur [Mills] is going to start in June holding other hearings—[39]

Smathers: That's right. Well, that's—

President Johnson: —and if we can just get this—They want to keep me from having my budget. They want me to keep my debt ceiling and my taxes, and they're going to work on that to give us a whipping.[40]

Smathers: Yeah.

President Johnson: But . . . don't let them do that.

Smathers: Well, we're not. We—I know we can hold them on the debt

---

36. Johnson was referring to a January 1964 budget estimate that assumed the 1964 tax cut would take effect on 1 February, when it actually had been delayed until 26 February. See Johnson to Kermit Gordon, 10:46 A.M., 26 May 1964, in McKee, *The Presidential Recordings, Johnson*, vol. 6, *April 14, 1964–May 31, 1964*, pp. 826–32.

37. Smathers proposed an unsuccessful amendment to cut the general telephone service tax from 10 percent to 5 percent. He succeeded, however, in repealing the excise tax on musical instruments. *Congressional Quarterly Almanac*, 1964, vol. 20, p. 542.

38. The existing extension of the excise tax structure would expire at the end of June 1964 (30 June).

39. Representative Wilbur Mills of Arkansas chaired the powerful House Ways and Means Committee, which controlled the initiation of all federal revenue-raising measures. Mills largely dictated the committee's actions, and thus exerted extensive control over the U.S. tax code. During the summer of 1964, the Ways and Means Committee held a series of hearings on the excise tax extension.

40. In the Senate, the Finance Committee had jurisdiction over legislation required to raise the legal limit on the federal debt. On 4 June, the House Ways and Means Committee would report legislation that increased the ceiling to $325 billion for the 1965 fiscal year, a $9 billion increase. Although Larry O'Brien reported that the administration should "expect no Republican support," the bill would pass the Senate quickly, and Johnson would sign it into law on 29 June. Lawrence F. O'Brien, "Memorandum To The President; Subject: Possible Items for Discussion at Leadership Breakfast," 2 June 1964, "Ex FG 400/MC 11/22/63–6/15/64" folder, Box 328, White House Central Files: Federal Government Operations, Lyndon B. Johnson Library; *Congressional Quarterly Almanac*, 1964, vol. 20, p. 582.

ceiling, and I think we can maneuver around on the taxes, and if they was going to take any off, why . . . this is why I put in the telephone thing. If I'm going to say, "Well, if any is coming off, just take off the telephone." Now, [Abraham] Ribicoff and his crowd don't want the telephone off particularly; they want to take off cosmetics and handbags and rouge. Phil Hart wants to take it off of automobiles. Vance Hartke wants to take it off musical instruments, and so it goes.[41] So if everybody's got one, then we can finally say, "Now look, my God, I'll give up mine, and you give up yours."

President Johnson: That's right. I'll leave that up to you. Now you do that for me.

Smathers: All right.

President Johnson: That'll be wonderful. Now, do you know any other news?

Smathers: No, I don't know any other news . . .

President Johnson: How's Dick [Russell] feeling?[42]

Smathers: Well, Dick's feeling pretty good. I just had lunch with him.

President Johnson: I never do see him. I haven't been to lunch yet; I've got to—

Smathers: Everybody's worried about South Vietnam, as you know, and there's no point in me telling you that.

President Johnson: Well, what do you think we ought to do? What do they . . . What do they think we ought to do?

Smathers: I tell you what: I don't think that they think we ought to commit a lot of people out there. I'm sure of that. I mean, if any way, it seems to me, you can get it referred to the . . . some international agency, because in the first place nobody really believes the South Vietnamese know whether or not they're Democrats, Republicans, capitalists, or Communists, or a goddamn thing. The second thing: They've long been indoctrinated by General [Douglas] MacArthur and others that we really shouldn't get on a . . . in a shooting war with the Chinese on the Chinese mainland or in that area.[43] Now, you say, "Well, you don't want to give it up." Well, that's right:

---

41. All three men were Democratic senators: Ribicoff from Connecticut, Hart from Michigan, and Hartke from Indiana.

42. The previous week, Johnson had held a lengthy conversation with Senator Richard Russell of Georgia. Johnson to Richard Russell, 10:55 A.M., 27 May 1964, in McKee, *The Presidential Recordings, Johnson*, vol. 6, *April 14, 1964–May 31, 1964*, pp. 871–85.

43. In the aftermath of the Korean War, General Douglas MacArthur (who had commanded U.S. forces in that conflict) had warned against committing U.S. troops to fight a land war in Asia. President Kennedy had cited MacArthur's views during discussions about a possible escalation of American military involvement in Southeast Asia. Fredrik Logevall, *Choosing War: The Lost Chance for Peace and Escalation of War in Vietnam* (Berkeley: University of California Press, 1999), p. 26.

You don't want to give it up. But on the other hand, they don't want to get in a war about that area. I think—

President Johnson: Well, then what do we do, though? That's right, we—

Smathers: I think that we just—

President Johnson: They're coming down, they're eating us up, and we either got to run or fight.

Smathers: Well, I think you better run to an international agency, and if they take it over—[John Foster] Dulles got us in there in '54 by bad judgment, and nobody thinks that we ought to fight a war in that area of the world.[44] And to start committing more and more has just got everybody really worried. Jack Knight wrote a damn good editorial yesterday.[45] He called me about three days before about it, said he was worried about it, what did I think was going to happen. I said, "Well, looks like to me that [Robert] McNamara sort of got the bit in his teeth. I have not been on Wayne Morse's side. I think it's unfair to call it 'McNamara's war,' but I'm afraid that the opinion is, in the executive branch of the government—they have to decide these things—that this is an essential area and that we're going to have to commit our own troops to it. And that—"[46]

President Johnson: [with Smathers acknowledging] That's basically what the Republicans say. Hickenlooper is down here, and that's what he said. We can't retreat because if we do, why, it'll be very disastrous for the United States to give up all of our interests [in] Southeast Asia because the next thing comes is Indonesia, 100 million people, and next thing comes is the Philippines. And the Chinese are very aggressive, and if you run from them, why, we'd have run out of Greece and Turkey a long time ago if we'd of run from [Soviet Premier Nikita] Khrushchev. Now, if we show some strength, why, we may have a chance to hold on. If we don't, why, we just throw in the flag, and we . . .

---

44. Dulles served as secretary of state under Dwight Eisenhower.

45. John Knight published the *Miami Herald.*

46. Senator Wayne Morse of Oregon had been an outspoken early opponent of U.S. military involvement in Vietnam. The first reference to Vietnam as "McNamara's war" recorded in the nation's major newspapers was a 30 March 1964 speech by Morse in which he called for the "repudiation" of the Johnson administration unless it ceased to support "the McNamara war." The phrase caught on so rapidly that by late April, McNamara himself responded by embracing the designation: "I don't object to its being called 'McNamara's war.' I think it is a very important war and I am pleased to be identified with it and do whatever I can to win it." "Morse Scores Role of U.S. in Vietnam," *New York Times,* 31 March 1964; "M'Namara Agrees to Call It His War," *New York Times,* 25 April 1964.

Smathers: Well, I would agree with that in certain areas—and God knows I'm no runner from the Communists—but they've got us at a big disadvantage. Nobody gives a damn about that area, generally, even though they probably should.

President Johnson: Yes, everybody . . . I think the people don't, but I think that it's a very important area. With India changing governments and with Indonesia what it is, they can really have two-thirds of the world there if we're not careful. It'll be another China.

Smathers: And I think that responsible Republicans ought to start making that clear, if you can get them to do it.

President Johnson: Well, Nixon has done it. He said that we ought to go in with North Vietnam. [Nelson] Rockefeller has done it.[47] [Barry] Goldwater has been wanting to drop atomic bombs.[48] They're all doing it. Now, I have refused to do it, and I'm trying every way in the world with every organization: with SEATO, with NATO, I've had my secretary of state—both of them, with the United Nations.[49] I went up to see them myself with the ICC Commission.[50] And I'm trying every way I can just to hold on and keep from getting run out. But they see a chance now, in an election year, and they think our people—they're reading Morse over here—and they think we want to get out. And I believe if I said, "Well, we'll pull out," God, I believe that they'd be up in arms on me. And I think if I say, "Well, we're going in," they would be up in arms too.

Smathers: Well, that's right. That's why—

President Johnson: So . . .

Smathers: —I agree that there's no easy way out of this if—I know

---

47. A potential contender for the Republican presidential nomination, Rockefeller served as governor of New York.

48. The leading candidate to challenge the President in the fall, Arizona Senator Goldwater had made a number of controversial foreign policy remarks.

49. Loosely modeled on the North Atlantic Treaty Organization (NATO), the Southeast Asia Treaty Organization (SEATO) provided for the mutual defense of non-Communist countries in Southeast Asia. Signatories included the United States, France, Great Britain, the Philippines, Thailand, Pakistan, Australia, and New Zealand. Cambodia, Laos, and South Vietnam could not sign the treaty because of the non-alliance provisions of the Geneva Convention of 1954, while India, Burma, and Indonesia chose not to sign. Stanley I. Kutler, ed., *Encyclopedia Of The Vietnam War* (New York: Charles Scribner's Sons, 1996), pp. 499–500.

50. Johnson was referring to the International Control Commission (formally known as the International Commission for Supervision and Control), which had been established to oversee the neutrality agreements for Southeast Asia created under the 1954 Geneva Accords. The specific context of the remark was probably Canadian diplomat Blair Seaborn's upcoming mission to deliver a message from the U.S. government to the North Vietnamese government. Seaborn was the Canadian representative on the ICC (Canada held one of the three seats on the ICC).

that's what you'd like to do is to get it stabilized and then send it off and to have some kind of a neutrality efforts again. And . . . bring in . . . make those British and French and so on—they belong to SEATO—somehow get them in on it with us and assume some responsibility. Now, they're damn good about guiding things into international hearings and so on. If we can get this and stabilize it into an international hearing for a while, and then finally . . .

President Johnson: Well, that's what we did with Laos, and we got an agreement, and then the sons of bitches violate, you see, and . . .

Smathers: Yeah. Well, of course, our people apparently violated that first, or the rightists did anyway.

President Johnson: Well, no, we didn't. We didn't have anything to do with that. We're not in with the rightists. We laid it down and said they had to go back to Souvanna Phouma or to hell with them.[51]

Smathers: Yeah.

President Johnson: And the rightists, though, wanted to take over, but then they're kind of like they are . . . some of our oilmen in Texas, you know.

Smathers: Yeah. [*Johnson chuckles.*] Well, that's right. Well, it isn't an easy one, but I can assure you it is just the people generally that I talk to—and I talk to a good many in our state, of course—but you talk to many more. But anyway—

President Johnson: No, I don't. No, I don't.

Smathers: —they don't want to be run out, but on the other hand, they don't feel very—I heard Billy Graham on the program just the other night, and he usually stays out of these things pretty well, but he said, "I just don't understand why it is we can be so tough in that area of the world and how we can be so un-tough in Cuba."[52] Now, I think you've done well in Cuba. I think everything's coming along *fine* and as well as could be expected. But this is . . . They oversimplify it, as you know. And they get us fighting, and the way the hell its going out in South Vietnam when the people themselves don't want to fight, apparently. They don't

---

51. Smathers and Johnson were referring to the April right-wing coup attempt against the neutralist Laotian government. Laotian Premier Souvanna Phouma managed to maintain power by reaching an accommodation with the coup leaders, only to face renewed attacks by the Communist Pathet Lao. McKee, *The Presidential Recordings, Johnson*, vol. 6, *April 14, 1964–May 31, 1964*, pp. 97–99.

52. In a 22 May speech before the Southern Baptist Convention in Atlantic City, Graham urged the government to "get in with all we've got in Vietnam or get out." Paul L. Montgomery, "Baptists Oppose School Prayers," *New York Times*, 23 May 1964.

know what the hell they want to do. It is obviously not going to be a very well-accepted conclusion.

Now, I agree that that's not—in the final analysis, that can't guide you. You've got to do what you think in the long range is best for your country and the free world irrespective of what the hell people think. But . . . I don't know, if there's some way it could just be held in abeyance, or maybe this . . . again, it being—you've got it figured out better than I have—if just a real strong show of strength might stabilize it where nothing else would.

President Johnson: We're trying everything else, but I'm afraid that's not going to do it. I've got them out in Honolulu now trying to figure if [there is] anything else they can do.[53]

Smathers: Yeah. Well, God thanks you. I won't second-guess you on those . . .

President Johnson: I'll see you.

Smathers: All right.

President Johnson: Bye.

Smathers: Thank you.

3:20 P.M.: President Johnson read newspapers in the outer office and met briefly with Walter Jenkins.

3:30 P.M.: Returned to the White House Mansion and ate lunch alone.

4:26 P.M.: Unrecorded call to Senator Humphrey.

5:25 P.M.: Unrecorded call to McGeorge Bundy.

5:30 P.M.: Unrecorded call to Bill Moyers.

5:35 P.M.: Unrecorded call to George Reedy.

5:52 P.M.: Returned to the office, stopping en route in the Flower Garden to have picture taken with a Japanese journalist.

6:05 P.M.: Unrecorded call to McGeorge Bundy.

6:06 P.M.: Unrecorded call to Jack Valenti.

6:08 P.M.: Unrecorded call to Jack Valenti.

6:13 P.M.: Meeting with special assistant for science and technology, Dr. Donald Hornig.

President Johnson and Hornig discussed issues of long-term arms control and disarmament planning.

---

53. Johnson was referring to the meeting of top U.S. foreign policy and military officials taking place in Hawaii to reevaluate U.S. policy in Southeast Asia.

6:20 P.M.

From Walter Jenkins[54]

Johnson then recorded a call from Walter Jenkins, who reported on a background briefing on the President and First Lady's business interests that Johnson's friend and attorney Abe Fortas had just given to interested reporters from the *Washington Star*.[55] Jenkins indicated that Fortas believed he had successfully parried the reporters' questions, but this assessment proved premature, as the newspaper published a highly critical investigative piece by reporter John Barron on June 9.[56]

Walter Jenkins: . . . [*unclear*] people let after two hours. He's elated. He thinks that they're reconsidering the whole business. He said they took very careful notes, and . . . he—Abe [Fortas]—did most of the talking. He said he milked everything he had gotten from me, from Jesse [Kellam], and from Leonard [Marks].[57] And he said they were very much impressed. And [John] Barron said [at] one point, said, "Now, some of these things, I have your statement, and then I have other statements to the contrary from other people." And I said . . . Abe said, "Well, I'm just trying to give you the facts as best I understand them, and you'll have to evaluate them." And then [Charles] Seib said that "suppose we want to print what you're telling us. Can we attribute it to somebody?"[58] and Abe suggested that since this—they'd agreed this was for background, that they'd let him know if they decided they wanted to print anything [*unclear*] said, and then we'd . . . they'd talk about how to handle it. He said, "I think the impact was terrific." I told them what was in the wire from Naman, and they gave me the impression that they were going to check back with Naman because Barron felt it was something different from what he had

---

54. Tape WH6406.01, Citation #3605, Recordings of Telephone Conversations—White House Series, Recordings and Transcripts of Conversations and Meetings, Lyndon B. Johnson Library.
55. In 1963–64, the official title of the newspaper later known as the *Washington Star* was the *Evening Star* six days of the week and the *Sunday Star* on the seventh day. Since most references in the transcripts for this volume are either to the *Star* or the *Washington Star*, all citations of this newspaper will be to the *Washington Star*.
56. John Barron, "The Johnson Money," *Washington Star*, 9 June 1964.
57. Jenkins was referring to Jesse Kellam, the general manager of the Johnsons' television and radio stations, and to Washington telecommunications lawyer Leonard Marks, who in 1952 had advised the Johnsons to enter the Austin television market and subsequently represented their broadcasting interests.
58. Jenkins was referring to *Washington Star* reporter Charles B. Seib.

told him, that they had difficulty squaring it with what Naman had said.[59] On the Moses thing, he—[60]

President Johnson: All right. I would call Don and tell him that right now.

Jenkins: All right.

President Johnson: Next. [*Pauses.*] Moses.

Jenkins: Yes, sir. They said they . . . they say on the Moses, he read it to them and told them there had been no such incident whatsoever—

President Johnson: Diaries that are here too, he ought to point that out.

Jenkins: There just had been no such incident whatsoever. All right. And just as we were walking out, Barron turned around and said, "You know, the most important thing here in my whole story is the December incident."[61] I said, "Yes, I agree with you, and the burden of proof is very heavy on you. And with the President of the United States involved, it becomes tremendous, and it just didn't happen." And as [*unclear*] went through, I ticked off from page to page every place that came up about the FCC [Federal Communications Commission] giving special treatment. I had covered it very thoroughly once, but then I went back over it: that we had never asked for anything that was contested; that we had never gotten any special favors; we'd only asked for one once, and that

59. Wilfred Naman was a Texas attorney who had been a stockholder in KWTX, a station in the Waco, Texas, broadcast market that had been a rival to Johnson broadcast holdings in the area. In the 9 June *Washington Star* article, Naman recounted a complex series of 1955 negotiations between the two sides, the major television networks, and the FCC. Barron, "The Johnson Money."

60. C. Hamilton Moses was an executive with Midwest Video, the parent company of Capital Cable of Austin, Inc., of which Johnson-owned KTBC-TV held an option to purchase a controlling stock share. TV Cable, a rival Austin cable company, had recently complained to the FCC that in a 1963 filing to the commission, KTBC and Capital Cable had falsely claimed that KTBC-TV did not control Capital Cable. The rival company argued that this claim had contributed to an FCC ruling that placed it at a competitive disadvantage. In Barron's 9 June *Washington Star* article, Moses denied charges that President Johnson had illegally conferred with Midwest Video executives after the family business holdings had been placed in a blind trust shortly after he assumed the presidency in November 1963. The FCC eventually refused to overturn the ruling, and late in 1964, Capital Cable bought out TV Cable. Barron, "The Johnson Money"; Louis M. Kohlmeier, "FCC's Disclosure of Stock-Option Terms Clears Way for Decision in Austin TV Case," *Wall Street Journal,* 27 April 1964; "Lawyer for TV Cable Alleges Capital Cable and Johnson Family Station Misled FCC," *Wall Street Journal,* 29 April 1964; "Austin TV Company Takes Over A Rival," *New York Times,* 18 November 1964.

61. Jenkins was likely referring to a December 1954 incident, recounted in the Barron article, in which both the CBS and ABC networks chose to affiliate with the Johnson-owned (and newly FCC-licensed) KANG-TV station in the Waco market. The choice was a surprise, because KANG, a UHF station, was selected over rival KWTX, a VHF station, at a time when the networks were shifting to the VHF broadcast standard. Barron, "The Johnson Money."

was an expedited consideration, and it was denied. And . . . by the time I got through, there wasn't much left in the article. They said they had a big job of reconsideration to do on the whole article. We will have to see what happens now.

Leonard had given me a very helpful clipping from the *New York Times* that said that [in] places frequented by the President, installations of telephonic nature were permanently installed and mentioned his cousin [Oriole Bailey] as an example. I showed them this clipping to establish that the fact there was a telephone at [A.W.] Moursund's house didn't indicate in any way that it was there where they could talk business, and that it was there for any place that he—[62]

An operator conversation interrupts the recording.

  6:36 P.M.: The President discussed plans in the Cabinet Room for future press conferences with George Reedy, McGeorge Bundy, Bill Moyers, Jack Valenti, Horace Busby, Douglass Cater, and Deputy Assistant Secretary of State for Public Affairs James Greenfield.

  6:45 P.M.: Called the White House operator to request that Walter Jenkins join the meeting.

  7:33 P.M.: Returned to the Mansion to prepare for an evening State Dinner honoring Israeli Prime Minister Eshkol.

    This event featured a performance of "An Evening of Bach" by violinist Mischa Elman and the Swingle Singers.

---

62. The article specifically mentioned a phone installed in the home of Johnson's cousin, Oriole Bailey. Apparently, the *Washington Star* reporters had pursued the possibility that a phone installed in the Texas ranch home of Johnson friend and business partner A.W. Moursund indicated an intent to evade limitations on the President's control of his business interests, which had been placed in a blind trust codirected by Moursund. "President's Trips Stir Quite A Fuss," *New York Times*, 29 May 1964.

Tuesday, June 2, 1964

We've been saying to these congressional committees that we have been looking at these . . . all of these alternatives that we've been talking about, these four main alternatives, all along. The one we haven't been taking up for any serious study is the alternative of pulling out of Southeast Asia. But the other alternatives, we've been looking at. And that we're on the track of supporting the Vietnamese and giving— letting—giving them the chance to win that war. The other alternative of enlarging the war is a very serious one. We don't rule that out, but that that is . . . that's a very serious matter and that the President will be in touch with congressional leaders if we have to move that way. Now, that's what I've been saying in executive sessions.

—Dean Rusk to President Johnson

The outlines of the 1964 presidential campaign took on a more fixed form on June 2, as Arizona Senator Barry Goldwater won a surprise victory in the critical California primary. The win gave Goldwater the state's 86 delegates to the Republican National Convention and pushed him to within 30 of the total number of delegates necessary to secure the nomination. Although the ABC and CBS television networks projected Goldwater as the winner shortly after the polls closed, NBC, United Press International, and the Associated Press all refused to declare a winner in the contest because of the narrow margins that separated Goldwater and New York Governor Nelson Rockefeller. Goldwater would eventually be declared the winner on June 3 by a margin of 59,000 votes, most of which had been secured in Southern California.[1]

The California primary had important implications for the Democrats as well, as former White House Press Secretary Pierre Salinger defeated State Controller Alan Cranston for the party's nomination to run for the seat of cancer-stricken Senator Clair Engle. Salinger's victory represented a setback for California Governor Edmund G. Brown, who had backed Cranston in an unsuccessful struggle for dominance of the state party against State Assembly Speaker Jesse Unruh. The Johnson White House had attempted to remain neutral in the contest.[2] President Johnson would not learn of these results until late in the day.

Focused on the more immediate concerns of legislative tactics and news management, Johnson hosted his regular Tuesday morning breakfast with the Democratic House and Senate leaders and his key aides.[3] When the breakfast ended shortly after 10:00 A.M., the leaders accompanied Johnson to the Oval Office and remained there for a few minutes before departing.

Over the following 35 minutes, the President and many of his key advisers engaged in last-minute preparations for a previously unscheduled presidential press briefing that would take place shortly after 11:00. An article in the day's *Washington Post* had noted that Johnson had not held a press conference for an unprecedented three weeks and speculated that Johnson had either listened to critics who argued that his visibility had been so high as to risk overexposure or wanted to avoid difficult questions about Southeast Asia.[4] An insatiable reader of newspapers, the President would certainly have noticed the article.

10:25 A.M.: Unrecorded call to McGeorge Bundy.
10:29 A.M.: Unrecorded call to Bundy.
10:32 A.M.: Unrecorded call to Walter Jenkins.
10:36 A.M.: Unrecorded call to Jenkins.
10:37 A.M.: Meeting with Jenkins.

---

1. Lawrence E. Davies, "Goldwater Clings to Thin Lead in Bitter California Primary," *New York Times*, 3 June 1964; Charles Mohr, "California Vote Puts Goldwater Near Nomination," *New York Times*, 4 June 1964.
2. Gladwin Hill, "Salinger Winner in Bid for Senate," *New York Times*, 3 June 1964.
3. For the meeting agenda, see Lawrence F. O'Brien, "Memorandum To The President; Subject: Possible Items for Discussion at Leadership Breakfast," 2 June 1964, "Ex FG 400/ MC 11/22/63–6/15/64" folder, Box 328, White House Central Files: Federal Government Operations, Lyndon B. Johnson Library.
4. "LBJ's Talk Not Flowing So Freely," *Washington Post*, 2 June 1964.

10:40 A.M.: Unrecorded call to Bill Moyers.

10:42 A.M.: Meeting with Moyers, Bundy, and Jack Valenti.

10:55 A.M.: Unrecorded call to George Reedy.

11:01 A.M.

From George Reedy[5]

In the first recorded conversation of the day, Reedy informed the President that the press corps was ready to enter the office.

A scattered and mostly inaudible office conversation precedes the call.

Jack Valenti: George?

George Reedy: Yeah.

Valenti: What's the reply on [McGeorge] Bundy? He was going to talk to—

A brief interruption of the recording occurs.

Reedy: [*Unclear*] has not been notified yet.

President Johnson: All right.

Reedy: I'm ready to go anytime, sir.

President Johnson: All right. I'd bring them on in, then.

Reedy: Can I get the photographers in first and get them out of the way?

President Johnson: Yeah. Mm-hmm.

Reedy: OK.

President Johnson: But get them out in a minute or so. Get them on out.

Reedy: Right. I'll bring them right in, sir, as soon as I get them assembled in here.

President Johnson: All right.

Reedy: OK.

11:03 A.M.: Bill Moyers joined George Reedy, Jack Valenti, and Richard Goodwin in the office and all remained throughout the press conference.

5. Tape WH6406.01, Citation #3606, Recordings of Telephone Conversations—White House Series, Recordings and Transcripts of Conversations and Meetings, Lyndon B. Johnson Library.

11:05 A.M.: Reporters entered the office and gathered around the President's desk.

11:05 A.M.–11:30 A.M.: An unscheduled, unannounced press conference was held in the Oval Office.

Johnson made a lengthy statement that reasserted the United States' commitment to defend the nations of Southeast Asia "against Communist encroachment," summarized the latest domestic economic statistics, and restated the administration's position on the federal debt limit and the excise tax issue. He then fielded questions about the civil rights bill, the Medicare proposal, Robert F. Kennedy's rumored plans to run for the Senate from New York, reconnaissance flights over Cuba, and Wisconsin Representative Melvin R. Laird's recent charge that the administration planned to launch military strikes in North Vietnam (Johnson stated that Laird did not speak for the administration).

11:30 A.M.: Unrecorded call to Valenti.

11:31 A.M.: Valenti joined the President in the office.

11:32 A.M.: Unrecorded call to Reedy.

11:33 A.M.–11:44 A.M.: Meeting with Robert Meyner, former governor of New Jersey.

11:40 A.M.: Unrecorded call to Moyers while meeting with Meyner.

11:45 A.M.: Unrecorded call to Valenti.

11:55 A.M.: Departed for a meeting in the Cabinet Room and commented on the sound of his staff's clattering typewriters: "Goodness, that sounds good."

11:55 A.M.–12:15 P.M.: Meeting in the Cabinet Room with the Joint Committee of the United Italian American Labor Council and the Order of the Sons of Italy.

This group included officials of the United Textile Workers, the Amalgamated Clothing Workers, the International Ladies' Garment Workers' Union, and the Order of the Sons of Italy. The meeting was primarily ceremonial, as Johnson signed a new immigration bill and declared Columbus Day a national holiday.[6] Before beginning the ceremony, Johnson called the operator and requested ten cups of coffee.

---

6. The 1964 immigration reforms were of far less consequence than the Hart-Celler reforms passed the following year. The latter legislation transformed the U.S. immigration system and over the following generation remade the demographic face of the nation.

12:15 P.M.: Unrecorded call to Valenti.

12:20 P.M.: Special Assistant Ralph Dungan entered the office and introduced former Congressman Hamer Budge.[7]

12:21 P.M.–12:29 P.M.: Meeting with Budge and Dungan.

12:30 P.M.: Unrecorded call to Walter Jenkins.

12:32 P.M.: Dungan returned with William Jones, with whom he met until 12:51.

12:35 P.M.

To John McClellan[8]

With Jones and Dungan still in the office, Johnson made a call to Senator John L. McClellan of Arkansas. The conversation focused on an investigative report that had apparently undermined, if not eliminated, a candidate for a federal judgeship in Arkansas. Much of the conversation is closed under deed of gift restriction.

A brief, inaudible office conversation precedes the call.
John McClellan: Hello? Mr. President?
President Johnson: Yes?
McClellan: John McClellan.
President Johnson: Yes, John, how are you?
McClellan: All right. They said that you wanted to talk to me about—
President Johnson: Yeah, yeah.
McClellan: —this judgeship matter. Now, I just asked Jack [Valenti]—
President Johnson: Well, now, wait a minute—
McClellan: —to find out if it was all right for me to see whatever file you had—
President Johnson: Yeah . . . yeah.

---

7. Budge was a former Republican congressman from Idaho and a candidate for a vacant Republican position on the Securities and Exchange Commission. For plans to hold the meeting, see Johnson to Ralph Dungan, 11:21 A.M., 26 May 1964, in Guian A. McKee, ed., *The Presidential Recordings, Lyndon B. Johnson: Toward the Great Society, February 1, 1964–May 31, 1964,* vol. 6, *April 14, 1964–May 31, 1964* (New York: Norton, 2007), pp. 834–38. Also, George Reedy to Johnson, 12:02 P.M., 25 May 1964, ibid., pp. 812–14.
8. Tape WH6406.01, Citations #3608 and #3609, Recordings of Telephone Conversations— White House Series, Recordings and Transcripts of Conversations and Meetings, Lyndon B. Johnson Library.

McClellan: —whatever—if it wasn't confidential.

President Johnson: Yeah. I don't know whether it is or not, but anything I got, you can look at.

McClellan: All right.

President Johnson: I'd just . . . I'd treat it that way. I'd treat it as confidential, but you can come look at it anytime you want to.

McClellan: Well, Mr. President, I wonder if there's anything in there that I should know that would influence me—that ought to influence me—with respect to this appointment. All I've ever tried to get to this appointment—tell me what the hell is wrong—

President Johnson: Wait a minute; let me get it. It's on my desk, and I'm over here. Wait just a second.

McClellan: Well . . . [*Brief pause as Johnson goes away from the line and confers with someone.*]

President Johnson: Hello?

McClellan: Yes.

President Johnson: Um . . .

McClellan: Why don't you just let Jack show it to me, if it's all right?

President Johnson: That's all right. I'll be glad to; you just run by anytime you want to, and—

McClellan: All right. [*Unclear*]—

President Johnson: —if I'm here, I'd love to see you. . . .

McClellan: Just let Jack show it to me. That's all right. Now, Mr. President, you know I'd just as soon have Oren Harris back.[9] I'd [*unclear*] rather have Oren, but we can't do that now.

President Johnson: Mm-hmm, mm-hmm, mm-hmm.

McClellan: You know what I mean?

President Johnson: Mm-hmm.

McClellan: And a situation is developing down there [in Arkansas] where the workload is getting to where we need another court. And I've got—if I'm not going to do either of these things, see, I've got to begin to find us somebody down there that . . . to take this appointment. And I'm reluctant, goddamn it—Lyndon?

President Johnson: Yeah.

---

9. Representative Oren Harris was a Democrat from El Dorado, Arkansas, and the chairman of the House Committee on Interstate and Foreign Commerce. He had served in the House since 1941. McClellan's wish that Harris be considered for the federal judgeship would eventually be fulfilled: In February 1966, Harris resigned from Congress to accept an appointment as U.S. district judge for the Eastern and Western districts of Arkansas. *Biographical Directory of the United States Congress, 1774–Present*, http://bioguide.congress.gov/biosearch/biosearch.asp.

McClellan: I'm reluctant to go through the . . . Justice Department. I'll do it. I don't understand: I call down there, and I don't get any return calls sometimes, and I just don't know what the heck's going on.

Nine minutes and twenty-nine seconds excised under deed of gift restriction.

McClellan: Well, let me . . . Listen—Hello?

President Johnson: Yeah.

McClellan: You just hold it. I won't ask to see it now. What I'll do now, I'll go down state, and I'll check and see about submitting a name of someone else. And—

President Johnson: You do it. You get your—

McClellan: —of course, I'd rather have Oren Harris than anybody, but I can't ask him to quit—

President Johnson: I would too. . . . I would too.

McClellan: —that would be—undeservedly. Oren would be just fine. Well anyhow, let's just hold it in abeyance.

President Johnson: We'll just ride it, and we'll just do what you want done. You just try to get . . . I just want you-all to be pleased. You-all got to confirm him, and . . . don't say I told you this because I'm—

McClellan: Oh, I won't. . . . Oh, I won't. I always try. What I look— Goddamn, get the Justice Department to sit down with me and go over this thing and show me what the hell they said was wrong. Well, you give me—they never would talk to me about it, never did give it to me.

President Johnson: Well, don't you tell them I did because—

McClellan: No, I won't. I won't.

President Johnson: —you know they'll get a fight with the FBI, and . . .

McClellan: I won't, and let's forget about it, and I'll—

President Johnson: I just . . . Anything I've got you can have anytime you want it.

McClellan: Now listen: I'll begin working towards finding a candidate to submit.

President Johnson: That's good.

McClellan: I'll do that.

President Johnson: That's good.

McClellan: And in the meantime, I got your bill out this morning.[10]

---

10. Senator McClellan chaired the Senate Government Operations Committee, which on 4 June would report a bill to extend the Reorganization Act of 1949. This legislation gave the president authority to consolidate, transfer, or abolish federal agencies subject to a 60-day congressional review. It had expired on 1 June 1963, and the new bill reinstated it. *Congressional Quarterly Almanac,* 88th Cong., 2nd sess., 1964, vol. 20 (Washington, DC: Congressional Quarterly Service, 1965), p. 425.

President Johnson: Wonderful. That reorganization?

McClellan: Yeah. . . .

President Johnson: Good.

McClellan: I've been trying to get old [Wayne] Morse to relax.[11] He never—relent—he never would, and so I called the committee. I called it last week for today thinking this would be the best day to get a quorum, and I had a quorum. Just a quorum, nothing less. [*Both laugh.*] So I got it out.

President Johnson: Wonderful, John. Thank you.

McClellan: All right.

President Johnson: Now, you let me know what you want to do, and take your time, and whatever you want to do, we'll work out.

McClellan: All right, and I want you to know I appreciate this very much.

President Johnson: I know that. Well, you're entitled—

McClellan: I'll swear to everyone that if I could be goddamned—

President Johnson: You've been here the long—

McClellan: —sit down with me and go over it like . . . like they should. But just, come out [*unclear*], "We just can't do it." That doesn't add up to me.

President Johnson: I told them I wanted to see it, and they just sent me a summary. They say it's six inches thick, but I went over everything I've got with you, and I'll do whatever you think you ought to do on it.

McClellan: OK, Lyndon.

President Johnson: And I think you're entitled to plenty [of] consideration. You'll always get it as long as I'm here.

McClellan: All right.

President Johnson: Bye.

McClellan: Thank you kindly. Bye.

12:56 P.M.: Meeting in the office with Secretary of the Interior Stewart L. Udall, Budget Director Kermit Gordon, their under secretaries and assistant secretaries, Associate Counsel Lee White, and the administrator of the Bonneville Dam.

12:58 P.M.–1:01 P.M.: Greeted a group of people in the Cabinet Room who were meeting with Ralph Dungan.

Attendees included Edgar Kaiser of Kaiser Industries, Harold Linder of the Export-Import Bank, Indian industrialist

---

11. Wayne Morse was a Democratic senator from Oregon.

G. D. Berla, National Security Council staff member Robert
Komer, and attorney Lloyd Cutler.

1:01 P.M.–1:30 P.M.: Returned to the previous meeting being held in
the office.

1:40 P.M.: Unrecorded call to Walter Jenkins.

1:42 P.M.: Joined Jack Valenti for lunch in the White House Mansion,
followed by a nap.

3:30 P.M.: Unrecorded call from the Mansion to attorney Robert B.
Anderson, the former secretary of the Treasury, in New York.

3:30 P.M.: Returned to the office after stopping in the Cabinet Room
to meet two of daughter Lynda's professors from George
Washington University.

A series of brief recorded calls followed Johnson's return to the office. The
first was to McGeorge Bundy, who briefed the President on an upcoming
meeting with Israeli Prime Minister Levi Eshkol and offered advice on a
number of other matters, including Robert B. Anderson's recent meeting
with French President Charles de Gaulle.

3:56 P.M.

To McGeorge Bundy[12]

*Before informing him that Bundy is on the line, the secretary tells the
President that Robert Anderson has called.*

President Johnson: Mac? Who's going to carry on these discussions
[with Israeli Prime Minister Levi Eshkol] this afternoon? What are we
supposed to do?

McGeorge Bundy: You've got a memo from [Robert] Komer which
summarizes it.[13] Everybody's in a good mood, and the communiqué is

---

12. Tape WH6406.01, Citation #3610, Recordings of Telephone Conversations—White House
Series, Recordings and Transcripts of Conversations and Meetings, Lyndon B. Johnson Library.
13. A member of the National Security Council staff, Komer advised the President to push
Israeli Prime Minister Eshkol to reassure Egyptian President Nasser that Israel's Dimona
nuclear reactor was intended for peaceful purposes only and to accept international controls
on its nuclear program. This memorandum is summarized by the State Department historians
in "Memorandum from Robert W. Komer of the National Security Council Staff to President
Johnson," 3 June 1964, U.S. Department of State, *Foreign Relations of the United States* (*FRUS*),
1964–1968: Arab-Israeli Dispute, 1964–1967, ed. Harriet Dashiell Schwar (Washington, DC:
GPO, 2000), 18:n. 2.

agreed, and all you need to do is apply one more coat of paint to the Prime Minister, and it doesn't need to be long. Did you do that intelligence talk with him? Have you done that part?

President Johnson: Yeah.

Bundy: Well then, I think you really—it's a replay, Mr. President. It doesn't have to be long.

President Johnson: Well, tell the State people—

Bundy: The thing to do, I think, if you don't want to carry it heavy is not to have too much of a—to have ten minutes privately, and then bring him in and go back and forth in the Cabinet Room, and I'll tell the State people to be ready to take a lead.

President Johnson: All right. That's what we'll do, then. He'll come in here [in] ten minutes. I may run a little late. How late can I keep him? Five minutes?

Bundy: Oh, sure. Actually, the prompter the better, Mr. President, that you—It's better to have him prompt and get out early.

President Johnson: All right. Well, my problem is, I've got [Robert] Anderson calling me back on the other phone right now.

Bundy: Bob Anderson?

President Johnson: Yeah.

Bundy: Aye-aye.

President Johnson: He's rather insistent that we—

Bundy: I know he is.

President Johnson: —make that call [to French President Charles de Gaulle], and I don't . . . my instinct's against it—[14]

Bundy: I don't . . . I really don't think it matters. My instinct is not strong; I just—I was presenting his arguments. My own view is with George [Ball] going in on Friday afternoon, and with the language barrier, a nice, friendly, warm letter from you is just as good, Mr. President. I think that the old boy is using the telephone because he thinks *you* want to. He's never been fond of the telephone.

President Johnson: Mm-hmm. Mm-hmm.

Bundy: And in fact, the legend is he never uses it.

President Johnson: Mm-hmm. OK. . . .

Bundy: But Bob's a pretty determined fellow. [*Chuckles.*]

---

14. Anderson had received an unexpected invitation to meet the French president while in Europe the previous week. De Gaulle had requested an improvement in communications, and since his return Anderson had argued repeatedly that President Johnson should call de Gaulle. Johnson had spoken to Anderson slightly more than 20 minutes earlier. See McGeorge Bundy to Johnson, 1:04 P.M., 1 June 1964, in this volume.

President Johnson: You hear anything from out there [in Hono-lulu]?[15]

Bundy: No. You have no cables from out there, and we weren't planning any phone calls. They'll be back in tomorrow morning, but I *can* get you an overnight report, if you want one.

President Johnson: No . . . no.

Bundy: [I'd] just as soon let them finish their work, I think.

President Johnson: Yeah. OK.

Bundy: I thought that went very well this morning, Mr. President, and I think the tickers are very good.[16]

President Johnson: OK.

Bundy: [*Unclear.*]

President Johnson: [Melvin] Laird's saying that . . . Laird's saying that [Robert] McNamara has given them a plan for invasion of the north [Vietnam].[17] Well, all I said was that . . .

Bundy: You said you knew of no such plan.

President Johnson: That I knew of no such plan. I don't mean that I . . . that we haven't got plans for any contingency—

Bundy: Of course you have.

President Johnson: —but I've approved no plan to invade anything.

Bundy: Why don't you have George [Reedy] clarify that if you think it's worth it. I'll talk to him about it. But I think—I'd just leave it alone. I'd just leave it alone. I wouldn't get into an argument with Laird; he's too small.

President Johnson: OK.

Bundy: All right, sir.

Johnson next returned Robert B. Anderson's call. On the basis of a lunch that day with Dwight Eisenhower, under whom he had been a Cabinet member, Anderson suggested that it would be valuable for Johnson to consult with the former president about the situation in Southeast Asia.

---

15. Johnson was referring to the ongoing meetings of top U.S. national security officials in Hawaii.

16. Bundy was referring to the unscheduled press conference that the President had conducted earlier in the day.

17. Wisconsin Representative Melvin R. Laird's actual statement had been that the administration had prepared a plan for an attack on the north. Lewis Hawkins, "Plans for Viet Strike North Told," *Washington Post*, 1 June 1964.

3:59 P.M.

To Robert Anderson[18]

President Johnson: Hello?

Robert Anderson: Mr. President?

President Johnson: Yeah, Bob.

Anderson: I have been thinking over what you asked me about. Now, I had lunch today with President Eisenhower, and for the opposition you could not have a greater admirer than he is. Why don't you ask him to come down and talk to you about this thing in Southeast Asia?

President Johnson: [*Pauses.*] Well, I've given a lot of thought to that, and I rather think I ought to before we . . . I know we ought to before we make any . . . definite, hard plans to do more than we are doing. It's . . . the situation has not materially changed in the last 90 days under [Nguyen] Khanh's operation.[19] It's changed at home because they're writing articles about it and the Scripps Howard and others are kind of promoting a panic.[20] On the other hand, we're not getting anywhere with what we're doing.

Anderson: Yeah.

President Johnson: And I'm restless with that, and I don't want to get tied down in an Asiatic war. . . .

Anderson: [*Unclear*] I told you a while ago I think something's got to be done that's more than ordinary. Now, what that more than ordinary is, I don't know. But . . . I know that from having lunch with him today—and I have told him all the things you've told me. And he's a great admirer. And so I was just thinking over after I hung up the telephone talking to you.[21] He's going back to Gettysburg today. It just might be the solution to it.

President Johnson: Mm-hmm.

---

18. Tape WH6406.01, Citation #3611, Recordings of Telephone Conversations—White House Series, Recordings and Transcripts of Conversations and Meetings, Lyndon B. Johnson Library.

19. General Nguyen Khanh served as prime minister of the Republic of Vietnam (South Vietnam). Khanh had seized power in January from a military junta that itself had violently overthrown the government of Ngo Dinh Diem in November 1963.

20. Reporter Jim Lucas of the Scripps Howard Newspaper Alliance had recently written at least one critical article regarding the progress of the U.S. effort in South Vietnam. See Johnson to Richard Russell, 10:55 A.M., 27 May 1964, in McKee, *The Presidential Recordings, Johnson*, vol. 6, *April 14, 1964–May 31, 1964*, pp. 871–85.

21. Anderson was referring to an unrecorded telephone conversation that President Johnson and he had conducted 30 minutes earlier.

Anderson: And then you've got no ... Well, then you've got both sides.

President Johnson: Mm-hmm.

Anderson: Because after all, when you get over in a place like that, politics end.

President Johnson: It sure ought to.

Anderson: It sure ought to, and I think it will.

President Johnson: Mm-hmm.

Anderson: And this is the man that ... he's got a military background, a military history. I think he'd be very responsive, and I just got to thinking about it after you and I talked. Why don't you do it that way?

President Johnson: Hmm. OK, Bob, that's good. [*Sighs.*] When are you going to be down this way?

Anderson: Whenever you say. I will not be down there this week unless you want me to.

President Johnson: Mm-hmm.

Anderson: Now, I am preparing a reply to the letter that you got from our friend in Texarkana.

President Johnson: Mm-hmm.

Anderson: Walker [Stone] sent it up to me.[22]

President Johnson: Yeah.

Anderson: I'll get that back to you sometime in the next few days.

President Johnson: All right. I'm going up to the Coast Guard Academy tomorrow.[23] How far is that from where you are?

Anderson: Well, that's ... a hundred miles.[24]

President Johnson: Mm-hmm, mm-hmm.

Anderson: Now that I'm thinking of it, maybe 50.

President Johnson: Mm-hmm.

Anderson: But I'm always at your service, you know. I would think that what we ought to do is talk about it down there.

President Johnson: Mm-hmm.

Anderson: But I just happened to think that I was ... I had lunch with him today, and we talked about a lot of things. We talked about a lot of ... possibilities for American [*unclear*], and he's a great admirer. Really great admirer. And so afterwards, you and I had talked a while ago about this stuff. I said to myself, "Well, why in the world don't we just get both groups in here?"

---

22. Walker Stone was the editor in chief of the Scripps Howard newspaper chain.
23. The President would give the commencement address at the U.S. Coast Guard Academy in New London, Connecticut.
24. Anderson was in New York City.

President Johnson: I'm just thinking that maybe I could get a heli-copter to pick you up and fly over and come back down here with me, but maybe it'd be better just to meet directly.

Anderson: I think it would be better because if we did it that way, why, everything would be in public notice and all this sort of thing.

President Johnson: Yeah. OK, I'll probably give you a ring tomor-row.

Anderson: OK, my friend.

President Johnson: Bye.

Anderson: Thank you.

Johnson next placed a call to McGeorge Bundy, who called him back a few minutes later. Bundy updated the President on efforts to manage the reaction of Arab nations to the visit of Israeli Prime Minister Eshkol. Over the previous week, diplomats from most of the major Arab countries had publicly and privately criticized the Eshkol meeting, warning that it would undermine U.S.-Arab relations.[25] When Eshkol arrived on June 1, 13 of the Arab embassies issued a joint statement that condemned the visit and suggested, correctly, that the talks involved negotiations for the sale of military equipment to Israel. Although the administration denied the lat-ter claim, the meetings with the Israelis had advanced the arrangements for a secret U.S. sale of tanks to Israel through the United Kingdom and West Germany. Bundy reported on Under Secretary of State George Ball's meeting on the issue with the ambassadors from the 13 Arab countries.[26]

4:05 P.M.

From McGeorge Bundy[27]

President Johnson: Yeah?

McGeorge Bundy: He [George Ball] had them in. He had him for about a half an hour, and he gave them a pretty brisk talk about how this was a totally uncalled for effort to influence American opinion when a man

---

25. "Circular Telegram from the Department of State to Certain Posts," 26 May 1964, *FRUS, 1964–1968*, 18:143–44.

26. "U.S. Reprimands Arab Envoys for Criticism of Eshkol's visit," *New York Times*, 3 June 1964.

27. Tape WH6406.01, Citation #3612, Recordings of Telephone Conversations—White House Series, Recordings and Transcripts of Conversations and Meetings, Lyndon B. Johnson Library.

was here as the guest of the President of the United States. And they said well, they had always done it before when [former Israeli Prime Minister David] Ben Gurion came, and he said no, that they might have made informal comments, but this kind of concerted statement by a bunch of ambassadors accredited *to* the President of the United States—or rather by their press spokesman—was wholly unacceptable, and we took a very dim view of it.[28] And it was particularly offensive that they should have accused us of being subject to influence in an election year by any group of this kind, and he said the man who spoke up most in answer was the UAR [United Arab Republic] man, the man you had privately just a little while ago, but that he thought he was probably just trying to show his colleagues that [Gamel Abdel] Nasser's man was brave.[29] But he kept right after them, and they went out, he thought, fairly chastened. Now, we'll make no announcement to this effect, but we will plan to let it be known that we have expressed our dim view of this statement, unless you want it put more strongly than that.

President Johnson: That's good. That's fine. Did you go over the press conference? Was that all right?

Bundy: Yes, it's come out all right, Mr. President.

President Johnson: All right.

Bundy: No problem.

3:30 P.M.: Israeli Prime Minister Eshkol arrived at the Oval Office for his second private meeting with Johnson in two days.

4:11 P.M.

From McGeorge Bundy[30]

Bundy called once more as the meeting began, inquiring about whether George Ball's upcoming meeting with Charles de Gaulle should be announced to the press.

---

28. David Ben Gurion had been the founding prime minister of Israel; he held the office over several different periods, the last of which had concluded in 1963.

29. Bundy was referring to Ambassador Mustafa Kamel from the United Arab Republic, the loose coalition of Arab states headed by Egypt, of which Nasser was president. Kamel had met with President Johnson on 25 May.

30. Tape WH6406.01, Citation #3613, Recordings of Telephone Conversations—White House Series, Recordings and Transcripts of Conversations and Meetings, Lyndon B. Johnson Library.

A brief, unclear office conversation precedes the call.

President Johnson: Yeah?

McGeorge Bundy: Mr. President, you can do this yes or no. We have a clearance from the Elysée to announce [George] Ball's visit to [Charles] de Gaulle. I think we'd better do it now than have it look like it's a crisis coming out of Honolulu tomorrow. We can put it on George's [Reedy's] afternoon briefing, if you want. It would—

President Johnson: Yeah. That's all right.

Bundy: All right.

Johnson met privately with Prime Minister Eshkol for slightly less than 15 minutes. The State Department Office of the Historian has found no record of this meeting. The next day, however, National Security Council staff member Robert Komer reported to Johnson that "your soft sell to Eshkol connected a lot better than we realized yesterday." Komer was referring to the final meetings of the visit on the morning of June 3, in which Johnson did not participate, and in which the Israelis consented to International Atomic Energy Agency controls on its nuclear programs, including a controversial research effort to develop water desalination technology that employed nuclear power, and to a U.S. effort to mollify Nasser's concerns about the Dimona reactor.[31]

At 4:25, Johnson and Eshkol joined Komer, Under Secretary of State for Political Affairs W. Averell Harriman, U.S. Ambassador to Israel Walworth Barbour, Assistant Secretary of State for Near Eastern and South Asian Affairs Phillips Talbot, Israeli Deputy Defense Minister Shimon Peres, and a number of other Israeli officials in the Cabinet Room for a brief final meeting that appears to have been little more than a formality. The two heads of state issued a joint communiqué that endorsed the territorial integrity of all nations in the Middle East and opposed the use or threat of force by any nation in the region. The *New York Times* emphasized that the importance of the statement lay not in its actual content, but in the fact that its shared provenance demonstrated de facto U.S. support for Israel.[32]

4:31 P.M.: Unrecorded call to George Reedy.

4:34 P.M.: Unrecorded call to Jack Valenti.

4:35 P.M.: Unrecorded call to Reedy.

---

31. "Memorandum From Robert W. Komer of the National Security Council Staff to President Johnson," 3 June 1964, *FRUS, 1964–1968*, 18:163.

32. "U.S. Reprimands Arab Envoys."

4:36 P.M.: Brief meeting with Valenti and McGeorge Bundy.

4:38 P.M.: Walked with Bundy around the South Grounds, stopping to play with his dogs.

After returning to the office, Johnson received a call from Secretary of State Dean Rusk, who was in Honolulu for the meeting of top civilian and military officials on U.S. policy in Southeast Asia. Bundy joined the President on the line, and Valenti remained in the room. Rusk and Defense Secretary McNamara planned to hold a short news conference on the Honolulu discussions, and they felt that they needed to know how President Johnson had responded at his own press conference to questions about Representative Melvin Laird's recent charge that the administration planned to attack North Vietnam.[33] The conversation involved only a short discussion of the actual content of the Honolulu meetings.

4:55 P.M.

From Dean Rusk; President Johnson joined by McGeorge Bundy[34]

McGeorge Bundy: Hello, Dean?

Dean Rusk: Yes [*unclear*]—

Bundy: Mac Bundy. The President's coming right on.

Rusk: Right. [*Brief pause as the President comes on the line.*]

President Johnson: Hello?

Rusk: Mr. President?

President Johnson: Yes.

Rusk: Bob McNamara and I have the feel that we should have a brief backgrounder out here to try to cut down, if we can, some of the excitement about this meeting. We plan to have it in about an hour's time. But one of the questions we need to check with you on is this matter of your press conference statement and the way [Melvin] Laird tried to pick that up.[35] Now, this is a phony issue he's raised, because the departments of State and Defense have a responsibility of always looking at all contingencies that might develop in any situation, but the truth is that we have

---

33. Despite the Rusk-McNamara press conference, coverage of the meeting the following day was limited. Max Frankel, "Honolulu Parley on Asia Is Ended," *New York Times*, 3 June 1964.
34. Tape WH6406.01, Citation #3614, Recordings of Telephone Conversations—White House Series, Recordings and Transcripts of Conversations and Meetings, Lyndon B. Johnson Library.
35. See Johnson to McGeorge Bundy 3:56 P.M., 2 June 1964, in this chapter.

not put—laid before *you* any such plan as he was referring to for your consideration and approval. Now, what is your judgment as to how we ought to play that particular point out here?

President Johnson: I think that . . . if they get into the Laird question, I'd say Laird is talking about . . . contingencies and possibilities and . . . potentialities, and Johnson's talking—

Rusk: You're talking about approval [*unclear*].

President Johnson: —about a program and a decision.

Rusk: Yeah. Yeah.

President Johnson: And there's a good deal of difference between the two. We have plans for every . . . for every contingency, but that does not mean that that is an administration plan to go into North Vietnam.

Rusk: That's right, if [*unclear*]—

President Johnson: Now, McNamara—

Rusk: Those contingencies are not policy.

President Johnson: That's right. Now, McNamara's statement, which I have—

[*to Bundy*] Mac, see if you can get that to Jack [Valenti] right quick.

Bundy: Executive session.

President Johnson: [*with Rusk acknowledging*] In an executive session, he just says we've got a program for going into North Vietnam, and we're all ready. And Laird takes that as an administration program. And I imagine that General [Maxwell] Taylor has got a plan for Cuba, and maybe he's got one for Honolulu and Pearl Harbor.[36] But that doesn't mean that that's this administration. Now, what he said . . . Mr. Laird, over the weekend—"Mr. President . . ." over the weekend, Laird declared that the administration is preparing to move the Vietnam war into the north. Now, I don't know whether we're preparing to do that or not. I've got no preparations to do it on my desk. Now, you might recommend something like that down the road, but tha—not here. That's my feeling. So I said . . . I would say, "Mr. Laird is not as yet speaking for the administration. He might next year sometime. [To] my knowledge he has no authority to speak at this time."

[*reading from a transcript of the morning's press conference, with Rusk acknowledging*] "Question: 'Mr. President, does that mean that you expect the Republicans to win?' 'No, that means just what I said: He doesn't have any authority to speak for it now. He could at some other time.' 'Regardless of whether Mr. Laird is a spokesman or not, is there any

---

36. General Maxwell D. Taylor served as chairman of the Joint Chiefs of Staff.

substance to what he said?' President: 'I know of no plans that have been made to that effect.'" That is, to take the war into . . . move the Vietnam war into the north. Now, I think that's a truthful statement. I haven't got any plans to move it in there. I don't know what y'all are going to do. Now, here's what he's basing his on. So that ended. Then I replied again. . . . "I would say that Mr. Laird is not as yet speaking for the administration. He might next year," so on.[37]

Now, here's what McNamara said: "I think the committee might be interested to know—and I assume I can tell you this in confidence, since this is an executive session—that in the recommendations which we presented to the President on March 16 following our visit to South Vietnam at that time, we recommended that preparations be undertaken immediately to be in a position on specified period of notice to carry out the program of military action against North Vietnam, and those actions have been taken, and we are prepared. Now, this is a preparation for United States military action against North Vietnam. The action General [Nguyen] Khanh was referring to was action by South Vietnamese forces against North Vietnam. He is continuing to strengthen his air force. We're taking many actions to assist him to that end. He believes that he'll be prepared for air strikes, effective air strikes, by the end of the year."

Rusk: Yeah.

President Johnson: [*with Rusk acknowledging*] Now, McNamara is talking about planning on contingency and a decision being made. I'm talking about—I have no such plans to do that. Now, I might have them this afternoon; I might have them tomorrow. But I don't have them before me, and I haven't made them now, and he has no right to say that we're going into North Vietnam.

Rusk: Right, right. All right, well then . . . [*unclear*]—

President Johnson: I don't know who's—

Rusk: —gives me the line, and we'll—

President Johnson: I don't know who's right. It looks like that . . . It looks like he has a good basis for what he's saying. I think—

Rusk: Well—

Bundy: I think it's the difference, Dean, isn't it, between—we have a book full of contingency plans, but—

Rusk: That's the point.

Bundy: —we have no current plan for action.

---

37. For a full transcript of the press conference, see "The President's News Conference of June 2, 1964," *Public Papers of the Presidents of the United States: Lyndon B. Johnson, 1963–64* (Washington, DC: GPO, 1965) 1:733–39.

Rusk: Well, we've been saying . . . we've been saying to these congressional committees that we have been looking at these . . . all of these alternatives that we've been talking about, these four main alternatives, all along. The one we haven't been taking up for any serious study is the alternative of pulling out of Southeast Asia. But the other alternatives, we've been looking at. And that we're on the track of supporting the Vietnamese and giving—letting—giving them the chance to win that war. The other alternative of enlarging the war is a very serious one. We don't rule that out, but that that is . . . that's a very serious matter and that the President will be in touch with congressional leaders if we have to move that way. Now, that's what I've been saying in executive sessions.

President Johnson: [*with Rusk acknowledging*] Now, my statement is a little awkward: "I know of no plans that have been made to that effect." That is, to carry the war into Vietnam. Now, I don't mean that we haven't considered the alternative of going in there, and we haven't considered South Vietnamese planes going in there, and taking bombs, and whatnot. But I have approved no plans to carry the . . . and have made no plans at this stage to carry the war into North Vietnam. That's what I was trying to say.

Rusk: Right. Well, I think that gives us a difference, and that's the same difference that Bob McNamara and I feel . . . see out here. And we'll try to get that a little more perspective in a little backgrounder we have.

Bundy: What's your return plan?

Rusk: I beg your pardon?

Bundy: What's your timing for coming back?

Rusk: Well, the backgrounder would come in about an hour's time.

Bundy: Right.

Rusk: Now this is—one thing you should have in mind back there in terms of this meeting—this is at least the 14th meeting that has been held in Honolulu, plus a meeting with Admiral [Harry] Felt and Bob McNamara on five occasions when he's gone to Vietnam.[38]

Bundy: Yeah.

Rusk: So this is not a massive orgasm of something that is wholly new and in—different.

Bundy: Yeah. Yeah.

Rusk: So—

Bundy: We're not playing it any heavier than we can help [*unclear*], back here.

---

38. Admiral Felt served as commander in chief of the Pacific until February of 1964.

Rusk: Yeah. Well, I think we ought to play down any sort of notion of cataclysmic character of this meeting.

Bundy: Couldn't agree more.

President Johnson: Are y'all about through?

Rusk: Yes, sir. We'll be through—we'll be leaving here about 6 [P.M.] this afternoon and be there first thing in the morning.

President Johnson: All right. How . . . Are you reasonably well together?

Rusk: Well, I think I could answer you a little better in the afternoon. We want a private talk with [Henry] Cabot Lodge . . . this afternoon, and we'll try to pull things together with him.[39] But in general I think we're at the moment seeing it pretty much the same way. There may be one or two points we've got to straighten out with him and see what he really thinks about it.

President Johnson: You try to stay there until you wrap that thing up and y'all have . . . are one mind.

Rusk: All right. We'll try—we'll try our . . . do our best to.

President Johnson: All right.

Rusk: All right. Thanks.

President Johnson: Bye.

5:05 P.M.: Unrecorded call to Bill Moyers.

5:07 P.M.–5:11 P.M.: President Johnson met a group of West German newspapermen in the Rose Garden.

5:16 P.M.: Off-the-record meeting with Alex Rose and Timothy Castillo.[40]

5:41 P.M.: Unrecorded call to Walter Jenkins.

5:45 P.M.: Unrecorded call to Jenkins.

5:56 P.M.: Unrecorded call to George Reedy.

6:10 P.M.: Joined by Lady Bird Johnson and Rose, Castillo, State Department Protocol Chief Angier Biddle Duke, and their spouses, Johnson attended a reception at the Mayflower Hotel hosted in his honor by Prime Minister Eshkol.

---

39. Henry Cabot Lodge, a former Republican senator from Massachusetts and the 1960 Republican vice presidential nominee, served as U.S. ambassador to South Vietnam.

40. Alex Rose was the president of the United Hatters, Cap, and Millinery Workers International Union and the vice chair of the New York Liberal Party. He was also a close political ally of the President's. Timothy Castillo remains unidentified.

6:47 P.M.–7:21 P.M.: Attended with Lady Bird the 25th wedding anniversary party of their old friends Dale Miller and his wife at a suite in the hotel.

7:24 P.M.: Departed the Mayflower Hotel with Alex Rose and his wife.

7:35 P.M.–7:45 P.M.: Brief Stop at the Sheraton-Park Hotel to make a brief appearance at a Women's National Democratic Club dinner honoring Adlai Stevenson.

7:24 P.M.: Returned to the White House with the Roses, who then departed.

8:20 P.M.: Returned to the Mansion.

8:30 P.M.: Unrecorded call to Bill Moyers, and then dinner with Lady Bird Johnson.

10:30 P.M.: Unrecorded call to "The Usher."

Less mysteriously, Johnson received an unrecorded call from his former press secretary and current California Senate candidate Pierre Salinger at 12:01 A.M. In the state's primary election earlier in the day, Salinger had won the California Democratic senatorial nomination over State Controller Alan Cranston.

Wednesday, June 3, 1964

You know, I did [expect the Goldwater victory]. I did, but I couldn't get anybody else to believe it. I've been expecting it all along. The polls almost threw the thing off the last ten days, but I think it makes it awful easy for you if they're foolish enough to nominate him. Of course, I think it's easy any [unclear] under any circumstances regardless of who it is, but I think the . . . the state [California] just couldn't be better as far as you're concerned.
                                    —Jesse Unruh to President Johnson

A trip to the U.S. Coast Guard Academy in New London, Connecticut, occupied much of President Johnson's day on June 3. At the academy, Johnson gave the commencement address, inducted the graduating cadets into the Coast Guard, and helped to present both their degrees and their commissions. He also presided at the keel-laying ceremony for the nuclear submarine USS *Pargo* at the Electric Boat Company shipyard in Groton. The President returned to the White House at 3:25 P.M. and went immediately to the Mansion.

4:00 P.M.: Unrecorded call to Walter Jenkins.
4:06 P.M.: Unrecorded call to Jenkins, followed by a nap.
5:35 P.M.: Returned to the office.
5:50 P.M.: Made brief remarks in the Flower Garden before the official U.S. delegation to the ceremonies in Normandy, France, commemorating the 20th anniversary of D-Day and shook hands with members of the delegation.
   Retired General Omar Bradley headed the delegation.

6:00 P.M.–6:27 P.M.: Off-the-record meeting with the presidents of Monsanto Chemical, Dupont, and Union Carbide; McGeorge Bundy joined the meeting at 6:15.

6:26 P.M.: Unrecorded call to Jack Valenti.

6:32 P.M.: Received a briefing in the Cabinet Room on the recently concluded Honolulu meetings of civilian and military officials regarding U.S. policy options in Vietnam.

Secretary of State Dean Rusk, Secretary of Defense Robert McNamara, Chairman of the Joint Chiefs of Staff Maxwell Taylor, and others had just returned that morning from Honolulu. Other attendees at the briefing included National Security Adviser McGeorge Bundy, CIA Director John McCone, Under Secretary of State George Ball, and Assistant Secretary of State for Far Eastern Affairs William Bundy. The State Department's Office of the Historian has found no record of the meeting, and newspaper accounts provided only general indications of the issues discussed.[1]

At 6:50, Johnson excused himself from the briefing and called Jesse Unruh, the speaker of the California House of Representatives, to discuss the previous day's primary in the state. Barry Goldwater had won a narrow but crucial victory in the Republican presidential primary that placed him in a favorable position to secure the party's nomination. In the Democratic senatorial primary, former Kennedy-Johnson Press Secretary Pierre Salinger had defeated State Controller Alan Cranston. Salinger's win had been a victory for Unruh in an internal battle with Governor Pat Brown for dominance of the state party. Brown had endorsed Cranston as a means to restore his influence over the state party, which had diminished after he failed to deliver the state decisively for John F. Kennedy at the 1960 Democratic National Convention in Los Angeles. The Kennedy campaign had then turned to Unruh as its chief representative in California, and Kennedy had continued to rely on him after entering the White House. Reflecting this relationship, Unruh endorsed Salinger when he entered the race on March 19.[2] After receiving Unruh's analysis of the prospects for healing the rift in the party, Johnson sounded out the

---

1. Tad Szulc, "Johnson Confers on Asia Struggle," *New York Times*, 4 June 1964.
2. *Congressional Quarterly Weekly Report*, 15 November 1963, p. 1966; Bill Stout, "California Democrats: Battle Royale for the Senate," *The Reporter*, 7 May 1964.

California politician for his views on the West's continually contentious regional power and water issues.

6:50 P.M.

To Jesse Unruh[3]

President Johnson: Yes. How are you?

Jesse Unruh: [*Unclear*] I'm fine.

President Johnson: Good to hear you.

Unruh: How are you, sir?

President Johnson: Well, what do you think about things out there now?

Unruh: Well, I think it's a great victory for the people.

President Johnson: Good.

Unruh: Great victory for the people, and I think the . . . I think the state's in great shape for you, and we're just waiting for you to come out here in June to show you how much . . . how much it's in shape for you.[4]

President Johnson: Well, that's good. Did you expect this [Barry] Goldwater thing?

Unruh: You know, I did. I did, but I couldn't get anybody else to believe it. I've been expecting it all along. The polls almost [*Johnson whistles*] threw the thing off the last ten days, but I think it makes it awful easy for you if they're foolish enough to nominate him.[5] Of course, I think it's easy any [*unclear*] under any circumstances regardless of who it is, but I think the . . . the state just couldn't be better as far as you're concerned.

President Johnson: Mm-hmm. . . . Mm-hmm. That's good. What—

Unruh: Couldn't be better. Now, I'm willing to . . . I told Jack Valenti I'm going to suggest to the governor [Edmund "Pat" Brown] that he tender the olive branch to Sam Yorty so that we get everybody back

---

3. Tape WH6406.02, Citation #3615, Recordings of Telephone Conversations—White House Series, Recordings and Transcripts of Conversations and Meetings, Lyndon B. Johnson Library.
4. President Johnson would visit California, 19–21 June.
5. Polls during the final weeks of the campaign had projected that New York Governor Nelson Rockefeller would win the California primary. "Rockefeller Given Edge in Primary on Coast Today," *New York Times*, 2 June 1964.

under the tent. Sam ran a pretty good race out here considering the fact that he spent no money.[6]

President Johnson: Yeah . . . yeah.

Unruh: And it wasn't an anti-Johnson vote because he was as strongly for you as anybody was.

President Johnson: Mm-hmm.

Unruh: [*with Johnson acknowledging*] I think it's time we tried to pull everybody back, at least make the effort. If he doesn't want to come, that's another thing, but I think he'd come. I talked to him this morning. And he said gladly, without any question of a doubt, that he's all the way for you. So I thought the smart thing for us to do would be to try to pull him back in.

President Johnson: What do you know about this water thing, this tie-line, the electric line, with the electric companies and Bonneville and the city of Los Angeles?[7] Is that a good thing for us to go into?

Unruh: I think so.

President Johnson: Mm-hmm. Now, what do you know about this compromise worked out between Arizona and California on water?[8] Brown, they say—

Unruh: I'm not that . . . I'm not that conversant with it, so I hesitate to tell you anything, but it looks to me off what the papers and everything are saying out here that it would be a solid political settlement.

President Johnson: Mm-hmm. Well—

---

6. Like Unruh, Los Angeles Mayor Sam Yorty had clashed with Governor Brown. Yorty had fielded an unsuccessful rival slate of presidential nominators against Brown's slate. Both men had pledged their prospective delegations to President Johnson. "Salinger Winner in Bid for Senate," *New York Times*, 3 June 1964.

7. The planned West Coast Power Intertie would consist of four long-distance, super-high-voltage transmission lines that would relay surplus electrical power from the Pacific Northwest to Southern California and other large Southwestern markets. Legislation authorizing the project had passed the Senate and had been reported in the House the previous year, but had been delayed by disputes over the precise allocation of power. The project involved private electrical companies, local governments such as Los Angeles, and the Department of Interior's Bonneville Power Administration (which managed the dams in the Pacific Northwest). *Congressional Quarterly Almanac*, 88th Cong., 2nd sess., 1964, vol. 20 (Washington, DC: Congressional Quarterly Service, 1965), p. 47.

8. Johnson was referring to the Pacific Southwest Water Plan, under which the federal government would enlarge aqueducts in California to bring excess water from northern to Southern California to replace Colorado River water diverted to Arizona cities by a long-planned project of dam and aqueduct construction. For an analysis, see Kermit Gordon to Johnson, 10:04 A.M., 12 May 1964, in Guian A. McKee, ed., *The Presidential Recordings, Lyndon B. Johnson: Toward the Great Society, February 1, 1964–May 31, 1964*, vol. 6, *April 14, 1964–May 31, 1964* (New York: Norton, 2007), pp. 596–99.

Unruh: I don't know what [*unclear*]—

President Johnson: —they want me to come back by Arizona. I've got to agree to it pretty soon. Brown's had his man in here with Arizona. They've been fighting 40 years; now they say they're together. What they do, they really agree that Arizona will have its water, and California will have its water if there's enough left. And if there's not enough left, well, the federal government guarantees it to California. [*Chuckles.*] So they shift it over in our lap.

Unruh: Yeah.

President Johnson: But if we can get it settled after a fight for 40 years, it looks like it'd be good business between now and November.

Unruh: Yes . . .it would be one hell of a victory for you.

President Johnson: Mm-hmm.

Unruh: One great victory for you.

President Johnson: All right. If you're back here anytime, I wish you'd come stay all night and let me visit with you.

Unruh: I'll be very happy to, and I expect to be back sometime in the next two weeks.

President Johnson: OK.

Unruh: All right, Mr. President.

President Johnson: Thank you.

Unruh: Thank you. Bye.

After Johnson returned to the Cabinet Room meeting on Vietnam policy, George Reedy came in to ask if the press photographers could expect to take pictures at the conclusion of the briefing. Johnson said no, but asked Reedy to stay for the remainder of the meeting, which continued until 8:00 P.M. Secretary McNamara walked back to the Oval Office with the President. After McNamara left, Johnson played with his dogs on the South Grounds for a few minutes, and afterward was joined in the Oval Office by Jack Valenti. He then received a call from Bundy regarding the administration's plan for military aid to India. Indian Minister of Defense Y. B. Chavan had been in Washington in May to negotiate the agreement, which had been nearly complete when Chavan had to return to India following the death of Prime Minister Jawaharlal Nehru on May 27. Bundy indicated that the aid program had been scaled back so much that it included little that would provoke controversy and counseled that immediate approval would have symbolic value as a sign of support for Indian Prime Minister–elect Lal Bahadur Shastri.

8:07 P.M.

From McGeorge Bundy[9]

McGeorge Bundy: Mr. President, we have an agreement now with the Indians on military assistance which goes—falls short of and reserves for later discussion the one controversial item, which is the . . . high performance aircraft. And we would like to go ahead with this. State, Defense, and our office [National Security Council staff] are all agreed on it. It commits us no further than you've been committed before on the size and magnitude of the program, and we have moved the Indians back a long way. The urgency is simply that to make this affirmative noise at this stage is a good thing for the [Lal Bahadur] Shastri government and the [Y. B.] Chavan . . . visit.[10]

President Johnson: Let me see it tomorrow, what you propose. I want to know something about the India aid program and what we're doing there anyway. I agree with you that what we're going to do is—now's a good time to do it, but let me see it in the morning.[11]

Bundy: We can take it overnight?

President Johnson: Yeah.

Bundy: Right.

8:16 P.M.: Unrecorded call to Lady Bird Johnson.

8:17 P.M.: Unrecorded call to George Reedy.

8:50 P.M.: Unrecorded call to Walter Jenkins; the Daily Diary notes that the call continued for one hour and fifteen minutes.

---

9. Tape WH6406.02, Citation #3616, Recordings of Telephone Conversations—White House Series, Recordings and Transcripts of Conversations and Meetings, Lyndon B. Johnson Library.
10. Following Nehru's death on 27 May, Lal Bahadur Shastri had been elected leader of the Congress Party on 2 June. He would officially become prime minister on 9 June. India's minister of defense, Y. B. Chavan, had visited Washington in May to negotiate the India military aid program. Thomas F. Brady, "Shastri Backs Soviet View on Laos," *New York Times*, 3 June 1964.
11. For the material Johnson requested, see "Memorandum from Robert Komer of the National Security Council Staff and the President's Special Assistant for National Security Affairs (Bundy) to President Johnson," 4 June 1964, U.S. Department of State, *Foreign Relations of the United States (FRUS), 1964–1968: South Asia*, ed. Gabrielle S. Mallon and Louis J. Smith (Washington, DC: GPO, 2000), 25:116–17.

The Daily Diary indicates that the President spoke again to Lady Bird Johnson at 9:26 P.M. One of the two calls between the first couple was recorded, most likely the latter one.[12] Along with their dinner arrangements, the Johnsons discussed the President's plan to record a television show on "how I wooed the press" for George Reedy. Lady Bird reminded him that he would need to get "a special machine to get it." She was referring to the early television recorders that were manufactured by RCA.[13]

TIME UNKNOWN

To Lady Bird Johnson[14]

Lady Bird Johnson: Yes, dear.

President Johnson: What time do you want to eat?

Lady Bird Johnson: I'm ready anytime you are, dear, and I'll ask the kitchen how quickly they could be ready. When would you like to?

President Johnson: I'd say about 30, 40 minutes. I've got some things to sign and one, two things to do yet.

Lady Bird Johnson: All right.

President Johnson: Do you want to invite anybody to eat?

Lady Bird Johnson: No, I don't, but I'll be willing to have any—

President Johnson: All right. OK. That's good. Then we'll just go to bed early.

Lady Bird Johnson: Anybody that'd you'd like.

President Johnson: They've got a show on at 10:30 that . . . how I wooed the press. I want [George] Reedy to see it on television, so . . .

---

12. Although the call slip on the actual tape does not list the time that the call was made, the Daily Diary does indicate that the second call came from the First Lady to the President. The call slip, however, notes that the *recorded* call came *from* the President, suggesting that it could have been the 8:16 call and that the diary notation was not correct—and indicating that the first couple actually spoke just once during the evening. Aspects of the form and content of the conversation support such an interpretation, as does the diary's reference to the unrecorded Jenkins call continuing for over an hour.

13. The Ampex Electric and Manufacturing Company developed primitive television recorders in the 1940s and 1950s and licensed their system to RCA. In 1964, both the machines and the videotape they required were too expensive for mass market sales. http://encyclopedia.thefreedictionary.com/Ampex.

14. Tape WH6406.02, Citation #3617, Recordings of Telephone Conversations—White House Series, Recordings and Transcripts of Conversations and Meetings, Lyndon B. Johnson Library.

Lady Bird Johnson: Now, it takes a special machine to get it. Have you got that?

President Johnson: Yeah, I'm telling them to order it now.

Lady Bird Johnson: That's fine, because if you weren't I was going to.

President Johnson: [*Unclear*]—

Tape cuts off.

10:16 P.M.: The President said good night to secretary Vicki McCammon, still working in the office at 10:16, and returned to the Mansion.

10:20 P.M.: Joined Lady Bird Johnson for dinner.

Thursday, June 4, 1964

We are not suggesting that you ask him for a price cut, but that you tell him you've got a problem and would like to get his views on how it's to be handled. That is to say, he's got very high prof-its and higher than average productivity, and what is his view as to the appropriate way to handle it as between higher wages and lower prices and higher profits. Very tough case. It's a central case in the future of the economy's wage-price stability and that it's nice to be able to ask him on a social occasion.

—Walter Heller to President Johnson

Asia again dominated foreign events on June 4. There was news that the United States might support a Polish proposal for a six-nation sum-mit on the crisis in Laos as a substitute for the French idea of holding a new summit with all 14 of the nations that had signed the 1962 neutral-ity agreement. Meanwhile, a growing crisis in South Korea threatened the stability of the peninsula that had hosted the largest military con-flict of the 1950s. Student protests in 12 cities rocked the government of President Chung Hee Park. More than 1,200 arrests had followed the declaration of martial law on June 3.[1]

The day also brought new developments in Republican presidential politics. In the aftermath of Arizona Senator Barry Goldwater's upset victory in California two days before, New York Governor Nelson Rockefeller announced that while he would not pull out of the campaign, he would be willing to join a coalition in support of another more viable Republican

---

1. "Korean Protests Against Regime Flare in 12 Cities," *New York Times*, 5 June 1964.

moderate. Pennsylvania Governor William Scranton also announced—perhaps not coincidentally—that he would be willing to accept a convention draft as the party's nominee for vice president on a ticket with Rockefeller, but that he had no plans to challenge the New York governor for the top spot. Scranton was viewed by many Republicans as an exciting dark horse contender who might gain the united support of the party's moderates against Goldwater. Following the California victory, however, Goldwater would not be stopped by anyone in the Republican Party.[2]

On the morning of June 4, Johnson did not make or receive any phone calls until after arriving in the Oval Office at 11:15. His first call of the day came from George Reedy a few minutes after he reached the West Wing. Reedy wanted to go over material for his morning press briefing. The President had no interest in commenting for the press on any of the items on Reedy's agenda.

11:20 A.M.

From George Reedy[3]

George Reedy: Mr. President?

President Johnson: Yeah.

Reedy: I'm about ready to start my briefing, wanted to check in with you. They'll probably of course want some kind of a comment on California, which I don't think there should be.[4]

President Johnson: No.

Reedy: I have a query from Jack Horner of the [*Washington*] *Star* on the Jerry Kluttz column this morning, in which Jerry said that when you heard stories that pressure was being put on employees at GSA [General Services Administration] to buy tickets to the gala, that you fired off a note to Kermit Gordon, and that Kermit Gordon got in touch with Bernie Boutin, and that the whole result was a signed statement by all of these people—by both

---

2. Warren Weaver, "Rockefeller Seeks New Man to Halt Goldwater Drive," *New York Times*, 5 June 1964; Joseph A. Loftus, "Scranton Is Open to 2d-Place Draft," *New York Times*, 5 June 1964.

3. Tape WH6406.02, Citation #3618, Recordings of Telephone Conversations—White House Series, Recordings and Transcripts of Conversations and Meetings, Lyndon B. Johnson Library.

4. For discussion of the California primary, see Johnson to Jesse Unruh at 6:50 P.M., 3 June 1964, in this volume.

Kermit Gordon and Boutin—certifying that it's a fixed and firm GSA policy not to subject employees to pressure of any kind to buy tickets.[5]

President Johnson: I'd just say we have no comment on it.

Reedy: OK, sir. . . .

President Johnson: That'd just prolong the story, and . . .

Reedy: [*with President Johnson acknowledging*] That's right, and that's a standard story every year about the pressure. Even if they didn't have a $100 dinner, you'd have the story. Anything you want me to say, or anything this morning?

President Johnson: I don't think of it.

Reedy: Right sir, I'll just get them in, get them out, then.

President Johnson: OK.

Reedy: You bet, sir.

Johnson's next call came from Houston Harte, the publisher of a chain of Texas newspapers that covered many medium-sized Texas cities, including San Antonio, Corpus Christi, Abilene, and San Angelo. President Johnson viewed Harte as one of his closest allies in the media, as his newspapers frequently ran laudatory stories about Johnson's activities and those of his administration. In addition, Johnson aide Bill Moyers had once been a reporter for one of Harte's newspapers.[6] Harte called the President to discuss the administration's position on beef prices. Ranchers in Texas and elsewhere were suffering from low prices in the U.S. beef market, and Harte wanted to be able to explain the administration's policy to local critics. The U.S. cattle industry favored the imposition of new tariffs on imported beef, particularly from Australia and New Zealand, but despite pressure for tariffs from Congress, the administration opposed the idea because it feared that such measures would undermine the ongoing Kennedy Round of negotiations on the General Agreement on Tariffs and

---

5. Jerry Kluttz wrote a column for the *Washington Post* that focused on issues affecting federal employees. His 4 June 1964 column reported that when President Johnson learned that employees of the General Services Administration had been pressured to buy tickets for a Democratic fund-raiser at the Washington Armory the previous week (in violation of federal law), he personally ordered Budget Director Kermit Gordon to investigate and, if necessary, halt the process. Bernard Boutin was the administrator of GSA. Although the story was a small embarrassment, Kluttz depicted Johnson as having taken appropriate action once he became aware of the problem. Jerry Kluttz, "President Acts to Stop Pressure Fund-Raising," *Washington Post*, 4 June 1964.

6. "Harte, Houston," The Handbook of Texas Online, http://www.tsha.utexas.edu/handbook/online/articles/view/HH/fhaal.html.

Trade (GATT). Johnson informed Harte that the cause of the problem lay not in cheap imports, but in overproduction.

11:25 A.M.

From Houston Harte Sr.[7]

President Johnson: Hello?

Houston Harte Sr.: How are you this morning?

President Johnson: Fine.

Harte: I know you're kind of busy. I've got two or three questions I want to ask you right quick. I just talked to Trinity River up there in Canada yesterday. Fish are in the river. Now, I want to send you a fish, and I hope it's not against protocol.

President Johnson: [*chuckling*] No, I don't think so.

Harte: Huh?

President Johnson: I don't think so.

Harte: All right. Can I send it to Arthur just like I've been doing?

President Johnson: Yeah.

Harte: All right. All right.

Now, I got another deal here. [*Pauses.*] These cattle men are *really* singing the blues and raising the dickens, and, of course, although they know that this thing didn't happen overnight, you're the one that's getting credit for it because of the imports. Is there anything that I can say to them that will pacify them in any way?

President Johnson: Yeah. Yeah. Tell them if you published 100,000 papers in San Angelo, in a town of 50,000, you'd go broke right quick because nobody [is] there to buy the other 50,000, and you couldn't get a dime for them; they'd probably sell for a penny.

They had an average five years of 92 million.[8] They raised it to 106 million. They won't be controlled like anybody else. They don't want the government to have anything to do with them.

So they jumped up—every doctor in the country and every lawyer and every congressman and every president and every newspaper publisher buys himself a ranch. And he takes his deducts on it and he expenses it,

---

7. Tape WH6406.02, Citations #3620 and #3621, Recordings of Telephone Conversations—White House Series, Recordings and Transcripts of Conversations and Meetings, Lyndon B. Johnson Library.

8. Johnson was referring to the number of cattle produced for market by U.S. ranchers.

and he gets up to 106 million head of cattle when he only could use 90 million, and you got 16 million surplus. And that drives the price down just like it does in cotton and corn and newspapers and labor and anything else where you got a huge surplus.

Now, the imports now are less than they have been for a five-year average. We've got them limited from Australia and New—

Harte: Have you got that . . .

President Johnson: I've got that agreement.[9]

Harte: All right. We ought to have that—

President Johnson: Well, they, if you do—

Harte: You ought to have somebody send us that thing.

President Johnson: Well, if you do that kind of stuff, you get Australia and New Zealand in the same problem we are.[10]

Harte: Yeah.

President Johnson: Their government falls.

Harte: Yeah.

President Johnson: Because they want to ship it here. But the facts will leak out in time, and the only thing you can do about it is to do the best you can. We're trying to sell it abroad to Europe and France, and it's high as hell over there. They can't get enough of it. We're trying to divert Australia and New Zealand over there, but we didn't build this up, the cattlemen did it themselves. They won't take any controls, and when you . . . when an auto man there in San Angelo's got ten Fords and there ain't a market for but two, he has to lose his profit on them.[11]

Harte: That's right.

President Johnson: Now, if they would let us control it, why, we could keep it 90 million and they could all get their 30 cents, but they don't

---

9. See Johnson to Charles Murphy, 10:40 A.M., 5 May 1964, in Guian A. McKee, ed., *The Presidential Recordings, Lyndon B. Johnson: Toward the Great Society, February 1, 1964–May 31, 1964,* vol. 6, *April 14, 1964–May 31, 1964* (New York: Norton, 2007), pp. 456–59. The cattle industry blamed imports of foreign beef, particularly from Australia and New Zealand, for low domestic beef prices. Australia and New Zealand, however, had already placed voluntary limits on their beef exports to the United States. William M. Blair, "U.S. Acts to Spur Exports of Beef," *New York Times,* 5 May 1965; "Agriculture, General Legislation, 1964—Meat Imports," *Congress and the Nation 1945–1964: A Review of Government and Politics in the Postwar Years* (Washington, DC: Congressional Quarterly Inc., 1965), pp. 728–29.

10. Johnson was referring to demands from the beef industry and its congressional supporters for new tariffs on foreign beef. In August, Congress passed a limited meat tariff bill over the opposition of the administration. William M. Blair, "U.S. Acts to Spur Exports of Beef," *New York Times,* 5 May 1965; "Agriculture, General Legislation, 1964—Meat Imports," *Congress and the Nation,* pp. 728–29.

11. Harte was calling from San Angelo, Texas.

want to do that. They want freedom, but they bellyache. As soon as the price goes down, they want the government to raise it.

Now, we're buying every bit of the meat we can. We've got all these chain stores promoting it, all the newspaper editors, the society editors, and the food editors. We've had them all in. We've got consumption up 35 percent. And we are doing the best we can to work off this surplus, but you just can't go out and shoot it. We considered the government buying it up, but the meat—cattleman committee voted against that, said they don't want any government interference. We thought we'd go out and buy all these young heifers—they've got a bunch of yearling heifers . . .[12]

Harte: That's right.

President Johnson: . . . 6[00], 700 pounds.

Harte: That's well and fine.

President Johnson: And get them out of the way, but they all voted against that.

Harte: All right.

President Johnson: So you've got to find new markets.

Now, the imports haven't got a damn thing to do with them anyway, because they'd have this same problem without the imports. They're not 5 percent of it. That's the only thing, though, they've got to bellyache about. They can't bellyache about themselves raising it from 92 to 106 [million], so they've got to talk about a few little imports. But we've got the imports cut back. And the stuff that we are buying [is] over and above what we did before. For instance, we bought all of our meat before for our armed services abroad.

Harte: Yeah.

President Johnson: We got a million men overseas. They eat beef every day, except they have pork one day a week, and I cut that out now. So instead of buying it abroad, we pay 20, 25 percent more for it here and ship it abroad.[13] Considering what we're buying for our school lunch [program] and our defense, plus the reductions that Ireland and Mexico and New Zealand and Australia have voluntarily made, we're now importing less than we've imported over the five-year average. And if they had their law that they proposed, which would do nothing except make us a protectionist

---

12. See Johnson to Charles Murphy, and Orville Freeman to Johnson, at 10:40 A.M. and 6:05 P.M., respectively, 5 May 1964, in McKee, *The Presidential Recordings, Johnson*, vol. 6, *April 14, 1964–May 31, 1964*, pp. 456–59, 466–68.

13. For the shift in Defense Department policy regarding beef purchases, see Robert McNamara to Johnson, 6:10 P.M., 5 May 1964, in ibid., pp. 468–69.

nation, and we sell four billion surplus agriculture products—and we're wanting to sell meat right now to England and to France, and we think we've got a good market out for it—and pass[ing] a law would just ruin us with every other country in the world when we're trying to lower tariffs 50 percent.[14] For us to come in here and say we're going to bar any imports into the United States, but we're going to reserve the right to dump them everywhere else in the world . . .

Nevertheless, we've got the imports down below where they propose to put it by law, and [Orville] Freeman's testifying to that today.

Harte: Good. I think that'll . . . I think that'll have a marked effect on the way these people feel.

President Johnson: Every economist tells me that the only thing they can do, though, is to get rid of this meat and eat it up.

Harte: That's right. [*Unclear.*] [*Chuckles.*]

President Johnson: They've jumped from 92 to 106 million. And that's 14 million extra head.

Harte: Certainly is. Well, that's good. I'll pass—I'll at least tell all these guys to come in and cry on *my* shoulder.

President Johnson: Hmm. Well, if they would limit their production, they could hold their price up. But if they're going to increase their production by 10 percent, they've got to expect the price to fall because that extra 10 percent is what gluts the market and what makes it go down.

Harte: Well, you know the thing that they can't understand, of course, is that the price of the feed goes down, the price of the land goes *up*, and of course you know it's going up every day.

President Johnson: That's right, but that's because your doctors and everybody else wanted to buy it.

Harte: I guess that's right; I guess that's right. Now—

President Johnson: I got land that joins me that I wouldn't pay 50 cents for it. They wanted to lease it to me yesterday for $6 an acre a year. [*Harte chuckles.*] But these—everybody's got to have him a ranch, you know, to get free of his frustrations.

Harte: That's right. What do you think of the California situation?

President Johnson: Well, I think that it's a pretty intense fanatical group, and they poured *lots* of money in, and there's a bunch of screwballs in California, kind of like the Doctor [Francis] Townsend

---

14. Johnson was referring to the Kennedy Round of GATT negotiations that had begun in early May 1964.

group.[15] They're the [John] Birch societies. They've got 11 people nominated for Congress on the Birch ticket.[16] I don't know what it'll mean over the country. I think it'll probably mean the death of the Republican Party, and it'll kill out a bunch of congressmen and senators and governors and things like that if they keep going. He [Barry Goldwater] wants to drop atomic bombs on everybody, and I don't believe the people will stand for that. They may do it.

Harte: I think it's a fine thing for us. I think he's the easy man to beat.

President Johnson: I agree.

Harte: There may be somebody that's easier to beat, but I know he's *very* easy to beat.

President Johnson: I think so.

Harte: I think that you didn't have any trouble before. Now, when the Republicans have their convention, get through with it, I hope you're going to announce your choice for vice president. Of course, you know who I hope it will *not* be.

President Johnson: Yeah.

Harte: But I'm always wrong to give advice to you politically because I've got a record showing that I'm wrong.

President Johnson: I'd really like to have the job myself today. [*Both laugh.*]

Harte: Well, we don't want to make that swap. But you know your Secretary of Defense [Robert McNamara] is a lot [more] popular than I had any idea he was.

President Johnson: Yeah.

Harte: People have got a lot of confidence in him.

President Johnson: Yeah, he's a good man.

Harte: I'm not saying he's the man, but I'm saying that I'm amazed at the way people talk about him who I thought would cuss him because he's cold and efficient.

President Johnson: All right.

Harte: Well . . .

---

15. Johnson was referring to Dr. Francis Townsend of Long Beach, California, who during the Great Depression proposed a plan to give a monthly payment of $200 to every senior citizen in the United States on the condition that they spend it within the month. Although economists immediately discredited this "Townsend Plan," supporters of the idea formed local groups across the United States.

16. Johnson was referring to the far right-wing John Birch Society. For an analysis of Goldwater supporters in California, see Lisa McGirr, *Suburban Warriors: The Origins of the New American Right* (Princeton, NJ: Princeton University Press, 2001).

President Johnson: Now, the wool men are all coming in to see me this morning. They want me to support the wool act that gives them that subsidy again and agree to go down the line for it. I guess I . . . I guess—

Harte: Who all is going to be there?

President Johnson: The National Wool Growers Association, that's all I know.

Harte: I see. Well, as you know, I've—

President Johnson: Mr. [J. R.] Broadbent and Mr. [Edwin E.] Marsh are from Salt Lake City.[17]

Harte: Oh, I was hoping— [*unclear*] ask you if Lenore would be there because he's your friend.

President Johnson: Uh . . . they're not—

Harte: I've begged these guys to let me say something about who they put on these committees, but they won't . . . they think I'm not with them, and I guess I'm not.

President Johnson: They want to bar all wool from being imported too.

Harte: Oh, yes. Well, hell, they . . . They're not doing so bad. Lamb prices are pretty good.

President Johnson: Mm-hmm.

Harte: And they've been bad for the last two years, but they're pretty good now.

President Johnson: Mm-hmm. What do they—What's the lamb sell for?

Harte: Well, the price is up 16, 17 cents now.

President Johnson: Mm-hmm.

Harte: It has been below that. But . . . So, the sheep men here, since we've had this rain, all feel pretty good.

President Johnson: Mm-hmm. OK. Well, good luck to you.

Harte: Same to you.

President Johnson: Bye.

Harte: Bye.

11:34 A.M.: Unrecorded call to Jack Valenti.

11:34 A.M.: Meeting with Special Counsel Myer Feldman, Under

---

17. J. R. Broadbent and Edwin E. Marsh were the vice president and executive secretary, respectively, of the National Wool Growers Association. Johnson would meet with this group's officers at 11:45 A.M.

Secretary of Agriculture Charles Murphy, and Pan American Airlines President Juan Trippe.

11:45 A.M.: With Feldman and Murphy accompanying, meeting in the Cabinet Room with representatives of the National Wool Growers Association; joined by Democratic senators Mike Mansfield of Montana and Wayne Morse of Oregon, both of whom opposed the administration's positions on livestock tariffs and Southeast Asia.

11:48 A.M.: Read first editions of afternoon newspapers in the outer office.

12:06 P.M.: Unrecorded call from Walter Jenkins.

12:10 P.M.–12:24 P.M.: Met with NATO General Secretary Dirk U. Stikker.

12:25 P.M.–12:32 P.M.: White House physician Dr. George Burkley burned a wart off the President's finger.

12:36 P.M.: Unrecorded call to Valenti.

12:37 P.M.–12:50 P.M.: Off-the-record meeting with National Woman's Party President Emma Guffey Miller.

12:50 P.M.: Unrecorded call to Valenti.

12:52 P.M.: Cabinet Room meeting with the U.S. ambassadors to Somalia, Israel, and Portugal.

12:56 P.M.

From Dean Rusk[18]

Almost immediately, Johnson was called away from the meeting with the ambassadors to receive an urgent phone call from Dean Rusk. The Secretary of State's call raised a long-standing issue that had occupied little of the President's time in recent weeks. Since gaining its independence from Britain in 1960, the island of Cyprus had seen conflict between its majority Greek and minority Turkish ethnic groups. The Greek Cypriots hoped to annex the island to Greece, while the Turkish Cypriots sought an independent entity of their own. In a complicated peacekeeping arrangement, Britain, Greece, and Turkey all maintained bases on the island. Earlier in 1964, U.S. and British diplomatic efforts had narrowly averted a civil war after the Greek Cypriot president of the island, Archbishop

---

18. Tape WH6406.02, Citation #3623, Recordings of Telephone Conversations—White House Series, Recordings and Transcripts of Conversations and Meetings, Lyndon B. Johnson Library.

Makarios III, restricted the rights of the Turkish minority and attempted to advance the cause of unification with Greece.[19] Violence had continued on the island, however, and Rusk informed the President that the Turkish Cypriot leader Fazil Kutchuk planned to declare an independent state and that the Turkish government might intervene to support such a move. Rusk sought, and received, the President's approval for a strong diplomatic message to Turkey opposing any military action.[20]

President Johnson: Hello?

Dean Rusk: Mr. President—

President Johnson: Yes.

Rusk: —I'm sorry to bother you, but we've just had some flashes in indicating that [Fazil] Kutchuk, the Turkish separate leader, might declare a separate state on the island there and then ask for immediate Turkish intervention. And Ray Hare reports that the foreign minister told him that there's an important Cabinet meeting—meeting this evening, which is just about now, Turkish time—and that intervention was one of the things that could be decided.[21]

I'd like your authority to go through Hare, and the Turkish ambassador *here*, most insistently to the Turks that they must *not* intervene, that you had direct assurances from them on this, and that the most minimum we would expect is full consultation on any matter that evoked our own responsibilities for the security of countries in that part of the world.

President Johnson: Sure would. Sure.

Rusk: And then hit them very hard on it.

President Johnson: Sure.

Rusk: All right?

President Johnson: Thank you.

---

19. Johnson to George Ball, 6:35 P.M., 28 January 1964, *The Presidential Recordings, Lyndon B. Johnson: The Kennedy Assassination and the Transfer of Power, November 1963–January 1964*, vol. 3, *January 1964*, ed. Kent B. Germany and Robert David Johnson (New York: Norton, 2005), pp. 926–31.

20. Johnson's message led Turkey to withdraw its threat of military intervention. "Telegram from the Department of State to the Embassy in Turkey," 5 June 1964, *Foreign Relations of the United States (FRUS), 1964–1968: Cyprus, Greece, Turkey*, ed. James E. Miller (Washington, DC: 2000), 16:107–9; "Telegram from the Embassy in Turkey to the Department of State" 5 June 1964, ibid., 16:111; "Telegram From the Embassy in Cyprus to the Department of State", 6 June 1964, ibid., 16:112–13. For the aftermath, see Johnson to Dean Rusk, 6:30 P.M., 9 June 1964, in this volume.

21. Raymond A. Hare served as the U.S. ambassador to Turkey.

Rusk: Now, from you.
President Johnson: Bye.
Rusk: All right.

Rusk first called the Turkish ambassador to the United States and expressed the U.S. government's opposition to intervention. He then cabled Ambassador Hare in Ankara and instructed him to convey the same message to Turkish Prime Minister Ismet Inonu immediately, even if he had to call Inonu out of a cabinet meeting.[22]

> **1:00 P.M.–1:16 P.M.:** Meeting with Phan Huy Quat, the foreign minister of South Vietnam, along with the State Department's William Sullivan and NSC staff member Michael V. Forrestal.[23]

1:17 P.M.

To Lee White[24]

Immediately after Quat's departure, Johnson called Lee White to inquire about what he could expect in an upcoming meeting with Attorney General Robert Kennedy. Although developments in the civil rights field had been the President's primary concern in making the call, the conversation initially turned to Kennedy's ideas for reforming the athletic development programs of the U.S. Olympic movement. Johnson had discussed the subject with Kennedy in a recorded conversation on May 28.[25]

Broaching a more serious subject, White reported that a black student had been admitted to the University of Mississippi, where the court-ordered admission of James Meredith nearly two years before had provoked one of the major confrontations of the civil rights movement.

---

22. "Memorandum of Telephone Conversation," 4 June 1964, *FRUS, 1964–1968*, 16:104–5; "Telegram 1285 to Ankara, June 4, 1:15 P.M.," summarized in ibid.
23. "Memorandum of a Conversation, White House," 4 June 1964, *FRUS, 1964–1968: Vietnam 1964*, ed. Edward C. Keefer and Charles S. Sampson (Washington, DC: GPO, 1992), 1:447–48.
24. Tape WH6406.02, Citation #3624, Recordings of Telephone Conversations—White House Series, Recordings and Transcripts of Conversations and Meetings, Lyndon B. Johnson Library.
25. See Johnson to Robert Kennedy, 11:45 A.M., 28 May 1964, in McKee, *The Presidential Recordings, Johnson*, vol. 6, *April 14, 1964–May 31, 1964*, pp. 914–24.

Although White had few details, he predicted that the university would probably not fight the case, but that trouble might arise if students or white residents of the university town of Oxford, Mississippi, provoked a confrontation. White's assessment that the university had accepted the reality of a nondiscriminatory admissions policy would prove overly optimistic. On June 5, the State College Board ordered a delay in the admission of Cleveland Donald Jr. until a U.S. District Court judge ruled on the applicability to the case of the federal court order that had required the admission of James Meredith in October 1962. A court order barred Donald from campus until the case was decided. On June 10, however, Federal District Judge Harold Cox ordered the university to admit Donald, although he banned the new student from engaging in any civil rights activities.[26]

After holding the line for over a minute, the President comments to someone in the office: "Oh, hell, I don't know why I can't get anybody on the phone." He continues to hold until White is finally connected.

Lee White: Yes, sir.

President Johnson: Lee, the Attorney General's coming to see me, due at 1:00. Now, what problems do we have with him that I may need to know about on the racial thing and civil rights?

White: Well, there's quite a range of them, sir. I have a memo. It's a little long, but it's broken down into sections with subsections, and I think you might just glance through that. I can bring it right up to you.

President Johnson: All right. Now, do you know what he wants to talk about today?

White: I'm not sure. I believe the information I had was about the . . . General [James] Gavin and the Olympics.[27]

President Johnson: Yeah. Well, I've got a letter from him on that, and I'll just tell him to bring General Gavin on in. Who would handle that for us on our staff here, you?

---

26. "Mississippi U. Delays Negro's Admission," *New York Times*, 6 June 1964; "Negro Wins Entry at Mississippi U.," *New York Times*, 11 June 1964; "Negro Is Enrolled at Mississippi U.; Whites Are Calm," *New York Times*, 12 June 1964.

27. Kennedy had been lobbying for the formation of a committee to study improvements in mobilizing and training U.S. athletes for the Olympics. He had suggested that retired General James Gavin might head such a committee. See Johnson to Robert Kennedy, 11:45 A.M., 28 May 1964, in McKee, *The Presidential Recordings, Johnson*, vol. 6, *April 14, 1964–May 31, 1964*, pp. 914–24.

White: It had been Ted Reardon, and I've been checking around.[28] It looks like nobody else has quite fallen heir to it yet.

President Johnson: Well, why don't you take it?

White: All right, I will.

President Johnson: Take it, and just tell him, and I'll tell him too, and tell whoever's handling this for his department to—I don't—he suggests here that I may want to write General Gavin. I don't know enough about the movement. I'd suggest he just tell General Gavin that he'd like for us to get together and to bring General Gavin in.

White: Sure.

President Johnson: Whenever he's ready.

White: I'd say—you know, the whole thing's a pretty worthwhile undertaking, trying to move up that situation. Instead of being 8th and 10th in every international competition, to let our people really concentrate on making a good showing.

President Johnson: That's good. Anything else?

White: There . . . Yeah, there is something. I haven't been able to put it into a memo yet because it just came to me. But we've got a problem brewing in the University of Mississippi. A Negro student, we think, has been admitted. It's a little unclear because the university hasn't quite acted on his latest papers, but assuming that he is admitted, he will register on Monday and classes would begin on Tuesday. This would not be by court order, and there is no enforcement of the court order by the marshals or federal troops.

Some of the ways that we might move on this is to get in touch with the head of the university—perhaps with Governor [Paul] Johnson or maybe Senator [James] Eastland—to kind of get a feel for what the situation is and whether it's going to be smooth.[29] But the information is not quite hard. The Justice Department called this morning, and they've got a call in to this particular fellow's lawyer in Mississippi to see if they can get a little more data on who he is and what kind of a fellow he is and likely what problems are likely to arise.

But it's a . . . kind of a sneaky thing. We haven't heard anything about it until just yesterday afternoon. The kid could well be there Monday morning. So I've asked for as much information as I can get. I know that

---

28. Timothy Reardon had been President Kennedy's Cabinet secretary. He had resigned in February to accept a post as special assistant to the chairman of the FDIC. *Washington Post,* 5 February 1964.

29. White was referring to Mississippi's governor, Paul Johnson, and Senator James Eastland, both of whom were Democrats.

Burke Marshall is in Mississippi today.[30] He went down, I think, the night before last and was supposed to call. I haven't yet heard from him, but it does have the earmarks of a little bit of a crisis, and I don't know if the Attorney General has been brought up to date on that one yet.

President Johnson: Well, now, you think if he went in, what would provoke the crisis? They'd try to kick him out?

White: That—I don't think the university will; I think the university is all right. It's [*unclear*]—

President Johnson: Students?

White: —the people in the town and the students.

President Johnson: Mm-hmm.

White: The information we have is that the chancellor of the university has come long last to the decision that students ought to be considered on the basis of their ability, and he just plain doesn't want to have any more trouble if he personally can avoid it. So I think he's all right [given the] information we have. But we have not had any check with Governor Johnson on this to find out whether they will provide him the kind of protection that may be necessary. I'm sorry we don't have more information, but they didn't have it, and they're seeking it for us.

President Johnson: Well, now, who would be the one who would normally get in touch with Johnson? Burke Marshall?

White: Well, no, sir. I'd say that that's kind of one where either you might do it or conceivably the Attorney General. Burke *might*. He never had any dealings with Governor Johnson; he doesn't quite know him. He listened in on those phone conversations that President Kennedy had with him during the [James] Meredith crisis, but . . . some of the alternatives would be for Burke to talk to the chancellor or to talk to the—

President Johnson: I'd make him talk to him while he's down there today.

White: All right. Well, I have his number, and he's [*unclear*]—

President Johnson: I'd get ahold of him and tell him to explore that fully for you.

White: All right, I will.

President Johnson: And bring me the memo.

White: I will, sir.

---

30. Burke Marshall served as assistant attorney general for the civil rights division of the Justice Department.

1:26 P.M.–2:20 P.M.: Robert Kennedy entered the Oval Office at 1:26 and met with the President for nearly an hour.

2:21 P.M.: Unrecorded call to McGeorge Bundy.

2:25 P.M.: Unrecorded call to Bill Moyers.

2:26 P.M.: Unrecorded call to Jack Valenti.

2:27 P.M.: Walked around the South Grounds with his unofficial legal and political advisers Clark Clifford and Abe Fortas.

2:31 P.M.: Lunch in the White House Mansion with Clifford, Fortas, Moyers, and Valenti.

4:40 P.M.: Unrecorded call to Walter Jenkins from the Mansion.

4:44 P.M.: Unrecorded call from Jenkins.

5:11 P.M.: Unrecorded call from George Reedy.

5:35 P.M.–5:45 P.M.: Walked through the Mansion and called White House staff member Ashton Gonella to find a reception being hosted by Lady Bird Johnson, then made a brief appearance at the reception.

5:35 P.M.: Returned to the office.

Johnson then made a call to Council of Economic Advisers Chairman Walter Heller. On the phone with Robert McNamara, Heller arranged to return the President's call.

5:56 P.M.

To Walter Heller[31]

President Johnson: Yes, Walter.

Walter Heller: I was just on the phone with Bob McNamara on the—

President Johnson: I hope I didn't interrupt you.

Heller: Well, we were just about to reach *this* point. I was giving [*unclear*]—

President Johnson: Do you want to call me? Why don't you finish with him and then call me back here?

Heller: All right. May I do that?

---

31. Tape WH6406.02, Citation #3625, Recordings of Telephone Conversations—White House Series, Recordings and Transcripts of Conversations and Meetings, Lyndon B. Johnson Library.

President Johnson: Yeah. Yeah.

Heller: I'll do that, thank you.

6:00 P.M.: Unrecorded call to Jack Valenti.

6:15 P.M.

From Walter Heller[32]

Few economic issues presented a greater challenge to administration policymakers in 1964 than the upcoming negotiations between the United
Automobile Workers and the big three U.S. automakers. With the profits of the car companies approaching record levels, UAW President
Walter Reuther appeared poised to abandon his tentative acceptance of
the Johnson administration's wage guideposts unless the automakers
agreed to a price cut. CEA Chairman Walter Heller, Secretary of Defense
Robert McNamara, Secretary of Labor Willard Wirtz, and Secretary of
Commerce Luther Hodges had formed a committee to prepare the administration's strategy for the upcoming negotiations.[33] The committee had
met the previous day with General Motors Chairman Frederic Donner
to broach the question of a price cut. They had received no commitments,
but had not been rejected out of hand either. In this conversation, Heller
informed the President that he and McNamara thought an upcoming
state dinner honoring West German Chancellor Ludwig Erhard would
present an excellent opportunity for Johnson to raise the issue with
Donner. Johnson vehemently disagreed. Heller also asked about the
political implications of statements he had made in a *U.S. News & World
Report* article criticizing wage increases for the building trades unions
that exceeded the administration's guideposts and about economic measures the administration might employ in a recession. Johnson agreed
with Heller's approach in both cases.

---

32. Tape WH6406.02, Citation #3627, Recordings of Telephone Conversations—White House
Series, Recordings and Transcripts of Conversations and Meetings, Lyndon B. Johnson Library.
33. See Johnson to Willard Wirtz, 5:40 P.M., 21 May 1964, in McKee, *The Presidential Recordings,
Johnson,* vol. 6, *April 14, 1964–May 31, 1964,* pp. 799–803.

President Johnson: Yes, Doctor.

Walter Heller: Mr. President?

President Johnson: Yeah.

Heller: I am glad to be able to bring you a unified recommendation now on this automobile thing, and—

President Johnson: Just so it don't include me.

Heller: [*Laughs.*] Well, it includes Bob McNamara, and I tell you that's going some.[34] He thinks that this [Ludwig] Erhard dinner would be just the right kind of occasion.[35]

President Johnson: No, no. I ain't going to do that, now. I told y'all that the other day. I want you and Bill Wirtz to do what you can. I don't mind McNamara doing it, but I don't think I ought to do it. I got a good feeling on that, so don't try to shove me into it, now, because I don't want to do it.

Heller: Well, I . . . I thought that the . . .

President Johnson: I told Jack [Valenti] to tell you I wasn't going to do it. I told you the other day, but y'all—I didn't make it clear enough, I guess.

Heller: Well, but, Mr. President, I immediately then called [Frederic] Donner, and then we had this meeting yesterday.

President Johnson: Yeah, I saw that. I saw that.

Heller: And we thought that that was an awfully good . . . you know, first round on it. And we are not suggesting that you ask him for a price cut, but that you tell him you've got a problem and would like to get his views on how it's to be handled. That is to say, he's got very high profits and higher than average productivity, and what is his view as to the appropriate way to handle it as between higher wages and lower prices and higher profits. Very tough case. It's a central case in the future of the economy's wage-price stability and that it's nice to be able to ask him on a social occasion rather than . . .

President Johnson: I'd think that would be very distasteful to a fellow—invites you to your house to dinner, and then you start to politicking with him on a proposition that I doubt the wisdom of a president talking to him about anyway.

Heller: Well, I don't think we've got a . . . I think . . . I doubt very

---

34. Before joining the Kennedy administration, McNamara had been the chief executive officer of the Ford Motor Company.

35. West German Chancellor Ludwig Erhard would make an official visit to Washington on 12 June. Executives from the major U.S. automakers would attend a White House state dinner that evening in Erhard's honor.

much that we've got much of a chance of succeeding in this without you doing it. I think we have a reasonable chance of doing so if you do. And I realize, Mr. President, that this is a . . . this is a tough one. This is the, you know, this is the problem—

President Johnson: Well, I think we'll have to lose if it depends on my going to him and asking him to do this. I think we just have to approach it some other way or take what they've got—

Heller: Well, I thought this approach we had yesterday at which we didn't—I, you know, made very clear we're not requesting him for a price cut, but also made him very—

President Johnson: I think it's all right for y'all to talk to him all you want to. But I don't want you coming up with a recommendation that winds up—that might get me into it and calling him because I don't want the president doing that. If I do, I'll be doing it on everything [that] comes along, and I just don't want to do it. . . .

Heller: Well, you notice this is the first . . . other than patting some fellows on the back, this is the first time we've really recommended this because, of course, this is the . . . this is the nub. This is the one that really is going to determine—

President Johnson: Well, that's what I've got the Secretary of Labor and chairman of Council [of] Economic Advisers for. You-all are better informed than—

Heller: Yeah, but we . . . To use one of your expressions, we can't pee a drop compared with you.

President Johnson: Well, yes, you can. If y'all can't, I'm sure I can't. And I don't think I ought to. My judgment is that I just oughtn't to get into it, and I told you that the other day.

Heller: Well, I thought maybe I misunderstood you: I thought you wanted us to take sort of a first shot at—

President Johnson: No.

Heller: —first reading at it, and then see—

President Johnson: No, I'm a little . . . I question the wisdom of my doing it. First place, I don't think I have a chance to succeed.

Heller: Well, I . . .

President Johnson: Question my judgment. I just honestly don't, and—

Heller: Really? . . . Really? . . . Really?

President Johnson: —and I think that the fact that you-all didn't make any progress with him, it's a good indication—

Heller: Well, we thought we did. We thought that while they were, you know, they didn't go out of here convinced, they certainly didn't rear back and say, "This is ridiculous. It can't be done." Nothing of that kind at all.

President Johnson: Mm-hmm.

Heller: Their whole attitude was: We have big profits; we recognize it; we've got good productivity; we . . . this is something that we, you know, we have tough risks in this industry too. But at no time did they say that this was impossible or implied that they wouldn't do it. Now, at the same time they made no commitment that they would. Obviously, these fellows can't do that.

So, we thought that they were leaving the door open. And we just don't know of anybody, as I say, that can hold it open, keep it open, push it open further, except the president. And I don't think that Donner is going to react to anyone but the president. And that's why . . . I had thought, frankly, that a meeting in your office was the right thing. Bob thought that this chance for just . . . putting it in sort of a social setting was perhaps the better way to do it, but I see your point, that you don't like to invite somebody in and . . .

President Johnson: Say, "I want you to pay for your dinner, now, by giving me a price cut on your autos."

Heller: [*laughing*] Yeah. . . . And also, Bob thought that we ought to get—as he had earlier recommended—that we ought to get Clark Kerr and perhaps Ed Mason at Harvard in [*unclear*]—[36]

President Johnson: I told Bill Wirtz that a long time ago.

Heller: Yes.

President Johnson: Go on and call him immediately. Have you done that?

Heller: Yes, he's been called. We've sent the study out to him. Bob suggested that I draft for *you* a note indicating to you that you were very much interested in this and like to have him do that, and . . .

President Johnson: All right.

Heller: I don't know whether you . . . [I] mean, in other words, to make it sort of a presidential assignment to him.

President Johnson: All right.

Heller: Would you be willing to do that?

President Johnson: Yeah, yeah, yeah.

Heller: And Mason, too.

---

36. Clark Kerr was the chancellor of the University of California at Berkeley; Kerr was also one of the nation's leading experts in labor-management relations. Edward S. Mason was an economist at Harvard University who specialized in industrial organization. *New York Times*, 4 March 1992, 2 December 2003.

President Johnson: Yeah.

Heller: May I just—

President Johnson: Now, who is Mason?

Heller: Mason is one of the top economists in the country and very widely respected. Been in and out of Washington a great deal. He's at Harvard and is an expert in this whole field of industrial organization, and Bob thought it would be a good idea to have the two of them weigh in on this from somewhat different points of view in different parts of the country. Is that . . .

President Johnson: Yeah, that's all right.

Heller: OK.

President Johnson: Yeah.

Heller: May I quickly raise the other two questions with you?

President Johnson: Sure . . . sure.

Heller: One, I did an interview this morning with *U.S. News & World Report,* and in it I brought—there are two things I did that I would like to check with you quickly. One, I made a rather strong statement about the fact that the building trades unions have been exceeding the guidelines and that I think the—and you understand these are things I can edit out of it. That's why . . . That they have been presenting a problem with respect to the guidelines and excessive wage settlements. I think this is generally accepted by everyone, and we said we'd speak out when they flouted the public interest, and they sure are. And they're doing it right there in Detroit under the noses of the UAW, and I thought that . . . I hoped sometime you'd have a chance to make some comment on it, but I thought that it was entirely appropriate depending on the political aspect of it for me to say something in this interview. It would be printed in two or three weeks, I guess.

President Johnson: Yes, I think that's all right. Have you talked to Bill Wirtz about it?

Heller: I have not explicitly but will before it's published.

President Johnson: I think I would and see if he . . . so he doesn't come in and say that we've kicked over the bucket.

Heller: Oh, no. No, and—

President Johnson: I think I would.

Heller: We're working hand in glove, he and I, on this.

President Johnson: I think . . . But I mean on the—

Heller: Yeah. You bet.

President Johnson: —building trades, I think it's all right to say it, but I'd notify him, and . . .

Heller: All right.

President Johnson: . . . and if he['s] got any objections, let's hear it, but otherwise I think it's good.

Heller: You bet I will. . . . The other thing was that they quizzed me at some length about recessions and so forth. And I indicated that this administration was thinking ahead, that while things were in very good shape now and we foresaw further expansion as far as we could see, but a prudent administration had to think ahead to such contingencies and think about measures that ought to be considered when these contingencies came along. They said, "Well, like temporary tax cuts and public works and so forth?" And I said yes and made a few comments about it without making any commitments, of course. Is it a good idea to let them know that we're thinking along these lines and into the future this way?

President Johnson: Yes, I think so, if they don't scare people to death and don't put it out of context or something—

Heller: Oh, I . . . I think I thoroughly embedded it in an optimistic assessment of the economy and simply said, you know, when the sun is shining is the time to think about the rain.

President Johnson: I think that's good. I think you ought to take this labor statistics—I don't guess there's any way we can put it out. It's a shame, though—

Heller: Aren't they terrific?

President Johnson: Yeah, but it's a shame they go out Friday afternoon for Saturday morning paper.

Heller: Oh . . .

President Johnson: Why does it have to do that? Why don't they release them Friday for Sunday paper?

Heller: Well, I don't really know. I could call them and find out.

President Johnson: They got a rule on that?

Heller: I think they have a rule.

President Johnson: You see—

Heller: They've been awfully sticky about that.

President Johnson: If they—

Heller: Because the Saturday—

President Johnson: Well, I'd put it out Friday and just give them time to work it up for Sunday morning release because we got no circulation on Saturday. Nobody reads it, and they're the weak paper, and everything else. But I don't—

Heller: And, you know, it's the best validation yet of the workings of the tax cut. In particular, he tells labor that it looks as though—begins to look as though we were right about this tax cut being the best thing that could happen to them.

President Johnson: Yeah . . . yeah.

Heller: The other . . . the final thing, Mr. President, is not . . . Well, we have to think about this third council member for that day when I take off. And again, it's a matter of advance scheduling. We are sort of narrowing down in our thinking to a fellow at Yale who was here before as a staff member, a fellow named Arthur Okun. And, you know, these academic plans get made.[37] He's first-rate. He's an excellent forecaster and would round this council out quite well, and I just wondered how you want us to play this. Do you—

President Johnson: Well, I'd like to know something about it. Give me a page on him and let me look at it, and I'd be inclined to go along with your judgment.

Heller: Well, that would be fine. Should we check with Abe Ribicoff, or would you like to do that yourself?[38]

President Johnson: No, I would rather you do it.

Heller: All right.

President Johnson: Tell him I asked you to.

Heller: Will do, and you know I'm heading out to Minnesota after—I hope I have a chance to bring my daughter in for a moment tomorrow . . .

President Johnson: Love to.

Heller: Jack Valenti thought maybe about the time you're going to visit the Shah, and then I hope to hitch a ride back with you.[39]

President Johnson: That's good; that's wonderful.

Heller: Good.

President Johnson: When do I go out there?

Heller: I understand you're going out to Detroit on the 27th and Minneapolis on the 28th.

President Johnson: Well, now, you're not going to be gone from here to out—Are you taking off two or three weeks?

Heller: [*with President Johnson acknowledging*] Yeah, about three weeks. You had said to take the month of June off. But I'll be in touch. I'll—

President Johnson: Oh, all right. OK.

Heller: Anytime you need me.

President Johnson: Well, I'm going to miss you. I'm going to miss you.

---

37. Arthur Okun would replace Walter Heller on the CEA in 1965; he would become chairman of the CEA in 1968.
38. Abraham Ribicoff served as a Democratic senator from Connecticut.
39. Heller was referring to the Shah of Iran, who would visit the White House on 5 June.

Heller: [*chuckling*] Well . . .

President Johnson: Now, what's going to happen to this thing if we don't see Donner? Nothing?

Heller: Well, I'm afraid nothing. You see, that's the thing that I . . . I just see this thing just fizzling out. I . . . And I just think that one way or another . . . I can't imagine McNamara seeing him. I just can't imagine his putting himself in that position in the light of his role in the administration. Now, maybe you want to talk to him about that and see if he feels that he would want to. And I really can't see him dealing with anybody but the president. This is . . . I know that you get used right and left, and I'm not . . . and I don't do this lightly, Mr. President. I haven't suggested this in any other case, but I sure hope that this is one you'd give a little further thought to.

President Johnson: All right. OK. I'll see you tomorrow.

Heller: Thank you.

After the call from Heller, McGeorge Bundy and Walter Jenkins joined the President in the Oval Office.

> **6:30 P.M.–6:35 P.M.:** President Johnson met briefly with King Lejolan Kabua of the Marshall Islands, accompanied by top officials of his government and Congressman John Young of Texas.
>
> **7:00 P.M.:** Unrecorded call to Scripps Howard reporter Marshall McNeil (an old Texas friend).
>
> **7:25 P.M.:** Joined in the office by Special Assistant Douglass Cater, who remained with the President until 8:20.
>
> **7:35 P.M.:** Unrecorded call to McGeorge Bundy.
>
> **8:00 P.M.:** Bill Moyers joined the President and Cater.
>
> **8:40 P.M.:** Unrecorded call to Lady Bird Johnson.
>
> **8:48 P.M.:** Unrecorded call to Lady Bird Johnson.
>
> **9:00 P.M.:** Unrecorded call to Lady Bird Johnson.
>
> **9:05 P.M.:** Returned to the Mansion and left almost immediately with Lady Bird to attend a 30th birthday party and dinner for Bill Moyers at the home of journalist Max Freedman.
>
> **11:15 P.M.:** Bundy arrived and met with Johnson for five minutes in the presidential limousine.
>
> **11:20 P.M.:** The Johnsons left the party for the White House with Jack and Mary Margaret Valenti; they arrived at 11:34.

Friday, June 5, 1964

And now, the problem we've got is getting [Ralph] Yarborough
[to] beat this attractive young boy [George H. W.] Bush. And
he ought to quit fighting with [John] Connally and every
Democrat. If a man's got a Democratic label on, he ought to say
"Mister." And the only ones he ought to cuss is Republicans.

—President Johnson to Walter Reuther

On a day in which the Rolling Stones made their first U.S. concert appearance in San Bernardino, California, the U.S. Senate engaged in a series of strategic maneuvers about Senate Majority Leader Mike Mansfield's cloture petition on the civil rights bill. The main focus of the discussions concerned a request from a group of conservative Republican senators, led by Bourke Hickenlooper of Iowa, for consideration of three additional amendments to the legislation before the cloture vote took place. Hickenlooper and his colleagues remained formally uncommitted on the cloture question, and while the pro–civil rights leadership did not support the amendments, they agreed to a one-day delay on submission of the petition to allow for debate on the proposed changes. Any other move would have risked alienating the Hickenlooper group and turning their votes against cloture. Faced with the same constraint on the opposing side of the issue, Georgia Senator Richard Russell in turn asked for and received a day's delay in consideration of the arrangement between Hickenlooper and the leadership. As the latter agreement required the unanimous consent of the Senate before it could be implemented, any member of the anti–civil rights southern delegation could have blocked it with a single objection. The southerners, however, could no more afford to alienate the Hickenlooper group than could the leadership. The

Senate would debate the three amendments and vote on them early the following week.[1]

Among foreign policy concerns, Asia remained the world's most active trouble spot. In South Korea, additional student protests around the country brought the resignation of the chairman of the Democratic Republican Party, which dominated the government under President Chung Hee Park. In Laos, the Communist Pathet Lao staged new attacks on a city just north of the Plaine des Jarres that neutralist forces had retaken the week before. Meanwhile, at Paris's Elysée Palace, U.S. Under Secretary of State George W. Ball made little progress in discussions with French President Charles de Gaulle about differences in the two countries' policies regarding the defense of South Vietnam. De Gaulle argued that the situation in South Vietnam presented "primarily a political and psychological problem," as the United States would always remain a foreign power to the Vietnamese and that no amount of military or economic aid could change that reality. De Gaulle suggested that a better strategy would be a "worldwide conference" to pursue a diplomatic solution to the conflict. In response, Ball presented the administration's belief that any form of negotiation with the North Vietnamese and their Chinese backers would undermine the will of the South Vietnamese and could even lead to the total collapse of South Vietnam. Although the meeting ended cordially, it had delineated the stark differences between the United States and its colonial predecessor in Southeast Asia.[2]

At the White House, Lyndon Johnson awoke at 8:00 A.M., ate breakfast in bed, performed his physical exercises, and began his working day with a meeting with Jack Valenti. He then made a series of phone calls before leaving the Mansion.

---

1. One of the amendments changed the jury trial requirement in all cases of criminal contempt except those brought under the voting rights section of the act (Title I); another called for the elimination of funding for training school personnel in desegregation issues; a third called for the complete removal of Title VII, which contained the legislation's equal employment opportunity provisions. On 9 June, the first of the amendments passed, while the other two were easily defeated. E. W. Kenworthy, "G.O.P. Asks Delay on Closure Move in Rights Debate," *New York Times*, 6 June 1964; *Congressional Quarterly Almanac*, 88th Cong., 2nd Sess., 1964, vol. 20 (Washington, DC: Congressional Quarterly Service, 1965), pp. 366–67.
2. "Korean Party Chief Quits in Effort to Calm Rioters," *New York Times*, 6 June 1964; "Leftists in Laos Renew Offensive," *New York Times*, 6 June 1964; "Telegram from the Under Secretary of State (Ball) to the Department of State, Paris," 6 June 1964, U.S. Department of State, *Foreign Relations of the United States (FRUS), 1964–1968: Vietnam 1964*, ed. Edward C. Keefer and Charles S. Sampson (Washington, DC: GPO, 1992) 1:464–70.

9:29 A.M.: Unrecorded phone call to Walter Jenkins.

9:40 A.M.: Unrecorded phone call to Judge A.W. Moursund in Johnson City, Texas.

10:40 A.M.: The President attended a memorial service for former Indian Prime Minister Jawaharal Nehru at the Washington National Cathedral; Nehru's widow attended the service as well.

11:35 A.M.: Returned to the White House with Lady Bird Johnson and State Department Chief of Protocol Angier Biddle Duke.

11:50 A.M.–11:55 A.M.: Arrived at the West Wing, stopping briefly at Kenneth O'Donnell's office and then greeting Council of Economic Advisers Chairman Walter Heller and his daughter Kaaren in the Oval Office.[3]

12.00 P.M.: Greeted the Shah of Iran, Mohammed Reza Pahlavi, as he arrived at the White House by car.

   The President brought the Shah to the Oval Office, where he introduced him to the Hellers.

12:10 P.M.–12:31 P.M.: Met privately with the Shah.

12:31 P.M.–12:56 P.M.: Cabinet Room meeting with the Shah, Secretary of State Dean Rusk, Assistant Secretary of State for Near Eastern and South Asian Affairs Phillips Talbot, National Security Council staff member Robert Komer, and Iranian Ambassador to the U.S. Mahmoud Foroughi.[4]

Immediately following the meeting with the Shah, Johnson made calls to aides Richard Goodwin and Bill Moyers. Although neither the Daily Diary nor the call slip for the physical tape lists either conversation as having been recorded, one brief conversation, probably with Goodwin, does appear on the tape. Goodwin served primarily as one of Johnson's speechwriters, and the brief conversation focuses on changes to the draft of an upcoming speech, probably one of two to be given the next day to the International Ladies' Garment Workers' Union (ILGWU) in

---

3. In a recorded phone conversation the previous day, Heller had asked if he could bring his daughter to the White House to meet Johnson. See Walter Heller to Johnson, 6:15 P.M., 4 June 1964, in this volume.

4. For documents related to these meetings, see "Memorandum From Robert W. Komer of the National Security Council Staff to President Johnson," 5 June 1964; and "Memorandum From the Assistant Secretary of State for Near Eastern and South Asian Affairs (Talbot) to the Under Secretary of State for Political Affairs (Harriman)," 6 June 1964, *FRUS, 1964–1968: Iran*, ed. Nina D. Howland (Washington, DC: GPO, 1999) 22:72–75.

New York.[5] The President particularly noted that he wanted all references to presumptive Republican presidential nominee Barry Goldwater deleted.

12:58 P.M.

To Richard Goodwin[6]

President Johnson: . . . [*unclear*] books. And then each child we give $10 worth of stamps to buy his books, or something like that. But get all this anti-[Barry] Goldwater stuff out of there. I don't want to bring him up and start arguing with him, with all this bluster and bravado and all that stuff because it'll just build him up when we go to picking at him, and that's childish. So cut all that Goldwater stuff out of it [*unclear*] like you never heard of Goldwater. We're not concerned with him; we're not worried about him. We've got a positive, affirmative program. And then get it out in the next hour so when I get through with the Shah [Mohammed Reza Pahlavi] I can look at it.

Richard Goodwin: All right, fine. We'll do that right away.

President Johnson: Tell Bill [Moyers], if you can't get him, that's what I want done.

Goodwin: OK, fine.

President Johnson: And you do it. You do it. Get a little phonetic stuff in there, a little rhythm for me.

Goodwin: All right.

President Johnson: Jazz it up a little. It's a pretty good speech, but

---

5. "Remarks in New York City Upon Unveiling a Plaque in Honor of the 50th Anniversary of the ILGWU Health Center," 6 June 1964; and "Remarks in New York City to Members of the International Ladies Garment Workers Union," 6 June 1964, *Public Papers of the Presidents of the United States: Lyndon B. Johnson, 1963–64* (Washington, DC: GPO, 1965), 1:749–53.

6. The Lyndon B. Johnson Library lists Goodwin as the other participant in this call, but includes a question mark after the name; it lists the time as 12:58 P.M., also with a question mark. Based on this information, the Daily Diary, and a comparison of the speaker's voice in the recording with known examples of Goodwin's voice, an editorial decision was made to positively identify the conversation as the call to Goodwin listed in the diary. Tape WH6406.02, Citation #3628, Recordings of Telephone Conversations—White House Series, Recordings and Transcripts of Conversations and Meetings, Lyndon B. Johnson Library.

just jazz it up a little bit. But it's Hillman and all the Liberal Party, and they're going to be watching it from coast to coast.[7]

Goodwin: All right, I'll do that.

President Johnson: All right.

Goodwin: OK, fine—

A secretary interrupted to report that House Majority Leader Carl Albert was on the line. Johnson took the call from Albert. Their conversation focused on two issues of congressional strategy and politics: how to counter the efforts of House Rules Committee Chairman Howard Smith and of House Minority Leader Charles Halleck to slow or even block major items of administration legislation, particularly the Economic Opportunity Act; and the objections of two House Democrats to Johnson's choice for a Republican vacancy on the Securities and Exchange Commission.

1:00 P.M.

To Carl Albert[8]

President Johnson: Carl?

Carl Albert: Yes.

President Johnson: [Sargent] Shriver—have you heard what [Howard] Smith told Shriver?[9]

---

7. Johnson may have been referring here to Sidney Hillman, the influential former leader of the Amalgamated Clothing Workers who had died in 1946 after shaping the liberal left of the U.S. labor movement. The New York Liberal Party was a union-backed, left-liberal, political organization that provided a small but key swing vote in New York politics. Run by Alex Rose of the United Hatters, Cap, and Millinery Workers Union and David Dubinsky of the ILGWU, the Liberal Party had been formed during World War II when an anti-Communist group left the American Labor Party. Joshua Freeman, *Working Class New York: Life and Labor Since World War II* (New York: The New Press, 2000), pp. 56–57.

8. Tape WH6406.02, Citation #3629, Recordings of Telephone Conversations—White House Series, Recordings and Transcripts of Conversations and Meetings, Lyndon B. Johnson Library.

9. Brother-in-law of the Kennedys and director of the Peace Corps, Sargent Shriver headed the President's Task Force on Poverty, which had drafted the economic opportunity bill that formed the legislative center of the War on Poverty. After passage of the bill, Shriver would direct the Office of Economic Opportunity, the central implementation agency of the War on Poverty.

Albert: I heard this morning that he told him that he might not get the bill out until week after next.[10]

President Johnson: Yeah, he said the leadership wasn't in a hurry to get it out. They had more than they could take care of, and he couldn't do anything about it. Now—

Albert: Well, that isn't true.

President Johnson: That's just a part of the strategy, Carl. They're just screwing us to death every week, and we just—

Albert: I went to him and asked him to get it out yesterday, you know.

President Johnson: Well, I think you and [John] McCormack better—[11]

Albert: And then I—then I went—well, I've got a—I'm going to talk to him. I went to him then. I personally went to him and asked him if he'd get it out on Thursday of this week—that's yesterday—and he said, "No, I just can't do it." Said, "I'm already committed." And I said, "Well, will you get it out next week?" And he said yes, he would. So, I . . . Now, he . . . I felt that I had a commitment from him at least to get it up to where the others could get it out, if he didn't want to vote for it, next week. Now, I asked him *specifically.* He said, "Well, I'll get it out." I said, "Next week?" He said, "Yes, next week. I'll . . . " He didn't promise to vote for it, but he said he'd get it—[12]

President Johnson: I don't care whether he votes for it or not, but that's my number one bill. [*talking over Albert*] I'd rather have it than all the other bills put together.

Albert: We're not going to let that . . . We're going to get that bill.

President Johnson: I know, but I see him meeting with these people. I see [Charles] Halleck's people delaying the report for over a week.

Albert: I know.

President Johnson: I've just been suffering here for three damn months while they just screw us to death. I can't ever get it up. And I know when I'm being screwed: when I see Halleck and Smith and them

---

10. Smith would begin Rules Committee hearings on the economic opportunity bill on 16 June, but would not grant the bill a rule until 28 July.

11. Massachusetts Representative John McCormack served as Speaker of the House of Representatives.

12. For another indication that Smith had promised to consider the legislation the following week, see Lawrence F. O'Brien, "Memorandum To The President; Subject: Possible Items for Discussion at Leadership Breakfast," 2 June 1964, "Ex FG 400/MC 11/22/63–6/15/64" folder, Box 328, White House Central Files: Federal Government Operations, Lyndon B. Johnson Library.

just put us off week after week after week. Now, Cliff Davis told me three weeks ago we had about one more week on Appalachia.[13]

Albert: I talked to Cliff myself. Cliff, who—well, he's got to go back to Tennessee, listen. Now, I think we're going to get the pay bill next week.[14] I don't think—I think the Senate's going to report that bill—

President Johnson: Well, they say they're going to try to report it Monday or Tuesday, but they sent over a statement yesterday saying they'd vote for the 10,000 [dollars].[15] They thought that would be enough for the House to bring it up, but the thing I'm worried about is the big issue: this poverty bill, getting it passed in time for the Senate to act on it. And they are delaying it. You can see what they did on the floor. You can see what they did holding up the report for a week.[16]

Albert: Of course they did.

President Johnson: You see what they did by not letting the committee meet, not getting a quorum, and running off our people and getting their Democrats to saying that, "Well, we don't want to rush the Republicans." And then they say it's a political thing, that we're trying to do it for political sake. Well, hell, we're not—16 percent of our unemployment's among young people. And we're trying to move that 16 percent down and make taxpayers out of them instead of tax eaters.

Albert: I [*unclear*]—

President Johnson: But I've been on this thing now for six long months trying to get this bill up to where they can vote on it. I think we can get the votes to get it if we can do it. Now, I think you and the Speaker

---

13. Representative Cliff Davis, a Tennessee Democrat and member of the House Public Works Committee, strongly supported the administration's Appalachian development bill. In July, he would sponsor a revised version of the bill that took account of objections raised by members of the Public Works Committee. John D. Morris, "Appalachia Plan Gathers Support," *New York Times*, 30 April 1964; *Congressional Quarterly Almanac*, 1964, vol. 20, p. 291.

14. The federal pay bill would increase the salaries of all career, appointed, and elected federal employees, including members of Congress and federal judges. It had been rejected by the House in March, but congressional supporters and the administration had drafted a revised version that reduced the congressional pay raise and delayed it until after the November election. *Congressional Quarterly Almanac*, 1964, vol. 20, pp. 416–19.

15. The original version of the federal employees pay bill had included $10,000 congressional, Cabinet, and judicial pay raises, but the resubmitted version of the bill cut the raise to $7,500 in order to defuse resistance to the bill. The Senate restored the $10,000 raise for Cabinet members, and the House eventually agreed to the change in a conference committee. *Congressional Quarterly Almanac*, 1964, vol. 20, pp. 416–23.

16. The House Education and Labor Committee had approved the economic opportunity bill on 26 May; Representative Phil Landrum of Georgia, the Democratic floor leader for the legislation, had then introduced a "clean" version of the bill that was not reported until 3 June. *Congressional Quarterly Almanac*, 1964, vol. 20, p. 222.

ought to this afternoon sit down with Smith and tell him the President's called you—

Albert: I have planned to do it this afternoon to—

President Johnson: That's good, and then tell him, if necessary—

Albert: I had a note right here that I'm going to call Smith. I talked to [Phil] Landrum. He wants it nailed down next week if it's humanly possible. I called him and asked him if he was ready to go. He said he'd be here by—he said he's leaving town. I called—heard he was going to leave town, and I called him to be sure he didn't leave town if we needed him, and he says, "Well, I'm going to be back Monday," he said, "because Smith won't meet before Tuesday anyway." And I said, "Well . . ." And he gave me—I've got his phone: it's Jasper, Georgia, 692-3377, in case Smith should agree to meet on Monday, then I'll get him back here on Monday.

President Johnson: Well, I'm going to meet him at lunch today, and I just think you and John ought to tell him that we just need that Monday to be taken up next week without fail, if we don't do anything else. If they don't, damn it if I'm not going to turn this job over to somebody else. I just . . . poverty, I just fought my heart out for it, and each week, Halleck gives me another week postponement.

Albert: Well, you know we're going to get it out.

President Johnson: I don't know with Smith. I just think that they've had a meeting with these—

Albert: We're going to get it out [unclear].

President Johnson: —some of these conservatives like Omar Burleson and [John] Dowdy and that group, he's been meeting with them, and he's been meeting with Halleck, and Halleck told me that he wasn't going to let it come out if he could help it.[17]

Albert: I know he did. He told me that. He told me he was going to fight that poverty bill.

President Johnson: And he's fighting it with all he's worth, and he helped—making these political speeches about it, and I just think that we got to take them on and say, "By God, they stand for poverty, and they stand against progress, and they stand against helping the people." We just got to take them on and make everybody stand up on a party issue. If I need to, I'll call every Democrat down here and meet in the East Room with them and say, "Now, goddamn it, let's pass our program, or let's quit." We've got the votes up there if we just stand together, but they run off and join those Republicans.

---

17. Representatives Omar Burleson and John Dowdy were Texas Democrats.

Now, is Abe going to be here next week?[18]

Albert: His office told me he would, but he's still tired and worn out, and we . . . They told me he would be here, though, and that he would be here when the poverty bill came.

President Johnson: Now, Halleck recommended this boy . . . uh, uh, from Idaho—

Albert: Yeah.

President Johnson: —[Hamer] Budge for the Security [and Exchange] Commission. I put him on the security commission.[19]

Albert: Hamer Budge, he's about the meanest Republican. He's worse than Halleck; he's ten times meaner than Halleck.

President Johnson: That's right, but we can't name the Republicans for them. They let us name the Democrats, a good many of them, when they're in, [Sam] Rayburn and I.[20] And he wanted it, and I put him on the SEC, and the only one he can be mean to is the New York bankers.

Albert: Yeah.

President Johnson: And [Bernice] Sisk called down yesterday and raised hell about it—Bernie Sisk, and this boy, Ralph, whatever his name was out there that voted against us on everything. What's his name in Idaho?[21]

Albert: Oh . . .

President Johnson: Ralph Harding.

Albert: Ralph Harding.

President Johnson: [*talking over Albert*] And he's raising hell about it, so I think you just have to tell him that the Republicans are entitled to a minority membership on some of these commissions. That we look to the Republican leader in the Senate for one recommendation, Republican leader in the House for the other. That Halleck said this is the only recommendation he'd made, the only one he was going to make until it's filled. That he didn't specify where he had to be, but he wanted him taken care of because he'd done more to help him than any other man, and he had five years before he could retire. And so I've waited six months, and

---

18. The President may have been referring to Senator Abraham Ribicoff of Connecticut.

19. Johnson's nomination of former Idaho Republican Congressman Hamer Budge to the SEC was officially sent to the Senate on 5 June 1964. For background on this issue, see Johnson to Ralph Dungan, 11:21 A.M., 26 May 1964, in Guian A. McKee, ed., *The Presidential Recordings, Lyndon B. Johnson: Toward the Great Society, February 1, 1964–May 31, 1964*, vol. 6, *April 14, 1964–May 31, 1964* (New York: Norton, 2007), pp. 834–38.

20. Johnson was referring to former Speaker of the House Sam Rayburn of Texas.

21. Representative Bernie Sisk was a California Democrat; Representative Ralph Harding was an Idaho Democrat who had defeated Hamer Budge in a 1960 congressional race.

I've offered him three or four jobs, and he wouldn't take any of them. And finally, the SEC, I put an Oklahoma boy on there, and I'm going to put another one as chairman.[22] He can't hurt me any there. I don't care what he does to New York Wall Streeters. He can't be too mean to them, and I thought that I had to do it or just forget the minority representation.

Now, explain that to Sisk and Harding for me. Harding gave him a hell of a recommendation at FBI, said he was a fine man.

Albert: Yeah, well . . . Well, you had to do that. I told Harding yesterday it was a Republican vacancy, and that you did it—

President Johnson: Not a Democratic vacancy, and when they had a Democratic vacancy, they'd call up Rayburn, and call up me, and we'd meet, and we'd pick out—

Albert: You don't have to worry about Halleck—Harding anyway.

President Johnson: Well, he didn't vote with us on the farm bill, I noticed.

Albert: You never know when you're going to get him anyway, so why worry about somebody that—

President Johnson: Well, I was a little bit worried about Sisk.

Albert: Well, Sisk . . . Sisk will change. Sisk is impetuous; he's not just as . . . he's not, you know, he's one of the nicest people in the world; he's not one of the smartest people in—

President Johnson: Well, you just tell Sisk that Rayburn appointed them, and I appointed them under [President] Eisenhower, and Halleck's got the chance to appoint them now, and it can't be of any hurt to us, and that I waited six months, but I can't just refuse to consider him and that . . . I can't back out now, I've given him my word.

Albert: I won't have any trouble with Sisk. Now, Harding is another matter. I talked to Harding about this very thing yesterday. He came to me griping about it yesterday, and I told him just exactly what you said to me. I said, "Well, he gave it to him because Charlie Halleck wanted him to and it was a Republican vacancy and that had been a precedent."

President Johnson: All right. Now, Walter Jenkins said he talked to Sisk, and he thinks he's satisfied.

---

22. In March, Johnson had appointed Hugh F. Owens, who had previously served as chief administrative officer of the Oklahoma Securities Commission, to the SEC. The reference to the second Oklahoman is uncertain; later in the year, Johnson appointed Manuel F. Cohen, a New Yorker, to the post of SEC commissioner. "Johnson Names Hugh Owens to SEC Post; Laurence Walrath reappointed to the ICC," *Wall Street Journal*, 9 March 1964; "New Wall St. Watchdog," *New York Times*, 11 July 1964.

Albert: Sisk—

President Johnson: You call me after you and John talk to old man Smith.

Albert: All right.

President Johnson: OK.

1:10 P.M.: The President walked to the White House Mansion with Jack Valenti for a ceremonial exchange of gifts with Shah Mohammed Reza Pahlavi.

Johnson gave the Shah a lithograph of the signing of the American Declaration of Independence, a gold plaque, and a copy of his campaign book *A Time For Action* with a personal inscription to the Shah.

1:35 P.M.–2:45 P.M.: Attended a White House luncheon for the Shah.

2:50 P.M.: Accompanied a group of executives from Gulf Oil, Socony Oil, and Standard Oil and their wives—all of whom had presumably attended the luncheon with the Shah—to the White House living quarters.

3:44 P.M.: Unrecorded call to Carl Albert.

4:10 P.M.: Napped in the living quarters.

4:47 P.M.: Unrecorded call to George Reedy.

5:05 P.M.: Greeted members of a "Young Citizens for Johnson" group, escorted by Indiana Senator Birch Bayh, in the Flower Garden.

5:07 P.M.: Returned to the office.

5:11 P.M.: Cabinet Room meeting with leaders of the National Coal Policy Conference, a joint industry-labor group.

Attendees at the meeting included executives of major coal producers and railroads, union officials from the United Mine Workers, and West Virginia senators Jennings Randolph and Robert C. Byrd (both Democrats).

Before the meeting with the coal group began, the President received another call from Carl Albert, who updated him on the House leadership's efforts to contact Judge Howard Smith and urge him to schedule a committee hearing on the economic opportunity act. Smith had not yet responded to their request, and far more than in his earlier conversation with the President, Carl Albert expressed his irritation with the recalcitrant chairman of the Rules Committee.

5:12 P.M.

From Carl Albert[23]

Albert is on hold for approximately one minute and forty seconds while an operator contacts an office secretary, who then locates the President.

President Johnson: Yes, Carl. [*Noise can be heard in the background.*]

Carl Albert: The Speaker [John McCormack] and I have been trying again. I've sent Judge [Howard Smith] this telegram to his home, his office, his farm, and his committee:

"Dear Judge: You will remember that I had a telephone talk with you last week about giving a hearing on the rule for the antipoverty bill this week, and you told me you could not possibly do so, but you promised to do it next week, the week of June 8. The Speaker and I have tried and tried to reach you by telephone but have been unable to contact you, as we were advised you were on the way to your farm. The Speaker and I, as well as the President, all regard this as a matter of the highest priority and strongly urge that it be considered by your committee next week. In other words, I request that you keep the promise that you made me. I'm sending this telegram to you so you can make arrangements to change the agenda of your committee for next week to include this bill. Regards, Carl Albert."

President Johnson: Mm-hmm. Well, that's all you can do, and I'd have the Speaker put in a call and try to stay after him.

Albert: We've both got calls in for him right now.

President Johnson: That's good. . . . OK, my friend. I'd . . .

Albert: [*Unclear.*]

President Johnson: I'd tell the press that I'd hoped to bring it up and planned it.

Albert: Well, if he doesn't cooperate—if . . . I'm going to. I think I should give him a chance to answer and to comply with what *I* understood, and I honestly understood it because I didn't just say, "Now, Judge, will you do this?" I went back to him. The Speaker was present when I talked to him on the phone. I went back two or three times. I said, "Now, Judge, does that mean you'll do it next week?" You know, I cross-examined him and pinned him down probably a little more than he thought I should, but I did it to try to be sure we knew where we were, and *I* was sure in my own mind beyond any shadow of a doubt that he had promised me that while he couldn't do it this week, he would [*unclear*]—

---

23. Tape WH6406.02, Citation #3630, Recordings of Telephone Conversations—White House Series, Recordings and Transcripts of Conversations and Meetings, Lyndon B. Johnson Library.

President Johnson: You talk to him tomorrow or whenever you get him. Just tell him that you've conveyed that to me, and you're committed, and we expect it to be brought up, and then I'd just tell the papers today or tomorrow that—not quoting him at all—but that you expect to have it scheduled next week or early the following week for sure.

Albert: All right, sir.

President Johnson: OK.

Albert: Good.

With the Albert call completed, Lyndon Johnson called the White House operator to request 12 cups of coffee for the meeting, which he rejoined.

> **6:20 P.M.:** Representatives from the Oil, Chemical, and Atomic Workers International Union joined the coal policy meeting.
>
> **6:30 P.M.:** Went to Kenneth O'Donnell's office and shook hands with Bob McKinney, the publisher of the *Santa Fe New Mexican* and a former assistant secretary of interior during the Truman administration. It is not clear whether he returned to the coal meeting.
>
> **6:52 P.M.:** Meeting on Laos and Vietnam in the Situation Room (located in McGeorge Bundy's office) with Bundy, Robert McNamara, Dean Rusk, and Jack Valenti.[24]
>
> **7:32 P.M.:** Secretary Vicki McCammon delivered a message from the First Lady that their dinner guests for the evening, writer John Steinbeck and his wife, had arrived at the White House. At the conclusion of the meeting, Johnson and McNamara talked privately for an additional five minutes.
>
> **7:43 P.M.:** Returned to his office, shaved, and—with Jack Valenti and Bill Moyers in the office—went over a speech that he would give the following day.

Valenti and Moyers remained with President Johnson. When McCammon reminded him that he had a number "of pending phone calls on spindle," Johnson replied, "Honey, please try to get the operators and y'all ask them to talk to someone else. I just can't talk to everybody." Nonetheless, Johnson made an unrecorded call to Bundy, followed by a lengthy recorded conversation with United Auto Workers President Walter Reuther in Detroit.

---

24. For a briefing paper prepared for this meeting, see "Paper Prepared for the President by the Secretary of Defense (McNamara)," 5 June 1964, *FRUS, 1964–1968: Vietnam,* 1:461–64.

7:52 P.M.

From Walter Reuther[25]

Although Johnson and Reuther touched briefly on the UAW's pending negotiations with the major U.S. automakers, most of the call addressed the internal conflicts within the Texas Democratic Party. In a sometimes bitter divide that could be traced to the 1940s, the state party had split into a liberal faction organized behind Senator Ralph Yarborough and a conservative wing that aligned itself behind Governor and former Johnson aide John Connally. In the past, Lyndon Johnson had adroitly managed each faction to his own advantage. In 1956, he had aligned with the liberals after Governor Allan Shivers moved the party to the extreme right, only to depose them from the party power structure after Shivers had been defeated and it appeared that Yarborough might gain sufficient influence to challenge Johnson's own control. By the time Connally won the governorship in 1962, however, he had split with Johnson over civil rights, along with his desire to establish a political identity separate from his mentor. Johnson's differences with Yarborough and the liberal camp left his relations with that group little better. An attempt to unite the state party had been the primary rationale for John F. Kennedy's trip to Texas in November 1963.[26]

In the spring of 1964, Johnson feared that this internal division might threaten his own ability to carry Texas in the general election. In early May, Connally and Yarborough had each faced and defeated a challenger from the other faction in the state primary, although Johnson had managed to dissuade popular Congressman Joe Kilgore from running against Yarborough. With both nominations secured, the focus of the conflict shifted to the Texas delegation to the Democratic National Convention and the perennial question of whether it would be pledged to support the national party platform and ticket. Haunted by Shivers's 1952 endorsement of Eisenhower, Yarborough had staged a drive to secure liberal representation in the delegation. This effort had further alienated Connally and the conservatives, and Johnson feared that many of them might abandon the party and support Yarborough's Republican opponent, busi-

---

25. The call slip indicates that this call was from Reuther; the White House Daily Diary notes that it was placed by Johnson to Reuther, "returning his call." Tape WH6406.03, Citations #3631 and #3632, Recordings of Telephone Conversations—White House Series, Recordings and Transcripts of Conversations and Meetings, Lyndon B. Johnson Library.

26. Robert Dallek, *Flawed Giant: Lyndon Johnson and His Times* (New York: Oxford University Press, 1998), p. 46.

nessman George H. W. Bush. Although he was more concerned that the Democrats would lose Yarborough's vote in the Senate, Johnson worried that such a collapse of party cohesion would threaten even his own ability to win the state.

Although Johnson and Reuther discussed how Texas union leaders might be recruited to work for party unity, much of the conversation consisted of Johnson expressing his frustration with Yarborough for failing to recognize that the state delegation to the Atlantic City convention was not worth fighting for: The President alone would control selection of the Texas delegation, it would be pledged to him, and it would support the platform he approved. Further, Johnson would work tirelessly for Yarborough's own election, but could do little for him if he persisted in antagonizing the other, and larger, wing of the state party.

President Johnson: Hello.

Walter Reuther: Hello.

President Johnson: Hi, Walter.

Reuther: How are you?

President Johnson: Fine. I . . . Your labor boys have given me such a push today, I haven't been on the phone.[27] I just got through, and I'm going over and eat dinner [with] John Steinbeck, but I thought I'd better call you in between.

Reuther: Oh . . . I'll just take a minute of your time.

President Johnson: I had O. A. Knight in today and John Lewis and all of his coal workers, and so I've had a pretty rough day.[28]

Reuther: I see. . . . You've had a rough day, yeah. Well, I want to just say first that I was so proud of you at the U of M that day.[29] That was a tremendous job you did.

President Johnson: Well, thank you.

Reuther: And I was real proud.

President Johnson: Thank you, Walter.

Reuther: Now, what I'm calling you about, I'll just take a minute. I've

---

27. Johnson was referring to his meeting with the National Coal Policy Conference group.

28. O. A. Knight was the president of the Oil, Chemical, and Atomic Workers International Union; John L. Lewis was the president emeritus of the United Mine Workers of America; both had attended the National Coal Policy Conference meeting earlier in the day.

29. Reuther was referring to Johnson's 22 May commencement address at the University of Michigan. See McKee, *The Presidential Recordings, Johnson,* vol. 6, *April 14, 1964–May 31, 1964,* pp. 806–9.

been working with [Hiram] Moon and our boys on the Texas situation.[30] We've been trying to help put that together down there, you know, so that the [John] Connally forces and the [Ralph] Yarborough forces could work together and give you a united Texas, which we need. And I thought it was coming along, and then the other day, Ralph Yarborough called me, and Hank Brown, who's been trying to get me, and he wrote me a long letter. And I met this afternoon with our regional director, who's a fellow that Moon works under—Teddy Hawks—and I think it would be a great tragedy.[31] Those boys are talking about walking out of the convention down there and so forth, and I don't think there's really as much difference between them as they appear to be.

President Johnson: Mm-hmm.

Reuther: And Hank Brown and these fellows are talking about "well, they're fighting for your program, and the Connally forces won't go along with it."

President Johnson: Well, neither one of us know what our program is. It hasn't been written. The only thing they're doing, the damn fools are letting the Republicans sic them on . . .

Reuther: That's right.

President Johnson: They want to try to take the convention away from Connally, Walter, and they can't do it.

Reuther: Of course they can't!

President Johnson: He's got them beat 2 to 1. And Connally hasn't got a program or platform, and I haven't got one. We've got to write it up at . . . Atlantic City. We're going to write a platform, and then they're going to have another convention.

But all the Republicans are doing is, they've got a bunch of simpletons down there who really want to control this, and Yarborough is their agent. He votes right up here, but he [has] got absolutely no judgment. What he ought to be doing is getting every Democrat he can to support him because he's going to wind up getting in a fight and running half of them over to the Republicans.

Reuther: Yeah.

President Johnson: And there ain't damn thing in the world for him

---

30. Hiram Moon was a UAW international representative, who may have known Lyndon Johnson through shared ranching interests. "Billy Owens Tells Some of His Story," http:// www.uaw848.org/848-1962.htm.
31. H. S. "Hank" Brown was the president of the Texas AFL-CIO and a liberal activist; Theodore Hawks served as director of Region 5 of the UAW from December 1958 to August 1967. http://www.reuther.wayne.edu/collections/hefa_261-uaw-s4.htm. Region 5 included Texas, as well as most of the southwestern and western United States.

to gain. Every delegate that's come to that convention is going to be a carefully selected Lyndon Johnson man from who laid the chunk. [*Reuther acknowledges.*] And he's going to be ordered—instructed to vote for me all the way down the line. Now, what they're trying to make them do is say, "You give us a blank check to endorse a platform that hasn't been written."

Reuther: Yeah, well, I—

President Johnson: Now, they can't do that.

Reuther: Of course they can't.

President Johnson: And if they did, Connally would get beat by a Republican.

Reuther: Right. The point is that why can't there be somebody to work this thing out, because they're fighting over nothing. Now, number one, the important thing is to get that convention united to support all the Democratic candidates, starting with you.

President Johnson: Well, I'll tell you why. Mrs. [Frankie] Randolph through the years is a good soul, but she rules or ruins.[32] If she can't rule the roost, then she'll ruin it.

Reuther: That [*unclear*].

President Johnson: Now, they have tried to figure out—they went out . . . first thing they tried to do was beat Connally, which was a terrible mistake for them to do. They oughtn't be fighting with him.

Reuther: Right. . . . Of course not.

President Johnson: Then I got in a fight with Connally because he said, "Well, if they're going to beat me . . ."

Reuther: He'll beat Yarborough.

President Johnson: "I'm going to beat Yarborough."

Reuther: Sure.

President Johnson: Well, I said, "You can't do that." And he said, "Well, it's a hell of a thing to take my gun away from me and give them the gun to work on me with."

Reuther: Right.

---

32. Frankie Randolph was the heir to a Houston lumber and banking fortune and a leader of the liberal faction in the Texas Democratic Party during the 1950s and 1960s. A founder and the publisher of the liberal weekly newspaper the *Texas Observer*, she had been instrumental in Ralph Yarborough's 1957 election to the Senate. Although Randolph had worked with Johnson to break conservative Governor Allan Shivers's control of the state party in 1956, she had opposed his nomination for vice president at the 1960 convention and as a result lost her position as Texas national committeewoman. Ronnie Dugger, "Randolph, Frankie Carter." The Handbook of Texas Online. http://www.tsha.utexas.edu/handbook/online/articles/view/RR/fra34.html; Chandler Davidson, *Race And Class In Texas Politics* (Princeton, NJ: Princeton University Press, 1990), pp. 162–66.

President Johnson: "And you can't keep Don Yarborough out, but you can keep me out." Well, I made Joe Kilgore mad, and I made Connally mad, but I kept Yarborough from getting defeated, because any one of the group—Jim Wright, Joe Kilgore, any of them—would have defeated Yarborough.[33]

Reuther: That's right.

President Johnson: Connally had it right. But I said, "Why do I want to improve a situation when I get a man's vote 99 times out of a 100?[34] Why do I want to change that kind of a man?" And I appealed to Connally's intelligence, and he said, "Well, all right, but I'm still mad about it."

Reuther: Yeah.

President Johnson: Well, he didn't beat him. Now, soon as they got by that thing, they come out to start a fight and say, "OK. We can't run the convention. We've tried to beat you. We've lost, but now we're going to tell you that if you don't do it, we're going to embarrass the President by going up with a separate delegation." Well, Connally don't give a damn if they take a separate delegation, and I don't either as far as that's concerned—

Reuther: Well, it's [*unclear*].

President Johnson: —because they've got nothing to fight. I had Yarborough to lunch today at the White House.[35] I said, "Now, Ralph, why in the living *hell* do you want to fight about something that hasn't been written yet? If you want to fight about it, go into the September convention in Texas after we've had Atlantic City and try to blackball everybody that doesn't support our platform. I wouldn't give a damn what they supported. I'd say, 'You support Johnson, period.' Because we haven't written our platform. I don't know what it is I want to ask them to support."

Connally called me and said, "Now, what kind of a program are you

---

33. In January, Johnson had blocked a conservative challenge to Senator Ralph Yarborough from Representative Joe Kilgore, but had failed to convince Don Yarborough to drop his primary race against Governor Connally. As a result, the Connally faction had maintained its agreement with Johnson that Kilgore would not run, but had run Gordon McLendon in the senatorial primary to prevent the liberals from focusing all their resources against Connally. Representative Jim Wright was a moderate Texas Democrat who would eventually serve as Speaker of the House from 1987 to 1990. He is mentioned here as a stronger alternative to McLendon that the Connally faction could have run in the primary against Ralph Yarborough. See Walter Jenkins to Joe Kilgore, 1:20 P.M., 3 February 1964, Robert David Johnson and Kent B. Germany, eds., *The Presidential Recordings, Lyndon B. Johnson: Toward the Great Society, February 1, 1964–May 31, 1964*, vol. 4, *February 1 1964–March 8, 1964* (New York: Norton, 2007), pp. 78–83.

34. Johnson was referring to Ralph Yarborough's voting record in the Senate.

35. Yarborough had joined the official White House luncheon for the Shah of Iran.

advocating? What are you going to put in your platform? Are you going to balance the budget, or are you going to unbalance it?"[36] And I said, "Well, we're going to have a platform committee, and we're going to write a damn good platform." Well, he said, "Don't ask me, though, to write a blank check before we ever meet because that don't appeal to anybody."

Reuther: No. Well, I wondered what was Ralph Yarborough's reaction.

President Johnson: Well, Yarborough's reaction is that they're after him and they're going to beat him and Connally's after him, so he's got to fight Connally. Now, I've told Connally that he's got to get out there and get elected himself. He's got to support Yarborough. And all of us go together. I told Yarborough today, I said, "I'm with you money, marbles, and chalk, all the way, all the time. Now you tell me who you want me to call, what you want me to do, I'll do it." And he said, "Well, that's fine. I'll sure be in touch with you." But says, "They're really after me." Well, that's true: they are after him.

Reuther: Well, they're after each other—

President Johnson: He—

Reuther: —that's the problem. Why the hell did they let—

President Johnson: He—

Reuther: —Don Yarborough get in that race? That was a lot of damn nonsense.

President Johnson: Well . . . of course it was. It's awful. But we will get Connally and every conservative Democrat that's on that ticket and connected with them. They'll wind up voting for Johnson, voting for Connally, and voting for Yarborough. Now, the only one that's really important about it is the Yarborough thing. They're going to vote for me, the Democrats are, and it'll pull Yarborough over. But if he has a blood-letting, and he gets them all mad at him . . .

Reuther: That's right.

President Johnson: And what he ought to do is start fighting the living hell out of [George H. W.] Bush. That's the man to fight; not to fight Connally.[37] But they don't do that. And this is [the] history of Texas in the liberal movement. And that's why they always get back. We had them up to, when Connally was elected, where labor could make advances in Texas ten years ahead of what he'd done. They didn't wait two hours until they started threatening him.

---

36. Johnson's last recorded conversation with Governor Connally had been on 14 April, although Connally had visited the White House a week later.

37. George H. W. Bush, the future 41st president, would be Ralph Yarborough's unsuccessful opponent in the 1964 election.

Reuther: Yeah. Well, you know, our UAW boys supported him.

President Johnson: That's right. They have and the state—

Reuther: The problem down there now is our fellows are fine, but then you've got CWA [Communication Workers of America] and the steelworkers and some other people, and I'm—and Hank Brown is calling me, and I'm just trying to get these other fellows to act sensibly.

President Johnson: What they ought to do is this: They ought to realize that number one, Mr. Connally won the conventions. They had a contest over it. They got 2,700 votes, and he's got about 1,800 of them.

Reuther: Uh-huh.

President Johnson: That's number one. So they tried, and the majority didn't win, and they lost. They tried Don Yarborough, and they lost. Now, Connally's there. And the man that didn't lose was Ralph Yarborough, and the only reason he didn't lose is because we wouldn't let a man run against him and wouldn't let Connally, and Connally's given me some very bad publicity about it. They said Connally and I have fallen out, and all that kind of stuff. It's not true, but Connally didn't like my telling him that he just absolutely couldn't support Kilgore, and then Kilgore called here, and I was in a Cabinet meeting, and Walter Jenkins talked to him, and they had to make a decision—they had an hour before it announced— and Walter Jenkins told him that he thought it would be an insult to me if he announced.[38] So he went up and withdrew, and that gave Yarborough an unheard of opponent, and he damn near defeated him.[39]

And now, the problem we've got is getting Yarborough [to] beat this attractive young boy Bush. And he ought to quit fighting with Connally and every Democrat. If a man's got a Democratic label on, he ought to say "Mister." And the only ones he ought to cuss is Republicans. Hell, if I were him, I wouldn't go to a county convention; I wouldn't mess around the convention. The convention is going to be for his candidate for president. His candidate for president is going to win. He's going to have his program. It's going to do what Yarborough likes to vote for. So why does he want to get mixed off in the convention? He ought to try to win the senatorship; that's what we need.

Reuther: Is John Connally prepared to adopt a broad general state-

---

38. For this conversation, see Walter Jenkins to Joe Kilgore, 1:20 P.M., 3 February 1964, Johnson and Germany, *The Presidential Recordings, Johnson*, vol. 4, *February 1, 1964–March 8, 1964*, pp. 78–83; see also John Connally to Jack Valenti, 8:25 P.M.; Jack Valenti to Albert Thomas, 8:30 P.M.; Johnson to Jack Brooks, 8:35 P.M.; Johnson to Dick Maguire, 8:45 P.M.; Johnson to Ken O'Donnell, 8:50 P.M.; and Johnson to Jim Wright, 9:15 P.M., 3 February 1964, ibid., pp. 131–46, 148–57.

39. Ralph Yarborough's opponent in the 2 May Texas primary had been conservative radio network owner and broadcaster Gordon McLendon.

ment, which you say that they provide full support to the President and all the Democratic candidates?

President Johnson: I don't know. I don't know; I haven't talked to him.

Reuther: See, because if we could get an agreement on that, hell, that's all they need. They don't need anything else.

President Johnson: John Connally is prepared to bring that delega- tion up there and support me to . . . [*unclear*]. I'm prepared to tell John Connally and everybody down there that we've got to go all out to elect Yarborough, but I don't know whether I can keep them from just fighting at each other's throat because they're like two big pussycats.

Reuther: Oh, they're acting like boys. Don Yarborough calls me, and—

President Johnson: But Connally's been elected, and Connally's got the votes, and Connally's in charge, and I've got to have Connally to carry the state myself, and that they ought to recognize. And Connally got 71 percent of the votes against Don Yarborough and didn't halfway try and didn't halfway campaign.

Reuther: That's right.

President Johnson: And a year ago, he only beat him by 26,000, but that's what they've lost in a two-year period.[40]

Reuther: Yeah—

President Johnson: And they'll get it down to 81 percent if they keep on, but what they'll do, they'll wind up having [John] Tower in the Senate and having Bush in the Senate.[41] Now, that's the way they're going because Yarborough is a very weak candidate. Civil rights and union labor and the Negro thing is not the way to get elected in a state that elects Connally by 72 percent.

And Yarborough votes right, but he's handicapped in that state. Now, he wouldn't be handicapped in Michigan or New York, but he's handi- capped in Texas. Look what they did to [Carl] Elliott in Alabama: the only decent guy we had in the whole South on Rules Committee, and they beat him.[42] Now, they will beat John Young from Texas because he's

---

40. During his first run for governor of Texas in 1962, John Connally had defeated Don Yarborough by 26,000 votes in a primary runoff. "Yarborough Concedes Defeat in Texas Run- Off," *New York Times*, 5 June 1962.

41. Republican John Tower was first elected to the Senate from Texas in 1961 to fill the seat vacated by Johnson when he assumed the vice presidency. He would remain in the Senate until January 1985.

42. Representative Carl Elliott, an at-large Democratic congressman from Alabama, had been defeated in a nine-candidate, "last-man-out" primary runoff on 2 June. A moderate opponent of Governor George Wallace, Elliott had been targeted by segregationists in the state despite having voted against the civil rights bill. *New York Times*, 3, 4, and 5 June 1964.

voting with us 100 percent of the time, but give them two years, they'll get him.[43]

Now, what we got to do, the big thing that the liberal movement ought to do, it oughtn't to give a tinker's damn about who comes to convention or what they say about the platform. There's one thing they ought to care about: Are the people coming to that convention are going to be for Johnson? The answer's yes. Every damn one of them are going to be approved by me; that's number one. They're not going to send a man there that's not agreeable to me. So that the man that they claim they're for is going to have the delegation that he wants, that's number one. The second thing they ought to be concerned about is electing Ralph Yarborough, and put every energy and dollar and time they can in it, not run people off from him.[44]

Reuther: That's right.

President Johnson: All they're doing is making everybody not want to vote for Yarborough, almost including *me*.

Reuther: Well, you see, when I talked to Yarborough, when he called me, he said that Connally was deliberately trying to build up in order to deny him a resolution endorsing him at the state convention.

President Johnson: A resolution endorsing him ain't going to change him one damn vote.

Reuther: I know, but the point is, if they have a general resolution endorsing everyone, that's what the convention is for—

President Johnson: I don't know whether—

Reuther: —endorsing Democrats.

President Johnson: I don't know whether they're going to have one even endorsing me. All I know is I told them this: that I want every delegate to come to that national convention to be a Johnson man. Period.

Reuther: No, but why couldn't we try to bump some heads together down there, and I'd be glad to work on the labor end of the thing even though the UAW guys are not the problem. That number one, that the convention pledges full and wholehearted support to you and to all the Democratic candidates who've been nominated in Texas, and that means

---

43. Texas Democrat John Young would serve in the House until January 1979.

44. What Johnson outlined in this passage would prove to be the exact eventual outcome of the 1964 battle within the Texas party. Johnson and Connally controlled the state convention and selected a conservative delegation to the Democratic National Convention in Atlantic City. Chandler Davidson concludes, however, that this delegation, "in spite of [its] displeasure with the national party's liberal platform, did what an equally liberal delegation would have done—supported the Johnson-Humphrey ticket." Davidson, *Race And Class In Texas Politics,* pp. 166–67.

the Yarborough people support the Connally people, and vice versa.

President Johnson: Well, I would certainly be for that. I'm going to support everybody—

Reuther: [*Unclear*] it's a simple, simple goddamn proposition.

President Johnson: I'm going to support . . . I'm going to support everybody that's—

Reuther: That's what *you're* going to do, you're—

President Johnson: That's right, and I'm going to support him openly, and I'm going to help raise him money, and I'm going to throw down any corporation president I can and make him help him. But while I'm doing that, he's going to be off trying to start a fight.

Reuther: Well, I mean, I'm—and I think that that doesn't make any sense whatsoever.

President Johnson: And you and Dave McDonald and O. A. Knight had better just say, "Now, what we want you to do is we want that one vote in the Senate. And incidentally, we've got to have it for the cloture, and he doesn't know what he's going to do on it, and we've just got to have it, or we're liable to lose it."[45] Hubert [Humphrey] and I talked last night until midnight on that problem, and he's going down there this Sunday.[46] And it's a hard vote, but he can't turn back to labor, and he can't come back to the Negroes, and he can't join over the Dixiecrats.

Reuther: That's right, that's right.

President Johnson: But he hasn't, he's . . .

Reuther: You think in a situation like that, he wouldn't be trying to make more problems for himself.

President Johnson: He's done that all of his life, though. He's constitutional that way. That's why he ran five times before he got elected.[47] I do my best because he votes with me 100 percent. He votes with me better than you'd vote with me, and you can't get mad at a man that does that.

Reuther: No, except that you could think his tactics is wrong.

President Johnson: But he votes for me, then he goes right out and starts a fight with the first man that helps him, [doesn't] make a damn who it is. It'll be Hubert—Hubert told me last night he was about the

45. David J. McDonald was the president of the United Steelworkers of America, and one of Reuther's leading rivals. Nelson Lichtenstein, *The Most Dangerous Man in Detroit: Walter Reuther and the Fate of American Labor* (New York: Basic Books, 1995), p. 322.

46. The Daily Diary makes no mention of a conversation or meeting with Senator Hubert Humphrey of Minnesota on 4 June.

47. Ralph Yarborough had run unsuccessfully as the liberal candidate for the Texas Democratic gubernatorial nomination in 1952, 1954, and 1956; he had also lost a bid for state attorney general in 1938.

damnedest problem that he had ever had. And I had him in to lunch today, he and his wife, with the Shah of Iran [*slight chuckle*], and had him sitting at the head table, and I went up to him and I said, "Now, I want you to know, Ralph, I'm with you money, marbles, and chalk, and anything, anytime you want me to do, call Walter Jenkins and I'll pick up the phone and call them. Now, you go down there and run for yourself day and night because we cannot take two Republican senators from Texas."

Reuther: That's right.

President Johnson: He caused the first one, you know. He got in that thing and caused that, and now he's going to cause another one. Well, what he wants to do, he and Mrs. Randolph, they want to get down there and fight with Connally. Now, what in the hell do you want to fight with a man that has got 72 percent of the votes for?

Reuther: [*Chuckles.*] I don't know. Well, you see, two years ago when Connally was running, the state council down there were solidly against him.[48]

President Johnson: Yeah.

Reuther: And I sat down with Moon and our fellows, and I said, "This doesn't make sense. You're going to elect a Republican. You're going to turn the whole state administration over to the Republican Party, and that doesn't make sense." And so we fought to get the state convention to leave it up to each individual union. We then endorsed Connally, the UAW.

President Johnson: Yeah . . . that's right. Well, Connally is not as liberal and progressive as I want him to be.

Reuther: I understand.

President Johnson: But Connally is much more a representative of the Texas sentiment than *I* am. And . . .

Reuther: He's a hell of a lot better than the Republicans would give you.

President Johnson: And ten times better, and what we've got to do—my job is to get Connally to support Yarborough.

Reuther: Right.

President Johnson: Now, you know the first thing after this election, Connally called me up and said, "Well, I've got 72 percent of the vote." Two days later he called me up and said, "What have you got Ralph Yarborough down here looking to the secretary of state['s] office checking every one of my county chairman for?" And I said I never heard of it. "Well," he said, "he's got three men in there, and they're checking every certification to

---

48. Reuther was referring to the Texas AFL-CIO State Council.

see who my people are and what votes they got." And said, "Looks like, by God, when I didn't run a man against him and I didn't support McLendon and I let him eek out and just slip in that we wouldn't have anything to fight about now, and he's going to need me a lot more in November than I need *him*." And I said, "Well, I'll check into it." And I checked into it, and Yarborough was down to see if he could control the convention.

So he's picking that fight. He can't control the convention.

Reuther: Yeah. . . . Of course he can't.

President Johnson: It's going to be 2 to 1 [for] Connally. So then he's going to say, "Well, if you don't let us have our way even though we just got a third of the votes and although Don Yarborough just got 28 percent of them . . ."

Reuther: "We'll walk out."

President Johnson: "We'll walk out." Now, Connally don't give a damn.

Reuther: Of course he doesn't, he's got the machinery and the—

President Johnson: And, Walter, that's what's happened to us in Texas all these years. [Allan] Shivers was a CIO [Congress of Industrial Organizations] lawyer. He represented the oil field workers at Port Arthur. He was sympathetic to labor; he went to the Senate representing labor.[49] Connally went in there being very sympathetic to him. But when they get in, some of these extreme folks start fighting with them, and they rule or ruin them. And so they drive them over, and they get so extreme. Now, Connally is 20 degrees to the right [of] what he was when he was elected.

Reuther: Yeah. Well, I'll go to work on this thing. I—

President Johnson: I'll do my best, and—

Reuther: If the UAW guys were involved, there'd be no problem, but—

President Johnson: Well, your boy, I forgot his name, that died down there . . . you remember what . . . any . . .

Reuther: [*Unclear*] Cumus.[50]

---

49. Allan Shivers was governor of Texas from 1949 to 1957. During the 1930s, he had served in the Texas state senate, to which Johnson was referring here (Shivers never served in the U.S. Senate). A conservative Democrat who supported Senator Joseph McCarthy, Shivers called for the death penalty for Communists. In 1952, he deployed the Texas Democratic Party apparatus to work for Republican nominee Dwight Eisenhower. This led Johnson and Speaker of the House Sam Rayburn to form a temporary alliance with Frankie Randolph and the state party's liberal faction to deny Shivers the Democratic nomination in 1956. Davidson, *Race And Class In Texas Politics*, pp. 161–62.

50. Cumus is a phonetic spelling, and has not been identified.

President Johnson: Yeah, what's his name?

Reuther: Cumus.

President Johnson: Yeah.

Reuther: Yeah, he was a very fine [*unclear*]—

President Johnson: Well, he was at the convention that night—I was there speaking—and at the dinner, and Moon and all those boys are all right, and if they had listened to them, they'd be all right. Now, Dave McDonald has got some boys down there that let this woman [Frankie Randolph] lead them off. Now, she's a good woman and she's for our program, but she—

Reuther: The problem was the steelworkers, the oil workers, and the CWA—Joe Beirne's people. And they're just so goddamn bitter, they can't be sensible.[51]

President Johnson: Well, if I only had 28 percent, I'd be awfully careful who I'd challenge. Now, the only thing that . . . the one job that labor has got to do in Texas is not Johnson because they're all for him anyway; is not the Negroes [because] they're all for him anyway; not the Mexicans [because] they're all for him anyway. The one job they've got to get done is to get the moderate conservative Democrats to vote for Yarborough. They've got all the others: They've got all the oil-field workers, all the CWA, all the steelworkers, all the UAW including the president, but they haven't got the others that they need to win this race in November, and they oughtn't to run them off. They ought to try to get them. I'd kiss their butt every minute, and that's what I'm going to do. I bet I've seen 50 conservatives from that state and [to] every one of them I say, "Please let Yarborough come back to help *me.*"

Reuther: Yeah. That's right.

President Johnson: And . . . what happens in Atlantic City is not a matter of his concern at all because I'm going to be nominated.

Reuther: Sure.

President Johnson: What happens in Texas is a matter of great concern to me. And I'll carry him over in Texas if he just won't make himself [*Reuther attempts to interject*] so damned obnoxious.

Reuther: Right.

President Johnson: And he's a good man, and he votes right, and he feels right, except you've got to get him to vote for cloture. Now, that's . . . [*Reuther attempts to interject*]. You've got to let Dave

---

51. Joseph A. Beirne was president of the Communications Workers of America Union.

McDonald and CWA or some of them know that this vote last night, it looks like they've got about 24, and Hubert thinks we've got 41. That's 65. Now, we need 67. And we may lose one of those, but we've got to get Frank Clements [*sic*] agreed that this fellow [Herbert] Walters with Kennedy would vote *for* cloture. But now he won't vote for them, and Yarborough's doubtful, so we lost [Estes] Kefauver, and we lose Yarborough . . .[52]

Reuther: Yeah.

President Johnson: . . . why, we may lose that bill, and [*Reuther tries to interject*] we're within one or two votes of getting it, and I think that they've just got to tell him [Yarborough] that he just can't go back on the people [who] elected him.

Reuther: Right.

President Johnson: And somebody's got to get Mrs. Randolph to tell him, and the only one I know who can do that is the steelworkers.

Reuther: All right, I'll go to work on that right away.

President Johnson: Don't quote me on it, because I don't want him to think it, but I had that—

Reuther: This conversation is between us.

President Johnson: I will go 100 percent for Yarborough, and I'll raise him $100,000 if I have to. I'll do anything in the world to get him reelected. And if I had any power with him, I'd get him to quit fighting these other folks. Now, I'll fight with Connally. I've already fought with him . . .

Reuther: That's right.

President Johnson: . . . on Yarborough's . . . first campaign, but I'll fight with him again. And Connally's going to support the nominee, and he's going to support *him*, and I'll try to get him to say so by resolution. I imagine Connally thinks that what he's trying to do is hold these Dixiecrats and these conservative fellows from going over to the Republicans.

Reuther: Yeah.

---

52. Johnson was referring to the current breakdown of Senate Democratic and Republican votes in favor of cloture on the civil rights bill (44 Democrats and 27 Republicans eventually voted in favor of cloture). Along with Senator Yarborough of Texas, who did vote for cloture, Johnson was referring to Senator Herbert S. Walters of Tennessee, who had been appointed to the Senate by Tennessee Governor Frank Clement following the death of Senator Estes Kefauver in August 1963. A liberal and the party's 1956 vice presidential nominee, Kefauver had voted in favor of the 1957 Civil Rights Act and, Johnson assumed, would have been a safe vote for cloture. Walters, in contrast, voted against cloture. *Congressional Quarterly Almanac*, 1964, vol. 20, p. 678; Robert Mann, *The Walls of Jericho: Lyndon Johnson, Hubert Humphrey, Richard Russell, and the Struggle for Civil Rights* (New York: Harcourt, Brace, 1996).

President Johnson: He's trying to hold them in the Democratic Party.

Reuther: That's right. [*Unclear*]—

President Johnson: And when we don't hold them, we always lose. We didn't hold them in Dallas, so we got [Bruce] Alger. We didn't hold them in El Paso, so we got the boy [Ed Foreman] out there. We got defeated. And we didn't hold them in the Senate race, so we got John Tower.[53]

Reuther: That's right.

President Johnson: Unless we can hold some of those conservatives, if they go Republican with us, why then they'll beat us.

Reuther: Right.

President Johnson: OK, Walter.

Reuther: Well, let me, one thing—

President Johnson: Yeah.

Reuther: —one second. I'm coming to that [Ludwig] Erhard dinner that you—[54]

President Johnson: Yeah . . . yeah.

Reuther: —invited me to, and my wife has a problem that night, and I was just wondering whether I violate protocol if I bring my oldest daughter.

President Johnson: Hell, no. I'd rather have her than you or your wife. [*Reuther laughs.*] I've got two daughters, and I'm a daughter man.

Reuther: I shall bring her along.

President Johnson: You just bring her. Tell her that she got a special oral invitation from the President.

Reuther: Very good. Her name is Linda.

President Johnson: OK, that's wonderful.

Reuther: Very good.

President Johnson: Well, I got a Lynda too. How old is she?

Reuther: She's a senior at the University of Michigan.

President Johnson: Well, she must be 21 or [2]2. I've got one—

Reuther: She's 21.

President Johnson: I've got one that's going on—be 21 next March.

Reuther: She's 21.

President Johnson: Well, I'll see her.

---

53. Johnson was referring to Representative Bruce Alger, a Republican from Dallas who had been elected in 1954; he would be defeated in the 1964 Democratic landslide. Also referred to is Representative Ed Foreman, a Republican from Texas's 16th District, which included El Paso and Odessa; and Senator John Tower, who had won Johnson's former Senate seat with an upset victory in a 1961 special election.

54. West German Chancellor Ludwig Erhard was scheduled to make an official visit to Washington at the end of the next week (11–13 June).

Reuther: Very good.

President Johnson: Thank you, Walter.

Reuther: Thank you.

President Johnson: Say, what are you going—when are you getting started on your negotiation?

Reuther: Oh, we don't start until the 30th of June.

President Johnson: Well, I made a couple of passes at them urging them to reduce prices, but I haven't had much success.

Reuther: I did too. You saw the story in the *New York Times* today, if you get to it. I'm going to urge them strongly to cut prices.[55]

President Johnson: Mm-hmm. O[K]—

Reuther: I'm in your corner on that one.

President Johnson: All right.

Reuther: All the way.

President Johnson: Bye.

Reuther: Bye.

Johnson made three more calls before leaving for dinner with the Steinbecks, all of which were recorded. The first was to his adviser and Special Counsel Myer "Mike" Feldman, whom he asked to draft a memorandum outlining a new Cabinet committee on fuel policy.

8:17 P.M.

To Myer Feldman[56]

Scattered office conversation with Jack Valenti precedes the call.

President Johnson: Mike? I talked to [Robert] McNamara and told him I was going to make him chairman of a Cabinet committee on fuel policy.

Myer Feldman: Yes, sir.

President Johnson: I think he can be objective and can put some

---

55. Johnson and Reuther were discussing the upcoming contract negotiations between the UAW and the major automakers, as well as the administration's efforts to extract a price cut from the automakers. See Johnson to Willard Wirtz, 5:40 P.M., 21 May 1964, in McKee, *The Presidential Recordings, Johnson,* vol. 6, *April 14, 1964–May 31, 1964,* pp. 799–803; and Walter Heller to Johnson, 6:15 P.M., 4 June 1964, in this volume. For the newspaper article referred to by Reuther, see Damon Stetson, "Reuther to Seek Auto Price Cuts," *New York Times,* 5 June 1964.

56. Tape WH6406.03, Citation #3633, Recordings of Telephone Conversations—White House Series, Recordings and Transcripts of Conversations and Meetings, Lyndon B. Johnson Library.

staff and organize it and so forth. And I want to put on that committee: [Stewart] Udall . . .[57]

Feldman: Yes, sir.

President Johnson: And Commerce.

Feldman: Yes.

President Johnson: And Interior—Udall and Commerce, now wait a minute, and Labor.

Feldman: Yes, sir

President Johnson: And Secretary of State.

Feldman: Yes.

President Johnson: And the Council of Economic Advisers.

Feldman: All right.

President Johnson: That gives us six.

Feldman: Shall I draft an order to that effect?

President Johnson: Yeah . . . mm-hmm.

Feldman: All right.

President Johnson: And tell them what they're supposed to do and get in [and] come back with a report to us just as promptly as possible.

Feldman: Now, the kind of report you'll get will be not the kind the coal industry wants, I'm certain of that, but I think it's a good idea just the same. I'm certain that the kind of report you will get will call for the abolition of all controls, because we had a similar committee, only it was headed by OEP [Office of Emergency Planning], the office—and perhaps we should put [Edward] McDermott on this committee too.[58] About a year ago they filed a report calling for the abolition of—

President Johnson: Well, did he have Cabinet people on it too?

Feldman: He had representatives of them. He did not have a Cabinet-level committee; they were third- or fourth-level people. But I'm sure—

President Johnson: Well, we'll just tell Bill Wirtz.[59] Now, he ought to represent labor. And Council of Economic Advisers ought to be friendly to labor.

Feldman: Yes, sir.

President Johnson: And McNamara's not going to be unfriendly to them.

Feldman: No.

President Johnson: And Commerce will be friendly to them.

Feldman: Commerce will be friendly to [*unclear*].

---

57. Stewart Udall served as secretary of the interior.
58. Edward A. McDermott was the director of the federal Office of Emergency Planning.
59. Willard Wirtz served as secretary of labor.

President Johnson: So State Department won't be, and Interior probably won't be.

Feldman: That's right.

President Johnson: I don't know about OEP. I don't know whether to get them in there or not. I don't know how their attitude—they may just do the same.

Feldman: Well, they're . . . the OEP people will take the position of the Council of Economic Advisers. The Council of Economic Advisers will be violently against the position that was expressed this afternoon to you.[60] They believe that all controls ought to be off oil. They believe as much as possible should be imported because as an economic matter, the lower the cost, the better off the American industry is, and so I'm sure of their position.

President Johnson: Well, we better not put them on it, then.

Feldman: All right.

President Johnson: I wouldn't put them on it, then.

Feldman: Then the committee would be, then, with McNamara as chairman.

President Johnson: Chairman. Would be . . .

Feldman: McNamara.

President Johnson: Then Labor.

Feldman: Labor.

President Johnson: Interior and Commerce.

Feldman: Commerce and Interior.

President Johnson: Labor, Interior, and Commerce, and State.

Feldman: And State, yes, sir. All right, I'll . . . instead of putting it under the formality of an executive order, I'd like to suggest it simply be by memorandum.

President Johnson: That's right . . . that's right; that's all right.

Feldman: All right, sir, I'll do it.

President Johnson: OK. Fine. Bye.

Feldman: Yes, sir.

Johnson next returned an earlier call from Secretary of Agriculture Orville Freeman, who requested a meeting with the President sometime the following week to discuss possible appointments to the National Commission on Food Marketing. The authorizing legislation for this

---

60. Feldman was referring to the afternoon's meeting with the business-labor National Coal Policy Conference.

commission had just passed the House, although amendments there meant that the Senate would have to agree to an altered version of the bill. The commission would report on the development and operation of the food marketing system in the United States.

8:21 P.M.

To Orville Freeman[61]

Orville Freeman: . . . What I really wanted was just to ask you if over the weekend when you work out your schedule for next week, I'd appreciate it if I could have about a half an hour.

President Johnson: All right. It's commencement week.[62]

[*to Valenti, in the office*] Jack, do you know what my best days are next week?

Jack Valenti: Yes, sir. I can find that out for you.

President Johnson: [*to Valenti*] Run in there and get on the phone right quick. Run in and get on the phone right quick. [*Pause.*]

Freeman: We have . . . the marketing commission passed the House, as you probably noticed.

President Johnson: Yeah . . . yeah, but they got to go to conference now, because—

Freeman: They'll be going to conference. The House—

President Johnson: Can't you get the Senate just to agree to it and go on and pass it as they did?[63]

Freeman: I think we can improve it in conference, Mr. President, and . . .

President Johnson: Oh, hell, we're going to hell before we ever get the damn thing, though.

Freeman: Well . . .

---

61. Tape WH6406.03, Citation #3634, Recordings of Telephone Conversations—White House Series, Recordings and Transcripts of Conversations and Meetings, Lyndon B. Johnson Library.
62. The following week, Johnson would give commencement addresses at Swarthmore College on 8 June and Holy Cross College on 10 June.
63. The Senate had passed the Food Marketing Commission legislation on 18 May; the House passed an amended version of the bill on 4 June. As Johnson suggested, the Senate would approve the amended House version by voice vote on 19 June. *Congressional Quarterly Almanac,* 1964, vol. 20, pp. 142–43.

President Johnson: What do you need? You just got—you got a million and a half [dollars], that's more than the . . ."[64]

Freeman: Well, we could—if we have any problems in the Senate, why, we'll probably do this.

President Johnson: I'd just get them to agree to the House bill, and . . . right now while they've got civil rights on. If you don't, if you got a difference, and it has to go to conference, why you'll be there until we go to the convention, and then we won't get them appointed. I'd like to name them tomorrow. [*Freeman makes a barely audible comment.*] I don't know why in the hell the House let them change that. We got no leadership at all. We can't pass anything the same way in both places.

Freeman: Well, I agree.

President Johnson: It's just a damned outrage. Why'd they change it in the House?

Freeman: Oh, it was just a . . . they had to jockey around. As you say, they've always got to change it and be a little different. And we pushed them hard to try and have the two-year period, which is really needed, and a little more resources to work with.[65] It passed the Senate unanimously, you know, before, and this may not be. I'm watching it very closely. But I would like to discuss the appointment on that group with you. I do want to talk to you a little bit about this beef thing.[66] We've got a couple of other things I just want to bring you up to date on so that they're clearly in mind. So, I know you're busy and had a long day today, and I won't burden you with it now.

President Johnson: [*to Valenti*] What's the best day, Jack?

Valenti: I would say [*unclear*].

President Johnson: [*to Valenti*] Mr. Freeman wants to see me, and I want the best day to see him.

Valenti: All right. I'd say around 12:30 on Thursday.

President Johnson: [*to Freeman*] 12:30, Thursday, all right?

Freeman: Yes, sir, fine.

President Johnson: All right. OK.

Freeman: Thank you, Mr. President.

---

64. For background on the National Commission on Food Marketing, see Lawrence F. O'Brien, "Memorandum To The President; Subject: Possible Items for Discussion at Leadership Breakfast," 2 June 1964, "Ex FG 400/MC 11/22/63–6/15/64" folder, Box 328, White House Central Files: Federal Government Operations, Lyndon B. Johnson Library, p. 3.

65. The House version of the bill required a completed report by July 1965, rather than July 1966 as required in the Senate version. Ibid., p. 3.

66. See Houston Harte to Johnson, 11:25 A.M., 4 June 1965, in this volume.

Johnson's final recorded call of the day was to Cliff Carter, his longtime aide, adviser, and, in 1964, personal liaison to the Kennedy-dominated Democratic National Committee. Johnson berated Carter for scheduling too many events in Ohio, a state that he thought offered few fund-raising prospects, and for overloading his schedule with so many fund-raising events that the press had begun to raise questions.

8:26 P.M.

To Cliff Carter[67]

A brief office conversation precedes the call.
President Johnson: . . . [*unclear*].
Jack Valenti: I've heard you say that to me, sir.
President Johnson: [*Unclear.*]
Valenti: I wasn't in the meeting, Mr. President. Walter [Jenkins] and Cliff and Dick Maguire and Bill Moyers met.[68]
Recording of the conversation begins abruptly.
President Johnson: [*Unclear.*] They shouldn't tell [*unclear*] them that.
Cliff Carter: Yes, sir.

President Johnson: I don't know why you're trying to raise money in Ohio. By God, you can't even elect a constable out there. And they oughtn't to use the President on that kind of stuff. That's awful bad judgment. And I've been to Ohio and campaigned over it for years and never have made any progress, and I'm ready to wipe them out [as] far as I'm concerned. So I'd just tell whoever is telling you on Ohio that Ohio's off the list until they come in with their guarantee and bring it in and show us what they got.

Carter: Yes, sir.

President Johnson: So don't get us scheduled anymore for Columbus. I think *Detroit's* bad.[69] I don't think you-all know what you're doing when you schedule these things, and you just let some damned nincompoop put you in. But we're doing too many of them, I know that. And the

---

67. Tape WH6406.03, Citation #3635, Recordings of Telephone Conversations—White House Series, Recordings and Transcripts of Conversations and Meetings, Lyndon B. Johnson Library.
68. Richard "Dick" Maguire served as treasurer of the Democratic National Committee.
69. President Johnson would appear at a fund-raising dinner in Detroit on 26 June. "Remarks at a Fundraising Dinner in Detroit," 26 June 1964, *Public Papers, Johnson, 1963–64,* 1:819–23.

press briefings over here are sounding pretty bad. I'm just looking at one tonight on . . . Oh, hell, where is it?

[*reading quickly, apparently from a report from George Reedy*] "I was asked today about an engagement in Columbus." "For what date?" "The 17th." "Consequently, I can place up on the schedule's firm commitment or firm uncommitment." "What is?" "The fund-raising dinner." "I wasn't here this morning, but I read it, and I didn't see anything about Detroit." "Yes, Detroit's on there." "Did you say Detroit?" "Yes, it's on there after the 26th." "Columbus, then, would make five if you considered that the same day as Cleveland." "That is right: It would be five." "Is someone keeping a running total of how much money is collected from all these fund-raising affairs the President's going to?" "I would hope there's a treasurer keeping track of such a thing," George [Reedy] said.[70]

So Columbus, I'm not an Ohio man. Just tell them that they leaked it out there that I was coming, and they're not authorized to until we make a commitment, and that—don't make any more engagements or consider Ohio until I clear it.

Carter: Yes, sir.

President Johnson: OK.

Carter: Sure.

8:30 P.M.: President Johnson went to the Mansion with Jack Valenti for dinner with Lady Bird Johnson and the Steinbecks. The Daily Diary records no details about the dinner or any other activities of the evening.

9:36 P.M.: Unrecorded call to Judge Moursund in Texas.

---

70. Johnson would make a speech at the Communications Workers of America convention in Cleveland on 17 June and would attend a "Salute to President Johnson" dinner in Cleveland on 8 October. The event tentatively planned for Columbus did not take place. "Remarks in Cleveland at the Convention of the Communications Workers of America," 17 June 1964; and "Remarks at a 'Salute to President Johnson' Dinner in Cleveland," 8 October 1964, *Public Papers, Johnson, 1963–64,* 1:778–81, 2:1251–61.

Saturday, June 6, 1964

*Go ahead and read it to me. I just wanted you to leave it. I
don't want to be interrupted. I'm trying to get all this mail out.
I'm in a hurry. Go ahead.*

—President Johnson to Richard Nelson

The first Saturday in June proved to be more eventful, and historically
significant, than typical weekend days at the Johnson White House.
Just before 11:00 A.M., Johnson went to the West Wing for a meeting of
the National Security Council, stopping on the way to talk with paint-
ers working on the colonnade outside the offices. The Security Council
meeting had been called because Communist Pathet Lao forces had shot
down a U.S. reconnaissance plane operating over the Plaine des Jarres
in Laos. Secretary of Defense Robert McNamara informed the President
and the NSC about the situation and indicated that the pilot had been
observed to parachute out of the plane only to land in an area controlled
by the Pathet Lao. Rescue attempts had been unsuccessful. The incident raised the question of whether, how, and when the United States
would retaliate militarily. McNamara and the Joint Chiefs of Staff recommended that the reconnaissance flights continue immediately, with
a mission of two unarmed planes escorted by six to eight bombers. The
bombers would be authorized to attack the source of any ground fire
that the mission encountered. This recommendation met with approval,
although Air Force Chief of Staff Curtis LeMay and Lieutenant General
George Greene indicated that they personally would have preferred
a raid against the specific antiaircraft battery that had shot down the
plane. A discussion followed about what the reconnaissance flights,
which had resumed on May 22, had accomplished. A number of the NSC

members indicated that the flights had produced important intelligence about both Pathet Lao activities and the movement of material along supply routes from North Vietnam. In addition, the airborne U.S. presence had provided crucial political support for the neutralist government of Prince Souvanna Phouma, and might have intimidated the Pathet Lao into limiting their recent attacks. President Johnson, however, raised a crucial question about the implications of responding to the shootdown: "And what comes next?"[1] During the day, the White House made no official comments about the incident, although a State Department spokesman described the shootdown as a "serious" situation. The NSC meeting lasted until 11:15 A.M., after which Johnson returned to the White House Mansion with aides Jack Valenti and Douglass Cater and made an unrecorded call to Walter Jenkins.

President Johnson did not record any telephone conversations until late in the afternoon of June 6. Before the morning NSC meeting, he had received unrecorded calls from George Reedy, McGeorge Bundy, and Jenkins, and made unrecorded calls to Bill Moyers and Jenkins. Most of the President's afternoon would be occupied with a trip to New York, where he would appear at two events for the International Ladies' Garment Workers' Union.

11:33 A.M.: The President left the White House for Andrews Air Force Base and departed for New York on Air Force One.

12:25 P.M.: Arrived at Kennedy Airport.

12:35 P.M.: Departed for Manhattan by helicopter.

12:50 P.M.: Arrived at the West 30th Street heliport.

New York City Mayor Robert Wagner met the presidential party at the heliport.

12:53 P.M.: Motorcade to the New York City Union Health Center.

Along the way, Johnson stopped the motorcade so he could shake hands with members of a "Young Citizens for Johnson" group at the corner of 31st Street and 7th Avenue.[2]

1:03 P.M.: Arrived at the health center and greeted International Ladies' Garment Workers' Union President David Dubinsky.

The occasion for the visit was the 50th anniversary of the

---

1. "Summary Record of the 533d Meeting of the National Security Council," 6 June 1964, 10:45 A.M.; and "Memorandum for the Record," 6 June 1964, 10:45 A.M., U.S. Department of State, *Foreign Relations of the United States (FRUS), 1964–1968: Laos*, ed. Edward C. Keefer (Washington, DC: GPO, 1998), 28:141–44.

2. Damon Stetson, "President Appeals for an End to Bias; Salutes Union Here," *New York Times*, 7 June 1964.

health center, the first union-sponsored health facility in the United States.

1:20 P.M.: Unveiled a plaque honoring the health center and made a brief speech.[3]

2:30 P.M.: Departed the health center and greeted onlookers as he walked to the High School of Fashion Industries.

2:45 P.M.: Spoke briefly to the crowd gathered outside the school.

2:55 P.M.–3:50 P.M.: Following a speech by Mayor Wagner and an introduction by David Dubinsky, Johnson delivered a second, longer speech before departing for the heliport and Kennedy Airport.[4]

4:25 P.M.: Air Force One took off for Washington.

5:16 P.M.: Arrived at the White House and immediately placed an unrecorded call (probably from the Mansion) to secretary Vicki McCammon to ask if he had any calls to return.

5:18 P.M.: Unrecorded call to McGeorge Bundy to request his presence in the office.

5:20 P.M.: Arrived at the Oval Office with Jack Valenti and George Reedy.

5:24 P.M.: Met with Bundy and NSC staffer Michael Forrestal, who updated him on the loss of the U.S. reconnaissance plane over Laos.

5:34 P.M.: Unrecorded call from Lady Bird Johnson.

This call was followed a few minutes later by a recorded call from Douglass Cater, who asked for the President's opinion about a draft of a speech for the Holy Cross College commencement on June 10.

5:45 P.M.

From Douglass Cater[5]

Douglass Cater: [*Garbled recording*] over for a minute, or do you want to talk on the phone?

---

3. "Remarks in New York City Upon Unveiling a Plaque in Honor of the 50th Anniversary of the ILGWU Health Center," 6 June 1964, *Public Papers of the Presidents of the United States: Lyndon B. Johnson, 1963–64* (Washington, DC: GPO, 1965), 1:749–50.

4. "Remarks in New York City to Members of the International Ladies' Garment Workers' Union," 6 June 1964, ibid., 1:750–53.

5. Tape WH6406.03, Citation #3636, Recordings of Telephone Conversations—White House Series, Recordings and Transcripts of Conversations and Meetings, Lyndon B. Johnson Library.

President Johnson: I'd rather talk on the phone if you can.

Cater: Well, I've been giving some thought to this Holy Cross [address], and I had a good talk with Mac Bundy on it. We both feel that there is a way of giving this speech that would be particularly relevant to the situation that might be on next week. It does . . . it would pick up from Pope John [XXIII] and from President Kennedy's American University speech, but it would soberly address itself to the fact of the tensions that do exist in the world and the fact that we have to live with them, but that . . . and then we've got to face up to them.[6] But there are a number of things that need to be said, that look beyond, that would actually be very good in this connection. And this is what if—unless you are strongly opposed, I'd like to at least—

President Johnson: No, if you can do that, that's fine. I was just trying to agree with you this morning. I thought you said that it was on peace, and we didn't have any peace, and we better be worried about it.

Cater: No, sir. . . . I'm sorry. I made a basic mistake in trying to raise that in too brief a time. I didn't—I'm sorry, sir.

President Johnson: Yeah. . . . Well, you just send me what you got whenever you're ready to and let me look at it.

Cater: All right, sir.

President Johnson: OK.

Cater: Thank you.

5:50 P.M.: Unrecorded call to McGeorge Bundy.

6:25 P.M.: Unrecorded call to Jack Valenti.

6:34 P.M.: Unrecorded call to Walter Jenkins.

6:36 P.M.: Met with Valenti.

The President then received a call from Walter Jenkins's aide Richard Nelson, who needed approval of a sympathy cable being sent to an unidentified person. Irritated at the interruption, Johnson approved the cable but instructed Nelson to remove a sentence offering the President's personal assistance.

---

6. Kennedy's June 1963 American University speech had examined the possibility for world peace within the context of the cold war and announced that negotiations would begin toward a comprehensive test ban treaty and that the United States would cease all nuclear weapons tests as a gesture of good faith towards the success of the negotiations. "Commencement Address at American University in Washington," 10 June 1963, *Public Papers of the Presidents of the United States: John F. Kennedy, 1963* (Washington, DC: GPO, 1964), 1:459–64.

6:42 P.M.

From Richard Nelson[7]

President Johnson: Yes, Dick?

Richard Nelson: This is the cable, sir. If you approve it, we'll put it on the diplomatic cable and send it right up.

President Johnson: All right. . . . Go ahead and read it to me. I just wanted you to leave it. I don't want to be interrupted. I'm trying to get all this mail out. I'm in a hurry. Go ahead.

Nelson: [*reading*] "Mrs. [Lady Bird] Johnson and I were deeply saddened to learn of your father's death.[8] We wanted you to know that our thoughts and prayers were with you during this difficult time. If there is anything I can do personally to expedite your return to the United States or to assist you in any way, please contact me. With deepest sympathy, Lyndon Johnson."

President Johnson: I'd leave out that last sentence.

Nelson: All right.

President Johnson: Anything I can do personally, just cut that off.

Nelson: All right.

President Johnson: OK.

Nelson: Thank you, sir.

7:00 P.M.: Daughter Lynda stopped at the office with her date for the evening.

7:25 P.M.: President Johnson stopped on his way to the Mansion to get speech cards for the evening from Vicki McCammon.

7:30 P.M.: Asked McCammon to call Secretary of the Navy Paul H. Nitze, who was not available. The President then returned to the Mansion.

8:40 P.M.: Left with Jack Valenti to make an appearance at Gallaudet College's Centennial Banquet.[9]

8:46 P.M.: Spoke briefly and received a medallion from Gallaudet President Leonard M. Elstad.

---

7. Tape WH6406.03, Citation #3637, Recordings of Telephone Conversations—White House Series, Recordings and Transcripts of Conversations and Meetings, Lyndon B. Johnson Library.

8. The Johnson Library listing for the call suggests that the recipient of the cable could be U.S. Postmaster General John Gronouski.

9. Located in Washington, D.C., Gallaudet College is the nation's leading institution of higher education for the deaf.

9:05 P.M.: Departed Gallaudet alone and stopped at Jack and Mary Margaret Valenti's home, where he remained until 10:30.

10:37 P.M.: Returned to the White House.

The Daily Diary makes no further entries for June 6, but at 3:38 A.M. on the morning of June 7, Johnson made an unrecorded call from the Mansion to Michael Forrestal in the White House Situation Room. Although the diary provides no specific indication, the call likely involved the loss of a second U.S. plane in Laos.

Monday, June 8, 1964

The whole world will have the same worry: just as you put it,
"Where is the United States going, to war or not?"

—Michael Forrestal to President Johnson

As a new week began, the Johnson administration dealt with an intensification of the problems in Laos. The previous day, Pathet Lao forces had shot down a second U.S. aircraft, this one a fighter jet escorting an unarmed reconnaissance plane. In contrast to the first incident, a U.S. rescue mission reached the downed pilot before he could be captured by the Pathet Lao. The shootdown forced the United States to acknowledge for the first time that armed planes had participated in the reconnaissance missions over Laos. This admission created a diplomatic embarrassment because of the United States' previously strong rhetorical commitment to the Laotian neutrality provisions of the 1962 Geneva Accords, such that the U.S. ambassador to Laos even argued that it would have been preferable not to identify the downed aircraft specifically as a fighter plane.[1] Regardless of the diplomatic consequences of the armed flights, the loss of the second plane forced U.S. policymakers to come to a deci-

---

1. U.S. Ambassador Leonard Unger also opposed the idea of retaliatory bombing. In a telegram on 8 June, Unger noted that "I am deeply distressed over events of past several days and am apprehensive that all our careful work of past two years may be largely vitiated. . . . Have we come to decision that after two years of Communist violation of Geneva Accords and aggression in Laos, we are also taking off wraps?" "Telegram From the Embassy in Laos to the Department of State," 8 June 1964, U.S. Department of State, *Foreign Relations of the United States (FRUS), 1964–1968: Laos,* ed. Edward C. Keefer (Washington, DC: GPO, 1998), 28:150–52; Alvin Shuster, "Leftists in Laos Down 2D U.S. Jet Within 48 Hours," *New York Times,* 8 June 1964.

sion about whether and how to respond militarily to the loss of the U.S. planes. Bombing raids into Laos represented a significant escalation of U.S. military involvement in Southeast Asia, and along with discussion of the scope and specific targets of a potential mission, both President Johnson and Director of Central Intelligence John McCone raised the possibility in meetings on Sunday, June 7, that military action in Laos would send the United States "sliding down the slippery slope" toward a wider war in Southeast Asia.[2]

The weekend had also been a busy one on Capitol Hill, as the Senate gave unanimous consent to a motion to debate and vote on three Republican amendments to the civil rights bill before a Wednesday cloture vote to break the southern filibuster. Senate Majority Leader Mike Mansfield delayed filing a petition for the cloture vote until Monday to provide time for consideration of the amendments. Although the pro–civil rights Senate leadership from both parties opposed the three amendments, neither they nor the bill's segregationist opponents could afford to alienate the still uncommitted group of conservative Republicans who supported the changes. As a result, the consent motion met no opposition, and the Senate moved toward the first of a series of tremendously significant civil rights votes.[3]

Despite the pressures of the Laos crisis and Senate actions on civil rights, President Johnson's morning was occupied with a commencement address at Swarthmore College. After flying to Philadelphia and making a brief speech at the airport, Johnson took a short helicopter flight to the Swarthmore campus a few miles outside the city. He was greeted by Swarthmore's president, Courtney Smith, and then taken by motorcade to Smith's offices in the college's Parrish Hall. He met the day's other honorary degree recipients, who included Secretary General of the United Nations U Thant, economist and race relations expert Gunnar Myrdal, Nobel Prize–winning geneticist Hermann Muller, poet W. H. Auden, and theologian Alexander Purdy. Johnson dressed in academic regalia and participated in the procession to Swarthmore's Scott Outdoor Amphitheater for the 10:30 A.M. ceremony. The President's speech began at 11:15.[4] He

---

2. [John McCone] "Memorandum for the Record," 7 June 1964, Subject: Meeting on Sunday, June 7th, with the President, McNamara, Vance, Forrestal, Harriman, [U. Alexis] Johnson, William Bundy, Manning and McCone, *FRUS, 1964–1968*, 28:148–50.

3. E. W. Kenworthy, "Civil Rights Bloc Near Showdown on Scope of Bill," *New York Times*, 8 June 1964.

4. "Address at the Centennial Commencement of Swarthmore College," 8 June 1964, *Public Papers of the Presidents of the United States: Lyndon B. Johnson, 1963–64* (Washington, DC: GPO, 1965), 1:755–58.

departed immediately afterward, shaking hands with spectators along a fence at the college's athletic fields.

> **12:35 P.M.:** President Johnson returned to the White House.
>
> **1:45 P.M.:** Received a haircut from White House barber Dave Highly.
>
> **2:00 P.M.:** Unrecorded call to Jack Valenti. The President then attempted to take a nap.
>
> **2:02 P.M.:** Unrecorded call to Michael V. Forrestal, who was engaged with the question of how to respond to the loss of the two U.S. planes in Laos.
>
> **2:15 P.M.:** Unrecorded call to White House staffer Ashton Gonella. At this point, the President apparently fell asleep.
>
> **3:25 P.M.:** Unrecorded call to Walter Jenkins.

3:35 P.M.

To Michael Forrestal[5]

Ten minutes after the call to Jenkins, President Johnson made his first recorded call of the day to Michael Forrestal, who briefed him on the progress of an ongoing meeting (which the President would later join) in which the administration's most influential foreign policy officials were considering whether to conduct a retaliatory air strike in Laos.[6] Forrestal explained Ambassador to Laos Leonard Unger's opposition to an immediate U.S. attack on the antiaircraft batteries that had shot down the U.S. planes. Unger believed that a U.S. retaliatory raid, in combination with the revelation that U.S. fighter planes had accompanied the reconnaissance flights, would be interpreted by much of the world as a violation of the Laotian neutrality provisions of the Geneva Accords. Throughout the spring, the United States had argued that North Vietnam had violated the accords, and Unger felt that the costs of undermining this diplomatic position far outweighed the benefits of the demonstration of U.S. fortitude that the raid would provide.[7] Forrestal, however, reported that all of

---

5. Tape WH6406.03, Citation #3638, Recordings of Telephone Conversations—White House Series, Recordings and Transcripts of Conversations and Meetings, Lyndon B. Johnson Library.
6. For a summary of the meeting, see Bromley Smith, "Memorandum of Conference with President Johnson," 8 June 1964, *FRUS, 1964–1968*, 28:152–60.
7. Unger felt that if an attack were made, it should be conducted by the Laotian air force. Ibid.

the State Department and military figures gathered at the meeting, himself included, disagreed with Unger and felt that the United States had to strike back against the Pathet Lao antiaircraft installations. Johnson, at this point, remained unconvinced. He worried that aggressive action would send a message to both friends and enemies that the professed U.S. interest in a peaceful solution to the problems of Southeast Asia was little more than rhetoric. Nonetheless, the President indicated that he would probably accept his advisers' recommendations.

Michael Forrestal: Sir, we're in the room there. Everybody seems to be in agree—this is [Averell] Harriman and [Robert] McNamara, [U. Alexis] Johnson, [William] Bundy, and the whole State Department —are strongly of the view that this ought to go ahead today.[8] Mac Bundy feels that—this is on the basis of my talk with him and giving him [Leonard] Unger's telegram—that it probably would be a wise idea to delay another 24 hours in order to permit us to get all our ducks in order here in Washington and to get Unger in Laos more understanding of our problem.[9] No one in the meeting thinks we ought to wait an additional 24 hours.

President Johnson: Why? What is the urgency?

Forrestal: Their feeling is that psychologically, if you don't—if you delay another 24 hours, you detach, you separate the action of shooting down one of our planes from the action that answers it. They also feel that they would just rather not do it at all than delay. This is particularly Bob's feeling but supported also by Averell. They think that if you ... if you ... if you don't do it today, you will get ... a sufficient amount of time will have passed so that the incident in people's mind will have disappeared and sort of gotten less, and you won't have support for the action anywhere.

Now, John McCone and his representative—he's not here, but General [Marshall] Carter is—they raise a strong question: whether

---

8. Averell Harriman served as under secretary of state for political affairs, U. Alexis Johnson as his deputy; William Bundy, brother of McGeorge, served as assistant secretary of state for far eastern affairs.
9. Leonard Unger was the U.S. ambassador to Laos. For his opposition to air strikes against the Pathet Lao positions, see "Telegram From the Embassy in Laos to the Department of State, Vientiane," 8 June 1964; and Smith, "Memorandum of Conference With President Johnson," 8 June 1964, *FRUS, 1964–1968,* 28:150–60. For a summary of Bundy's own reservations, see "Memorandum From Michael V. Forrestal of the National Security Council Staff to President Johnson," 7 June 1964, ibid., 28:146.

this is really part of the scenario that we were talking about last week.[10] They say this is escalating too fast. It's an action which is really out of step. The answer to that that the State Department gives very strongly is, the whole purpose of doing this is to give Hanoi one very strong signal now. [Blair] Seaborn, the Canadian, is on his way to Hanoi.[11] He *needs* to have something to back him up when he gets there, and this is the best time to do it, and we have the opportunity. So they want rather strongly to go ahead.

President Johnson: We're violating the [Geneva] Accords to do it, aren't we?

Forrestal: Yes, sir, we are. And—

President Johnson: We've already violated them in sending an armed plane in there, haven't we?

Forrestal: No, sir. We take the pos[ition] . . . Well, the armed plane . . . Yes, we have, sir, that's right. Technically, we have violated by sending the armed plane, *not* by sending the reconnaissance plane in.

President Johnson: No, that's right, by sending the armed plane.

Forrestal: By sending the armed plane. And, of course, we also claim that they have violat—they are in continuous violation of the accords, and so on and so on.

President Johnson: Yeah, I know that. . . . I know. They've been . . . all the time.

Forrestal: Yeah.

President Johnson: But this is the first time we've really violated it.

Forrestal: This is really the—this is Unger's whole point: This is the biggest signal we've ever given that we are sort of about to junk the accords. The answer to that, that the State Department makes now, is that this is only to be done once, it's a one-shot—sort of—operation; we are not going to continue this kind of thing afterwards.

Bob McNamara agrees that we should not run any more dangerous reconnaissance missions over the Plain of Jars. Instead we will move to another kind of action, the kind that had been discussed before, such as fleet movements outside of Southeast Asia and various other things that are on that list of things which are not in violation of the accords.

---

10. Lieutenant General Marshall S. Carter served as deputy director of the Central Intelligence Agency under Director John A. McCone. Forrestal was referring to the previous week's discussions, in both Honolulu and Washington, about whether to escalate U.S. military actions against North Vietnam. A decision had been reached to delay bombing raids or other increases in engagement.

11. Blair Seaborn had served as the Canadian commissioner to the International Supervision and Control Commission in April 1964.

Harriman makes the point that . . . he doesn't think—well, he says that Souvanna [Phouma] can't possibly approve of this.[12] We oughtn't to go back and ask his permission to do it. He can't possibly give it. But that his judgment is that Souvanna will probably not revolt, although he says he defers to Unger's judgment in the field. Unger *is* worried about Souvanna's reaction.

I must say I'm having a hard time arguing for the delay because all we get by delay is opportunity to think a little bit more here ourselves. We don't . . . Nothing's going to happen in the next 24 hours that will help us make this decision. More likely, it will be a little bit more difficult tomorrow to do it because of the cooling off of the situation.

President Johnson: I don't see what we get out of it, though. I don't think that the . . . expected—this signal is . . . the result we get there is going to be worth throwing away the position that we have that we want to follow the accords, and we want peace, and we're not seeking war. Looks like to me we're just going in and starting it.

Forrestal: Well, it's going to look—there is that, sir, no question, that that . . . that there's going to be that element. I think myself that the signal may be a little stronger than you suspect because it . . . just because we've never done it before and because it hurts—it's going to hurt our friends just as much . . . probably more than it's going to hurt Hanoi, but it's bound to hurt Hanoi somewhat. It's going to make them worried because it does suggest the United States may be about to embark on some different policy, and they're not quite sure where it may lead.

Of course you pay the cost of that because your friends have the same worry. The whole world will have the same worry: just as you put it, "Where is the United States going, to war or not?"

President Johnson: They want me to come over there, don't they?[13]

Forrestal: They haven't asked for you, sir, but I think you probably should on this point because this is not—a napalm is out of the question. We aren't talking about it.

President Johnson: Yeah.

Forrestal: It's—decided not to do it, and I really feel you should—

President Johnson: Do you have any Joint Chiefs [of Staff] there?

Forrestal: We have one, sir, [Earle] Wheeler, General Wheeler, who's pretty good.

---

12. Prince Souvanna Phouma was the prime minister and minister of defense in the neutralist Laotian government.
13. Johnson would join the meeting at 4:00 P.M.

President Johnson: Mm-hmm.

Forrestal: We have Carter, the CIA, State Department people all of whom you know, and [William] Colby and [Chester] Cooper from CIA too. [John] McNaughton and McNamara from Defense.[14]

President Johnson: What does [Dean] Rusk say?

Forrestal: Rusk is inclined to say go ahead, but he's very much, as Harriman put it, he's . . . he sees both sides of it. He's inclined to say go ahead. He's not as clear in his mind as Harriman or Alex Johnson or Bill Bundy, all of whom think we ought to go.

President Johnson: OK, I'll see you.

Forrestal: Right, sir.

3:55 P.M.: After speaking to Michael Forrestal outside the Cabinet Room, Johnson arrived at the Oval Office.

3:55 P.M.: Joined the meeting on Laos in the Cabinet Room.

By the time the President arrived, the participants in the Cabinet Room session had reached a rough consensus that Unger's objections focused too narrowly on Laos, and that the primary reason to stage an attack consisted of the tough message that would be delivered to Hanoi. Johnson raised the question of whether the benefits of an attack outweighed the costs of an international perception that the United States had violated the Geneva Accords. McNamara suggested that the accords permitted a retaliatory strike, while others argued that the Communist forces had altered the situation with their own violations of the accords. Unconvinced, Johnson stated that he was "bothered" by "throwing to the winds the Geneva Accords," and also worried that the U.S. action might be opposed by Souvanna Phouma's neutralist government. After a discussion of follow-up options and the costs of delaying a decision for 24 hours, Johnson left the room after receiving a note which probably informed him that he had received a call from Senator Richard Russell of Georgia. Johnson called Russell immediately. The Georgia senator's aggressively stated view that the United States had no choice but to go forward with

---

14. General Earle C. Wheeler was the chief of staff for the U.S. Army (and would succeed Maxwell Taylor as chairman of the JCS in July); William E. Colby was the chief of the Central Intelligence Agency's Far East Division; Chester Cooper was a CIA staff member who would join the NSC staff in November 1964; John T. McNaughton served as assistant secretary of defense for international security affairs.

the attack and should probably have done so already may have played a part in the President's eventual decision. Interestingly, the conversation did not touch on the charged topic of the Senate's pending action on the civil rights filibuster, an issue about which the President and his friend and mentor were on opposing sides.

4:35 P.M.

To Richard Russell[15]

President Johnson: Dick?

Richard Russell: Yes, sir.

President Johnson: How are you?

Russell: Very well. How are you?

President Johnson: Fine. You've seen what's happened to these planes the last two days?

Russell: Yes, sir.

President Johnson: Our people are pretty unanimous that they ought to go in there and notify Hanoi by taking out this antiaircraft battery.

Russell: Do they know where it is?

President Johnson: Yeah.

Russell: I think they—I thought they ought to have already taken it out, then.

President Johnson: Well, they had to get that boy last night. And they were shooting the hell out of us all around it, and they had to pick him up because he was on that fighter escort armed, and we didn't want him prisoner.

Russell: Did they get both the boys?

President Johnson: No, they got the one that was armed in the fighter escort, but they haven't gotten the other one yet.

Russell: What kind of antiaircraft battery is it?

President Johnson: Thirty-seven millimeter, they think.

Russell: Golly, that's not much. Our people must have been flying pretty low.

---

15. Tape WH6406.03, Citation #3639, Recordings of Telephone Conversations—White House Series, Recordings and Transcripts of Conversations and Meetings, Lyndon B. Johnson Library.

President Johnson: We do: 5[00], 600 feet.

Russell: Oh, I see. Yeah.

President Johnson: But they say that's less danger than 1,500.

Russell: Well, I would think so.

President Johnson: They have given instructions. The ambassador [Leonard Unger] is very much against it. He says it'll escalate it, that it'll likely cause us to lose the government, but the . . . all the Joint Chiefs [of Staff] and [Robert] McNamara—

Russell: I thought this was in Laos.

President Johnson: This is. This is. But they think Souvanna Phouma would be very much against going in with armed planes and start shooting and . . .

Russell: Well, I thought they had asked just to do that reconnaissance for them.

President Johnson: They'd asked us to do the reconnaissance, but they hadn't asked us to start destroying any batteries.[16]

Russell: Well, God Almighty, if they go to shooting at us, what'd they expect us to do?

President Johnson: Well, that's the question. Now, the orders have been given, and they're about ready to go—the Joint Chiefs, the State Department. There's been some level of questioning in the State Department, but [Dean] Rusk, on balance, says that this ought to be done. But the ambassador feels that you're violating the Geneva Accords and you're now getting yourself in the same position that the other side's in. They've been violating them all along, but now we're going in violating them. And if they knock a bunch of these planes out, we might be in pretty bad position. On the other hand, all of our military people and most of our political people feel definitely, and my own instinct is to hit back when I'm hit. Now—

Russell: Well [*unclear*], we want to be sure and know where it is and be sure and knock it out. It would be a very great tragedy if we went in there and failed.

President Johnson: Well, they think they can do it. [Curtis] LeMay says he's practically certain; we go in with Air Force people instead of Navy people.[17]

Russell: Well, I wouldn't bet on the Air Force people being any bet-

---

16. Souvanna Phouma had opposed a retaliatory strike by the United States. "Telegram From the Embassy in Laos to the Department of State, Vientiane," 8 June 1964, *FRUS, 1964–1968*, 28:150–52.

17. General Curtis LeMay was chief of staff of the Air Force.

ter. Those Navy pilots, Marine pilots, are the best ones on that low-flying rocket attack that we've got. They're better than the Air Force.[18]

President Johnson: Mm-hmm. I think they've all pretty well agreed that . . . that these planes that we've moved in—Air Force planes and Air Force pilots—they've have had a little more experience in this particular type of stuff.

Russell: Where are they going to strike from?

President Johnson: South Vietnam.

Russell: Well, that brings on complications. Of course . . . wouldn't it be better to have them strike from the carriers?

President Johnson: They don't think so. They think that they're more accurate and better this way, better planes—

Russell: That may be, but we haven't invited them in so much if we strike from the Navy, from the sea, as we have if we strike from a base there in South Vietnam. But I'm sure all that's been taken into consideration. See, if we strike from the sea, why, we're striking from our own base, and we're not involving the South Vietnamese. But if we strike from a base there, then we're inviting them right in there to retaliate on us.

President Johnson: Anyway, you think in light of what's happened, it's . . . we haven't got much choice, have we?

Russell: No, if we're going to keep up the missions. Of course we've got to protect our people. We might as well just knock them out.

President Johnson: Mm-hmm. OK, I just wanted to talk to you before we went.

Russell: All right.

President Johnson: Thank you. I'll talk to you later.

Russell: All right, sir. Thank you.

The President returned to the meeting and raised Russell's point about the potential dangers of attacking from South Vietnam rather than from a U.S. aircraft carrier. His advisers countered that the Communists had no viable means for a retaliatory air attack on South Vietnam, and that the ground-based Air Force would be more effective in carrying out the action. Deputy CIA Director General Marshall Carter raised a final objection, arguing for a 24- to 48-hour delay to at least provide Ambassador

---

18. Russell's specific knowledge about the aerial capabilities of different branches of the military derived from his service as chairman of the Senate Committee on the Armed Services.

Unger with full information.[19] The argument that the United States had to send a strong message to Hanoi, however, could not be resisted by the foreign policy advisers assembled by the Kennedy-Johnson administration. President Johnson told his advisers that he "had doubts about the action," but gave the order to attack.

As the President returned to his office at 4:55, the time in Laos (an 11-hour time difference) was 3:55 A.M. on June 9. Chinese radio reports claimed that six U.S. planes attacked at dawn along the eastern edge of the Plaine des Jarres, dropping 12 bombs and 2 rockets. The planes also flew over Pathet Lao headquarters at Khang Khay. In addition, the Chinese reports claimed that two of the U.S. planes sustained damage.[20] As these events unfolded, President Johnson stayed in frequent contact with Michael Forrestal and other advisers.

> **5:02 P.M.:** Unrecorded call to Jack Valenti.
>
> **5:05 P.M.:** Unrecorded call to Walter Jenkins.
>
> **5:10 P.M.:** Unrecorded call to Michael Forrestal.
>
> **5:14 P.M.:** Oval Office meeting with Forrestal.
>
> **5:21 P.M.:** Unrecorded call to Bill Moyers.
>
> **5:40 P.M.:** Unrecorded call to Moyers.
>
> **5:46 P.M.:** Unrecorded call to Forrestal.
>
> **5:48 P.M.:** Unrecorded call to George Reedy.
>
> **5:55 P.M.:** Unrecorded call to Valenti.
>
> **5:58 P.M.–6:06 P.M.:** Off-the-record meeting with Rhode Island Senator Claiborne Pell.
>
> **6:09 P.M.–6:12 P.M.:** Off-the-record meeting in the Cabinet Room with the U.S. ambassadors to Cambodia and to Syria.
>
> **6:15 P.M.:** Unrecorded call to Jenkins.
>
> **6:21 P.M.–7:20 P.M.:** Meeting with Ken O'Donnell and Larry O'Brien.
>
> **6:30 P.M.:** Unrecorded call to Moyers.
>
> **7:40 P.M.:** Unrecorded call to Valenti.
>
> **7:45 P.M.:** Joined in the lounge by Valenti.
>
> **7:55 P.M.:** Unrecorded call to Reedy.
>
> **8:10 P.M.:** Unrecorded call to Lynda Johnson.
>
> **8:30 P.M.:** Returned to the White House Mansion.

---

19. As this advice was not taken, Secretary of State Rusk sent an apologetic telegram to Unger that explained the decision and the failure to notify him in advance of the raid. "Telegram From the Department of State to the Embassy in Laos," 8 June 1964, *FRUS, 1964–1968*, 28:161–63.
20. Hedrick Smith, "U.S. Jet Attack on Leftist Base in Laos Reported," *New York Times*, 10 June 1964.

8:40 P.M.: Dinner in the Mansion with Lady Bird Johnson, Lynda, and two of Lynda's friends.

9:25 P.M.: Unrecorded call to Moyers.

10:45 P.M.: Unrecorded call from Texas rancher, businessman, and Johnson friend Wesley West, who was staying at Washington's Mayflower Hotel.

The quiet nature of the President's evening belied the momentous step that he had taken that afternoon in ordering the U.S. bombing of targets in Laos. The direct engagement of U.S. forces in a combat role, rather than as advisers who accompanied troops of other nations into combat, represented a significant escalation of U.S. involvement in the spiraling conflict in Southeast Asia. While the Laotian raid of June 8–9, 1964, did not by itself mark an inescapable military commitment for the United States, it did bring President Johnson much farther out onto "the slippery slope" about which his director of Central Intelligence had warned earlier in the day. The consequences of this decision and others like it in the coming months would reverberate throughout the remainder of Lyndon Johnson's presidency.

Tuesday, June 9, 1964

[It would] be just a miracle getting this bill. I mean, who could have thought a year ago that we'd get this bill?
— Robert Kennedy to President Johnson

Although rumors had circulated in Washington about the U.S. bombing raid on the Pathet Lao positions, the first official reports of the action came over Radio Peking, a Chinese government news agency. Late editions of U.S. newspapers, as well as the nightly news broadcasts, carried the story. Much of Lyndon Johnson's day on June 9 would be occupied by briefing congressional leaders on his decision and its consequences.[1]

Elsewhere in the United States, the pending presidential campaign continued to occupy the attention of politicians and political strategists, particularly in the Republican Party. On June 7, former President Dwight Eisenhower had encouraged Pennsylvania Governor William Scranton to make a late entry into the campaign for the Republican nomination in order to unify opponents of Arizona Senator Barry Goldwater around a single candidate. Under heavy pressure from Goldwater supporters, Eisenhower withdrew his advice to Scranton on June 8. Speaking at the National Governors Conference in Cleveland the following day, however, Eisenhower's former vice president, Richard Nixon, launched his own anti-Goldwater maneuver. Nixon, who himself had been the party's 1960 nominee, urged Michigan Governor George Romney to enter the race as the candidate of moderate Republicanism. Romney responded with a statement that he was not a candidate, but made no indication about how

---

1. Bernard Gwertzman, "U.S. Jets Hit Reds in Laos, China Says," *Washington Star*, 9 June 1964.

he would view a convention effort to draft him as the party's nominee.[2]

Regardless of the travails of the opposition party, the day also brought heightened political concerns for Lyndon Johnson, as the *Washington Star* published a lengthy article assessing the Johnson family's business and financial holdings. The article detailed allegations that Johnson had previously used his position as a powerful senator to influence federal regulators charged with overseeing Lady Bird Johnson's TV and radio holdings. While the article remained inconclusive in its assessment of such charges, the story represented the latest in a string of such journalistic investigations, all of which worried the President as he faced a reelection campaign.

> **7:00 A.M.:** President Johnson woke and had tea in bed, performed his exercises, dressed, and went downstairs with Lady Bird and Lynda Johnson.
>
> **8:06 A.M.:** Unrecorded call to Robert McNamara.
>
> **8:14 A.M.:** Unrecorded call to Assistant Secretary of State for Inter-American Affairs Thomas Mann.
>
> **8:45 A.M.:** Joined Democratic congressional leaders for the regular Tuesday morning breakfast meeting.
>
> Lady Bird and Lynda Johnson accompanied the President to greet members of the leadership group prior to the start of the meeting.

Time Unknown

Between Carl Albert and His Office Secretary[3]

At some point during the meeting, House Majority Leader Carl Albert of Oklahoma called his office to ask about the arrival in Washington of Fred Harris, the Oklahoma state senator who had just received the Democratic nomination for the U.S. Senate.[4]

---

2. Joseph A. Loftus, "Curb on Scranton Is Laid to a Shift by Eisenhower," *New York Times*, 9 June 1964; Earl Mazo, "Nixon Urges Romney Race to Block Goldwater Drive," *New York Times*, 10 June 1964.

3. Tape WH6406.03, Citation #3640, Recordings of Telephone Conversations—White House Series, Recordings and Transcripts of Conversations and Meetings, Lyndon B. Johnson Library.

4. See Johnson to Fred Harris, 6:10 P.M., 28 May 1964, in Guian A. McKee, ed., *The Presidential Recordings, Lyndon B. Johnson: Toward the Great Society, February 1, 1964–May 31, 1964*, vol. 6, *April 14, 1964–May 31, 1964* (New York: Norton, 2007), pp. 928–30.

9:35 A.M.: With the breakfast meeting concluded, the leadership accompanied Johnson to the Oval Office before proceeding to the Fish Room for a press briefing. The President remained in the office, where he met with Special Assistant for Congressional Relations Larry O'Brien and took a call from Press Secretary George Reedy.

9:50 A.M.

From George Reedy[5]

Reedy inquired about whether U.S. arms negotiators at the ongoing 17-nation Geneva disarmament conference could issue an official statement about U.S. policy positions.[6]

President Johnson: [*to someone in the office*] . . . will never admit [*unclear*] in order. But I'd list them with poverty. I'd list them with debt limit, taxes, and poverty.

[*on phone*] Yes?

Office Secretary: Congressman [Wilbur] Mills is out of his office for just a moment. We left word, and George Reedy is on 9-0.

George Reedy: Mr. President, Ned Nordis is calling me from Geneva about this statement. He says that [William] Foster is going to go on in ten minutes with it unless we say no, and the . . .[7]

President Johnson: I'll try to see if I can get back to you in two minutes. My judgment is no, it oughtn't to be.

Reedy: OK.

President Johnson: And I'd just tell him to hold it unless you . . . hear from you.

Reedy: Right. Shall do, sir.

President Johnson: Bye.

5. Tape WH6406.03, Citation #3641, Recordings of Telephone Conversations—White House Series, Recordings and Transcripts of Conversations and Meetings, Lyndon B. Johnson Library.
6. The Geneva conference had resumed on 9 June. "Foster in Geneva," *Washington Post*, 19 January 1964; "U.S. to Press Plea for Atomic Curbs," *New York Times*, 7 June 1964.
7. William C. Foster served as the director of the Arms Control and Disarmament Agency and headed the U.S. delegation to the Geneva conference. Ned Nordis remains unidentified.

Representative Wilbur Mills of Arkansas, the powerful chairman of the House Ways and Means Committee, returned an earlier call from the President.

9:55 A.M.

From Wilbur Mills[8]

Mills informed Johnson about the status of the committee's work on the federal debt ceiling and excise tax legislation and indicated his concerns about the implications of possible increases in Social Security payroll taxes that would finance the administration's proposed Medicare program. Johnson in turn took the opportunity to emphasize the social and historical importance of the health care initiative. Although he had consistently opposed the Medicare legislation, largely because of concerns that it would undermine the actuarial soundness of Social Security, Mills was now seeking a compromise position that would advance some form of health care insurance legislation while both protecting Social Security and saving political face for members of the Ways and Means Committee, who had previously opposed the administration's proposals. Although later in the month Mills would abandon this attempt and implement a series of parliamentary maneuvers to block Medicare for the year, he would broker a compromise in 1965 that led to the enactment not only of Medicare but also Medicaid, the primary federal health care program for impoverished Americans.[9]

An unclear office conversation precedes the call.
Wilbur Mills: Good morning.
President Johnson: You doing all right?
Mills: Yes, sir. I see you're still busy.
President Johnson: Well, you've got lots of problems that I . . . this clock this week with our debt and our taxes. Do you feel reasonably comfortable about them?

---

8. Tape WH6406.03, Citation #3642, Recordings of Telephone Conversations—White House Series, Recordings and Transcripts of Conversations and Meetings, Lyndon B. Johnson Library.
9. Julian Zelizer, *Taxing America: Wilbur D. Mills, Congress, and the State, 1945–1975* (New York: Cambridge University Press, 1998), pp. 212–54.

Mills: I do about the debt ceiling, but I'm a little concerned about this motion of [John] Byrnes on these excise . . . retail excise taxes.[10]

President Johnson: Mm-hmm.

Mills: [*Unclear*]—

President Johnson: Let me ask you if you'd do this quietly: kind of look over that House, have your clerk do it or somebody, and let's take the Democrats that might be pressured into going against us that we might save—like [John] Fogarty or the Rhode Island boys or some of that kind of stuff, Massachusetts—and give me a list and let me see if some of our folks could quietly talk to them.[11]

Mills: I'll have that list this afternoon.

President Johnson: Just put it in plain, blank paper, and I'll have Larry O'Brien drop by your office late this afternoon to pick it up.

Mills: That will be fine.

President Johnson: How are you doing on your Mills bill?[12]

Mills: I don't know. It looks like we're getting ready to vote. We've looked at a great number of possibilities. One of the things that disturbs me a little bit is this present increase in these taxes on Social Security . . .

President Johnson: Mm-hmm.

Mills: . . . going into effect in '66 and '68. Now, part of what we may end up doing is spacing that a little bit better than [it] is under present law.

President Johnson: Mm-hmm.

Mills: I'm afraid of the reaction to . . . 2 or 2.5 billion dollar take from the working people and on $4,800 of income right at the time when we may begin to soften a little in the economy. I don't know whether you've talked to Walter [Heller] and others about it, but this could make it impossible for us to carry forward with a balanced budget at that time.[13]

President Johnson: Mm-hmm. Well, I trust your judgment, and I think it . . .

Mills: Existing law. . . . I say that's existing law I'm talking about.

President Johnson: Yeah . . . yeah, I know that.

Mills: If we can make some changes in that and spread this tax to where the full effect is not in '68 but in, say, '70 or '72 or ['7]3, I think we're better off.

---

10. John Byrnes was a representative from Wisconsin and the ranking Republican on the Ways and Means Committee.

11. John Fogarty served as a Democratic representative from Rhode Island.

12. Johnson was referring to the Medicare legislation in a way that flattered the Ways and Means Committee chairman by acknowledging his determinative influence on the bill's fate.

13. Mills was referring to Council of Economic Advisers Chairman Walter Heller.

President Johnson: Mm-hmm. Well, I think that we've got this thing wrapped up and all of us in good shape if we can have anything that's reasonable in that field. I spoke in New York and Pennsylvania in the last two days, and as of now—and it can change mighty quick—but as of now, we're in the best shape that I believe we could be in. And I'll tell you this: The most important . . . the most single, most important popular thing is the bill you're working on. There's no question in my mind about it. If you get something you can possibly live with and defend that these people will not kick over the bucket with, that'll mean more than *all* the bills we've passed put together, and I think it'll mean more to posterity and to you and to me.

So I'm not trying to go into details, and I'm not trying to write a new section every morning, or title—I just let it go since I talked to you last time and haven't done anything—but I've looked at some of the stuff that's being considered from the press and other people, and it looks like to me that you're approaching it right and that you're getting in shape. And I just say this: that there's not anything that's happened in my six months, or that will happen in my whole term in my judgment that will mean more to us as a party or me or you as individuals than this piece of legislation.

Now you . . . the details of it, if you don't know more about it than I do, like Mr. [Sam] Rayburn used to say, "We've wasted a hell of a lot of money on West Point, if these generals don't know more than I do."[14] Now, if you don't know more about Ways and Means [Committee] than I do, you haven't been applying yourself, and I know you have. But you work it out, and anything you want me to do, let me know. And any [of] these . . . if you want Walter or [Douglas] Dillon or anybody to give us any estimates, let's do it.[15] Let's make it sound and solid, but let's move in this direction, and it'll be a bill that you and your folks will never forget, and I'll come in and applaud you.

Mills: Well, we're making every effort to do something.

President Johnson: Well, grind something out of there.

Mills: Well . . .

President Johnson: And let me know anything that I need to know.

Mills: All right, sir.

President Johnson: And be sure to give me that list.

Mills: I'll do it.

---

14. Sam Rayburn, Democrat of Texas, had been Speaker of the House and a mentor of Johnson.
15. Johnson was referring to Secretary of the Treasury Douglas Dillon.

President Johnson: Thank you, Wilbur.

Mills: Thanks so much. Bye.

The President next received a call from Special Assistant for National Security Affairs McGeorge Bundy, with whom he discussed the statement on disarmament proposed by the U.S. negotiators at the Geneva conference.[16]

10:00 A.M.

From McGeorge Bundy[17]

Office Secretary: Mr. Bundy, may I tell the President where you are?

McGeorge Bundy: I'm calling from a phone booth. I'm five minutes from the office.

Office Secretary: Thank you.

President Johnson: . . . [*unclear*] on Social Security [*a buzzer sounds*] because he's afraid it'll take too much out of the consumer's pocket right now. He didn't know whether I'd talked to Walter or not. I guess he means Walter Heller.

[*on phone*] Yes?

Office Secretary: Calling from a phone booth five minutes away is Mr. Bundy, on 9-3.

President Johnson: Mac?

Bundy: Yes, sir.

President Johnson: They've got some statement on disarmament— have you read it?—that they want to release in Geneva?

Bundy: I haven't seen the second form of it, Mr. President. They sent it for redrafting by the experts.

President Johnson: Well, in the light of what happened last night and others, I don't know whether it's very appropriate for us to be lecturing people on disarmament this morning or not [*Bundy acknowledges*], but they're going to issue a statement unless we let them know in five min-

---

16. See George Reedy to Johnson, 9:50 A.M., 9 June 1964, in this chapter.

17. Tape WH6406.03, Citation #3643, Recordings of Telephone Conversations—White House Series, Recordings and Transcripts of Conversations and Meetings, Lyndon B. Johnson Library.

utes.[18] It's always under a gun: These little jerks call up and say, "If you don't tell me no, I'll be gone in five minutes."

Bundy: Mr. President, we can hold it up, and I'll stop it until we have a look at it.

President Johnson: Well, wait a minute, let me read it to you.

Bundy: Right.

President Johnson: [*reading*] "President Johnson today instructed [William] Foster to make every effort at the Geneva disarmament conference to find safeguarded alternatives to the arms race. Mr. Foster heads the U.S. delegation to [the] conference. The President said, 'We have taken the first steps down the pathway to peace. Last year saw the Test Ban Treaty, the direct communications link, the U.N. resolution against nuclear weapons in space. This year both the Soviet Union and the United States have announced reduction in production of fissionable material for nuclear weapons.[19] Each of these steps points in the direction of a more peaceful world. Each moves us a small way down the long and difficult road to such a world. We must not hesitate now, to [*sic*] journey has been begun. We must redouble our efforts until it's completed.'

"In January, President Johnson presented specific proposals for further steps to the conference. Today, he instructed Mr. Foster to set forth in Geneva our plans for the procedures necessary to verify compliance with a number of his January proposals in order to reach early agreement on it. [The] United States has long believed that inspection or other procedures for verification are necessary for significant arms control and disarmament measures to be taken. The President reemphasized his determination to pursue safeguard agreements which would permit such action. They would be important first of all for peace, but they would also permit us [to] devote more of our energies and resources to building a greater society for all mankind."

I don't think it says anything. I don't know what this verified compli—

Bundy: No, I would be inclined, Mr. President, in light of today's events, to change two sentences: The one where we talk about a peaceful world, I would say simply toward effective arms control and disarmament.

President Johnson: Well, now, let me see, if you want to rewrite it now, because they're going in five minutes if we don't call them. Where is it now?

Bundy: Well, Mr. President, if I were you, I'd say hold, and we'll give

---

18. The President was referring to the U.S. bombing raid on Laos the day before.
19. McKee, *The Presidential Recordings, Johnson,* vol. 6, *April 14, 1964–May 31, 1964,* pp. 99–100.

them a corrected version in half an hour. I'll be in the office in five minutes, and I'll fix it up.

President Johnson: All right, OK. . . . Well, they say, though, they can't
do it but ten minutes. You reckon he's just got one spot he can do it?

Bundy: I don't think so for a minute, Mr. President.

President Johnson: OK.

Bundy: I think that's putting our fingers . . . putting their hands . . . putting us to a gun that they shouldn't do.

President Johnson: Right. . . . All right . . . all right.

Bundy: All right, sir.

> **10:02 A.M.–10:16 A.M.:** President Johnson placed calls to George
> Reedy (10:02) and to Special Assistant Walter Jenkins (10:06
> and 10:14).

10:16 A.M.

From George Reedy[20]

Johnson next received a call from his press secretary, during which he
complained about being interrupted by someone entering the office. The
substance of the conversation involved procedures and timing for releasing advance copies of Johnson's speeches to the White House press corps.

George Reedy: Mr. President?

President Johnson: Yeah?

Reedy: Wanted to be positive about this. [McGeorge] Bundy has sent
me the statement with a number of small changes in it: "peace" changed to
"disarmament," "a more peaceful world" changed to "effective control of
arms." He's added lines saying that you instructed Mr. [William] Foster
to set forth our plans for the procedures necessary to—

President Johnson: Call me. Wait a minute.

*[apparently addressing someone who has entered the room, probably Jack
Valenti]* Wait a minute. Here . . . Just call me, now, when you want to talk
to me. I'm busy. Don't want you tying up—

---

20. Tape WH6406.03, Citation #3644, Recordings of Telephone Conversations—White House
Series, Recordings and Transcripts of Conversations and Meetings, Lyndon B. Johnson Library.

Reedy: I want to be sure that you have seen this.

President Johnson: George, that's what I've been trying to stop with the Kennedy people butting in here.

Jack Valenti: Yes, sir.

President Johnson: Haven't I told you-all that?

Valenti: Yes, sir.

President Johnson: All right.

[*resuming with Reedy*] OK, now go back to the thought, where I was before I got interrupted. I am trying to follow you, but somebody busted in the door just like it . . . Where?

Reedy: Right, sir. Bundy sent me the statement with the changes. In which he's changed "peace" to "disarmament," "a more effective . . . a more peaceful world" to "effective control of arms," one or two other very minor changes, and I wanted to be sure that you had seen that before I call Geneva.

President Johnson: Yeah, I haven't seen it, but go on and call them and get it out. I don't think it's worth a damn, but go ahead. That's all right with me.

Reedy: OK, sir. . . . You bet.

President Johnson: Now, George, you get some sign before you issue any statement in my name or any speech in my name that I have approved something, and don't ever issue anything over two hours in advance anymore. You've accommodated all these folks and ruined me. Every one of them. None of them thank you, and none of them appreciate that you gave it two-sided. But I read every story this morning, and practically every one— the whole story was written on the changes we made in a speech that I have not approved and have not clipped and was issued without my knowledge, without a damned thing. And you have no right to issue anything that I don't approve of. [*President Johnson pounds something, probably his desk.*]

Reedy: That's why I'm calling you direct on the phone, sir.

President Johnson: All right, OK. But you ought to have done it last Saturday.[21]

Reedy: I will call you direct on anything.

President Johnson: Say, "I'm getting ready to issue your speech, that you have not seen, and is it OK?"

Reedy: I'm calling you direct on everything.

President Johnson: Just don't do it anymore. And tell these reporters that they damn sure didn't play it fair with you, that you gave it to them

---

21. On Saturday, 6 June, Johnson had made two speeches in New York City at events for the International Ladies' Garment Workers' Union. He also made a brief speech that evening at Gallaudet University.

Saturday and they wrote the whole story on change, and next time you don't have to give it to them at all.

Reedy: OK, sir.

President Johnson: All you do is serve their convenience. I don't give a piss whether I get it in the afternoon paper or not. I couldn't care less. [*Unclear*]—anyway, if you can't give it to them at 8:00 and get it in the afternoon paper, I don't know what the hell they're doing. Why did they go up there? They could every damn one file their story. And all you had to do is hand it to them when they got on the plane, Sunday, Monday morning, but—just like you did, and every one of them had it and wrote their stories, but wrote the story about the dumbbell trick we pulled, about "we have to bury [Barry] Goldwater."[22] And then also read the speeches very carefully, and if there's anything can be interpreted as hitting at Goldwater, call it to my attention.

Reedy: OK, sir.

President Johnson: All right.

10:25 A.M.–10:56 A.M.: Unrecorded calls to Bill Moyers (10:25 and 10:31), Jack Valenti (10:30), Walter Jenkins (10:51), and George Reedy (10:56).

11:05 A.M.: Meeting with McGeorge Bundy in the office.

11:50 A.M.: Unrecorded call to Valenti.

11:51 A.M.–11:56 A.M.: Off-the-record meeting in the Cabinet Room with the Church of Jesus Christ of Latter-day Saints Eastern Mission President Bill Burton and Utah Senator Frank E. Moss.

Burton presented the President with copies of the Book of Mormon, a biblical concordance and reference, and two histories (one of them illustrated) of the Mormon Church.

12:10 P.M.: Unrecorded call to Jenkins.

12:12 P.M.–12:16 P.M.: Meeting with United States–Puerto Rican Commission.

Johnson made brief remarks to the members of the commission.

12:20 P.M.: Unrecorded call to Valenti.

12:23 P.M.: Meeting with Representative Sam Stratton of New York.

The President autographed a baseball for the National Baseball Hall of Fame in Cooperstown, New York.

---

22. Arizona Senator Barry Goldwater had emerged as the leading candidate for the Republican presidential nomination.

12:25 P.M.

From Robert Kennedy[23]

The President then received a call from Attorney General Robert Kennedy, who urged him to inform members of Congress about the previous day's bombing of a Pathet Lao antiaircraft battery in Laos. Considering the possibility of future military escalations in Southeast Asia, particularly against North Vietnam, Johnson and Kennedy also weighed the eventual necessity of a congressional resolution on the use of force—or even a formal declaration of war—in the region and considered the political and strategic consequences of such a course. In early August, the Gulf of Tonkin Resolution would provide congressional sanction for military action in Vietnam and, in its skirting of the constitutional authority of Congress to declare war, would become one of the most controversial legacies of the Johnson administration.

Scattered, unclear office conversation precedes the call in which someone mentions Woodrow Wilson and in which some unidentified visitors arrive at the Oval Office.

President Johnson: Hello?

Robert Kennedy: Oh, Mr. President?

President Johnson: Hi, Bobby.

Kennedy: How are you?

President Johnson: Fine.

Kennedy: [*with the President acknowledging*] I was just talking, Mr. President, to Mac Bundy on the phone. I heard of this incident of last night, and I asked him if the congressional people had been informed about it. And he didn't think that they probably had.

President Johnson: No.

Kennedy: And, you know, it's going to come out from the Chinese, and it's going to come out in other ways [*the President acknowledges*], and I thought it was rather . . . a matter that would be well if it was handled . . .

President Johnson: Yeah . . . yeah. Yeah, I think so. Some of them have been, but it hasn't been done as a group.

---

23. Tape WH6406.03, Citation #3646, Recordings of Telephone Conversations—White House Series, Recordings and Transcripts of Conversations and Meetings, Lyndon B. Johnson Library.

Kennedy: Yeah, because—

President Johnson: And I don't know whether the Republicans would bring it out and leak it or not. That's a great question.

Kennedy: But of course the Chinese will talk about it.

President Johnson: Yeah.

Kennedy: And the Russians will talk about it, and it's going to be a . . . you know, it's going—I would think you can expect that it's going to be a . . . Within 24 hours it'll be worldwide, and if we had done it without telling anybody in the United States, they're all going to wonder—you know, I would think that that's going to be a problem.

The second thing is it seems to me that somebody should be working on how it will be handled with the public because the Chinese obviously will say something about it. You know, what are we going to say, and then . . . and what the . . . and whether we'd repeat it, and—

President Johnson: I raised that question with them, and I've got another meeting at 1:00 where I'll raise it again.[24] They . . . the boy in the State Department and [Robert] McNamara both have had that question put to them by me. [*Kennedy acknowledges.*] What's the man over there that runs their publicity?

Kennedy: Where? [Arthur] Sylvester?[25]

President Johnson: No, in State.

Kennedy: Bob Manning?[26]

President Johnson: Manning, yeah.

Kennedy: He's a good man.

President Johnson: And I think he's been one of the best.

Kennedy: Yes.

President Johnson: His feeling was that we shouldn't do anything about it. My feeling was that we ought to go ahead and say something. McNamara agreed with him.

Kennedy: I would agree with you.

President Johnson: [*with Kennedy acknowledging*] I'm seeing them at 1:00 again, and we took the ball the other day and said that we had taken this action and announced it ourselves, and I thought got by with . . . pretty

---

24. President Johnson would have a 1:00 P.M. lunch meeting with McNamara, Bundy, and Secretary of State Dean Rusk.

25. Arthur Sylvester was assistant secretary of defense for public affairs and served as the equivalent of the Defense Department's press secretary.

26. Robert J. Manning was the assistant secretary of state for public affairs and served as the equivalent of the State Department's press secretary.

well with the other two flights.[27] It doesn't look like they got much results last night, what they did. Have you analyzed it?

Kennedy: I haven't. I just, you know, I just heard about it on the telephone. But—

President Johnson: Are you going to meet with them anytime today or tomorrow?

Kennedy: I hadn't heard of it.

President Johnson: I told Mac Bundy [to] get you because we've got to see where we go from here. What . . . they have no real—

Kennedy: Yeah. . . . No, that's right.

President Johnson: —plans. McNamara and [Dean] Rusk are both . . . were rather insistent on going through with this one, although the ambassador [Leonard Unger] raised some grave questions which concerned me: (a) the reaction in the world, and (b) Souvanna's [Phouma's] reaction. But they felt that unless we showed some strength and made some kind of reply that it would be very bad for us, and we went ahead.[28] But they were confident they could knock this battery out. They didn't. And I think it shows us that we can't rely too much on air power on some of these things.

Kennedy: No . . . no. No, I think that's a real lesson. The other—I had, you know—they . . . about four or five days ago, we went through the plan for Vietnam, and I had some serious questions about it, but . . . but perhaps they're going to have some other discussions with you. But, I mean, for instance, the congressional part of it and getting a congressional resolution, I think it poses all kinds of problems if we're going ahead on that.

President Johnson: It will. . . . You can't do anything about that until you get rid of this problem we've got up there now, and the question is— whether you ought to try is a difficult one, and I don't know how you can conduct much offensive without some authority.

Kennedy: Yeah.

President Johnson: We had the United Nations behind us, but we had a very divided country, and a lot of hell, and we finally really lost—the Democrats did—on the Korea thing.

Kennedy: Yeah, that's right.

---

27. Johnson was probably referring to the previous day's acknowledgment that fighter planes had participated in reconnaissance missions over Laos after one had been shot down on 7 June. See the introduction to 8 June in this volume.

28. Leonard Unger served as U.S. ambassador to Laos. Prince Souvanna Phouma was the country's neutralist Prime Minister. For Unger's objections, see the introduction to 8 June in this volume.

President Johnson: I'm fearful that if we move without any authority of the Congress that the resentment would be pretty widespread and would involve a lot of people who would normally be with us if we asked for the authority. On the other hand, I would shudder to think if they debated it for a long period of time, and they're likely to do that. So neither choice is very good.

Kennedy: Yeah, because I think . . . No. I think that they'll start asking. It seems likely that they'll start asking somebody to spell out exactly what's going to happen. And if you—we drop bombs in, and they retaliate, will we eventually bomb Hanoi, and all that kind of business. And what—the answers to that, to those questions, are *so* difficult to give, particularly if you're giving it to a lot of people, the antagonistic.

President Johnson: All right. Now, if you don't . . . That's all true.

Kennedy: Yeah.

President Johnson: And you can't go into the details of your—

Kennedy: No.

President Johnson: —plans and you just have to tell them that, but if you take the other route . . .

Kennedy: Well, the other—

President Johnson: . . . then they ask you, "By what authority, what executive order do you declare war?"

Kennedy: Yeah. The other—well, I guess you really don't need . . . from their explanation at least—and I haven't looked into it—but it's not essential that . . . it's not necessary constitutionally. But the alternative to that—especially if that's going to be very harmful—the alternative, of course, is for you and Secretary McNamara and Secretary Rusk at the appropriate time to start bringing in the labor leaders and the business leaders and the congressional leaders and talk with them on, you know, sort of as if it was a National Security Council meeting and that you are briefing them, and this is what we have to do at this time, and that if you have to take any further steps that you'll inform them, and that you'll keep them advised. And rally, and bring in some of the newspapers, and bring in some of the television people just to—

President Johnson: [*with Kennedy acknowledging*] And I think probably talk to the country about why we're there and how we're there and what we've confronted there and what we may do before you submit a resolution, because I don't . . . I have doubts about what would happen to it right now.

Kennedy: Well, that's what I think.

President Johnson: I think they'd just talk and develop a big divided type here at home.

Kennedy: That's what I think. . . . That's what I think, and then there'll be—some people will say we're not doing enough; the others will say it's too much. There'll be some people saying . . . you know, all you need is 15 of them up there that are doing that, and I think it's just . . . unless the ground's laid, is really going to be unpleasant.

President Johnson: Does this jury amendment bother you any this morning?[29]

Kennedy: No, I think it makes it much more difficult, but, hell, we can live with it.

President Johnson: Mm-hmm. Does it help you any on cloture?

Kennedy: Yes.

President Johnson: Mm-hmm. You think cloture is decided now, don't you?

Kennedy: It looks that way.

President Johnson: Mm-hmm.

Kennedy: It certainly appears that way. [It would] be just a miracle getting this bill. I mean, who could have thought a year ago that we'd get this bill?

President Johnson: Well, it'll be a wonderful thing. Now, are you going to—you're making your plans on who we ought to call in to follow through on it?[30]

---

29. Johnson was referring to an amendment, sponsored by Kentucky Senator Thruston B. Morton, that would entitle defendants to a jury trial in criminal contempt cases brought under all sections of the civil rights bill except Title I (Voting Rights); in Title I criminal contempt cases, judges would have discretion over whether to allow a jury trial, although sentences in cases without a jury trial could not exceed 30 days in prison or a fine of $300 (preserving the core of the compromise over the issue in the 1957 Civil Rights Act). The Senate leadership had proposed an amendment on 24 April that would have given judges discretion over whether to allow criminal contempt jury trials under all titles of the bill while limiting penalties in nonjury trial cases. Civil rights supporters opposed jury trials in civil rights cases on the grounds that southern juries would be unlikely to convict white defendants. Kennedy's lack of concern about the Morton amendment reflected his belief that most violations of the Civil Rights Act could be tried as civil contempt cases, in which the prosecution simply sought compliance with the law (as opposed to criminal contempt cases, in which the goal was punishment for violation of the law) and in which jury trials were not permissible. The Morton amendment passed in a narrow 51–48 vote, clearing the way for a vote on cloture the next day. "Jury Trial Amendment And How Senate Voted," *Washington Post*, 10 June 1964; E. W. Kenworthy, "Senate Defeats 3 Moves to Curb Civil Rights Bill," *New York Times*, 10 June 1964; *Congressional Quarterly Almanac*, 88th Cong., 2nd sess., 1964, vol. 20 (Washington, DC: Congressional Quarterly Service, 1965), pp. 360–61, 366–67.

30. Johnson was probably referring to the anticipated expansion of the Justice Department's Civil Rights Division that would be needed to enforce the civil rights bill once it passed. One estimate suggested that the division would require "40 to 50 more lawyers." Anthony Lewis, "U.S. Powers Are Limited in Dealing with Civil Rights Strife," *New York Times*, 28 June 1964.

Kennedy: Yeah. . . . Yes, we are.

President Johnson: Now, should we do that between the time it goes from the Senate to the House and by the time we sign it? Or should we wait until after we sign it?

Kennedy: I think, probably, at least the feeling has been to wait until after we sign it.

President Johnson: [*with Kennedy acknowledging*] All right. Now you give thought to that, because we could move when the Senate messages it over to the House because it's a pretty forgone conclusion then.

Kennedy: That's right . . . that's right.

President Johnson: I assume, though, that Rules Committee will hold hearings for a while and try to delay it, won't they?

Kennedy: I guess so.

President Johnson: The Republicans are committed enough, though, they'll give you a rule, won't they?

Kennedy: Yes, that's right.

President Johnson: Uh . . .

Kennedy: That's right.

President Johnson: OK, now, [John] Stennis wants to see me about politics in Mississippi.[31] I assume it's about this marshal. Have you already gone and appointed him?

Kennedy: Well, that's—Yes. I think—

President Johnson: Then I think we ought to go in to him—with him, all this stuff you told me, don't you think so?

Kennedy: That'd be fine. The other problem he wants about the judge, Mr. President.

President Johnson: Well, what's—the Fifth Circuit?

Kennedy: Yes.[32]

President Johnson: Well, now, what—

---

31. John Stennis was a Democratic senator from Mississippi.

32. Johnson and Kennedy were referring to a vacancy on the U.S. Fifth Circuit Court of Appeals created by the death of Judge Ben F. Cameron. The Fifth Circuit has jurisdiction over Mississippi, Georgia, Florida, Alabama, Louisiana, and Texas, and it had maintained a 5–4 majority in support of the Supreme Court's rulings on civil rights issues. Each state in the circuit was represented on the court, and Cameron had been from Mississippi. He was also a hard-line segregationist. In addition, Mississippi Senator James Eastland chaired the Senate Judiciary Committee and, with input from Senator Stennis, would control the confirmation process of any judge, particularly one nominated for an ostensibly Mississippi seat. This meant that President Johnson faced significant pressure to name a judge from Mississippi. Many observers expected Eastland and Stennis to push for the nomination of a segregationist. Drew Pearson, "Will LBJ Bow to Sen. Eastland?" *Washington Post*, 16 December 1964; Fred P. Graham, "Coleman Picked for Court," *New York Times*, 13 May 1965.

Kennedy: And they want to have a judge from Mississippi, and we're still looking into it. It's awfully tough, you know, to get somebody down there who would be acceptable.

President Johnson: If we don't find somebody acceptable, though, they won't confirm him. I . . .

Kennedy: No. The only thing is that you take him from another state.

President Johnson: What I did was . . . that old Fifth Circuit, I remember that Roosevelt appointed [James] Allred, who had been a federal judge and resigned, to the circuit court several years after he resigned, or several months.[33] And there's been a Louisiana vacancy, and [Allen] Ellender took the position that it was really Louisiana's place, and the Senate stood behind him and overrode Roosevelt.[34]

Kennedy: Hmm.

President Johnson: Now, you may have another situation like that in Mississippi, unless we got the race thing in it, unless we just said, "Well, because of civil rights, we've got to go outside the state." You might get northern people to support you and not recognize this individual loyalty to the state.

Kennedy: Yeah. . . . They said—he said—Stennis said to me that he'd take [James] Coleman.[35]

President Johnson: Well, Coleman won't have it, though—

Kennedy: I know.

President Johnson: —I understood. I'd be for Coleman.

Kennedy: Yeah, I know. Of course, that would be . . . I mean, if Coleman at least . . . you could get Coleman to do it for a few years anyway.

President Johnson: Well . . .

Kennedy: You know, get us all beyond this.

President Johnson: Do you think we ought to try to do that?

Kennedy: Well, he'd be fine, you know. He'd be acceptable, and that

---

33. A former governor of Texas, James V. Allred was appointed in 1939 by Franklin Roosevelt to the U.S. District Court for the Southern District of Texas and served until resigning in 1942 to pursue the Fifth Circuit judgeship; unsuccessful, he served on the U.S. District Court again in the Southern District of Texas after being nominated by Harry Truman in 1949 until his death in 1959.

34. Allen Ellender had been a Democratic senator from Louisiana since 1937.

35. A former judge, state attorney general, and governor of Mississippi, and in 1964 a member of Mississippi's state house of representatives, James (J. P.) Coleman would be appointed to the U.S. Court of Appeals for the Fifth Circuit in 1965 and serve there until 1984. Although acceptable to senators Eastland and Stennis and opposed by some civil rights leaders, Coleman had a generally moderate reputation on civil rights, had supported John F. Kennedy for President in 1960, and represented a compromise nominee. Graham, "Coleman Picked for Court"; Rowland Evans and Robert Novak, "Inside Report," *Washington Post*, 7 July 1965.

would be . . . that would be—and I think it's going to be awful tough to take anybody else.

President Johnson: Would [James] Eastland take Coleman?

Kennedy: Well, Stennis said he'd take Coleman, so I assume—

President Johnson: That *he* would?

Kennedy: Yeah.

President Johnson: Or both of them would?

Kennedy: Well, the way he talked was that Coleman would be fine. He said, "It's my appointment, and the first person I wanted was Coleman."

President Johnson: All right, OK. If it's his appointment, that would just be fine with me because I think he's a good person.

Kennedy: Yeah, very.

President Johnson: I heard the President [Kennedy] offer him the secretary of the Army, and he just said he couldn't do it because he hadn't been in the Army, and he wouldn't do it.

Kennedy: That was very noble.

President Johnson: Yeah.

OK, I sure want you to get with these fellows. I tell them every day, and I want you and . . . if they're having any meetings this afternoon, after . . . or in the morning. Mac Bundy told me this morning that they were going to have executive meetings until Thursday and come in with some recommendations on Thursday. And I'll get back in touch with him, and you—

Kennedy: Yeah. Can I give you one other—

President Johnson: Oh, yeah, FBI, I talked to them.

Kennedy: Oh, yes.

President Johnson: And they said they'd get us a report in by the 1st, and I followed [*unclear*] in your memo.

Kennedy: Yeah. Well, that's terrific. The other person, Mr. President, who's got some sense on these matters, is . . . you know, again, none of us are always right, but who's got some sense and has had a good deal of experience is Douglas Dillon, so—

President Johnson: Yes, I've told them that. I've told them that every day.

Kennedy: Yeah.

President Johnson: OK.

Kennedy: Bye, Mr. President.

Immediately after the conclusion of his conversation with the Attorney General, Johnson took a call from Reedy.

12:31 P.M.

From George Reedy[36]

Although Reedy had called to clear the release of a statement on Puerto Rico (presumably in reference to the President's earlier meeting with the United States–Puerto Rican Commission), Johnson immediately turned the conversation to a story about the Johnson family business interests that had just appeared in the *Washington Star*. The *Star*'s investigation was the latest in a string of journalistic efforts to explore the business operations of the President and First Lady for wrongdoing—efforts which Johnson unfailingly viewed as hostile. Along with the well-known stories of the Johnsons' acquisition of their TV and radio stations and Lyndon Johnson's possible efforts to use his influence to gain favorable rulings from the Federal Communications Commission, the *Star* story opened a number of new investigative angles. It emphasized that most of the Johnson family fortune had been built up *after* Lyndon Johnson entered the U.S. Senate, argued that Johnson had been actively involved in managing the businesses—in contrast to widespread popular impressions that Lady Bird Johnson had run them independently—and suggested that the Johnsons had actively consulted with the managers of the supposedly blind trust that had been established to manage the businesses after Johnson assumed the presidency in November 1963. Johnson strongly objected to the article and indicated that he believed that it had been planted by Robert F. Kennedy and his supporters—despite the friendly and collegial tone he had maintained during the conversation with the Attorney General only minutes before.[37]

George Reedy: Mr. President, Lee White has just brought me back this Puerto Rican statement.[38]
President Johnson: Mm-hmm.
Reedy: Should I put it out?
President Johnson: Yeah.
Reedy: OK, sir.

---

36. Tape WH6406.04, Citations #3647 and #3648, Recordings of Telephone Conversations—White House Series, Recordings and Transcripts of Conversations and Meetings, Lyndon B. Johnson Library.
37. John Barron, "The Johnson Money," *Washington Star*, 9 June 1964.
38. Lee C. White served as associate counsel to the President and was one of Johnson's key advisers on civil rights issues.

President Johnson: Now, I don't think there's much in that. I think you ought to go away in your bathroom or someplace, take the [*Washington*] *Star*, read this [John] Barron story, because it's a very vicious—

Reedy: Yes, sir. . . . It is.

President Johnson: —a mean one, and it's planted, and I rather think that we'll have to say that it's untrue, but I think if we go to getting into it, then we bring it right in here and start debating it.

Reedy: Right.

President Johnson: And I don't know how to avoid that. But we have not met with them, at any time—that's a pure planted lie. They claim we met with [George] Morrell and [C. Hamilton] Moses.[39] Both of them denied it in [a] telegram. Now they come along and say that members of the board of directors say that Morrell told them that. Although they didn't tell us that before—

Reedy: Mm-hmm.

President Johnson: —and we showed them that it was a plant, that it was not true. We showed them Moses said he hadn't met with us, and we showed them the other hadn't.

Now they've got a presidential aide telephoning him.[40] We didn't do that; that's all untrue. But I don't know how you can do it. They submit it to you, and you tell them what to do. They didn't have the presidential aide in here, this is a new addition.[41]

Reedy: Yeah, there are a lot of things that are new in it.

President Johnson: We told . . . We told them a lot of things that, like Kingsbery, wasn't true, that we didn't negotiate. It doesn't make any difference, we had a right to, not anything wrong with our buying a radio

---

39. George Morrell and C. Hamilton Moses were executives with Midwest Video, a Little Rock, Arkansas, company that owned Capital Cable, an Austin, Texas, cable company. The Johnsons' Texas Broadcasting Company held a two-year option to purchase a 50 percent share in Capital Cable, which had recently benefited from an FCC ruling that denied a vital regulatory exemption to a competing company, TV Cable of Austin. The *Star* article alleged that Lyndon and Lady Bird Johnson had met with Morrell and Moses at the LBJ Ranch during the 1963 Christmas holidays to discuss the option and other business issues—after the blind trust had been established. The executives and Johnson attorney Abe Fortas denied that any such meeting took place. Barron, "The Johnson Money."

40. The *Star* article claimed that in the days following the assassination of John F. Kennedy, an unnamed Johnson aide had telephoned Midwest Video to convey the message that the new President remained interested in the purchase option in Capital Cable.

41. The *Star* had apparently submitted a draft of the article to the White House. For discussion of an earlier meeting between representatives of the newspaper and Abe Fortas, see Walter Jenkins to Johnson, 6:20 P.M., 1 June 1964, in this volume.

station from Mr. [Wesley] West.[42] But we just told them it didn't happen. We designated a lawyer, and he's the one that negotiated and did the [voir] dire, but he . . . and we got a letter from him saying that, but I don't guess you can ever answer it.[43]

Reedy: No.

President Johnson: Now, we've got to think about the strategy, and Abe's [Fortas's] in New York. You ought to read the story, and then you ought to try to talk to Abe and see what you think ought to be done. What is your reaction as to what ought to be done?

Reedy: First of all, the most damaging thing in it is that 9 million [dollar] figure.[44] Because that's the sort of thing that's going to get picked up. The rest of it, I think, is too complicated for anybody to read or understand [*Johnson acknowledges*], but that 9 million is going to make a big splash.

Second, my immediate impulse is that we've got to ride it out, but I want to go over it again once more. I've read it, and there's an awful lot of stuff that I could pick to pieces in it even with my limited knowledge. But before I give you a reas—a judgment I really want to sit down and do some thinking, because I think this can be serious. But the thing that everybody's going to leap to immediately is that 9 million because that sounds like a hell of a lot of money to John Doe on the street.

President Johnson: And I think the bad part is that, I think this is . . . I think is unquestionably these opponents of ours for the nomination.[45]

Reedy: No doubt.

President Johnson: I think that there's no question but what Bobby [Kennedy] and this group have got the *Star*, that they're using it, and the play they give it is . . . it's most unusual for the *Star* to do anything like that at all.

Reedy: Yes. And they've spent a lot of dough on this. They've obvi-

---

42. The Johnsons had purchased their share of Austin's KTBC television station in 1943 from their friend Wesley West, a conservative Democrat. The *Star* article claimed that Austin businessman E. G. Kingsbery had been interested in purchasing the station but agreed to let Johnson acquire it after learning of the congressman's interest. Kingsbery also told the *Star* that Johnson had spent Christmas 1942 at West's ranch negotiating the purchase.

43. Voir dire is a preliminary examination of prospective jurors or witnesses under oath to determine their competence or suitability.

44. The *Star* article estimated that the total Johnson holdings were worth at least $9 million. Barron, "The Johnson Money." A report earlier in the year placed their net worth (including debts) at $7 million. "The Story of the Johnson Family Fortune," *U.S. News & World Report*, 4 May 1964, p. 38.

45. Johnson feared that Robert F. Kennedy and his supporters would attempt to wrest the Democratic nomination from Johnson at the August Democratic National Convention in Atlantic City.

ously done an awful lot of work and research for a story that just as a news story isn't quite worth it for them.

President Johnson: [*softly*] Mm-hmm. . . . Mm-hmm. Mm-hmm.

Reedy: This is . . . They had to spend an awful lot of expense money in Barron, and they got to examine an awful lot of records, and I'll bet they've had libel lawyers go over this several times, but . . .

President Johnson: Well, it looks like that they'd have to prove . . . they quoted Fortas denying it, but they go ahead and allege that three stockholders say it, and it looks like to me they'd have to prove these stock-holders say it. If we proved it otherwise, they damage us by alleging this. I don't know whether we could prove damage or not, but . . .

Reedy: I don't—I think that your problem there is going to be if they carry the denial. And they're going to say, "Well, it was alleged here and denied here," but that usually covers any . . . any libel suit. And of course the big thing about libel is you've got to prove damage, and that's almost impossible for a public figure to prove under the current interpretations of what is libel.

[*with the President acknowledging*] Actually, almost any public figure is libel-proof as far as the papers are concerned. You can say almost anything about him. Because I've been through that a number of times in Washington. A businessman can sue at the drop of a hat—

President Johnson: Well, won't all your wires pick this up?

Reedy: I think they will. I think they'll pick up the 9 million [dollars] and write brief stories.[46] I don't think they'll pick up too much of it because it's complicated, but I think they'll pick up enough to get—

President Johnson: He doesn't really allege any wrongdoing anywhere.

Reedy: Nowhere. Nowhere.

President Johnson: And says the commission says that there [was] never any.

Reedy: That's right. They don't allege wrongdoing anywhere.

President Johnson: Just a kind of a biographical sketch for the Republican National Committee, that's what it is.

Reedy: Right.

President Johnson: And our Democratic opponents.

Reedy: All they do, they leave an inference. They say you've got a hell of a lot of money. They don't even say that directly, but I'm talking about the way the average man will read it. That you've got a lot of dough, and

---

46. As Reedy expected, the lead of the Associated Press summary of the *Star* article featured the $9 million figure. "Johnson Fortune Put at $9 Million," *New York Times*, 10 June 1964.

you made that dough when you were in Congress, and that you were a member of the Commerce Committee, which had a lot to do with it.

And the trouble is that when you start looking at it . . . when you start nit-picking at it, they can claim they've been fair. Now, they haven't been, but they can claim they've been. For instance, on this stuff about . . . that letter that you sent to the FCC [Federal Communications Commission], which wasn't a letter—I'm familiar with the whole thing—but just the files, say they contain one letter of him forwarding an appeal from a constituent together with the request that the issue raised be decided on its merits. Now, actually that whole paragraph is, standing all by itself, a fair paragraph, but you put it in with all the rest of this gunk, and it . . . Well.

President Johnson: Well, that was an error that Gene Latimer and [*unclear*] made in the office . . .[47]

Reedy: I remember.

President Johnson: . . . in putting a buck slip on.[48] I had orders not to even submit anything to him.

Reedy: I remember when young Neil MacNeil dug that one up, and of course he wasn't even as fair as the *Star* story was.[49] He just said you'd intervened in this case.

President Johnson: Mm-hmm . . . mm-hmm. [*Pauses.*] All right. Now, have you read the story?

Reedy: Yes, sir, I want to read it once more, though—

President Johnson: I sure—I'd read it and mark it as I went through very carefully. Then I'd try to talk to Walter [Jenkins] and find out where Abe Fortas is, and . . . he's in New York, see if you can't talk to him.

Reedy: Right.

President Johnson: See what you think you ought to say—

Reedy: Right.

---

47. Gene Latimer had been a member of a high school debate team coached by Lyndon Johnson during the future President's tenure as a teacher. Latimer later worked as an aide to Johnson, first in the office of Representative Richard Kleberg and later, on Johnson's own staff. Transcript, Gene Latimer Oral History Interview, 17 August 1971, by David G. McComb, Lyndon B. Johnson Library.

48. A "buck slip" is a routing form that indicates where and to whom a document should be sent.

49. Neil MacNeil was a congressional reporter for *Time* magazine. In 1964, he started the weekly show *Neil MacNeil Reports* on the Washington public television station WETA, one of the first serious political news and analysis programs on television. It eventually became the long-running PBS program *Washington Week in Review*. Reedy referred to him here as "young Neil MacNeil" because his father, of the same name, had been a longtime reporter and editor for the *New York Times*. Bruce Weber, "Neil MacNeil, Among First of TV Reporters on Congress, Dies at 85," *New York Times*, 12 June 2008.

President Johnson: —at your briefing because I imagine they'll ask you about it before—

Reedy: They will ask me about it.

President Johnson: What would you be inclined to say?

Reedy: My inclination is merely to say that this is a—I have no jurisdiction whatsoever, and just refer them to the trustees, or refer them to Abe Fortas.[50] I think Abe handled himself very well as I go through this thing. But this is one of those situations where it doesn't matter how well you handle yourself, which means that the best thing to do is to play it tight.

President Johnson: I wish they hadn't quoted him. I wish they'd just said the counsel for the trustees. They don't quote the other people, good many times.

Reedy: That's right. But everything that I see that he said I think is pretty good. [*Pauses.*] They've changed it around a little bit. "Mr. Fortas states that his information is that the Johnson purchase of the station was handled entirely by a lawyer and family friend, the late Alvin Wirtz."[51] They might just have said, "Mr. Fortas stated that the purchase was handled entirely by Alvin Wirtz," which would be the same thing but doesn't sound defensive.

President Johnson: Mm-hmm. [*Long pause.*] Now, the *Star* is not a [Barry] Goldwater paper, not a mean, Republican paper, and always has been friendly to me.

Reedy: No. . . . Right.

President Johnson: Until the last three or four months. Until—I guess, until I became President.

Reedy: And you know the weird thing about it is that most of their people—

President Johnson: And they came in and told Pierre [Salinger] that they were going to write this story, and Pierre knew all about it.[52] That's why I think Bobby Kennedy owns it.

Reedy: That is unusual. I was at a party Sunday, given by Charlie Seib, and—[53]

---

50. On 29 November 1963, the Johnson family business interests had been placed in a blind trust managed by A.W. Moursund and J. W. Bullion, two longtime Johnson friends and advisers. Barron, "The Johnson Money."

51. Alvin J. Wirtz had been a lawyer, Texas state senator, and an early political mentor to Lyndon Johnson. Merle Miller, *Lyndon: An Oral Biography* (New York: Ballantine Books, 1980), p. 744.

52. Pierre Salinger had been President Kennedy's press secretary and had continued in that role for President Johnson until resigning on 19 March 1964 to run for the Senate from California.

53. Charles B. Seib was a reporter for the *Washington Star*.

President Johnson: Did he invite you?

Reedy: Yes. Oh, yes. It was mostly *Star* people: Dick Fryklund and Charlie Seib and Newbold Noyes.[54] They were all very friendly, except Newbold Noyes, and I wouldn't say he was unfriendly, but just a . . . little cold. Of course, I've known Charlie for many years.

President Johnson: Mm-hmm. Well, he made the decision, Seib did, but he got Noyes and them to approve it beforehand. But he was very wrought when he found out that I hadn't seen these people, and Abe assured him that I hadn't, and . . . then they went back, and they talked to some of the directors who claimed somebody had told them that they'd seen them.

Reedy: Well, I have a hunch from the way Charlie talked to me Sunday, he may have gotten overruled on a couple of things. He didn't talk specifically about this article. The only thing he said to me was that he had a good session with Abe Fortas, who's a very convincing man. And he said, "A very honest man; he just laid the facts out for us."

President Johnson: Mm-hmm. [*A telephone rings in the background.*] What was the point of the party, just social?

Reedy: Just a reception that Charlie gave.

President Johnson: For whom?

Reedy: Did not—I shouldn't have said reception, just a party that . . . he had a lot of people, about . . . oh, maybe a hundred people, mostly newspapermen.

President Johnson: Mm-hmm. . . . Mm-hmm. All right, now, if you had to answer it now and suppose the *New York Times* say[s] the *Star's* got a big two-page story on this thing, what comment do you have to make?[55]

Reedy: I would just refer them to the trustees.

President Johnson: I think what I'd say is the President stated when he entered the—when he took the—shortly after he took the oath, that he had no television holdings and that Mrs. [Lady Bird] Johnson and his family had placed all of theirs in trust, as . . . had other presidents. The lawyers say the trust is one of the tightest ever drawn. And that's the only comment I have to make on it. Maybe you want to improve on it.[56]

---

54. Newbold Noyes Jr. was the editor of the *Washington Star*; Richard Fryklund was a reporter for the *Star*.

55. The *New York Times* published the Associated Press's summary of the *Star's* story in its back pages the next day. "Johnson Fortune Put at $9 Million," *New York Times*, 10 June 1964.

56. For Reedy's response to the *Star* story, see "Johnson Fortune Put at $9 Million," *New York Times*, 10 June 1964.

Reedy: Well, I'm going . . . I'll go over it with Abe. [*Pauses.*] But after seeing it, I really believe the less we say, the better.

President Johnson: OK.

Reedy: You bet, sir.

12:44 P.M.

From Carl Albert[57]

Johnson spoke next with House Majority Leader Carl Albert about the probability that House Rules Committee Chairman Howard Smith of Virginia would issue rules for the economic opportunity bill and the Senate-passed civil rights bill. Smith was a frequent administration foe. In addition, as he had indicated to Robert Kennedy that he would do, the President also informed Albert about the bombing raid in Laos.

Carl Albert: . . . he told Ed Edmondson, he said he'd get ahold of Howard [Edmondson] just as soon as he could.[58]

President Johnson: All right. Now, we have a message here, "Edmondson strongly indicates he will now support cloture because of the jury trial amendment."[59]

Albert: Yes. Well, that's good.

President Johnson: It was adopted, the jury trial.

Albert: Yes, I know it was.

President Johnson: So . . . Well, that's good. Did he indicate how long it might take on poverty?[60]

Albert: No, he didn't, but all—what we've got to do is have our horses

---

57. Tape WH6406.04, Citation #3649, Recordings of Telephone Conversations—White House Series, Recordings and Transcripts of Conversations and Meetings, Lyndon B. Johnson Library.

58. Edmond Edmondson was, like Albert, a Democratic representative from Oklahoma. The reference to "Howard" is probably to Senator J. Howard Edmondson of Oklahoma (the brother of Representative Edmondson). Representative Howard Smith of Virginia, the recalcitrant chair of the House Rules Committee, is also referred to a few moments later.

59. This reference is to Senator Edmondson. For the jury trial amendment to the civil rights bill, see Robert Kennedy to Johnson, 12:25 P.M., 9 June 1964, in this chapter.

60. Johnson was referring to the need to get a rule for floor debate on the economic opportunity bill, the legislative centerpiece of the proposed War on Poverty, from House Rules Committee Chairman Howard Smith. The powerful chairman had already delayed hearings on the bill and would not actually grant a rule until 28 July. See Johnson to Carl Albert, 1:00 P.M., 5 June 1964, in this volume.

there. But I would think that he would want a reasonable time, but not an unreasonable time. I would think—

President Johnson: Think he might get it where you might take it up Thursday?

Albert: Well, I doubt *that*, because we've got the debt ceiling we'll probably have to take up on Thursday, and that's probably one reason he's bringing it up that week to make it . . . you know, to give him a little play on the debt ceiling.

But I think he'll—I feel that they'll get it out if we can keep our members there, but this gives us something to shoot at. We got to get [Richard] Bolling back, and got to be sure that Tip O'Neill stays here.[61] And I would think once started, that he would lose control of it except maybe for a little bit of minor delaying tactics. So I think we're over the big hurdle as far as the Rules Committee is concerned.

President Johnson: Mm-hmm.

Albert: I think we can get it up the following week.

President Johnson: Mm-hmm. OK. Now, is there anything we need to do on the Bollings, and—

Albert: That'll be ahead of civil . . . that'll be ahead of the civil rights conference.

President Johnson: Will you have to go to Rules Committee with civil rights? You will.[62]

Albert: Yes, sir. Yes, sir, and that'll be tougher.

President Johnson: But the Republicans will help you get a rule there, won't they?

Albert: Well, they will unless they can . . . unless they decide they don't want it before the convention, you know.

President Johnson: They will wa—

Albert: I think they would.

President Johnson: They'll want it before the convention.

Albert: They don't know, right now, whether they want it before or after the convention. We're at their *mercy* on that because we can't get [Carl] Elliott and Jim Trimble, you know, Judge Smith and [*unclear*].[63]

---

61. Richard Bolling was a Democratic representative from Missouri; Thomas "Tip" O'Neill was a Democratic representative from Massachusetts; both served on the House Rules Committee.
62. Johnson was referring to the need to get a new rule for House consideration of the amended Senate version of the civil rights bill. The House had passed its version of the bill on 10 February 1964.
63. Both Democratic representatives and members of the Rules Committee, Carl Elliott was from Alabama and James Trimble was from Arkansas. Albert worried that as southerners, both would likely vote with Chairman Smith against granting a rule for the amended civil rights bill.

President Johnson: Couldn't you get them if you had to have them now on a rule? Elliott being defeated?[64]

Albert: I think we could get Trimble.

President Johnson: Trimble's always indicated he'd go if he had to.

Albert: We'd get Trimble if we had to have him. I don't know whether we'd get Elliott or not, though. He might feel that he would . . .[65]

President Johnson: Just let them vote on it.

Albert: He might . . . I don't know.

President Johnson: Incidentally, I told [John] McCormack. I told McCormack you could tell him that I'd . . . anything he wanted us to do for him, I'd try to help him.

Albert: Yes, sir.

President Johnson: Elliott. So you ought to know that.

Albert: All right, sir.

President Johnson: Carl?

Albert: Yes, sir.

President Johnson: [with Albert acknowledging] Last night—this is very confidential—but last night, we had to go in and respond to this battery in Laos and try to knock it out, and we injured it. We didn't lose any planes, but we did fire back at them. We've lost two planes over there in the last few days, and last night we went in to take the battery out, and I think you ought to know it.

Albert: Well, I think you had no alternative.

President Johnson: We hadn't, but I wanted them to say that I'd talked to you.

Albert: All right, sir.

President Johnson: OK.

Albert: Bye.

---

64. Despite voting against the civil rights bill in the House, Carl Elliott was a relative moderate and an opponent of the state's archsegregationist Governor George Wallace. Targeted by segregationists, Elliott had been defeated in a nine-candidate, "last-man-out" primary runoff on 2 June. The bizarre runoff had been necessitated by the Alabama legislature's failure to complete a redistricting plan. Claude Sitton, "Right Wing Gains in Southern Vote," *New York Times*, 3 June 1964; Marjorie Hunter, "Alabama Liberal's Defeat Is a Blow to Johnson," *New York Times*, 5 June 1964.

65. Both Trimble and Elliott eventually voted with Chairman Smith against a rule for the amended civil rights bill. Nonetheless, the bill cleared the committee easily. *Congressional Quarterly Almanac*, 1964, vol. 20, p. 377.

12:50 *P.M.*

To John McCormack[66]

After the Albert conversation concluded, the President called Speaker of the House John McCormack and briefed him about the Laos situation.

The President is on hold for approximately three and a half minutes while waiting for McCormack to come from the floor of the House.
John McCormack: Yes, Mr. President.

President Johnson: I called you Sunday afternoon to tell you about this thing we had the discussion about the other day, and I didn't get any answer at your apartment, and I couldn't talk to you again about it this morning.[67]

McCormack: Yeah, we were . . . [*unclear*] Harriet and I went down to Harpers Ferry.[68]

President Johnson: We went in there last night to take out this battery that had shot down these two planes, and we destroyed some buildings and maybe took out—had a partial success in taking out one of the guns. Secretary of State [Dean Rusk] and Secretary of Defense [Robert McNamara] and the Joint Chiefs [of Staff] all felt like that after they shot down two planes that we had to make some response. If we didn't, why, we just . . . destroy ourselves. So, we did that, and our planes came back uninjured and all back at their base.

Now, we can't say anything about it. I'm going to meet with them again at 1:00—Secretary of State and Secretary of Defense. I have a regular Tuesday luncheon with them, and I don't know who we ought to discuss this with, if anyone. I imagine the Chinese, who are speaking for them, will issue a press release some time or other.

But we do not plan any further expeditions. We'll make a survey about once a week to see their location so we can't get caught off guard, but we have answered them now and shown that we mean business, but—and I stayed awake most of the night hoping that these planes would come back, and 1:30 [A.M.] they went off and 3:00 they got back. But there are

---

66. Tape WH6406.04, Citation #3650, Recordings of Telephone Conversations—White House Series, Recordings and Transcripts of Conversations and Meetings, Lyndon B. Johnson Library.
67. Johnson was referring to the morning's legislative leaders breakfast at the White House.
68. Harriet was McCormack's spouse. McCormack was referring to the town of Harpers Ferry, West Virginia, located along the Potomac River northwest of Washington.

ten of them, [and] they're all back safe. And they partially destroyed the battery that was giving us this trouble with these 37-millimeter Russian guns. And that's where we stand now.

McCormack: Mm-hmm.

President Johnson: Would it be your thought we ought to talk to [Charles] Halleck and any of the Republicans about it?[69] [*Pauses.*] A great—

McCormack: Well, it's bound to come out. I would think so because of the [*unclear*].

President Johnson: I had the feeling that I ought to send McNamara to see the Armed Services [Committee] people, and I ought to send Rusk to see the Foreign Affairs [Committee] people, but they got that bill on the floor today.[70] But we've got to keep it to a very limited group; if we don't, it would greatly injure our interests by their talking about it.

McCormack: Yeah, and the worst of that is when you get a group like that, you know what democracies are.

President Johnson: Yeah, they want to—

McCormack: Yet, on the other hand, it's bound, I suppose, is bound to come out from elsewhere. From the Chinese angle.

President Johnson: Yeah.

McCormack: I don't know, Mr. President, but I would think there are certain things that you've got to—all we can do is rely on—

President Johnson: My judgment is that we ought to talk to Halleck and we ought to talk to [Les] Arends and we ought to talk to the ranking Republican on Foreign Affairs.[71] Who is that?

McCormack: Uh . . . Mrs. [Frances] Bolton.[72]

President Johnson: Mrs. Bolton.

McCormack: Wait a minute. Wait a minute, Mr. President. [*Sounds of pages rustling.*] Yeah, Mrs. Bolton.

President Johnson: I believe it ought to be kept to that, and they ought to be sworn to secrecy.

McCormack: I agree with you.

President Johnson: You think it over, and we'll talk later in the afternoon, and don't discuss it with anyone.

---

69. A Republican from Indiana, Charles Halleck was minority leader of the House.

70. Johnson was referring to the foreign aid authorization bill.

71. Leslie Arends was a Republican from Illinois and the minority whip in the House.

72. As the result of a special election upon the death of her husband, Chester Bolton, Frances Bolton became a Republican representative from Ohio in 1940 and served until January 1969. Her son Oliver was also a Republican representative from Ohio in the 88th Congress.

McCormack: No.

President Johnson: I'm going to discuss it with you and Carl [Albert] and [Mike] Mansfield and [Hubert] Humphrey, and we'll try to keep it to that.

McCormack: All right . . .

President Johnson: OK.

McCormack: And I . . . Carl's meeting with the California delegation at 1:30, and I suggested that if he runs into any difficulty there, that he have them talk with someone that can talk with you, is that all right?

President Johnson: Yes, sir. Yes, sir. Yeah.

McCormack: Because, you see—well, you know what happens.

President Johnson: Yeah, I know that.

McCormack: [*Unclear*] the Senate, goddamn it, is.

President Johnson: Just tell them . . . I know it. But, I tell you, they . . .

McCormack: [*with the President acknowledging*] And you've got your friends in the House here, you know that. Carl and I and [Hale] Boggs,[73] and . . . but they're . . . the hell, we have our problems over here, and it's . . . the feeling is, "Well, if we pass the bill over there, the Senate won't do it," don't you see? And then we're left holding the bag and everything else.

Now, Joe Waggonner just come up to me.[74] He's for the bill. He told me that he talked with the chief counsel of the Senate committee, and they say there won't be a bill out tomorrow. That's all I know, is just what he told me. So I . . . if it can be done, this is the week to get it up.

President Johnson: Yeah, it ought to be, that's for sure.

McCormack: On the other hand, we've got to iron out certain things here in the House.

President Johnson: I sure think it ought to come up in the House, and I think if it does, we'll pass in the Senate, but if we don't, why—you be your own judge. If they call me, I'll talk to them.

McCormack: All right.

President Johnson: All right.

McCormack: Fine.

---

73. Hale Boggs was a Democratic representative from Louisiana and the House majority whip. McCormack's comments here may have been in reference to the federal pay bill.
74. Joseph Waggonner was a Democratic representative from Louisiana.

12:56 P.M.

To Mike Mansfield[75]

Continuing with his efforts to notify key congressional leaders about the bombing raid in Laos, Johnson called Mike Mansfield. The Senate majority leader had privately begun to express doubts about the direction of U.S. policy in Southeast Asia.

The President is on hold for almost two minutes while waiting for Mansfield to come to the line.
President Johnson: Mike?
Mike Mansfield: Yes, sir.
President Johnson: All right, this is quite confidential, but I want you to know it, and I want to get your advice on who else we ought to talk to.
Mansfield: OK.
President Johnson: [*with Mansfield acknowledging throughout*] This morning at 3:00, our Air Force planes went in to this battery that had knocked down our two planes, that—this antiaircraft battery of 37-millimeter Russian guns—in an attempt to destroy it. They had about a 50 percent success. Shot at it with rockets and bombs in Laos and returned to their base. We got them back about—little after 3:00. I wasn't in a position much to talk there in that meeting because all the employees and everybody else this morning and you were rushing to get back up there.[76] But they returned to their base, and I'd say it's only a partial success.

Now, the Joint Chiefs [of Staff], and the Secretary of State, and Averell Harriman, and Alexis Johnson, and the head of the Vietnam-Laos task force, and Bill Bundy, [Robert] McNamara, shall like, in light of their knocking down two of our planes—we couldn't do it the day before because we were searching for this pilot who we picked up yesterday— but that if we didn't, that this was a test of us and they'd just start moving

---

75. Tape WH6406.04, Citations #3651 and #3652, Recordings of Telephone Conversations— White House Series, Recordings and Transcripts of Conversations and Meetings, Lyndon B. Johnson Library.
76. Johnson was referring to the morning's legislative leaders breakfast.

again and confront us with a fait accompli before we could do much about it and this—we had to give this signal to Hanoi.[77]

Now we've done it. We don't plan to do it anymore. We planned to try to take pictures. And we're trying to work out with Souvanna [Phouma] what he wants and hope that we can hold things as they are and try to have this Polish conference.[78] I have submitted all the things that you've suggested to me, and I've got [Adlai] Stevenson down there and got him to suggest all the things.[79] They don't have very much of a plan. We can't go in there with the ground troops; the air forces don't get the job done and can't get it done. We are trying every way we know how to appeal to Hanoi and to Peiping. We have told [Charles] de Gaulle that we are very anxious to follow any conference route that we can, that we are very anxious to follow any planned neutralization we can.[80] He agrees with us that . . . that would be desirable. That's what he's suggested all along, but we've got to keep our strength there and show that we will react in order to have them where they'll talk to us at all. Otherwise, they just think they don't need to.

We have very confidentially talked to the Canadians on this ICC [International Commission for Supervision and Control] and asked them to go to Hanoi and say to Hanoi that we're willing to pull out of there and get out of there and stay out of there if they'll just quit overrunning South

---

77. Averell Harriman was secretary of state for political affairs; U. Alexis Johnson served as Harriman's deputy until July, when he became the deputy ambassador to Vietnam. William Bundy, brother of McGeorge, was assistant secretary of state for far eastern affairs.

78. In late May, the government of Poland had proposed a six-nation conference to assess the situation in Laos and possibly establish terms for reconvening the larger Geneva Conference that in 1962 had established a national unity government in the country. Participating countries would include Britain, the Soviet Union, Canada, India, Poland, and representatives of the major Laotian factions—but not the United States or China. While the United States opposed reconvening the Geneva Conference, U.S. officials saw the Polish conference as a useful way to reduce tensions while also delaying a larger Geneva Conference. The opposition of France and China, however, threatened to block the Polish proposal. Paul Underwood, "Six-Nation Talks on Laos Proposed," *New York Times*, 29 May 1964; Flora Lewis, "Britain, Greece Squabble about Intervention over Cyprus Draft Law," *Washington Post*, 4 June 1964; "Draft Paper Prepared for a White House Meeting," 10 June 1964, U.S. Department of State, *Foreign Relations of the United States (FRUS), 1964–1968: Laos*, ed. Edward C. Keefer (Washington, DC: GPO, 1998), 28:167–69; Fredrik Logevall, *Choosing War: The Lost Chance for Peace and the Escalation of War in Vietnam* (Berkeley: University of California Press, 1999), pp. 214–16.

79. Adlai Stevenson was the U.S. representative to the United Nations.

80. French President Charles de Gaulle had recommended the neutralization of Vietnam and the reconvening of the Geneva Conference (although France opposed the idea of a limited, intermediate conference as proposed by Poland). In contrast to Johnson's statements here, the United States opposed both ideas. Logevall, *Choosing War*, pp. 129–32; Lewis, "Britain, Greece Squabble about Intervention Over Cyprus Draft Law."

Vietnam.[81] And that we may actually be able to work with them and help them better their lot. But we don't want anything over there. We've got no interest there; we've got no objective there; we don't want to dominate anybody. If they'll just quit advancing, why, then we can get out. We don't know how much that goes, but . . . that's about the situation.

Now, I—we talked to [Bourke] Hickenlooper and all the Republicans.[82] Hickenlooper felt like we had to respond and—this was a week or so ago, I told you about it at the time—that we, he—and none of them objected— that he thought that we had to go in and show some strength. If we didn't, they'd run us out, and that would be a catastrophe. Now, I haven't agreed to that yet because I can't see any very firm plans, and I don't want to get in a land war in Asia.

Mansfield: No, sir.

President Johnson: So I have held it back for three or four weeks, and now I don't know who I ought to discuss what we're doing with up there. My guess would be [Richard] Russell and Hickenlooper and [Leverett] Saltonstall from Armed Services and Foreign Relations; you and [Hubert] Humphrey, the leadership, and [Everett] Dirksen, and probably [J. William] Fulbright and the ranking Republican—who is that?[83]

Mansfield: [George] Aiken.[84]

President Johnson: Aiken?

Mansfield: Yeah.

President Johnson: And keep them up to date.

---

81. Johnson was referring to a proposed mission to North Vietnam that would be headed by senior Canadian diplomat Blair Seaborn. The goal of such a mission would be to deliver three messages to the North Vietnamese leadership: first, that the United States remained determined to defend South Vietnam; second, that continued North Vietnamese intervention in the South would lead to an escalation of the war, potentially including direct strikes against the North; and third, that the United States would provide aid for North Vietnam if the latter withdrew support for the Vietcong guerrillas. Canadian Prime Minister Lester "Mike" Pearson had readily agreed to the idea of a Seaborn mission during a 30 April meeting with Secretary of State Rusk and had discussed the details with President Johnson in a 28 May meeting. "Memorandum for the Record of a Conversation Between President Johnson and Prime Minister Pearson, Hilton Hotel, New York, May 28, 1964, 6:15–6:45 P.M.," *FRUS, 1964–1968: Vietnam 1964*, ed. Edward C. Keefer and Charles S. Sampson (Washington, DC: GPO, 1992), 1:394–96.

82. Bourke Hickenlooper was a Republican senator from Iowa and the ranking minority member of the Senate Foreign Relations Committee.

83. Democrat Richard Russell of Georgia served as the chairman of the Senate Armed Services Committee. Massachusetts Republican Leverett Saltonstall was the ranking minority member of that committee. Senate Minority Leader Everett Dirksen was a Republican from Illinois. Democratic Senator J. William Fulbright of Arkansas was chairman of the Committee on Foreign Relations.

84. Senator George Aiken of Vermont was the ranking Republican on the Foreign Relations Committee.

Mansfield: Yes, sir.

President Johnson: Do you have any suggestions on who we ought to talk to? I thought I'd send [Dean] Rusk and McNamara. McNamara would talk to Russell and them, and Rusk to talk to the others.

Mansfield: Mm-hmm. I think the best thing to do would be if you talked to them all together.

President Johnson: It always gets out.

Mansfield: Mm-hmm.

President Johnson: And I noticed these personal conferences with Rusk and McNamara, they don't attach that much importance to them, and we don't want to blow it up.

Mansfield: I see.

President Johnson: Because we sure don't want to give any indications that we're getting involved in a war. I've been playing it down, if you'll notice.

Mansfield: Mm-hmm. Well, I think—

President Johnson: If you notice after the Honolulu meeting, I've tried to draw away from this thing that we're invading the North.[85]

Mansfield: And you did it very successfully. But I think, Mr. President, even if there is a leak, it would be better if you'd do it rather than the others—with the others in attendance of course—because it'll get out anyway. And it's a matter of ego as far as some of these people are concerned. And I think you ought to lay it out just like you did now, and so far as I'm concerned, I think you've done everything right.

President Johnson: Well . . . you-all are voting this afternoon, aren't you?[86]

Mansfield: Yes, sir. But . . .

President Johnson: And if you come down, that'll sure get in the papers, and that will be notifying them what we're doing.

Mansfield: [*with President Johnson acknowledging*] That's right. Well, of course, you have to decide that. It's just my suggestion as to what should be done. The only thing is, if you want them to—we ought to be through with these things by 7:00 tonight—drop in briefly for 10 or 15 minutes. But you've got to decide that, and I . . . no matter what you say it's OK. You want to send the others up, all right.

---

85. Johnson was referring to a meeting of the administration's leading foreign policy and military officials that had been held on 1 and 2 June near Honolulu to discuss future policy in Southeast Asia, including whether to escalate U.S. military actions against North Vietnam. A decision had been reached to delay bombing raids or other increases in engagement.
86. The Senate on 9 June would vote on three amendments to the civil rights bill.

President Johnson: OK. God bless you.

Mansfield: OK, Mr. President.

President Johnson: How do—You think this helped you on cloture, this vote, don't you?[87]

Mansfield: I do indeed.

President Johnson: Are you going to adopt the other amendments?

Mansfield: No, I think the others will be defeated.[88] At least I hope so because we were . . . the other—the fourth amendment carried by less votes than we had anticipated.

President Johnson: OK, my friend.

Mansfield: Yes, sir.

President Johnson: Thank you, Mike.

Mansfield: Thank you, Mr. President.

1:05 P.M.: Secretary of Defense Robert McNamara joined Johnson in the Oval Office.

1:06 P.M.

To Hubert Humphrey[89]

The next in Johnson's series of calls to congressional leaders went to Senate Majority Whip Hubert Humphrey of Minnesota.

President Johnson: We lost these two planes in Laos. Our folks went in there about 3:00 this morning—that is, the day before yesterday and the day before you read about them. We went in about 3:00 this morning and tried to take out that battery, and we had a partial success. And our

---

87. Johnson was referring to the jury trial amendment to the civil rights bill that had been approved earlier in the day. See Robert Kennedy to Johnson, 12:25 P.M., 9 June 1964, in this chapter.

88. Later in the day, the Senate would defeat three amendments to the civil rights bill. The first (sponsored by Bourke Hickenlooper of Iowa) would have eliminated funding under Title IV for colleges to provide training for school officials in managing school desegregation issues; another (sponsored by Sam Ervin of North Carolina) would have eliminated Title VII, which banned employment desegregation; a third (sponsored by Norris Cotton of New Hampshire) would have limited the application of Title VII to firms and unions with at least 100 workers.

89. Tape WH6406.04, Citation #3653, Recordings of Telephone Conversations—White House Series, Recordings and Transcripts of Conversations and Meetings, Lyndon B. Johnson Library.

planes returned safely. I don't know—we don't want to tell them what we're doing. We felt like we had to respond.

Hubert Humphrey: Right.

President Johnson: The Secretary of State [Dean Rusk] and Secretary of Defense [Robert McNamara] and Joint Chiefs thought that this was the minimum; a good many thought we ought to do a good deal more. We have . . . I couldn't talk to you-all publicly with all those people there this morning. I talked to Mike [Mansfield] over the phone a moment ago, and I've talked to [John] McCormack and [Carl] Albert.

I don't want us to be responsible for escalating this thing and announcing these things and appear that we are on a bombing rampage, because we're not. We just had to answer their knocking down two planes with some kind of response.

Humphrey: Yes, sir.

President Johnson: And we did, and we got back, and while we didn't get everything we went after, we didn't lose anything, and we did make the response.

Now, the question comes is what is the wise thing. McNamara is going to talk to [Richard] Russell and [Leverett] Saltonstall; I've talked to you and Mansfield. Mansfield thinks we ought to call these people to the White House. I think that escalates it and makes it too important, and it announces to the enemy what we're doing. We're just doing that too much these days.

Humphrey: I agree with that.

President Johnson: So, I rather think that [I] probably ought to call [Everett] Dirksen on the phone and [Bourke] Hickenlooper, or maybe send [Dean] Rusk up to see Dirksen and Hickenlooper. Let McNamara see the two Armed Services [Committee members], and you and Mike have been talked to, and the leadership of the House have been talked to. But it's kind of like making an atomic bomb: If you go to telling everybody, why, you'll lose the war.

Humphrey: [*with the President acknowledging*] I would suggest that you send both Rusk and McNamara to those persons together. It just seems to me that the two of them coming together is more impressive and has a tendency to give everybody sort of an equal treatment. Plus the fact McNamara's a little firmer, and Rusk can give a little . . . little touch to it.

President Johnson: OK.

Humphrey: That'd be my view of it. I mean, with Dirksen and Hick, Dirksen is not on the Foreign Relations [Committee], but he's key.

President Johnson: Well, do you—Would you think they ought to be done together? Are they getting along that well these days?

Humphrey: No, I'd send them to talk to them separately.
President Johnson: Mm–hmm. OK.
Humphrey: Individually.
President Johnson: All right.
Humphrey: Yeah.
President Johnson: OK.
Humphrey: But I don't think you could do anything less than you've done right now.
President Johnson: OK.
Humphrey: Yes, sir.
President Johnson: Bye.
Humphrey: Bye, sir.

1:11 P.M.: Unrecorded call to George Reedy.
1:15 P.M.: McGeorge Bundy joined the President and Secretary Robert McNamara; they walked to the Mansion, where they were joined by Secretary Dean Rusk for lunch.
2:31 P.M.–4:10 P.M.: Unrecorded calls, all at the Mansion, from Hale Boggs (2:31), from John McCormack (3:00), to Walter Jenkins (3:06, 3:21, and 4:05), to Jack Valenti (3:27 and 3:36), to George Reedy (3:55), and to White House staff member Ashton Gonella (4:10).
4:32 P.M.: Returned to the office.

4:37 P.M.

From George Reedy[90]

A few minutes after President Johnson arrived back at the Oval Office, George Reedy called to update him on the afternoon's press briefing and, in particular, the White House press corps' response to the *Washington Star* story about the Johnson family's business interests.

Reedy is on hold for approximately forty seconds before the President comes to the line.

---

90. Tape WH6406.04, Citation #3655, Recordings of Telephone Conversations—White House Series, Recordings and Transcripts of Conversations and Meetings, Lyndon B. Johnson Library.

President Johnson: Yeah?

George Reedy: Mr. President?

President Johnson: Mm-hmm.

Reedy: They hit me with one question.

President Johnson: Who did, the AP [Associated Press]?

Reedy: No, not the AP, I got hit with it in the press briefing.

President Johnson: I thought the AP was going to—

Reedy: By Dan Rather.[91]

President Johnson: Uh-huh.

Reedy: And I almost got by without any questions, but Helen Thomas popped in with the [*Washington*] *Star*.[92] So I gave them the statement. And they started to pepper me with a bunch of questions, most of which I just referred to the trustees, but then they said, "Well, what does he do with his own salary?" Now, I had a dim recollection that Pierre [Salinger] had said something about it. And I didn't want to answer that question until I'd had a chance to talk to you.

President Johnson: What do I do with my own salary?

Reedy: Yeah, you live on it is the answer, isn't it, sir? [*Slight chuckle from the President.*] I mean, that's the only income you have.

President Johnson: No, I have some other income from government bonds.

Reedy: Well . . . Yeah, but their idea is do you donate your salary to charity, or something like that.

President Johnson: No, just tell that I use it to live on and meet the expenses of my family and school and my girls. But I don't think that's properly their business what I do with my salary, do you?

Reedy: I don't think it is, but they've asked the question.

President Johnson: Who has?

Reedy: Dan Rather of . . . Dan Rather was the one who asked it.

President Johnson: Well, I would just ask him—just tell him that I don't invest it in anything, I just have it. I've had six months of it. We have pretty heavy expenses that . . . with our family.

Reedy: Mm-hmm. [*Pauses.*] I think the thing that's done it is this wealth figure.[93] They keep . . .

President Johnson: Well, I don't see—it looks like to me that that's almost insulting, is "what do you do with your salary, George?"

---

91. Dan Rather was a White House correspondent for CBS News who had gained prominence for his coverage of the assassination of President Kennedy.

92. Helen Thomas was a United Press International (UPI) White House correspondent.

93. The *Star* article had estimated the Johnsons' total wealth at $9 million. Barron, "The Johnson Money."

Reedy: I think it is too. I think it's very insulting, but there's . . . my saying that's an insulting question doesn't help us any.

President Johnson: No. No, I'd say he lives off of it.

Reedy: Right.

President Johnson: And . . . I don't know what it is after taxes.[94] You better ask Walter [Jenkins] what our salary is after taxes, but . . . I'd say, "He lives off of it. He's made no investments, and he lives off of it."

Reedy: Right. [*Pause.*]

President Johnson: What I've done with it, two things: I've lived off of it and paid . . . made payments on debts I owe.[95] [*Chuckles.*]

Reedy: Yeah, and also the . . . obviously, this is a damned expensive proposition.

President Johnson: Well, you get into that, though, and—

Reedy: I know it.

President Johnson: —they go to studying that.

Reedy: I'm not going to.

President Johnson: No, I'd say, "He lives off of it, and he has a few notes at banks that he's made some payments on, but he has no investments of any kind."

Reedy: Right.

President Johnson: "And if he had any surplus left over, he invested it in government bond."

Reedy: Mm-hmm.

President Johnson: "And municipal bond."

Reedy: Right.

President Johnson: Now, what other questions? What—Did Helen Thomas ask you about the *Star* story?

Reedy: Yeah, they were just all set to walk out of the room when she said, "How about these published reports in the *Star* of the great Johnson wealth?" And so I . . .

---

94. In 1964, the President's salary was $100,000, plus a $50,000 expense account (before taxes). At this income level, the marginal tax rate (following the 1964 tax cut) in the category "married filing separately" was 76.5 percent; for "married filing jointly," 71 percent (the blind trust retained all earnings of Lady Bird Johnson's holdings); for "head of household," 74 percent. Johnson's final rate would have varied depending on exemptions and deductions. Michael Nelson, ed., *Guide to the Presidency*, 3rd ed. (Washington, DC: CQ Press, 2002), 2:978; Sumeet Sagoo, ed., *Facts and Figures on Government Finance*, 38th ed. (Washington, DC: The Tax Foundation, 2005), p. 106.

95. A report earlier in the year estimated the Johnsons' debts to be $683,000, "mostly on land and livestock." "The Story of the Johnson Family Fortune," *U.S. News & World Report*, 4 May 1964, p. 38.

President Johnson: Well, that would have been a good time to say, "I haven't read it."

Reedy: Well, I couldn't because it's . . .

President Johnson: Mm-hmm.

Reedy: They know I've read it, sir. And so I gave them that statement, and then the . . .

President Johnson: Hurry, because I've got [Carl] Albert on one line and [Bernice] Sisk on one.[96] Just say, "Well—

Reedy: Yeah. . . . [*Unclear.*] Then they started to pepper me on, "Does he get any income from this," and I said, "Well, these were not his holdings. These were holdings of Mrs. [Lady Bird] Johnson and his family."

President Johnson: Yeah, and nobody gets any income. The trust provides, and none of it can be paid to anybody. Mrs. Johnson, the children, none of them can get it until I'm out of public office.

Reedy: Right. Well, I'll go on out and just talk [to] them—inform the—straighten them out on this salary thing, but I did not want to do that without talking to you first.

President Johnson: I'd just say, "He lives off of it, and if he has any surplus, [*slight chuckle*] he has a few notes at the bank that he pays, and that I don't want to say this on the record, but this is a purely imaginary, blown-up figure that" . . . Well, you can't get into that, but it is. It's just a purely pumped-up one.

Reedy: It is.

President Johnson: My total financial statement's less than a half-million dollars. Everything I own. And I would guess hers is less than 4 [million dollars].

Reedy: Right. That's obvious from the story that they've just pulled this out of thin air.

President Johnson: Yeah, it is.

Reedy: If anybody reads the story carefully enough, which I don't think they will.

President Johnson: Mm-hmm. Well, can't you call Helen, and—I mean Rather, and just tell him that . . . [*Chuckles.*] "I don't know, Dan. What do you do with your money? But the President lives off of his."

Reedy: Right.

President Johnson: "Takes his to live, and he has . . . no income from any business or any investment of any other kind."

Reedy: Right.

President Johnson: "And under the trust, Mrs. Johnson can draw no

---

96. Bernie Sisk was a Democratic representative from California.

income from any of her properties. So this is what he and Mrs. Johnson and two daughters live off of."

Reedy: Mm-hmm. Right.

President Johnson: "And when you consider 80 percent [tax] bracket, the 100,000 [dollars] we make, why, it probably takes 20[000], 25[000 dollars]."[97]

Reedy: Right.

President Johnson: OK.

Reedy: You bet, sir.

4:44 P.M.

To Carl Albert[98]

Following the conversation with Reedy, the President spoke with House Majority Leader Carl Albert for the second time that day, this time about managing a series of issues including appointments and the federal pay, foreign aid, and poverty bills.

President Johnson: Well, I didn't—the White House doesn't know anything about it. Did he call down here?[99]

Carl Albert: I understood he did, and he was told you were in session with [Robert] McNamara or somebody.

President Johnson: All right. I have been. Do you know who he talked to? I guess not.

Albert: No, I don't know.

President Johnson: Well, I got a note here that he wants to raise hell about [Hamer] Budge being appointed [to the SEC] and tell me who to appoint on—[100]

---

97. Prior to the 1964 tax cut, a couple filing jointly with an income of $150,000 would have had an 81 percent tax rate. Sagoo, ed., *Facts and Figures on Government Finance*, p. 105.

98. Tape WH6406.04, Citations #3656 and #3657, Recordings of Telephone Conversations— White House Series, Recordings and Transcripts of Conversations and Meetings, Lyndon B. Johnson Library.

99. Johnson was referring to California representative Bernie Sisk, who had attempted to reach the President earlier in the afternoon.

100. On 5 June, Johnson had announced the nomination of former Idaho Republican Congressman Hamer Budge to fill a Republican vacancy on the Securities and Exchange Commission. Congressman Sisk had objected to the nomination. See Johnson to Carl Albert, 1:00 P.M., 5 June 1964, in this volume; Eileen Shanahan, "Johnson Appoints a Republican to Fill a Vacancy on the S.E.C.," *New York Times*, 6 June 1964.

Albert: No . . . no. . . . No, I've talked to him. I think that's all—no, he wanted to talk to you only . . . he, I think he—

President Johnson: Wants me to keep—appoint a Republican on the FTC [Federal Trade Commission].

Albert: No. I—My opinion is that what he indicated was that we agree—we got an agreement out of the California delegation they would support this pay bill, and they were putting it down to follow this foreign aid bill, which will probably be Thursday of this week.[101]

President Johnson: Good. How you coming on foreign aid? They being mean to you?

Albert: No, not up to now. And we're just in general debate, and it's kind of petered out. They're about to finish up there.

President Johnson: I think you ought to tell George Mahon that he ought to watch this, that these things are much more serious in Southeast Asia than the public knows, and we can't advertise to the Chinese Communists what we're doing.[102]

Albert: That's right.

President Johnson: But we're having to use a good deal of defense money that we don't have now for the aid bill in there in South Vietnam and Laos.

Albert: Right. I—

President Johnson: We're sending carriers and sending planes and sending everything else. Our boys are getting shot at: We've had two planes shot down this week. And if they want Otto [Passman] to defend them, all right, but if they want me to defend them, they better give me some wherewithal.[103]

Albert: All right. Well, then I think all that [Bernie] Sisk probably— I talked to Sisk, you know, you told me to—

---

101. The federal pay bill would increase the salaries of all career, appointed, and elected federal employees, including members of Congress and federal judges. It had been rejected by the House on 12 March. Congressional supporters of the bill, however, had worked with the administration to craft a revised version of the pay bill that reduced the congressional pay raise and delayed it until after the November election. *Congressional Quarterly Almanac*, 1964, vol. 20, pp. 416–19. The foreign aid authorization bill was under debate on the House floor, where it received almost entirely favorable treatment. Felix Belair Jr., "House Expected to Vote Full Aid Asked by Johnson," *New York Times*, 10 June 1964.

102. George Mahon was a Democratic representative from Texas and the chairman of the House Appropriations Committee, which would have jurisdiction over the actual appropriation of funds in the foreign aid bill.

103. A Democratic representative from Louisiana, Otto Passman was a powerful, vocal, and often effective opponent of foreign aid. He chaired the House Appropriations Committee's Subcommittee on Foreign Operations, which held hearings on the foreign aid appropriations bill.

President Johnson: Yeah.

Albert: —about the . . . this Budge appointment. I told him that you were . . . did that because Charlie Halleck recommended it and that that was pretty much a precedent, and he seemed to be all right. Now, he did say something about this other, this Ross—I didn't [*Johnson acknowledges*] pay much attention—but I think all he wanted to talk to you about was the . . . that the California delegation hoped you would continue your efforts to get the Senate committee to report a $10,000 bill.[104]

President Johnson: OK, I'll do that.

Albert: Now listen, just one other thing: The Speaker [John McCormack] has talked to Tip O'Neill, and Tip's going to leave next Tuesday night. If they don't finish that bill on Tuesday [*the President chuckles*] before the committee . . .[105]

President Johnson: Well, I'll just let them nominate somebody else. I ain't going to—

Albert: Isn't that fine.

President Johnson: [*speaking over Albert*] I ain't going to kiss any more congressmen's ass. I decided this morning, I don't even think we ought to be meeting at breakfast. We don't do a thing. We just find things that—everybody comes in and finds the thing that's wrong. It's meat or it's something else. I don't believe we get anywhere. I['m] just tired.

Albert: It'd be fine with us all. . . . Well, I just don't understand. He said he's taking his wife and going to Europe.

President Johnson: Well, he has—

---

104. Albert may have been referring to Charles Ross, who had been suggested by Vermont Senator Winston Prouty to be reappointed to the Federal Power Commission. See Johnson to Winston Prouty, 10:24 A.M., 27 May 1964, in McKee, *The Presidential Recordings, Johnson,* vol. 6, *April 14, 1964–May 31, 1964,* p. 862. Albert's comment about a "$10,000 bill" was probably a reference to the amount of the congressional pay raise in the initial pay bill; after the bill's defeat in March, the revised version included only a $7,500 congressional raise. *Congressional Quarterly Almanac,* 1964, vol. 20, p. 416.

105. Albert was referring to the economic opportunity (or poverty) bill, the core legislation of the President's proposed War on Poverty. The bill had been reported by the House Education and Labor Committee on 3 June but still required a rule for floor debate from the House Rules Committee, of which Massachusetts Democratic Representative Tip O'Neill was a member. The Rules Committee planned to hold hearings and potentially vote on the poverty bill the following week. O'Neill's absence would make it more difficult to get the bill through the committee. For the administration's earlier difficulties with O'Neill on the poverty bill, see Johnson to Carl Albert, 2:20 P.M., 11 May 1964; Johnson to John McCormack, 2:36 P.M., 11 May 1964; Johnson to Larry O'Brien, 2.52 P.M., 11 May 1964; and Johnson to Sargent Shriver, 2:45 P.M., 13 May 1964, in McKee, ed., *The Presidential Recordings, Johnson,* vol. 6, *April 14, 1964–May 31, 1964,* pp. 522–28, 557–77, 622–28.

Albert: I said, "Is Tip mad?" He said, "No, this thing in the paper was all wrong," the Speaker said, but the Speaker . . . But how are we going to pass a bill out if we don't have our votes *[unclear]*?

President Johnson: You can't; you can't. Just have to talk to the Speaker and see if he can do anything about it. If not, just give it up. I don't care, Carl. I'm in the humor today to tell them I won't have a nomination. I'm just not. I just listen there . . . *[Unclear comment by Albert.]* My staff's embarrassed to come to those breakfasts. Some of them told me this morning, said they don't think we ought to have them anymore. The Speaker starts talking about all the things that are wrong with the pay bill, then somebody else talks about what's wrong. I have to manage to get these recommendations together; I have to manage to get the budget; I have to manage to submit them to the Congress; and then I—God, I have to go to calling all these congressmen, individually. Now, that's *[the]* leader's job and y'all's, and I can't do it.

Albert: We call them all the time.

President Johnson: Yeah.

Albert: *[Unclear]* and I spent—I bet I talk to a hundred congressmen a day.

President Johnson: Well, you got to get Tip O'Neill back, and you got to get Dick Bolling back, and I'm just . . . I'm not going to do it.

Albert: I'm working on Dick right now, myself, personally.

President Johnson: Well, I'd go tell the Speaker about it, and just tell him if he wants the poverty bill to fail because Tip O'Neill's gone, why, that's all right, that's what can do, and . . .

Albert: I asked the Speaker, myself, to go see Tip, and he went and saw him. Then he called and that was his report. Well, my gosh, I don't know. If the Speaker can't do anything with him, what can I do?

President Johnson: No, nobody. I'd just let him go, and we'll just let him go and let the whole damn thing go.

I've got Bernie on the other line, and I'll talk to him.

Albert: All right, sir.

President Johnson: Bye.

Albert: Bye.

4:48 P.M.

To Bernie Sisk[106]

As he had just indicated to Albert, Johnson was connected almost immediately on a call to Representative Bernie Sisk of California. The conversation bore out Albert's expectation that Sisk wanted only to convey the California Democratic congressional delegation's support for the pay bill and its opposition to any reduction in the original $10,000 congressional pay raise—which in a revised and resubmitted version of the bill would be cut to $7,500.

Bernie Sisk: And we just passed a resolution, and which—this was a part of it that I convey to you that we are receding from our position on the salary bill in order to go along with you and try to get it passed as quickly as possible, Mr. President.

The delegation . . . I—frankly, our delegation felt very strongly on this, and on the other hand, they *do* want to go along, and . . . with the presentations made by Larry O'Brien and others, we understood your concern and your desire to get it passed as quickly as possible. So the delegation has gone along, as I say [*slight chuckle*], to play ball and to support you and, of course, in the hopes that the Senate will go ahead and come through with the 10,000—

President Johnson: I'll do everything I can to get them to do that, and I think they will. The committee indicates that they're prepared to do it as soon as they get it out. I appreciate it very much, and I'm grateful for your calling [*unclear*], Bernie. Bye.

Sisk: Well, I just wanted to let you know because, as I say, this was part of—

President Johnson: Well . . . well.

Sisk: —the request that we convey to you that—

President Johnson: You thank them for—

Sisk: —our desire to go along, and—

President Johnson: You thank them for me, and I'm glad you've been a Johnson man all along, and I'll try to be worthy of it.

Sisk: Well, we'll be in there pitching.

President Johnson: Thank you, boy.

---

106. Tape WH6406.04, Citation #3658, Recordings of Telephone Conversations—White House Series, Recordings and Transcripts of Conversations and Meetings, Lyndon B. Johnson Library.

Sisk: Thanks a lot, Mr. President.
President Johnson: Bye.

4:50 P.M.: Unrecorded call to Bill Moyers.

4:55 P.M.

To Karl Mundt[107]

Johnson next returned an earlier call from Republican Senator Karl Mundt of South Dakota. Mundt informed the President that he would vote for cloture on the civil rights bill.

A brief office conversation with Jack Valenti about the schedule precedes the call.
President Johnson: Yes, Karl?
Karl Mundt: Oh, Lyndon?
President Johnson: Yeah.
Mundt: Thanks for calling back. I just thought I'd call you up as an old friend and tell you that I'm going to vote for your doggone cloture motion tomorrow.
President Johnson: Well, good, Karl, good.
Mundt: And you're the first one I've told, so I thought I'd tell it to you.
President Johnson: Well, thank you, my friend. Well, I appreciate that.
Mundt: Yeah. I mean—I appreciate you didn't call me up and give me the old Texas twist, so I could come and tell you myself—that's better.
President Johnson: [*Chuckles.*] I haven't called a human, Karl. I haven't called a human. Now, I . . .
Mundt: Haven't you really?
President Johnson: No, I don't do that. I just talk to my friends once in a while about general things, but I'm not calling anybody to ask them to vote for anything. I saw [Everett] Dirksen said I was an arm-twister one time, but I haven't really done that. I—

---

107. Tape WH6406.04, Citation #3659, Recordings of Telephone Conversations—White House Series, Recordings and Transcripts of Conversations and Meetings, Lyndon B. Johnson Library.

Mundt: Well, this is . . . a devilish, ticklish issue for a state like mine, but I figure, holy cow, if I believe in majority rule, sometime I got to face up to the votes.

President Johnson: Yeah, that's right. Well, you're fine. I appreciate you calling me, my friend.

Mundt: OK. Just thought I'd let you know.

President Johnson: Thank you.

Mundt: You bet.

President Johnson: Bye.

4:57 P.M.: Unrecorded call to Jack Valenti.

4:58 P.M.

To Larry O'Brien[108]

Johnson called Larry O'Brien to inform him of the problems that Tip O'Neill's travel plans posed for the poverty bill and of Karl Mundt's intentions regarding the cloture vote.

President Johnson: . . . things. On the Tip O'Neill thing, he's told [John] McCormack and all of them that he's leaving, and I guess he wants to be kissed, and as far as I'm concerned he can just leave and kill the bill if—

Larry O'Brien: No, he's—

President Johnson: —if he feels that way about it. I'm tired of this cheap, dirty, low-down blackmail, and—

O'Brien: No, I think it's in shape.

President Johnson: Well, he just told the Speaker, according to Carl Albert, he's going to leave anyway.

O'Brien: No, he's going to leave Tuesday night.

President Johnson: Well, they won't have it out Tuesday night, will they?

---

108. Tape WH6406.04, Citation #3660, Recordings of Telephone Conversations—White House Series, Recordings and Transcripts of Conversations and Meetings, Lyndon B. Johnson Library.

O'Brien: Yeah. We've been talking to [Phillip] Landrum.[109] They're going to take it up Tuesday morning, and Landrum feels that he's already working on the witnesses to be sure that ours are held to bare bones and that—and he's going—he's further exploring having an afternoon session of the committee if necessary. And I'm just convinced that we're going to get the rule that day, or if we have to go in the next day, that we'll just have Tip stay.[110]

President Johnson: That's good. Now, Karl Mundt called me and said that he wanted us to know—he hadn't told anybody else—but he's going to vote with his President on cloture.

O'Brien: Wonderful.

President Johnson: How is the thing lining up?

O'Brien: Yeah, it's lining up well. You got my note on the report of the steelworkers?

President Johnson: Yeah. Is that final now on our friends?

O'Brien: Yep.

President Johnson: OK.

O'Brien: Right.

President Johnson: Bye.

O'Brien: OK, Mr. President.

4:59 P.M.: President Johnson greeted visitors in the Oval Office.

5:00 P.M.: Welcomed Danish Prime Minister Jens Otto Krag at the White House Colonnade and showed him the White House Flower Garden; Johnson and Krag then went to the Oval Office for a brief private meeting.

5:12 P.M.: McGeorge Bundy joined Johnson and Krag in the Oval Office.

5:51 P.M.: Krag, Johnson, and Bundy proceeded to the Cabinet Room for a meeting with the Danish ambassador and representatives from the State Department's section on northern European affairs. On the way to the Cabinet Room, Johnson introduced Krag to members of his office staff.

---

109. Democrat Phil Landrum of Georgia served as floor manager for the economic opportunity bill in the House.

110. The Rules Committee hearings on the poverty bill would actually begin on Tuesday, 16 June, and continue through Thursday, 18 June; the committee then delayed a vote on a rule until late July. *Congressional Quarterly Almanac*, 1964, vol. 20, p. 226.

6:06 P.M.

To George Reedy[111]

With the meeting in the Cabinet Room still in progress, the President made a call to George Reedy, who followed up on an earlier discussion of the *Washington Star* story about the Johnsons' business and financial interests.

A brief office conversation precedes the call.
President Johnson: Got a nice, attractive girl's been waiting for you to . . . see you tonight, so you better get freshened up. Get a lot of rest.
Unidentified: I'll do my best. [*Someone chuckles.*]
President Johnson: I've been hearing good reports from my wife . . . my daughter.
The operator interrupts to report on her efforts to reach Reedy.
President Johnson: George?
George Reedy: Yes, sir.
President Johnson: Any news?
Reedy: I've spent the time with the PIOs [Public Information Officers], got a few ideas in case you want a press conference Wednesday or Thursday.
President Johnson: All right. What did you do with [Dan] Rather?
The operator picks up the line.
Hello, I'm on.
Reedy: [*with the President acknowledging*] I told all of them, because the question had been asked in front of all of them, that obviously you . . . that your salary was the income for you and your family, and that obviously no income was coming in from the trust. And I said you might get a little bit here and there from some municipals and bonds of that nature. [*Someone in the background can be heard addressing the President.*] But that this was your income, and that you were meeting all of your expenses and everything else out of it.
President Johnson: Mm-hmm. Sounds all right.
Reedy: And . . . that part really wasn't too much trouble. I think it was just a question that they tossed in without thinking about it.

---

111. Tape WH6406.04, Citation #3661, Recordings of Telephone Conversations—White House Series, Recordings and Transcripts of Conversations and Meetings, Lyndon B. Johnson Library.

President Johnson: Mm-hmm.

Reedy: But nevertheless it was asked, and it was there.

President Johnson: Is that all of it?

Reedy: Yes, sir.

President Johnson: Now, the Prime Minister [of Denmark] is here; you got any press around that would like to interview him before he leaves?

Reedy: I would think so, yes, sir.

President Johnson: All right, get them in—[*unclear comment by Reedy*]—get them in here.

Reedy: Right.

President Johnson: Where should he come, your office, or . . .

Reedy: I'll come on up to my office if he'll meet me there. I'm downstairs down in the Situation Room.

President Johnson: Where do you prefer, George, out in the lobby or the office?

Reedy: I prefer my office for him.

President Johnson: All right, OK.

Reedy: You bet.

6:15 P.M.: After the meeting in the Cabinet Room concluded, Johnson and McGeorge Bundy remained in the room and held a private discussion.

6:20 P.M.

To Robert McNamara[112]

Johnson placed a call to Robert McNamara, who along with Dean Rusk had spent much of the afternoon briefing key members of Congress about the U.S. bombing raid in Laos. McNamara updated the President on the congressmen's reactions. Republican Senator Leverett Saltonstall and Democratic Congressman George Mahon had expressed serious concerns about U.S. public opinion regarding the Southeast Asia situation. This led McNamara and Johnson to consider how the American

---

112. Tape WH6406.04, Citation #3663, Recordings of Telephone Conversations—White House Series, Recordings and Transcripts of Conversations and Meetings, Lyndon B. Johnson Library.

public's understanding of the strategic rationale behind administration policy might be increased. More significantly, Johnson read a letter from Senate Majority Leader Mike Mansfield that raised doubts about the strategic significance of Southeast Asia and the desirability of continued U.S. military engagement in the region. Although the President and his defense secretary interpreted Mansfield's position as focusing on the need to better inform the public about the strategic rationale for U.S. policy, the letter actually presaged the eventual emergence of overt opposition to the Vietnam War among leading Democratic lawmakers such as Mansfield.

President Johnson: Hello?

Robert McNamara: Yes, Mr. President.

President Johnson: How'd you get along with the Congress today?

McNamara: They . . . Senator [Richard] Russell didn't want to meet with us because he said you had talked to him. [Leverett] Saltonstall is concerned as to where we're going; he doesn't think the American people know why we're in Vietnam. He wasn't particularly concerned about the reconnaissance flights. [Carl] Vinson and [Les] Arends, I reported to you. . . .[113]

President Johnson: What do you answer Saltonstall? Why don't you tell him [John Foster] Dulles got us in there?[114]

McNamara: [*with the President acknowledging*] Well, Saltonstall [*unclear*] says he knows why we got in and he's generally in favor of being there, but he doesn't think the people understand, and . . . they ask him questions indicating that they don't understand. What he's saying is we ought to tell the America people why we're there and explain to them why Southeast Asia is important to us, but many of his constituents think it is not. I think that he's right in a sense that we're going to have to do more work on making clear to the American people why this is important to us.

President Johnson: I do too, I do too.

---

113. A Democratic representative from Georgia, Carl Vinson was the chairman of the Committee on Armed Services.

114. John Foster Dulles served as secretary of state for Dwight Eisenhower from 1953 to 1959. Johnson was referring to Dulles's role in establishing a U.S. commitment to the government of South Vietnam following the defeat of the French in 1954. Specifically, Dulles had pushed for the formation of the Southeast Asia Treaty Organization (SEATO), which provided for collective action against aggression. Along with the United States, signatories to the treaty included Australia, Britain, France, New Zealand, Pakistan, the Philippines, and Thailand.

McNamara: No question in my mind about it. This is the kind of thing that Bob Manning has got to emphasize and all of us have got to spend more time on.

[*with the President acknowledging*] George Mahon is a little timid. He's just . . . uncertain about the whole situation. He's not concerned about the reconnaissance flights per se, he's just worried about the situation in Southeast Asia and the criticism that he thinks is going to be directed at the government because of it. I think in that respect he reflects a substantial body of public opinion. He's a rather timid person anyhow, and he's simply reflecting the fears of many of his own constituents.

President Johnson: Anything else?

McNamara: No, sir, that's all.

President Johnson: I've been trying to evaluate this thing. We haven't taken any real serious losses, and we can't put our finger on anything that's . . . really justifies this acceleration of and escalation of public sentiment that it's going to hell in a hack since you were out there in March. Is that a buildup of our critics largely? Have we fed that? Where does it come from [that] we're losing? Is that the [Jim] Lucas stories coming out of there?[115] . . . We'll—

McNamara: No, I think it's the appraisal . . . if you went to the—

President Johnson: You take this country, now, is all concerned that we've lost Southeast Asia, [that] we're in a hell of a shape. Now, where did that come from?

McNamara: All right. Well, I think it came from two things: If you went to Sherman Kent and the estimators in CIA and said, "How's the situation today in South Vietnam versus three months ago or four months ago?" I think they would say it's worse.[116] And therefore—

President Johnson: Now, that's not what [Henry Cabot] Lodge and [Nguyen] Khanh think, is it?[117] They think it's a little better, don't they?

---

115. Jim Lucas was a reporter for the Scripps Howard Newspaper Alliance. In early May, he had reported that two U.S. pilots had been killed as a result of mechanical failures on their T38 fighter jets. The article charged that the planes were obsolete and had not been properly maintained. *Life* and *U.S. News & World Report* soon printed letters that the pilot had written to his wife before his death in which he complained about inadequate support and low morale. "We Are Losing, Morale Is Bad . . . If They'd Give Us Good Planes," *U.S. News & World Report*, 4 May 1964; "McNamara Faces Quiz on Obsolete Plane Use," *Washington Post*, 13 May 1964; "Sylvester Scores Magazine on Vietnam Letters," *New York Times*, 23 May 1964.

116. Sherman Kent was the chairman of the Board of National Estimates of the Central Intelligence Agency. For his assessment of the situation as of 9 June 1964, see Sherman Kent, "Memorandum From the Board of National Estimates to the Director of Central Intelligence (McCone)," 9 June 1964, *FRUS, 1964–1968*, 1:484–87.

117. Henry Cabot Lodge was U.S. ambassador to South Vietnam. Major General Nguyen Khanh was Prime Minister of the country.

McNamara: Well . . . I don't think they really believe that, Mr. President. No, sir. I think that they both would indicate it's a very weak situation. I think they think it's better in the sense that it's better to have Khanh there than it was four or five months ago to have that committee running it.[118]

But I think Lodge is personally very much concerned about it. The very fact that he's constantly pushing for pressure on the North, military pressure on the North. And of course that letter that he sent in today that we read at lunch was . . . the primary purpose of that was to tell you that he thinks you ought to go ahead and apply military pressure on the North. What he was saying is, "Don't be scared away from my plan to apply military pressure on the North by the thought of putting in seven divisions. We should never think of putting in seven divisions; it isn't necessary. You ought to apply military pressure anyhow."[119] And this is Lodge's way of saying that things are in pretty bad shape.

Now, my point is that the CIA estimators, Lodge, many of the rest of us, in private would say that things are not good; they've gotten worse. And you see it in the desertion rates; you see it in the morale; you see it in the difficulty to recruit people; you see it in the gradual loss of population control. Now, while we say this in private and not public, there are facts available in the public domain over there that find their way in the press, and I think this is one way that our people get this feeling of the fact we're not moving ahead. The second way is the clear case of Laos, where the Pathet Lao just advanced on the ground—and it was in the last three weeks—and have kept their gains. Now, I think it's these two events that lead the people to feel a sense of pessimism about Southeast Asia.

President Johnson: I got while I was talking to you . . . I have a note from [Mike] Mansfield, which is interesting.[120] [*reading*]

"What follows is in the context of my full support for whatever deci-

---

118. Major General Nguyen Khanh had become Prime Minister of South Vietnam in January 1964 after leading a coup against the military junta that had ruled since the November 1963 murder of Ngo Dinh Diem.

119. Although probably not the document referred to by McNamara, a 5 June letter from the ambassador to the President outlined the difficulties involved in "committing seven divisions of the U.S. Army to the mainland of Southeast Asia." Lodge wrote that "it is a largely U.S. venture of unlimited possibilities which could put us on a slope along which we slide into a bottomless pit." In contrast, he added, "I still have faith that naval and air power, with clearly limited and very specific actions on the ground, can give us what we need . . . . there ought to be a way to apply American power to North Viet-nam and in addition use the threat of our tremendous superiority in overall military power to keep the Chinese communists at bay." Henry Cabot Lodge to the President, 5 June 1964, "Folder 4: Vietnam Memos vol. XI 6/1–13/64," Country File: Vietnam, Box 5, National Security File, Lyndon B. Johnson Library.

120. For the letter, see "To: The President; From: Senator Mike Mansfield," 9 June 1964, ibid.

sions you may have to take under the awesome responsibilities of your office. You alone have all the facts and considerations. You alone make the decisions. The Senate, we can only give you, in the last analysis, our trust, our support [and] such independent thoughts as may occur to us from time to time in the hope that they may be constructive.

"You know far better than I how delicate a maneuver was, first, the reconnaissance flights, second, the bombing of [the] antiaircraft sites in Laos. These two steps have opened up the immediate possibility of a far more direct U.S. military involvement in Laos than we now have in Vietnam.

"I presume that the reconnaissance flights were designed primarily as a show of U.S. determination [and] as an aid of some sort for the government of Laos. Nevertheless, they did lead to the shooting down of the U.S. planes and then to the U.S. bombing of antiaircraft sites.

"Clearly this process of action and reaction can continue and grow deeper. It may be that circumstances require that the process continue and deepen. Only you are in a position to make that determination in light of the whole of the interests of the nation. But I gather from our conversation that a deepening of the involvement is not what you believe desirable or necessary in terms of the nation's interest.[121] You indicated to me that the bombing of sites was not to be repeated. But you cannot count on the absence of the need for repetitions of bombing so long as [the] reconnaissance flights continue over Laos.[122] What happens if other U.S. reconnaissance planes are shot down? Having once taken out antiaircraft sites by bombing, are we not to repeat the operation? And if we cannot stop the attrition by air, must we not do it by land force or suffer the consequences?[123] I think it is most dangerous to assume that if reconnaissance flights continue, additional planes will not be shot at and, if they fly low enough, [that] some will not be brought down.

"The basic reality remains: If it's not in the national interest to become deeply involved in a military sense on the Laotian front, we will avoid those actions which [can] compel us, even against our inclination or expectation, to become more deeply involved.[124] We will avoid further

---

121. For the telephone conversation, see Johnson to Mike Mansfield, 12:56 P.M., 9 June 1964, in this chapter.
122. Mansfield underlined this sentence in the actual letter. "To: The President; From: Senator Mike Mansfield," 9 June 1964, "Folder 4: Vietnam Memos vol. XI 6/1–13/64," Country File: Vietnam, Box 5, National Security File, Lyndon B. Johnson Library, p. 2.
123. The letter actually referred to "the ignominious consequences." Ibid.
124. The phrase "even against our inclination or expectation" was underlined in the letter. Ibid., p. 3.

unilateral commitments and actions and take every possible initiative to bring about a peaceful settlement. But if our interests justify, in the last analysis, to become fully involved in Southeast Asia mainland, then there is no issue. What must be done will be done.

"My own views are well-known. On the basis of my limited knowledge I do not conclude that our national interests are served by deep military involvement in Southeast Asia. But in this situation, what I or any other Senator may conclude is secondary. The responsibility rests with you, and we can only give you our support [in] whatever decisions you [may] make.

"If the decision must be for continuance of the course which is leading to deeper involvement, however, I would most respectfully suggest the basis for these decisions must be made much clearer and more persuasive to the people of the nation than has heretofore been the case. [In] my judgment, public attitudes are far from understanding, much less accepting, even the limited degree of our present involvement in Southeast Asia."

So what he comes out and says [is] that he thinks we ought to get out of there, which we can't and not going to, and if we don't, then we've got to educate the people as to why we're in there.

McNamara: That's right. Well, I think he's absolutely right: If we're going to stay in there, if we're going to go particularly up the escalating chain, we're going to have to educate the people, Mr. President. We haven't done so yet. I'm not sure now is exactly the right time.

President Johnson: No, and I think if you start doing it, they're going to be hollering, "You're a warmonger."

McNamara: That's right. I completely agree with you. So this is the major reason—

President Johnson: I think that's the horn the Republicans would like to get us on.

McNamara: That's right.

President Johnson: Now, if we could do something in the way of social work, in the way of our hospitals, in the way of our province program, in the way of our fertilizer, in the way of remaking that area out there, and giving them some hope and something to fight for, and put some of our own people into their units and do a little better job of fighting without material escalation for the next few months, that's what we ought to do.

McNamara: This is . . . Mr. President, this is what I call my "eight critical province program," and I—that's what we laid out. We finally sent it out to Lodge by cable three nights ago—Friday, I guess it was—and it was that to which he replied this morning: step H and I on there that involves the use of 580 additional U.S. personnel in these critical provinces, and it was that step that he objected to. Or at least he said he wanted to make it perfectly clear he hadn't agreed to it. He's going to comment further in later cables. So we've just got to push like hell on this.

President Johnson: Well, I wonder why we don't come right back to a cable to him? Why don't you draft one—send it over to State, from State to him, or from me to him—saying that we have felt since '61 that one of the great problems there was giving those people something to fight for, and we recommended that to Diem in '61 when I was out there and got his agreement that he would do more of it, and that he didn't do enough of it and soon enough.[125] And that's one of the big problems we have, and we deeply believe in it and feel that it's got to be done and urge him to carry out what we want done.

McNamara: He said in his cable he would respond more fully when he'd gone over the detailed plan. I think it might be wise, in view of our relations with him, to give him a day or so to do that.[126]

President Johnson: All right, may be.

McNamara: And—

President Johnson: I've got a report, I don't know what it says, but I know it goes into that a good deal. It was made in '61, and I could hang it on that and just say, "I personally recommended this in '61, and I want to reiterate what I'd like to see done, and I hope I can have your cooperation in doing it."

McNamara: Well, it gets you on the line, though, of putting more Americans in Vietnam, and this is one of the issues he could charge against you or the administration: We've got too many Americans there trying to run the country, take over, and causing resentment among the Vietnamese. He's already had a kickback from Khanh and Deputy Prime Minister [Nguyen Xuan] Oanh on the four men he put in the government.[127] And I'm sure this is in his mind here on this 500. I think it'd be better if you kept out of it and let us handle it with him.

---

125. Johnson was referring to his 1961 vice presidential trip to Asia, in which he visited South Vietnam.

126. Johnson and his foreign policy team had frequently been frustrated by Lodge's inability or unwillingness to carry out decisions made in Washington, as well as his poor relations both with subordinates at the embassy and with the U.S. military command in South Vietnam. In addition, many observers anticipated that Lodge would soon resign in order to return to the United States and pursue the Republican presidential nomination. For the administration's difficulties with the ambassador, see Johnson to Richard Russell, 10:55 A.M., 27 May 1964; and Johnson to Robert Kennedy, 11:45 A.M., 28 May 1964, in McKee, *The Presidential Recordings, Johnson*, vol. 6, *April 14, 1964–May 31, 1964*, pp. 871–85, 914–25.

127. Nguyen Xuan Oanh became Vietnamese minister of finance and vice minister for economy following the coup in February.

President Johnson: All right.

McNamara: And I'll make a note on my pad: two days from now, if we don't get a favorable reply, to go back to him on this.

President Johnson: OK. All right.

McNamara: All right, sir. Thank you.

President Johnson: Bye.

6:30 P.M.

To Dean Rusk[128]

Johnson made an immediate call to Secretary of State Rusk for his opinion of the congressional reaction to the raid on Laos. The conversation, however, quickly turned to the ongoing crisis on the divided island nation of Cyprus, where Greek and Turkish Cypriots remained caught in a bitter struggle to determine the future of the island.[129] The previous week, the Turkish Cypriot leader, Cyprus Vice President Fazil Kutchuk, had explored the possibility of declaring an independent state, potentially with the aid of limited Turkish military intervention on the island. Greek Cypriot leader Archbishop Makarios III, who held the presidency of Cyprus, accused Kutchuk of planning the partition of Cyprus and claimed that he had effectively given up the vice presidency during conflicts earlier in the year. A strongly worded message from President Johnson led Turkish President Ismet Inonu to withdraw the threat of Turkish military action—but also increased U.S. diplomatic involvement in the crisis.[130]

Despite this de-escalation of the previous week's tensions, the situation in Cyprus remained highly uncertain and was complicated by the upcoming June 26 expiration of an agreement that had sent United Nations

---

128. Tape WH6406.05, Citations #3664 and #3665, Recordings of Telephone Conversations—White House Series, Recordings and Transcripts of Conversations and Meetings, Lyndon B. Johnson Library.

129. For background on Cyprus, see Johnson to George Ball, 6:35 P.M., 28 January 1964, Kent B. Germany and Robert David Johnson, eds., *The Presidential Recordings, Lyndon B. Johnson: The Kennedy Assassination and the Transfer of Power, November 1963–January 1964*, vol. 3, *January 1964* (New York: Norton, 2005), pp. 926–31.

130. "Telegram from the Department of State to the Embassy in Turkey," 5 June 1964, 12:15 A.M., *FRUS, 1964–1968: Cyprus, Greece, Turkey*, ed. James E. Miller (Washington, DC: GPO, 2000), 16:107–10; "Telegram from the Embassy in Turkey to the Department of State," 5 June 1964, 7:00 P.M., ibid., 16:111; "Telegram from the Embassy in Cyprus to the Department of State," 6 June 1964, 1:00 P.M., ibid., 16:112–13; Dean Rusk to Johnson, 12:56 P.M., 4 June 1964, in this volume.

peacekeepers to the island. Britain, in particular, had indicated a desire to reduce its troop commitment to the peacekeeping force after incidents of harassment of British troops and their families on the island, as well as diplomatic disagreements with the government of Greece. Ireland and Finland, the other participants in the U.N. force, had explicitly reserved the right to withdraw after June 26.[131]

Beginning on June 8, U.S. and British diplomats had conferred in London about both the future of the peacekeeping force and the direction of Anglo-American policy towards Cyprus more generally. Under Secretary of State George Ball had participated in the initial London meetings on Cyprus (and a number of other key issues).[132] In this call, Bundy and Johnson discussed whether Ball should return to Washington for additional assessment of the Cyprus situation before proceeding to Athens for meetings with Greek Prime Minister George Papandreou. They also assessed whether Johnson should encourage a diplomatically problematic visit to Washington by Turkish President Ismet Inonu.

President Johnson: Hello? Mr. Secretary?

Dean Rusk: Hello?

President Johnson: How'd you get along?

Rusk: All right with [J. William] Fulbright, [Bourke] Hickenlooper, and [Everett] Dirksen. I was not able to get ahold of [Charles] Halleck, who's out of town, and Bill Bundy was up with the House Foreign Affairs Committee, and I will check with them. I haven't been able to reach them this afternoon.[133]

President Johnson: All right.

Rusk: But the others were all right, they had no problem.

President Johnson: All right. Now—

Rusk: Now, I've got a call in for George Ball, the . . . Mr. President, I think the problem here is that we need to get him back to be sure that

---

131. "Treatment of Britons Scored," *New York Times,* 2 June 1964; "Cyprus Exit Is Desired by British," *Washington Post,* 3 June 1964; "Cyprus Turks' Chief Scored by Makarios," *New York Times,* 4 June 1964; Flora Lewis, "Britain, Greece Squabble about Intervention over Cyprus Draft Law," *Washington Post,* 4 June 1964.

132. "Telegram from the Embassy in the United Kingdom to the Department of State," 9 June 1964, *FRUS, 1964–1968,* 16:117–18; Flora Lewis, "Ball Checks with Top Britons on His Way to Geneva Parley," *Washington Post,* 9 June 1964.

133. Rusk had met with the senators late that afternoon as part of the administration's effort to inform key congressional leaders about the raid on a Pathet Lao antiaircraft base in Laos.

we're all on the same track here and to see where we're going. That's my concern about that. If he goes to Athens at this point, it could stimulate a good deal of excitement without putting one foot forward. I don't think Ball is in a position yet to begin to move toward a solution to this thing. And we—our talks in London have not produced enough agreement between us and the British about how we proceed here.[134] I just think that since he now is not planning to stop off in London but he was planning to come right on back, that we better let him do it even though by the weekend we might want to send him out to the area.

President Johnson: All right. Now, what's he . . . if he can't produce it while he's over there, how's he going to produce it here?

Rusk: Well, I think that—

President Johnson: With the British.

Rusk: I think the point is that we . . . that you and he and I and our people working on this should come to a final conclusion on what we ought to shoot for, and there's not a conclusion on that at the moment, and we . . . the conclusion that they've been talking about in London is something that would almost guarantee the Turks would intervene, and this is what concerns me.[135]

President Johnson: [*softly*] Mm-hmm.

Rusk: We're not giving the Turks enough of a break here in the kind of solution that they've been talking about . . . in London.

President Johnson: Well, now, is it necessary for him to get back here to do that? Is he an integral part of our . . .

Rusk: [*with President Johnson acknowledging*] Well, I think that it would be extremely helpful to me because he's our most experienced man on this problem and could take a real leadership on it.

President Johnson: I think it's a lot bigger problem to send him after he gets back over there than let him go while he's there, don't you?

Rusk: Mm-hmm. Well . . .

President Johnson: Looks like it's just a routine thing if he's there

---

134. Most of the substantive discussions at the London talks actually took place after Under Secretary of State George Ball had departed for the ongoing trade negotiations in Geneva. For the limited progress on the future of British participation in the U.N. peacekeeping force in Cyprus, see "Telegram from the Embassy in the United Kingdom to the Department of State," 9 June 1964, *FRUS, 1964–1968*, 16:117–18.

135. While the United States opposed either Turkish military intervention in Cyprus or partition of the island into separate Greek and Turkish Cypriot-controlled zones, it favored a strong guarantee for the rights of the Turkish Cypriot minority in a "unitary, Greek [Cypriot]-run state, closely associated with Greece." "Telegram from the Embassy in Cyprus to the Department of State," 6 June 1964, *FRUS, 1964–1968*, 16:112–13.

now. He's been touring all over the continent, but . . .[136]

Rusk: There is another piece of information on this: The Greek Cypriot foreign minister has just arrived in New York to ask for a [U.N.] Security Council meeting on this subject.[137] So that is likely to take the play away from other matters here for a brief time.

President Johnson: Mm-hmm. Well, is that good?

Rusk: [*Pause.*] I think so, sir. I . . .

President Johnson: Looks like we need some time to get some solutions, don't we?

Rusk: Yeah, well, I think we do need some time here. This is one of the most—

President Johnson: I'll defer to your judgment. If I were secretary of state, I'd send him to Greece and say, "Now, Mr. Prime Minister, here's what happened: We were notified that they were going in and invade that night. We prevailed on them not to do it. We don't think that things are going as they ought to there, and we're very concerned about what's going to happen. So we . . . our people are concerned, and we appeal to you to exercise whatever influence you've got with [Archbishop] Makarios to try to let the United Nations work this thing out for you instead of shooting at them and arresting them and capturing them and running off with them.[138] And we just think if you don't take some leadership here and move in as we had to move in with Turkey, that this is going to be a very bloody bath, and . . ."

Now, I don't know what other specific proposals other than urging him to do that, but it seems to me that then that would give us something to say to the Turks that we've made an appeal to him and personally sent our man. Now, if you think he ought to come on back before he does that, why . . .

Rusk: I think that if you said that to the Greek ambassador when he brings you that message, that that would be . . . that would have the

---

136. Ball would travel to Athens on 10 June and then make a stop in Ankara to meet with Turkish leaders on 11 June. Afterward, he returned to London for additional meetings with British officials about the Cyprus crisis. "Memorandum From the Under Secretary of State (Ball) to President Johnson," 11 June 1964, *FRUS, 1964–1968*, 16:132–34; "Ball's Mission Lifts Cyprus Peace Hopes," *Washington Post*, 12 June 1964.

137. A Greek Cypriot, Spyros Kyprianou served as foreign minister of Cyprus. Later in the month, the U.N. Security Council debated extension of the peacekeeping mission but did not hold the wider debate on "the Turkish government threat of military intervention in Cyprus" that Kyprianou requested. "Cyprus Asks U.N. to Score Turk 'Threat'," *Washington Post*, 10 June 1964; "Turks Balk at U.N. No-Invasion Pledge," *Washington Post*, 20 June 1964.

138. Archbishop Makarios III was President of Cyprus. Johnson was referring to the harassment of U.N. peacekeeping forces by the Greek Cypriot government.

greatest weight and influence in Athens.[139] But let me talk to George Ball and get his judgment on this point. Right.

President Johnson: All right . . . OK. . . . That's good, and I don't think, though, that [Ismet] Inonu's going to think that's much, for me to talk to his little ambassador here.[140] I think if he thinks that this man's crossed the waters and gone to Athens and put the heat on them just like we put on the Turks, that he'll think that we're sincere and genuine and we're really working at it and not gone to sleep on it.

Rusk: Yes, now, there's a press report out of Ankara that Inonu is replying and conditionally accepting your invitation.[141] I don't know what that kind of a press leak means, but if he were to come here in the next few days, I think that that would be an important step.

President Johnson: Well, I look at it the other way: I think the last thing we want him to do is let me be the peacemaker and let it wind up on my lap. I think that we ought to carry it right to Ankara and to Athens. Now, that's my country boy approach to it.

Rusk: Right.

President Johnson: And I think that we got in trouble the other night when we suggested to him that if he—I couldn't come over there, but I'd be glad to see him.[142] But we were absolutely desperate, and I let that go.

Rusk: Right.

President Johnson: But when I got home and thought about it a little bit, I thought, "Now, what in the hell's Lyndon Johnson doing inviting this big mess right in his lap? Bad enough for George Ball to go to him and see him without the President calling him over here, because I have no solution. I can't propose anything. He'd come over here looking for heaven, and he'd find hell."

Rusk: Well, his message, if it is a conditional message, will probably

139. Alexander A. Matsas served as the Greek ambassador to the United States.

140. Ismet Inonu was President of Turkey; Melih Esenbel was the Turkish ambassador to the United States.

141. At the conclusion of his 5 June 1964 message urging Inonu not to intervene in Cyprus, Johnson had invited the Turkish President to Washington for talks. "Telegram From the Department of State to the Embassy in Turkey," 5 June 1964, *FRUS, 1964–1968*, 16:107–10.

142. Johnson had noted that the constitutional situation in the United States, meaning the lack of any provision for appointment of a new vice president following the succession of a sitting vice president to the presidency, prevented him from making diplomatic trips outside the United States. "Telegram From the Department of State to the Embassy in Turkey," 5 June 1964, *FRUS, 1964–1968*, 16:107–10. Despite Johnson's reluctance to increase his personal involvement—and risk his prestige—in the Cyprus crisis, he would hold White House talks with Inonu on 22–23 June and with Greek Prime Minister George Papandreou on 24 June. "Memorandum of Conversation," 22 June 1964, *FRUS, 1964–1968*, 16:146–48; "Memorandum of Conversation," 23 June 1964, ibid., 16:148–51; "Memorandum of Conversation," 24 June 1964, ibid., 16:151–55.

have that kind of thing in it and would be the basis for deferring it until we get some further feeling out of this, but—

President Johnson: [*with Rusk acknowledging*] Mm-hmm. . . . Well, my feeling is—and I don't want to be arbitrary, and I won't be a bit disappointed if he comes on—but I think you ought to let him know that I think in the light of this strong message that I sent to the Turks that I need to follow through with the Greeks, and the easiest and simplest and least noticed way to do it is while he's there to spend two hours doing it. Then I wouldn't hesitate the slightest to say to them, "Now, we're going on and appeal to the Turks to hold this thing in abeyance," and he could go tell the Turks what he'd done. And although you wouldn't have any final solution or division, you would have [at] least kept faith and made an effort and followed through on what I told him in this wire instead of him saying we went off and went to sleep.

Rusk: Right. Well, let me talk to George this evening.

President Johnson: OK.

Rusk: Right, thank you.

President Johnson: Bye.

6:40 P.M.: The President talked with Lee White, first in the outer office and then in the Oval Office.

6:45 P.M.: Unrecorded call to Bill Moyers.

6:51 P.M.

From McGeorge Bundy[143]

The recording system captured a brief segment of a phone conversation in which the President and McGeorge Bundy discussed the itinerary for George Ball's travels in his effort to defuse the Cyprus crisis.

McGeorge Bundy: . . . [*unclear*].

President Johnson: What about to Ankara?

Bundy: Well, if he goes to Athens, he must certainly go on to Ankara and say what he's done.

---

143. Tape WH6406.05, Citation #3666, Recordings of Telephone Conversations—White House Series, Recordings and Transcripts of Conversations and Meetings, Lyndon B. Johnson Library.

President Johnson: Well, does he know that?

Bundy: Yes, I think so, Mr. President.

President Johnson: Are you coming to the [Jens Otto] Krag dinner?

Bundy: No, sir.

President Johnson: Uh-huh. OK. All right.

Bundy: Right.

President Johnson: Bye.

6:55 P.M.: Unrecorded call to George Reedy.

7:01 P.M.: Unrecorded call to Bill Moyers.

7:03 P.M.

To Hubert Humphrey[144]

Johnson called Senator Hubert Humphrey to discuss the current head count on the next day's Senate cloture vote on the civil rights bill, as well as the status of the administration's poverty and pay bills in Senate committees.

President Johnson: Hubert?

Hubert Humphrey: [Mr. Pres]ident.

President Johnson: Tell me, do you have a reliable count on your cloture?

Humphrey: Yeah, I think that my reliable count shows a minimum of 68 votes, and I'm just going to have—go over it here again with one of the staff fellows then, because we're going to be in session practically all night. I guess we got some boys who are going to hold us in session. We had a little parliamentary snafu here, but we got it all cleared up. So I think we're all right. You—can I . . . I'm going to be here for some time, can I call back one of your men and let you know?

President Johnson: Yeah, I'm going to . . . Call Lee White. I'm going to have to be at a dinner at 7:40 to meet the Prime Minister [of Denmark], but I'll—if you call Lee White . . .

---

144. Tape WH6406.05, Citation #3667, Recordings of Telephone Conversations—White House Series, Recordings and Transcripts of Conversations and Meetings, Lyndon B. Johnson Library.

Humphrey: Yeah.

President Johnson: How are you counting [Carl] Hayden?[145] Against us, aren't you?

Humphrey: Yes, sir.

President Johnson: All right.

Humphrey: I'm counting him against. I was hopeful that he—he gave us a couple of good votes today. I'm counting some—we got some Republicans that come in that sound pretty good. [Karl] Mundt.

President Johnson: Mundt called me and told me he was going to do it. What are they . . . counted [Ralph] Yarborough?[146]

Humphrey: Yarborough, count him, yes.

President Johnson: Well, now, I know what the steelworkers told you, but our information is that they weren't quite that sure.

Humphrey: Well, I'll put the arm on him again. He told me he was going to go.

President Johnson: Yarborough told you?

Humphrey: Yeah.

President Johnson: Today?

Humphrey: Yeah.

President Johnson: Well, that's all right, then. I thought that's what he'd do.

Humphrey: Yeah.

President Johnson: But if he told you.

Humphrey: Yeah. And the other . . . I haven't gotten any commitment out of [J. Howard] Edmondson yet.[147] But the boys tell me that it looks good. I've asked some of the people to contact his brother. I've been after Edmondson two or three times. And since that jury trial amendment got in, I thought that might pull him through, and I think it does, because he was so anxious about it.

President Johnson: But you think we're safe?

Humphrey: Yes, sir. That's my . . . I'm just pawing around here for some papers, but as I see it now, we have 68 votes.

President Johnson: How many of those are Democrats?

---

145. Carl Hayden was a Democratic senator from Arizona and president pro tempore of the Senate. On 10 June, he would vote against cloture on the principle that filibusters were necessary to protect small states.

146. Ralph Yarborough was a Democratic senator from Texas; he would vote in favor of cloture.

147. J. Howard Edmondson was a Democratic senator from Oklahoma. Senator Edmondson would vote in favor of cloture.

Humphrey: Forty-two. [*Pause.*]

President Johnson: Well, the Republicans are doing a little better than we are, aren't they?

Humphrey: Yes, sir. [Everett] Dirksen says he—Dirksen tells me he's got 28 votes. But I don't think he has. I think he's got 26.

President Johnson: And how many do they have, 36?

Humphrey: They've got 33 members of the Senate.

President Johnson: Thirty-three?

Humphrey: Yeah. [*Unidentified person in office with the President also says "Yeah."*] He's losing seven.

President Johnson: I know three of them is [Edwin] Mechem and [John] Tower and [Barry] Goldwater.[148]

Humphrey: Mechem, Tower, Goldwater . . . [Milward] Simpson, and . . . let me see.[149] Those are the four and one more; let me . . . one more, see—

President Johnson: What about [Wallace] Bennett?[150]

Humphrey: Huh?

President Johnson: Bennett?

Humphrey: Bennett is wobbly. That's the fifth one that we counted out, but he's wobbly. It's looks fairly—it looks like a possibility. But Mechem, Tower, Goldwater, Simpson, Bennett, and, let's see, who the hell is the other one—Possibly, yeah, the other one I had was [Bourke] Hickenlooper . . .[151]

President Johnson: And [Roman] Hruska?[152]

Humphrey: No, Hruska's with us. [Peter] Dominick is with us. Mundt is with us. [Leonard] Jordan of Idaho is with us. The other possibility I saw was John Williams of Delaware.[153] So that would leave . . . that would leave 26.

President Johnson: I believe Williams will go with us.

Humphrey: I think he will. I think Williams and Bennett will go; that's

---

148. Senator Edwin Mechem was a Republican from New Mexico; he would vote against cloture. Senator John Tower was a Texas Republican; he would vote against cloture. Senator Barry Goldwater would also vote against cloture.

149. Milward Simpson was a Republican senator from Wyoming; he would vote against cloture.

150. Republican Senator Wallace Bennett represented Utah and would vote against cloture.

151. Senator Hickenlooper of Iowa would vote in favor of cloture.

152. Senator Roman Hruska was a Republican from Nebraska; he would vote in favor of cloture.

153. Peter Dominick was a Republican senator from Colorado; he would vote in favor of cloture, as would Mundt, Jordan, and Williams.

what Dirksen's planning on. Giving him 28, which he thinks he's got; I think he's got 26, just to be a little gun-shy and careful.

President Johnson: OK. All right.

Humphrey: Now, I want you to know I've had a meeting over here with [Sargent] Shriver and [Pat] McNamara.[154]

President Johnson: Yeah?

Humphrey: And we've agreed to the following: that this week, there will be a meeting of his subcommittee—McNamara's subcommittee—at which they will establish the outline and procedure on this bill.[155] They will immediately send letters out to all witnesses saying that they've testified in the House, and that we would like to incorporate their testimony in the Senate proceedings, and if they have any additional comments, we would welcome that. And then while the House is . . . we'll also get the review of the House bill as modified as it come from committee, the latest analysis of it. We'll then . . . after the House gets a rule and votes on the bill, the House bill will be brought over here, and at that time if any senator wishes to call witnesses, the witnesses will be called. McNamara doesn't want to call a lot of witnesses because he's afraid that if he takes the initiative, that the Goldwater crowd will just be loading them up with hundreds of them. And we want to try to get this bill out of committee and get it on the calendar, but to permit, if need be, by the vote of the committee, certain witnesses to be called. [*Pauses briefly.*] Is that agreeable?

President Johnson: Well, I think that . . . that's not the way I'd do it. You're going to have to have the four Cabinet officers; you can't ignore them.[156]

---

154. Peace Corps Director Sargent Shriver headed the presidential task force that had drafted the economic opportunity bill; he would later serve as the first director of the Office of Economic Opportunity, the central implementation agency of the War on Poverty. Senator Pat McNamara, a Michigan Democrat, chaired the Senate Labor and Public Welfare Committee that had jurisdiction over the economic opportunity bill in the Senate.

155. The Senate Labor and Public Welfare Committee had established a select subcommittee that on 17, 18, 23, and 25 June would hold hearings on the economic opportunity bill. *Congressional Quarterly Almanac*, 1964, vol. 20, p. 224.

156. Johnson was referring to the Cabinet secretaries that had some form of departmental interest in the War on Poverty legislation; six secretaries had actually testified in the House hearings: Secretary of Defense Robert McNamara; Secretary of Health, Education, and Welfare Anthony Celebrezze; Secretary of Labor Willard Wirtz; Secretary of Commerce Luther Hodges; Secretary of Agriculture Orville Freeman; Attorney General Robert F. Kennedy (who had chaired the President's Committee on Juvenile Delinquency, which had developed much of the conceptual framework for the War on Poverty); and Secretary of the Interior Stewart L. Udall. *Congressional Quarterly Almanac*, 1964, vol. 20, pp. 216–18.

Humphrey: I told . . . I told McNamara that. He's just stubborn as hell. I told him that. I said that we ought to get all those Cabinet officers over here, and he said, "Well, they've already testified," he said, "and we'll just incorporate their testimony into the record."

President Johnson: All right. OK, if he can get by with that, that—

Humphrey: And I said, "Well I'm not going to let you do that alone, Mac. You've got to hold a committee meeting and decide whether or not that satisfies the committee." So we've agreed that Thursday or Friday of this week, such a committee meeting will be held at which he will outline this procedure and get an official approval of the procedure by a vote of the committee.

President Johnson: All right. Now, what are you going to do . . . what are you going to do about the pay bill?

Humphrey: Well, that goddamn Olin Johnston, I cannot—both Mike [Mansfield] and I have pleaded with him today to get this bill out, and they say, "Well, we're going through it. We're trying to do the best we can."[157] They had some prayer breakfast he was supposed to attend tomorrow, and the leader, Mike, told him, said, "Hellfire, you had—we got you a plane to take some of those fellows out to Cleveland and got them on back here for you so they could be here for your meeting today, and now you want to have a prayer breakfast. Why don't you hold that prayer breakfast another day and get that bill out?" Well, he just . . . he just won't . . . [laughing] he just won't give us a solid commitment. And I've been at him, and—

President Johnson: Didn't he give you a commitment he'd report that bill right away if I'd name his judges?[158] You told me he did.

Humphrey: Yes, he did, Mr. President. He not only told me that, but he's told me three times that he'd report this bill out. He told me that he'd report it out Monday, this week. [Sighs.] He's just a weakling, that's all. I hate to say it on this stuff, but he just doesn't . . . when [Mike] Monroney and a few of them stand up there and raise hell, why, he lets them get by with it.[159] But I'll be on his back. I'm going to have to be here, I guess,

---

157. A Democratic senator from South Carolina, Olin Johnston was the chairman of the Committee on Post Office and Civil Service, which had jurisdiction over the pay bill.

158. On 14 April, President Johnson had agreed to appoint two of Johnston's preferred candidates for vacant judgeships on the South Carolina Federal District Court if the senator would report the pay bill quickly. See Johnson to Olin Johnston, 1:40 P.M., 14 April 1964, in McKee, *The Presidential Recordings, Johnson*, vol. 6, *April 14, 1964–May 31, 1964*, pp. 35–39.

159. Mike Monroney was a Democratic senator from Oklahoma and would succeed Johnston as chairman of the Committee on Post Office and Civil Service in the next (89th) Congress.

most of the night. They're going to have an all-night session around here. I don't know why, but some of the boys decided—

President Johnson: Why don't you go tell him that you made a firm commitment here, and the House has held it and held it and held it, and you got him his two judges, and you thought he'd keep his word?

Humphrey: I have, Mr. President. I'll do it again and again. I'll do everything I can except go over to that committee and become a member of it.

President Johnson: Do you reckon that Dirksen can help you with Olin?

Humphrey: Well, we had Dirksen working on his Republican members, and I personally think that what's going on is that Monroney is just asking a lot of questions à la Albert Gore style and that the chairman of the committee is just messing around.[160] [*Pauses.*] That's the way it adds up.

President Johnson: OK.

Humphrey: Well, we'll . . . I'll report to Lee White. Is he at the White House?

President Johnson: Yeah.

Humphrey: I'll double-check it out, Mr. President.

7:12 P.M.

From Willard Wirtz[161]

Secretary of Labor Willard Wirtz called the President to update him on discussions with General Motors Chairman Frederic Donner about the upcoming negotiations between the big three automakers and the United Auto Workers (UAW). The Johnson administration hoped to persuade the automakers that a price cut on new automobiles would head off UAW demands for wage increases in excess of the administration's 3.2 percent guidepost for such raises; based on productivity gains, such wage guideposts formed the central component of Johnson's anti-inflation policy. CEA Chairman Walter Heller had suggested that the President broach the question of a price cut with Donner at an upcoming

---

160. Albert Gore, father of the future vice president Albert Gore Jr., was a Democratic senator from Tennessee.
161. Tape WH6406.05, Citation #3668, Recordings of Telephone Conversations—White House Series, Recordings and Transcripts of Conversations and Meetings, Lyndon B. Johnson Library.

state dinner for West German Chancellor Ludwig Erhard. Wirtz offered the opinion, which Johnson agreed with, that such an overture would be inappropriate.[162]

President Johnson: [*to someone in the office*] . . . all afternoon. I didn't see him, and I know—[*unclear, buzzer is sounding*]—wants to do anything he can to help you. I know he knows you're going to help him on everything you can. I know he wants to help you. But he is worried about the state of California in [an] election year, and he doesn't want any fight developing out there, and [Edmund "Pat"] Brown is not the whole state.[163]

The President answers the buzzer and is informed that Wirtz is returning his call. The call is then connected.

President Johnson: Yes.

Willard Wirtz: Hello, Mr. President.

President Johnson: Yeah.

Wirtz: I'm talking to [Frederic] Donner about the automobile case.

President Johnson: Mm-hmm.

Wirtz: I've talked with [Robert] McNamara, again with Walter Heller, to Louis [Seaton], Clark Kerr, and this fellow [Ed] Mason.[164] Now, I think that my reactions add up almost exactly to what Bob McNamara suggested to you, and I'm not sure there's any point in doing anything more than confirm that. I would think the likelihood of getting anything on it is very light and would think that to raise the question would be all right, but to put anything on the line in terms of any kind of direct request would not at this point be good judgment.

President Johnson: Mm-hmm. . . . Well, what should I say to him? I hate to bludgeon a fellow that comes to dinner—I mean a social event.

Wirtz: I don't believe there's any point in it; just none at all. I understood Bob McNamara suggested simply to be to refer to the fact that we had been looking at this and we're concerned about the fact that the productivity figures seem to suggest a situation which the guidelines pointed

---

162. For Heller's suggestion, see Walter Heller to Johnson, 6:15 P.M., 4 June 1964, in this volume.

163. Edmund "Pat" Brown was the Democratic governor of California.

164. Louis G. Seaton was a vice president of General Motors and a top negotiator for GM with the UAW; Clark Kerr was a leading industrial relations expert and the chancellor of the University of California at Berkeley; Ed Mason was an economist at Harvard University who specialized in industrial organization.

in the direction of . . . oh, I don't know whether I'd even mention a price decrease, but I certainly would not go beyond that. I just—

President Johnson: Well, say what now?

Wirtz: Well, if you say anything at all, I'd simply ask for whatever reaction he—

President Johnson: Well, (a) would you say anything at all?

Wirtz: If I were you and just as a matter of my own personal advice, I would not, Mr. President.

President Johnson: All right.

Wirtz: Now, I think that Walter Heller and, to a lesser degree, Bob McNamara would have a slightly different view on that, and I give you a . . .

President Johnson: Now, Bob doesn't think it would do a bit of good. He's just trying to satisfy Walter that something can be done.

Wirtz: Oh, well . . . Oh, if that's it, frankly, we had as strong a talk with [Louis] Seaton, who's their industrial relations man, as we could have without making a direct request, and frankly, I read that conversation as indicating almost no possibility. And furthermore, if I were bargaining for General Motors, what I would say to the directors would be, "If you're ready to get any sort of a price decrease in mind, save it and let me use it in connection with the negotiations when they come up." [*Johnson acknowledges.*] That'd be the sensible thing to do. So if that's . . . if Bob's is simply a . . . Well, this makes it quite easy: As far as I'm concerned, I don't think there's enough justifica—enough reason to expect this to even raise it.

President Johnson: OK, Bill.

Wirtz: OK.

President Johnson: Bye.

Wirtz: Right. Bye.

7:25 P.M.

To George Reedy[165]

Apparently looking over a transcript of the day's press briefing, Johnson asked his press secretary for clarification regarding the questions that had

---

165. Tape WH6406.05, Citation #3669, Recordings of Telephone Conversations—White House Series, Recordings and Transcripts of Conversations and Meetings, Lyndon B. Johnson Library.

been raised about Johnson's salary in the aftermath of the day's *Washington Post* story. Only a short segment of the conversation was recorded.

President Johnson: Who is this—no . . . do you say that "the present question of his salary is dealt with at previous briefings," is that [Dan] Rather?

George Reedy: No, sir, that was raised originally by . . . that particular question came from Bob Young of the *Chicago Tribune*.

The recording ends.

> **7:30 P.M.:** Unrecorded call to Walter Jenkins.
>
> **7:35 P.M.:** President Johnson returned to the White House Mansion.
>
> **8:00 P.M.:** Received Danish Prime Minister Otto Jens Krag and his wife, the Danish actress Helle Virkner, upstairs in the White House.
>
> **8:35 P.M.:** Went to the East Room with Lady Bird Johnson, Krag, and Virkner to receive guests for the state dinner.
>
> **8:50 P.M.:** Commenced the state dinner in honor of Krag and Virkner; dancing followed the dinner, beginning at 10:20 P.M.
>
> **12:55 A.M.:** Returned to the White House living quarters with Lady Bird Johnson.

Wednesday, June 10, 1964

We've just got to tell him to have some sense. These goddamn folks that can't do anything without talking, I don't under-stand it. They just got to get publicity, haven't they? They've got him "rushing frantically," that's the whole air, and they just . . . Can't they take a presidential request and go on and fulfill it without doing a lot of talk?

—President Johnson to McGeorge Bundy

The 10th of June 1964 brought an unprecedented triumph for the civil rights movement and its supporters. Just after 11:00 A.M., as the temperatures outside soared towards a high of 100 degrees, the U.S. Senate voted 71–29 to end debate on the civil rights bill (four votes more than the 67 required), bringing to a close the 75-day filibuster maintained by southern Democrats. No cloture petition on a civil rights bill had ever succeeded, despite 12 attempts on previous bills.

Before the vote, only the Senate leaders and the chief spokesmen for the two sides spoke. Majority Leader Mike Mansfield of Montana noted that "the Senate now stands at the crossroads of history, and the time for decision is at hand." Georgia Senator Richard Russell, the leader of the filibuster, spoke next and charged that the bill violated states' rights and the separation of powers and warned, in a comment that foreshadowed reactionary politics for much of the remainder of the century, that passage of the civil rights bill would be followed by "new demands for enactment of further legislation in this field, such as laws requiring open housing and the 'busing' of children." Russell also argued that "this is not, and cannot be, a moral question; however it may be considered, it is a political question." Majority Whip Hubert Humphrey, who served as floor leader for the bill, quoted Shakespeare, citing Henry V's speech before the Battle of Agincourt: "Crispin Crispian shall ne'er go by / From this day to the ending of the world / But we in it shall be remembered." Continuing, the Minnesotan called on the Senate "to make that dream of full freedom, full justice, and full citizenship for every American a reality by their votes on this day, and it will be remembered until the ending of the world." Minority Leader Everett Dirksen of Illinois, who had held together a critical but tenuous block of pro–civil rights Republican senators, applied Victor Hugo's observation that "stronger than all the armies is an idea whose time has come" to the civil rights issue: "The time has come for equality of opportunity in government, in education, and in employment. It will not be stayed or denied. It is here." He also observed that "nothing is eternal except change," and directly contradicted Russell with the observation that the civil rights issue was "essentially moral in character. . . . nor is it the first time in our history that an issue with moral connotations and implications has swept away the resistance, the fulminations, the legalistic speeches, the ardent but dubious arguments, the lamentations and thought patterns of an earlier generation." In a dramatic moment during the voting, California Senator Clair Engle, terminally ill with brain cancer, entered the chamber in a wheelchair. Unable to speak, he nodded his head and pointed weakly to his eye (signaling an "aye" vote) when the roll call reached his name.[1]

Within minutes, the vote had concluded, and the primary obstacle to the most sweeping change in U.S. race relations since the Civil War had been removed. Over the remainder of the day, the Senate decisively rejected two amendments from southern senators that would have significantly weakened the bill.[2] Achievement of cloture, however, had little immediate effect on the escalating conflict over civil rights, as a white mob in St. Augustine, Florida, attacked a march led by the Reverend Martin Luther King Jr. Meanwhile, King and his allies contemplated submitting a request that federal marshals be sent to the city.[3]

---

1. *Congressional Record* [hereafter *Cong. Rec.*], 88th Cong., 2d sess., 1964, 110, pt. 10:13307–10, 13319–20, 13327; Marjorie Hunter, "Packed Senate Galleries Tense; 10-Minute Vote Makes History," *New York Times*, 11 June 1964.

2. Hunter, "Packed Senate Galleries Tense; 10-Minute Vote Makes History"; E. W. Kenworthy, "Senate Invokes Closure on Rights Bill, 71 to 29, Ending 75 Day Filibuster," *New York Times*, 11 June 1964.

3. "King Set to Ask LBJ to Send Marshals to St. Augustine," *Washington Post*, 11 June 1964.

8:00 A.M.: The President flew by helicopter from the White House Ellipse to Washington National Airport, accompanied by Jack Valenti and members of the White House staff.

8:05 A.M.: Departed on a flight from Washington National Airport to Worcester, Massachusetts, to attend graduation ceremonies at Holy Cross College.

9:40 A.M.: Arrived at Worcester Municipal Airport; greeted at the airport by Massachusetts Governor Endicott Peabody, Worcester Mayor Paul V. Mullaney, and other local officials.

10:00 A.M.–10:34 A.M.: Traveled by motorcade from the airport to Holy Cross College.

At one point, Johnson halted the motorcade to shake hands with people in the crowd along the route.

10:34 A.M.: Arrived at Holy Cross football stadium; met by the president (Very Reverend Raymond J. Swords, S.J.) and trustees of Holy Cross College; proceeded to the "robing room" to prepare for ceremony; posed for pictures with other honorary degree recipients and graduate student Robert Smith, a resident of Washington, D.C.

11:25 A.M.: Entered the stadium with President Swords, as the Catholic Youth Council Band performed "Ruffles and Flourishes" and "Hail to the Chief."

11:32 A.M.: After welcoming remarks from Governor Peabody, President Johnson delivered the commencement address.

Partway through the speech, the President received a note from an aide and announced the results of the Senate cloture vote. The crowd responded with a standing ovation.[4]

12:10 P.M.–12:31 P.M.: Motorcade returned to Worcester Municipal Airport; made one stop en route for Johnson to shake hands with disabled children.

12:38 P.M.: Departed Worcester Municipal Airport.

2:28 P.M.: Arrived at Washington National Airport.

2:35 P.M.: Arrived by helicopter at the White House Ellipse; President Johnson went to the White House Mansion.

2:55 P.M.: Unrecorded call from Mansion to Walter Jenkins.

3:15 P.M.: Received a rubdown in the bedroom.

---

4. Taylor Branch, *Pillar of Fire: America in the King Years 1963–65* (New York: Touchstone, 1998), p. 336.

4:00 P.M.: Conducted a meeting in the bedroom with Lady Bird Johnson and Judge A.W. Moursund (codirector of the blind trust that oversaw the Johnsons' financial and business interests during his presidency).

4:31 P.M.: Unrecorded call from the Mansion to George Reedy.

4:36 P.M.: Unrecorded call from the Mansion to Lee White.

4:40 P.M.: Unrecorded call from the Mansion to Representative Adam Clayton Powell, in Puerto Rico.

4:46 P.M.: Unrecorded call from the Mansion to Arizona Senator Carl Hayden.

5:00 P.M.: Unrecorded call from the Mansion to McGeorge Bundy.

5:30 P.M.: Attended an East Room reception for the Presidential Scholars, 121 academically promising high school students from around the United States who had been chosen by a presidential commission for special presidential recognition. The scholars each received a presidential medallion from Johnson, who also made brief remarks.[5]

6:20 P.M.: Proceeded to the Oval Office with Jack Valenti.

6:23 P.M.: Met with McGeorge Bundy.

6:30 P.M.: Attorney General Robert Kennedy joined Bundy and the President in the Oval Office. The White House Daily Diary noted that as Kennedy "walks in the door . . . the President says, 'Hello, hero.' The AG replies, 'Wasn't that good?' "—referring to the cloture vote curbing the civil rights debate.

6:40 P.M.

From Larry O'Brien[6]

With Kennedy (and possibly Bundy) still in the office, Johnson received a call from Special Assistant for Congressional Liaison Larry O'Brien regarding the status of the House vote on the foreign aid authorization bill.

---

5. For background on the Presidential Scholars program, see Johnson to Milton Eisenhower, 16 April 1964, 11:35 A.M., in Guian A. McKee, ed., *The Presidential Recordings, Lyndon B. Johnson: Toward the Great Society, February 1, 1964–May 31, 1964*, vol. 6, *April 14, 1964–May 31, 1964* (New York: Norton, 2007), pp. 58–61.

6. Tape WH6406.05, Citation #3670, Recordings of Telephone Conversations—White House Series, Recordings and Transcripts of Conversations and Meetings, Lyndon B. Johnson Library.

Robert F. Kennedy can be heard in the office before the call.

President Johnson: Good or bad news. It's Mr. O'Brien.

[*on phone*] Hello?

Larry O'Brien: Hi, Mr. President.

President Johnson: I made a speech about you today and got loud and vociferous applause.

O'Brien: [*chuckling*] Couldn't have been about me, I wouldn't get that even in Worcester.[7]

President Johnson: I said I had [Kenneth] O'Donnell and O'Brien and . . . in my staff, and I figured out if you couldn't join them, why . . . you couldn't beat them, you better join them.[8]

O'Brien: [*laughing*] That's pretty good.

President Johnson: What's happened on the Hill?

O'Brien: Well, they just defeated the motion to recommit, 211 to 193.

President Johnson: 211 to 193. Well, that's wonderful.

O'Brien: Yeah. . . . But now the roll call is on, and final pass is now.

President Johnson: Well, you hit the ground standing up. They didn't touch it then, did they?

O'Brien: Nope.

President Johnson: Well, congratulations.

O'Brien: No, not at all. God, I just had my fingers crossed. Boy, these . . . foreign aid is the toughest thing in the world.

President Johnson: Yes, it is. Now, we got to get to work on that appropriation. I'll have to . . . Speaker [John McCormack] called me and suggested that I have the Ways and Means [Committee] Democrats down. I told him I didn't think I'd better do that, after I told him you'd asked me to call [Wilbur] Mills earlier in the day, and . . .[9]

O'Brien: Yeah . . . yeah. Well, I talked to Mills this afternoon again, and he asked me if I would stop by tomorrow afternoon, midafternoon, and have a private talk with him. Now, he was saying, "Well, I don't know, it looks awfully tough" and all that. And I said, "God, I'll be happy

---

7. O'Brien was a native of nearby Springfield, Massachusetts.

8. Special Assistant Kenneth O'Donnell had served as appointments secretary for President Kennedy. Although he still held that title under Johnson, O'Donnell occupied a diminished role because Special Assistant Jack Valenti had taken over most of the responsibilities that O'Donnell had handled for Kennedy. O'Donnell resigned from the White House staff in January 1965. "Goodwin Named Aide to Johnson," *New York Times*, 11 December 1964; "Text of President's News Conference at Texas Ranch," *Washington Post*, 17 January 1965.

9. A Democratic representative from Arkansas, Wilbur Mills served as the chair of the Ways and Means Committee.

to sit right down with you now." "No," he said, "I'd rather do it tomorrow afternoon," he said.

President Johnson: Did he ever give you those names of the excise tax people we need to see?[10]

O'Brien: Yeah, well, Chuck Daly has those, and we're culling them.[11] My God, they have 41 names plus 10—you know, the usual thing. So . . . I'm not going to disturb you with that for a little while. Let us break it down and do every damn thing we can with our people, and then let's see what's left.

President Johnson: Attorney General's here and said that you let him down a little bit. He thought he'd get 79 instead of 71.[12]

O'Brien: Well, tell him that he was always that kind of a fellow.

President Johnson: [*laughing*] OK. Good-bye.

O'Brien: OK.

President Johnson: [*to Kennedy, before hanging up*] He said that— *The recording ends.*

Time Unknown

To Lee White[13]

At some point between the end of the O'Brien conversation and a call to Marie Fehmer at 7:03 P.M., Johnson made a call to Special Assistant Lee White. The conversation addressed the growing civil rights crisis in St. Augustine, Florida. The year 1964 marked the 400th anniversary of St. Augustine's founding as a Spanish colony. As plans for extensive commemorations later in the year went forward, Martin Luther King Jr.'s Southern Christian Leadership Conference (SCLC) had selected the city for an integration drive, choosing it in part because of the publicity that the anniversary celebrations would garner. A rented beach home where

---

10. Johnson was referring to an upcoming bill to extend for one year the existing federal excise taxes on "cigarettes, distilled spirits, beer, wines, automobiles, auto parts and accessories, general telephone service and passenger travel by air." *Congressional Quarterly Almanac*, 88th Cong., 2nd sess., 1964, vol. 20 (Washington, DC: Congressional Quarterly Service, 1965), p. 540.

11. Chuck Daly was an aide to Larry O'Brien; he later served as vice president of Harvard University and the University of Chicago. Transcript, Lawrence F. O'Brien Oral History Interview I, 18 September 1985, by Michael L. Gillette, Lyndon B. Johnson Library, pp. 22–23.

12. Johnson was referring to the Senate's 71–29 vote in favor of cloture on the civil rights bill.

13. Tape WH6406.05, Citation #3671, Recordings of Telephone Conversations—White House Series, Recordings and Transcripts of Conversations and Meetings, Lyndon B. Johnson Library.

King stayed during his periodic trips to join the protests had been shot into on May 29 and then ransacked by vandals on June 7 (King was not in St. Augustine at the time of either incident), while SCLC aide Andrew Young and other marchers had been beaten by a white mob during a march on June 9. In addition, King had received a number of threats to kill him if he returned to the city. Despite the threats, King had arrived in St. Augustine earlier in the day amid a coordinated effort to pressure federal officials into providing direct protection for the minister and pressuring state and local officials to accept some form of talks that would lead to a negotiated compromise.[14] The President asked White about a telegram on the matter from King himself.

By the time of the conversation, King had already participated in a march in St. Augustine that was met by what the New York Times described as "a white mob, screaming oaths and hurling bricks." The Florida state police, who had just been called into the city, lost control of the situation for a time, but the incident did lead to the first arrests of whites since the St. Augustine campaign began.[15]

President Johnson: [on the speakerphone] Lee?

Lee White: Yes, Mr. President.

President Johnson: I noticed Martin Luther King at 4:24 [P.M.]. UPI [United Press International] says he's sending us a letter. [reading] "He will ask President Johnson to send federal marshals in the city to preserve law and order."[16]

White: I saw that same thing, but I'm not aware that we've received that kind of a telegram from him.

President Johnson: Well, you watch those wires when they come in here and be right on them. White—[reading] "King said he would urge in a telegram to Johnson not only protection but also personal intervention by the President to open communication between the white and Negro communities."[17]

White: I have got a copy of that right in front of me here, and he has, indeed, promised to do so. We don't have that; what we do have is

14. For a detailed account of the civil rights movement in St. Augustine, see Branch, *Pillar of Fire*, pp. 324–27, 334–40. See also Johnson to George Smathers, 2:48 P.M., 1 June 1964, in this volume; "Dr. King's Beach Cottage Is Ransacked by Vandals," *New York Times*, 9 June 1964; "King Set to Ask LBJ to Send Marshals to St. Augustine," *Washington Post*, 11 June 1964.
15. John Herbers, "Police Rout Mob at St. Augustine," *New York Times*, 11 June 1964.
16. "King Set to Ask LBJ to Send Marshals to St. Augustine," *Washington Post*, 11 June 1964.
17. Ibid.

a telegram from Wyatt Walker, one of his aides, saying that the Justice Department has not taken proper precautionary measures to safeguard the life of Dr. King.[18] He's—

President Johnson: Why don't you get in touch with Burke Marshall, and you-all do whatever you need to, and acknowledge those telegrams promptly, and take whatever action you think is indicated.[19]

White: All right. Well, what I have done is dictated a telegram for my reply saying that we have been in touch with Governor [Farris] Bryant, who advises that he has dispatched state officials to the scene in St. Augustine adequate to control the situation and has promised to keep us advised.[20] Now, I don't know if I can send that without checking with the governor, but that's the way I would propose to do if it meets with your approval.

President Johnson: All right. Well, you check with the governor, and . . . You propose to check with him first?

White: Yes, sir, before I sent it. I wouldn't think it would be fair to do it without telling him.

President Johnson: Yeah. . . . I sure would, but I'd tell him to try to open up that communication down there, because we catch hell if they don't.

White: He said he was going to talk to the mayor after I talked to him today.[21] He said it sounded worth trying, and that he would be in touch with the mayor, who he says is a fine fellow and a sensible and reasonable man who might be able to pull it off.

President Johnson: [Did] you talk to George Smathers?[22]

White: Not yet.

President Johnson: Don't you think you ought to?

White: Well, I guess I ought to. He's got a lot of influence with this fellow [Herb] Wolfe.[23]

President Johnson: Didn't I tell you last night to call him and tell him you'd call at my request?

---

18. Reverend Wyatt Tee Walker was executive director of the Southern Christian Leadership Conference.

19. Burke Marshall served as assistant attorney general in the Civil Rights Division of the Justice Department.

20. Farris Bryant was the Democratic governor of Florida.

21. Dr. Joseph A. Shelley served as mayor of St. Augustine.

22. Democrat George Smathers was the junior senator from Florida.

23. Herbert Wolfe was a prominent St. Augustine businessman and local political baron who had been a key fund-raiser for Senator Smathers and the President. He was also chairing the extensive effort to celebrate St. Augustine's 400th anniversary.

White: I thought that was to wait until we found out what happened with the governor.

President Johnson: Oh no, go on and call him and tell him to get ahold of Herb Wolfe, and just tell him that we don't want to embarrass him, but this thing's bad and he's wiring . . . He's sending in troops, and he better get ahold of him and open up some communication down there.

White: OK, I'll call him this evening.

President Johnson: Then call the governor too.

White: All right, I will.

President Johnson: All right.

White: All right.

President Johnson: Let me know only if you can't get the job done, if you get into some hitch. But you get Burke Marshall on it. Let's watch it, now.

White: OK.

President Johnson: Bye.

6:54 P.M.: Attorney General Robert Kennedy departed.

6:55 P.M. and 6:58 P.M.: Unrecorded calls to George Reedy.

7:03 P.M.

From Marie Fehmer[24]

Secretary Marie Fehmer called the President to relay a report on the passage of the foreign aid authorization bill in the House.

President Johnson: Yes?

Marie Fehmer: Claude Desautels just called saying that the House just passed the foreign aid bill: 230 yeas, 175 nays.[25]

President Johnson: 230 to 175?

Fehmer: Yes, sir.

---

24. Tape WH6406.05, Citation #3672, Recordings of Telephone Conversations—White House Series, Recordings and Transcripts of Conversations and Meetings, Lyndon B. Johnson Library.
25. Claude Desautels was Larry O'Brien's administrative assistant.

7:05 P.M.

Office Conversation with George Reedy[26]

Immediately after the call from Fehmer, the recording system captured an office conversation between Johnson and Press Secretary George Reedy about the preparation of a press release on the passage of the foreign aid authorization bill.

George Reedy: Mr. President, you asked for me?

President Johnson: Yeah, I just said to get that statement quick as you can. They just passed it—

Reedy: I'll get it right into you, sir—

President Johnson: —230 to175.

Reedy: Right. The girl can type—and type it, and it will be in the box in 30 seconds.

Unidentified: Here it is now, sir.

Reedy: I haven't showed a copy yet. [*Long pause.*]

President Johnson: Fine.

Reedy: OK, sir, I'll [*unclear*]—

President Johnson: See if you—yeah, mm-hmm. [*Pause.*] That's 175 to 230; that's 55 votes.

Reedy: Uh . . . that's right.

President Johnson: By margin more than 50 votes, I'd put that in.

Reedy: OK.

President Johnson: So it shows that it's really a victory.

Reedy: Right.

---

26. Tape WH6406.05, Citation #3673, Recordings of Telephone Conversations—White House Series, Recordings and Transcripts of Conversations and Meetings, Lyndon B. Johnson Library.

TIME UNKNOWN

Between Office Secretary and Jack Valenti[27]

At some point during this time period, the recording system also captured a brief segment of office conversation between a secretary and Special Assistant Jack Valenti.

Office Secretary: Hello?

Jack Valenti: Honey, I've got to see him before he leaves, if he sneaks out that door.

Office Secretary: OK. Sure try.

7:20 P.M.: President Johnson met briefly with Attorney General Robert Kennedy, who then accompanied the President to a party on the White House south lawn that Lynda Johnson had organized for the presidential scholars.

7:35 P.M.: Appointment in the office lounge with tailors Tom Hickey and Gino Porro.

7:40 P.M.–8:00 P.M.: Unrecorded calls from lounge to Speaker of the House John McCormack (7:40), Senate Majority Whip Hubert Humphrey (7:50), House Majority Leader Carl Albert (7:55), and Senate Majority Leader Mike Mansfield (8:00).

8:02 P.M.

From McGeorge Bundy[28]

Johnson recorded a call from McGeorge Bundy regarding a submission to the night-reading folder. The President complained about the hyperbolic manner in which the State Department had announced that George Ball would travel to Athens and Ankara in an effort to ease the Cyprus crisis. Bundy indicated that Ball himself had likely been responsible for the announcement.

---

27. Tape WH6406.05, Citation #3675, Recordings of Telephone Conversations—White House Series, Recordings and Transcripts of Conversations and Meetings, Lyndon B. Johnson Library.
28. Tape WH6406.05, Citation #3676, Recordings of Telephone Conversations—White House Series, Recordings and Transcripts of Conversations and Meetings, Lyndon B. Johnson Library.

A brief conversation between secretaries regarding whether the President is on his private line precedes the call.

McGeorge Bundy: I was going to say I'm sending you a memo for the night reading wrapping up the situation as it is at the end of the day today.[29] There's nothing on the immediate international ticker that we need to worry about. We can't tell what to do about—what you might say at a press conference until we see the morning papers and see how it's being played, but we'll have something ready, if you'll want to be ready to go in the afternoon.

President Johnson: All right. I'm sorry that State put out that I was rushing [George] Ball over there. I thought what I had in mind was Ball would go and tell the Greeks that, but I didn't—

Bundy: That broke from Geneva, Mr. President. Ball must have done that himself.

President Johnson: [*with Bundy acknowledging*] Yeah, he did. We've just got to tell him to have some sense. These goddamn folks that can't do anything without talking, I don't understand it. They just got to get publicity, haven't they? They've got him "rushing frantically," that's the whole air, and they just . . .[30] Can't they take a presidential request and go on and fulfill it without doing a lot of talk?

Bundy: Well, I don't think there's pain in it, Mr. President, because I think this myself: that there's some advantage in having this be a visible trip and it obviously couldn't have been off [*unclear*]—

President Johnson: Well, I think it will . . . of course, it'll be visible, but you don't have to do it in—

Bundy: Don't need to boast about it.

President Johnson: [*with Bundy acknowledging*] That's right, and don't have to be in a hurry, and don't have to have the President frantic, and all that kind—

Bundy: Certainly, the President oughtn't to be frantic. Nobody's . . . the President is never frantic.

---

29. Bundy's memorandum summarized the day's meetings on the situation in Southeast Asia, which the President had not attended. "Memorandum From the President's Special Assistant for National Security Affairs (Bundy) to the President," 10 June 1964, U.S. Department of State, *Foreign Relations of the United States (FRUS), 1964–1968: Vietnam 1964*, ed. Edward C. Keefer and Charles S. Sampson (Washington, DC: GPO, 1992), 1:496–97.

30. Although coverage of the Bundy mission in major newspapers on 10–11 June indicated that Johnson viewed the Cyprus situation with "extreme gravity," none of it described the President as "frantic." "Ball Flies to Athens in Crisis," *Washington Star*, 11 June 1964; Sydney Gruson, "U.S. Prepares 'Measures' to Bar Turk-Greek War," *New York Times*, 11 June 1964; "Ball Takes LBJ Message to Athens and Ankara," *Washington Post*, 11 June 1964.

President Johnson: No . . . no. OK.
Bundy: [*chuckling*] Right, sir.
President Johnson: Bye.

8:06 P.M.–8:30 P.M.: Unrecorded calls to Senate Minority Leader Everett Dirksen (8:06, from the lounge), Marie Fehmer (8:20), Lady Bird Johnson (8:26), and Representative Thomas E. Morgan of Pennsylvania (8:30, from the lounge).

8:50 P.M.: The President returned to the White House living quarters on the second floor.

9:25 P.M.: Dinner with Lady Bird Johnson, Mrs. J. Hugh Powell, and Judge and Mrs. A.W. Moursund.

9:45 P.M.: Unrecorded call from the Mansion to Senator Ralph Yarborough of Texas.

9:55 P.M.: Accompanied Lady Bird Johnson to the White House South Lawn for close of presidential scholars party.

10:20 P.M.: Returned to the White House Mansion.

10:25 P.M.: Unrecorded call from the Mansion to Admiral David L. McDonald, chief of naval operations.

Thursday, June 11, 1964

> *But we're just doing fine except for this damn Vietnam thing.*
> —President Johnson to Richard Russell

One day after the Senate voted to close debate on the civil rights bill, the deepening crisis in St. Augustine demonstrated once again the wider stakes in the civil rights debate. Following a night of violent mob attacks on civil rights marchers (although Florida state troopers had, for the first time, moved to protect the marchers), Martin Luther King Jr. attempted to gain entry to a segregated, beachfront restaurant in a deliberate attempt to be arrested in order to show solidarity with local activists who had already been jailed. While King debated with the restaurant's owner, a white customer angrily pushed him out of the way and entered the building. As King and his aides had expected, the sheriff soon arrived and arrested King, fellow civil rights activist (and Southern Christian Leadership Conference vice president) Reverend Ralph Abernathy, and three other activists. Tensions in the city remained so high that city workers removed decorative bricks in a park next to St. Augustine's Old Slave Market lest they be turned into projectiles by white counterprotestors. Such measures, along with the presence of hundreds of state troopers, proved effective. Authorities succeeded in establishing a barrier between an evening civil rights march held in the aftermath of King's arrest and white crowds eager to attack the marchers. As King waited in jail, however, he and his advisers remained deeply uncertain of their next steps in the St. Augustine campaign.[1]

---

1. John Herbers, "Martin Luther King and 17 Others Jailed Trying to Integrate St. Augustine Restaurant," *New York Times*, 12 June 1964; Taylor Branch, *Pillar of Fire: America in the King Years 1963–65* (New York: Touchstone, 1998), pp. 338–40.

8:30 A.M.: Johnson woke and met with Jack Valenti.[2]
9:32 A.M.: Unrecorded call from the Mansion to Abe Fortas.
10:55 A.M.: Unrecorded call from the Mansion to McGeorge Bundy.

Time Unknown

To Adam Clayton Powell[3]

At some point before 11:00 A.M., Johnson placed a call to Representative Adam Clayton Powell, a congressman from Harlem since 1945 and one of the most powerful black politicians in the United States. Powell chaired the House Education and Labor Committee, which on June 3 had reported the economic opportunity bill that would form the legislative cornerstone of the War on Poverty. Powell and Johnson discussed the distribution of anti-poverty funds to Harlem, touching briefly on the role that Powell himself would play in relation to New York Mayor Robert Wagner. Although not specifically referred to in this conversation, Powell would largely control the Harlem Youth Opportunities Unlimited–Associated Community Teams (HARYOU-ACT) organization that would receive most of Harlem's early War on Poverty funding.[4] After originating as a demonstration project funded by the President's Committee on Juvenile Delinquency and Youth Crime—the Robert Kennedy–run project that formed a precursor for the War on Poverty—HARYOU-ACT would emerge over the following year as one of the War on Poverty's most controversial projects. Critics charged that HARYOU-ACT mismanaged funds, supported radical organizations and militant projects, and served the political interests of Adam Clayton Powell.[5]

Adam Clayton Powell: Hello?
President Johnson: Yes, go ahead.

---

2. The Daily Diary notes that due to running 35 minutes late, President Johnson skipped his exercises.
3. Tape WH6406.05, Citation #3678, Recordings of Telephone Conversations—White House Series, Recordings and Transcripts of Conversations and Meetings, Lyndon B. Johnson Library.
4. In May, Johnson had personally announced that HARYOU-ACT would receive a $1 million grant under the Juvenile Delinquency and Youth Offenses Control Act of 1961. *Congressional Quarterly Almanac*, 88th Cong., 2nd sess., 1964, vol. 20 (Washington, DC: Congressional Quarterly Service, 1965), p. 256.
5. OEO, "The Office of Economic Opportunity During the Administration of President Lyndon B. Johnson; November 1963–January 1969," 1969, "Volume I, Part I; Narrative History" folder, Box 1, Special Files: Administrative Histories, Lyndon B. Johnson Library, pp. 103–23.

Powell: This is Adam.

President Johnson: Yes, sir. Go, go—

Powell: [*Unclear*] me.

President Johnson: Go ahead.

Powell: Hello?

President Johnson: Yes?

Powell: I thought you were calling *me.*

President Johnson: Well, they called me—your secretary did—and said you were trying to reach me, and you wanted me to ca—

Powell: [I] spoke to Jack Valenti last night.

President Johnson: Oh, OK.

Powell: And I told Jack Valenti the problem.

President Johnson: Yeah.

Powell: And the problem is that Mayor [Robert] Wagner and myself can work out this thing together . . . on New York City. That's that War on Poverty allocation to Harlem?

President Johnson: Yeah?

Powell: And so I saw Bob a week ago Sunday, and we decided that we would meet again this Sunday past or next Sunday.

President Johnson: Fine, Adam. I just got in, and I got a note here at 1:15, "Congressman Powell's secretary called [*unclear comment by Powell*] saying a very urgent matter, please call him immediately."

Powell: You can talk . . . Talk to our friend Jack Valenti. I talked to him last night; he's got all the dope.

President Johnson: All right.

Powell: How you feeling?

President Johnson: Fine, I just came back from Massachusetts.[6]

Powell: Yeah?

President Johnson: All I know, I saw in the paper . . . Wagner, when I was up in New York, he didn't talk to me about it or didn't mention it, but I said, "I saw in the paper where you want to talk to me about some project. Now, that's under Dave Hackett at the department."[7]

---

6. Johnson was referring to his trip to Worcester, Massachusetts, the previous day for the commencement exercises at Holy Cross College.

7. David Hackett had served as executive director of the President's Committee on Juvenile Delinquency and Youth Crime under Attorney General Robert F. Kennedy and was a key member of Sargent Shriver's poverty task force that had drafted the economic opportunity bill. He had been one of a group of task force members who were instrumental in shaping the idea of community action that quickly emerged as one of the most innovative and controversial features of the War on Poverty. OEO, "The Office of Economic Opportunity During the Administration of President Lyndon B. Johnson," pp. 143–56.

Powell: That's right. [*Unclear*] to call him, and he wants to put a man in there.

President Johnson: So—

Powell: But they don't know—

President Johnson: I told him I didn't know anything about it and didn't have anything to do with it. He ought to talk to Hackett about it, and whenever you-all—

Powell: [*Unclear*] knows the story.

President Johnson: Whenever you-all get ready—

Powell: This is six months.

President Johnson: Whenever you-all get ready, you-all talk to Hackett about it.

Powell: [*with the President acknowledging*] Yeah, yeah. Now, we got a rule for juvenile delinquency on Monday.[8] We get War on Poverty before the Rules Committee Tuesday.

President Johnson: Now don't let them filibuster on that. Just make a very brief statement—

Powell: [*Unclear*] problem there.

President Johnson: Make a brief statement, make them vote on it, because one of the fellows is leaving Tuesday afternoon.[9]

Powell: That's what I told [Phil] Landrum too.[10] "Don't talk; just say hello and good-bye."

President Johnson: Good luck.

Powell: OK.

President Johnson: Bye.

Powell: Hope you feel well now, Mr. Pres—

---

8. Johnson was referring to the reauthorization bill for the Juvenile Delinquency and Youth Offenses Control Act of 1961, which the House of Representatives would pass on 16 June. The bill extended the act for two years, provided $10 million for funding in 1965, and created a new $5 million demonstration program in Washington, D.C. The 1961 act had funded the creation of pilot projects to experiment with juvenile delinquency prevention. *Congressional Quarterly Almanac,* 1964, vol. 20, p. 256.

9. Johnson was probably referring to Massachusetts Representative Tip O'Neill, a member of the House Rules Committee (and a key Democratic vote) who was scheduled to leave Washington late on Tuesday, 16 June. See Johnson to Carl Albert, 4:44 P.M., 9 June 1964; and Johnson to Larry O'Brien, 4:58 P.M., 9 June 1964, in this volume.

10. Representative Phillip Landrum of Georgia was the floor leader for the economic opportunity bill.

11:00 A.M.

To William Bustamante; President Johnson
joined by Lady Bird Johnson[11]

At an undetermined time after the Powell conversation, the President and Lady Bird Johnson extended get-well wishes to Jamaican Prime Minister William Bustamante. In April, President Johnson had arranged for Bustamante to have cataract surgery at Washington's Walter Reed Army Hospital.[12] This conversation appears to address an unrelated ailment.

President Johnson: . . . mighty happy that you're doing so well, and if there's anything in the world I can do.

William Bustamante: I know. What I want you to do for me is to top the poll in November.

President Johnson: Well, I'm going to do my best—

Bustamante: [*chuckling*] Yes.

President Johnson: —if—You say a prayer for me, will you?

Bustamante: [*Unclear*] I will.

President Johnson: Mrs. Johnson and Lynda Bird wanted to send their regards.

Bustamante: Thanks very much.

President Johnson: And—

Bustamante: Give ours to Lady Bird and the girls.

President Johnson: All right. Now, here's—

Bustamante: I want you to top that poll. [*Chuckles.*]

President Johnson: All right, we're going to try. Here's Lady Bird, wants to say hello to you.

Bustamante: Hello?

Lady Bird Johnson: Mr. Prime Minister?

Bustamante: Hello, Lady Bird, I hope to see you back in Jamaica.

Lady Bird Johnson: Oh . . . oh, bless you.

Bustamante: And we are praying that the President tops the poll in November and [*Lady Bird laughs*] this absolutely sincere.

---

11. Tape WH6406.05, Citation #3679, Recordings of Telephone Conversations—White House Series, Recordings and Transcripts of Conversations and Meetings, Lyndon B. Johnson Library.
12. See Johnson to William Bustamante, 6:29 P.M., 14 April 1964, in Guian A. McKee, ed., *The Presidential Recordings, Lyndon B. Johnson: Toward the Great Society, February 1, 1964–May 31, 1964*, vol. 6, *April 14, 1964–May 31, 1964* (New York: Norton, 2007), p. 45.

Lady Bird Johnson: Oh, thank you. Listen, I know this trouble's not going to get a man like you down, and I'm delighted that you're getting along well.

Bustamante: Oh, no—all right. I'm just as good as I was before.

Lady Bird Johnson: That's great.

Bustamante: In fact, I'm better. [*Lady Bird chuckles and Bustamante joins her.*]

Lady Bird Johnson: And we'll look forward to seeing you sometime.

Bustamante: OK. Good luck, good health, and regards to the girls.

President Johnson: All right, now, you let me know if there's anything I can do for you, anytime.

Bustamante: OK.

President Johnson: Good-bye.

Bustamante: Good luck.

11:02 A.M.–11:21 A.M.: Unrecorded calls from the Mansion to Senator George Smathers of Florida (11:02), George Reedy (11:09), former Kentucky Senator Earle C. Clements (11:20),[13] and Walter Jenkins (11:21).

11:40 A.M.: President Johnson shook hands in the Oval Room of the Mansion with delegates to the Equal Pay Conference, an event focused on ending wage inequality between men and women; the conference was sponsored by the Department of Labor and the National Committee for Equal Pay, a coalition of labor unions and women's groups.[14]

11:52 A.M.: Addressed the Equal Pay Conference on the White House South Lawn.

12:04 P.M.: Took Secretary of Labor Willard Wirtz to the Mansion to show him a picture of the President's birthplace. Wirtz then accompanied Johnson to the Oval Office.

12:12 P.M.: Photographs taken, off the record, by a *National Geographic* photographer.

---

13. Clements had served as Senate majority whip when Johnson was majority leader. His daughter, Bess Abell, served on Lady Bird Johnson's staff.

14. The conference also officially marked the first anniversary of the implementation of the Equal Pay Act of 1963, which prohibited sex-based wage and salary discrimination. "Johnson Suggests G.O.P. Pick Woman," *New York Times*, 12 June 1964.

12:26 P.M.

To Richard Russell[15]

The President called Georgia Senator Richard Russell to consult on the selection of a replacement for U.S. Ambassador to South Vietnam Henry Cabot Lodge, who according to most political observers would soon return to the United States to challenge Arizona Senator Barry Goldwater's presumed nomination as the Republican Party's 1964 presidential candidate. A former Massachusetts senator, Lodge had been Richard Nixon's running mate in the 1960 election. He had won an upset victory over Goldwater in the March 10 New Hampshire primary—despite having neither declared his candidacy nor returned to the United States to campaign. In a gesture of bipartisanship, President Kennedy had appointed Lodge—who he had defeated not only in 1960 but also for a U.S. Senate seat in 1952—to the ambassadorship in 1963. Since coming to office, however, Johnson had found Lodge to be tremendously difficult to work with because of his tendency to centralize control over all U.S. operations in South Vietnam and his refusal to work with other U.S. officials. Still, because of his suspicions about Lodge's political ambitions, President Johnson had thought it wise to keep him in Saigon. Most recently, during a lengthy conversation in late May, the President had clearly expressed his concerns about the ambassador to Russell, who thus needed little explanation of the situation in this conversation.[16] While Russell evaluated prospective candidates for the post, he offered no new alternatives. Although the conversation repeatedly returned to the ambassadorship, Johnson and Russell also touched on a range of other issues.

The previous day, Senator Russell had suffered a significant, although expected, political defeat when the Senate voted in favor of closing debate on the civil rights bill, an action that ended the Russell-led filibuster and removed one of the primary remaining obstacles to passage of the legislation. Despite their stark differences on civil rights, Johnson and Russell remained close, and the Georgia senator continued to be a trusted source of advice for the President.

---

15. Tape WH6406.05, Citations #3680 and #3681, Recordings of Telephone Conversations—White House Series, Recordings and Transcripts of Conversations and Meetings, Lyndon B. Johnson Library.
16. Johnson to Richard Russell, 10:55 A.M., 27 May 1964, in McKee, *The Presidential Recordings, Johnson*, vol. 6, *April 14, 1964–May 31, 1964*, pp. 871–85.

President Johnson: Dick?

Richard Russell: Yes, sir.

President Johnson: I want you to do a little heavy thinking for me today. I don't want anybody to know this but the two of us. I think [Henry Cabot] Lodge is . . . He hasn't been willing to do anything out there, and I think he's coming out within the next few days or weeks. I need to pick the best man in America to succeed him. I don't know who that is. I can't find anybody in my government. [*Unclear comment by Russell.*] [Dean] Rusk is willing to do it, and I don't think he's the man, and I don't think I can afford to let him go. [Robert] McNamara's anxious to do it, the same thing. [McGeorge] Bundy, the same thing. I can't let any of them go here because I've got too many damn serious problems. I need a Lucius Clay 25 years ago.[17]

They . . . We're making some little progress in our province program, and we've been doing a little better the last few weeks because the folks think they got some little something to hope for and to live for. We're doing a little with the school and the hospital here and there. They're getting a little better, and we haven't done bad, but Lodge won't let any of these folks really do anything. He won't let anybody broadcast hope because he handles all radio, television, newspaper himself. He won't let anybody get out [and] do any of this economic work because he thinks that we've got too many Americans now.

So we need a top man, and . . . I can't take anybody from the Cabinet. I've looked over every single ambassador we've got: George McGhee and [Charles "Chip"] Bohlen and [David] Bruce, and none of them fit the specifications.[18] The man we need is a man that's a pretty good diplomat and a hell of a good administrator that can help this government and make some decisions for them and lead them and that can put in a good economic program and get those people doing something themselves and, at the same time, work with our military. We think we've got the best man we can get in [William] Westmoreland.[19] Now, that man needs a combination

---

17. Like Russell, a native of Georgia, Lucius Clay graduated from West Point and embarked upon a successful military and civilian career. Before retiring from the Army in 1949, General Clay served in the Corps of Engineers, was in charge of materiel in World War II, and in 1947 became commander in chief of U.S. forces in Europe and military governor of the U.S. zone in Germany. As John Kennedy's personal representative in Germany he gave the order to send U.S. tanks to "Checkpoint Charlie" during the construction of the Berlin Wall in 1961. At the time of this conversation, Clay was 67 years old. "Lucius Clay Dies, Led Berlin Airlift," *New York Times*, 17 April 1978.

18. George McGhee, Charles "Chip" Bohlen, and David Bruce were the U.S. ambassadors to Germany, France, and the United Kingdom, respectively.

19. General William Westmoreland served as deputy commander of the Military Assistance Command for Vietnam; he would become commander on 19 June.

of military and economic experience and must be a good administrator. The best that anybody's come up with now, I'm down to George—

Russell: It'll be hard to find that kind of man [*unclear*]—

President Johnson: George Ball. The best we've got in the government's George Ball, who's probably first, and Averell Harriman.[20] And we just can't send Walter Jenkins, so we've got to send somebody. And I don't know where they are. I need a good . . . Lucius Clay 25 years ago. He's too old, and he wouldn't go now, and tired. [J. Lawton] Collins I don't guess would be the man, would he?[21]

Russell: [*softly*] No.

President Johnson: All of my men are too old, the retired ones like [General Omar] Bradley and Collins and Clay.[22]

Russell: Collins is as old as Clay, I'd think.

President Johnson: Yeah. I saw him the other day, and he didn't look good, but he was here with the D-day group that took off.[23] [George Whelan] Anderson, my administration wouldn't have him: They think he's just a puffed up, attractive physically fellow, but he's not much to him, as chief of naval operations.[24]

Russell: He's pretty good man.

President Johnson: You think so?

Russell: Yes, sir, I do. He's a pretty good man, but I don't know. He grates on the State Department people. They never have liked him. I don't think I'd select him for that reason. They . . . I don't know. I don't know why the hell they ever sent Lodge out there—

President Johnson: Well, they did, and—

---

20. A veteran diplomat, former governor of New York, and scion of one of the wealthiest families in the United States, W. Averell Harriman served as under secretary of state for political affairs.

21. General J. Lawton Collins served as commanding general of the 25th Infantry Division at Guadalcanal and of the VII Corps during the Normandy Invasion. He was chief of staff of the Army during the Korean War and was a special U.S. ambassador to Vietnam during the Eisenhower administration (1954–55).

22. General Omar Bradley served in North Africa and oversaw the Omaha Beach landing on D-Day. He later directed the Veterans Administration for President Truman, succeeded Eisenhower as chief of staff of the Army, and became the first chairman of the Joint Chiefs of Staff.

23. Collins was a member of the official U.S. delegation that would travel to Normandy, France, to participate in ceremonies marking the 20th anniversary of D-Day. Omar Bradley headed the delegation. Johnson had met with the delegation in the Rose Garden on 3 June, prior to their departure for France.

24. Admiral George Whelan Anderson had served as chief of naval operations from 1961 to 1963. Clashes with Defense Secretary Robert McNamara led to his removal from the position. President Kennedy then appointed him to the post of U.S. ambassador to Portugal. Bruce Lambert, "Adm. George W. Anderson, 85; Was in Charge of Cuba Blockade," *New York Times*, 22 March 1992.

Russell: —it makes it doubly difficult to succeed him. If you had a career man out there, it wouldn't be any problem. But now you've got to get a man that somebody knows and that's got some sales [*unclear*].

President Johnson: Somebody just gave me a thought, and I don't guess he'd think of doing it, but what about [John] McCone?[25] I just thought of that while I was talking to you. No human's ever mentioned him, but since Rusk is willing to do it and since McNamara is willing to do it. You think it would be very bad for McNamara, don't you?

Russell: Yeah, I don't see hardly how . . . how you . . . he could afford to do that.

President Johnson: He's the most valuable man I got in the Cabinet on everything.

Russell: He's . . .

President Johnson: I have him work—

Russell: You need him here in the first place, and in the second place, all this business about "McNamara's war" would be accentuated if you sent him out there.[26] Nobody's paying any attention to it now, but they might if he went out there. And . . .

President Johnson: Have you had any dealings with George—

Russell: I don't think . . . don't think you can spare him.

President Johnson: Have you—

Russell: George Ball, could you spare him? He's a consistent fellow.

President Johnson: Yes, I could. . . . I could. I just . . . They say he's no administrator, but they say this AID [Agency for International Development] man, [William] Gaud, G-a-u-d, is the best administrator in the government.[27] He's a former businessman and tough and able, and he's the deputy for AID, and they say we ought to just jerk him out of there and send him out yonder.

Russell: Ball is a tough fellow and a good man. I . . . without any further thought, I'd say Ball could fill the bill. Ball is a[n] exceptionally

---

25. John McCone served as director of Central Intelligence.

26. In a 30 March 1964 speech, Oregon Senator Wayne Morse had called for the "repudiation" of the Johnson administration unless it ceased to support "the McNamara war." This was the first recorded use of the phrase in the nation's major newspapers, but it caught on so rapidly that by late April, McNamara responded by embracing the designation: "I don't object to its being called 'McNamara's war.' I think it is a very important war and I am pleased to be identified with it and do whatever I can to win it." "Morse Scores Role of U.S. in Vietnam," *New York Times*, 31 March 1964; "M'Namara Agrees to Call It His War," *New York Times*, 25 April 1964.

27. William S. Gaud served as deputy administrator of the State Department's Agency for International Development (AID).

strong character. He's a . . . and he's a man—he's an observant man, too. He knows what's going on, where he is.

President Johnson: He went to Greece and Turkey, and Greece just made him a stump speech and didn't get a goddamn where. They're just insisting on backing [Archbishop] Makarios, and they're going to ruin the . . . run the Turks back up a wall, and they're going to go in and invade, and we're going to have a bloody war. I stopped an invasion the other night. They already had the ships ready to go.[28]

Russell: I don't see how the Turks have put up with what they have over there.

President Johnson: I don't either. . . . And I sent Ball back to talk to both of them yesterday, and Inonu is just doing his best, wants to come see me in June, June 22 or something.[29] And we can't settle it. They've got to settle it between themselves, and they've got to have some kind of a formula that both of them can agree to and won't humiliate either. They just don't do it. The Greeks just make a stump speech and say they got to support Makarios, and the Greeks can't take it, and Inonu's—that government's in danger, threatened, because he's listening to me and stopped the invasion. And he's not going to listen to me next time.

Russell: McCone and [Sargent] Shriver and all those boys are Catholics. If you could get a good strong Catholic, it would help out there.

President Johnson: Shriver's got to run the poverty program and get me some talent. He's good at selecting good men for government and now, damn it, I need them by the dozens. I wish you'd find some good, young men in Georgia. Trouble is, every damn one of your folks want to stay there and be a [unclear] like Bobby [Russell].[30] We need some of those folks coming out and doing these things. I got me a good ambassador in the Dominican Republic from your place, but he's an old . . . career one, been gone a long time from Georgia.[31]

Russell: Yeah, Tap's a good boy.

---

28. Archbishop Makarios III was the leader of the Greek Cypriots and the President of Cyprus. Johnson was referring to his efforts to dissuade Turkey from invading Cyprus to support the possible establishment of an independent state for the island's Turkish minority. See Johnson to Dean Rusk, 6:30 P.M., 9 June 1964, in this volume.

29. Johnson mispronounced the Prime Minister of Turkey's last name here and a few sentences later.

30. Bobby Russell was the senator's nephew and a state judge in Georgia.

31. Johnson was referring to W. Tapley Bennett Jr., the U.S. ambassador to the Dominican Republic. Johnson and Russell had talked about Bennett at length in January 1964. See Kent B. Germany and Robert David Johnson, eds., *The Presidential Recordings, Lyndon B. Johnson: The Kennedy Assassination and the Transfer of Power, November 1963–January 1964*, vol. 3, *January 1964* (New York: Norton, 2005), pp. 654–55, 662–64, 683, 1007.

President Johnson: We need some folks with some common sense that adjusted to what's happening in the world, and we just haven't got many of them. The only place I can go is [to] professors. The last recommendation I got is the best man to send to Vietnam was Clark Kerr, the president of the University of California. I don't know him, but they say he's the ablest man in that whole country.

Russell: I don't know him either.

President Johnson: Said he'd built a school of a 100,000.[32] He's able, and he's tough, and he'd do this if I insisted.

Russell: I would think some. I don't know . . .

President Johnson: What's your impression of McCone?

Russell: Oh, McCone can do the job. He's getting old, but he's still tough-fibered as hell. I don't—I doubt whether he'd want to go out there or not, but he might. I guess he'd do anything nearly to get rid of Lodge; he despises him. He feels like—

President Johnson: Well, he has been a miserable failure.

Russell: —[*unclear*]—Well, they ought to [have] known he was going to be when they sent him out there.

President Johnson: And this damn State Department, I can't stop them from talking. They're infiltrated worse than MacArthur said they had, and they put out one this morning that we—yesterday and last night—that somebody over there said that we had suspended flights.[33] Well, we hadn't scheduled any. We just sent one in there to answer what they'd done and answer it damn quick, and then we didn't schedule any more. We haven't suspended some that hadn't been scheduled, but it makes it look like we started a program and then quit it. We started one

---

32. Clark Kerr had served as the president of the University of California system since 1958 (previously, he had been the chancellor of the system's flagship Berkeley campus). During his tenure, Kerr had overseen a massive expansion of the U.C. system, including the addition of three new campuses. A graduate of Swarthmore College and a Quaker who had once worked on an American Friends Service Committee "peace caravan" in support of the League of Nations, Kerr was thus an ironic choice as a candidate for an ambassadorship that would consist in large part of overseeing the diplomatic dimensions of an American military effort. Grace Hechinger, "Clark Kerr, Leading Public Educator and Former Head of California's Universities, Dies at 92," *New York Times*, 2 December 2003; Clark Kerr, *The Gold and the Blue: A Personal Memoir of the University of California, 1949–1967* (Los Angeles: University of California Press, 2001).

33. Johnson was almost certainly referring to Senator Joseph McCarthy, who in 1950 had claimed that the U.S. State Department had been infiltrated by Communist agents. As Johnson indicated, major newspapers had carried stories that the United States had suspended reconnaissance flights "over Laos . . . in deference to objections by Premier Souvanna Phouma." Hedrick Smith, "Temporary Halt in Laos Flights Ordered by U.S.," *New York Times*, 11 June 1964; "Laos Flights May Resume," *Washington Star*, 11 June 1964.

of going in there, and we went in and came out. And we think it had a good reaction, don't you?

Russell: Apparently so.

President Johnson: Mm-hmm. Looks—

Russell: It's surprising that these Chinese Reds haven't been hollering like hell about it.

President Johnson: Well, they came out this morning and said that this was a very dangerous game we were playing.[34]

Russell: Oh, they did?

President Johnson: Mm-hmm.

Russell: Yeah.

President Johnson: They're going to have to do something about it if we keep it up. They notified us they'd come in this morning if we didn't stop it.

Russell: I thought they'd be going to the . . . United Nations and all that if it bothered them—

President Johnson: Well, I think that they . . . I think they're doing some of that, and that's all right for them to go. We want some conferences. I do. I'm confronted with a . . . I don't believe the American people ever want me to run. If I lose it, I think that they'll say I've lost the . . . I've pulled in, and at the same time, I don't want to commit us to a war, and I'm in a hell of a shape. I can't do . . . I just don't know.

Russell: Well, we're just like the damn cow over a fence out there in Vietnam.

President Johnson: That's right, and Laos, and I've got a study being made now by the experts, which I want you to come over some night and have a drink and see how important the two of them are. Whether Malaysia will necessarily go and India will go, and how much it'll hurt our prestige if we just got out and let some conference fail or something.[35]

Russell: I know all those arguments.

President Johnson: But they say that . . . well, a fellow like A.W. Moursund said to me last night, said, "Goddamn, there's not anything [that will] destroy you as quick as pulling out and pulling up stakes and running, that America wants, by God, prestige and power, and they don't want . . ." I said, "Yeah, but I don't want to—"

---

34. For the Chinese statement, which warned that any extension of U.S. military activities in Laos would meet with a "powerful rebuff," see Seymour Topping, "Red China Warns U.S. on Laos War," *New York Times*, 11 June 1964.

35. Johnson was referring here to the idea that unless Communist expansion in a region such as Southeast Asia was immediately checked, one state after another would fall in succession.

Russell: [*Unclear*] what anybody's saying.

President Johnson: "I don't want to kill these folks." He said, "I don't give a damn," said, "they didn't want to kill them in Korea, but," said, "if you don't stand up for America, there's nothing that a fellow in Johnson City or Georgia or any other place will—they'll forgive you for everything except being weak."

Russell: Well, there's a lot in that. There's a whole lot in that, and . . .

President Johnson: [Barry] Goldwater and all of them raising hell about, "Go on, let's . . . hot pursuit; let's go in and bomb them."

Russell: Yeah. . . . I ran into Chan [*unclear*] the other day. He said, "[*Unclear*] God, hell, why don't we just go on in there in Vietnam and Laos and clean that situation up?"

President Johnson: You can't clean it up; that's the hell of it.

Russell: I said, "My God, Chan, it would take a half a million men. They'd be bogged down in there for 10 years," and [he said], "Oh, hell no, they'd be [*unclear*]"—

President Johnson: Well, we never did clean Korea up yet!

Russell: [*chuckling*] No, it ain't clean yet. We're right where we started, except for 70,000 of them buried over there.[36]

President Johnson: Now, Dick, you think every time you can get your mind off of other things, think about some men. You're bound to run into them testifying or something.[37]

Russell: I'll try, Mr. President. I've got a hell of a lot on my mind, but I'll try to think of—[38]

President Johnson: You haven't got anybody in Georgia that's top-flight?

---

36. U.S. casualties during the Korean war included 33,741 battle deaths, 2,833 "nonhostile deaths," and 103,284 wounded. For many years, the Department of Defense listed the battle deaths total as approximately 54,246; in 2000, however, research indicated that this figure included 17,672 military deaths during the Korean War period *outside* of the Korean theater itself, and the totals for the war itself were revised downward. Washington Headquarters Services, Directorate for Information Operations and Reports, "Korean War—Casualty Summary; As of June 15, 2004," http://web1.whs.osd.mil/mmid/CASUALTY/KOREA.pdf; Steve Vogel, "Death Miscount Etched into History; American Fatalities Outside of Korea Included in War Toll," *Washington Post*, 25 June 2000.

37. Senator Russell chaired the Senate Armed Services Committee and would thus have been familiar with many officials in the military and foreign service through their testimony in committee hearings.

38. Along with leading the just-concluded Senate filibuster against the civil rights bill, Russell was serving on the Warren Commission, the body charged with investigating the assassination of President Kennedy. The commission would make its final report in September 1964. Morton Mintz, "Warren Commission Combined Men of Diverse Talents and Views," *Washington Post*, 28 September 1964.

Russell: I don't think of anyone in the moment that I would . . .

President Johnson: I've looked at every man I've got in Texas, and I can't think of a single one I know, and my great weakness in this job is that I just don't know these other people. The Kennedys, they know every damn fellow in the country or have got somebody that knows them. They're out [at] these universities and every place in the country, in New York, and Chicago, and . . .

Russell: I never did know just how they made all those connections.

President Johnson: Well, this damn Shriver knows everybody. He's the fellow, you know, that get [*sic*] Phil Landrum to handle poverty. That's a damn smart thing to do. We never would have a pro[gram]—

But we're just doing fine except for this damn Vietnam thing. We're just doing wonderful. Every index, the businessmen are going wonderful. They're up 12, 14 percent investment over last year. The tax bill has just worked out wonderfully.[39]

Russell: We're in a boom period [*unclear*]—

President Johnson: The married people, only 2.6 percent of the married people are unemployed; 97.4 got jobs. There's 16 percent of these youngsters, and I'll have all them employed when I give them a job where they can stay in high school, give them a job where they can stay in college, and give them a job at one of these camps, and I'll cover that 16 percent when I get my other program, but . . . everything's doing—[40]

Russell: Well, a lot of that's not firm unemployment at all.

President Johnson: No, it's kids that are dropping out of school and then they're going on a [welfare] roll. But I'll take care of that with my poverty, just by organizing it all. We've got the money in these various departments: Labor and HEW [Health, Education, and Welfare] and Justice. Justice has got a juvenile delinquency program; Labor's got a retraining program; HEW's got an education program. I'm going to put all of them in one, and put one top administrator, and really get some

---

39. Johnson was referring to the $11.5 billion reduction in personal and corporate taxes that his administration had successfully navigated through Congress in January and February 1964. An annual survey of business plans for capital expenditures released in April indicated that U.S. businesses planned to increase spending on plants and equipment by 12 percent over 1963, up from a projection of 4 percent in a survey taken in April 1963. Manufacturers planned an 18 percent increase. *17th Annual McGraw-Hill Survey; Business' Plans For New Plants and Equipment* (New York: McGraw-Hill, Department of Economics, 1964), pp. 1–2.

40. Johnson was referring to his economic opportunity bill, the legislative core of his proposed War on Poverty. The Job Corps component of the program (Title I) would establish camps where unemployed young people could receive remedial education and job training. *Congressional Quarterly Almanac*, 1964, vol. 20, pp. 210–11.

results, go in and clear up these damn rolls. And I'll do it with only 300 million [dollars] more than was in the budget anyway, last year.[41]

Russell: Well, I hope so.

President Johnson: Well, that's—I've got 900 million [dollars] and 600 million's already in the budget last year for this stuff—

Russell: Mm-hmm.

President Johnson: —but it's being scattered around, and we get no credit for it. We don't dramatize it, and they don't know it.

Russell: Well, there has been a good deal . . . been a lot of comment on it. I think it's more widely understood than you perhaps [*unclear*]—

President Johnson: Well, I was down in Kentucky the other day. We've got 50 kids there that are teaching beauty culture, how to fix Lynda's [Johnson's] hair, and they're all going out and get jobs at 50, 60 dollars a week in another three months. They've been at it now for about a year. I had 50 auto mechanics in the same building, and those kids from all over the mountain. They're teaching them how to tear down a differential and put it back together, and they'll get jobs.[42] Now, that's what we ought to do instead of paying out 4 billion [dollars] a year on relief . . . for nothing. They don't have to work. To hell with this unemployment compensation relief.

But I've got to find a man for Vietnam, and I don't know . . .

Russell: [*coughing*] Well, I'll try to think.

President Johnson: You wouldn't send Clay—

Russell: [*Unclear.*]

President Johnson: You wouldn't try Clay, would you?

Russell: I haven't seen Clay in the last three or four years, Mr. President. Sometimes these fellows start breaking mighty fast; I don't know. Last time I saw him, he was full of vigor, but I haven't seen him in four years now.

---

41. Johnson was referring again to the economic opportunity bill and portraying it as primarily a reorganization of existing social service programs. Contrary to Johnson's claims, the bill created a series of new antipoverty initiatives and a new executive agency, the Office of Economic Opportunity, to oversee their implementation (a few programs were delegated to the Department of Labor and the Department of Health, Education, and Welfare). James T. Patterson, *America's Struggle Against Poverty 1900–1994* (Cambridge, MA: Harvard University Press, 1994), pp. 133–43; Michael L. Gillette, *Launching the War on Poverty: An Oral History* (New York: Twayne Publishers, 1996).

42. Johnson had traveled to Kentucky on 24 April as part of the first of two tours of high-poverty regions of Appalachia. "Remarks at the Johnson County Courthouse, Paintsville, Kentucky," 24 April 1964, *Public Papers of the Presidents of the United States: Lyndon B. Johnson, 1963–64* (Washington, DC: GPO, 1965), 1:543–44.

President Johnson: What would you think of Westmoreland for both places?

Russell: I think highly of that. I was going to suggest that. I made a note here when I was talking to you. See if Westmoreland couldn't fill both of them. He's a topflight man. [*Coughs violently.*]

President Johnson: Well, I see you're still having trouble with your damn cough, aren't you?

Russell: Yes, I certainly am.[43]

President Johnson: Well, take care of yourself, and I love you, and be good.

Russell: Westmoreland, he can do the job if you want a military man, if there's any way you can handle it where he can do both of them.

President Johnson: All right. Let me ask you this: What would you tell these Greeks now? Just tell them they've got to get with the Turks and do something or they all going to hell in a hack?

Russell: Well, I think I'd tell them if they wasn't willing to come to some reasonable agreement there, that you'd just have to pursue a hands-off policy, and I think that will scare the hell out of them. They're counting on us supporting them; the Greeks are. [*Pause.*]

President Johnson: [*with Russell acknowledging*] Now, one other thing. Carl Hayden is crying and just shoving me and just demanding that I send up a budget estimate on his Arizona thing.[44] And I'm just so scared it's going to screw me in California that I don't know what to do. He's got a little agreement with [Edmund "Pat"] Brown, but he hasn't

---

43. The 66-year-old senator suffered from emphysema and died from respiratory complications in 1971.

44. Carl Hayden, a Democratic senator from Arizona and president pro tempore of the Senate, had been pushing for federal funding for the Central Arizona Project, which would construct a series of dams and aqueducts to divert Colorado River water for urban uses in rapidly growing areas of Arizona. The massive project had been blocked since the 1940s by opposition from California, which would have lost Colorado River water rights allocated to it under earlier agreements. The Kennedy administration had developed a compromise regional water plan known as the Pacific Southwest Water Plan that allocated water resources on a cooperative basis and minimized interstate competition. In particular, the federal government would subsidize the cost of diverting excess water from northern to Southern California to compensate for the Colorado River water that would be redirected by the Central Arizona Project. For background and additional conversations on the topic, see Edmund G. "Pat" Brown to Johnson, 3:31 P.M., 6 April 1964, in David S. Shreve and Robert David Johnson, eds., *The Presidential Recordings, Lyndon B. Johnson: Toward the Great Society, February 1, 1964–May 31, 1964,* vol. 5, *March 9, 1964–April 13, 1964* (New York: Norton, 2007), pp. 734–40; Kermit Gordon to Johnson, 10:04 A.M., 12 May 1964, in McKee, *The Presidential Recordings, Johnson,* vol. 6, *April 14, 1964–May 31, 1964,* pp. 596–99; and Johnson to Jesse Unruh, 6:50 P.M., 3 June 1964, in this volume.

got one with [Pierre] Salinger and the *Los Angeles Times*, and [Thomas] Kuchel and all of them are raising hell about it.[45]

Russell: Lot of dynamite in that.

President Johnson: And it's just awful. And he just cries with me *every* day. And I just put off and run and dodge and hide, and I can't kill him, and I hate to get involved in that damn thing again. He does have the governor of California. He won his lawsuit, and he got the governor, and they've worked out a plan.[46] It don't cost me much money this year, and not much next year. And over the whole affair, the [Bureau of the] Budget said it's a sound project, that it'll pay back, but I think it kind of messes up my image a little bit.[47]

Russell: It'll sound mighty big when you get that total figure out there and go to throwing [*unclear*].

President Johnson: Yeah, and it'll sound pretty big if California goes to giving me hell. I need those electoral votes.

Russell: That's what I'm talking about.

President Johnson: Well, how do you look at this political thing?

Russell: Oh, I think it'd . . . I can't see the slightest difficulty anywhere now.

President Johnson: Goldwater said yesterday he had three issues. Southeast Asia, he's going to make that an issue; I don't know how he can. That the results of the civil rights bill would be an issue. I've got to get the leaders in here after that bill's passed. I don't know how to do it, but what would happen if I asked you senators to come in and give us advice and try to help us see that it was put into effect the right way, would that be a bad move?

Russell: [*chuckling*] I don't know how anybody up here could tell you much.

---

45. Pat Brown served as governor of California, while Thomas Kuchel was a Republican senator from the state. Press Secretary Pierre Salinger had left the Johnson administration earlier in the year to run for the Senate in California with the backing of Jesse Unruh, the Speaker of the house in the California House of Representatives and Brown's rival for control of the state party. Gladwin Hill, "Salinger Winner in Bid for Senate," *New York Times*, 3 June 1964.

46. The compromise Pacific Southwest Water Plan had been motivated in part by the June 1963 Supreme Court case of *Arizona v. California*, in which the court allocated a fixed, specific amount of water to each state in the lower Colorado basin according to a formula that in effect granted Arizona the right to build the Central Arizona Project. The Court based these allocations, however, on outdated estimates of annual water flow, which meant that the Interior Department would have to allocate annual shortfalls among the states. Kermit Gordon to Johnson, 10:04 A.M., 12 May 1964, in McKee, *The Presidential Recordings, Johnson*, vol. 6, *April 14, 1964–May 31, 1964*, pp. 596–99.

47. Since taking office, Johnson had worked to cut unnecessary spending and create an image of fiscal frugality.

President Johnson: Are governors, senators and governors—I think I've got to have some leaders to kind of help take charge because we're going to be worse after the bill than it was before if we don't.

Russell: Yeah [*unclear*]—

President Johnson: And they're demanding I send troops in. Last night, St. Augustine just raising hell, and I told them, "Go call the governor [Farris Bryant].[48] Tell the governor to send his highway patrol in, his national guard, that I didn't want to take over a state, that I" . . . So they did, but I don't know whether he did or not.[49] He's a pretty good little governor, but he's tough as a boot.

Russell: Yeah, Farris is a pretty tough little fellow. He had the state police over there for a while.

President Johnson: Well, I know it, but he's off running around this governors' conference, and they're threatening Martin Luther King, and he's down there wanting to get shot.[50]

Russell: Yeah, he don't want to get shot, except by a fellow with—who's got a camera in his hand. [*The President chuckles.*] That's the only way he wants to get shot. Some fellow's got a Kodak can shoot him.

President Johnson: Well, I see you and John Stennis got your pictures all over the paper.[51] You ought to open your eyes, though, goddamn them, make them quit taking with [*unclear*]. You took that picture like Lyndon Johnson, having my eyes shut.

Russell: [*Chuckles.*] Well, I . . . I'm not very photogenic as you are.

President Johnson: Somebody said you made a hell of a speech yesterday, closing it up.[52] Were you proud of it?

Russell: Yeah, I was, perhaps, except they got it so screwed up that I couldn't recognize the stenographer's notes. It said they'd all got worn out over here at Bob Byrd's one-man effort, and that [*the President chuck-*

---

48. Farris Bryant served as the Democratic governor of Florida from 1961 to 1965.

49. Governor Bryant had deployed the Florida State Police to St. Augustine on 10 June. John Herbers, "Police Rout Mob at St. Augustine," *New York Times*, 11 June 1964.

50. Farris Bryant was attending the 56th Annual National Governors' Conference in Cleveland. Douglas B. Cornell, "Governors End Conference with GOP Show Sidetracked," *Washington Post*, 11 June 1964. On 11 June, Martin Luther King Jr. and 12 or 13 other civil rights protestors were arrested for attempting to integrate a St. Augustine restaurant. "King Arrested in St. Augustine Racial Protest," *Washington Post*, 12 June 1964; Taylor Branch, *Pillar of Fire: America in the King Years 1963–65* (New York: Touchstone, 1998), pp. 338–40.

51. John Stennis was a Democratic senator from Mississippi.

52. Johnson was referring to Senator Russell's final speech before the successful cloture vote on 10 June. Without any apparent recognition of the irony in his choice of words, the defeated segregationist had referred to civil rights supporters as a "lynch mob." He had also argued that the rationales for the bill were similar to those for "a purely socialistic or communistic system." *Congressional Quarterly Almanac*, 1964, vol. 20, pp. 367–69.

les] I got the damn notes back, and I couldn't remember a word I'd said, and I finally just threw them on the floor and told Bill Bates to try to make them make some sense, and . . .[53]

President Johnson: Bob Byrd just stood to the last, didn't he?

Russell: Yeah, he sure did.

President Johnson: He's a tough little—

Russell: He's tough as hell.

President Johnson: He's a good little boy—

Russell: Yes, he—

President Johnson: Good little boy. I had old John Lewis and all of his coal men in last week for him just to try to help him a little bit.[54]

Well, I'll think about McCone and Ball and Westmoreland, and you try to give me two more names in the next 48 hours.

Russell: Well, I'll try to, but—

President Johnson: OK.

Russell: —out of those three, Westmoreland is the best man. He's tough, he's smart as hell, he understands human nature, yet he's an excellent officer. And he's a scholar, too.

President Johnson: How did the Congress react to our going in and doing this bombing?[55]

Russell: They don't know about it.

President Johnson: Mm-hmm.

Russell: Not over a dozen know about it, but I think all of them would approve of it if they did.

President Johnson: Well, now, we're going to continue these reconnaissance flights as needed and as we must have them, and we're going to send in armed people, and if they shoot at us, we're going to shoot back.

Russell: Well, that's just like A.W. told you, that's the American inclination. I—

President Johnson: Well, now, [Mike] Mansfield's got a—

---

53. Robert Byrd was a Democratic senator from West Virginia, a position he would hold until his death in June 2010. On the final night of the filibuster, Byrd had delivered a 14-hour, 13-minute speech against the civil rights bill—still more than ten hours short of Strom Thurmond's record, set during debate over the 1957 Civil Rights Act. Bill Bates remains unidentified. See Johnson to Robert Byrd, 4:55 P.M., 10 April 1964, in Shreve and Johnson, *The Presidential Recordings, Johnson*, vol. 5, *March 9, 1964–April 13, 1964*, pp. 956–62.

54. John L. Lewis was president of the Congress of Industrial Organizations (CIO) from 1937 to 1940 and of the United Mine Workers from 1920 until 1960. Both Senator Byrd and John Lewis had attended a meeting of the National Coal Policy Committee at the White House on 5 June.

55. Johnson was referring to the recent U.S. bombing of a Pathet Lao antiaircraft battery in Laos. Johnson had called the congressional leadership on 9 June to inform them of the raid.

Russell: —sometimes think we go too far on it, but—

President Johnson: Mansfield's got a four-page memo saying that I'm getting ourselves involved, and I'm going to get in another war if I do it anymore.[56]

Russell: Yeah. Yeah, he's taking that attitude down there all the way. And I, in a way, share some of his fears.

President Johnson: I do too, but the fear the other way is more.

Russell: I don't know what in the hell to do. I didn't ever want to get messed up down there. I do not agree with those brain trusters who say that this thing has got tremendous strategic and economic value and that we'll lose everything in Southeast . . . in Asia, if we lose Vietnam.[57] I don't think that's true. But I think as a practical matter, we're in there, and I don't know how the hell you can tell the American people you're coming out. There's just no way to do it. They'll think that you've just been whipped and you've been run, you're scared. And it'd be disastrous.

President Johnson: I think that I've got to say that we're—I didn't get you in here, but we're in here by treaty and we can't—our national honor is at stake, and if this treaty is no good, none of them are any good. Therefore, we . . . we've . . . we've . . . we're there, and being there, we've got to conduct ourselves like men. That's number one. Number two, in our own revolution, we wanted freedom, and we naturally look with other people—sympathy with other people who want freedom, and if he'll leave them alone and give them freedom, we'll get out tomorrow. That's the second thing. The third thing, I think that we've got to try to find some proposal some way that . . . like Eisenhower worked out in Korea that we can—

Russell: I wouldn't eliminate the United Nations or some agreement because if . . . I think the people, if you get some sort of agreement all the way around, would understand it, and I don't think that they're some—so damned opposed to . . . they . . . to the United Nations getting in there, and I don't think they'd be opposed to coming out. I don't think American

---

56. "To: The President; From: Senator Mike Mansfield," 9 June 1964, "Folder 4: Vietnam Memos vol. XI: 6/1–13/64," Country File: Vietnam, Box 5, National Security File, Lyndon B. Johnson Library. For a discussion of the Mansfield memorandum, see Johnson to Robert McNamara, 6:20 P.M., 9 June 1964, in this volume.

57. Russell was most likely referring to members of the Kennedy foreign policy team, particularly Robert McNamara and William and McGeorge Bundy, who had shaped U.S. policy in Southeast Asia and had backgrounds either in academia or in highly technical areas of business management.

people want to stay in there. They got enough sense to realize it's just a matter of face that we just can't walk off and leave those people down there [*unclear*] some agreement.

President Johnson: That's right, but . . . U Thant says he won't have anything to do with that part of the world.[58] He just says, "No, we can't do it."

Russell: Who's that?

President Johnson: U Thant of the United Nations.

Russell: Oh. Well, why in the hell does he say that? Ain't he from Burma himself?

President Johnson: Well . . . Yeah, yeah, yeah. Well, but he doesn't want to.

Think about my man, and I'll talk to you in a day or two.

Russell: All right, sir.

President Johnson: Bye.

12:45 P.M.: Unrecorded call to McGeorge Bundy.
12:55 P.M.: Unrecorded call to Bill Moyers.

12:58 P.M.

From McGeorge Bundy[59]

Special Assistant for National Security Affairs Bundy called the President with an apparent follow-up to their unrecorded conversation a few minutes before. He informed the President about the State Department's assessment of the advisability of a possible U.S. threat to hurt the Greek tourist industry by imposing travel warnings unless Greece moderated its policy on the Cyprus conflict. Johnson would meet with Greek Prime Minister George Papandreou at the White House on June 24, and the conversation may have involved the development of a talking point for that meeting.

---

58. A native of Burma (now officially known as Myanmar) in Southeast Asia, U Thant served as secretary-general of the United Nations from 1961 to 1971.
59. Tape WH6406.05, Citation #3682, Recordings of Telephone Conversations—White House Series, Recordings and Transcripts of Conversations and Meetings, Lyndon B. Johnson Library.

Bundy is on hold for approximately 50 seconds.

McGeorge Bundy: I talked to Phil Talbot.[60] The Secretary of State is out on business at the moment in . . . hosting a luncheon. The . . . he says the worry he has about the tourist threat is simply that we might not in fact be able to carry it through and that the Greek response would be, "Hell, it's only the Turkish threat to invade that's creating danger." I think, myself, that isn't quite right because I think you can say, "Look, you people are driving them into this corner, and while this tension is high, obviously there *is* a question, and there may come a point at which our people will have to respond to questions saying that we don't whole-heartedly recommend travel." I wouldn't make it as a threat. I think *that* is correct because the Greeks would feel that we were browbeating them and it was the Turks who were sinning. Whatever may be the rights and wrongs, that would be—as a fact, that the tension may in fact feed back upon both our people and their economies, I think it is worth saying.

President Johnson: All right.

Bundy: Yes, sir.

1:00 P.M.: Unrecorded call to Bill Moyers.

1:02 P.M.: Unrecorded call to Jack Valenti.

1:02 P.M.–1:32 P.M.: Off-the-record meeting with Greek Ambassador to the United States Alexander A. Matsas, Assistant Secretary of State Phillips Talbot, and National Security Council staff member Robert W. Komer.

1:40 P.M.: Lady Bird Johnson entered the Oval Office to ask about Johnson's lunch plans.

1:42 P.M.–1:45 P.M.: Off-the-record meeting with International Telephone and Telegraph Company (ITT) President Harold S. Geneen and Senator Vance Hartke of Indiana.

1:47 P.M.–2:07 P.M.: Off-the-record meeting with Senator Mike Monroney of Oklahoma and Oklahoma Democratic senatorial nominee Fred R. Harris and his wife; pictures taken by Cecil Stoughton.

2:06 P.M.: Unrecorded call to George Reedy.

2:11 P.M.: Attempted to return to the Mansion for lunch, but was stopped by Valenti, who informed him that he still had another visitor to see in the office.

2:13 P.M.: Off-the-record meeting with John Miller Baer, a former North Dakota congressman (1917–1921) and a political car-

---

60. Phillips Talbot was assistant secretary of state for Near Eastern and South Asian affairs.

toonist and journalist for union publications. Baer presented the President with an original cartoon.

2:15 P.M.: Went to the White House Mansion for lunch with Lady Bird Johnson, Mrs. J. Hugh Powell, and Mrs. A.W. Moursund.

2:30 P.M.: Returned to the office. Read newspapers in the outer office before entering the Oval Office.

2:36 P.M.: Unrecorded call to Reedy.

2:40 P.M.: Reedy joined the President and went over the transcript for the day's press briefing.

3:02 P.M.: Unrecorded call to Moyers.

3:05 P.M.

To Dorothy Nichols[61]

The President initially requested that a call be placed to Special Assistant and speechwriter Horace Busby, who was unavailable. Johnson spoke instead with secretary Dorothy Nichols and asked her if she knew whether Busby had been talking to members of the press such as *Time*'s Hugh Sidey about the internal workings of the White House office and, specifically, about Johnson's speechwriting team. Nichols attempted, in vain, to defend Busby.

President Johnson: Dorothy?

Dorothy Nichols: Hello. Yes, sir.

President Johnson: Has Hugh Sidey been in that office in the last week?[62]

Nichols: No, sir.

President Johnson: Have you heard from him? Has he called?

Nichols: He has called. I do not know whether Buzz [Horace Busby] has talked to him or not.

President Johnson: He says that he got the story from Buzz about Dick Goodwin writing a lot of speeches, and specific ones, and it just guts me.[63]

---

61. Tape WH6406.05, Citation #3683, Recordings of Telephone Conversations—White House Series, Recordings and Transcripts of Conversations and Meetings, Lyndon B. Johnson Library.
62. Hugh Sidey was a Washington correspondent for *Time* magazine.
63. Richard Goodwin was a speechwriter for both presidents Kennedy and Johnson. Johnson may have been referring to an article about Johnson's staff in the 29 May issue of *Time*, which noted that "Goodwin cranks out major texts in far less time than Kennedy's Ted Sorensen did, and Johnson insists that he does it with just as much style." "The New Team," *Time*, 29 May 1964, pp. 18–19.

And Joe Kraft says the same thing, and I just can't believe Buzz would do me that way, but—[64]

Nichols: I don't think he ever would do that. I've never heard him say *anything* like that.

President Johnson: Has Joe Kraft called or been around there?

Nichols: No, sir, not to my knowledge.

President Johnson: Mm-hmm. Where is Buzz now?

Nichols: Oh . . . Buzz is . . . had a luncheon appointment with Tom Wicker . . . today.[65]

President Johnson: Mm-hmm. [*Pauses.*] Well, he's seeing a press, and it's just causing us all kinds of trouble over here. And he doesn't know what's going on, and he's speculating, and he's telling them things, and I guess he's going to be prominent with them, but it hurts us. I wished he'd stay away from the press. He's not with the press office, and it just creates a hell of a problem for me. I don't know what to—how to avoid it. I've told him to please be careful and not do this.

Nichols: Mr. Johnson, I know they're after *him*, but I did not know he was—

President Johnson: Well, if he's going to lunch with them.

Nichols: —telling *them* anything.

President Johnson: Well, you see, if he's going to lunch with them, honey, he's got to say something.

Nichols: Yeah.

President Johnson: You know that. When you go out with a man, you're going to say something to him. And that's what he's doing. Tom Wicker just gave us a hell of a lecture over here, and poor George [Reedy] is trying to do the best he can and doing a good job, and there are people just cutting us to pieces from our outsiders, and it's my own people, and I don't believe they know they're doing it. Liz [Carpenter] gave a big story out about Dick Goodwin going to the [LBJ] Ranch in his tuxedo and gave it to Les [Carpenter].[66] Les wrote it up, and now *Time*'s doing a

---

64. Joe Kraft was a columnist for the *Washington Star* who was known to be sympathetic to Robert F. Kennedy and, more generally, a critic of the Johnson administration from the left. See Dean Rusk to Johnson, 12:47 P.M., 13 February 1964, in Germany and Johnson, *The Presidential Recordings, Johnson, vol. 3, January 1964*, p. 460.

65. Tom Wicker was a member of the White House press corps from the *New York Times*.

66. Liz Carpenter served as Lady Bird Johnson's press secretary. Leslie Carpenter was a reporter for the *Washington Post*. He had recently written that during the June fund-raiser in New York City, Johnson had invited Richard Goodwin to join him for a trip to the LBJ Ranch immediately after the event. Goodwin accompanied the President to Texas even though he had no clothes other than the tuxedo that he had worn to the fund-raiser. Leslie Carpenter, "Washington Beat . . . ," *Washington Post*, 6 June 1964.

special article on Dick Goodwin, and they got the information from Buzz, according to *Time.*

Nichols: On Goodwin?

President Johnson: Yeah, that Goodwin wrote the Michigan speech and Goodwin wrote this other speech, and he's telling them—[67]

Nichols: Mr. Johnson, I have heard him say that he's not writing speeches. I have . . . I just can't *believe* he's saying to any of them—

President Johnson: That's what—

Nichols: —that somebody else is writing speeches.

President Johnson: Well, he oughtn't to. He ought to just say he knows nothing about that.

Nichols: He's been—

President Johnson: And last week he told them, though, that he was a Rose Garden specialist and admitted that he had written one in the Rose Garden.

Nichols: Well . . .

President Johnson: For one of the little—

Nichols: Never in my hearing has he ever said anything he did. He's been very . . .

President Johnson: Sure oughtn't to, and I'd stay away from them. If I were him, I'd just tell them I've got another lunch. Tell him I'll buy his lunch if he's got to go to them.

Nichols: I think this is the first time he has been to lunch—well, it's the first time he's been to lunch. The guy goes through the day without lunch most of the time.

President Johnson: Mm-hmm. [*Whistles.*]

Nichols: And has refused over and over again to see people who have called him up, press people. He's been avoiding them like the plague, and I don't know if he's seen them—

President Johnson: Mm-hmm. . . . Sure wish he would. I wish he'd—

Nichols: If he's seen them and talked to them, it is not in the office, it has not been at lunch.

President Johnson: Well, I don't care where it is, if he talks to Hugh Sidey.

Nichols: I know.

---

67. Johnson was referring to his highly acclaimed commencement address at the University of Michigan on 22 May, which had been written primarily by Goodwin. The speech marked Johnson's first extended explication of the term *Great Society.* See Conclusion to 21 May 1964 in McKee, *The Presidential Recordings, Johnson,* vol. 6, *April 14, 1964–May 31, 1964,* p. 806–9.

President Johnson: Hugh's quoting him, and I believe that—I don't believe he'd just be deliberately lying.

Nichols: Well . . . I would tell him—

President Johnson: Not anything . . . not anything you and I can do about it, and I wouldn't tell him anything. I'll talk to him. You tell him I want to talk to him as soon as he comes in and don't discuss any of this conversation with him.

Nichols: All right, sir—

President Johnson: I just, I just—

Nichols: —that would be better, I know.

President Johnson: Yeah . . . yeah. But I'm going to have to either let him go, or stop it, or lock the door on him or something. I just got to keep my little amateurs away from these newspaper people telling them what's happening.

Nichols: I'm completely shocked with what you've told me, Mr. President. I'm just—

President Johnson: I am too, but—

Nichols: I just thought he was doing . . . leaning over backwards to keep him out of the press.

President Johnson: Well . . . each one of the people like to talk to the press, you know. They just like to, plain do. And they told me, and I knew Hugh Sidey talked to him, or he wouldn't have said he talked to him.

Nichols: Oh, dear.

President Johnson: And . . .

Nichols: He's been right here through the day, as I say. And turned down calls from people. And talk and . . . finally take the call and not accept the invitation to lunch, and so on. I guess they're after him pretty much, but—

President Johnson: They are. They're going to get him and get Goodwin. They're going to be the first two to go because he's talking, and I think he might be a little hurt that Goodwin's doing some of my speeches. Maybe he's a little jealous, I don't know.

Nichols: I don't think so, Mr. President.

President Johnson: Well, he sure oughtn't to be telling that.

Nichols: Um . . .

President Johnson: Anyway, I've got to see Sidey in 10 minutes, and I'll—

Nichols: In 10 minutes?

President Johnson: —do my best, and just let him go, and maybe he'll get back by the middle of the afternoon; 3:10's a hell of a time to be at lunch anyway. And if he comes in, though, anytime, tell him to call me.

Nichols: Right.
President Johnson: Thank you, darling.
Nichols: All right.
President Johnson: And don't talk about the details.
Nichols: Right.

3:10 P.M.

From George Reedy[68]

Almost immediately, George Reedy called to report that Hugh Sidey was in the office and asking about the Johnson administration's speechwriting process.

President Johnson: Yes?
Office Secretary: We have a rush memo from Bill [Moyers] and two new polls. Can we bring them in?
President Johnson: Yeah, I've seen them, but bring them on in.
Office Secretary: All right. George Reedy's on 9-0.
President Johnson: Yes, George.
George Reedy: Mr. President, Hugh Sidey is here and asking me about Mr. [Richard] Goodwin's role. I was wondering if he could come back and see you—
President Johnson: Role in what?
Reedy: As a speechwriter, as an adviser in the White House.
President Johnson: Well, tell him he's neither, but I'll be glad to talk to him about what he does if it's any of his business, any of his interest.
Reedy: OK, sir.
President Johnson: Bring him on in.
Reedy: You bet.
President Johnson: [*to someone in the office*] Hurry up, honey, right quick. George is coming in [*unclear*].

3:12 P.M.: Met with *Time*'s Hugh Sidey and George Reedy.

---

68. Tape WH6406.05, Citation #3684, Recordings of Telephone Conversations—White House Series, Recordings and Transcripts of Conversations and Meetings, Lyndon B. Johnson Library.

3:19 P.M.

From Olin Johnston; preceded by Office Conversation
with Hugh Sidey and George Reedy[69]

With Hugh Sidey and George Reedy still in the office, President Johnson took a call from South Carolina Senator Olin Johnston, who offered an encouraging report on the prospects for passage of the federal pay bill and inquired about the successor to Internal Revenue Service (IRS) Commissioner Mortimer Caplin.

Before a secretary notified Johnson of the call, the recording system captured a segment of Johnson's comments to Sidey about the administration's speechwriting process and the responsibilities of various members of Johnson's staff. The specific subject under dispute consisted of the authorship of Johnson's important May 22 "Great Society" speech at the University of Michigan.

President Johnson: [*to Hugh Sidey, in the office*] . . . got to have [George] Ball, got to [*buzzer sounds*] have [Sargent] Shriver, call them together. He never is called on as I know of, as an adviser on policy questions. He makes suggestions that are a result of research of agreements that we've made. Every day I have 10 to 20 meetings, and I have to be briefed for each one of them, and I ask various staff members. Horace Busby brings me certain memos, but he doesn't turn out any speeches. This boy does the same thing. Both of them are pretty competent folks, but I wouldn't say that they're either advisers as such because I've got a department that handles each specific thing. If it's national defense or foreign policy, it's [McGeorge] Bundy. If it's legislation, it's [Larry] O'Brien. If it's [Theodore] Sorensen's work, general counsel, it's Mike Feldman.[70] He writes some speeches; he prepares all of my orders; he does primarily what Sorensen did. He reviews the notes that we put together, after I sit down with Bill Moyer[s] and Jack Valenti and George [Reedy] and say, "Here's what I'd like to do at San Francisco next week." And I

---

69. Tape WH6406.06, Citation #3685, Recordings of Telephone Conversations—White House Series, Recordings and Transcripts of Conversations and Meetings, Lyndon B. Johnson Library.
70. Ted Sorensen had served as special counsel and a speechwriter to President Kennedy beginning in 1961. After staying on for Johnson in the immediate aftermath of the assassination, he left the administration at the beginning of 1964 to become, with President Johnson's help, the president of the Motion Picture Association. Myer "Mike" Feldman had taken over many of Sorensen's responsibilities.

did that this morning for an hour with Jack Valenti, and he just writes them down. Then we get the material from whatever . . . it may be Atomic Energy [Committee] we want it from, or it may be Council of Economic Advisers we want it from. Jack pulls it together and . . .

[*on phone*] Hello?

Office Secretary: Senator Olin Johnston is calling you from the floor. He's not on the phone yet.

President Johnson: All right. Get him on—put him on.

An exchange between the secretary and operator attempting to connect Johnston with the President ensues. The recording resumes with the office conversation.

President Johnson: Whoever led you to believe this [*unclear*] on the outside and didn't know.

Hugh Sidey: Yeah.

President Johnson: I'm sure that nobody [*unclear, followed by an unclear comment by someone in the room*]. I can tell you the Ann Arbor speech came as a result of a book I read and some work that I did with Barbara Ward, if that satisfies you.[71] Dick Goodwin, as far as I know, never saw it.[72]

Sidey: Right.

President Johnson: It doesn't make any difference, but I just want to show you that somebody's trying to tear us apart from you, and I resent that to be—hell. So that people on the outside, the edge, they want to appear that they know something that they don't know.

Sidey: Well, not [*unclear*] will talk to me on [*unclear*] matters.

President Johnson: Well, because they ought to be working. That's not their job to spend their time telling *Time* about who does what. I'll tell them if they want to know.

[*on phone*] Hello? Hi, Senator, glad to hear you.

Olin Johnston: Just fine. I want you to know that we're going to pass this bill over here in the Senate, but the Republicans have been away several times there wasn't a one [*unclear*]—[73]

---

71. Also known as Lady Jackson, Barbara Ward was a British economist and the author of *The Rich Nations and the Poor Nations*, a study of poverty in the developing world that had influenced President Johnson. Johnson required his staff to read Ward's book. Philip Geyelin, *Lyndon B. Johnson and the World* (New York: Praeger, 1966), pp. 38–39.

72. This comment was almost certainly inaccurate; the Ann Arbor "Great Society" speech had been drafted by Goodwin, with input from Bill Moyers and historian (and Johnson adviser) Eric Goldman. Eric Goldman, *The Tragedy of Lyndon Johnson* (New York: Dell Publishing, 1968), pp. 194–95; Merle Miller, *Lyndon: An Oral Biography* (New York: G.P. Putnam's Sons, 1980), pp. 483–84.

73. Johnston was referring to the federal pay bill. The South Carolina senator chaired the Senate Committee on the Post Office and Civil Service, which had jurisdiction over the bill.

President Johnson: I know that, I know that.

Johnston: So they're trying to put the rub on us, and—

President Johnson: That's right.

Johnston: —we need to get them to go along with us.

President Johnson: I sure hope you can.

Johnston: We will. Another thing I was calling about: I was talking to [Sam] Ervin and [B. Everett] Jordan, my colleague here, about a matter.[74] Have you selected—and, why, if you have, of course, let's just close the door—in [Mortimer] Caplin's place?[75]

President Johnson: Yes.

Johnston: You have?

President Johnson: Yeah.

Johnston: I didn't know. They had—

President Johnson: Yeah. . . . Yeah, I've done that before he left, before he even announced it.

Johnston: [*with Johnson acknowledging*] I see. Well, that's the only thing I wanted to know. If you hadn't, there's a boy in North Carolina who's been chairman down there that's pretty active in politics.

President Johnson: I have, Olin, and I appreciate it, and I'll be in touch with you, and we'll talk about some of these things, but that's already behind us.

Johnston: Good. All right, then.

President Johnson: Thank you, my friend.

Johnston: Good.

President Johnson: Go on, get that out this week.

Johnston: We'll do our best.

President Johnson: All right.

---

74. Sam Ervin and B. Everett Jordan were Democratic senators from North Carolina.

75. Appointed by President Kennedy in 1961, Mortimer Caplin was resigning as commissioner of the Internal Revenue Service. Vance Hartke, the Democratic senator from Indiana, had also called about this appointment. See Hartke to Johnson, 12:06 P.M., 6 May 1964, in McKee, *The Presidential Recordings, Johnson*, vol. 6, *April 14, 1964–May 31, 1964*, pp. 489–90. IRS Chief Counsel Sheldon S. Cohen would replace Caplin as commissioner.

3:55 P.M.

From Larry O'Brien and Wilbur Mills[76]

While still meeting with Sidey and Reedy, Johnson received a call from Special Assistant for Congressional Relations Larry O'Brien, who informed him that the House had just passed the federal pay bill. O'Brien was with Arkansas Congressman Wilbur Mills, and much of the call consisted of a conversation between the President and the powerful House Ways and Means Committee chairman that focused primarily on legislative and policy strategies for advancing some combination of health care legislation and amendments to Social Security. Mills was seeking a compromise position that would advance some form of health care legislation through the Ways and Means Committee and the full House, while also allowing those members who had previously opposed the administration-backed King-Anderson Medicare bill to save face while still supporting the bill. He also appeared to hope that the Senate might pass a stronger version of the legislation, which could then be the basis for final legislation after minor modification in conference committee. Ultimately, however, Mills would not throw his full support to Medicare until 1965. As he had in a June 9 conversation with Mills, the President sought to convince the chairman of the legislation's social and political merits, as well as its centrality for both men's historical legacy.[77]

President Johnson: . . . the little . . . by joining the little countries [*unclear*]—[*buzzer sounds*]—and taking young people who'll go [*unclear*].
    Unidentified: [*Unclear.*]
    President Johnson: But . . .
    Unidentified: [*Unclear*]—
    President Johnson: Looking at it [*unclear*] in this office, [*unclear*].
    Unidentified: [*Unclear*], thank you.
    President Johnson: I haven't spent . . . [Richard] Goodwin spent one day on the [LBJ] Ranch with . . . the ranch surrounding it, because we were going down—I was going to the University of Texas, and I wanted

---

76. Tape WH6406.06, Citations #3686 and #3687, Recordings of Telephone Conversations—White House Series, Recordings and Transcripts of Conversations and Meetings, Lyndon B. Johnson Library.
77. Wilbur Mills to Johnson, 9:55 A.M., 9 June 1964, in this volume.

him like [Ted] Sorensen to have a chance to see the ranch, like I had George [Reedy] down, like I've had you down. He's one that had never seen it and is working. Had him down.

The President answers the secretary's page, who reports that Larry O'Brien is on the line.

President Johnson: Yeah? Yes, sir.

Larry O'Brien: Well, the pay bill has passed: 243–157.

President Johnson: Congratulations! Congratulations! That's wonderful. 243 to 157.

O'Brien: That's right.

President Johnson: All right, now that—

O'Brien: I'm meeting here with a mutual friend of ours who just walked in off the floor. I'd like to have him say hello to you.

President Johnson: I want to talk to him, but wait just a minute now. That gives you your . . . That gives you your tax bill, your civil rights bill, your farm bill, your pay bill. Now, you get me a rule on poverty next week, and we're really moving. When you going to get it reported in the Senate, your pay bill?

O'Brien: Well, we'll . . . [*Johnson attempts to speak*]. Things [have] been getting a little sticky over there, you know.

President Johnson: Mike Monroney told me this morning the vote's 72 against 10,000 [dollars].[78]

O'Brien: Well, he . . .

President Johnson: And O[lin]—

O'Brien: It's [*unclear*] that he's done a good job of lobbying the damn committee.

President Johnson: All right, that's what he told me. He was in here and said they'd never report 10,000. I told him they had to, we committed to.

O'Brien: Yeah.

President Johnson: But Olin Johnston called me and wanted to name a big Cabinet officer or sub-Cabinet officer. I told him we had no vacancy, but then he said he's going to get the bill out, and I said, "When?" He said, "Pretty soon." I said, "Please do it this week." I called Mike and asked— Mike Mansfield—and asked him to try to come in a little later and let

---

78. Mike Monroney was a Democratic senator from Oklahoma. He had met with the President earlier in the day. The original version of the federal employees pay bill had included $10,000 congressional, Cabinet, and judicial pay raises, but the resubmitted version of the bill cut the raise to $7,500 in order to blunt opposition to the bill. *Congressional Quarterly Almanac*, 1964, vol. 20, pp. 416–19.

them have a morning or two this week to report this pay bill now before the opposition builds up to it.

O'Brien: Yeah, yeah.

President Johnson: Let me talk to who—who you got there?

O'Brien: Wilbur Mills.

President Johnson: Wonderful, wonderful!

O'Brien: I'll put him right on, Mr. President.

President Johnson: All right, are you going—are y'all going to come to see me together, or are you going to wait sometime?

O'Brien: Well, we'll see—

President Johnson: All right.

O'Brien: —they just walked in. They just finished the roll call, so we haven't chatted yet.

President Johnson: All right. . . . All right, OK.

Wilbur Mills: Yes, sir. You feeling all right?

President Johnson: I'm just feeling good. Did your wife ever get all right?[79]

Mills: [*with the President acknowledging*] Oh, she's able to do some things. Still not back completely yet, but she's a lot better.

President Johnson: I went up to Massachusetts yesterday and had a . . .

Mills: Glad to see you were up there.

President Johnson: Had a mighty good meeting.

Did you see the little Negro girl from Little Rock that was here yesterday?[80]

Mills: No . . . Bill Fulbright and I were supposed to have had lunch with them yesterday or the day before—yesterday—and neither one of us could attend.[81] We had to send our administrative assistants to eat with them. But they were both—both of them were very much impressed with all three of these—

President Johnson: You sure would have been proud of Arkansas.

Mills: Yeah.

President Johnson: Now, just . . . you and Bill Fulbright, and the Rhodes scholar, and the Harvard graduate, why, you'd have looked a—that little girl was integrating the first group, and I was out there last

---

79. Clarine "Polly" Mills had been ill for several months.
80. Johnson was referring to Jacquelyn Faye Evans, who had received one of the presidential scholar awards given at a White House reception the previous day. Evans had been one of the small group of African American students who in 1960 had integrated Little Rock High School under the protection of federal troops. She had earned straight A's and won a scholarship to Radcliffe College. "'A Nourishing of Excellence,'" *Time*, 12 June 1964, p. 59.
81. J. William Fulbright was a Democratic senator from Arkansas.

night about 10:30 when they about finished up. Lady Bird and I went out to tell them good night and thank them for coming, and she was on the front row right with "A" begins with Arkansas, and . . . I talked to her, and she was as cultured as she can be and smart as a whip, and I was real proud of her.

Mills: Well, she—I understand, she's smart as a—

President Johnson: Well, you had—

Mills: —[*unclear*] three.

President Johnson: You had three.

Mills: Yes, two of them were [*unclear*].

President Johnson: You know, we hear a lot about football players.

Mills: Yeah.

President Johnson: But the old boy got up last night telling a little joke, and he said, "Well, I'm so proud to come down here and give my talent." But said, "Heretofore, I've always given it to the heroes, the football players." And said, "They're back home driving beer trucks now." And said, "I'm glad to be out here with the people who are going to own the city." [*Laughs.*]

Mills: Now, incidentally, we're coming up Wednesday and Thursday this week, I understand, on our excise and debt ceiling.[82]

President Johnson: We got a list from you, and we're going to work that list very care—

Mills: Well, I think we're in good shape, fairly good shape on all that. There's some of them that maybe you can touch that none of the rest of us could do . . . not that whole list, now, I don't want to worry you with all that because Larry and Walter [Jenkins] and the rest of them can make some of them. [*President Johnson covers the telephone receiver, muffling his voice.*] But I've picked up some that I had on the list already.

President Johnson: [*Makes a muffled, unclear comment to someone in the office.*] Wilbur?

Mills: Yes.

President Johnson: I got a poll in Vermont that I've just looked at, and do you know what my weakest point is?

Mills: What is it?

President Johnson: We've done nothing for the old folks.

Mills: I know it, now. We've got—

---

82. Mills was referring to the upcoming House votes on bills authorizing a one-year extension of the federal excise tax and a $9 billion increase in the federal debt limit. *Congressional Quarterly Almanac*, 1964, vol. 20, pp. 540, 582.

President Johnson: It's not on any particular part of the old folks, *all* the old folks, and I've got two—

Mills: Yeah. . . . [*Unclear*] do something about it. Now, I've got in mind that this cash benefit increase is going to be worth a whole lot, and then, too, I want to lower the age—and I've already talked to the Secretary about it—for widows only where they can begin drawing a benefit at age 60, which suits him all right, he said.[83] They'd draw on an actuarially reduced amount, which wouldn't cost any more. Labor would go along with that. They don't like to have us do it if it's going to cost any more.

And then, too, I want to set up a category under public assistance—you think about it—of aid to widows who are 50 years, 55, something like that or older, who are unemployed.

President Johnson: Mm-hmm.

Mills: Now, we've got a provision in the Aid to Dependent Children to take care of the unemployed father.[84] You remember that?

President Johnson: Mm-hmm, mm-hmm.

Mills: [*with the President acknowledging*] We did that just a year or two ago. This is a . . . would be a state program in which the state would start it. We would participate just like we do with old-age assistance.

But I think one of the most serious problems we've got is the problem of the woman who's left a widow at 50, 55, 60 years of age [*the President whispers "OK" to someone*] who's never had a job, wouldn't know how to go about getting one. Nobody wants her, and she can't be trained to anything. Now, what's she going to do, die before she can get her Social Security at 62? That's her present question. And I want to—whatever we do on Social Security, I want to put some things like that in this year. I believe it would help us.

---

83. Mills was probably referring to Secretary of Health, Education, and Welfare Anthony Celebrezze, or possibly Secretary of Labor Willard Wirtz. As passed by the House of Representatives, the Social Security Amendments of 1964 would have granted a 5 percent increase in monthly Social Security payments. The amendments were adopted after the Ways and Means Committee on 24 June delayed a vote on Medicaid for the year. Later in the summer, the Senate passed the Medicare bill, but a conference committee was unable to work out a compromise between the two Social Security–related bills, leading to the demise for the year of both Medicare and the Social Security Amendments. *Congressional Quarterly Almanac*, 1964, vol. 20, pp. 234–40.

84. Mills was referring to the Aid to Families With Dependent Children–Unemployed Parent (AFDC-UP) program, which extended eligibility for the primary federal welfare program to any unemployed parent, whether male or female. It had been established in 1961. Previously, AFDC had covered only families with a dead or absent parent (usually male). *Congressional Quarterly Almanac*, 87th Cong., 1st sess., 1961, vol. 17 (Washington, DC: Congressional Quarterly Service, 1962), pp. 280–82.

President Johnson: And find some way to do something on [the] medical thing. Just a little.

Mills: Well, that's [*unclear*] up to [Robert M.] Ball, now, on—[85]

President Johnson: Well, you've got—if you go for it, you got 13 votes and—

Mills: Yeah.

President Johnson: —[can] probably get 14. Right, Democrats. You get 14 out of 15 Democrats, that's about as strong as you'll ever get.[86]

Let me read you this. "Providing jobs: favorable, 59. Selected national issues, their importance, and President Johnson's job rating on them." This was taken in June '64 by Oliver Quayle, a survey of the presidential race in Michigan.[87] Now, I want to just give you a summary, but I believe . . . I believe a good deal of this. [*Pauses.*]

Mills: Let me ask you—

President Johnson: "Johnson, all voters, 57; [Henry Cabot] Lodge, 43." This is Michigan. "Johnson-Nixon, 60; Johnson, 60, Nixon, 40. Johnson, 84, [Barry] Goldwater, 16." Now, that is . . . that is in Michigan in June. Now, they say, "Give us the issues and how you rank him." "To provide jobs"—I guess that's our tax bill and other things—"59, favorable, 41, unfavorable. Lowering taxes: 67, favorable; 33, unfavorable. Keeping the economy healthful: 71, favorable, 29, unfavorable. Working for peace and disarmament: 74 and 26. Handling [Nikita] Khrushchev and the Russians: 61, 39. Maintaining a strong defense: 76, 24. Obtaining unity among our allies: 54, 46. Supporting the United Nations: 73, 27. [*deliberately*] More help for older people: 43, favorable, 57, unfavorable."

Mills: Yeah. Mm-hmm. May be true of us everywhere.

President Johnson: "Congressional reform: favorable, 43; 57, unfavorable. Latin American relations: 52, favorable; 48, unfavorable. Handling Panama: 66 to 34. Catching the Russians in space: 63 to 37." That's what I've been strong on, you see. But more help for older people—that's Michigan.

[*to someone in the office*] Do you know what day in June?

---

85. Robert M. Ball served as commissioner of the Social Security Administration and was deeply involved in the negotiations over the Medicare bill. Along with Mills, Ball was one of the leading experts on the Social Security system. Edward D. Berkowitz, *Robert Ball and the Politics of Social Security* (Madison: University of Wisconsin Press, 2003).

86. Johnson was referring to Democrats on the House Ways and Means Committee, which had jurisdiction over the administration's Medicare bill.

87. Oliver Quayle was a prominent pollster whose work was frequently employed by the White House. Robert Dallek, *Flawed Giant: Lyndon Johnson and His Times 1961–1973* (New York: Oxford University Press, 1998).

Mills: What day?

Walter Jenkins: The last ten days [*unclear*].

President Johnson: I've got two that are coming out Sunday, June the 14th from Gallup.[88] And what people like and what they dislike. "Handling civil rights, 6 percent, dislike; handling foreign policy, 4 percent; poverty, 2 percent dislike; personal conduct: driving fast, pulling dogs' ears [*Mills chuckles*], et cetera. Bobby Baker"—that, this is a major part of the Republican campaign—"2 percent dislike it. Nothing I dislike, 68 percent." [*Laughs, and Mills joins in.*]

Mills: That's pretty good.

President Johnson: What they like: "His personality, 20; experience, 10; dynamic approach, 8; War on Poverty, 5; domestic policies, generally, 34; other answers, 14; no opinion, 4. Is there anything you particularly like about the President? What? Is there anything you particularly dislike? [*reading quickly*] Chief among the lists of strong likes are his personality, his character, he's admired, honesty, friendly, dignity, as well as for desire to help everyone. The reasons cited second [*unclear*] most often [by] this group are those who have helped sustain the President's high popularity ever since he took office after the death of Kennedy. These are his political experience, his dynamic approach to the job, his carrying out the Kennedy policies. Specific programs, policies [of the] Johnson administration such as civil rights, foreign policy, come high on the list. The following tables show the percentage of persons who voiced particular likes and dislikes," and then that lists them.

"Percent President Johnson's popularity holds steady in the latest survey and that shows: approve, 74" . . . No—"latest figures in the trend since Johnson: Do you approve or disapprove of the way Johnson's handling the job: Approve, 79; disapprove, 3; no opinion, 18."

That's unbelievable, isn't it?

Mills: Yes, it is. On this thing, now, here's what I've been trying to do: is to get something that we could say was so different from the [Cecil] King bill itself that those of us who have repeatedly said we wouldn't vote for the King bill could vote for it.[89]

President Johnson: That's exactly right. That's what you've got to do, if you ever make it acceptable.

---

88. George Gallup ran the nation's most prominent polling organization.

89. Representative Cecil R. King, a California Democrat, had sponsored the administration's Medicare bill in the House. New Mexico Democrat Clinton Anderson had sponsored it in the Senate, and it was commonly referred to as the King-Anderson bill. Mills and others on the Ways and Means Committee had opposed the bill. *Congressional Quarterly Almanac*, 1964, vol. 20, p. 232.

Mills: That's right. Now, I'm going to lay it hold for a week, think about it some more, and give the departments an opportunity to think with me, and have these excise taxes on the 15th, 16th, and possibly the morning of the 17th. Then the excise tax bill and the debt ceiling bill on the floor Wednesday and Thursday of next week, so we'll be busy anyway.

President Johnson: Mm-hmm.

Mills: We get back on this Social Security bill, then, the 22nd of June, and I'm going to wind it up that week to where we can have it reported, whatever it is, and ready for House action perhaps even before the Republican convention.[90] We can decide on that, whether we take it up before or after. But we can get—we can wrap—we've got most of our language written so that there won't be a long delay from the time we make our final decision—

President Johnson: If you do that, that'll do more for us this year than any other single thing that we'll do except your tax bill, and that's already behind us. But it'll be the most positive, affirmative, future thing that we'll have.

Mills: Now, let me ask you this to get your judgment on it.

President Johnson: I'd rank it number one.

Mills: If we pass a . . . if I can't get something that I can get more than 13 votes on—I told you in the beginning, and I thought you and I both felt that it ought to get more than that—[91]

President Johnson: God, what percentage you want, 13 out of 15. That's 90 percent, isn't it?

Mills: Yeah, but I mean 13 out of 25.

President Johnson: Oh, no! No, no. Well, you don't ever expect to get the Republicans. They're going to be against *any* proposal I make. All of them against poverty. Every single one of them.

Mills: But they're not always against Social Security. I've got them in a bind if they vote against reporting this bill.

President Johnson: They won't always be against the other either, if you ever give them a taste of it, I'll tell you this. They all voted against Social Security when we enacted it—[92]

Mills: I know.

---

90. The Republican National Convention was set to begin on 13 July in San Francisco.
91. Mills was referring to his desire to have more than a minimum 13–12 majority on the House Ways and Means Committee for a major bill such as Medicare. For a discussion of this position and its implications, see Earle Clements to Johnson, 4:18 P.M., 11 June 1964, in this chapter.
92. Medicare would be an extension of the broad Social Security program.

President Johnson: —when we started it, but they won't do it if you give them a taste of it.

Mills: No, I know that. And they all want to be for these cash benefits, you see.

President Johnson: Mm-hmm.

Mills: This increase in cash benefits, and that's going to—that too is very helpful. The Secretary said yesterday in the committee before we quit that what we're talking about is the last—this three-prong approach he calls it, which would have some hospitalizations connected with Social Security, this cash benefit increase, plus improvements of the Kerr-Mills. [*Unclear*]—[93]

President Johnson: I'd be for all three of those, if you could put that fourth one in on it, your 13. If you didn't, I'd wait until I could get them all together because I think if you don't, why, you just murder the other one, and I think the other one's what's got the sex appeal.[94]

Mills: They have now . . . if we didn't put it in, what—would the Senate put it in?

President Johnson: I don't think so.

Mills: You don't?

President Johnson: I think that—I don't—I doubt they'd ever even take it up. I imagine if you don't get that out until July the 1st, I'll have to get them back here between conventions to handle it.[95] And I just—I would do that if you had it because I think it's the best thing that we can have for 50 states, and I've been in a good many of them and I'm going to a bunch more this weekend.

When I get back next week from California, I will have been in states

---

93. Mills was referring to a compromise proposal apparently made by HEW Secretary Celebrezze. Sponsored by Wilbur Mills and Oklahoma Senator Robert Kerr, the Kerr-Mills Act had been passed by Congress in 1960. It established a program of federal matching grants to state programs that provided means-tested health care coverage for the indigent elderly who could not meet their medical bills but who did not qualify for public assistance. The Kerr-Mills Act gave states discretion about coverage levels, eligibility requirements, and whether to create a program at all. By 1965, nine states had not passed the state programs that could receive Kerr-Mills funds, and most of the remaining states provided highly limited benefits under the program. Julian Zelizer, *Taxing America: Wilbur D. Mills, Congress, and the State, 1945–1975* (New York: Cambridge University Press, 1998).

94. Although Johnson's meaning is somewhat uncertain in this passage, he appears to be referring (here and in the exchange with Mills about the Senate that follows) to the necessity of including hospitalization provisions in any compromise legislative package. Removal of the "sex appeal" of hospitalization insurance would "murder" the overall Medicare bill to such an extent that the Senate would not even consider it. See Zelizer, *Taxing America*, pp. 225–26.

95. The Democratic National Convention in Atlantic City, New Jersey, would begin on 24 August.

that have a hundred million population in the first six months of this year. Like yesterday in Massachusetts, like the day before in Pennsylvania. And when I get through with Michigan and California—I've already been to Michigan and to California too—when I get through with them, this last run, I'll have a hundred million. My judgment is, that is by far the most popular thing that we've ever touched and will do us more good than all the other put together, and I'd put taxes and civil rights and poverty and education bills, all of which we will have passed, I don't think they're in this one's comparison.

Mills: You remember what President Roosevelt said: You don't get any mileage politically out of taxes.

President Johnson: Well, I think we are because we're having prosperity.

Mills: Well, that part, yes, but . . .

President Johnson: I think if you've got—I think that you've got . . . you've got unemployment down to 2.6 [percent] for married men. [*Mills acknowledges.*] So 97.4 married men have jobs, and by God, they show it. Yesterday I saw 200,000 in Worcester, Massachusetts. Every single one of them, Wilbur, were frown—were smiling. Now, when I was here in Hoover's administration, they were frowning and cussing and spitting. But they were all smiling yesterday, and you can sure get a . . . and if you hadn't have passed that tax bill, and hadn't passed a good one, why, we wouldn't have that kind of a sentiment.

Mills: Well, I agree with you.

President Johnson: Look at this poll, now, in six months that I come in, a Democratic administration before an election: December, 79; January, 80; February, 75; March, 73; May, 75; June, 74. Now, we've run from 79 to 74 in 6 months, of all this hectic—problem, and that—the reason it is, people are happy with the prosperity.

Mills: You find that no matter where you go, don't you?

President Johnson: Yes, sir; every place. And if you'll give me that bill, I'll underwrite it, and I'll give you 25, 50 more Democrats too. You just give me the one you were talking about the other day, and . . . you just— I think we can get 14 out of your 15; that's about as unanimous you can get on anything that's controversial.[96] Then I think that you can get 250 votes out there in the House proper, maybe more. I think you'll get 40 or 50 from their side.

Mills: Oh, I can get more than that.

President Johnson: And, if you—

---

96. Johnson was referring, once again, to votes on the Ways and Means Committee.

Mills: [*Unclear.*]

President Johnson: If you get . . . if you get this moderate thing that you're talking about, we'll go to town, and we'll improve it as the years go on, but that'll be the biggest day you ever had and you ever did for your country, I can tell you that. And all these other things are important, but that's the important one.

Mills: Well, we're still working.

President Johnson: OK.

Mills: Fine.

President Johnson: Bye.

Mills: Bye.

4:18 P.M.

From Earle Clements[97]

Johnson's next call came from former Kentucky Governor and Senator Earle Clements, who updated the President on his own conversations about the Medicare bill with Kentucky Representative John Watts, a Democrat and a key swing vote on the House Ways and Means Committee. Watts had apparently expounded on the strategy that Wilbur Mills hinted at in the preceding conversation—finding a face-saving compromise in the Ways and Means Committee and then securing a stronger final bill through conference committee consideration of a Senate-passed version of the full King-Anderson bill favored by the administration.[98] Within weeks, Watts would turn against even the limited version of the bill, undermining the support that Mills needed and leading to the committee's abandonment of Medicare for 1964. The Senate, however, would pass the bill as a rider on the year's Social Security bill, leading to a showdown (over actuarial soundness) rather than a compromise with Mills.[99]

Earle Clements: [*with the President acknowledging*] . . . bill's passed, and goes over and the Senate puts the Anderson-King bill on it, that they

97. Tape WH6406.06, Citation #3690, Recordings of Telephone Conversations—White House Series, Recordings and Transcripts of Conversations and Meetings, Lyndon B. Johnson Library.
98. Larry O'Brien and Wilbur Mills to Johnson, 3:55 P.M., 11 June 1964, in this chapter.
99. Zelizer, *Taxing America*, pp. 225–30; *Congressional Quarterly Almanac*, 1964, vol. 20, pp. 234–40.

can get the bill you're talking about approved in the House by the confer-ees. May have no value at all.

President Johnson: Is he one of the conferees?[100]

Clements: [*with the President acknowledging*] He's not, but he says the conferees will agree to it, including Wilbur [Mills]. He says as a matter of fact the people, if the bill is tough enough in the Senate, that the people in the medical field will be hollering for them to try to save them through compromise.[101] I know that seems like a long, roundabout procedure. . . .

President Johnson: Well, that may [be] what we have to do. I've always got that to fall back on. [*Chuckles.*]

Clements: Well, that's . . . Now, I pick up another thing up there: that you might not have 12 votes on the Democratic side without Wilbur.

President Johnson: Mm-hmm. May be. Wilbur just talked to me about 10 minutes ago. He said he doesn't want to report a bill with just 13 out of 25 [*unclear comment by Clements*], and he implied that he . . . I told him, I said, "You make the 13th, and I think we can get you another." And I said, "You ought to have 14, and we can pass it with 250 votes in the House." "Oh," he said, "you get more than that in the House, but I just don't like to bring out something with 13 on it." He asked me what would happen if we brought out a regular bill that's to old folks and Kerr-Mills and so forth and let them put King-Anderson on it over there—

Clements: I see.

President Johnson: —then he moderated it.[102] And I said, "Well, I would hope you'd moderate it before you send it through." But I imagine that what you say is what he's going to do.

Clements: Well, I'll tell you what: I think that it takes both of them off of the lam, and I'm not sure that Wilbur's—and these things happen often times—I'm not sure that he's being quite as frank with you . . .[103]

President Johnson: Well, he didn't tell me that this other fellow, but that's what our people thought, and . . .

Clements: Well, actually, I can just give you this, and I believe this to be true: that [*chuckling*] Wilbur said to John [Watts], "For God's sakes, don't you let Clements outtalk you. Put me in a hell of a shape." [*Both laugh.*] Hear what I'm saying? That didn't happen today, that happened

---

100. Johnson and Clements were referring to Representative John C. Watts of Kentucky, a Democrat and a member of the House Ways and Means Committee.

101. The American Medical Association had conducted an extended campaign against Medicare.

102. In his conversation with Johnson, Mills had only implied that this would be his strategy.

103. As Clements suggested, Mills would soon abandon his effort to find a compromise on Medicare.

last week. But this fellow . . . this fellow, except for this commitment he's got out, now, he's going to vote for the pay bill this afternoon.

President Johnson: It's passed: 230 to a 100, and—

Clements: Yeah. . . . I'm saying he was one of them.

President Johnson: Good, that's wonderful.

Clements: And others that had had long commitments out, they agreed that they would give a live pair to somebody who couldn't be here and was for it.[104]

President Johnson: Good.

Clements: But Watts is going to—Watts will do damn near anything, my friend, that you want him to do, and we can make him—if you decide to go this other route, we can make an ally out of him, and by God he can, I think, can get this thing done.

President Johnson: You mean putting it on the Senate?

Clements: Yeah.

President Johnson: Let me try it. I'll get in touch with you.

Clements: All right.

President Johnson: Thank you, Earle, I'm awful grateful.

Clements: I'm at your service.

President Johnson: I know it.

Clements: God bless you.

President Johnson: Yeah.

Clements: Bye.

4:21 P.M.

From Hale Boggs[105]

House Majority Whip Hale Boggs called the President to report the final vote total on the federal employees pay bill.

Hale Boggs: . . . seven.

President Johnson: Two, what?

---

104. "Pairing off" is a legislative device that allows a member of Congress to miss a roll call vote without affecting the vote's outcome. A member who planned to be absent would pair off with a lawmaker from the opposing side who agreed to withhold their vote. Both positions would be listed in the *Congressional Record* as part of the pair.

105. Tape WH6406.06, Citation #3691, Recordings of Telephone Conversations—White House Series, Recordings and Transcripts of Conversations and Meetings, Lyndon B. Johnson Library.

Boggs: 243 to 157.

President Johnson: Isn't that wonderful?

Boggs: Eighty-six folks. Terrific. [*The President laughs, and Boggs joins in.*]

President Johnson: Hale, you tell them that we don't take a defeat the first time, we keep fighting.

Boggs: Hell, yes. Look, I knew we could pass this thing this week, and that's why I kept pressing.

President Johnson: Well, I pressed it, my friend, pretty hard.

Boggs: We had a pretty good week this week, don't you think?

President Johnson: Yeah.

Boggs: Huh?

President Johnson: Yeah, we've got to get the poverty bill out Tuesday, that's the key.

Boggs: Oh, we'll get it out Tuesday, and we'll pass it the week after next.[106]

President Johnson: I don't know whether we will or not. They tell [me] Tip O'Neill's leaving to go to Europe or something.[107]

Boggs: Well, we'll have to keep him here, Mr. President.

President Johnson: I hope so. I'm proud of you and wonderful.

Boggs: Thank you, Mr. President.

President Johnson: Bye.

Boggs: Bye.

4:26 P.M.

From Edmund G. "Pat" Brown[108]

California Governor Pat Brown called to reassure the President of his commitment to the Pacific Southwest Water Plan and to outline a strategy for negating opposition to the project in Southern California.[109]

---

106. Boggs's assessment of the prospects for quick passage of the economic opportunity bill proved unduly optimistic. The House Rules Committee would not grant the bill a rule until 28 July, and the House would not pass it until 8 August. *Congressional Quarterly Almanac,* 1964, vol. 20, p. 226.

107. See Johnson to Adam Clayton Powell, time unknown, 11 June 1964, in this chapter.

108. Tape WH6406.06, Citation #3692, Recordings of Telephone Conversations—White House Series, Recordings and Transcripts of Conversations and Meetings, Lyndon B. Johnson Library.

109. For background on this issue, see Johnson to Jesse Unruh, 6:50 P.M., 3 June 1964, in this volume; and Johnson to Richard Russell, 12:26 P.M., 11 June 1964, in this chapter.

President Johnson: Lyndon Johnson. Hello?

Edmund G. "Pat" Brown: Hello, Mr. President?

President Johnson: Yes, sir. How are you, Pat?

Brown: Fine. How are you?

President Johnson: Doing good. I hope you are. We just passed our pay bill, and we got our civil rights through yesterday, so we've been doing pretty good.

Brown: And it looks like you did pretty good on your foreign aid, too.

President Johnson: Yeah, we did all right there.

Brown: You're doing great, and the Republicans did fine at the governor's conference, too.[110]

President Johnson: Well . . .

Brown: They did very well. By the way, this isn't what I called you for, but take a look if you have time on Sunday to *Issues and Answers.*[111] Bill Lawrence questions me and Governor [Mark] Hatfield of Oregon, and I think you might be interested in some of my replies where they took you on a little bit, where Governor Hatfield took you on. So if you get a chance Sunday, listen to it, will you?

President Johnson: Mm-hmm. I sure will.

Brown: But the other—here's what I wanted to talk to you about, this water thing . . . here in California. I've been working very closely with Senator [Carl] Hayden, and we suggested a compromise that he accepted, and I really think it's a good thing, and I think it would tie you in to the whole western water development as I told you when I sat there.[112]

Now, there are some irreconcilables in the Southern California that do not approve this. I want to be frank with you, and I haven't been able to get Tommy Kuchel to go along with this either, and he's been very critical of me for working with Senator Hayden rather than with him, but . . . he—these Southern California people, Mr. President, what they want to do is to hold up that Central Arizona Project so that they can continue to . . . to take more water out of that stream. Now, I'm telling you this very, very frankly. I wouldn't want to be quoted on it.

President Johnson: I know that.

Brown: They're take—they want to . . . they want to fight [the]

---

110. Brown was referring to an unsuccessful attempt by Republican governors attending the National Governors' Conference in Cleveland to agree on a moderate candidate to challenge presumptive Republic presidential nominee Barry Goldwater. Douglas B. Cornell, "Governors End Conference with GOP Show Sidetracked," *Washington Post*, 11 June 1964.

111. *Issues and Answers* was a Sunday morning public affairs program on ABC News.

112. Governor Brown had met with President Johnson on 25 April 1964.

Central Arizona [Project], and if they do, they'll continue to get more water than the Supreme Court gave them, and that's their strategy. But I will not go along with that because I want to work with a California and Arizona and Nevada to build that whole southwest area down there, and I'm just . . . I understand that Senator Hayden, our people said that he feels that I haven't gone along. I was supposed to fly back there and tell you this.

President Johnson: No, no, he told—I told him yesterday that you were strong for this, and I just want to be positive that I didn't make . . . have a lot of people in California splitting up and fighting it because I was going to catch unshirted hell for [a] 3 billion-dollar proposition right here before—when we're talking economy, where I had sent in a budget estimate up there and saying the budget approved this kind of a project because if there's not water there for California, then the federal government really underwrites getting it for them. And that means that I've got to go and find that . . . that's going to be a hell of a problem. So I told him I better let my [Bureau of the] Budget try to look at it, and I hope that he could get Kuchel aboard so we don't have a war when we get it to the Congress because I don't think he'll pass it if all this California group goes against it.

Brown: Well, the whole northern California group will be for it and some of the Southern California congressmen. I'll tell you what I'm working on to really take—

President Johnson: The congressmen, somebody told me, were meeting tomorrow. Do you know—

Brown: They're going to meet on Saturday, yeah. They—

President Johnson: That's [Chester] Holifield. Holifield's got a group of them meeting.[113] Now, is he going to be for us or against us?

Brown: I think he's going to be for it, and I'll tell you another one where, if we really get this, then you can come out for it without fear of these Southern California irreconcilables: that is the . . . the *Los Angeles Times.*

President Johnson: Well, now, somebody told me they hadn't made up their mind.

Brown: Well, they haven't, but I'm going to take my water engineer out there on Monday. I talked to Norman Chandler a half hour ago on the phone.[114] I talked to him for an hour and recommended . . . practically

---

113. Chet Holifield was a Democratic representative from the 19th District of California, which was in Los Angeles.
114. Norman Chandler was the publisher of the *Los Angeles Times.*

begged him to come out for them because I told him it meant the whole development of the Southwest. And they . . . they asked me to have my water engineer, and they'd have the people in Southern California that were opposed to it, into their office to talk with the editorial policy.

Now, if they come out for it, I don't think you have to have any fear of political repercussions from Southern California. You—there's some that you won't get, but they're not for you anyway.

President Johnson: All right.

Brown: And they never will be, and they've never been for me.

President Johnson: Why don't you call me after you get through with that meeting?

Brown: All righty, I'll do that. What—

President Johnson: That'll be Monday? That'll be—

Brown: I think our delegation did pretty good out here. We beat that [Sam] Yorty, 2½ to 1.[115]

President Johnson: Yeah, well, that's—well, you did a good job, Pat.

Brown: And we're all going to be . . . we're all going to be behind Pierre [Salinger] in this thing.[116] I was sorry to lose that one.

President Johnson: I know that. I know.

Brown: But Pierre is . . . I—He had a lot of glamour, and when Jackie [Kennedy] came out for him and when Mrs. [Lucretia] Engle came out for him, I just couldn't . . . I just couldn't overcome that.[117] It was just [*Johnson acknowledges*] too strong.

President Johnson: Well, y'all work it out and get together, and let's have a big victory in November. We can beat this [Barry] Goldwater to pieces, can't we?

Brown: [*with passion*] Oh, God, I mean, it'll be tragic. But I don't over—I don't underestimate anybody. We're going to . . . we're going

---

115. Los Angeles Mayor Sam Yorty was a conservative Democrat who opposed Governor Brown on civil rights issues. In 1960, he had supported Richard Nixon over Kennedy; in 1966 he would challenge Brown in the California Democratic gubernatorial primary and then decline to endorse the governor in the fall contest against Republican gubernatorial nominee Ronald Reagan. David S. Broder, "Kennedy Focuses on 'Backlash,'" *Washington Post*, 23 October 1966; Don Terry, "Sam Yorty, Maverick Mayor of Los Angeles, Dies at 88," *New York Times*, 6 June 1988.

116. Brown had supported Alan Cranston, the losing candidate in the recent California Democratic senatorial primary won by former Kennedy and Johnson Press Secretary Pierre Salinger. The primary had provoked a bitter split in the state Democratic Party. See Pierre Salinger to Johnson, 12:55 P.M., 26 April 1964, in McKee, *The Presidential Recordings, Johnson*, vol. 6, *April 14, 1964–May 31, 1964*, pp. 227–28.

117. Salinger was running for the Senate seat made vacant by the ill health of Democrat Clair Engle (who would die on 30 July 1964). Lucretia Engle, the senator's wife, had endorsed Salinger in late May. John H. Averill, "Wife's Role in Engle Drama Is Criticized," *Washington Post*, 1 May 1964; "Mrs. Engle Endorses Salinger," *Washington Post*, 29 May 1964.

to . . . I'm going to . . . we're going to run like you're running against the toughest man that ever [*unclear*]—

President Johnson: I'll see you next week.[118] You get those Democratic dinners together, and you give me a ring after your meeting Monday.

Brown: Fine and dandy, thank you.

President Johnson: Bye.

Brown: Bye.

4:28 P.M.

From Stephen Smith[119]

Stephen Smith, the husband of Jean Kennedy Smith and the brother-in-law of John, Robert, and Edward Kennedy, called the President to thank him for agreeing to attend a June 16 New York fund-raising dinner for the John F. Kennedy Library. Smith, who more than any other Kennedy maintained cordial relations with the President, was leading the campaign to raise funds for the establishment of the library.[120]

Stephen Smith: Hello?

President Johnson: Hi, Steve.

Smith: Oh, Mr. President?

President Johnson: How you doing?

Smith: I'm doing just fine. I'm sorry to bother you—

President Johnson: Why don't you come and see me?

Smith: You know, your wife was good enough to call and say that you were coming up, and—

President Johnson: Yeah.

Smith: —[*unclear*] and I wanted to be very frank. I was so overwhelmed because, God, I know what a burden it is for you to make that trip up here, that I told her that . . . obviously, if you could come, it's just

---

118. Johnson would visit California the following week, from 19–21 June.

119. Tape WH6406.06, Citations #3693 and #3694, Recordings of Telephone Conversations—White House Series, Recordings and Transcripts of Conversations and Meetings, Lyndon B. Johnson Library.

120. In May 1961, the two men and their wives had traveled through Southeast Asia on a highly successful public diplomacy mission for President Kennedy. See Johnson to Stephen Smith, 12:27 P.M., 11 May 1964, in McKee, *The Presidential Recordings, Johnson*, vol. 6, *April 14, 1964–May 31, 1964*, pp. 541–46.

wonderful, and it makes that evening, you know, a fantastic success. But I was just so embarrassed to think that both of you have to make that great effort, particularly with the problems you've got on your mind these days.

President Johnson: I want to do anything I can, anyway I can to be helpful, and—

Smith: Well, you've been terrifically helpful, and I send all these damn things down there to you because, you know, I don't want not to. On the other hand, I don't—

President Johnson: I'll tell you how I felt about it, Steve. I have a meeting with about 300 of the congressmen that night that I'd accepted two months ago. It's what they call gymnasium night. President Kennedy never missed one, and I always went with him. And everybody that goes to the House gymnasium, they have an annual dinner, and it was set for the same night as this. So the thing came in—your invitation came in, and I told Lady Bird to hold up and see if I could get out of it, and so I talked to a couple of my friends up there and they said well, they just sure hoped I'd come, and they wouldn't give me any satisfactory answer, and I procrastinated.

This morning, she handed it to me again and said, "I've got to have a firm yes or no," and I said, "I believe that President Kennedy's watching everything I do from heaven. I think that God Almighty has a way of directing these things, and he took him ahead of us so he could get things lined up for some of the rest of us [who] haven't got much chance. And they're having this meeting to carry on what he was trying to do, and they're calling a roll and they get to Johnson, they say absent. And I don't want to ever have that done, so you just call them and tell them we'll be there and bring whoever we can that will . . . else be helpful." So that's the story, and that's the way I feel about it, and I'm coming just beca—

Smith: Well, that's marvelous.

President Johnson: I'm coming just because I want to.

Smith: That's marvelous of you, and I hope, I hope you'd tell me—I was just so taken . . . surprised, and, you know, because, God, it's a hell of a burden for you to come up here.

President Johnson: No, it's not.

Smith: You're awful nice to do it, and it'll make it just a great affair.

President Johnson: If it was a Johnson dinner and in honor of my wife and I had been called ahead, he'd be there and you would too.

Smith: Well, you're awful nice, and we'll look forward to seeing you.

President Johnson: You tell—

Smith: I just want to say we're all damn appreciative to see you really—

President Johnson: You call Ken O'Donnell or Jack Valenti and anybody that wants to come from here.

Smith: I think Chief Justice [Earl Warren] and Bob McNamara, a few others are coming, so I'll do just that.

President Johnson: You just call them and tell them that we want them all to be our guests, and—

Smith: Listen, if you find on Wednesday that, you know, that things there are . . . certainly everybody understands here.

President Johnson: No, no.

Smith: It's just a major effort for you to do it and awful kind.

President Johnson: No, it's not. No, no. It's already made; I've already told them.

Smith: Fine.

President Johnson: And I'm going to be there. Tell your sweet girl hello, and you just call Ken O'Donnell or Jack Valenti and say put these on the list so we'll know who's coming. We can haul 35.

Smith: Many, many thanks.

President Johnson: Thank you, Steve.

Smith: OK.

President Johnson: Let me know anything else I can do, and come see me when you're down here. I get lonesome.

Smith: [*chuckling*] Oh, all right.

President Johnson: Do that.

Smith: OK.

President Johnson: Bye.

Smith: Bye.

4:31 P.M.

From David McDonald[121]

The president of the United Steelworkers of America union called from New York City with good news about a pet project of Johnson's that dated back to the Kennedy administration. As chair of the President's Committee on Equal Employment Opportunity under Kennedy, Johnson had initiated

---

121. Tape WH6406.06, Citation #3695, Recordings of Telephone Conversations—White House Series, Recordings and Transcripts of Conversations and Meetings, Lyndon B. Johnson Library.

the Plans for Progress program to encourage major U.S. companies to adopt voluntary plans to hire more minority workers. Heading the initiative was Hobart Taylor Jr, a black Texas attorney close to Johnson.[122]

President Johnson: Yes?

David McDonald: Mr. President?

President Johnson: Yes.

McDonald: This is Dave.

President Johnson: Yeah.

McDonald: I just wanted you to know that an hour and a half or so ago, we signed a Plans for Progress joint agreement with the 11 basic steel companies.

President Johnson: Wonderful.

McDonald: The guts of American steel industry, the whole—well, about 98 percent of it.

President Johnson: That's wonderful.

McDonald: And we are going to release a statement on Monday morning, for Monday morning's papers.

President Johnson: Wonderful.

McDonald: And your man, Mr. [Hobart] Taylor . . .

President Johnson: Wonderful.

McDonald: . . . will be telling you about it. Conrad Cooper of the industry—of U.S. Steel—is calling him.[123]

President Johnson: Wonderful.

McDonald: But I wanted to let you know in advance so that in case there's any comment that you want to make . . . after the release on Monday.

President Johnson: I'll sure do it, Dave, and I appreciate your calling me, and I think it's a wonderful step, and I appreciate it.

McDonald: This has never happened—nothing like this has happened before.

President Johnson: Well, we're making real progress, and we all got to get together as soon as we get this bill passed so we can implement it and get it accepted by the people that got to accept it.

McDonald: [*with Johnson acknowledging*] That's right, sir. And this is a step for acceptance by the steel industry and the steelworkers union

---

122. See Germany and Johnson, *The Presidential Recordings, Johnson*, vol. 3, *January 1964*, pp. 567, 706.

123. R. Conrad Cooper served as executive vice president of U.S. Steel.

working together, and we have a lot of ideas for promotion after the bill is passed. And I'd appreciate it if, after the release on Monday morning, perhaps at your conference—or you know how you handle it through George Reedy and so forth—after the release, which will be in the papers on Monday morning, you might say something.

President Johnson: I'll do it. . . . I'll do it, Dave.

McDonald: Thanks a million.

President Johnson: Bye. Bye.

McDonald: Good luck.

4:32 P.M.: Unrecorded call to George Reedy.

4:36 P.M.: Unrecorded call to Bill Moyers.

TIME UNKNOWN

With White House Operator[124]

While waiting for the operator to place a call to an unidentified person (probably the call to Mike Mansfield that follows at 4:56 P.M.), Johnson discussed the results of a new Gallup poll on his job approval ratings with Jack Valenti.[125]

President Johnson: White are 72, and nonwhite, 82.

Jack Valenti: Look at the Jews and the Catholics.

President Johnson: College is 71 to 20; high school is 76, 13; grade school is 72, 11. Republicans 62 to 22, Democrats are 82 to 8. [*Pauses.*]

Valenti: Jews and Negroes and Catholics—

President Johnson: Sixty-two percent of the Republicans approve of the job I'm doing—that ought to be pointed out. I don't know why he doesn't. [*Long pause.*] East, 80 to 10; Midwest, 77, 11; South, 65 to 18; Far West, 71 to 16. Traditional business, 72; white collar, 73; manual, 77; farmers—

White House Operator: Mr. President?

---

124. Tape WH6406.06, Citation #3696, Recordings of Telephone Conversations—White House Series, Recordings and Transcripts of Conversations and Meetings, Lyndon B. Johnson Library. 125. For the complete poll, see George H. Gallup, *The Gallup Poll: Public Opinion 1935–1971*, vol. 3 (New York: Random House, 1972), pp. 1885–86.

President Johnson: Yes?

White House Operator: The secretary's checked both offices and the floor; he's not around. Can I have her still check further?

President Johnson: I sure do. Tell her it's very urgent.

White House Operator: I surely will.

President Johnson: I want to talk to him in the next five minutes if she knows any place to locate him.

White House Operator: All right, sir, I'll tell her.

President Johnson: Tell her he may be in the gymnasium.

White House Operator: I'll tell her.

President Johnson: I sure do want to talk to him, and I'm waiting to go to Security Council before I do.

White House Operator: Right, I'll tell her.

4:54 P.M.: The President joined Secretary of State Dean Rusk, Robert McNamara, and McGeorge Bundy in the Cabinet Room and brought them back to the Oval Office.

4:56 P.M.

To Mike Mansfield[126]

The President called the Senate majority leader to discuss the timing and arrangements for a trip to tour flood damage in Montana, as well as to visit other western states that he hoped to carry in the fall election. Mansfield's immediate options for travel were limited because of debates and voting on amendments to the civil rights bill.

Before Mansfield is connected, the recorder picks up a brief unclear office conversation and the efforts of Vicki McCammon, one of Johnson's secretaries, to connect the President. In the exchange, an unidentified male says, "Those dogs are taking advantage."

President Johnson: Can you get off tomorrow?

Mike Mansfield: No, sir. We've got this bill, and we're getting the amendments rolling, and I can't. No Democrats can, if I can help it.

---

126. Tape WH6406.06, Citation #3697, Recordings of Telephone Conversations—White House Series, Recordings and Transcripts of Conversations and Meetings, Lyndon B. Johnson Library.

President Johnson: Mm-hmm. [*Pauses and sighs.*] How late are you going to be in?

Mansfield: Eight o'clock.

President Johnson: [*Pauses.*] Hmm. [*Pauses again.*] All right. I had this feeling that I might take you and anybody you wanted to take, fly out of here tomorrow about early as we could—maybe noon or something—and fly up to Montana and see what we could see by dark tomorrow night.

Mansfield: Well, I'd love to, Mr. President, but you've got this bill here, which means a lot to you and the country.

President Johnson: Yes, that's right. . . . That's right, and they'll be voting tomorrow afternoon, you think.

Mansfield: Yes, sir. And I'm planning on bringing them in Saturday too, and there's a lot of people—

President Johnson: That's what I mean. I'm talking about Saturday. I thought tomorrow's Sat—I'm talking about Saturday afternoon, Saturday evening.

Mansfield: Yes, my intention is to bring them in Saturday and come in about 10:00 and stay until 6, 7, or 8 [P.M.]. That's my intention.

President Johnson: And you think they'll be voting at 3, 4, and 5 [P.M.], along in there. So the only day we could get off would be Sunday then, isn't it?

Mansfield: Yes, sir.

President Johnson: Well, I might do it Sunday and come back Monday morning and send you on back in Sunday night.

Mansfield: Are you really—

President Johnson: I'd like—I thought I'd like to go to Montana, and maybe go to Salt Lake City and to the Omaha base for a briefing. I could do all three of them, but I'd like to point it to Montana.

Mansfield: Oh, good.

President Johnson: [*with Mansfield acknowledging*] And the plan they suggested for me was to leave here at a little after noon on Saturday, fly to Montana, inspect the flood damage, and go on to Salt Lake City Saturday night. Go to Omaha [on] Sunday and have lunch, receive a briefing, and come back Sunday afternoon. And they said this problem may be that Senator Mansfield might have difficulty getting away from Washington on Saturday afternoon.

Mansfield: Yes, sir.

President Johnson: Think about it, and we'll talk later.

Mansfield: OK, sir.

President Johnson: And don't say anything to anybody but yourself because I don't want it to get out.

Mansfield: OK. . . . Bye, Mr. President. Thank you.

President Johnson: You think, though, that you [can] go Sunday, but you can't go Saturday— that your thinking?

Mansfield: Yes, sir.

President Johnson: OK.

Mansfield: Thank you, sir.

TIME UNKNOWN

To Bob Manning[127]

Johnson next called Assistant Secretary of State for Public Affairs Bob Manning to review responsibilities for releasing sensitive military and diplomatic news to the press. His motivation in making the call came from an incident at George Reedy's noon press briefing in which reporters had aggressively questioned the press secretary about U.S. policy in Southeast Asia (and to a lesser extent in Cyprus). The thrust of the questions had been that the White House was attempting to limit news about the U.S. role in the region's deepening conflicts in order to protect Johnson during an election year.[128] In this call, Johnson indicated that Reedy simply lacked the knowledge about "operational" details of U.S. policy to answer specific questions and indicated that spokespeople at the Department of State and the Department of Defense should diffuse the issue by offering more expansive press briefings on developments in Southeast Asia.

Unidentified: Bob?

Bob Manning: All right.

President Johnson: [*to unidentified*] Is this Bob Manning?

Manning: Yeah.

President Johnson: Bob?

Manning: Yes, Mr. President.

President Johnson: [*with Manning acknowledging*] I think you and [Arthur] Sylvester ought to say to your press that "someone here has left

---

127. Tape WH6406.06, Citation #3698, Recordings of Telephone Conversations—White House Series, Recordings and Transcripts of Conversations and Meetings, Lyndon B. Johnson Library.
128. For a hostile account of the press conference, see Douglas Kiker, "White House Blackout on Asia News," *New York Herald Tribune*, 12 June 1964.

the impression with the White House that we are referring questions to the White House.[129] We have never done that. Neither of us have done it. We want the record to show that. All operational questions are answered here. White House doesn't do that, and we're glad to answer anything we can. They've told about these planes that went over, and we're the first ones to make the announcement. They were shot down, and what happened to the pilot, and everything else about it.[130] And White House doesn't come out with those announcements. They were made by the [Defense] Department. We've told them—[George]Ball told them about going to Turkey and to Greece, and he told them before he went."[131] He told them too damn much. He just made a stump speech. He talked big before he got over there, and then he got kind of like a lamb after he got there, but they're saying we don't tell them anything—

The recording of the conversation is briefly interrupted by an exchange in which Walter Jenkins asks Vicki McCammon for Juanita Roberts.

President Johnson: . . . Defense, and it hasn't been done in State.

Manning: And I've instructed two of them to go and read the transcripts just to refresh themselves, and one of them called back and said, "Well, I agree, and we'll"—this is the UP [United Press]—"and we'll change our story." But you're—we'll make the point again, Mr. President, because I think it deserves being made—

President Johnson: And tell Sylvester that too, because they were just inhuman to this poor fellow in his noon briefing.[132]

Manning: I know, I talked with him right after, and it's just, I think, inexcusable because we have *not* been referring them back, and I'll see that they get it straight. I told Dick today to tell them that the buck stops here as far as we're concerned on this, in the course of this pilot thing, and we're not passing it off to anybody.[133]

President Johnson: They go ahead further and say, "The President has refused to answer because he doesn't want to be unpopular on a—with

---

129. Arthur Sylvester served as assistant secretary of defense for public affairs, which was the Defense Department's equivalent of a press secretary.

130. Johnson was referring to the loss of two U.S. planes on reconnaissance flights over Laos the previous week. See introductions to 6 June 1964 and 8 June 1964 in this volume.

131. For Assistant Secretary of State George Ball's recent mission to Turkey and Greece to discuss the Cyprus crisis, see Johnson to Dean Rusk, 6:30 P.M., 9 June 1964; and McGeorge Bundy to Johnson, 6:30 P.M., 10 June 1964, in this volume.

132. Johnson was referring to Press Secretary George Reedy.

133. Manning was probably referring to Richard I. Phillips, director of the State Department's Office of News.

a—doesn't want to be connected with an unpopular war."[134] [*Manning laughs.*] OK.

Manning: All right. Thank you, Mr. President, I'll do that.

5:13 P.M.: Dean Rusk departed.

5:45 P.M.: McGeorge Bundy departed.

6:00 P.M.: Unrecorded call to Bill Moyers.

6:06 P.M.: Unrecorded call to Jack Valenti.

6:07 P.M.: Unrecorded call to Moyers.

6:08 P.M.: Unrecorded call to Valenti.

6:09 P.M.: Mississippi Senator John Stennis arrived for a meeting.

6:11 P.M.

To Robert Kennedy[135]

While still meeting with Senator Stennis, President Johnson called Attorney General Robert Kennedy to thank him for a letter offering to go to Vietnam, presumably as a replacement for Ambassador Henry Cabot Lodge. Despite the long-standing antipathy between the two, most political observers believed that Kennedy remained on Johnson's short list of potential vice presidential nominees.

A brief, unclear office conversation with John Stennis precedes the call.

President Johnson: Hello?

Robert Kennedy: Mr. President.

President Johnson: I'm with some folks. I just wanted you to know that the nicest thing to happen to me since I've been here is your note, and I appreciate it—

Kennedy: Well, thank you.

President Johnson: —so very, very much. And I can't think of letting

---

134. Johnson was likely reading from a transcript of Reedy's press briefing. A similar question would be quoted in the *New York Herald Tribune* story the following day. Kiker, "White House Blackout on Asia News."

135. Tape WH6406.06, Citation #3699, Recordings of Telephone Conversations—White House Series, Recordings and Transcripts of Conversations and Meetings, Lyndon B. Johnson Library.

you do that, but you've got to help me with who we do get, and we got to get him pretty soon. We'll talk about it in the next few hours, but I think we're in better shape than we've ever been, when that letter come in . . .

Kennedy: [*Unclear.*]

President Johnson: . . . and I wanted you to know that I'll sleep better tonight.

Kennedy: Thank you very much, Mr. President.

President Johnson: I appreciate it more than you'll ever know.

Kennedy: Oh, well, that's very nice.

President Johnson: And you're a great, great guy, or you wouldn't write that kind of letter.

Kennedy: Thank you very much.

President Johnson: Good-bye.

Kennedy: Bye.

6:40 P.M.–6:51 P.M.: President Johnson met with Under Secretary of State George W. Ball.

6:50 P.M.: Unrecorded call to Lynda Johnson.

7:00 P.M.: Unrecorded call to former Arizona Senator Ernest McFarland.

7:05 P.M.

To Thomas Mann[136]

Johnson's next call went to Assistant Secretary of State for Inter-American Affairs Thomas Mann, who updated him on key issues involving Latin America and Mexico.[137]

President Johnson: Tom, how are you?

---

136. Tape WH6406.07, Citations #3702, #3703, and #3704, Recordings of Telephone Conversations—White House Series, Recordings and Transcripts of Conversations and Meetings, Lyndon B. Johnson Library.
137. Mann also held the titles of special assistant to the President for Latin American affairs and U.S. coordinator for the Alliance for Progress. The Alliance for Progress was a Kennedy-initiated effort to promote political reform and economic development in Latin America.

Thomas Mann: [*Unrecorded segment*]—got back from the Hill. Talking to Cooley about sugar with Charlie Murphy.[138]

President Johnson: Mm-hmm. What are our problems now? You got the [Juscelino] Kubitschek problem in Brazil.[139] What are the hot ones in . . . you got election in Chile.

Mann: Got an election in Chile in September.

President Johnson: All right.

Mann: We've got this foreign ministers meeting, which will probably take place in July on this Cuban—Venezuelan accusation against Cuba.[140]

President Johnson: Are you—have you got that worked out where you're going to get the kind of resolution that you want?

Mann: Well, we're going to get a, I think, a fairly good one. We're having trouble with Mexico. Chile, because of its elections in September, is probably going to vote against it, but we think Brazil and Argentina will come along. We've been working on—haggling over words. [Ellsworth] Bunker is working on it almost full time.[141] I was talking when you called with the Mexican about it, trying to get him to [*unclear*], to—

President Johnson: Who do you talk to? Who [do] you mean, "the Mexican?"

---

138. Representative Harold D. Cooley was a North Carolina Democrat and chairman of the House Agriculture Committee; Charles Murphy was under secretary of agriculture.

139. Juscelino Kubitschek had been President of Brazil from 1956 to 1961, during which time he oversaw the construction of the country's new capital city, Brasília. A right-wing coup in early April had overthrown the elected government of Brazil headed by the leftist president, João Goulart; the new President, General Humberto Castelo Branco, had stripped Kubitschek and other possible opponents of all political rights for ten years. Although the military government claimed that the Kubitschek action was taken because of past corruption (others stripped of their rights were accused of Communist associations), the former President had already accepted the presidential nomination of the Social Democratic Party and announced that despite the coup he intended to run in the presidential elections scheduled for the following year. The suspension of Kubitschek's rights marked a key step in Brazil's slide towards military dictatorship, with the support of the Johnson administration. "Telegram from the Embassy in Brazil to the Department of State," 10 June 1964, U.S. Department of State, *Foreign Relations of the United States (FRUS), 1964–1968: South and Central America; Mexico*, ed. David C. Geyer and David H. Herschler (Washington, DC: GPO, 2004), 31:467–70; "Brazil: Forward Economics . . ." & ". . . Backward Politics," *New York Times*, 10 June 1964.

140. Venezuela had requested a meeting of the foreign ministers of the Organization of American States to consider the application of sanctions to Cuba for supplying weapons to Communist rebels fighting to overthrow Venezuela's government. The meeting would take place in July and would result in a series of diplomatic and economic sanctions against Cuba. "O.A.S. Votes July 21 Parley to Apply Sanctions on Cuba," *New York Times*, 27 June 1964; Tad Szulc, "20 Nations Sign Cuban Sanctions," *New York Times*, 27 July 1964.

141. Ellsworth Bunker was the U.S. representative on the Council of the Organization of American States (OAS). On 26 July, Mexico, Chile, Bolivia, and Uruguay would vote against the Cuba sanctions. Szulc, "20 Nations Sign Cuban Sanctions," *New York Times*, 27 July 1964.

Mann: [Vicente] Sanchez-Gavito.

President Johnson: Yeah, mm-hmm.

Mann: Their OAS [Organization of American States] ambassador.

President Johnson: Is he pretty difficult?

Mann: [*with the President acknowledging*] No, he's on our side, but he's having trouble at home because of politics down there. Their basic problem is Lombardo Toledano and [Lazaro] Cardenas.[142] And trying to keep the party from splitting. It's an internal problem, really. We're fiddling with words that everybody can live with and which—

President Johnson: When does that come up?

Mann: [*with the President acknowledging*] We think the first . . . within the first . . . it'll be after the elections, which in Mexico, which I believe are—it's on a Sunday—I think the 6th of July, the 5th of July.

President Johnson: Any question about the Mexican election?

Mann: No. No, there's no question at all there. They've had some disturbances. You know, the Commies are growing up in Mexicali. That's a serious problem for us, Mr. President, but I think we're making progress.

President Johnson: How—did you get [Carl] Hayden to agree to what you want to do on that water thing?[143]

Mann: Well . . . we're still waiting for word from him, but the Secretary's [Rusk's] going to see him again tomorrow.[144]

---

142. Lombardo Toledano was the leader of Mexico's Marxist *Partido Popular Socialista* (PPS), and a supporter of Fidel Castro. In 1964, the PPS created a split in the Mexican left wing when it endorsed Gustavo Diaz Ordaz, the candidate of the dominant *Partido Revolucionario Institucional* (PRI) in the 1964 Mexican presidential campaign. Lazaro Cardenas had fought in the Mexican Revolution, served as President of Mexico from 1934 to 1940, and had participated in the establishment of the leftist National Liberation Movement. In June 1964, Cardenas angered many of his leftist allies by appearing at a rally with Ordaz. Paul P. Kennedy, "Cardenas Angers Mexico Leftists," *New York Times*, 21 June 1964; Kennedy, "Red Farm Group Splits in Mexico," *New York Times*, 18 October 1964; James C. Tanner, "Mexico & Cuba; Why Diplomatic Tie Between Them Still Seems Firm," *Wall Street Journal*, 17 December 1964.

143. Johnson was referring to the Pacific Southwest Water Plan; Arizona Senator Carl Hayden had played a key part in the long political and judicial process that had produced the plan. For background on this issue, see Johnson to Jesse Unruh, 6:50 P.M., 3 June 1964, in this volume; Johnson to Richard Russell, 12:26 P.M., 11 June 1964; and Edmund G. "Pat" Brown to Johnson, 4:26 P.M., 11 June 1964, in this chapter.

144. Mann was presumably referring to Secretary of State Dean Rusk. Mexico and the United States. had been engaged in an ongoing discussion of Colorado River water rights, including annual flow levels and the level of salinity in the water reaching Mexico. Standards in each of these areas had been defined in a 1944 treaty that left neither nation satisfied. Construction of the dams and irrigation channels of the Pacific Southwest Water Plan, and in particular the Central Arizona Project component of the plan, would have a significant effect on both the flow levels and water quality of the Colorado River as it reached Mexico. McGeorge Bundy, "Memorandum from the President's Special Assistant for National Security Affairs (Bundy) to Secretary of State Rusk and Secretary of the Interior Udall," 6 April 1965, *FRUS, 1964–1968*, 31:749–51.

President Johnson: He told me, Hayden told me yesterday that he had agreed to go along with the State Department.

Mann: Well, I think what he's . . . I think what he's doing is waiting on some kind of a political commitment from your office about the Central Arizona Project.

President Johnson: That's right, but he told me he'd agreed to go along with y'all on the other one. And I want to be sure it's satisfactory before I agree with him.

Mann: Well, I think maybe that's where we are. That's the last word I had at noon today, that . . . I'll talk to the Secretary about it in the morning if I may, and—

President Johnson: You be positive about that and tell him that he already told me he'd go with the Secretary. The Secretary ought to tell him that the President says that you told him you were going with us.

Mann: I think he may infer back, yes, but this is a package deal, and where is—

President Johnson: He never has made it conditional that way, never has put it on that basis.

Mann: That—

President Johnson: He's just said, "I've already helped you, now you help me."

Mann: All right. Well, let me—I'll see the Secretary in the morning.

President Johnson: All right.

Mann: Tell him that it's not conditional, and push him.

President Johnson: No. . . . No, that's right. I'm trying to . . . trying . . .

Mann: We have a lot of potential problems. For example, Uruguay has five presidents, as you know. And they're just in a hell of a mess because they can't manage their affairs very well. Their growth rate is now down below their birth rate. The Kubitschek thing, the . . . is bad. We'll get some flack on that for two weeks, but the general trend, we think after June 15 they can no longer do this. The law—their power to designate new people expires then. We are urging them to set up an appeals procedure—Kubitschek and all of the others—so they'll have a chance for their day in court to be heard, know the charges against them, and so forth.[145] I don't think we'll get anywhere, but I would think the Brazilian thing will get better, starting in about two weeks. I think it'll look pretty good in 30 days.

---

145. For U.S. talks with the military government in Brazil about the revocation of political rights, see "Telegram from the Embassy in Brazil to the Department of State," 10 June 1964, *FRUS, 1964–1968,* 31:467–70.

President Johnson: You got any more hot spots?

Mann: We've got lots of headaches . . .

President Johnson: What's happening in the Dominican Republic?

Mann: Well, they've just reached an agreement with the [International] Monetary Fund, and we're now negotiating with them on trying to get them to take the self-help measures that they have to take. They've got lots of problems: It takes them seven cents, which is absurd, to produce sugar, and the world price is now around five [cents], and futures are about four-five. So they have to fire a lot of people and get more efficient and increase agricultural production. They've got to find a way to hold elections. And—

Approximately ten seconds excised as classified information and under deed of gift restriction.[146]

Mann: But things are moving along pretty well.

We've got problems nearly everywhere. Costa Rica's in trouble. Their . . . they claim there's a 35 percent loss of foreign exchange in their coffee exports and, I think, it's sugar. And we're going to work on that because the President will be up here to see *you*, and we'll fill you in on that before he gets here. Panama is rocking along. They haven't started talking yet, but they will presumably next week. [Jorge] Illueca I think is coming in on Monday, back from Panama.[147]

President Johnson: What do we hear from our ambassador down there?[148] Is he doing all right?

Mann: I think he's done a fine job, and you made a good selection. I say that without qualification: He's exercised good judgment; he's been calm, and he's been tough when he had to be tough. I . . . he'll be up this week.

By the way, early next week, we'll have about seven ambassadors. You said you wanted to meet with them.

President Johnson: Yeah . . . yeah.

Mann: Any time next week you're ready, we'll bring about seven over there.

President Johnson: All right. . . . All right, you just stay after Jack [Valenti], make him give you a date. Just hound him every day. Because we just—the ones that raise the most hell get the most sugar.

Mann: All right, I . . . [*chuckles*] I'll stay on the phone and raise hell.

---

146. A transcript of the excised material may be found in "Telephone Conversation Between President Johnson and the Assistant Secretary of State for Inter-American Affairs (Mann)," 11 June 1964, *FRUS, 1964–1968,* 31:44.

147. Jorge E. Illueca served as a special Panamanian representative to the U.S.-Panama negotiations over potential revisions to the disputed Panama Canal Treaty.

148. Jack Hood Vaughn served as U.S. ambassador to Panama.

President Johnson: And you're too good and too nice, so you just give him hell. Just tell him every day you got to call him the next day and get your date so you'll know what you're doing.

Mann: All right, will do.

President Johnson: And then you get me a briefing paper, so I can . . . tell me what I can say to them, and . . . What can I say that we've done in this hemisphere now that's improved the situation? What've we got to that we can point to with pride? Besides pointing to with alarm.

Mann: Well, we're going to send you over a memo with . . . that's in preparation now, under the Alliance [for Progress] side. Where we're weaker than in any other place, Mr. President, is on trade. The aid thing is going good as you know, thanks to you. You'll hear more complaints, I think, on trade: about sugar and coffee and things that they need to live . . . to sell in order to live. But I think, on the whole, that—

President Johnson: Can we say that these six months are better than the last six months before we came in?

Mann: I think we can. I believe it is.

President Johnson: Well, how—why—how, why are they better? How are they better now than they were six—

Mann: We're going to give you about 12 points on the aid side, and we'll scratch around and find some other general points on . . .

President Johnson: From March, though, if you're just making a general statement: from March to November, period. In November [until] now, what's the difference?

Mann: All right. Let us think about that.

The remaining 15 minutes and 25 seconds excised as classified information and under deed of gift restriction.[149]

7:35 P.M.: Unrecorded call from Walter Jenkins.

7:35 P.M.: The President returned to the White House Mansion, accompanied by McGeorge Bundy.

9:30 P.M.: Off-the-record dinner with the Time., Inc., founder and editorial chairman Henry Luce, along with Time, Inc., editor in chief Hedley Donovan, *Time* reporter Hugh Sidey, *Life* magazine editor John Steele, and Bundy.

1:40 A.M., June 12: Retired for the night.

---

149. A transcript of the excised material may be found in "Telephone Conversation Between President Johnson and the Assistant Secretary of State for Inter-American Affairs (Mann)," 11 June 1964, *FRUS, 1964–1968,* 31:45–50.

Friday, June 12, 1964

They're doing a great disservice to the American people by leaving the impression that their government's got something to hide and something to conceal, and we're misleading them and we're playing politics with it. And I think they'll get that impression over if we don't open up and repeat what our policy is and get a question planted, "Well, what is our policy? Why don't you tell us our policy?" And then let him tell them.

—President Johnson to Dean Rusk

Following Barry Goldwater's victory in the June 2 California Republican primary, moderate members of the party had privately scrambled to shape a strategy that might yet block the conservative Arizona senator's nearly inevitable nomination for the presidency. Those efforts came to fruition on June 12, as Pennsylvania Governor William Scranton declared his candidacy, arguing that the party would go to San Francisco the following month "to hold a convention, not a coronation" and asking fellow Republicans, in an implicit critique of Goldwater, "Can we pretend, even to ourselves, that it is possible for us to stand with one foot in the 20th century and the other in the 19th?" Seeking to unify anti-Goldwater Republicans around a single alternative, Scranton soon gained endorsement from leaders of the unofficial campaign to draft U.S. Ambassador to South Vietnam Henry Cabot Lodge, a former Massachusetts senator and 1960 vice presidential nominee. Even more significantly, former President Eisenhower effectively ended his previous neutrality in the race by declaring that he viewed Scranton's run as "good for the health and vigor of the party" and noting that he had "long admired" the governor. Former Vice President and 1960 Republican presidential nominee Richard Nixon, in contrast, stated that he would remain neutral, perhaps positioning himself as an acceptable alternative should the upcoming convention in San Francisco become deadlocked between Goldwater and Scranton. Similarly, New York Governor Nelson Rockefeller indicated that he would not yield to Scranton in seeking the support of the party's moderates and liberals.[1]

Meanwhile in Washington, the Senate overwhelmingly rejected a proposal from Georgia Senator Richard Russell to make implementation of the civil rights bill dependent on the outcome of a national referendum. Three other southern amendments that would have weakened the legislation met a similar fate.[2] As the day closed, a visiting Ku Klux Klan leader headed an anti–civil rights march in St. Augustine, Florida. At one point, African Americans greeted the segregationist marchers with the hymn "I Love Everybody, I Love Everybody In My Heart." Earlier in the day, additional civil rights supporters had arrived by bus from Georgia, Alabama, and North Carolina to aid the campaign in the city, and approximately 60 activists were arrested and placed in the county jail that already held Martin Luther King Jr.[3]

7:30 A.M.: Johnson woke, met with A.W. Moursund and Jack Valenti, and did his exercises.

8:45 A.M.: Unrecorded call to Moursund.

10:10 A.M.: Arrived at the office, accompanied by Valenti.

10:15 A.M.: Unrecorded call to Walter Jenkins.

10:34 A.M.

From Luther Hodges[4]

Secretary of Commerce Luther Hodges called to discuss the President's meeting later in the morning with West German Chancellor Ludwig

---

1. "Transcript of Scranton's Address," *New York Times*, 13 June 1964; Felix Belair Jr., "Eisenhower Hails Scranton's Move," *New York Times*, 13 June 1964; Ronald Sullivan, "Nixon Is Neutral in Scranton Move," *New York Times*, 13 June 1964; David Halberstam, "Rockefeller Hails Scranton's Move," *New York Times*, 13 June 1964.
2. E. W. Kenworthy, "Rights Backers Bar Referendum Asked BY Russell," *New York Times*, 13 June 1964.
3. Late in the evening, King was moved to Duvall County Jail in Jacksonville. John Herbers, "200 Whites March at St. Augustine," *New York Times*, 13 June 1964; Taylor Branch, *Pillar of Fire: America in the King Years 1963–65* (New York: Touchstone, 1998), pp. 343–45.
4. Tape WH6406.07, Citation #3705, Recordings of Telephone Conversations—White House Series, Recordings and Transcripts of Conversations and Meetings, Lyndon B. Johnson Library.

Erhard. The conversation turned, however, to Hodges' upcoming meeting with reporters in Virginia, during which he would discuss the implementation of the civil rights bill, and to the latest poll showing Johnson's high job approval ratings.

Luther Hodges: Hello?

President Johnson: Yeah.

Hodges: You going to see Mr. [Ludwig] Erhard this morning?

President Johnson: Yeah.

Hodges: I talked to him pretty fully about this Kennedy Round and the grain prices, which you're acquainted with I'm sure.[5]

President Johnson: Mm-hmm.

One minute and thirty-one seconds excised as classified information.

President Johnson: That's good. I'm sorry I missed you last night, but they're just murdering me these days.

Hodges: Well, I know that, and the early part of the week, when it's a little more convenient, I'd like to give you some impressions you and I will understand each other on—in these contacts abroad.

President Johnson: All right . . . that's good. . . . That's fine.

Hodges: One thing more: I'm going to see over a hundred press men— this is following your advice of getting in the southern states. I'm starting with the toughest one, Virginia, tomorrow.

President Johnson: Uh-huh . . . Good.

Hodges: About a hundred press men, and it's going to be political, and they're going to ask questions. I did want one statement from you if you want to give me your advice. Should we say this is going to be a tough campaign, assuming [Barry] Goldwater, or should we try to play it down the middle?

President Johnson: No, I'd play it in the middle.

Hodges: Uh-huh. Well, I—

---

5. Hodges was referring to the Kennedy Round of talks on the General Agreement on Tariffs and Trade (GATT), which had begun in May. With the support of the British and Canadian delegations, U.S. Special Representative for Trade Negotiations Christian A. Herter sought a 50 percent reduction in most tariffs, as authorized by the Kennedy administration's Trade Expansion Act of 1962 (the impetus for the trade talks and the reason for the "Kennedy Round" moniker for the negotiations). With elections pending in 1965, West Germany had resisted accepting a single price for grain produced in the European common market—a necessary precondition to a cut in tariffs on agricultural commodities. Richard E. Mooney, "Geneva Meeting on Tariffs Open; Success in Doubt," *New York Times,* 4 May 1964; "Comart Stalled on Common Grain Price," *Washington Post,* 21 May 1964.

President Johnson: I'd say every campaign is [a] problem, and we can't take anything for granted, and we're going to work hard, but the poll coming out Sunday shows that we . . . 74 percent approve our record.[6]

Hodges: That's good.

President Johnson: And in the East it's 80, 10. In the South, it's 65, 35.

Hodges: Well, I think that'll—

President Johnson: [*to someone in the office*] Sixty-two what?

[*on phone*] Sixty-two percent of the Republicans are for me, approve our record.

Hodges: Well, that's . . . Well, I thought we—

President Johnson: I think that's a pretty good thing to point out in the South that even, that . . .

Hodges: Will that be available that time by tomorrow?

President Johnson: It's Friday, June the 12th, it comes out.

Hodges: Mm-hmm. That's today.

President Johnson: And it's in the [*Washington*] Post, part of it, this morning.[7]

Hodges: Fine.

President Johnson: It doesn't have the whole breakdown.

Hodges: Well, then, I can use that. I didn't want to . . . I didn't want to say too much against Goldwater or to say that this thing was going to be so tough against him. I don't want to make his candidacy respectable, that's my problem.

President Johnson: I'm 80, 10 in the East, with 10 percent undecided; 77, 11 in the Midwest, with 12 undecided.

Hodges: [*repeating back, as though taking notes*] 77, 11.

President Johnson: 65, 18 in the South, with 17 undecided.

Hodges: All right, sir.

President Johnson: 71, 16 in the far West, with 13 undecided.

Hodges: Right, sir.

President Johnson: I've got 78 percent of the young people, 21 to 29; 75 percent of 30 to 49, and 71 over 50. Protestants, I've got 71; Catholics, 81; Jews, 83. [*Unclear comment by Hodges.*] Cities over 500,000, 77 percent; cities, 50 to 500, 77 percent; towns, 2,500 to 50,000, 70 percent; under 2,500, 72; farms, 65.

Hodges: Well, that's wonderful, Mr. President.

President Johnson: Negroes, 82 percent.

---

6. For the full poll results, see George H. Gallup, *The Gallup Poll: Public Opinion 1935–1971*, vol. 3 (New York: Random House, 1972), pp. 1885–86.

7. "74% Approve Way Johnson Handles Job," *Washington Post*, 12 June 1964.

Hodges: Good for you, sir. I'll do the best I can for you.
President Johnson: Thank you.
Hodges: Thank you.

10:40 A.M.: The President shook hands and took a picture with Chief Ellis Hendrix, a military aide who was retiring.

10:55 A.M.: Was joined in the Oval Office by Under Secretary of State George Ball.

10:56 A.M.: Unrecorded call to Press Secretary George Reedy.

10:57 A.M.–11:10 A.M.: Meeting with Ball and Reedy.

11:14 A.M.: Unrecorded call to Jack Valenti.

11:19 A.M.: Unrecorded call to National Security Adviser McGeorge Bundy.

11:25 A.M.: Called and then fed dogs, Him and Her, on the West Wing porch.

11:30 A.M.: Greeted West German Chancellor Ludwig Erhard at the White House driveway, and then met with Erhard and two interpreters in the Oval Office.

12:40 P.M.: Cabinet Room meeting with Erhard and top U.S. and West German policymakers.

12:50 P.M.: Pictures with Erhard on steps leading to White House flower garden.

12:52 P.M.: Returned to the office.

12:53 P.M.: Unrecorded call to Reedy's office to request a transcript of a briefing from Ball; spoke to Juanita Roberts.

1:00 P.M.–1:27 P.M.: Off-the-record meeting with Secretary of Agriculture Orville Freeman and Under Secretary of Agriculture Charles Murphy.

1:32 P.M.: Unrecorded call to Reedy.

1:43 P.M.

To Dean Rusk[8]

Following up on his conversation the previous day with Assistant Secretary of State for Public Affairs Bob Manning, Johnson called Secretary

---

8. Tape WH6406.07, Citation #3707, Recordings of Telephone Conversations—White House Series, Recordings and Transcripts of Conversations and Meetings, Lyndon B. Johnson Library.

of State Dean Rusk and urged him to increase the amount of specific, detailed content in the State Department's news briefings.[9] Johnson had become concerned about the issue after White House Press Secretary George Reedy had faced intense, hostile questioning about U.S. policy in Southeast Asia during a press briefing at the White House the day before.

President Johnson: [*with Rusk acknowledging*] Take all the information that we get, and all you can get, all you can put out, so that [Richard I.] Phillips has got some substantive stuff to give them and that he's clear on what our policy is, what it was ten years ago.[10] And it may be modified or changed or go forward or go backwards. What it is, we'll announce it, but until then this is the policy, and then restate the policy. People help themselves. And . . . say let nobody mistake what our policy is. It's been announced and repeated and repeated and repeated. And let him have some substance to his briefing that'll relieve a lot of pressure over here.

Dean Rusk: All right, sir, fine. I'll get after that and see that he gets a little more stuff to talk about.

President Johnson: They're doing a great disservice to the American people by leaving the impression that their government's got something to hide and something to conceal, and we're misleading them and we're playing politics with it.[11] And I think they'll get that impression over if we don't open up and repeat what our policy is and get a question planted, "Well, what is our policy? Why don't you tell us our policy?" And then let him tell them.

Rusk: Right. Right.

President Johnson: And get that pretty fully on the wire, so these little nitpickers over here can learn something from it.

Rusk: Fine, I'll do that.

President Johnson: And see that you got coordination from [Arthur] Sylvester's group over there [in the Defense Department] too.[12] I noticed

---

9. Johnson to Bob Manning, time unknown, 11 June 1964, in this volume.

10. Johnson was referring to Richard I. Phillips, director of the State Department's Office of News.

11. Johnson was likely referring to Douglas Kiker's hostile article in the day's *New York Herald Tribune*, which asserted, in essence, what the President described in this passage. See Douglas Kiker, "White House Blackout on Asia News," *New York Herald Tribune*, 12 June 1964.

12. Arthur Sylvester served as assistant secretary of defense for public affairs.

there's some good news coming in: They ran into 25 Communists and killed them yesterday, coming down from Laos.[13]

Rusk: Right.

President Johnson: Maybe they can get us some news from out in the field.

Rusk: Right, sir. All right, I'll get right up to that.

President Johnson: Bye.

1:53 P.M.: Unrecorded call to Lady Bird Johnson.

1:54 P.M.

To George Ball[14]

On June 11, in one of their regular joint press conferences that had become known to Washington humorists as the "Ev and Charlie show," Senate Minority Leader Everett Dirksen and House Minority Leader Charles Halleck had criticized a recently signed treaty between the United States and Russia that outlined provisions under which each superpower would establish new consulates in the major cities of the other nation. Dirksen, in particular, raised concerns that such offices would provide new opportunities for Soviet espionage in the United States and warned that Senate Republicans would give the treaty close scrutiny before approving it. The Illinois senator also cited warnings by FBI Director J. Edgar Hoover and Attorney General Robert F. Kennedy about the extent of ongoing Soviet spying within the United States.[15] In this call, Johnson urged Under Secretary of State Ball to assuage Dirksen's concerns in order to preempt any political gains that the Republicans might derive from the issue. Acting on the advice of Senator William Fulbright, however, Johnson on June 23 decided to defer submission of the treaty to the Senate until

---

13. Johnson was referring to an incident in a mountainous region of South Vietnam near the Laotian border in which South Vietnamese troops attacked a convoy of Vietcong entering the country from Laos. The Associated Press reported that 27 Vietcong were killed. "Saigon Troops Kill 27 Reds in Convoy at Laos Border," *New York Times*, 13 June 1964.

14. Tape WH6406.07, Citation #3709, Recordings of Telephone Conversations—White House Series, Recordings and Transcripts of Conversations and Meetings, Lyndon B. Johnson Library.

15. "G.O.P. Chiefs Wary on Soviet Treaty," *New York Times*, 12 June 1964. For the "Ev and Charlie Show," see "Sen. Dirksen Made Light of in Blackouts," *Washington Post*, 12 June 1964.

early 1965, and it did not actually receive Senate confirmation until March 1967.[16]

Johnson also spoke to Ball about the problems with press coverage that he had just discussed with Dean Rusk. Speaking about the issue more specifically than he had in the Rusk call, Johnson commented on Douglas Kiker's front-page story in the day's *New York Herald Tribune*, which claimed that "there is a total news blackout at the White House on the extent of new U.S. involvement, plans, and policies in Southeast Asia" and speculated that the White House had implemented this policy because of concerns that the region "could blow up in [the President's] face during an election year." The basis for the story was the June 11 press briefing in which George Reedy had faced hostile questions about his inability, or unwillingness, to answer detailed questions about U.S. policy in the region.[17] Johnson asked Ball to insure that State Department public affairs personnel increased the detail of their briefings on Southeast Asia to defuse the charge and take pressure off of Reedy. The incident marked an early step towards the eventual "credibility gap" that, along with failures in public communication and repeated setbacks on the ground, would ultimately undermine the Johnson administration's efforts to build public support for the Vietnam war.

George Ball: Hello?

President Johnson: George, I see [Everett] Dirksen is raising grave questions about the consular agreement, and looks like they may make a little politics about us being soft on Russia.

Ball: Right.

President Johnson: His objection, he says, is that we are giving them too many places to spy from: Chicago and New York and around the country. I think you ought to carefully read his press transcript yesterday and go up and see him and take the best people with you—or get [Dean] Rusk to—and try to nip it in the bud and compliment him on what he did

---

16. "Telegram From the Department of State to the Embassy in the Soviet Union," 24 June 1964; and "Memorandum of Conversation; Subject: Wortham Case; Participants: Soviet Ambassador Anatoliy [*sic*] F. Dobrynin, Deputy Under Secretary Foy D. Kohler," 10 March 1967, in U.S. Department of State, *Foreign Relations of the United States (FRUS), 1964–1968: Soviet Union,* ed. David C. Humphrey and Charles S. Sampson (Washington, DC: GPO, 2001), 14:94–95, 465–66.

17. Kiker, "White House Blackout on Asia News."

on the nuclear treaty and point out that this is definitely in the best interests of America before we get a big issue blown up there.[18]

Ball: All right, we'll certainly move on that. I rather think Dean has already, but, in any event, I'll check with him and we'll do it.

President Johnson: Well, he didn't do any good if he did because he just blasted hell out of us yesterday.

Ball: Yeah.

President Johnson: In the morning papers.

Ball: Well, we'll get right on it. You know, the fact is that this treaty doesn't commit us to consulate any particular places—that's all to be negotiated out yet. So that there's nothing in the treaty that commits us to let them be in *any* place. That's something that we'll all . . . we'll have to talk about right after the treaty's signed. It simply sets up the ground rules.

President Johnson: Well, I would—

Ball: We'll work it out with Dirksen, I think.

President Johnson: I would have [Richard I.] Phillips ask the question. Somebody plant a question [and] ask him.

Ball: All right.

President Johnson: This does, according to what Dirksen says, and then they'll explain it and say, "Obviously, it's not clear on the Hill what it does do and that the treaty is very much in our interest" and got to answer what they said at their political conference yesterday.

Ball: We'll get it out.

President Johnson: Now, George, I think the next few days . . . We've been done a great disservice by the [*New York*] *Herald Tribune*, a fellow lying about the State Department referring him back to the White House.[19]

Ball: Yeah.

President Johnson: He's left the impression [with] the American people that we're trying to cover up and hide something, so I think that

---

18. Johnson was referring to the Limited Nuclear Test Ban Treaty between the United States, the Soviet Union, and more than 100 other countries. The treaty, which the Senate ratified in October 1963, prohibited all aboveground and underwater nuclear tests and permitted only limited underground tests. After initially opposing the treaty, Senator Dirksen had shifted his position and voted with the administration. "Foreign Aid Gets Big Assist from Dirksen; Senate Likely to Pass Program This Week," *Wall Street Journal,* 11 November 1963; *Congressional Quarterly Almanac,* 88th Cong., 2nd sess., 1964, vol. 20 (Washington, DC: Congressional Quarterly Service, 1965), pp. 250–54.

19. The author of the story was the *Herald Tribune*'s White House correspondent, Douglas Kiker.

everything that you can conceive of that could go to Phillips for his briefings ought to go, and he ought to be as full as he can in the national interest so he can keep them off our neck over here.

Ball: We'll push everything out we can, Mr. President.

President Johnson: All right. Thank you.

Ball: All right. Bye.

2:08 P.M.: President Johnson returned to the Mansion for lunch.

2:10 P.M.: Unrecorded call to Jack Valenti, who joined him for
lunch.

2:11 P.M.: Unrecorded call to Larry O'Brien.

2:32 P.M.: Unrecorded call to House Majority Leader Carl Albert of
Oklahoma.

2:51 P.M.: Unrecorded call to Walter Jenkins.

3:20 P.M.: Unrecorded call to Jenkins.

3:10 P.M.–4:00 P.M.: Took a nap.

4:15 P.M.

From John Connally[20]

After the President woke from his nap, a call from Texas Governor John
Connally presented the most politically sensitive task of the day. Connally
led the conservative faction in the feuding Texas state Democratic Party
and he called Johnson to discuss the political implications of the upcoming Texas Democratic convention, which would take place in Houston on
June 16 and which would select the state's delegation to the Democratic
National Convention.[21] Two key disputes between Connally's conservatives and Senator Ralph Yarborough's liberals threatened to disrupt
the convention—and, potentially, embarrass the President. First, the
makeup of delegations from seven Texas counties remained in dispute,
with Houston and especially San Antonio the most heavily contested
and—because of their size—the most significant. Johnson feared that if
the convention credentials committee refused to seat the liberal delegate

20. Tape WH6406.07, Citation #3711, Recordings of Telephone Conversations—White House
Series, Recordings and Transcripts of Conversations and Meetings, Lyndon B. Johnson Library.
21. For background on the liberal-conservative rift in the Texas Democratic Party, see Walter
Reuther to Johnson, 7:52 P.M., 5 June 1964, in this volume.

slates from San Antonio and Houston, the liberal faction might walk out and stage a rump convention that would select a rival delegation to the national convention. Second, Yarborough and the liberals wanted to endorse not only President Johnson, but also his specific platform, including Medicare, the War on Poverty, and, most explosively, civil rights. Connally—who was running for reelection himself in November—and the conservatives preferred to endorse Johnson but not his platform, largely because of continued segregationist opposition in the state to civil rights. Johnson and the governor, who had a complicated political relationship, discussed these delicate issues carefully.[22]

President Johnson's priority was to remain neutral in the dispute and to fend off any further intraparty conflict that might cost the Democrats Yarborough's Senate seat or, potentially, even Texas's electoral college votes in the presidential election. In the conversation, he thus offered Connally a solution to the platform issue that in effect recognized the governor's political need to maintain formal loyalty to the President while separating himself from the specifics of Johnson's agenda. In the end, the Connally forces would prevail at the convention and seat the conservative delegations from the contested cities. Although liberals from Houston and San Antonio did walk out, a rump convention never formed. Instead, party leaders brokered a compromise in which the San Antonio liberal delegation would present its complaints to the national credentials committee in Atlantic City, and Connally would accept a general endorsement of President Johnson's goals (although not the specific platform)—but Connally would control the Texas delegation to the national convention.[23]

President Johnson: Hello?

John Connally: How you doing?

President Johnson: Fine, Johnny.

Connally: I had two or three things I want to tell you.

President Johnson: Sure.

Connally: One, I don't know whether you know, they elected me chairman of the Caucus of Democratic Governors in Cleveland the other day.

President Johnson: Good, wonderful.

---

22. "White House Denies Texas 'Peace Team'," *Washington Post*, 16 June 1964; Ronnie Dugger, "Connally's Slate Wins Texas Seats," *Washington Post*, 17 June 1964.
23. Dugger, "Connally's Slate Wins Texas Seats."

Connally: [*with Johnson acknowledging throughout*] And we'll have a vice chairman and an executive committee that I'm going to name. I haven't named them yet. It'll probably be Al Rosellini from Washington; probably be Frank Morrison of Nebraska; probably [Albertis] Harrison of Virginia or Carl Sanders [of Georgia]; and probably Dick Hughes in New Jersey.[24]

Beyond that, I want to know if you had any thoughts on the committeeman and the committeewoman. It's not going to be easy. I haven't done anything except just think about it, and I'm reversing the procedure almost. I've thought about all the qualifications that *I* think they ought to have. Certainly one is to support you and be your friend, be mine, although that's less important, actually. Beyond that, they've got to have the money to travel and interest to do it and ability to do it, to raise money and be of some support. I just don't think we ought to have a drone that we're honoring.

I thought about Adele Locke as a committeewoman, maybe Frank Erwin as a committeeman. If I move Frank Erwin up, though, I've got to put . . . probably put Marvin Watson in as the state chairman.[25] But I . . . there's no . . . I haven't done anything about it, I haven't talked to anybody about it.

And beyond that, I just wondered if you had any thoughts on the convention down here.

President Johnson: [*softly*] No . . . no.

---

24. All Democratic governors, Albert D. Rosellini served Washington from 1957 to 1965, Frank B. Morrison served Nebraska from 1961 to 1967, Albertis S. Harrison Jr. served Virginia from 1962 to 1966, Carl B. Sanders served Georgia from 1963 to 1967, and Richard J. Hughes served New Jersey from 1962 to 1970.

25. Connally was referring to his selections for Texas representatives to the Democratic National Committee, who would replace two moderate Democrats. Adele Locke was the wife of Connally ally and former state Democratic Party chairman Eugene Locke. Dugger, "Connally's Slate Wins Texas Seats." Frank Erwin was an Austin attorney and one of the most influential figures in Texas politics. In 1964, he was state Democratic Party chairman, a member of the University of Texas's Board of Regents, and one of Connally's closest advisers. Frank Erwin to Johnson, 1:25 P.M., 1 February 1964, in Robert David Johnson and Kent B. Germany, eds., *The Presidential Recordings, Lyndon B. Johnson: Toward the Great Society, February 1, 1964–May 31, 1964*, vol. 4, *February 1, 1964–March 8, 1964* (New York: Norton, 2007), pp. 25–35. Marvin Watson was a Texas businessman, a member of the conservative faction of the state Democratic Party, and a long-standing ally of both Johnson and Governor Connally. He would soon replace Erwin as state Democratic chairman. In 1965, after serving on the 1964 Johnson campaign staff, he would become a special assistant to Johnson; in 1966, he would become chief of staff. W. Marvin Watson with Sherwin Markman, *Chief of Staff: Lyndon Johnson and His Presidency* (New York: St. Martin's Press, 2004).

Connally: I think we're going to have a good convention, although Maury Maverick and Bill Kilgarlin are raising hell, and—[26]

President Johnson: I had a mean column in the news yesterday up here, that I was calling all the labor leaders and giving them hell and telling them that . . . pull them out [of] the convention. I haven't called a human; I didn't even know about it, but some labor man down there had called up here and put it in John Herling's column in the news.[27]

Now, I haven't heard anything about it. I'd just do what I thought was right, and on the program . . .

Connally: Right. . . . We're not going—

President Johnson: I'd say I'm a Democrat and going to support the nominees, but . . . I'll . . . I'll talk about our platform and their platform at the September convention after we see theirs, and . . .

Connally: I thought we'd have two resolutions: one praising you and endorsing you and your leadership, and the other one just say support the nominees from courthouse to the White House.

President Johnson: That's good.

Connally: And that's all.

President Johnson: That's good.

Connally: I ain't going to have one even praising me or anybody else. I just thought we'd have those . . . probably those two—no, we'll have a third one eulogizing Kennedy.

President Johnson: That's good. That's fine.

Connally: And beyond that, I don't—I think it's a hell of a lot of talk. I don't think you've got any problems. I don't know of any that we have, other than that.

President Johnson: They say they're going to have two conventions if—who won in Dallas—in San Antonio and Houston? Where are they contested, San Antonio?

Connally: I don't think there's any question but what the . . . Bill Kilgarlin, what I call the liberal group, won in Houston. I don't think

26. Maury Maverick was a well-known Texas civil rights and civil liberties lawyer and a leader of the liberal faction in the state's Democratic Party. David Uhler, "Maury Maverick 1921–2003; Champion of underdogs was S.A. icon; Bearer of a historic name and of liberals' banner, he was 82," *San Antonio Express-News*, 29 January 2003. William Kilgarlin was a Houston attorney and former member of the Texas state legislature; from 1962 to 1966, he served as the Harris County (Houston) Democratic chairman; he later served on the Texas Supreme Court. http://www.ischool.utexas.edu/kilgarlin/kilgarlin_bios.php.

27. John Herling was a columnist with the National Newspaper Syndicate, a group of union-based newspapers; he also published *John Herling's Labor Letter*. Walter P. Reuther Library of Urban and Labor Affairs, Collections. http://www.reuther.wayne.edu/collections/hefa_1259 .htm.

there's any question, but what Cliff Cassidy and the conservatives won in Dallas. San Antonio was damn close. John Peace and his boys didn't get a fair shake—they wouldn't even hear them, wouldn't even let them present a case before the credentials committee. And just—they didn't get to be heard at all. Just wouldn't hear them on some of the precincts that they had contested. [*Johnson acknowledges.*] San Antonio's the only one—and this I say to you in confidence because they—I haven't said anything to anybody.

President Johnson: Yeah.

Connally: But I don't think there's any question but what the liberals won Houston, conservatives won Dallas, and I think they'll be seated in that way. And San Antonio, I don't know. It's a damn close call in San Antonio. John Peace said he had it won, said it took 1,118, I believe, and he said he'd have had 1,250. Course the other side says they won. We've got a contest in Randall and Hutchinson. There are seven counties in all, but they don't amount to much.

But I have not fully gone into the facts. We're asking each of them to submit briefs in all the contested counties. But I don't think there's any county except one that's really of any importance, and that's Bexar County [San Antonio]. Randall, however, they claim up there that the liberals won by a few votes, but the reason they did is because they stole one of the . . . stole *the* biggest precinct in the county, which would have made the difference in the convention, and I don't know. [*Johnson acknowledges.*] Of course, the other side said they didn't. But there's seven counties all told—

President Johnson: Well, if they had them all, it doesn't make any difference, does it?

Connally: No. No. No. I think—We figured it every way under the sun. We can't figure any way but a 2 to 1 giving them everything.

President Johnson: Mm-hmm.

Connally: Give them all the counties, and . . . so, I don't think there's any problem.

President Johnson: [William] Scranton announced today, and I don't know what that's going to be.[28] I don't know—I believe [Barry] Goldwater looks pretty good, but he may not have.

---

28. William Scranton was the Republican governor of Pennsylvania and the preferred choice of liberal and moderate Republicans who hoped to block the party's nomination of Arizona Senator Barry Goldwater for president. Scranton formally announced his candidacy on 12 June. John D. Morris, "Scranton Enters G.O.P. Contest under a 'Progressive' Banner; Scorns the Views of Goldwater," *New York Times*, 13 June 1964.

Connally: I think Goldwater—my interpretation of it is that what they've done, they've just thrown Scranton in the breech in order to protect themselves a little bit on the theory he voted against cloture and they didn't want the whole Republican Party, in effect, to go by default *after* that vote.[29]

[with the President acknowledging] My judgment is if he had voted *for* cloture, Scranton would never have announced. That'd be my guess. And that what they're doing, they just feel like now they *have* to put somebody else in the arena with him so that they don't all get tarred with endorsing his position on cloture. That'd be my interpretation, but I don't know whether that's right or not. Scranton didn't indicate to me out in Cleveland that he's a damned bit interested, and I think it resulted from the stimulant that arose from this vote that he cast.

President Johnson: You go on and do what's right and run it the way you want to, and I know it'll be all right.

Connally: Well, ain't nobody going but your friends, and they're going to be for you for president and whoever in the hell who you want for vice president, and they ain't going to raise hell about your program or anything else. I just—as you know, I don't want to endorse it now because we don't know what the hell it is.

President Johnson: I'd say, "I'm endorsing him and *[unclear comment by Connally]* if he had a program, I'd be glad to endorse that. I haven't seen his program, don't know what it is, and he doesn't know himself. And *[as]* a matter of fact, I think that he's still working it out in Congress, and whenever he *[is]* ready to submit it to anybody, we'll be the first ones to look at it."

Connally: That's fine.

President Johnson: I'd just . . . I'd just say that I . . . They . . . "I'm going to be on the *[chuckling]* platform committee and I want to help write the program." That's what I'd tell them. I'd just say, "There ain't no program yet, and . . . I'm going to be on the platform committee and help write it."

Connally: Incidentally, the *[unclear]* poll came out today.

President Johnson: What does it show?

Connally: It shows you at an all-time high of 84 percent.

President Johnson: Mmm.

Connally: It shows me at . . .

---

29. Goldwater had voted against cloture of debate on the civil rights bill and would vote against the bill itself a few weeks later.

President Johnson: That's 74 in the nation, Sunday.

Connally: Yeah.

President Johnson: Gallup's coming out Sunday, 74.

Connally: And shows me 82.

President Johnson: God Almighty. Well, that's wonderful.

Connally: Highest of any governor since they've started keeping it in 1940. Highest was 79, and you had 84 and I had 82.

President Johnson: Well, I don't believe we're that good, do you?

Connally: No. [*laughing*] No, I don't believe we're that good.

President Johnson: [*Chuckles slightly.*] Well—

Connally: Congratulations on your foreign aid bill, and congratulations on cloture.

President Johnson: Well, thank you, my friend. We're doing our best we can, and . . .

Connally: Well, you're doing a hell of a job. I don't know any . . . any problems.

Incidentally, the next time Frank Morrison calls, if you don't mind, tell Jack [Valenti] or Walter [Jenkins], somebody, to put him through to you if you possibly can talk to him.

President Johnson: All right. . . . Yeah, I didn't know he'd called.

Connally: I know it. He's called up there four or five times, he says.

President Johnson: Mm-hmm. I'll do it.

Connally: OK.

President Johnson: All right.

Connally: Bye.

4:24 P.M.: The President returned to the office.

4:25 P.M.–4:32 P.M.: Meeting with Special Assistant David Lawrence, the former Pittsburgh mayor and Pennsylvania governor who headed the President's Committee on Equal Opportunity in Housing.

4:34 P.M.: Met Chancellor Erhard in the Cabinet Room and took him to the porch for a picture with Peace Corps Director and antipoverty committee chairman Sargent Shriver.

4:37 P.M.–5:23 P.M.: With Erhard, returned to the Cabinet Room for a meeting with leading U.S. and West German officials.

5:25 P.M.: Unrecorded call to George Reedy.

5:26 P.M.

To Orville Freeman[30]

After returning to the office, the President called Secretary of Agriculture Orville Freeman and discussed efforts by journalists to probe the significance of changes in budget estimates and overall spending for federal agricultural programs.

Orville Freeman: . . . memoranda on these budget and personnel figures that we discussed.

President Johnson: Good, all right.

Freeman: And that ought to be in—[*Freeman coughs*] excuse me—Jack's [Valenti's] hands by now. And I also ran down the reporters that have been snooping around here to get a fix on what they're working on, and we'll try and handle this business.

Briefly, if you've got a moment and you're interested, there are two things that they're trying to shoot at: First, the Commodity Credit Corporation spends one year and goes up to restore capital the next. Because we are not restoring as much capital in the fiscal '65 budget as we spent in the year fiscal '64, they're contending there's something questionable about this.[31] Obviously, that's nonsense, because it could just as easily mean we're going to spend less in '65 than we did in '64 and didn't need it. So that means nothing. Secondly, our estimates—or the general estimates for fiscal '65—have been increased. How much, I don't think anyone knows; they'd like to find out.

But these are just pure horseback estimates. They really mean very, very little because we don't know what the hell's going to happen in the weather or anything else. And I just talked with Kermit [Gordon] and said, "I don't think we ought to even talk about these estimates. Why

---

30. Tape WH6406.07, Citation #3712, Recordings of Telephone Conversations—White House Series, Recordings and Transcripts of Conversations and Meetings, Lyndon B. Johnson Library.
31. The Commodity Credit Corporation managed federal price support programs for agricultural commodities and the food-for-peace program that distributed surplus U.S. agricultural products among U.S.-allied countries. In the past, the CCC had received full reimbursement of any losses it sustained in these programs, but the fiscal 1965 budget provided for only partial reimbursement, with the difference to be made up as necessary by supplemental appropriations or a new program of interest-free credit for the agency. This led to a reduction of more than $975.4 million in the CCC's fiscal 1965 budget. *Congressional Quarterly Almanac*, 1964, vol. 20, p. 195.

should we open ourselves to exposure on something that is just pure guesses at this point anyway?"

President Johnson: I'd just tell them that near as I can tell that the best estimate you've got is the one you've already made.

Freeman: Yes, sir, and stay with it. And that that would be the one we made last January, and . . .[32]

President Johnson: That's right.

Freeman: And that's what I—

President Johnson: Don't let them use you to murder me.

Freeman: Well, that's exactly what I'm trying to stop, but, you see, we've had this system over the years to have a midyear—in this case it would be one updated estimate. And this is now the estimate that . . . being updated now. The one Kermit talked about and was released out of the White House about two weeks ago was an increased estimate.[33] But it doesn't mean a damn thing because that's for a whole year ahead, and in our business, with these crops and weather uncertainties, well, we ought not to give ourselves that kind of exposure. I just talked to him about it, and so I think we ought to just stand on what we made initially.

Forty-seven seconds excised as classified information.

Freeman: . . . do.

President Johnson: OK.

Freeman: Very good, sir.

5:36 P.M.: Off-the-record meeting with Attorney General Robert F. Kennedy and General James Gavin. Kennedy remained in the office until 6:34 P.M.; Gavin departed at 5:57 P.M.

6:02 P.M.: Unrecorded call to Walter Jenkins.

6:10 P.M.: Unrecorded call to Jenkins.

---

32. Freeman was referring to the funds allocated to agricultural programs in Johnson's January 1964 budget proposal (for fiscal 1965)—a total of approximately $5.1 billion. "Annual Budget Message to the Congress, Fiscal Year 1965," 21 January 1964, *Public Papers of the Presidents of the United States: Lyndon B. Johnson, 1963–64* (Washington, DC: GPO, 1965), 1:187.

33. Released on 30 May, the midyear budget estimate projected possible increases in agricultural spending (over the January estimate) of $1 billion for fiscal 1964 and $800 million for fiscal 1965. William M. Blair, "Rise Is Forecast in Farm Spending," *New York Times*, 31 May 1964.

6:21 P.M.

From George Reedy[34]

Press Secretary Reedy called to discuss the scheduling of a meeting the next day with an unidentified person.

George Reedy: . . . tomorrow if you're going to see him, I'll [*unclear*]—

President Johnson: I don't know, but I would say around 12 [P.M.], and we might see him earlier if we're going to see him at all. I don't know, but you'd better see Mac Bundy and State and see what you can get from them, and Defense.

Reedy: I've got . . . [*unclear*]—

President Johnson: For tomorrow. And I'll talk to you about it in the morning.

Reedy: Right. OK, sir.

President Johnson: All right.

6:22 P.M.: Unrecorded call from Walter Jenkins.

6:25 P.M.

To Myer Feldman[35]

With Attorney General Kennedy still in the office, Johnson placed a call to Special Counsel Mike Feldman to discuss an investigation by the Senate Government Operations Committee into a possible defense contracting scandal.

A brief, unclear office conversation precedes the call.
President Johnson: Mike?
Myer Feldman: Yes, Mr. President.

---

34. Tape WH6406.07, Citation #3714, Recordings of Telephone Conversations—White House Series, Recordings and Transcripts of Conversations and Meetings, Lyndon B. Johnson Library.
35. Tape WH6406.07, Citation #3716, Recordings of Telephone Conversations—White House Series, Recordings and Transcripts of Conversations and Meetings, Lyndon B. Johnson Library.

President Johnson: We have a situation involving a former operation of Colonel Kelly and some of his staff. Are you familiar with that operation?

Feldman: No, I'm not.

President Johnson: Did you know a Colonel Kelly that coordinated between us and the Defense Department on contracts?

Feldman: Yes. . . . Yes, I did, but I don't know any—

President Johnson: Did you ever hear of a fellow named Pericles? P-e-r-i-c-l-e-s?

Feldman: No, I didn't. I thought—Ron Linton was the fellow that I dealt most with.[36]

President Johnson: Who?

Feldman: Ron Linton, who left and went over to the Senate committee.

President Johnson: Well, this fellow's gone to AID [Agency For International Development], and he's involved in some trouble, and John McClellan's after him, and we need to have the facts developed here, and I want you to talk to the Attorney General and get his ideas about what to do and then carry them out.[37]

Feldman: All right, I will, Mr. President.

President Johnson: He'll be up to see you in a minute or call you.

Feldman: All right.

Time Unknown

Office Conversation with Robert Kennedy[38]

The recording system captured a brief section of mostly unintelligible office conversation, probably between the President and Robert F. Kennedy.

---

36. Ron M. Linton served as chief clerk and staff director for the Senate Committee on Public Works. Pericles remains unidentified.

37. John McClellan, Democrat from Arkansas, was the chairman of the Senate Committee on Government Operations.

38. Tape WH6406.07, Citation #3717, Recordings of Telephone Conversations—White House Series, Recordings and Transcripts of Conversations and Meetings, Lyndon B. Johnson Library.

TIME UNKNOWN

From Jane Leahy to Vicki McCammon[39]

Robert Kennedy's secretary called the White House with a message for the Attorney General. She stated that "it's very important that he call here before he leaves the White House." McCammon then relayed the message to another secretary at the White House.

TIME UNKNOWN

With Vicki McCammon[40]

An unclear office conversation continues before the call.
President Johnson: . . . well, get somebody to talk to him, and if we have to, I guess we just ride it out and do nothing. Is that right?
[*on phone*] Hello?
Vicki McCammon: Mr. President, Mac Kilduff is here with a statement that he and George [Reedy] would like to release on your meeting with General [James] Gavin and the Attorney General.[41] Could he show it to you?
President Johnson: Wait just [*unclear*].
General! General, wait just a minute.[42]
[*on phone*] Yeah, bring it on in.
McCammon: Thank you, sir. [*Pause.*]
President Johnson: [*on another telephone line*] [*Unclear.*] Tell the Attorney General. Catch him if you can for me. [*Long pause.*]
[*to someone in office*] Wait just a minute.
Unidentified: All right, sir. [*Long pause.*]
President Johnson: [*Unclear.*]

---

39. Tape WH6406.07, Citations #3718 and #3719, Recordings of Telephone Conversations—White House Series, Recordings and Transcripts of Conversations and Meetings, Lyndon B. Johnson Library.
40. Tape WH6406.07, Citation #3721, Recordings of Telephone Conversations—White House Series, Recordings and Transcripts of Conversations and Meetings, Lyndon B. Johnson Library.
41. Malcolm Kilduff served as assistant press secretary.
42. Johnson occasionally referred to Attorney General Kennedy as "general," so given the context of this comment it is probable that he is referring to Kennedy rather than General Gavin; in addition, the White House Daily Diary indicates that Gavin left at 5:57 P.M., probably prior to this call.

TIME UNKNOWN

With Vicki McCammon[43]

President Johnson: Hello?
Vicki McCammon: Mr. President, George Reedy is asking if he can put on a photo lid.[44]
President Johnson: Yeah.
McCammon: All right, sir. Thank you.
George Reedy: Hello?
McCammon: He said yes.
Reedy: [*to someone in office*] Photo lid.

TIME UNKNOWN

Between Vicki McCammon and Office Secretary[45]

The recording system captured a brief segment of a conversation in which Vicki McCammon discussed a message for Attorney General Kennedy that had been received from his office.

6:36 P.M.–7:03 P.M.: Meeting with Pennsylvania Senator Joseph S. Clark.

7:00 P.M.

To Larry O'Brien[46]

Perhaps on the basis of his conversation with Senator Clark, whose state would benefit significantly from the bill (and who remained in the office

---

43. Tape WH6406.07, Citation #3723, Recordings of Telephone Conversations—White House Series, Recordings and Transcripts of Conversations and Meetings, Lyndon B. Johnson Library.
44. A "lid" was generally a reference to a notice from the press secretary to the White House press corps that no more news would be forthcoming and that they could file their stories. In this case, it appeared to refer to opportunities for photographs of the President with any visitors.
45. Tape WH6406.07, Citation #3724, Recordings of Telephone Conversations—White House Series, Recordings and Transcripts of Conversations and Meetings, Lyndon B. Johnson Library.
46. Tape WH6406.08, Citation #3728, Recordings of Telephone Conversations—White House Series, Recordings and Transcripts of Conversations and Meetings, Lyndon B. Johnson Library.

at the time of the call), President Johnson called Special Assistant for Congressional Relations Larry O'Brien to ask about the current head count in the House on the urban mass transportation bill. The transit bill provided $375 million in federal matching grants to local and state governments for the development of regional mass transit systems.[47]

Larry O'Brien: Hello?

President Johnson: How many Republican votes you got for the mass transit [bill]?

O'Brien: They're calling 40 Republicans maximum, and the hard count that we have seen from the lobbyists puts it at 35.

President Johnson: All right. How many Democrats?

O'Brien: About 165.

President Johnson: Well, you can pass it, then.

O'Brien: No, you can't, not with 165 and 35.

President Johnson: That's 200.

O'Brien: Yeah. Not enough.

President Johnson: Well, they . . . Well, do you have over 400 voting on these roll calls these days?

O'Brien: Yeah. We hit 400 or slightly better.

President Johnson: How many you need to be sure?

O'Brien: They should be able to bring us a completely firm list of 40 to 45 Republicans that will calendar it.

President Johnson: I've got one from Joe Clark. He's sitting here listening to you.

O'Brien: Yeah.

President Johnson: I've got one with 40 names on it, and he says right where they came from: [Jesse] Younger, San Francisco Bay area, AMA; [Charles] Gubser, San Francisco Transit Authority—[48]

O'Brien: I have that list.

President Johnson: You have those 40?

O'Brien: Yeah. I head-counted this with the lobbyists twice. But the 40, I will buy the Pennsylvania names on the list, but there are some of the others that are slightly question mark, and I've discussed this with the leadership, with Speaker [John] McCormack yesterday afternoon, Carl Albert and Hale Boggs today. And I have told them that there's been an improve-

---

47. *Congressional Quarterly Almanac*, 1964, vol. 20, p. 556.
48. Representatives J. Arthur Younger and Charles Gubser were Republicans from California. Johnson's reference to "AMA" remains unidentified.

ment in this situation over the last two weeks, that it was not in good shape two weeks ago. It's in reasonable shape now, but not quite where it should be to calendar it, and that they should, however, look into this thing and give it some further consideration, which we are going to do Tuesday afternoon. In the meantime, this . . . [David] Henderson and these fellows have been told they've got to scratch around a little bit harder.[49]

President Johnson: Mmm. So what you really need is another 10 votes?

O'Brien: That's right. And we have another 10 votes on that list, then we go with it. And they can get them.

President Johnson: You—

O'Brien: They can get them. Now, hell, they just haven't gotten the votes they should get, the Pennsylvania Railroad and the rest of these people. Christ, I thought they had some real zip. They've got the power; they can get the votes. We started four weeks ago with these fellows, and I sat over here in this municipal association office with the railroad people and everyone else, and they had 24 Republicans and were demanding we calendar the damn bill.

Now they've got it up to 35 to 40. [William] Widnall is only claiming 35, and he's the Republican leader in this fight, and so let's say 35.[50] I'll bet you on a recommit motion tomorrow morning, they'd have 22. You know.

President Johnson: You don't think it's 35 firm, then, you—

O'Brien: No, I want to . . . they ought to publish the list and have each fellow publicly say he's for the bill. Maybe they ought to arrange the railroad and the municipal league and others. Why the hell don't they get these fellows to send a letter to the leadership up there demanding that the thing be calendared—that's a good bit of evidence they'll support it. See, the Republican Policy Committee has taken a position against this bill.

President Johnson: Well, if we got 40 Republicans for it, why don't [we] try to get them to get a letter to the Republican Policy Committee and ask them to . . .

O'Brien: That's very good, and that the Republicans in the Pennsylvania delegation are the strongest people for it. There's a letter from [William] Scranton to [Robert] Corbett urging enactment of this bill.[51] And by God, that's fine, except that they go into a Republican policy meeting

---

49. David Henderson was a Democratic representative from North Carolina and a member of the House Committee on Public Works.
50. William Widnall was a Republican representative from New Jersey.
51. Robert Corbett was a Republican representative from Pennsylvania.

and the Republicans take an official position against the bill. Now, that, generally, we have found in the past scares off some of these boys. They're well-meaning until that happens.

But hell, I . . . that bill, as you know, Mr. President, you've been anxious as the devil to see this pass now for months, and so have I and everyone involved. And goddamn, we'll calendar as soon as we have them.

President Johnson: Why couldn't we get a letter to . . . Why couldn't we get a letter to the Speaker and . . . say this bill has been given a rule and we heard your—we believe in it, we favor it, and we urge you to schedule the earliest possible date? Would that be too much trouble? And then ask these 40 to sign it?

O'Brien: Not a bit. We could try that. Now, Carl Albert tried to sit down with Widnall this afternoon, and he couldn't locate him, and he left a message at Widnall's office that he wants Widnall in *his* office Monday morning with his list, solid names, where he is willing to have Carl Albert have a copy of the list presented by Widnall that Albert can show to all concerned that are interested as an official list of Republican supporters on the recommit and on the passage.

President Johnson: All right.

O'Brien: And I . . . we've actually devoted a good deal of time the last couple of days to discussions on this, and I must say it's gone from what appeared to be limbo three or four weeks ago to a live product. But Christ, I think they want a bill rather than a show of force next week where they fall on their can and set mass transit back five years, so . . . if you calendar that damn thing—There's no question about it, we're going to calendar it. The Speaker told me last night, he said, "If it turns out we don't have the votes we're going to calendar it because," he said, "hell, we should have an up or down on this in this session of Congress. We're definitely going to." Said, "I'd like to pick an opportune time when we also can pass it."

President Johnson: All right, you got a rule on it, haven't we?

O'Brien: Yep.

President Johnson: Now, what is the situation on poverty now, any developments today?

O'Brien: [Pat] McNamara is going to conduct his hearings next Wednesday, Thursday, and Friday in the Senate.[52] He feels that he can clean the bill right out of committee in three days, that the administration side of it, probably even taking a look at that the first day, and if

---

52. A Democrat from Michigan, Patrick McNamara chaired the Select Subcommittee on Poverty of the Senate Committee on Labor and Public Welfare. The subcommittee would hold hearings on the administration's economic opportunity bill.

[Sargent] Shriver can go solo, or practically solo, as a witness, they could clean it out faster than that. He'll have that bill out of the committee.

President Johnson: All right. Now, what about the rule in the House?

O'Brien: I talked to [Tip] O'Neill at length again.[53] And O'Neill said to me, "Let me just say this, O'Brien," he said, "my wife is 50 years of age this coming week, and we've been married 25 years. And for 10 years I told her on the day of her . . . our wedding anniversary and her birthday at 50 and 25 respectively, we would be in Paris, and that's where we're going to be." [*The President chuckles.*] Now, he said, "By God, you've knocked one week off my vacation now." He said, "I was supposed to go on from Paris to Rome and a couple of other spots." Now, he said, "Damn it all, I'm leaving here at 7:30 next Tuesday night. I will be sitting in the committee room for the executive session on the poverty bill the following Tuesday morning at 10 A.M., and you have my vote on it, period." So, that's as far as I got with him.

President Johnson: Mm-hmm. All right. Any other news?

O'Brien: [*chuckling*] No. Let's see. I'm looking for a piece of good news. I can't find one right now. [*Laughs.*]

President Johnson: OK, God bless you.

O'Brien: OK, Mr. President.

President Johnson: Bye.

7:05 P.M.: Unrecorded call to Walter Jenkins.

7:17 P.M.–7:21 P.M.: Meeting in the lounge with Special Assistant Douglass Cater.

7:25 P.M.: Unrecorded call to Jenkins.

7:26 P.M.

From Robert Kennedy[54]

The Attorney General called with the suggestion that Terry Sanford, the progressive governor of North Carolina, would be a strong choice to replace Henry Cabot Lodge as U.S. ambassador to South Vietnam.

---

53. Thomas "Tip" O'Neill was a Democratic representative from Massachusetts and a member of the House Rules Committee.
54. Tape WH6406.08, Citation #3731, Recordings of Telephone Conversations—White House Series, Recordings and Transcripts of Conversations and Meetings, Lyndon B. Johnson Library.

Robert Kennedy: Hello?

President Johnson: Hi, General.

Kennedy: You know what another suggestion for Vietnam . . .

President Johnson: Good.

Kennedy: . . . is Terry Sanford.

President Johnson: [*Pauses.*] All right.

Kennedy: You know he was a paratrooper.

President Johnson: No, I didn't know that. I know he's got a lot of social consciousness and a damned able, good man.

Kennedy: And he was a good administrator. He was a paratrooper during the war, in the 82nd Airborne, and so he's had some military experience. I think he's got . . . he had a damn good war record, and he's a good administrator, and he's got the touch with people.

President Johnson: Yes, he has, and he's for people too.

Kennedy: Yeah.

President Johnson: They need somebody out there. That's—

Kennedy: [*with the President acknowledging*] George Ball just is never going to be able to get that across. You know, he's awful good in a . . . but he's not going to be able to excite people. I think that somebody like Terry Sanford or [Carl] Sanders, you know, one of those people, somebody that's had that political experience. Anyway, I thought he—

President Johnson: Thank you. It's a good—it's an excellent suggestion. We'll give it some thought.

Kennedy: Worth thinking about.

President Johnson: Fine.

Kennedy: OK.

President Johnson: Thank you.

7:35 P.M.

From Robert McNamara[55]

The Secretary of Defense called to brief the President on plans for resumed U.S. reconnaissance flights over Laos. These would be the first such flights since two U.S. planes had been shot down the previous week, leading to a U.S. bombing raid on an antiaircraft battery controlled by the

---

55. Tape WH6406.08, Citation #3732, Recordings of Telephone Conversations—White House Series, Recordings and Transcripts of Conversations and Meetings, Lyndon B. Johnson Library.

Communist Pathet Lao. Johnson then asked McNamara about the Defense Department's own inquiries into the activities of a colonel accused of illegally awarding defense contracts.

Robert McNamara: . . . and you approved another reconnaissance mission over Laos. I wanted to tell you we worked out the details today with the State Department. We're all in agreement on them. It would leave tomorrow night, some time roughly around 11:00 in the evening our time, and would consist of one reconnaissance plane and up to four escorts, a maximum total of five aircraft, to go over the . . . certain of the supply routes in the panhandle. It would stay away from the Plaine des Jarres and from any area in which we know there are antiaircraft replacements. It would seek a safe entry route and a safe exit route. The purpose would be to minimize life while at the same time carrying out reconnaissance.

President Johnson: That's good. Now, are you on top of this . . .

Eleven seconds excised under deed of gift restriction.

McNamara: Yes, sir.

President Johnson: You told them to fire him—

McNamara: Yes, sir.

President Johnson: —and [Eugene] Zuckert told them to fire him, and they didn't do it?[56]

McNamara: That's correct.

President Johnson: Uh-huh. Well, looks like it's . . . you ought to be sure that Cy [Vance] stays right on top of that, now.[57]

McNamara: [*Unclear*] . . . both Cy and I are on it, Mr. President. I have a full investigator's report in my own safe on this. I started it myself.

President Johnson: Well, I want you to put a letter of mine in your safe that I talked to you about on . . . about the 24th on all contracts.

McNamara: I issued . . . I came back here that day and spoke to the secretaries [of the Armed Services], and I believe I have a note in our file. I'll dig that up tomorrow.

President Johnson: Well, if not, I've got a letter I want you—to get you even ahead of that, right after—when I saw you in the EOB [Executive Office Building]. I'm looking at my diary to see what day it was.

---

56. General Eugene Zuckert was secretary of the Air Force. "Him" is probably a reference to a Colonel Kelly who was under investigation for alleged improprieties in the awarding of defense contracts.

57. Cyrus Vance was deputy secretary of defense.

McNamara: I'd be delighted to, Mr. President.

President Johnson: OK, all right.

McNamara: And I have *twice* talked to the secretaries personally about this, and I told them that you said that you told me that if anyone in the White House ever said that you said anything about a contract that it was a damn lie.

President Johnson: Or anybody else over here.

McNamara: Or anybody else.

President Johnson: What—I'm not worried about myself, but I am worried about anybody else.

McNamara: No, no, I said anyone in the White House.

President Johnson: That's right; that's right.

McNamara: That's exactly what I told the secretary, that you said that anyone in the White House that said you said anything about it was a damn lie.

President Johnson: Well, here's what I'm saying, [*reading quickly*] "Confirming our conversation, I wish to advise you that it is and will be my practice to commit the award of government contracts and matters incidental thereto to the appropriate departments and agencies concerned. I expect the officials of various agencies charged with this responsibility to scrupulously comply with all applicable laws and regulations, to observe and require observance to the high standards of probity and dedication to public interest. I shall make no recommendations nor suggestions respect[ing] the contracts, awards, and negotiations. I shall not permit any person on the staff at the White House to do so. If at any time anyone connected to the White House should endeavor to interfere on behalf of any person or company or otherwise to affect the award, I ask this be promptly reported to me so I can take action to separate such a person [from] my staff."

McNamara: I think it's excellent. Excellent. We have a pretty good record on this—

Three seconds excised under deed of gift restriction.

McNamara: . . . case, Mr. President. I handle it myself, and I—

President Johnson: When you ordered him fired, why in the hell wasn't he fired?

McNamara: Well, I'll tell you why sometime. I think that . . .

President Johnson: Mm-hmm, mm-hmm. Well . . .

McNamara: There was a little cell in here, as a matter of fact, and—

President Johnson: I know that, and I heard it, and I told Walter [Jenkins] we didn't want any of that stuff as soon as we came in here.

McNamara: Well . . . Well, this was cleaned out before you came in, I think. Yes, it was.

Thirteen seconds excised under deed of gift restriction.

McNamara: It's a nasty situation. The trouble here is that [John] McClellan's digging around here, you know, trying to find some dirt on the—

President Johnson: That'll reopen the whole thing, you see.

McNamara: That's right—

Twenty seconds excised under deed of gift restriction.

McNamara: And when I heard about it—I happened to hear about it through a friend at Ford that I hired at Ford Motor Company 15 years ago, and he called and gave us the information, and within an hour after we got the information, I had the inspector general of the Air Force in my office and set up a full-scale investigation. And the moment we completed it, which was maybe four or five weeks after that, I issued orders to have him fired. So I think the top level of the [Defense] Department is clean, and whatever happened underneath, which we're digging in now, won't make much of a story.

President Johnson: OK. All right.

McNamara: Thank you, Mr. President.

President Johnson: Say?

McNamara: Yes?

President Johnson: You look into what you can get with your inspectors and investigators on Terry Sanford, the governor of North Carolina. He's a pretty attractive fellow, and he may be the fellow that we're talking about.[58]

McNamara: All right, I'll do so.

President Johnson: You know, out—

McNamara: Yeah, sure. Sure, I know him. I know who you are talking about.

7:56 P.M.: President Johnson returned to the White House Mansion to prepare for dinner honoring Chancellor Erhard.

Vickie McCammon ran after the President through the colonnade to give him his prepared remarks for the evening.

---

58. Johnson was referring to the possibility of naming North Carolina Governor Terry Sanford to replace Henry Cabot Lodge as U.S. ambassador to South Vietnam. See the preceding conversation, Robert Kennedy to Johnson, 7:26 P.M., 12 June 1964, in this chapter.

According to the Daily Diary, the President replied, "Oh, good. Thank you, honey, you just caught me in time. I've only got ten minutes before Erhard arrives."

7:57 P.M.: With Lady Bird Johnson, greeted Chancellor Erhard at the North Portico of the White House.

8:00 P.M.: The Johnsons took Erhard and his party to the second floor of the White House.

8:15 P.M.: Received dinner guests in the White House East Room.

8:40 P.M.: Dinner for Chancellor Erhard in the White House flower garden, including a formal exchange of toasts and remarks by both leaders.

10:20 P.M.: Dinner guests retired to the White House ground floor for coffee and liqueurs.

10:45 P.M.: Entertainment on the South Grounds.

11:20 P.M.: Chancellor Erhard left the White House.

11:40 P.M.: President Johnson went to the second floor of the White House.

12:30 A.M., June 13: The President went to bed.

Saturday, June 13, 1964

The biggest load I carry is the fact I'm from Texas.

—President Johnson to Robert McNamara

While the Republican Party scrambled to assess the implications of Pennsylvania Governor William Scranton's late challenge to Arizona Senator Barry Goldwater's presumptive nomination as the party's presidential candidate, Lyndon Johnson enjoyed a relatively quiet Saturday at the White House.[1] Meanwhile, the Senate easily defeated a series of amendments designed to weaken the voting rights provisions of the civil rights bill, and the Chinese government called for a new round of Geneva talks to address the continuing conflict in Laos.[2] The President also received some slightly equivocal good news in a Gallup Poll, which reported that while 68 percent of respondents said there was nothing they disliked about him, 34 percent said there was nothing they particularly *liked*, either.[3]

10:55 A.M.: The President woke up.
11:15 A.M.: Unrecorded call from McGeorge Bundy.
11:25 A.M.: Unrecorded call to George Reedy.
11:30 A.M.: Unrecorded call to Bundy.
11:46 A.M.: Unrecorded call from Jack Valenti.

---

1. Earl Mazo, "Rivals Report Goldwater Is Losing Delegates," *New York Times*, 14 June 1964.
2. E. W. Kenworthy, "Rights Bloc Bars Curbs on Voting," *New York Times*, 14 June 1964; Seymour Topping, "Peking Demands Emergency Talk on Crisis in Laos," *New York Times*, 14 June 1964.
3. George Gallup, "68% Can See Nothing in Johnson to Dislike," *Washington Post*, 14 June 1964.

12:16 P.M.: Unrecorded call to Lee White.

12:40 P.M.: Unrecorded call to Larry O'Brien.

1:14 P.M.: Unrecorded call to Reedy.

1:50 P.M.: Unrecorded call to Valenti.

2:00 P.M.: Unrecorded call from Reedy.

3:10 P.M.: Unrecorded call to Walter Jenkins.

4:05 P.M.: Unrecorded call to Special Assistant David Lawrence in Pittsburgh, Pennsylvania.

4:35 P.M.: Went to the Oval Office and reviewed pictures and newspapers on secretary Gerri Whittington's desk.

4:55 P.M.: Malcolm Kilduff delivered press clippings and a copy of a briefing prepared by Secretary of State Dean Rusk.

4:56 P.M.

From Ashton Gonella[4]

In his first recorded call of the day, Johnson and White House staff member Ashton Gonella discussed the guest list for the evening's dinner with a group of Texas congressmen and their wives.

Ashton Gonella: . . . at Gunston Hall and gave her the list of the people who have accepted for tonight. There are 12. She wants to know if you want to add any more, or what. We've got two Johnsons, two [Walter] Jenkins . . .

President Johnson: Well, wait a minute. OK, go slow. Where are you?

Gonella: I'm at home.

President Johnson: All right, go ahead now.

Gonella: Two Johnsons, two Jenkins.

President Johnson: Now, your husband is not chasing you around? You're going so fast. Go ahead now. [*Gonella chuckles.*] Next?

Gonella: Two [Robert] Caseys.

President Johnson: Two Caseys. That's six.

---

4. Tape WH6406.08, Citation #3733, Recordings of Telephone Conversations—White House Series, Recordings and Transcripts of Conversations and Meetings, Lyndon B. Johnson Library.

Gonella: Beck—

President Johnson: Two [Lindley] Beckworths, that's eight.

Gonella: Two [Joe] Pools.

President Johnson: Two who? Pools, that's 10.

Gonella: One Doris Powell.

President Johnson: All right.

Gonella: One Walter Rogers.

President Johnson: All right.

Gonella: Now, that's 12. Now, I called Walter and he said he would suggest, and in this order, if you want to add anyone: Congressman and Mrs. [Bob] Poage . . .

President Johnson: Who turned us down?

Gonella: The Clark Thompsons are in North Carolina. Congressman [Olin "Tiger"] Teague is out of town, and the [Joe] Kilgores regretted to Mrs. Johnson, but I don't know what the reason was. I think they also are out of town.

President Johnson: Mm-hmm. All right, now, who are the next ones?

Gonella: And Walter suggests Poage and then [Graham] Purcell. Now, do you want to increase it from—

President Johnson: Yeah, I would do that, and then [the Jake] Pickles.

Gonella: And then Pickles.

President Johnson: I'd put Poages, Pickles, and Purcells, and what would that give you? That's 17, wouldn't it?

Gonella: No, sir. 12, 14, 16, *18*.

President Johnson: All right. Well—

Gonella: The table cannot hold any more than 18.

President Johnson: All right, that's what I'd do. That's [*unclear*] . . . I'd go with the Poages and the Pickles and the Purcells, and if you haven't got any more, have you got anybody else besides on the list, if those can't come?

Gonella: No, sir, that's all.

President Johnson: All right, call those right now.

Gonella: All right, fine.

President Johnson: OK.

Gonella: Thank you. Bye.

5:00 P.M.: Jack Valenti arrived in the office.

5:07 P.M.

To Robert McNamara[5]

The President called the Secretary of Defense to inquire about wire service reports that Chairman of the Joint Chiefs of Staff General Maxwell D. Taylor had cut short a European vacation and returned to Washington for "urgent consultations on the Southeast Asia crisis." The conversation soon turned towards an assessment of the overall strategic situation in the region. The issue had taken on somewhat pressing relevance, as five of the administration's top foreign policy officials had prepared policy papers on the situation, which would be reviewed in a high-level meeting the following Monday. Finally, Johnson and McNamara discussed possible replacements for Henry Cabot Lodge, the outgoing U.S. ambassador in Saigon.

President Johnson: [*in the office to someone while holding for McNamara*] Leave that open, honey, that's all right.

Unidentified: All right, sir.

Long pause, and then the operator comes on to clarify whether the President was asking for Senator Pat McNamara. The call to Secretary McNamara is then connected.

President Johnson: Bob?

Robert McNamara: Yes, Mr. President.

President Johnson: I see the AP [Associated Press] says that General [Maxwell] Taylor is hurrying home, left abruptly, from his vacation and the assumption is that President Johnson has called him back for urgent consultations on the Southeast Asia crisis.[6]

McNamara: Well, it isn't true; he's coming home exactly on the schedule he planned several weeks ago.

President Johnson: [*with McNamara acknowledging*] Well, I think somebody ought to call AP and tell them their 158 is completely an error, that he . . . Has he been on a vacation?

McNamara: No—well, he probably had a couple of days vacation. He went over there for the SHAPE exercise.[7]

---

5. Tape WH6406.08, Citation #3734, Recordings of Telephone Conversations—White House Series, Recordings and Transcripts of Conversations and Meetings, Lyndon B. Johnson Library.
6. For the AP story, see "Gen. Taylor Ends Trip Abruptly," *Washington Star*, 13 June 1964.
7. McNamara was referring to the Supreme Headquarters Allied Powers Europe, which was the NATO military headquarters.

President Johnson: Well, they say "abruptly ended his European vacation—"

McNamara: Well—

President Johnson: "—ahead of schedule and left for Washington, and the assumption is on Johnson's order for urgent consultations on the Southeast Asia crisis."

McNamara: Well, we'll correct it, Mr. President.

President Johnson: "The aide said he would be . . . have a quiet— would have spent a quiet weekend in Switzerland. They were scheduled to fly to Rome Monday, but—"

McNamara: Oh, that's right, he was supposed to have Saturday and Sunday in Switzerland, I think, Mr. President. He's due in, I believe, at 8:00, Monday morning.

President Johnson: And it says, "They were scheduled to fly to Rome Monday, before returning to Washington."

McNamara: No, I don't think so. I think his plan was always to come back at 8:00. Oh, I know what it was: *I* was supposed to be in Rome on Monday, and I canceled my trip. Oh, that's what they're talking about. I was to meet with [Giulio] Andreotti, the Italian defense minister, Monday and Tuesday, and about two or three weeks ago I canceled it, just believing this wasn't a good time to be out of Washington, and Max was going to meet me in Rome on Monday morning.

President Johnson: Well, I think maybe what you better do, then, is tell AP that there's not anything to this at all, we haven't called him home, we have no urgent consultations, and we have no crisis. And we're not going to let them make one for us.[8]

McNamara: Right.

President Johnson: Have you seen the UP [United Press] on the Air Force jet fighters?[9]

McNamara: Yes, I did. [Charles] Corddry's report.[10]

President Johnson: Yeah.

---

8. Taylor would in fact attend an important meeting on Southeast Asia policy on Monday, 15 June. See "Memorandum from the President's Special Assistant for National Security Affairs (Bundy) to the Secretary of State and the Secretary of Defense (McNamara)," 15 June 1964, U.S. Department of State, *Foreign Relations of the United States (FRUS), 1964–1968: Vietnam 1964*, ed. Edward C. Keefer and Charles S. Sampson (Washington, DC: GPO, 1992), 1:500.

9. The UPI story reported Chinese claims that on 7 June, "American jet fighters" had fired rockets into the town of Khang Khay, the headquarters of the Pathet Lao, and that on 11 June, "American-made" T-28 fighters belonging to the Royal Lao Air Force had killed one member of the Chinese Economic and Cultural Mission and injured five others during a raid over the town. "Viet Minh Seen in Laos, U.S. Resumes Flights," *Washington Post*, 13 June 1964.

10. Charles W. Corddry was a Washington correspondent for United Press International.

McNamara: Yeah, he got his story from somebody in the Pentagon, I think. I can't be absolutely sure of that, but that's my guess. We checked this afternoon on others and no one else had it, although others have been calling in since Corddry had it. We thought it was a group of [Mark] Watson of the *Baltimore Sun,* Corddry and Lloyd Norman of *Newsweek,* and several others that meet together that got some kind of a off-the-record briefing, but it turned out not to be the case. I don't know where Corddry got his.

President Johnson: Does he cover the Pentagon?

McNamara: He does, yes.

President Johnson: You have any suspicion[s]?

McNamara: No, I don't, although I've been trying to check up this afternoon, but I haven't found out yet. My first suspicion proved an error.

President Johnson: Looks like an Air Force story to me.

McNamara: Well, probably, although I'm not entirely sure. Could have been from the Joint [Chiefs of] Staff. Not many in the Air Force know much about this. I think it's more likely to have been out of the Joint Staff.

President Johnson: Are you a little bit shook up about them hitting the . . . killing some Red Chinese and hitting an air base—installation ten miles away?

McNamara: No. No, I think that's to be expected from air operations, Mr. President. I don't know that we killed any Red Chinese. It was the Red Chinese that said we did. I thought it was interesting they admitted they had Chinese in there, even though they called them economic advisers.[11]

President Johnson: Yeah.

Eight seconds excised as classified information and under deed of gift restriction.

President Johnson: What time do we get word tonight that they're back?[12]

---

11. U.S. analysis of reconnaissance photographs, as well as the statements of the Air Force pilots, confirmed that a flight of four U.S. planes had mistakenly attacked a fort at Khang Khay, rather than their assigned target at Xieng Khouang. This was the location of the Chinese economic and cultural mission where the Chinese government claimed that one of its mission staff had been killed and five had been wounded. "Memorandum From the President's Special Assistant for National Security Affairs (Bundy) to President Johnson," 12 June 1964, *FRUS, 1964–1968: Laos,* ed. Edward C. Keefer (Washington, DC: GPO, 1998), 28:184.

12. Johnson was referring to the day's reconnaissance flights over Laos.

McNamara: Well, they should take off around 11:30 our time, that's the present plan. Now, that may shift as the evening goes along as weather reports change, but—

President Johnson: From the same bases?

McNamara: One that the—recon plane takes off from Ton Son Knut if I—which is outside of Saigon—and the three or four fighters take off from Da Nang, which is about a 150 miles north of Saigon. Then the recon plane flies north and rendezvous with the fighters above Da Nang, and they go in from there. Then they come out, and it should take about two and eight-tenths hours, they estimate, so they should be landing some time around roughly 2:30 in the morning, Sunday morning, our time.

President Johnson: When do you get your word?

McNamara: About that time. Around 3:00, I would think, maybe 3:15.

President Johnson: What if they run into Chinese planes?

Thirty-two seconds excised as classified information and under deed of gift restriction.

President Johnson: All right. Now . . . Are we doing anything at all to keep Laos from gradually going away?

McNamara: Well . . .

President Johnson: And losing it?

McNamara: It's a very slippery slope we're on, Mr. President. I just finished talking to Mac [Bundy] a few minutes ago, and Bill Bundy and Mac and I have been all working and talking about this, and we're just not ready yet to talk to you.[13] We have some papers prepared, but they don't guarantee Laos won't slip away.[14] And some of the proposals that are being made that *might* have some effect of that kind are really more extreme, I think, than are warranted under the circumstances or than

---

13. William Bundy, McGeorge's brother, was assistant secretary of state for Far Eastern affairs.

14. For these papers, which were considered at a high-level meeting at the State Department on 15 June, see "Memorandum from the President's Special Assistant for National Security Affairs (Bundy) to the Secretary of State and the Secretary of Defense (McNamara)," 15 June 1964, *FRUS, Vietnam 1964*, 1:500; "Memorandum Prepared for a Meeting at the Department of State," 15 June 1964, ibid., 1:516–18; W. E. Colby, "Memorandum for the Record," 15 June 1964, *FRUS, 1964–1968: Laos*, 28:185–87; C. L. Cooper, "Memorandum from the Assistant Deputy Director for Policy Support, Directorate of Intelligence (Cooper) to Director of Central Intelligence McCone; Subject—A Course of Action for Laos," 15 June 1964, ibid., 28:188–91; "Memorandum from the Permanent Representative to the United Nations (Stevenson) to President," 16 June 1964, ibid., 28:191–92.

you would find acceptable.[15] It'll be, I think, Monday afternoon, Tuesday morning before we really have something that's worth your while looking at.

President Johnson: Did we get a—didn't we get a good report from South Vietnam yesterday? Didn't they run into a bunch of Communists and kill 25 or 30 of them?[16]

McNamara: Yes . . . yes, but that's just an isolated incident, Mr. President. I think on the whole the report from South Vietnam that came in—the weekly report that was issued yesterday—was not very encouraging. The pacification efforts, particularly in the South, are not progressing satisfactorily. Even in the North we're not making very much progress. Quang Nai province, which is in the North, is almost totally overrun by the Vietcong. The only city that is said—or the only area—that is said to be fully under the control of the government is the province capital itself, so I wouldn't put too much encouragement on that report of the capture of those men entering from Laos.

President Johnson: I had a suggestion that we give consideration to the governor of North Carolina [Terry Sanford].[17] I like him, and he's an able young fellow, and he's socially conscious, and he was a paratrooper, but I got to thinking that I'm not sure we ought to get a southern governor, even though his attitude's good, and send him into a place like Vietnam. I think they might say we're sending a segregationist, and it might cause us trouble in the whole area.

McNamara: You mentioned that to me this morning, Mr. President, asked me to check on it. I did today. I made several checks. I asked Mac to make one, as a matter of fact, and on the whole the checks were quite favorable. But I, for a different reason, am disinclined to recommend that he be put in there. I don't know that his segregationist tendencies or reputation would affect it, but—

President Johnson: He doesn't have any. He's against it.

McNamara: I know—

President Johnson: I don't have any either, but I'm from Texas, and it's the biggest load I carry is the fact I'm from Texas.

McNamara: Right, and I think this would tar him in that area, but

---

15. For a possible example of a "more extreme" proposal, see the memorandum by C. L. Cooper in the preceding note, as well as a sharp critique by Michael Forrestal in "Memorandum from Michael V. Forrestal of the National Security Council Staff to the President's Special Assistant for National Security Affairs (Bundy)," 12 June 1964, *FRUS, 1964–1968: Laos*, 28:185.

16. "Saigon Troops Kill 27 Reds in Convoy at Laos Border," *New York Times*, 13 June 1964.

17. This suggestion came from Attorney General Kennedy. See Robert F. Kennedy to Johnson, 7:26 P.M., 12 June 1964, in this volume.

more than that, I don't think he's had any experience whatsoever in foreign affairs, and I think it would be a terrible handicap for a man to step into that complicated environment without such experience. And I think it'd be very difficult for people back here to appraise his judgment when they know he didn't have any such experience.

President Johnson: Now, Bobby [Kennedy] thinks that it'd be a terrible mistake to put [George] Ball in there. Said he's a good lawyer, but he just has no initiative or imagination of his own.

McNamara: I think he's got lots of imagination, very little administrative ability, but that he could do the job. I would certainly recommend Ball over Sanford. I'd recommend [Nicholas] Katzenbach over Sanford, I think. I don't know how Bobby would compare the two.

President Johnson: Do you have any more thoughts? Would you recommend [William] Westmoreland over them all?[18]

McNamara: Well, he's always a last possibility, Mr. President. I don't think I would recommend him over Ball. I think I'd recommend Ball over Westmoreland.

President Johnson: Is he still your top choice, Ball?

McNamara: At the moment, yes, sir. [*Pause.*]

President Johnson: When do we have to make a decision?

McNamara: Oh, I think you've got another two weeks easily. We assume that [Henry Cabot] Lodge wouldn't move out until, let's say, mid-August, and I wouldn't think he'd want to have this leak publicly until after the Republican convention.[19] So you wouldn't want to do anything publicly until the 20th of July, and in between roughly the first of July and the 20th, you'd be working with the man on a quiet basis.

President Johnson: You know Ball pretty well, better than I do, in these meetings. What's his weakness? Does he shoot from the hip a little?

McNamara: Once in a while, that's right. He reasons very well, but comes to the wrong conclusion. Now, this is an occasional situation. We all do it occasionally. I think he [does] a little more than others, perhaps. Then, as I say, he's not a good administrator. But he *will* use staff, he will listen to people that work for him or work with him, and if we associate him with a lot of able individuals, which I would strongly recommend—

---

18. General William Westmoreland was the deputy commander of the U.S. Military Assistance Command for Vietnam and would become the commander on 20 June, replacing the retiring general Paul D. Harkins.

19. The Republican National Convention would be held in San Francisco from 13–16 July. Lodge would in fact resign as ambassador much sooner, on 23 June, in order to campaign for the nomination of Pennsylvania Governor William Scranton as the Republican candidate for President.

President Johnson: You ought to be making up that list, Bob.

McNamara: I have. I've got the list made, and I've got five people on it. And I would certainly like to see every one of them go out there.

President Johnson: You think that Ball would go if we just urged him to?

McNamara: I'm not at all sure he would. I don't mean to say he wouldn't do what you ask him to, but this is not a post that anyone's going to jump at, and I think him least of all.

President Johnson: That's what I'm afraid of. What would you think about Bob Anderson?[20] How well do you know him?

McNamara: I don't know him well, Mr. President. What I hear of him, of course, is very good. Everyone I've ever talked to about him speaks very highly of him, and I would . . . I understand his health isn't very good, and Saigon's not a very healthy place.

President Johnson: Mm-hmm.

McNamara: I don't know very much about his health, but I've heard this in recent weeks.

President Johnson: You going to be in town tomorrow?

McNamara: Yes, sir, I am.

President Johnson: I'll call you tomorrow.

McNamara: Very good. Thank you. I'll check on AP immediately.

5:20 P.M.: The President signed mail and read clippings from the press ticker.

5:50 P.M.: Met with Malcolm Kilduff to discuss a statement about Office of Emergency Planning Director Ed McDermott's upcoming tour of flooded regions of Montana with Senator Mike Mansfield.[21] Kilduff departed at 5:56 P.M.

6:00 P.M.: Unrecorded call to Walter Jenkins.

6:01 P.M.: Went to Jenkins's office.

---

20. Former owner of the Texas Broadcasting Company (1939–1943) and secretary of the Navy (1953–1954), deputy secretary of defense (1954–1955), and secretary of the Treasury (1957–1961) in the Eisenhower administration, Robert B. Anderson had been appointed by President Johnson in April as a special representative for the United States in negotiations with Panama on the future of the canal treaty.

21. "Flood Tour Scheduled," *New York Times*, 14 June 1964.

6:45 P.M.

To Richard Nelson[22]

This entire 59-second call, concerning White House office policy, is closed under deed of gift restriction.

6:50 P.M.: Yolanda Boozer informed Johnson that Ashton Gonella had called with the information that Congressman and Mrs. Pickle would attend the evening's dinner, but that the Purcells and Pogues would not.

6:30 P.M.: [*Exact chronology is uncertain.*][23] Swam in the White House pool and then ate dinner with Mrs. Johnson, Mr. and Mrs. Walter Jenkins, Congressman and Mrs. Pool, Congressman and Mrs. Casey, Congressman and Mrs. Lindsey Blackworth, Mrs. Doris Parnell, Congressman Walter Rogers, and Congressman and Mrs. Pickle.

7:05 P.M.: Unrecorded call to Senator Joseph Clark in Philadelphia, Pennsylvania.

9:35 P.M.: Unrecorded call from Lynda Bird Johnson in Honolulu, Hawaii.

9:50 P.M.: With Mrs. Johnson and guests, attended screenings of *Mr. President* and *The Unsinkable Molly Brown* in the White House theater.

12:15 A.M.: Retired for the evening.

---

22. Tape WH6406.08, Citation #3735, Recordings of Telephone Conversations—White House Series, Recordings and Transcripts of Conversations and Meetings, Lyndon B. Johnson Library.
23. The Daily Diary entry for these events follows the preceding 6:50 P.M. entry, but is listed as 6:30 P.M., with the notation "carded" to the left of the time.

Monday, June 15, 1964

Mac, you know the way I feel about Taylor is this: I believe the . . . from what I've seen the seven months I've been in here, that the most challenging and most dangerous military problem we have is out there. He's our top military man. He's respected in the world and here at home. And I'm not sure that the administration has as much respect on Vietnam as Taylor would have on Vietnam. I believe anything that his name is signed to would have a . . . would carry some weight with nearly anyone. If Westmoreland's as good as they say he is, well maybe . . . maybe Westmoreland can help him if he's got any problem with his age.

—President Johnson to McGeorge Bundy

On Sunday, June 14, as much of official Washington continued to assess the implications of the civil rights bill, the President's Committee on Equal Employment Opportunity, 11 large steel companies, and the United Steelworkers of America announced a voluntary agreement to undertake racially inclusive hiring in the nation's steel industry. Implemented under the committee's Plans for Progress program, the agreement marked a significant advance in eliminating overt forms of racial discrimination in the industry's hiring practices. Yet it also suggested the great challenges that the United States faced in overcoming the economic consequences of centuries of slavery and racial discrimination—regardless of the passage of the civil rights bill.[1]

The next day, the start of a new workweek brought developments of

---

1. "Steel Signs Pact on Job Equality," *New York Times*, 15 June 1964.

immediate political consequence for Lyndon Johnson, as New York Governor Nelson Rockefeller ended his candidacy for the Republican presidential nomination and pledged his support to Pennsylvania Governor William Scranton. Meanwhile, presumptive Republican nominee and Arizona Senator Barry Goldwater failed in a joint effort with southern Democrats to remove Title II of the civil rights bill, which outlawed segregation in public accommodations. Overseas, Henry Cabot Lodge denied reports that he planned to resign as U.S. ambassador to South Vietnam, and China once again warned the United States against making additional bombing raids into Laos.[2]

8:00 A.M.: President Johnson woke, ate breakfast in bed, met with Jack Valenti, completed his exercises, and had a blood sample taken from his arm.

9:26 A.M.: Unrecorded call from Secretary Dean Rusk.

9:55 A.M.: Unrecorded call to McGeorge Bundy.

10:15 A.M.: Unrecorded call from Secretary Robert McNamara.

10:25 A.M.: Unrecorded call to Bundy.

10:30 A.M.: Unrecorded call to Congressman Carl Vinson of Georgia.

10:40 A.M.: Unrecorded call to Walter Jenkins.

10:55 A.M.: Unrecorded call to Horace Busby.

11:00 A.M.: Unrecorded call to Senator Richard B. Russell.

11:50 A.M.: Arrived in the Oval Office.

11:55 A.M.: Unrecorded call to Jenkins.

12:00 P.M.: Unrecorded call to George Reedy.

12:04 P.M.: Unrecorded call to Bill Moyers.

12:16 P.M.: Unrecorded call to Reedy.

12:57 P.M.: Unrecorded call to the operator to request Reedy's immediate presence in the Cabinet Room.

1:05 P.M.: Received the Federal New Jersey Tercentenary Commission.

1:20 P.M.: Unrecorded call to Valenti.

1:25 P.M.: Received U.S. Ambassador to Senegal Mercer Cook, U.S. Ambassador to Mali William Handley, U.S. Ambassador to Togo William Witman, and National Security Council member Bill Brubeck.

---

2. Joseph Lelyveld, "Rockefeller Gives Up Race, Aids Scranton," *New York Times,* 16 June 1964; Max Frankel, "Lodge Resigning; Expected Home for Convention," *New York Times,* 15 June 1964; Peter Grose, "Lodge Denies Plan to Quit As Envoy," *New York Times,* 16 June 1964; Seymour Topping, "Peking Warns U.S. Risks Retaliation with Laos Flights," *New York Times,* 16 June 1964.

1:40 P.M.: Unrecorded call from Jenkins.

1:45 P.M.: Met with Lee White.

1:48 P.M.

From George Mahon[3]

Louisiana Representative Otto Passman chaired the House Appropriations Committee's Subcommittee on Foreign Operations, a position that had allowed him to become Congress's most outspoken and effective opponent of foreign aid. For almost a decade, Passman had succeeded in exacting significant cuts in the President's annual foreign aid requests, regardless of which political party held the White House. In 1964, however, Lyndon Johnson had decided to challenge this power by submitting a "bare-bones" request based on what Passman had actually approved the previous year and by placing this request within the framework of a frugal overall budget that he carefully limited to $100 billion—900 million less than President Kennedy's fiscal 1964 budget proposal and $500 million less than actual fiscal 1964 estimated spending.[4]

On June 9, the House had passed the foreign aid authorization bill, which approved specific aid programs, but the administration still had to convince Congress to pass an appropriations bill that would actually fund those programs. In this conversation, Johnson and Appropriations Committee Chairman George Mahon discussed how they might block Passman's efforts to cut spending in the appropriations bill. A Texas Democrat and close Johnson ally, Mahon had succeeded to the chairmanship in May following the death of Clarence Cannon, Passman's mentor and also a determined opponent not only of foreign aid, but of much of Lyndon Johnson's agenda.[5] Although far from certain at the time of this conversation, the ensuing fight would, as Mahon put it here, "break Passman's back," as the subcommittee chairman failed to make significant

---

3. Tape WH6406.08, Citation #3736, Recordings of Telephone Conversations—White House Series, Recordings and Transcripts of Conversations and Meetings, Lyndon B. Johnson Library.

4. "Annual Budget Message to the Congress, Fiscal Year 1965," 21 January 1965, *Public Papers of the Presidents of the United States: Lyndon B. Johnson, 1963–64* (Washington, DC: GPO, 1965), 1:132.

5. Rowland Evans and Robert Novak, "Inside Report . . . Black Days for Otto," *Washington Post,* 22 May 1964; Richard Pearson, "Ex-Rep. Otto Passman, Foe of Foreign Aid, Dies," *Washington Post,* 14 August 1988.

cuts in the foreign aid appropriation. He would never again regain the aura of invulnerability that he had once possessed on the aid issue.[6]

President Johnson: [*to someone in office*] If I carry out his plan, it'd be better. I think [*unclear, the buzzer sounds*] the Attorney General's got to call him [*unclear*]. That damn fool can't keep his mouth shut about anything.

[*on phone*] Hello?

The Mahon call is then connected.

President Johnson: Yes.

George Mahon: Mr. President?

President Johnson: Yes, George.

Mahon: I am going to have a meeting of the defense . . . of the foreign aid subcommittee, Democratic members. I'm going to save everything I can out of this foreign aid bill. Now, we have cut every budget this year, and we always make some cuts. I understand fully about what—

President Johnson: Well, I'll send you a revised estimate, if you want to cut it. You want me to add something to it for you to cut out?

Mahon: No, you can't do it at this late date. But, you see, I can't make . . . I'm more or less in the minority. I'm trying to get my boys together and I'm trying to break [Otto] Passman's back, and I'm just going to—I'm really working on this deal. But it's . . . they're going to have to take a little cut. There [is] going to have to be a little face-saving for Passman and for the subcommittee, and . . .

President Johnson: Well, I'll send another supplement. You know, I have made a pledge in a speech before the Associated Press editors that I'd get a bare-bones, down to every dollar, at the minimal we thought we could get, and if we didn't get it, we'd ask for supplementals, and just keep asking for them until the Congress—[7]

Mahon: Yes.

President Johnson: —refused them and let them make it very clear that they're the ones that's costing . . . the problem. Now, I think that's what we ought to do. Just let me ask for whatever supplementals—

Mahon: Well, but you—

President Johnson: —you think you got to have as a cushion.

---

6. *Congressional Quarterly Almanac*, 88th Cong., 2nd sess., 1964, vol. 20 (Washington, DC: Congressional Quarterly Service, 1965), p. 312.

7. For this speech, see "Remarks on Foreign Affairs at the Associated Press Luncheon in New York City," 20 April 1964, *Public Papers, Johnson, 1963–64*, 1:493–500.

Mahon: You won't want to ask for—

President Johnson: We thought we believe[d] in an honest budget and we ought to submit the minimum. That's what we did. Kennedy submitted four and a half—

Mahon: You did, and you did a wonderful job on this, but my problem is now to reverse the Appropriations Committee of 50 members that has been slashing and slashing for the years. I can't turn them all around suddenly in one bite.

Now, there's no doubt but what this is a good budget, and the House approved it, and they're going to make some cut. I can't hold the line completely, you see. And I think that—I'm going to hold it to the very lowest line I . . . to the highest line I can, and I'm going to have the Democratic members together this afternoon, I hope, or in the morning, and it's just a matter of breaking Otto's back or holding to some extent, but they won't go the whole way with me.

Now, I need to ask you—you see my point here. [*Johnson acknowledges.*] They've cut everything else a little here and there, not much. Now, Otto and I—had a knock-down, drag-out with him last week or the week before: "Well, I need to see the President. I need to see the President," and so on. Well, he talks about 45 minutes without stopping, you get nothing out of him, and it's up to him if he wants to see the President, and I don't know what his view is or desire is now, but I'm going to, as I say, during the afternoon, I'm going to have a confrontation with him.

President Johnson: Mm-hmm.

Mahon: And if he says, "I want to see the President. I want to see the President," what must I tell him [*unclear*]?

President Johnson: Say, "The President said the last time he saw you, he was fully misrepresented to the press and that he doesn't think that they ought to have meetings like that that misrepresent his position." I saw him at the Speaker's [John McCormack's] insistence, and I swore then that I'd never see him again if I never got another dime because he just goes out and lies on you and tells things that he says and things that you say that are just not correct at all, and I do not have any respect or any trust in the fellow.

Mahon: No, I don't either. I have the same . . . I have the same feeling, and . . . But I think what I'll say to him, "Well, now, if you want to see the President, that's up to you. That's not my problem," don't you see?

President Johnson: Mm-hmm . . . mm-hmm. I think that's right.

Mahon: And then you can just be unavailable, or whatever you think.

President Johnson: Yeah. . . . Yeah, yeah. . . . That's good.

Mahon: But as you say, he, you know, he honeys around with the

Speaker and so forth. I told the Speaker the other day that . . . he said, "I think Otto's going to soften up and be OK." I said, "Mr. Speaker, the only thing's going to soften him up is we've got to have the votes, and we've got [*unclear comment by Johnson*]—that's the only way we—"

President Johnson: The Speaker got him in here last year and destroyed me with him, and I told him I would never see him again.

Mahon: Well, I—

President Johnson: That's what Eisenhower said about him, and that's what Kennedy said about him.

Mahon: Yeah.

President Johnson: Ain't no use of destroying him. He has no character, and we know that from this deal on his woman.

Mahon: Yeah, I know.

President Johnson: And . . .

Mahon: Well, I'll tell you I . . . I have not talked to him alone because I don't want to be—have him go off and quote you—well, he quoted McCormack, you see, he misquoted you, he misquoted President [*Johnson acknowledges*] Kennedy, and so forth.

Well, I wanted to get the feel on that. And I'll do my dead-level best to hold this to—

President Johnson: You ought to sit down and talk to Dave Bell about it.[8] Now, Dave Bell—

Mahon: Oh, I'm going to.

President Johnson: —and them all thought I made a mistake. They all thought I ought to put the padding in, and I hate the Congress to prove I ought to because I thought that because of the 100 billion [dollar] thing that I could have an honest budget. But if—

Mahon: I understand.

President Johnson: —you've got to have a padding in it to get it out, why, I'll put it in. I'll [*unclear*]. If I'm here—

Mahon: Well, before—

President Johnson: —next year, I'll make it up to 5 billion [dollars] and let them cut the billion out of it, and let them be heroes. But I thought since they allowed 3½ [billion dollars] themselves and said that this was what is needed, that I'd just take the position this is all Congress would allow, and although I needed 4½ [billion dollars] and I wanted 4½, that Congress wouldn't allow over 3½, so I just asked for 3½. No use asking 4½ if they're going to cut it anyway.

---

8. David Bell was administrator for USAID (United States Agency for International Development), one of the primary federal agencies charged with implementing foreign aid programs.

Mahon: That's right.

President Johnson: And then I wouldn't get me a billion extra on my total figure.

Mahon: On your budget. Let me ask you this . . .

President Johnson: But I said in the Associated Press that every dollar Congress cuts out I'm going to ask for it in a supplemental. And send a message up, and just as soon as I get this bill, I'm going to come right back and say, "Now, I asked you honestly, and I cut it a billion more than you had last year, and I gave you just what you gave us, what you admitted we needed."

Mahon: Yes.

President Johnson: "And I think this is a phony cut and it ought to be put back. And it's just to play to the galleries to show that" . . . so forth. Now . . .

Mahon: Well, now, let me ask you this: If you would say what you have said to me to this full Democratic group . . .

President Johnson: I'll be glad to, be glad to. [*Mahon attempts to speak.*] If you just get them together and say, "Now, we're in a war. We've got a problem." I'm getting ready to make some very drastic decisions, and just say, "We've got problems, and we've got them all over the country." We've got them in Latin America that would just chill your backbone when you talk about them.[9] We've got an election coming up in Chile, right in the middle of it.

Mahon: That's right.

President Johnson: We've got a wobbly situation in Brazil. We've got bad confiscation in Argentina. We've got problems in Peru. We've got both prime ministers of Greece and Turkey . . . are on their way here to see us. Both of them are big participants in these funds. One of the reasons the Greek government failed is because we cut the hell out of the [Constantine] Caramanlis, and we've driven the best man we had out of the Greece government out because of Otto Passman.[10] That's the first thing.

I went over there, and at Kennedy's instruction, because Otto had butchered us up, told him that he'd have to take it. He said, "All right. Now, if you cut me, that'll mean my government will fall. And I'm giving you men for $400 a year that cost you $4,000."

Mahon: Yeah.

---

9. For the situation in Latin America, see Johnson to Thomas Mann, 7:05 P.M., 11 June 1964, in this volume.

10. Constantine Caramanlis had been Prime Minister of Greece from 1961 to 1963. For the conflict between Greece and Turkey over Cyprus, see Johnson to Dean Rusk, 6:30 P.M., 9 June 1964, in this volume.

President Johnson: But I did it anyway, and that was the most painful thing I ever did was to cut out defense assistance from the Greek government when they got the best fighting soldier. But now, both of them are getting ready to go at each other.

We've got a very precarious situation in Vietnam. We had more people killed, twice as many killed out there last week as we've had before, and we killed a—fewer people ourselves. We've got—the *New York Times* has got a front-page story: [Henry Cabot] Lodge is coming back here.[11] We've got to reorganize our whole operation out there in Laos and in Vietnam and in India. And we got a new Prime Minister in India, and we got—the Pakistanis are trying to get along with them now, and we've got to help both of them any way we can or think about giving up the 4[00] or 500 million people in India.[12]

Mahon: We can't do that.

President Johnson: We've got Malaya problems. We've got all of them.

Now, Otto's going to run foreign policy. We've just got to let him get out. Hell, I don't have to be nominated, I'll tell them. But I don't mind saying to him the problems I have. This is ½ of 1 [0.5] percent of our total gross national product. This is 3½ percent of our whole budget. Hell . . . defense, you're spending 20, 15 times as much on defense, and this is the way we're trying to keep these million men overseas *out* of a war.

Mahon: Well, now, let's talk just a minute here. If you could say to the—

President Johnson: No use talking to Otto, though. I'll talk to the rest of them, but Otto, he just goes to shouting at you and hollering, and there ain't no—

Mahon: Yeah, that's right. . . . Now, our problem is, if we . . . I'm going to touch base with them all this afternoon. Now, if we could come down there, if we could not take too much of your time, at some time, maybe late in the evening, or . . .

President Johnson: [*with Mahon acknowledging*] You come any time you want to. If you want to, I'll have these defense . . . these men that you set

---

11. The *Times* article reported that Lodge would return to the United States one day before the start of the Republican National Convention in San Francisco and that he would aid Governor Scranton in his late bid to block Barry Goldwater's nomination. Frankel, "Lodge Resigning," *New York Times*, 15 June 1964.

12. Indian Prime Minister Jawaharlal Nehru had died on 27 May. Lal Bahadur Shastri had succeeded Nehru as Prime Minister. See McGeorge Bundy to Johnson, 8:07 P.M., 3 June 1964, in this volume; also, "Nehru, a 'Queer Mixture of East and West,' Led the Struggle for a Modern India," *New York Times*, 28 May 1964.

up under the last foreign aid bill, this businessman's committee—they're volunteers; they're going out [in] this country. I had David Rockefeller in here this morning, had the president of Xerox Corporation this morning, had Dan Kimball, had all these businessmen in here that are sending out people to handle our foreign aid bill in a businesslike way.[13] It was set up as an amendment last year. I'd get half a dozen of those in here, get your—

Mahon: Well, you don't . . . I—you don't need anybody but you.

President Johnson: All right. OK.

Mahon: If you would say—

President Johnson: Yes.

Mahon: —to the full . . . I don't know whether we would want the Republicans or not, but it probably would—if we just come down there for a little touch-base with you before we mark this up, I think it might be helpful, because breaking Otto's back is not easy because these boys have been eating out of his hand. He's been leading them around by the nose, and I can't break them 100 percent on the first time, I don't believe. It remains to be seen what I can do. Are you going to be in town for the next couple days?

President Johnson: Yes, sir. . . . Yes, sir, be here all week. I'll see you anytime you want to and late in the evening or early in the morning. I'll have the businessmen in. I'll have anybody you want in.

Mahon: [*with the President acknowledging*] I don't think we need anybody but you. That's my feeling about it. It's just a . . . It's just a thing—

President Johnson: How many men you got on the committee?

Mahon: Oh, about six, seven.

President Johnson: Mm-hmm, I'd just sure bring them. That's the subcommittee.

Mahon: We'd have to bring Otto, though. But I would just tell Otto that we came down to listen to the President, and we would listen to the President, and then we would . . . that'd be it.

President Johnson: All right. I think you ought to talk to Jerry Ford ahead of time.[14] Now, Jerry said last year that he got committed before he knew it. Now—

Mahon: Oh, well, I've talked to Jerry Ford three or four times already.

---

13. David Rockefeller was the president of Chase Manhattan Bank; Dan Kimball was the chairman of Aerojet-General Corporation; Sol M. Linowitz was the president of the Xerox Corporation. All were members of the International Executive Service Corps with whom Johnson had met earlier in the afternoon.

14. In 1964, future president Gerald R. Ford was a Republican representative from Michigan and an influential minority member of the House Appropriations Committee's Subcommittee on Foreign Operations.

President Johnson: Was he—

Mahon: And Jerry is not going to go with us 100 percent, no. No, he's not—they're playing a little politics.

President Johnson: Hmm.

Mahon: He's going 100 percent on military, but not on the other.

President Johnson: Hmm.

Mahon: I'm rather of the opinion that if all of us went down, it might be best because, you see, [Silvio] Conte is strong, he's—Conte's told me, he said, "George, I'll go for the budget estimate 100 percent and I'll support you in every way I can."[15] I can't get that promise out of Jerry. Gary . . . Vaughan Gary—[*unclear attempted interjection by the President*]—Vaughan Gary.[16] Now, Bill Natcher, he just can't reverse himself 100 percent, he says, and so on.[17]

President Johnson: Well, he's not reversing himself. I'm giving him just what he had last year.

Mahon: That's right, but—

President Johnson: I'm not asking him to reverse himself at all. [*Unclear*]—

Mahon: This is Otto's out if he would just say, and that's what I'm trying to get him to say, "Well, at last I've achieved success: They've sent a budget down here that is bare bones, and I'm glad to approve it," and blah, blah. This is . . . this is his out, and he'll take this out if I can confront him with the votes, don't you see. That's my problem.

President Johnson: Mm-hmm.

Mahon: And I will be in touch with you.

President Johnson: Now, Jamie Whitten told me that if we had to, set up that little gimmick that he's got in agriculture, and he and Natcher would go with me.[18]

Mahon: Well, that's phony, but if—heck, it suits me if they'll go—

President Johnson: Well . . . you just ask him if that's true, if he'll go with us, and then tell Dave Bell that let's amend it to put that language in it and let . . . require 500 million [dollars] of it to go back to the [Bureau of

15. Silvio Conte was a Republican representative from Massachusetts.

16. Vaughan Gary was a Democratic representative from Virginia.

17. William Natcher was a Democratic representative from Kentucky.

18. Jamie Whitten was a Democratic representative from Mississippi. For the President's conversation with Whitten on this topic, see Johnson to Jamie Whitten, 4:31 P.M., 26 May 1964, in Guian A. McKee, ed., *The Presidential Recordings, Lyndon B. Johnson: Toward the Great Society, February 1, 1964–May 31, 1964*, vol. 6, *April 14, 1964–May 31, 1964* (New York: Norton, 2007), pp. 852–55; and the President's follow-up to Kermit Gordon at 3:40 P.M., 27 May 1964, in ibid., pp. 897–900.

the] Budget and the Budget will take every item of it—economic aid, 200 million, whatever they want to cut, 500 million—and he won't advance a dollar of it until they make a case for it to him, and do it just like they do REA [Rural Electrification Administration].

Mahon: Yes. Now, this may . . . if I can get . . . if I can get Passman to go with this—

President Johnson: Whitten told me that he and Natcher would go with that.

Mahon: Yeah. Well, Whitten is . . . Whitten is . . . Whitten always votes against *all* foreign aid.

President Johnson: That's right, but just tell him that you understand he called me, that I called you and asked you to try to put into effect what he wants to do, that he said he and Natcher would go with us if we do it. Tell him that I've also, as soon as we get this election behind me, are going to try to do something to help the Mississippi congress[men].

Mahon: Yeah. That's good; that's good. I'll be in touch. I'll be in touch.

President Johnson: And just tell him, what is his formula now, and you can call Elmer Staats and he'll give you the formula.[19] The formula is—

Mahon: Oh, I've talked to Elmer. Elmer's been in my office.

President Johnson: He just—

Mahon: I've been through all of this.

President Johnson: Well, set up 500 million [dollars] of that economic aid that requires them . . . just give them 500 [million] less than they're asking. But 500 [million] more will come in when they justify it to the director of the budget [Kermit Gordon].

Mahon: Yes.

President Johnson: And that gives Otto an out.

Mahon: A little face-saving, yeah. Yeah. And of course, the fact—the face-saving of the whole thing is that we've got the budget down to where we thought it ought to be.

President Johnson: Kennedy asked four-nine [$4.9 billion], [*the recording skips*] six months and came up and asked for four-five [$4.5 billion], then I came along and asked for three-five [$3.5 billion].

Mahon: Yeah, that's right. That's right. Well, I hate to trouble you with this—

President Johnson: OK. I think you—

Mahon: —but this is very important to you, and I—

---

19. Elmer Staats served as deputy budget director.

President Johnson: It's very important to the world. You'll be winning a silver star if you do this one.

Mahon: OK, I'll do my best.

President Johnson: Bye. Bye, George.

Mahon: I'll do—

2:10 P.M.

From Larry O'Brien[20]

Apparently returning an earlier call from the President, Larry O'Brien updated Johnson on California Representative Bernie Sisk's unhappiness about recent or pending appointments to Republican positions on the Securities and Exchange Commission and Federal Power Commission.[21]

President Johnson: Larry?

Larry O'Brien: Hello?

President Johnson: Larry?

O'Brien: Yes, Mr. President.

President Johnson: I just was calling about that memo I noticed on my desk about [Bernie] Sisk—

O'Brien: Oh, yeah.

President Johnson: —being upset about the Republican appointees, [Hamer] Budge and the power commission man.[22]

[*with O'Brien acknowledging*] Well, now, I don't know who desig-

---

20. Tape WH6406.08, Citation #3737, Recordings of Telephone Conversations—White House Series, Recordings and Transcripts of Conversations and Meetings, Lyndon B. Johnson Library.
21. For this issue, see Johnson to Carl Albert, 1:00 P.M., 5 June 1964; and Johnson to Carl Albert, 4:44 P.M., 9 June 1964, in this volume; Eileen Shanahan, "Johnson Appoints a Republican to Fill a Vacancy on the S.E.C.," *New York Times*, 6 June 1964.
22. Johnson had appointed former Idaho Congressman Hamer Budge to a Republican position on the Securities and Exchange Commission on 6 June. For this issue, see Johnson to Carl Albert, 1:00 P.M., 5 June 1964; and Johnson to Carl Albert, 4:44 P.M., 9 June 1964, in this volume; Eileen Shanahan, "Johnson Appoints a Republican to Fill a Vacancy on the S.E.C.," *New York Times*, 6 June 1964. Johnson was also considering the possible reappointment of Vermont's Charles R. Ross to a Republican slot on the Federal Power Commission. Ross, a moderate Republican oriented towards consumer protection, was strongly opposed by Senate Minority Leader Everett Dirksen and lobbyists for the oil and gas industries. See Johnson to Mike Manatos, 6:11 P.M., 20 May 1964, in McKee, *The Presidential Recordings, Johnson*, vol. 6, *April 14, 1964–May 31, 1964*, pp. 776–78; "Unexpected Vacancy on SEC May Soften Squeeze on President," *Wall Street Journal*, 6 August 1964.

nated Sisk to handle my Republican appointments for me, but I wouldn't get . . . I wouldn't let him get into that at all. Just say, "That's probably a matter out of your field. You have enough to do on Democratic appointments without getting into the Republican appointments."

O'Brien: No, I agree. I think—Didn't I mention in the memo something about a project?

President Johnson: Yeah. Oh yeah, he's got—

O'Brien: That's really what I think [*unclear*].

President Johnson: [*with O'Brien acknowledging throughout*] Well, he says, he threatens the other two because of that, that he wants a payoff of $157 million.[23] And it's silly. The budget's up; I couldn't break it through. If I did I'd have 10 billion [dollars] going up. So we'll consider it for next year, and . . . but we're not going to be blackmailed if we don't ever get a poverty bill. He can stick it up his ass, tell him.

O'Brien: All right. I didn't know whether that project—frankly, I should have checked it out more carefully, I guess—I didn't know whether there was any kind of a little piece of that that could stay alive through this year, but—

President Johnson: [*with O'Brien acknowledging throughout*] It's alive. It's a project—it's a new start for 157 million [dollars], and we just couldn't do it because we've got a tight budget. We might be able to put it in next year—I wouldn't want to make a commitment—but it's a possibility, and we will consider it for next year. But we had to cut hundreds of them out.

O'Brien: Yeah. That's fair enough.

President Johnson: All right.

O'Brien: That's the way I'll give it to him.

President Johnson: Now, what is your schedule . . . what are we going to talk to these folks about in the morning?[24] Do we do any good by talking to them in your judgment?

O'Brien: Yeah, well, what I—as I told you Saturday, what I will have before you this afternoon is our specific list of what has to be completed in this session, and it will be spelled out carefully. There'll be a copy of it on plain stationery without any identification for each one of them if you want to distribute it to them.

---

23. Johnson and O'Brien were referring to Sisk's efforts to secure funding for the Westlands Water District Project, a massive irrigation project in California's Central Valley—and Sisk's congressional district. See Johnson to Elmer Staats, 9:44 A.M., 16 June 1964, in this volume.
24. On Tuesday mornings the President typically had a breakfast meeting with the legislative leaders. The President had questioned the efficacy of these meetings with Carl Albert the week before. See Johnson to Carl Albert, 4:44 P.M., 9 June 1964, in this volume.

President Johnson: That's good.

O'Brien: And I would say that that list is our checklist and we want to, as rapidly as possible, draw a line through each item, and that they can complete all these items in the eight or nine weeks of legislative activity between now and Labor Day. And I think it's a pretty good list, and I'd like to go over it with you later today. . . .

President Johnson: OK.

O'Brien: All right?

President Johnson: Fine.

O'Brien: All right, Mr. President.

2:15 P.M.: President Johnson met with Lee White.

2:30 P.M.: Went to the White House pool with Clark Clifford and Jack Valenti.

3:05 P.M.: Returned to the Mansion and lunched with Clifford and Valenti.

3:30 P.M.: Unrecorded call to Walter Jenkins.

4:46 P.M.: Unrecorded call to Bill Moyers.

5:00 P.M.: Unrecorded call to Valenti.

5:01 P.M.: Unrecorded call from George Reedy.

5:02 P.M.: Unrecorded call to McGeorge Bundy.

5:05 P.M.: Unrecorded call from Bundy.

5:10 P.M.: Returned to the Oval Office.

5:22 P.M.: Presented a Presidential Medallion to CIA Director John McCone.

5:25 P.M.

From George Reedy[25]

Between 5:25 and 5:45 P.M., the President and his press secretary exchanged three calls about a United Press International query regarding New York City Mayor Robert F. Wagner's unauthorized statement that Johnson would travel to the city the next day.

---

25. Tape WH6406.08, Citation #3738, Recordings of Telephone Conversations—White House Series, Recordings and Transcripts of Conversations and Meetings, Lyndon B. Johnson Library.

Before the conversation, the President laughs with an unidentified person, presumably Director of Central Intelligence McCone, who is in the office.

President Johnson: Yeah?

George Reedy: Mr. President, UPI [United Press International] has asked me about a report that Mayor [Robert] Wagner says you're going to New York tomorrow.

President Johnson: Well, I don't know what Mayor Wagner is talking about. [*Pauses.*] Just ask him to give you more details, and see what the mayor . . . I haven't talked to the mayor; I don't know what he's talking about.

Reedy: Right.

President Johnson: Just—I wouldn't tell them I'd talked to me at all. Just say before you go in you'd like to know what the mayor's talking about, what he has in mind. And as far as you know, I haven't talked to him.

Reedy: Right.

President Johnson: Telephone girls tell you that I haven't talked to him and haven't been in communication with him. I don't know what he's talking about. I guess it's the fool Secret Service told him I want to go up to the Kennedy dinner tomorrow night.[26] But now, I imagine that's what he's done.

Reedy: Right. OK, sir. [*Pause.*]

President Johnson: Are they in a press conference, or is this just a query?

Reedy: No, it was during the . . . I called them in to tell them about [George] Papandreou.[27] And they asked me that question while I was telling them about Papandreou.

President Johnson: Mm-hmm. OK. Who was this, this morning that said the same thing to you that they did the other day, that they bucked it back here to you?

Reedy: That was Ron Nessen.[28]

President Johnson: Well, is he lying?

Reedy: I think he was just repeating the conversation the other day. I just told him flatly it hadn't happened, and let it go at that.

President Johnson: Mm-hmm. OK.

Reedy: You bet, sir.

---

26. Johnson was referring to the 11 June fund-raising dinner of the John F. Kennedy Library. He would attend the dinner. See Stephen Smith to Johnson, 4:28 P.M., 11 June 1964, in this volume.
27. Greek Premier George Papandreou had accepted an invitation to visit Johnson in Washington, primarily to discuss the Cyprus crisis. "Athens Confirms Visit," *New York Times,* 16 June 1964.
28. Ronald H. Nessen was a Washington correspondent for NBC News.

5:32 P.M.

From George Reedy[29]

An office conversation with John McCone precedes the call.
John McCone: I believe I . . . I believe I [*unclear*]—
President Johnson: I can't send . . . I can't send Bobby [Kennedy]. Here's the letter, which I thought was unusual and made me feel better about the administration. I haven't showed it to one human. You're the first one.
The secretary interrupts to report that Reedy is on the line.
President Johnson: Yeah?
George Reedy: UPI [United Press International] just has a message from the New York bureau which says, "Mayor [Robert] Wagner said in a speech today that the President is coming to New York tomorrow. Is that right," question mark. [*Pause.*]
President Johnson: Well, I don't know. I've been talking about going up to the Kennedy dinner, but it's off the record, it's a private dinner. It's got nothing in it to . . . I haven't talked to Wagner at all. Why don't you call Wagner and tell him you've got that query and you know nothing about it and what is the story?
Reedy: Right.
President Johnson: And then say, "Please, for God sakes, Bob, if you're going to announce these things, tell us."
Reedy: Right, I'll call him right now.
President Johnson: Just tell him I have no firm date to come and what is he talking about?
Reedy: Right.
President Johnson: And say, "For God sakes"—like Hubert Humphrey, I don't know what's wrong with them. Now, I want to go up there to that dinner, but . . . OK.
Reedy: You bet, sir.

5:35 P.M.: Unrecorded call to Jack Valenti.

---

29. Tape WH6406.08, Citation #3739, Recordings of Telephone Conversations—White House Series, Recordings and Transcripts of Conversations and Meetings, Lyndon B. Johnson Library.

5:45 P.M.

From George Reedy[30]

An office conversation with Jack Valenti precedes the call.

Jack Valenti: . . . been done for mental retardation in the last two years than in the last 200—is that a correct statement?

President Johnson: No, it's more than just [*unclear*]. [*Pause.*]

Valenti: Who gave you that statement? [*Pause.*] More has been done within the government, is that what you're saying?

President Johnson: [*Unclear*] statement, that's all it was, [*unclear*].

Valenti: Where is your support for your first statement?

The secretary interrupts to report that Reedy is on the line.

President Johnson: Yeah?

George Reedy: Just talked to Bob Wagner. He says he apologizes deeply, that he was at a meeting of the Democratic State Committee and his police force had just told him that you were coming up tomorrow and he'd assumed that it was a thing that had been announced. And he said he was just talking off-the-cuff to the Democratic State Committee, and he mentioned it. He said he assumes now some newspapermen were there, although he didn't know. And he said he'll do whatever we tell him to do. Said he'll try to kill it. Of course, he can't really kill it, he's just got to go ahead and say it's . . .

President Johnson: No, he's a goddamn fool, the son of a bitch. If I wanted it announced, I'd say so.

All right, now you call that Secret Service and eat his ass out like nobody's business and tell them that we ain't ever going into New York for *nothing* if they can't go—if they've got to have me announce publicly, and then just tell UP you've got no comment, that we have no definite plans as yet.

Reedy: Right.

President Johnson: Because I don't know whether I'll go or not. But these sons of bitches, I get so mad. Those bastards, I'm going to call him right now and tell him myself, and then you call him.

Reedy: Right.

---

30. Tape WH6406.08, Citation #3742, Recordings of Telephone Conversations—White House Series, Recordings and Transcripts of Conversations and Meetings, Lyndon B. Johnson Library.

5:50 P.M.

To Floyd Boring[31]

Johnson berated Secret Service Agent Floyd Boring about the leak of information regarding the New York City trip.

Another office conversation with Valenti precedes the call.
President Johnson: Who did you tell on Secret Service we was going?
Jack Valenti: The only man, Floyd Boring, the only one I talked to.
President Johnson: Who is Floyd Boring?
Valenti: He is one of Jim Rowley's men on the White House detail.[32]
President Johnson: All right. See if you can get the son of a bitch on the phone here. Those bastards, I'm going to have to quit telling *you* I'm going [*unclear*]—
The operator interrupts to report that she has Boring on the line.
President Johnson: Mr. Boring?
Floyd Boring: Yes, sir.
President Johnson: Why in the *hell* do I have to be humiliated by giving y'all a day's notice I'm going to New York? You've had the mayor announce up there publicly now that I'm going.
Boring: Oh, my God [*unclear*]—
President Johnson: And I'm not going to tell you a goddamn thing because y'all can't keep a secret, you've got to tell every cop in the world. Now, I'm going to start leaving at 4:30 in the afternoon if you keep doing me this way.
Boring: All right, sir.
President Johnson: I just—How do you expect me to operate? The mayor got up and made a public speech today at lunch announcing my arrival in New York. And I told Jack Valenti to tell you-all and keep it just as confidential as you can.
Boring: I know that, sir.
President Johnson: Well, call the chief of police up there and tell him you damn near got fired on account of it.

---

31. Tape WH6406.08, Citation #3743, Recordings of Telephone Conversations—White House Series, Recordings and Transcripts of Conversations and Meetings, Lyndon B. Johnson Library.
32. James J. Rowley served as chief of the United States Secret Service. President Johnson despised the Secret Service's encroachments on his freedom of movement. Transcript, Marie Fehmer Chiarodo Oral History Interview III, 8/16/1972, by Michael L. Gillette, Lyndon B. Johnson Library, p. 5.

Boring: All right, I certainly will, sir.

President Johnson: And just tell him that we cannot do it, and if he wants to keep us out of New York, keep out. And quit announcing how many men he's assigning to me.

Boring: All right sir, I'll do that.

President Johnson: It's causing trouble all over the country, and I'm just going to get a law passed or something that, by God, will make it a felony for you fellows to tell this.

Boring: All right, sir.

President Johnson: I give you a little notice and then you, by God, you just go wild: You'll have 5,000 up there standing man-to-man with a gun [*unclear*] and drawn. And it's the damnedest disgrace I ever saw with all those little tin soldiers lined up there. I asked Bob Wagner the other day, "Why have you got 200 men here at a helicopter? [*Pauses.*] They're liable to fall down and let a gun go off and kill themselves." But now, when he gets up and starts announcing it in a public speech because I wanted y'all to have a chance to tell your wife or get a suitcase tonight—

Boring: Yes, sir; yes, sir.

President Johnson: —if you need it. And then you-all go tell them, and then they tell the mayor, and the mayor tells the world.

Boring: I'm going to call—

President Johnson: So I'm going to try to cancel my trip out. Tell him there's nothing definite on it at all and that I'm in the humor of not going at all if you have to tell him.

Boring: I'm sorry this happened—

President Johnson: And you just—well, you just tell him—I'm sorry too, but it keeps happening. This is not the first time.[33]

Boring: Yes, sir . . . yes, sir.

President Johnson: Last time they had 5,000—they gave out an announcement—5,000 police to guard me. I don't want stuff like that. [*Hangs up.*]

Boring: Yes, sir.

5:51 P.M.: President Johnson spoke to the Kennedy Foundation Mental Retardation Group in the Flower Garden.

6:01 P.M.: Returned to the Oval Office.

---

33. For earlier examples of Johnson's irritation with the Secret Service, see Johnson to James Rowley, 3:32 P.M. and 5:05 P.M., 13 May 1964, in McKee, *The Presidential Recordings, Johnson*, vol. 6, *April 14, 1964–May 31, 1964*, pp. 630–32, 669–70.

6:10 P.M.: Met with Jack Valenti and Cliff Carter.

6:26 P.M.: Met with Ralph Dungan.

6:40 P.M.: Unrecorded call to Bill Moyers.

6:55 P.M.: Unrecorded call to George Reedy.

6:57 P.M.: Received a group of Southwest Texas State Teacher's College alumni in the Cabinet Room.

7:00 P.M.: Returned to the office.

7:01 P.M.: Unrecorded call to Reedy.

7:02 P.M.

To Lee White[34]

Senate Majority Whip Hubert Humphrey of Minnesota, the floor leader for the civil rights bill, had publicly suggested on June 14 that President Johnson should call a national conference to examine "how we implement this law on the state and local and Federal level and how we back it up by community action and community support."[35] In this call, the President and Associate Counsel Lee White discussed their mutual misgivings about the idea. Although the connection to Humphrey's proposal is uncertain, Johnson did eventually hold a White House conference on civil rights in June 1966 under very different circumstances, including extensive urban unrest, an increasingly unpopular war in Vietnam, and greater budgetary constraint.[36]

President Johnson: AP [Associated Press] ticker 178 says Senator [Olin] Johnston took issue at [Hubert] Humphrey's suggestion—they got a fight started on Humphrey's conference.[37] So you better get a copy of it: 1-7-8—

Lee White: 1-7-8?

President Johnson: Yeah.

White: Uh-huh.

---

34. Tape WH6406.08, Citation #3744, Recordings of Telephone Conversations—White House Series, Recordings and Transcripts of Conversations and Meetings, Lyndon B. Johnson Library.

35. "Focus on Rights Shifts to House," *New York Times*, 15 June 1964; Susanna McBee, "National Conference on Rights Suggested," *Washington Post*, 15 June 1964.

36. Robert Dallek, *Flawed Giant: Lyndon Johnson and His Times 1961–1973* (New York: Oxford University Press, 1998), pp. 222–26, 327–29.

37. Olin Johnston was a Democratic senator from South Carolina.

President Johnson: Says that Johnston saying any massive—he says that, statement: [*reading*] "Governors and mayors have no more responsibility or obligation to enforce the bill than they would have to enforce regulations, federal aviation, internal revenue, or the customs service."

White: I'll be darned. I talked to Burke Marshall this afternoon about it, and all of those fellows assumed when they saw the story this morning that it had been cleared here, and none of them had ever heard of it before.[38] Isn't that discouraging? And now this just makes it miserable.

President Johnson: Yeah . . . yeah.

White: If they start issue—fighting about that.

President Johnson: Yeah. I'd call Humphrey if I were you and just—

White: All right.

President Johnson: —tell him that you've seen it, and you're handling it. We're planning it, but we don't know what the hell to do now that we've got a fight going with senators and others, and we don't believe any of them would come if we had the meeting. I don't want to call it.

White: I'm not sure if I were a southern governor, I would. Frankly.

President Johnson: No, they wouldn't come at all.

White: No. All right, I will call him and let you know what he says, sir.

President Johnson: But just tell him that you don't believe they'll come, and we have that problem, and we don't know what to know— What does Burke Marshall say we ought to do?

White: Well, he was kind of nonplussed just as I was and said that he would talk to Bob [Kennedy] about it this afternoon and see what they could do. He could see some disadvantage in it being a Justice Department operation, but he could also understand clearly the awkward spot that you were put in by that story. He wasn't sure how widely it'd been played, but now, even if it hadn't been played before—

President Johnson: I saw it in the papers this morning, yeah.

White: Boy, this is going to play it up all over, especially in the South. I'd say that . . . I'd say that makes it virtually impossible to—

President Johnson: I would say it would be just about like Jim Eastland calling together Roy Wilkins and them for [*White chuckles*] Humphrey to call together this group.[39]

---

38. Burke Marshall served as assistant attorney general in the Civil Rights Division of the Justice Department.

39. James Eastland was a Democratic senator from Mississippi and a dedicated segregationist. Roy Wilkins was the executive secretary of the National Association for the Advancement of Colored People (NAACP).

White: Yeah. Just about. [*Chuckles.*] It's a pretty good analogy. They'd be about as responsive.

President Johnson: You try to work them out—work us out of it, some way. I'll attend, but you try to work us out on your own. I don't want to get the Attorney General offended at me. I agreed to have the meeting.

White: Oh, no, he's not—no, no, he is—

President Johnson: I agreed to have the meeting, but I don't want to have it now. . . .

White: Sure.

President Johnson: And just be Humphrey's puppet. I just can't afford to because I think they'll ridicule me to death.

White: I would think so, and—

President Johnson: And so you try to get Burke Marshall to find some other way to get away from it.

White: All right. We might even think about letting some of the outside organizations sponsor their own meetings. Let them call it and be here, and then you could just drop by.

President Johnson: Well, I don't need to if it's an outside organization, maybe. Let the officials of the government, maybe the conciliation service, or the Attorney General, or Humphrey and them, or whoever it is.

White: All right, we ought to come up with a few alternatives and let you take a look at them.

President Johnson: Thank you, my friend.

White: Thank you, sir.

7:05 P.M.: Unrecorded call to George Reedy.
7:15 P.M.: Unrecorded call to Walter Jenkins.

7:35 P.M.

From Walter Jenkins[40]

In this call Walter Jenkins updated President Johnson on a new round of inquiries from the *Wall Street Journal* and *U.S. News & World Report*

---

40. Tape WH6406.09, Citation #3745, Recordings of Telephone Conversations—White House Series, Recordings and Transcripts of Conversations and Meetings, Lyndon B. Johnson Library.

regarding the Johnsons' business and financial interests, particularly the Johnson's philanthropic foundation.[41] The original conversation slip for this call at the Johnson Library is marked "Do Not Transcribe" (a note to the White House secretaries), "Not Supposed To Record," and "RE LBJ Foundation."

Walter Jenkins: You alone?

President Johnson: Yeah. Jack's [Valenti's] with me.

Jenkins: Well, yeah. He had a call from Bob Phinney this afternoon who said [Louis] Kohlmeier of the *Wall Street Journal* was in his office today wanting to see the [LBJ] Foundation tax returns, which they ... are entitled to see pages three and four—receipts and disbursements on foundations.[42] He let him see two years: '61 and '62. And he's coming back tomorrow. He said he wanted to see the rest of them, and they're getting them from the Fort Worth warehouse.

And then we got a call, long distance, later in the afternoon from Bob MacDougal of the *U.S. News & World Report* saying if Phinney did, that he wanted to have to see the same information.[43] Didn't know the other fellow was there, but that's what he asked to see. And said he was flying down, would be there tomorrow, and would like to see the same material. [*Pauses.*]

President Johnson: Well, what's that—what's wrong with it?

Jenkins: Nothing wrong with it, just wanted us to know it. He says he assumes Bob knows what he's talking about, that he had to show it to him. But he says, "I'm going to check that with Sheldon [Cohen] to see whether he does."[44] Bob told him that on foundations, those two pages— that's the receipts, that money received and the money expended—

---

41. For background on this issue, see George Reedy to Johnson, 12:31 P.M., 9 June 1964, in this volume.

42. Johnson friend Robert L. Phinney was an Austin, Texas, businessman who had served as the Austin district director of the New Deal's Works Progress Administration, as postmaster of Austin, as director of internal revenue in the First District of Texas, and as an executive with radio station KVET, which he started with a group of partners that included John Connally. Transcript, Robert Lorin Phinney Oral History Interview, 19 September 1968, by Paul Bolton, Lyndon B. Johnson Library. Louis M. Kohlmeier was a reporter for the *Wall Street Journal* and the author of a series of stories on the Johnson family fortune. The series would win him the 1965 Pulitzer Prize for reporting on national affairs. "Kohlmeier of Wall Street Journal Awarded Pulitzer Prize for Johnson Wealth Series," *Wall Street Journal*, 4 May 1965.

43. In May, *U.S. News & World Report* had published an investigative article about the Johnson finances and business operations. "The Story of the Johnson Family Fortune," *U.S. News & World Report*, 4 May 1964, pp. 38–42.

44. Sheldon S. Cohen was the chief counsel of the Internal Revenue Service.

President Johnson: Show who gives it to them?

Jenkins: Not on the form itself, but Bob told him that there was a form attached. There was a schedule attached to one of them one year, the way it was filed, that did show it. Bob thinks he saw that too, and [Jesse] Kellam said he told him, said, "Well, now, you better find out for sure whether he's entitled to see that or not.[45] If he isn't, take it off and not show him any more. Or tell him that that's . . . That he was not supposed to have seen, that that was . . ." The form itself only shows amounts and not names.

President Johnson: Well, what will it show, 30[000], 40,000 [dollars] a year or something?

Jenkins: Oh, it'll show that much from you and then lower than that from the company.

President Johnson: Mm-hmm.

Jenkins: More like—

President Johnson: What does it show [as] disbursement?

Jenkins: Small ones.

President Johnson: Mm-hmm.

Jenkins: To united funds and colleges and gift things that . . . churches and so on [that] Mrs. [Lady Bird] Johnson has indicated interest in. Of course, the answer is they're trying to build up their corpus so they'll have enough income from it to really do some good.

President Johnson: Mm-hmm. Well, is there anything wrong with that?

Jenkins: I don't think so. I just thought maybe I better hold him and tell you in case you had any comment to make on it. I thought I'd talk to Sheldon tonight.

President Johnson: No, but why in the hell didn't he tell us when the fellow asked for permission to come in instead of after it's over with?

Jenkins: Well, I agree with that.

President Johnson: And tell Bob that that's what he's supposed to do.

Jenkins: All right.

President Johnson: Tell Jesse to tell him that. Then get ahold of Sheldon. . . . I just can't believe that they'd turn over the Kennedy Foundation, Ford Foundation, every contribution they got and every disbursement they made. I just can't believe that. Because if they do, they can tell what your income tax is. Because they know that you can't give over 5 percent if you gave so and so.

---

45. Jesse Kellam was the general manager of the Johnsons' television and radio stations and a codirector of the blind trust that managed the family's business interests.

Jenkins: That's right. [*Pauses.*] They can tell certainly what the maximum it could be was.

President Johnson: Mm-hmm.

Jenkins: I mean the minimum it could be.

President Johnson: Mm-hmm.

Jenkins: Could be more than that because you don't have to give the total amount that you *can* give, but I think they'd assume that you would.

He also asked me if A.W. [Moursund] had called me. I said no. He said A.W. is in Houston. He talked to him awhile ago, and A.W. had told him that John [Connally] had talked to him about being temporary chairman, that he thought probably he was going to talk to us about it.[46]

President Johnson: Please don't. God, I wish you'd get A.W. out of that. If he does, just tell him, "Please don't do it." Tell Jesse to tell A.W., "Please don't get mixed up in that convention."

Jenkins: All right. [*Pause.*]

President Johnson: Because it just gets me involved in [it].

Jenkins: He also mentions Liz's [Carpenter's] Falcon [*unclear*] still being on the books and thinks we ought to sell it to her. If you don't have any objection, I'll go ahead and do that.[47]

President Johnson: Yeah.

Jenkins: That book value is down to where it would be a very good bargain for her.

President Johnson: Well, I don't know whether she can afford to sell it. You better—it's appraised value, isn't it? That last . . .

Jenkins: That's what they held at that last go-around.

President Johnson: I think we better just let it go back to the company unless she has to have it. I don't want to do—I don't care about doing them any more favors.

Jenkins: All right. [*Pauses.*] All right, I'll—I'm holding him, so I'll go back—

President Johnson: Because you sell it to Carpenter, that'll get you in more trouble, you see.

---

46. Jenkins was referring to the Texas State Democratic Convention, which would take place in Houston on 16 June. Johnson's friend A.W. Moursund, who with Jesse Kellam served as codirector of the blind trust that managed the Johnson assets, would serve as temporary chairman of the convention—despite the President's wishes expressed in the passage that followed. Ronnie Dugger, "Connally's Slate Wins Texas Seats," *Washington Post*, 17 June 1964. For background, see John Connally to Johnson, 4:15 P.M., 12 June 1964, in this volume.

47. Liz Carpenter served as Lady Bird Johnson's press secretary. Her "Falcon" was presumably an automobile owned by the Texas Broadcasting Corporation.

Jenkins: Yes, sir.

President Johnson: And I think that I'd . . . I'd tell him—you go back so he's not paying—OK.

Jenkins: All right, sir.

President Johnson: Is that all?

Jenkins: That's all, sir.

7:35 P.M.: Jack Valenti arrived in the office.

7:45 P.M.: Unrecorded call to Bill Moyers.

7:46 P.M.: Unrecorded call to Walter Jenkins.

7:48 P.M.: Jenkins arrived in the office.

7:55 P.M.

Between Carol Agger and Walter Jenkins[48]

In this recording of a short segment of a longer conversation, Jenkins spoke briefly to close Johnson adviser and attorney (and future Supreme Court Justice) Abe Fortas. He then asked Carol Agger, who was Fortas's wife and herself a prominent Washington attorney, about the law governing access to the tax records of the Johnson foundation. The question was in direct reference to the conversation that Jenkins had just completed with the President.

Abe Fortas: She's right here. Just a minute, Walter.

Fortas's wife then comes on the line.

Carol Agger: Hello?

Walter Jenkins: Carol?

Agger: Yes, Walter.

Jenkins: How are you?

Agger: I'm fine.

Jenkins: [*with Agger acknowledging*] We had a call this afternoon from Jesse [Kellam], and he had been told informally by the district director that this afternoon [Louis] Kohlmeier of the *Wall Street Journal* came in and asked to see the returns for the . . . what was the LBJ Foundation,

---

48. Tape WH6406.09, Citation #3747, Recordings of Telephone Conversations—White House Series, Recordings and Transcripts of Conversations and Meetings, Lyndon B. Johnson Library.

now the Johnson City Foundation. And that he had shown them '61 and '62—which they had on file readily—pages three and four, which he says under their rules they're entitled to see. And that's receipts and disbursements.

Agger: That's right.

Jenkins: He then asked to see the rest of them, and so they're getting them from Fort Worth, and he's going to show the rest—

Agger: What years were there—'60?

Jenkins: '61 and '62 is the ones they had.

Agger: Mm-hmm. Mm-hmm.

Jenkins: And that they plan to show him the rest of them as soon as they get them. Then this afternoon late he had a long—

The recording ends abruptly.

7:56 P.M.

From McGeorge Bundy[49]

In a front-page article in the day's *New York Times*, influential foreign affairs correspondent Max Frankel had reported that U.S. Ambassador to South Vietnam Henry Cabot Lodge would return to the United States in July.[50] Earlier in the year, Lodge had been widely expected to make a bid for the Republican presidential nomination (and had even indicated that he would accept a draft), but Frankel reported that Lodge would support Pennsylvania Governor William Scranton's challenge to Barry Goldwater's presumptive nomination.[51] In this conversation, Johnson and McGeorge Bundy speculated on the possible source of Frankel's story and reviewed candidates to replace Lodge as ambassador.

---

49. Tape WH6406.09, Citation #3748, Recordings of Telephone Conversations—White House Series, Recordings and Transcripts of Conversations and Meetings, Lyndon B. Johnson Library.

50. Max Frankel, "Lodge Resigning; Expected Home for Convention," *New York Times*, 15 June 1964. For the Lodge situation, see Johnson to Richard Russell, 10:55 A.M., 27 May 1964, in McKee, *The Presidential Recordings, Johnson*, vol. 6, *April 14, 1964–May 31, 1964*, pp. 871–85; Johnson to Richard Russell, 12:26 P.M., 11 June 1964; and Robert Kennedy to Johnson, 7:26 P.M., 12 June 1964, in this volume.

51. Max Frankel, "Lodge Resigning; Expected Home for Convention." Lodge would officially inform the President of his intent to resign in an 18 June telegram. "Telegram from the Ambassador in Vietnam (Lodge) to the Department of State," 18 June 1964, U.S. Department of State, *Foreign Relations of the United States (FRUS), 1964–1968: Vietnam*, ed. Edward C. Keefer and Charles S. Sampson (Washington, DC: GPO, 1992), 1:521–22.

McGeorge Bundy: . . . [Max] Frankel had been so damn near the bone. I just found that out when I saw the—finally caught up with this baby. We have no evidences, none whatever after a day of hunting, as to where or how. The Secretary [Dean Rusk] will want to tell you more at lunch tomorrow of how he's gone about it.

We have been up and down the names and numbers of the possible next man, and I think you'll find at lunch tomorrow that everybody is quite—that Dean and Bob [McNamara] and I all think that your best bet is in fact [Roswell] Gilpatric, and that maybe he's [*unclear*]—[52]

President Johnson: He's out. I couldn't name him at all. I can't name Gilpatric.[53]

Bundy: You're sure of that, Mr. President?

President Johnson: Mm-hmm. Yeah.

Bundy: You . . .

President Johnson: [*softly*] Yeah, yeah. I'm not going to—I can't name him.

Bundy: Well, then we have to—

President Johnson: I'd be afraid to—

Bundy: We have to go back to the boards. We have assumed that whatever might have been his political trouble before, any man leaving a very fat and fancy practice for the most dangerous job in the government would be . . . get more cheers than groans.

President Johnson: Mm-hmm. . . . No, I'll tell you what I'm about: I'm just pretty confident that it ought to be [Maxwell] Taylor.[54]

Bundy: Well, we're—for different reasons—we're all in varying ways

---

52. Until he resigned in January to return to private law practice, Roswell Gilpatric had been deputy secretary of defense.

53. Although the Justice Department had cleared him of any wrongdoing, Gilpatric had been accused of a conflict of interest in the award of a contract for the TFX (F-111) fighter aircraft to the General Dynamics Corporation. Gilpatric had done extensive legal work for General Dynamics, and after he joined the Defense Department, his former firm had become the company's chief counsel. In making the award, Gilpatric had overruled the recommendation of Navy and Air Force technical analysts who favored Boeing's design for the plane. Gilpatric and Robert McNamara argued that the decision reflected their preference for a single design that could be modified for use by the Air Force and Navy, a feature that General Dynamics provided but Boeing did not. In addition, Gilpatric had been accused of participating in a Pentagon effort to discredit Senator John McClellan's investigation of the TFX contract. For Johnson, the affair was particularly problematic because General Dynamics was based in his home state of Texas, thus raising questions about his own possible involvement. Still plagued by the ongoing Bobby Baker investigation, Johnson remained deeply concerned that any hint of additional corruption might jeopardize his reelection. "Changes at the Pentagon," *New York Times*, 11 January 1964; *Congressional Quarterly Almanac*, 1964, vol. 20, pp. 1089–97.

54. General Maxwell D. Taylor served as chairman of the Joint Chiefs of Staff; he would eventually be selected for the ambassadorship.

and for quite different reasons, Rusk and McNamara both think that would be a mistake.

President Johnson: I want to hear them out on it. But that's who—

Bundy: Of course you do . . . of course you do.

President Johnson: —that's who I'd be for. I wouldn't name Gilpatric. I like him, and I'm for him, but I wouldn't send him to that job. I think it'd just be hari-kari, just be political suicide.

Bundy: Mm-hmm. Mm-hmm. Well, I'm astonished at your judgment. Well, we must argue it out again tomorrow.

President Johnson: Yeah.

Bundy: And there—

President Johnson: What are their objections to Taylor?

Bundy: One, that he is physically weary.

President Johnson: Well, he'll be less weary there than he is here, running every goddamn day to every conference they got in the world.

Bundy: He's got a . . . not a—I don't know whether it's a bum ticker, but he's—

President Johnson: Yeah.

Bundy: —had a warning. And Rusk feels that a second military man and military men in the one and the two spots is a bad signal, both internationally and in some ways locally.[55]

President Johnson: That's a military job, though.

Bundy: Uh . . . Well, Bob would agree with you on that; Rusk would not.

President Johnson: Mm-hmm.

Bundy: And I would not, because I myself very much doubt that he has the sense of—I think you'd have a backward . . . you'd lose ground, and it would be said that you lost it because of a militaristic process and a failure to understand the politics of it.

The thing that worries me most, though, is simply that this man— this is a man of ebbing energy.[56] I just think it's a fact that he is. And I think the fact is you need a hell of a commander on that spot. I would rather put [William] Westmoreland in charge of everything than send Max out. That's an acceptable solution from McNamara's point of view. Either of them is. He's perfectly willing. He, I think, feels as I do that Ros is first-rate and that there is *not* a political vulnerability, but we'd defer obviously to your judgment on that.

---

55. Bundy was referring to General William Westmoreland, the new head of the U.S. Military Assistance Command in South Vietnam.
56. Contrary to Bundy's assessment, Taylor would live until 1987.

President Johnson: Yeah. I made up my mind on Ros. I don't need anything on him. I just don't . . . I don't think that's the thing to do. I just think that that would invite *all* . . . It would make a real partisan war out of it, and I don't want that to happen. And I think we've got to have somebody that's got great stature to avoid it, and I don't think Alex Johnson, George Ball will do it.[57]

Bundy: No. . . . The top of McNamara's list is [John] McCloy, and I can certainly find out in the most discreet way whether he would go, if you think it's worth doing.[58]

President Johnson: Well, I think it's worth doing. I . . . I just have the feeling that the people of this country have more confidence with Taylor out there than any man that's going to be available to us that I've heard of. I don't believe they know McCloy enough. I believe the people of the world—I don't think they're going to think that Max Taylor is a [Curtis] LeMay.[59] I don't think they will—

Bundy: No, of course they're not going to think that . . .

President Johnson: —look at it in that regard at all.

Bundy: . . . they're not going to think that.

President Johnson: They're going to look at him as a reasonable, fair, good man that has respect of everybody, and I think it's going to show that we mean business without having to bluff and bluster a lot. I think it means we got our best man that we put out there. And I've talked to three or four groups about it, and every person I talk to says the same thing—outside of our own little shop.

Bundy: Mm-hmm. Mm-hmm. Mm-hmm. Mm-hmm.

President Johnson: And they're people that have had a lot of dealings with the different ones and have—

Bundy: Sure.

President Johnson: —have pretty good judgments on them. I'm going to have dinner with [J. William] Fulbright tonight.[60] I'm going to ask him what he thinks.

Bundy: Well, then it's going to leak. But never mind.

---

57. U. Alexis Johnson was the deputy under secretary for political affairs.
58. A New York lawyer and adviser to presidents Kennedy and Johnson, John McCloy had served as assistant secretary of war (1940–1945), president of the World Bank (1947–1949), and high commissioner of occupied Germany (1949–1952).
59. Air Force Chief of Staff General Curtis E. LeMay had served as chief of the Strategic Air Command (SAC) and was a virulent cold warrior. He would retire in 1965 and in 1968 would be the running mate of segregationist Democrat and Alabama Governor George Wallace.
60. A Democratic senator from Arkansas, J. William Fulbright chaired the Committee on Foreign Relations.

President Johnson: You think so?

Bundy: It will be decided within 24 hours. Well, no, I think he can keep his peace for a day or two. That's about all. And I think you'll have it decided in that length of time.

President Johnson: Uh . . .

Bundy: No, I don't think *quite* that, Mr. President. He—unless he gets asked by some newspaperman he fully trusts, that kind of thing. I say that because it happened so many times in the last three or four years.

President Johnson: Well, I don't want—

Bundy: I think—

President Johnson: —to discuss it with him, then.

Bundy: I think . . . I think he needs to be in the act. No, I think he'd probably—I think he'd keep his mouth shut for you. For the length of time you need. For the length of time you need, because you've got to decide this right away anyhow.

President Johnson: Well, if I had to decide tonight, I want to hear them, hear everything they've got to say, but I've decided, and Taylor [*unclear*]—

Bundy: Well, I've told you the essence of it both ways, and . . . I don't, you know, I couldn't pass judgment on the politics of it, but it does *surprise* me that you're so negative on Ros on that [*unclear*].

President Johnson: I'm for Ros, but I'm just not for him on that place.

Bundy: I understand. You're talking about the specific ground and specific place.

President Johnson: Mm-hmm . . . mm-hmm.

Bundy: Yeah. Yeah.

President Johnson: And he's just left, and he's gone up there, and now he's coming back. I think that . . . I'd rather have Ball than Ros.

Bundy: Mm-hmm. Mm-hmm.

President Johnson: And they tell me that *Ros* is no administrator.

Bundy: No, I don't think that's right.

President Johnson: Well, McNamara told me. I asked him what his weakest point was, and he said administration.

Bundy: Well, Bob would be a better judge, but I think his use of staff and [*a buzzer sounds*]—I would have thought very well of, without being direct[ly]—now his handling of White House business, of the President's business, or of staff business for the NSC [National Security Council] and all that was excellent when I saw him . . .

President Johnson: Mm-hmm.

Bundy: . . . and it was alert, and he used his people, and he knew what he was saying.

President Johnson: Mm-hmm.

Bundy: Uh . . . Well, that's the sum and substance of it. The names and numbers—the other names and numbers aren't very interesting, I don't think, that people have thought up during the course of the day.

President Johnson: Who are they?

Bundy: Well, people like George Woods, who you'd never pry loose from the [World] Bank and who's had no previous experience in the area, although he has a hell of a reputation.[61] Gene Black, who's again got a great reputation, but I think is genuinely a tired man.[62] Younger people . . . Fred Eaton.[63] I don't think he would be up to it. He would have a certain Republican protective coloration. Howard Petersen up in the Philadelphia banking area, who, again, was Bob Patterson's junior, and, again, very respectable figure.[64] I don't think *he* has quite the size we're looking for. Among the military, the only two that McNamara would recommend to you are either Taylor or Westmoreland.

That's the up and down, the names that have been added that make much sense. I think . . . I think—the more I think of George Ball, the more I think you need him where he is more than you need him there, and that there are . . . I wouldn't be too worried about Bobby's [Kennedy's] wariness of him because I don't think that's decisive. I don't think—I think Bobby would cover that pretty well.

President Johnson: Mac, you know the way I feel about Taylor is this: I believe the . . . from what I've seen the seven months I've been in here, that the most challenging and most dangerous military problem we have is out there. He's our top military man. He's respected in the world and here at home. And I'm not sure that the administration has as much respect on Vietnam as Taylor would have on Vietnam. I believe anything that his name is signed to would have a . . . would carry some weight with nearly anyone. If Westmoreland's as good as they say he is, well maybe . . . maybe Westmoreland can help him if he's got any problem with his age. But I don't—

---

61. George D. Woods served as the fourth president of the World Bank from 1963 to 1968. He was also chairman of the board of FirstBoston, one of the country's largest investment banking firms. "George D. Woods, 81, Dies; Ex-President of World Bank," *New York Times*, 21 August 1982.

62. Eugene R. Black, Woods's predecessor, had been World Bank president from 1949 to 1962. "Eugene R. Black Dies at 93; Ex-President of World Bank," *New York Times*, 21 February 1992.

63. Frederick M. Eaton was a partner in the New York law firm of Shearman and Sterling and Wright. During the Eisenhower administration, he had served as chairman of the U.S. delegation to the "committee-of-ten" negotiations on disarmament. "Fred Eaton to Head Disarmament Group," *Washington Post*, 4 December 1959.

64. Howard Petersen was president of Fidelity Philadelphia Trust Company.

Bundy: I think you're right.

President Johnson: I don't think he would if he's sitting there—

Bundy: I think that—

President Johnson: —in a hotel or—

Bundy: Mr. President, I don't think you . . . I don't think anyone can argue with you that the immediate prestige and safety impact of this is better than any other single appointment you can make. On the real merits, I would say you are . . . This is a tired man with a . . .

President Johnson: Well, your—

Bundy: . . . with an uncertain health problem, and I myself do *not* believe that in fact he has ever understood that war. I think this is just the painful truth.

President Johnson: Well, it's a good place for him to get to understand it then, because—

Bundy: Well, Mr. President, men at 62½ who are tired are not an easy bet for that. I think what you're getting is—

President Johnson: Well, I'm going to see one that you—

Bundy: —great protection and no harm.

President Johnson: You're bringing one over here for an hour and a half within the next week that's 82.[65]

Bundy: [*Both laugh.*] I don't describe the ages of foreigners, Mr. President, and I certainly don't want to sound as if only people under . . . only people your age and under are worth having, but I . . . This is—I'm only describing the way—All the people who've watched him operate have been worried about how quickly he tires. This is just a fact.

President Johnson: Well, I think one of the reasons is that they run him. I can't—I can't run. When I go to this damn Los Angeles thing I'll be constipated; I'll skip three hours; I'll get up at 7:00 in the morning, and—[66]

Bundy: We haven't thought of sending you, Mr. President, but that's a perfect solution. [*Chuckles.*]

President Johnson: No, but I'm just telling you one of the problems of his is just traveling the whole time. Every time I hear from him, he's just on tour.

---

65. Johnson was probably referring to Turkish President Ismet Inonu, who would turn 80 in 1964 and would visit the White House later in the month. Greek Prime Minister George Papandreou, who would also visit, was 64.

66. President Johnson would travel to California from 19–21 June.

Bundy: [*amused*] I'll grant you that . . . I'll grant you that; I'll grant you that.

President Johnson: He's touring, and . . .

Bundy: Yeah, yeah.

President Johnson: That'll kill anybody—a man that just travels the whole time.

Bundy: Yeah . . .yeah, yeah.

President Johnson: And I believe that . . . I believe . . . I believe he'll be easier there than he will fighting with LeMay here.

Bundy: Well, I'll tell you this: that of course if this is where your mind settles, it can be done, and we will . . . and it can—the basic solution, then, is fundamentally in the staffing and in the instructions. . . .

President Johnson: [*softly*] Mm-hmm. Mm-hmm.

Bundy: But . . .

President Johnson: That's the way I want it to come out unless they've got some awfully good reason. And if they've got some reason that I don't know about. If he has to—

Bundy: I haven't told you a thing you haven't heard.

President Johnson: If he has to—

Bundy: I think—

President Johnson: If he has to spend most of his day taking medicine, why I don't know about it, but . . .

Bundy: I don't think it's that bad.

President Johnson: What I have seen, I would . . . I would put him way out in front of anything that's been suggested up to now. And we'll talk about it tomorrow, then.

Bundy: Right.

I'll give you one more bit of trouble. I never could—

President Johnson: What was the first thing you were talking about? I didn't understand . . .

Bundy: [*with the President acknowledging*] This Frankel story. I mean, it's perfectly extraordinary.

President Johnson: Yeah, well, what do you think happened to it?

Bundy: I . . . Mr. President, you'd better talk to Dean Rusk because he's the only man who knows the exact history of the dispatch—

President Johnson: [*with Bundy acknowledging*] He said it came out of the channel, and was brought to his office by some code man and given to his most trusted assistant, who sees everything, and they're the only ones saw it.

Bundy: That is certainly the picture that we understand. My own conclusion from that is—since I think it's always *most* improbable that these things come from code messages—my own conclusion from that is that somehow some other way [Henry Cabot] Lodge gave a signal of this to the [*New York*] *Times.* I don't think we can . . . there's a little confirmation in that, in that . . . his answering cable to the Secretary's request for a denial was, "We'll of course deny as you suggest," which doesn't sound as if, you know, "My God, how can you people be so irresponsible, and I'll certainly deny it, and why didn't you," you know. I have a hunch that Lodge, for one reason or another, wished to be—decide his own timing, and decide it on this. Although I must say it sorts ill with his messages to us about protecting his intentions.

President Johnson: Mm-hmm.

Bundy: I don't see any other explanation that doesn't imply either that Dean Rusk can't trust his assistant, which I doubt, or that there's a wiretap into his office, which I doubt, or that there's a disloyal code clerk, which, again, I doubt.

President Johnson: Well, it's something that we sure ought to be awfully careful about because I looked today at two or three items in *Newsweek,* and we narrowed them down to only three people knowing them around here. They're just about as limited as they could be, and they know them.

Bundy: Yeah.

President Johnson: I'm getting very suspicious.

Bundy: Yeah.

President Johnson: And the hell of it is, Mac, two or three of these are just . . . just things that . . .

Bundy: You—

President Johnson: That *my* people knew. No. No, Bill Moyer[s] knew them, and Jack Valenti knew them. And the three of us are about [the] only ones that know them, and they've got them in there.

Bundy: I bet you a cookie more than those three, Mr. President. It's just not *possible* from what I know of your people that they just—they wouldn't—(a) they don't get trapped, and (b) they don't talk.

President Johnson: No, that's why we think something else. I just don't know.

Bundy: Something else. Something funny; something funny.

President Johnson: OK.

Bundy: Right, sir.

President Johnson: Bye.

8:20 P.M.: President Johnson returned to the Mansion with Jack Valenti.

8:30 P.M.: Called secretary Yolanda Boozer and requested a memo from Larry O'Brien and copies of *Time* and *Life* magazines.

9:15 P.M.: Dined with Mrs. Johnson, Valenti, columnist Joe Alsop and his wife, and Clark Clifford and his wife.

11:45 P.M.: Retired for the night.

Tuesday, June 16, 1964

I'd say, Mr. President, it's so monumental. It's equivalent to a . . . signing an emancipation proclamation, and it ought to just have all of the possible attention that you could focus on it.

—Lee White to President Johnson

At the Texas State Democratic Convention in Houston, conservative Democrats led by Governor John Connally retained control of the convention despite a walkout by liberals who protested the convention's refusal to seat a delegation of their allies from San Antonio. As expected, the Connally-led convention endorsed President Johnson but not his programs. The liberal faction had argued that the convention should support the President's policies as well as his candidacy.[1]

Meeting in Dallas the same day, the Texas State Republican Convention on June 16 pledged all 56 of its convention delegates to Barry Goldwater, theoretically giving the Arizona senator enough support at the upcoming national Republican convention in San Francisco to secure the party's nomination for president. Few of the delegates, however, were firmly bound to Goldwater, and significant doubts remained about whether he could block efforts by moderate Republicans to sway delegates in favor of Pennsylvania Governor William Scranton. Along with the continuing internecine strife among Republicans, the day brought more good news for President Johnson, as the Labor Department announced significant increases in industrial output, employment, and personal income for the

---

1. Ronnie Dugger, "Connally's Slate Wins Texas Seats," *Washington Post*, 17 June 1964. For background, see John Connally to Johnson, 4:15 P.M., 12 June 1964; and Walter Jenkins to Johnson, 7:35 P.M., 15 June 1964, both in this volume.

month of May, and the Senate defeated 34 hostile southern amendments to the civil rights bill in a series of roll-call votes. This action brought the bill to within days of a final Senate vote.[2] The wider civil rights situation remained tense, however, as police in St. Augustine sent an additional 50 civil rights protestors to jail after a series of sit-ins at lunch counters and restaurants.[3]

7:00 A.M.: Johnson woke, met with Jack Valenti, and completed his physical exercise routine.

8:45 A.M.: Attended the legislative leaders breakfast, with Speaker John McCormack, Senator Carl Hayden, Senator Hubert Humphrey, Congressman Carl Albert, Congressman Hale Boggs, Walter Jenkins, Bill Moyers, Lawrence O'Brien, Kenneth O'Donnell, George Reedy, and Jack Valenti.

9:30 A.M.: Arrived at the Oval Office with the legislative leaders.

9:36 A.M.: Unrecorded call to McGeorge Bundy.

9:44 A.M.

To Elmer Staats[4]

Johnson called Deputy Budget Director Elmer Staats with instructions to placate California Representative Bernie Sisk by informing him that the Westlands Water District irrigation project would receive "sympathetic" consideration during the next budget cycle.[5] Located on the flat, arid plain to the southeast of Fresno, California, the 600,000 acre Westlands district would become the nation's largest irrigation project. An expansion of the existing Central Valley water project, Westlands would consist of a series of "dams, reservoirs, canals, and pumping stations" that would transfer water from reservoirs in the Sierra Nevada mountains to the Sacramento River delta and then on to the Central Valley for use

---

2. Charles Mohr, "Goldwater Over Top If He Keeps All Votes," *New York Times*, 17 June 1964; Carroll Kilpatrick, "Scranton Backers Report Inroads on Barry's Strength," *Washington Post*, 17 June 1964; Eileen Shanahan, "Jobs, Production and Income Made New Gains in May," *New York Times*, 17 June 1964; E. W. Kenworthy, "Senate Speed-Up Puts Rights Bill Near Final Vote," *New York Times*, 17 June 1964.

3. "St. Augustine Jails 50 More Negroes," *Washington Post*, 17 June 1964.

4. Tape WH6406.09, Citation #3749, Recordings of Telephone Conversations—White House Series, Recordings and Transcripts of Conversations and Meetings, Lyndon B. Johnson Library.

5. For Sisk's discontent, see Larry O'Brien to Johnson, 2:10 P.M., 15 June 1964, in this volume.

in agricultural irrigation. Sisk, whose Fresno-based district included the Westlands area, had lobbied for the project since he entered Congress in 1955. As Johnson indicated, funding for the Westlands project would be included in the Public Works Appropriations Act for fiscal 1966.[6]

President Johnson: Elmer, are you familiar with this [Bernie] Sisk project in California?

Elmer Staats: Yeah . . . the Westlands irrigation project?

President Johnson: Yeah.

Staats: Yes.

President Johnson: Can you talk to him and tell him we'll give it serious consideration for '66? Is it a justified project?

Staats: Oh, yes. It's a good project, Mr. President—

President Johnson: Tell him we'll give it—tell him I'll talk to him, and I want to sympathetically consider it in '66. We can't do anything about it now. You get ahold of Larry O'Brien and go up and talk to him about it and see if you can get him in line.

Staats: OK. We considered this, as you may recall, last fall—

President Johnson: Yeah.

Staats: —but it was just such a big project, $157 million, that we are giving our preference to the smaller projects—

President Johnson: Tell him I just . . . I wouldn't explain to him what happened, I'd—

Staats: No.

President Johnson: —just tell him we're in trouble. But we'll . . . On his account, I'm willing to give it serious consideration in '66. And . . .

Staats: Be all right for him—

President Johnson: You talk to Larry about it. I don't want to get a letter. I don't want to be committing it, but . . .

Staats: Yeah. Well, now, how about his using it publicly? Could he use any indication from us, public [*unclear*]—

President Johnson: Well, if he's got to. Has he got any need for it?

Staats: Well—

President Johnson: Has he got an opponent?

---

6. Austin Scott, "Dividing the Land: Monopolies Stifle Small Farmers," *Washington Post*, 26 May 1975; Glen Martin, "The California Water Wars Water Flowing to Farms, Not Fish," *San Francisco Chronicle*, 23 October 2005; Eric Brazil, "Central Valley Irrigation District Fights to Save Arid Farmland, Despite Cost to Taxpayers," *San Francisco Chronicle*, 29 January 2001; *Congressional Quarterly Almanac*, 89th Cong., 1st sess., 1965, vol. 21 (Washington, DC: Congressional Quarterly Service, 1966), pp. 741–42.

Staats: We'd have to find out.

President Johnson: Yeah.

Staats: [*Unclear*] I understand from Larry that he's not in serious trouble [*unclear*]—[7]

President Johnson: All right. I wouldn't do it, then. [*Staats acknowledges.*] I'd just tell him that I want him to know [that if] he's interested in it, I'm going to seriously consider it, and before I turn it down, I'll have him in to see me, if I do turn it down.

Staats: OK.

President Johnson: Otherwise, I'll approve it.

Staats: I'll get ahold of Larry. I'm—

President Johnson: You tell—OK.

Staats: —[*unclear*]. All right. Thank you.

9:45 A.M.: Senator Mike Mansfield arrived in the office.

9:55 A.M.

To Robert McNamara[8]

The President next spoke with the Secretary of Defense and discussed possible replacements for Ambassador Henry Cabot Lodge in South Vietnam. As he had in the conversation with McGeorge Bundy the day before, Johnson indicated that he strongly preferred Chairman of the Joint Chiefs of Staff Maxwell Taylor. In contrast to what Bundy had said, McNamara agreed.

President Johnson: Bob?

Robert McNamara: Good morning, Mr. President.

President Johnson: How are you?

McNamara: I'm just fine. Yourself, sir?

President Johnson: Pretty good.

---

7. Bernie Sisk would be reelected in 1964 with 66.8 percent of the vote in California's 16th District. *Congressional Quarterly Almanac*, 88th Cong., 2nd sess., 1964, vol. 20 (Washington, DC: Congressional Quarterly Service, 1965), p. 1027.

8. Tape WH6406.09, Citation #3750, Recordings of Telephone Conversations—White House Series, Recordings and Transcripts of Conversations and Meetings, Lyndon B. Johnson Library.

Now, I've been talking to some folks about our possibilities and been talking to Mac [Bundy] last night and this morning.[9] He told me some of you-all's talks. And the more I talk to people, the more I consider it, the more I'm convinced that if . . . that we ought to really give every possible test to [Maxwell] Taylor. And every possible consideration. He seems to me to be the person that can give us the best . . . He knows what's going on and can give us the best protection with all the forces that want to make that a political war.

McNamara: Yeah. Yeah.

President Johnson: I think that . . .

McNamara: He's better in that respect than Ros [Gilpatric], that I grant you.[10]

President Johnson: Oh, they just start making speeches on Ros. The lead on the story . . . one fellow said to me the lead on the story would be: "Former under secretary of defense who was involved in the TFX contract was named by Johnson today to succeed [Henry Cabot] Lodge."[11] And then every damn speaker would be up raising hell about "here's the man that's running the war out there" and so on and so forth.

Now, they can't say much about Taylor. They can't question his military judgment; they can't question his experience; they can't question his patriotism, his knowledge. And they might say he's a little old, but I don't think any of them *feel* that way.

McNamara: No, I don't think they'll say that, Mr. President. I think what they'd say is you're putting it in the hands of a military officer—

President Johnson: [*talking over McNamara*] [Wayne] Morse and them would say that, but nearly everybody thinks that's what it is, and everybody—[12]

McNamara: Well, I was just going to say, I don't think that's bad. That's the only thing they'll say, I believe.

---

9. See McGeorge Bundy to Johnson, 7:56 P.M., 15 June 1964, in this volume.

10. Roswell Gilpatric had served as deputy secretary of defense before resigning in January 1964 to return to private law practice.

11. For the significance of the TFX contract, see McGeorge Bundy to Johnson, 7:56 P.M., 15 June 1964, in this volume.

12. Wayne Morse, the Democratic senator from Oregon, had been critical of Johnson's policies in Southeast Asia. In August he would be one of only two senators to vote against the Gulf of Tonkin Resolution. (The other was Democrat Ernest Gruening of Alaska.) See Johnson to Robert McNamara, 10:58 A.M., 27 April 1964, in Guian A. McKee, ed., *The Presidential Recordings, Lyndon B. Johnson: Toward the Great Society, February 1, 1964–May 31, 1964*, vol. 6, *April 14, 1964–May 31, 1964* (New York: Norton, 2007), pp. 234–37; Fredrik Logevall, *Choosing War: The Lost Chance for Peace and the Escalation of War in Vietnam* (Berkeley: University of California Press, 1999), pp. 136–39.

President Johnson: I just—

McNamara: No, I would lean to Max on this issue. I think Mac leans to Ros, but I—

President Johnson: He does very much, and he says that he thinks that you and [Dean] Rusk do, but I just—

McNamara: No.

President Johnson: —staying awake at night thinking—

McNamara: No.

President Johnson: —about it, and I've—

McNamara: Let me tell you, I lean to Max with one qualification: I think . . . we ought to really probe his personal situation, make damn sure this is all right for him. He—that man has sacrificed his life for this country almost, and I just hate to see us do anything that was really too much of a penalty for him to assume here. He told me yesterday, though, that he wanted to be considered for the job. Those were his exact words.

President Johnson: I have this feeling, Bob. I don't know whether you do or not. But I believe that a man in Saigon, staying there seven days a week, around there is [in] better shape than he is flying all over the damn world and missing the clocks and [*McNamara laughs*] getting constipated and staying up at nights and under strains—

McNamara: [*Unclear.*]

President Johnson: —and fighting with [Curtis] LeMay and so on and so forth.

McNamara: Yeah, you might be right.

President Johnson: I'll tell you one thing: With a cable . . . with his name signed to it, would have a hell of a lot more weight in a lot of circles than any other name I know of.

McNamara: I agree with you. I completely agree with you.

President Johnson: Well, now, you think about that because we, we've got to do something. I was with some folks last night, and they think that we're about to lose the greatest race that the United States has ever lost and be the first time that we've ever turned a tail and then shoved out of a place and come home and said we've given up the Pacific.[13]

Now, I don't think it's that bad, but a lot of people do, and I think we're going to have to make a decision pretty promptly, and we're going to have to send him out there and then kind of support what he thinks we ought to do.

---

13. Johnson had dined the previous evening with the influential syndicated newspaper columnist Joe Alsop and Washington attorney, adviser, and President's Foreign Intelligence Advisory Board chairman, Clark Clifford.

McNamara: Well, I just don't believe we *can* be pushed out of there, Mr. President. We just can't allow it to be done. You wouldn't want to go down in history as having that, and I [*unclear*]—

President Johnson: Not at all. How are we going to avoid it, though?

McNamara: Well, I—

President Johnson: Suppose your government collapsed today and another one came in and said to get the hell out. What do we do? [*Pauses.*] You see my—

McNamara: Oh, I—It's a tickly situation. You know how I felt about it. But I don't think we're quite at that point. I don't believe the government is going to collapse today, and I think if we continue to show some signs of firmness in Laos and in that area, it won't collapse. And I think putting Max out there, as a matter of fact, is a sign of firmness. [Nguyen] Khanh will appreciate it.[14] The people, I think, in Vietnam will interpret it as a [*unclear*]—

President Johnson: I think everybody in the world would look—I think everybody in the world would look at it and say, "These folks mean business."

McNamara: I favor this. Mac and . . . I don't really know how Dean feels on it, but Mac favors Ros, but I favor Max. With the single qualification that—

President Johnson: Well, that's who we're going to put if we don't run into more static than I anticipate. That's what I . . . I've thought about it now for two full days and nights. I called you last night, and they said they gave you a number, and I didn't want to interrupt you, and . . . But I thought about it Sunday and yesterday, and I . . . I'm just convinced that's the best thing of the people we have. And you explore—

McNamara: Well, I've thought a lot about it. I haven't talked to anyone on the Hill about this. Obviously, I didn't want to do so until you—

President Johnson: I talked to [Mike] Mansfield, and I talked to [Richard] Russell, and I talk—[15]

McNamara: What did Mansfield say?

President Johnson: He said by far the best man, and he'd have more

---

14. Major General Nguyen Khanh was Prime Minister of South Vietnam.

15. Mike Mansfield, Democrat of Montana and Senate majority leader, had recently written a memorandum to the President on his views on the Vietnam situation (which did not address the Lodge replacement); the two had also spoken on the phone on 9 June. See Johnson to Mike Mansfield, 12:56 P.M., 9 June 1964; and Johnson to Robert McNamara, 6:20 P.M., 9 June 1964, in this volume. The President had spoken with Richard Russell, the Democratic senator from Georgia and chairman of the Armed Services Committee, on the topic of Lodge's replacement on 11 June. Johnson to Richard Russell, 12:26 P.M., 11 June 1964, in this volume.

confidence in him and just said the other was out of the question. We just couldn't think of naming Gilpatric.

McNamara: What did Russell say about it?

President Johnson: [*with McNamara acknowledging*] Said that Taylor was by far the best man. I didn't tell [Carl] Vinson any—what I was thinking, or Russell either, and I just listed a number of people and said, "Which one would you select?"[16] And all of them selected Taylor without any question. I don't want the other boys down here to know that because it has a way of—

McNamara: Sure [*unclear*].

President Johnson: —getting in columns that I confer with my old congressional buddies, but I know Russell and Vinson can have a lot to do with helping us, and I just like to have their feeling. And they all just say right off the bat that they don't go very strong for [George] Ball. They like Gilpatric and think he's a good under secretary, but they think that he doesn't have the stature in the United States that that man ought to have following Lodge. [*Pauses.*] They all think you'd be the best man, but it would be hari-kari to send you out there . . .

McNamara: Well, I—

President Johnson: From my standpoint.

McNamara: I want you to know, Mr. President, I'm prepared to go. I've talked to Marg[e] about it, and Marge is prepared to go, and [*unclear*].[17]

President Johnson: Well, you're not going, so you just [*McNamara chuckles*] get ready to . . . Let's—you talk to him again today, and before we get over here at lunch, and see how he feels, and see . . . I think that you ought to tell him that he can write a blank check on us here, and—

McNamara: OK.

President Johnson: —just . . . let's get him the best people we can, and let's start assembling them.

McNamara: Very good.

President Johnson: OK.

McNamara: Thank you.

10:07 A.M.: Unrecorded call to Jack Valenti.

---

16. Carl Vinson, Democrat of Georgia, chaired the House Committee on Armed Services.
17. McNamara was referring to his wife, Margaret, to whom he had been married since 1940.

10:13 A.M.

To Lee White[18]

President Johnson next called Associate Counsel Lee White for an update on the civil rights protests in St. Augustine, Florida. White reported that Governor Bryant had made a strong commitment to keep order and limit violence in the city. Although White did not make the explicit comparison, the contrast between Florida and the other Deep South states such as Alabama and Mississippi—where state and local authorities ignored or even abetted segregationist violence and even murder against civil rights protestors in the spring and summer of 1964—demonstrated the significant difference that a governor could make and even that local leadership could make.

Johnson also asked White how the signing ceremony for the Civil Rights Act should be handled. White responded that the law had as much significance as the emancipation proclamation and should be treated with full dignity and ceremony. He also pointed out that the ceremony would offer Johnson the chance to speak to the nation, to urge calm as the legislation went into effect, and to reemphasize the basic American concepts of fairness and justice that formed the core of the legislation.

President Johnson: Lee?

Lee White: Yes, Mr. President.

President Johnson: How is St. Augustine?

White: Everything we hear down there, it's going very well. The governor felt obliged, even after he had moved his own troops in, to push and press the county sheriff, and just announced that—[19]

President Johnson: Wait just a second; somebody's buzzing me. Just a second.

White: All right, sir. [*Brief pause while Johnson goes away from the line.*]

President Johnson: Hello?

White: Yes?

President Johnson: Yeah, go ahead.

---

18. Tape WH6406.09, Citations #3751 and #3752, Recordings of Telephone Conversations—White House Series, Recordings and Transcripts of Conversations and Meetings, Lyndon B. Johnson Library.

19. White was referring to Florida Governor Farris Bryant, a Democrat.

White: He's . . . Governor [Farris] Bryant's said he was going to maintain law and order. He wasn't certain he was happy the way that the county was doing it, and so he's put some of his special people right into the county machinery. It sounds like a peculiar arrangement, but it's just further evidence of his intense desire to control the situation, and it is under control.

I've had no definite reports about negotiations, but all of the indicators are that it's possible that they're going to reach an accord on the—I don't want to say demands—but the request or the grievances of the Negro community, so that at the moment, it seems to be perfectly in control.

President Johnson: Is [Martin Luther] King satisfied with our reply and our talking to the governor? His man, I noticed, was over talking to . . . raising hell over with Burke Marshall.[20]

White: Uh . . . On Saturday, at your request, or your suggestion, I called Wyatt Walker—returned that call of his.

President Johnson: Yeah.

White: And he said two things: One, that they had to admit that the law enforcement was perfect. They had absolutely no complaints on that score, that the governor had indeed brought the situation into perfect control, and there was . . . they were . . . I don't know if the word was grateful, but certainly there was no complaint. Secondly, with regard to the . . .

President Johnson: They were aware that we had talked to him, though, aren't they?

White: [*with the President acknowledging*] Oh, yes. They're clearly aware. I tried to . . . I didn't want to maximize it, but he knew that we'd been involved in it. And then the second point he said was that . . . He wanted to reiterate the point in King's telegrams that when you were there as vice president, you had agreed to see to it that the two communities were in—had a dialogue going.[21] And I said well, on that point, I wasn't going to comment. I didn't know from—I hadn't discussed with you what conversations had taken place last year, but all I knew was we

---

20. Burke Marshall served as assistant attorney general in the Civil Rights Division of the Justice Department. Johnson may have been referring to a meeting between Marshall and King adviser Wyatt Walker. Taylor Branch, *Pillar of Fire: America in the King Years 1963–65* (New York: Touchstone, 1998), p. 351.

21. While still vice president, Johnson had visited St. Augustine in 1963. King had recently sent a telegram requesting federal protection while in St. Augustine in which he had attempted to establish a negotiation process between white officials and local civil rights leaders. "King Set to Ask LBJ to Send Marshals to St. Augustine," *Washington Post*, 11 June 1964; Johnson to Lee White, time unknown, 10 June 1964, in this volume.

had pretty good reports and that it was my own personal view that the less we appeared to be trying to push any decision down there, the more likely they were to receive it.

President Johnson: [*with White acknowledging*] And on that other point, let's don't let him get out of line there.[22] What they agreed to do: I accepted a meeting to go down there and speak. They came in and opposed my speaking. I asked them what they wanted me to do. They said they wanted it integrated—the meeting, the banquet meeting—and that they would like for the local official—the mayor or whoever it was—to agree—the local head of the commission, I've forgotten which—to agree that they would talk to them about how—the future.

So I talked to them, and they agreed to meet with them, which they did after my meeting. I don't know—they didn't agree to anything specific; I didn't propose anything specific. They did integrate the meeting. So they did the two things they agreed to do. They didn't agree to integrate the town or to change the thing or to any sweeping reform, they just agreed that they'd let Negroes come for the first time to the hotel to eat at the dinner I spoke to and that they would talk to them about what their demands were.

White: And both of those things took place.

President Johnson: And both those things took place.

White: Well, I—

President Johnson: So I—

White: [*with the President acknowledging*] I would assume it's best to continue to ignore it and not get into a shouting match with them. I'm delighted to know that's the case because those guys love to press and push beyond recognition.

I talked to Senator [Hubert] Humphrey briefly, and he said that he hoped that there was no . . . difficulty would arise from that [statement about the civil rights conference], but he tried to explain—exactly what happened was that he had made this for a local TV network in Minnesota.[23] Two reporters that he had questioning him were from the *Baltimore Sun* and from the *Washington Post.* He assumed that they were the only two papers that read it.[24] He hadn't seen it in any other paper,

---

22. In the passage that followed, Johnson discussed his memory of the commitments that he had made during his 1963 St. Augustine trip.

23. Earlier in the week, Senator Humphrey of Minnesota had been quoted as calling for a White House conference on implementation of the civil rights bill. Johnson to Lee White, 7:02 P.M., 15 June 1964, in this volume.

24. This claim was incorrect. The *New York Times*, and presumably many other papers, ran the story. "Focus on Rights Shifts to House," *New York Times*, 15 June 1964.

including Minnesota. And he said that even there in the *Post* story there was some sort of a distortion of it because he did not urge that a meeting be held by you but suggested that he understood that this was under consideration *by* you, and he wasn't trying to be presumptuous and said he would send over the transcript, which would make that clear.[25]

President Johnson: Well, get it, and let's look at it and see what we [can] do about it.

White: And he said he was sure that this sort of thing is . . . was really only [the] two papers that carried it were the two reporters who interviewed him.

President Johnson: Well, I don't think so. I saw it in a bunch of papers the next morning.

White: But—

President Johnson: AP [Associated Press] picked it up and carried it, but I don't [*unclear*] . . .

White: Well, I think Senator [Olin] Johnston may have fanned it a little bit yesterday.[26] But . . .

President Johnson: [Doesn't] make any difference whether it's one or one hundred. He oughtn't to be telling me what to do through the goddamn local network out in Minnesota or here either.

White: Well, in his—the way he puts it, he wasn't telling you, and when the transcript comes over we'll have a little better idea about how it—whether he did get treated unfairly by the paper.

President Johnson: [*softly*] Mm-hmm . . . mm-hmm.

White: And he said he would send that over today.

President Johnson: All right.

White: OK, sir.

President Johnson: Now, what are we going to do about this meeting?

White: I am kind of waiting to hear from the Justice Department now in terms of, you know, how they . . . whether they want to make it theirs or propose some alternative way of doing it. But as far as everybody is concerned, regardless of this Humphrey business, some series of meetings—even if they don't start for a week or 10 days—would be extremely useful.

---

25. For the *Post* story, see Susanna McBee, "National Conference on Rights Suggested," *Washington Post,* 15 June 1964.

26. Senator Olin Johnston was a South Carolina Democrat; on 15 June, he had objected to Humphrey's suggestion of a conference and stated that state and local officials were not responsible for enforcing the Civil Rights Act. See Johnson to Lee White, 7:02 P.M., 15 June 1964, in this volume.

President Johnson: What do you think we ought to do about the signing ceremony if we ever get to that point? Do you think we—

White: Well, I'm—

President Johnson: —ought to have a statement, or do you think we ought to quietly sign it, or do you think we ought to have a big hullabaloo about it, or what?

White: I'd say, Mr. President, it's so monumental. It's equivalent to a . . . signing an emancipation proclamation, and it ought to just have all of the possible attention that you could focus on it. It's *so* significant in terms of . . . now you've got the legislative branch joining the judicial and the executive: people who are elected in every corner of the country with people who are appointed and people who serve for life. And it just strikes me as being the last piece to show that this country is truly matching its responsibilities now and that . . . I would think that it deserves some real niche in history and may even provide an opportunity for you to address the nation for five or ten minutes, asking people to understand it and to try to . . . go along with its very simple and its very basic appeals to justice and to fairness, to equality, and to the conscience.

I would—I know that when President Kennedy signed the housing order, executive order on housing, it was done really in almost in the dark of the night.[27] He just interrupted a little letter he was writing to sign it, but he had such a sense of history, as he was . . . he decided he couldn't quite sign such a momentous thing without some record of it and had Cecil Stoughton come in and take a few shots of him doing it.[28] But the timing was such on that one he really wanted to slide it by.

This one is so major and so much in the public eye I would think that there would even be criticism if it were done without any ceremony. Some people who devoted a lot of time and energy to it I should think would want to be . . . some little participation in such a momentous act . . .

President Johnson: Where are you going to stop it?

White: You mean in terms of who comes in?

President Johnson: Mm-hmm . . . mm-hmm.

---

27. On 10 November 1962, President Kennedy had signed Executive Order Number 11063, which banned racial discrimination in any new housing built with federal funding, finance, or subsidy (thus including mortgage insurance for suburban single-family homes as well as public housing). Enforcement of the order, however, proved highly inconsistent. Roger Biles, "Public Housing and the Postwar Urban Renaissance, 1949–1973," in *From Tenements To The Taylor Homes: In Search of an Urban Housing Policy in Twentieth Century America*, ed. John F. Bauman, Roger Biles, and Kristin M. Szylvian (University Park: Pennsylvania State University Press, 2000), p. 151.

28. Cecil Stoughton was a White House photographer.

White: Well, if you do it on national television you could stop it pretty short at some congressional leadership. Because then everybody is in effect participating in it. I should think that'd make it easier. If you do it without television cameras, why then there's a little problem. There'll be considerable jockeying by congressional people who will want to be there and some of the civil rights leaders and groups that have really devoted a lot of energy to it.

I could list a few alternative possibilities. My own reaction is that it's just tailor-made for the kind of a talk that you could make that would just show the—make the difference between the way President Eisenhower responded to that Supreme Court decision in 1954 when it was sort of a grudging willingness to enforce the law without even saying that he thought the law was right as they had interpreted it.[29] And I think that this provides an opportunity to . . . for you, as president of *all* the people, to take a few moments of their time to impress upon them what they can do to make this thing work and why it's right and the moral basis for it.

President Johnson: Well, get busy working up your statement. Let's try to keep it to 5[00] or 600 words.

White: All right, and I won't tell anyone, just to see how long it takes for this to leak out.

President Johnson: Yeah . . . [*White chuckles.*] No one will know it but me and you.

White: All right, sir.

President Johnson: OK.

10:25 A.M.: Unrecorded call to Jack Valenti.

---

29. The civil rights issue generated a significant fault line within the Eisenhower administration, as Attorney General Herbert Brownell urged the President to pursue new civil rights legislation while Chief of Staff Sherwin Adams argued that the administration should avoid any significant action. In the aftermath of the *Brown* decision, Eisenhower had called for enforcement of the ruling, but made no public comment on the significance or moral dimensions of the underlying issues. Privately, he told an aide that "the Supreme Court decision set back progress in the South at least fifteen years" and worried that rapid integration would lead to the collapse of order in the schools. Eventually, however, Eisenhower submitted the nation's first civil rights legislation since reconstruction and, with the significant assistance of Senate Majority Leader Lyndon Johnson, secured its passage in 1957. Allan Wolk, *The Presidency and Black Civil Rights: Eisenhower to Nixon* (Rutherford, NJ: Fairleigh Dickinson University Press, 1971), pp. 221–22; Taylor Branch, *Parting the Waters: America in the King Years 1954–63* (New York: Simon & Schuster, 1988), pp. 113, 180–83.

10:26 A.M.

To Larry O'Brien[30]

The recording system captured a brief segment of a conversation between Johnson and Larry O'Brien. The specific topic cannot be determined.

Larry O'Brien: . . . just verbally.
President Johnson: Yeah.
O'Brien: And they'll . . . and it's [*unclear*]—
President Johnson: I didn't say it was irrevocable.
O'Brien: Yeah . . . right.
President Johnson: Because I don't know, but I would do it, everything else equal, unless something comes up that I don't know about.
O'Brien: Well, he should be pleased with that.
President Johnson: OK.
O'Brien: Thank you, Mr. President.

10:28 A.M. : Unrecorded call to Walter Jenkins.
10:33 A.M.: Jack Valenti arrived in the office.
10:36 A.M.: Unrecorded call to George Reedy.
10:58 A.M.: Jenkins arrived in the office.
11:10 A.M.: President Johnson met with U.S. Ambassador to India Chester Bowles and Bob Komer for an off-the-record discussion of American holdings of Indian currency. Bowles and Komer left at 11:36.

11:30 A.M.

From John McCormack[31]

Johnson received a call from Speaker of the House John McCormack, who briefed him on current head counts for the urban mass transportation

---

30. Tape WH6406.09, Citation #3753, Recordings of Telephone Conversations—White House Series, Recordings and Transcripts of Conversations and Meetings, Lyndon B. Johnson Library.
31. Tape WH6406.09, Citation #3754, Recordings of Telephone Conversations—White House Series, Recordings and Transcripts of Conversations and Meetings, Lyndon B. Johnson Library.

bill and assessed the political implications of scheduling the bill prior to the Republican National Convention.[32] Shortly after the McCormack conversation, the President called Larry O'Brien to inform him about the Speaker's views.

A brief, unclear office conversation precedes the call.

Carl Albert: Mr. President, here's—this is Carl—here's the Speaker.

John McCormack: Hello, Mr. President.

President Johnson: Mm-hmm. Yeah?

McCormack: On the mass transit, we've had [William] Widnall in here, and we've gone over, and he thinks that they'll get close to 40 Republican votes.[33] Now, of course there's all calculated risk, as you and I know. But he says that they're holding pretty fast, and that's about all we can rely on. And then the report I get from outside sources is pretty much the same. My judgment is that we ought to bring it up before the Republican convention.[34] [*Pauses.*]

President Johnson: Fine.

McCormack: It might—because it'd be a sort of a pre-Republican convention fight because [William] Scranton's strong for it, don't you see?

President Johnson: Mm-hmm.

McCormack: And then we can start organizing and just try and put—force it into operation to get [Nelson] Rockefeller to come in, and he ought to be interested in it, and [George] Romney and see what others.[35] But this could be in a sense, say, a pre-Republican convention test [*unclear*].

President Johnson: Good. You—I'll tell Larry [O'Brien] to get in touch with you, and you-all work out whatever you think's best.

McCormack: Yeah . . . What we've got to do is work on *our* side because Larry . . . Hale [Boggs] says about 160 Democrats; Larry says 168; I think we can up that 10 or 15 easily.

President Johnson: All right.

McCormack: With the right work done.

President Johnson: Good.

McCormack: And it might be—and with the effective work done

---

32. For the mass transit bill, see Johnson to Larry O'Brien, 7:00 P.M., 12 June 1964, in this volume.
33. William Widnall was a Republican representative from New Jersey.
34. The Republican National Convention would be held in San Francisco from 13–16 July.
35. Nelson A. Rockefeller served as the Republican governor of New York from 1959 to 1973; George W. Romney served as the Republican governor of Michigan from 1963 to 1969.

because . . . [Charles] Halleck will work like hell to block, and so forth and so on, but according to Widnall, we—I was going to bring it up anyway, don't you see?[36] Give them a political motive for [*unclear*] later on, but I wanted to *win* like . . . But I would think that—Widnall thinks it's best before the convention, and that's my judgment I've formed over the weekend.

President Johnson: Mm-hmm.

McCormack: Is that all right—

President Johnson: Yeah, you talk to Larry and whatever you-all agree on is good by me.

McCormack: In other words, it's all right if we put it down for next week.

President Johnson: Yeah. You talk to Larry about it. I don't want to be agreeing to something that he doesn't know about. I'll have him talk to you, and whatever you-all agree on is OK by me.

McCormack: All right, Mr. President.

President Johnson: OK.

McCormack: Good-bye.

11:37 A.M.: Off-the-record meeting with David Lilienthal, chairman of the board of the Development and Resources Corporation, to discuss the latter's recently completed travels in Iran.

TIME UNKNOWN

To Larry O'Brien[37]

Larry O'Brien: Hello?

President Johnson: Larry—

O'Brien: Yes, Mr. President.

President Johnson: —the Speaker wants to bring up mass transit next week. He says [William] Scranton and [Nelson] Rockefeller are both for it. [William] Widnall said he got 40-odd votes. They would be shifting if they don't bring it up.

---

36. Representative Charles Halleck of Indiana served as House minority leader.

37. Tape WH6406.09, Citation #3755, Recordings of Telephone Conversations—White House Series, Recordings and Transcripts of Conversations and Meetings, Lyndon B. Johnson Library.

O'Brien: Mm-hmm.

President Johnson: I told him to get with you, and whatever you-all agreed on is OK by me.

O'Brien: Very good.

President Johnson: Thank you.

O'Brien: Thank you, Mr. President.

11:40 A.M.

From Stephen Smith[38]

Stephen Smith, brother-in-law of the Kennedys, called the President to check on his plans following the evening's New York fund-raising dinner for the Kennedy Library.

The secretary announces Smith's call, and the President asks her to stay on the line.

President Johnson: Hello?

Stephen Smith: Yes, Mr. President?

President Johnson: Hi, Steve.

Smith: Hi. I'm sorry to bother you. I just . . . I didn't know what your plans were. If there was any chance you were going to stay overnight, why, I hope that perhaps you and Mrs. [Lady Bird] Johnson would stop by the house for a few minutes after the [Kennedy] dinner. But . . .

President Johnson: Steve, we'd love to. We're coming back, though . . .

Smith: Yeah, well, that's it. Well, why don't we see what time we are, and I think, you know . . . gosh, it's going to be late as it is, but I just thought if there was a chance you were staying that we'd hope you'd be able to come over. If you're going back, I think it makes [it] too late.[39]

President Johnson: Well, we'll see what time we get through and how we're feeling, and I sure do thank you and appreciate it.

Smith: All right. . . . Oh, well . . . but we'll leave it that way and see what it looks like.

---

38. Tape WH6406.09, Citation #3756, Recordings of Telephone Conversations—White House Series, Recordings and Transcripts of Conversations and Meetings, Lyndon B. Johnson Library.
39. As Smith anticipated, the President would return to Washington immediately after the dinner.

President Johnson: That'll be fine, my friend.
Smith: All right. Look forward to seeing you!
President Johnson: Bye.
Smith: Fine. Bye-bye.
President Johnson: Bye.

11:53 A.M.: Unrecorded call to Walter Jenkins.

11:55 A.M.: Jack Valenti arrived in the office.

11:56 A.M.: Jenkins arrived in the office.

12:06 P.M.: President Johnson stopped in the outer office after the departure of Valenti and Jenkins to talk with McGeorge Bundy about the agenda for the imminent National Security Council meeting.

12:07 P.M.: Went to the Cabinet Room with Bundy and George Reedy for the National Security Council meeting.

1:07 P.M.: Walked to the Mansion after the meeting for lunch with Bundy, Secretary of State Dean Rusk, and Secretary of Defense Robert McNamara.

2:50 P.M.: Unrecorded call to Secretary of Agriculture Orville Freeman.

2:56 P.M.: Unrecorded call to Bill Moyers.

3:21 P.M.: Unrecorded call from Lynda Bird Johnson.

4:36 P.M.: Unrecorded call to Jenkins.

4:37 P.M.: Unrecorded call to Valenti.

4:38 P.M.: Unrecorded call to Secretary Rusk, returning his call.

5:30 P.M.: Unrecorded call to Jenkins.

5:42 P.M.: Departed by helicopter with Mrs. Johnson for Andrews Air Force Base, arriving at 5:51 P.M.

5:59 P.M.: Air Force One took off, en route to New York City.

6:00 P.M.: Unrecorded call to Valenti from Air Force One.

6:40 P.M.: Landed in New York, where Deputy Mayor Edward F. Cavanagh escorted him to the presidential limousine.

6:50 P.M.: Departed for the St. Regis Hotel.

7:22 P.M.: Arrived at the St. Regis Hotel and went to the 20th-floor ballroom for a reception.

8:10 P.M.: Attended a dinner with Mrs. Johnson given by Mr. and Mrs. Stephen E. Smith and the Board of Trustees of the John Fitzgerald Kennedy Memorial Library in honor of Mrs. John F. Kennedy.

10:50 P.M.: Departed for JFK International Airport.

11:29 P.M.: Departed for Washington on board Air Force One, arriving in Washington at 12:05 A.M.

12:11 A.M.: Boarded a helicopter to the White House, where they arrived at 12:24 A.M.

12:45 A.M.: Retired to his bedroom for the evening.

Wednesday, June 17, 1964

The Lord will strike me dead for saying anything in favor of Mr. [Charles] de Gaulle, but I've always believed that, in the long run, his experience, or France's experience, is right: that nothing big can be done there over a long period of time without the acquiescence of China. Now, there's no sense in talking about long-range things because we've got a short-range thing, and we can't do anything about it except go on doing what we're doing now. I don't think we got any easy options: We can't get out, and we can't go smashing into China à la Mr. Goldwater.

—James "Scotty" Reston to President Johnson

The U.S. Senate took yet another crucial step towards passage of the civil rights bill on June 17, as it easily approved the substitution of the Mansfield-Dirksen bill for the civil rights bill that the House of Representatives had approved in February. Named after the Senate majority and minority leaders, the substitute contained the lengthy series of amendments that the Senate leadership had worked out over the previous three months in delicate negotiations with uncommitted senators from both parties, as well as with the White House and Justice Department. Acceptance of the amended substitute bill cleared the way for a final Senate vote on the legislation after more than 80 days of debate, negotiation, and filibuster in the Senate. Faced with the difficult prospect of voting on the civil rights legislation in the midst of a presidential campaign, presumptive Republican presidential nominee Barry Goldwater indicated that he had not yet decided how he would vote.[1]

---

1. Robert C. Albright, "Draft of Rights Bill Approved, 76 to 18," *Washington Post*, 18 June 1964; Charles Mohr, "Goldwater Scans Rights Bill Stand," *New York Times*, 18 June 1964.

7:35 A.M.: After waking and eating breakfast in bed, the President met with Jack Valenti and exercised.

9:21 A.M.: Unrecorded call to Governor Carl Sanders in Atlanta, Georgia.

10:10 A.M.: Unrecorded call to Judge Bobby Russell in Atlanta, Georgia.

10:15 A.M.: Unrecorded call to Secretary of the Treasury Douglas Dillon.

10:16 A.M.: Unrecorded call to Walter Jenkins.

10:32 A.M.: Unrecorded call to Ralph McGill in Atlanta, Georgia.

10:40 A.M.: Unrecorded call from Jenkins.

10:43 A.M.: Went to the Diplomatic Reception Room and greeted Illinois Congressman and Mrs. Dan Rostenkowski, Chicago Alderman Matthew J. Danaher, and other guests, including an unidentified group of children.

10:47 A.M.: Unrecorded call to Mrs. Arthur Krock.

10:53 A.M.: Boarded a helicopter and flew to Andrews Air Force Base accompanied by Secretary of Health, Education, and Welfare Anthony Celebrezze, Valenti, and members of military and Secret Service entourage.

11:05 A.M.: Unrecorded call to Burke Marshall from Air Force One.

11:09 A.M.: Boarded Air Force One with the presidential party and departed for Cleveland, Ohio.

11:40 A.M.

Between Ralph McGill and Juanita Roberts[2]

While the President was away from the White House, the taping system recorded a conversation between the publisher of the *Atlanta Journal-Constitution* and Johnson's chief secretary, Juanita Roberts. Ralph McGill, a liberal and Johnson ally, called to dictate a section of a letter to the President that detailed his recommendation for the director of the new Community Relations Service (CRS) that would be created by the Civil Rights Act.[3] Established by Title X of the legislation, the CRS was

---

2. Tape WH6406.09, Citation #3757, Recordings of Telephone Conversations—White House Series, Recordings and Transcripts of Conversations and Meetings, Lyndon B. Johnson Library.
3. For McGill's political orientation, see Robert Mann, *The Walls of Jericho: Lyndon Johnson, Hubert Humphrey, Richard Russell, and the Struggle For Civil Rights* (New York: Harcourt Brace, 1996), pp.41, 70.

designed to pursue federal conciliation of civil rights disputes in local communities, preferably though private mechanisms involving existing agencies. McGill's suggestion for CRS director would not be chosen, as the position eventually went to former Florida governor Leroy Collins.[4]

The dictated material was part of a longer letter that outlined strategies for reaching out to southern governors and business leaders following passage of the civil rights bill.[5]

Ralph McGill: Hello?

Juanita Roberts: Hello?

McGill: This is Ralph McGill.

Roberts: Yes, sir.

McGill: The editor of the *Atlanta [Journal]-Constitution.*

Roberts: Yes, sir.

McGill: The President called me this morning for some information . . .

Roberts: All right.

McGill: Said he would try to call me this afternoon or in the morning, but I have it now. I thought I'd like to dictate it so he can have it on his return.

Roberts: All right.

McGill: And this is personal and confidential.

Roberts: Yes, sir.

McGill: [*dictating*] "Dear Mr. President" . . .

Roberts: Mm-hmm.

McGill: "Here is a quick report on Harold Walker."

Roberts: All right.

McGill: "He is the son of Clifford M. Walker."

Roberts: How do you spell "gim"?[6]

McGill: M. M as in—

Roberts: M, as in Mary.

McGill: Yes.

Roberts: All right.

---

4. *Congressional Quarterly Almanac,* 88th Cong., 2nd sess., 1964, vol. 20 (Washington, DC: Congressional Quarterly Service, 1965), pp. 342, 378.
5. Ralph McGill, "Dear Mr. President," 18 June 1964, "HU 2 5/25/64–7/16/64" folder, Box 2, White House Central Files: Human Rights, Lyndon B. Johnson Library.
6. "Gim" is spelled phonetically and reflects Roberts's misunderstanding of McGill's pronunciation of "M."

McGill: "Walker, who was elected governor in 1922, and again in 1924. At that time the state had two-year terms; it now has four-year terms."

Roberts: All right.

McGill: "Mr. Walker came in . . . at a time of deficits and some turmoil caused by Tom Watson, who had been elected to the Senate in 1920."[7]

Roberts: Mm-hmm. [*Pause.*]

McGill: Wait just a minute.

"In the same campaign, Governor Walker had run second in a campaign for the governorship. His administration . . . was largely ineffective because of the great divisions in the state, but he was a highly respected man of complete honesty but with almost no political experience. He was a businessman. He had been a businessman-farmer."

Roberts: Mm-hmm.

McGill: New paragraph: "Harold Walker, his son, is about 47 years of age. He was for some time a member of a law firm of which James V"—V as in victory . . .

Roberts: Mm-hmm.

McGill: "Carmichael" . . .

Roberts: Mm-hmm.

McGill: . . . "now president of Scripto pencil company and a director of the Lockheed company" . . .

Roberts: Mm-hmm.

McGill: . . . was a senior member."

Roberts: Mm-hmm.

McGill: "Walker is highly regarded. He is the soul of honor and is honest and able."

Roberts: Mm-hmm.

McGill: "The Lockheed people think most highly of him."

Roberts: Mm-hmm.

McGill: "He has had considerable success for Lockheed in negotiating labor and race problems."

Roberts: Mm-hmm.

McGill: "He is a quiet"—"He is of quiet disposition . . . but this might be helpful in the sort of situations in which he would have to operate. He's not a table-pounder, but his ability to get people to listen" . . .

---

7. Tom Watson was among the leaders of the Populist Party in the late nineteenth century. By 1920, his political focus had shifted from agrarian reform to race-baiting, anti-Semitism, and anti-Catholicism, a platform which won him election to the U.S. Senate from Georgia during the turbulent aftermath of World War I. Edward Ayers, *The Promise of the New South: Life After Reconstruction* (New York: Oxford University Press, 1992), pp, 229, 261–62, 270–98, 411–13.

Roberts: Mm–hmm.

McGill: . . . "and to negotiate has been very well demonstrated. Lockheed credits him with the success they've had in their own operation."

Roberts: Mm–hmm.

McGill: "I feel sure that Lockheed would arrange to give him a leave if the job under consideration requires his full time"—"requires him full time."

Roberts: Mm–hmm.

McGill: "Mr. James V. Carmichael told me this morning that he as the director would be glad to help out in this matter if it was necessary."

Roberts: All right.

McGill: "Walker is married, has a family, and is" . . . Well, I should have put that up in the other part up there. If you'd just stick that up there with some of the other details, that he's married and has a family and is . . .

Roberts: All right.

McGill: . . . and is "highly regarded by his neighbors."

New paragraph: "I thought I would simply telephone this up and have it waiting for you when you returned rather than having to telephone me about it. I will . . . I'm thinking over the other problem we discussed and will try to have some ideas on it."[8]

Roberts: All right.

McGill: "Best regards."

Roberts: Yes, sir.

McGill: "Ralph McGill."

Roberts: All right.

McGill: "*Atlanta Constitution.*"

Roberts: All right.

McGill: Thank you very much.

Roberts: You're so welcome, Mr.—[*unclear comment by McGill*]— McGill. Mm–hmm. Bye.

12:00 P.M.: The President was greeted by Mayor Ralph S. Locher as he arrived at Cleveland Hopkins Airport.

Johnson spoke briefly and then greeted members of the public who had gathered in a fenced-in area of the airport.

---

8. Johnson had visited Atlanta on 7–8 May; McGill may have been referring to discussions during that trip.

12:18 P.M.: Left the airport and took a helicopter to Edgewater Park in Cleveland.

12:30 P.M.: Departed Edgewater Park by motorcade and stopped at Cleveland's Public Square to shake hands with onlookers.

1:00 P.M.: Arrived at the Communications Workers of America Convention in the Cleveland Public Auditorium and spoke for 20 minutes, beginning at 1:15.

1:40 P.M.: Returned to the motorcade and departed for Edgewater Park, where he boarded the helicopter for the brief flight back to the airport.

2:10 P.M.: Arrived back at Cleveland Hopkins.

2:15 P.M.: Unrecorded call to Tom Vail, a staff attorney for the congressional Joint Committee on Internal Revenue, from Air Force One.

2:18 P.M.: Departed for Washington, D.C., on Air Force One, arriving at 2:59 P.M.

2:38 P.M.: Unrecorded call to *Cleveland Press* Editor Louis Seltzer in Cleveland, Ohio, from Air Force One.

3:04 P.M.: Departed by helicopter for the White House, arriving at 3:14 P.M. He then remained at the Mansion.

3:35 P.M.: Unrecorded call to Walter Jenkins.

3:55 P.M.: Unrecorded call to Secretary of Defense Robert McNamara.

4:06 P.M.: Unrecorded call to Jenkins.

4:36 P.M.: Unrecorded call to Attorney General Robert Kennedy in New York City.

5:40 P.M.: Unrecorded call to Jenkins.

5:45 P.M.: Unrecorded call to Larry O'Brien.

5:57 P.M.: Unrecorded call to George Reedy.

6:00 P.M.: Unrecorded call to Jenkins.

6:14 P.M.: Unrecorded call to McNamara.

6:30 P.M.: Arrived in the Oval Office accompanied by Jenkins.

6:36 P.M.

From George Reedy[9]

Press Secretary Reedy called to ask for instructions about how to handle reporters' questions about the President's conversation with Attorney General Robert Kennedy, which had taken place the previous evening during a limousine ride back to Kennedy International Airport following a Kennedy Library fund-raiser. With rumors circulating that Kennedy would be nominated for vice president, become the next U.S. ambassador to South Vietnam, or run for the Senate from New York (as he eventually did), the semiprivate conversation had sparked rampant political speculation.

President Johnson: Yeah?

George Reedy: Two things: Tom Wicker came in to see me.[10] He said that the New York papers today carried stories saying that Bobby Kennedy rode back with you last night from the hotel to the airport and had a long conversation. And the New York papers are speculating on politics and that sort of thing.[11]

President Johnson: Well, tell him it wasn't mentioned. We've never— I've never discussed politics with him since I've been President.

Reedy: Right. Well, Tom said that both the Attorney General and Ed Guthman told them no, there was no discussion of politics—[12]

President Johnson: [*Unclear.*]

Reedy: —and what you did discuss was civil rights, but the Attorney General is reluctant to even let them do it for background without . . .

President Johnson: No, just tell him there was nothing said that was of public interest at all, that I must be able to ride to the airport [*chuckling*]—

Reedy: Mm-hmm.

President Johnson: —without getting in any controversy, and that there was absolutely nothing said that is of any consequence or of any

---

9. Tape WH6406.09, Citation #3758, Recordings of Telephone Conversations—White House Series, Recordings and Transcripts of Conversations and Meetings, Lyndon B. Johnson Library.
10. Tom Wicker was a White House correspondent for the *New York Times*.
11. Kennedy had in fact ridden back to the airport with the President, as had Chief Justice of the Supreme Court Earl Warren and Burke Marshall.
12. Edwin O. Guthman was director of public information for the Department of Justice.

public interest or that . . . it in no way touched on politics of any kind. Never have. He hasn't raised it with me, and I've never raised it with him.

Reedy: Right. Well, then you don't want me to tell him that [*unclear*]—

President Johnson: Hell, no, I don't want to tell him! I didn't discuss civil rights.

Reedy: Yeah . . . right. OK, sir.

Now, number two: Jack Rosenthal called me from the Justice Department. He's Ed Guthman's assistant.

President Johnson: Mm-hmm.

Reedy: He said that Dom Bonafede of the [*New York*] *Herald Tribune* called him and wanted to know whether they had an attorney, James H. Rowe, registered as a lobbyist for a Haitian sugar outfit. Of course, those are public records, and there is a James H. Rowe registered for a Haitian sugar organization.[13] And Bonafede said, "Is he also a man that has dealings with the White House?" And Rosenthal said, "Well, I know nothing about him." Apparently Rosenthal does not know Jim Rowe. But Rosenthal called me and said that "I thought you should know this: that they're apparently going to try to tie Mr. Rowe up, whoever he is, with—"

President Johnson: Call Jim Rowe and tell him that because he represents the *Herald Tribune*.

Reedy: Right.

President Johnson: And tell them they wanted to know if he didn't have a lot of relations with the White House, and I think that he ought to call . . . Who's the guy owns it? Jock Whitney.[14] And tell him that he has been in the White House once with a group of 20.

Reedy: Right. OK, sir.

President Johnson: Since I've been President. He's seen me once with a group of 25 and that they don't need to go to work on that.

Reedy: Right. OK, sir.

---

13. James H. Rowe was an influential Washington attorney and a former special assistant to Franklin D. Roosevelt who had helped Johnson, as a young congressman from Texas, gain Roosevelt's attention and support. A strong supporter of civil rights and a staunch anti-Communist, Rowe had engaged in a series of feuds with Johnson in the intervening years. The two had reconciled after Johnson became President. Taylor Branch, *Pillar of Fire: America in the King Years 1963–65* (New York: Touchstone, 1998), pp. 187–88.

14. John Hay "Jock" Whitney was the publisher of the *New York Herald Tribune*. A wealthy New York society figure and former ambassador to Britain, Whitney had purchased the newspaper in 1958 in an ultimately futile attempt to save it. The *Herald Tribune* ceased publication in 1966, although Whitney became the first chairman of a *New York Times*–led consortium that published the *International Herald Tribune* worldwide. "John Hay Whitney Dies at 77; Publisher Led in Many Fields," *New York Times*, 9 February 1982.

President Johnson: And he's never asked me for anything, and I appointed him to serve on a committee studying Puerto Rico.[15]

Reedy: Right.

President Johnson: But he's not a . . . Tell Jim that, and tell him I think he ought to call Jock Whitney and tell Jock Whitney what they're trying to do.

Reedy: Right.

President Johnson: All right.

Reedy: You bet, sir.

6:38 P.M.

From McGeorge Bundy[16]

The President immediately received another call regarding the ongoing speculation about Robert Kennedy's future. In the morning's *New York Times,* columnist James "Scotty" Reston had published an article claiming that Johnson planned to name Kennedy ambassador to South Vietnam as a replacement for Henry Cabot Lodge. The administration had already informed the *Times* that the story was inaccurate, and Reston had called McGeorge Bundy to share a draft of a follow-up article that would report the denials. Bundy then called the President to share what Reston had told him.[17]

McGeorge Bundy: . . . [James "Scotty" Reston] called me. Bobby [Kennedy] talked to him.

President Johnson: Mm-hmm.

Bundy: And he read me the way he proposes to write this and asked me to comment on it. I think he's done it very well and that it reflects credit on all concerned, but there is one aspect of it that I want to check with you personally, Mr. President, because I think your judgment will be better than mine.

Let me give you an outline of what he's said, that . . . it is that the

---

15. Johnson had appointed Rowe to the United States–Puerto Rican Commission.
16. Tape WH6406.09, Citation #3759, Recordings of Telephone Conversations—White House Series, Recordings and Transcripts of Conversations and Meetings, Lyndon B. Johnson Library.
17. James Reston, "Washington—The Latest Capital Rumor: Kennedy to Saigon," *New York Times,* 17 June 1964; Reston, "Johnson Declines an Offer of Kennedy Aid in Saigon," *New York Times,* 18 June 1964.

Attorney General has let it be known that—or it is understood that the Attorney General will not be recommended by the President, or nominated by the President, in the event that [Henry Cabot] Lodge comes home. The two men are known to have talked about it. It is known that the Attorney General offered to go. The President is known to have expressed his view that in terms of qualifications, the Attorney General is about the best man for the job."[18]

President Johnson: No, no. No, no. I don't want to say that at all.

Bundy: You don't want to say that.

President Johnson: [*with Bundy acknowledging*] I haven't said anything like that. I told the Attorney General to please call Scotty Reston and tell him he wrote me and told me that he—

Bundy: That part I—

President Johnson: [*with Bundy acknowledging*]—if he was a resignation that he was available to go, that he would volunteer to go. And I immediately called him and told him under no circumstances would I consider him for the task. Period. That I would need him here and didn't want him to think of going. Now, that's all I want them to say because I don't want to say that I considered him the best-qualified man for the post—

Bundy: That's fine.

President Johnson: —because I frankly don't.

Bundy: Oh, I thought you'd said that to me one time.

President Johnson: Yeah . . . yeah. No, no.

Bundy: I'm the source of that.

President Johnson: No. No, no.

Bundy: The other thing he's hanging it on is the . . . your unwillingness to put a man whose family have been in such danger in danger himself.

President Johnson: Not at all. I don't want to say that at all. That hasn't got anything to do with it. I just told him when I got his letter that it was a fine thing, that I appreciated it very much, but I couldn't under any circumstances consider him.

Bundy: Mm-hmm.

President Johnson: He asked me today if I wouldn't consider you, and I said no.[19]

Bundy: Yeah, that's—

President Johnson: Bobby told me that again. I just—

---

18. For Reston's follow-up, see James Reston, "Johnson Declines an Offer of Kennedy Aid in Saigon," ibid.

19. The President had made an unrecorded call to Kennedy earlier in the afternoon.

Bundy: I put him up to that.

President Johnson: I told him no, but . . . I think that we got all we can do here, but I just wish that by God a responsible guy like Scotty would before he goes saying things—

Bundy: Now, Mr. President, let me hasten to say that he is going on what I told him is my opinion, and he's turning it into your opinion. And he's given me a fair shot at it, and I think I can shoot it down.

President Johnson: Well, he didn't give us a fair one on that one this morning—

Bundy: No, he surely didn't.

President Johnson: —because if he did, I'd have told him—

Bundy: No, he didn't.

President Johnson: —just what happened: that we're not considering him.

Bundy: No.

President Johnson: What I would like for him to say is that the rumors that he was being considered for this thing are completely out of the question. I don't want Bobby or anybody else to get a lot of feeling in the country that I'm trying to send him—banish him to the isle.[20]

Bundy: Yeah. What is your reason for not considering him, then? What shall I say to Reston on that?

President Johnson: My reason for not considering him is that I want him to stay right where he is.

Bundy: Mm-hmm. [*Pauses.*] Nothing else.

President Johnson: I think it'd just be controversial as hell on the Hill—that's another good reason.

Bundy: Yeah.

President Johnson: But I don't want to say that. I don't want to cut the guy.

Bundy: No . . . no . . . no, no. No, you can't say that.

President Johnson: The same reason . . . there's a lot of reasons that . . . just like the . . . [Roswell] Gilpatric thing would not go good.[21]

Bundy: Sure . . . sure. Sure, sure. Sure.

President Johnson: And . . . same problems we have on the vice

---

20. Reston's column that morning had mentioned that some Kennedy allies saw the possible ambassadorial appointment as a way to remove Bobby Kennedy from the domestic political situation and block any move to nominate him as Johnson's running mate—or even as an alternative Democratic presidential nominee.

21. For Johnson's assessment of former Deputy Secretary of Defense Roswell Gilpatric as a potential successor to Lodge, see McGeorge Bundy to Johnson, 7:56 P.M., 15 June 1964; and Johnson to Robert McNamara, 9:55 A.M., 16 June 1964, in this volume.

presidency. Bobby's a very, very controversial character in this country, and . . .

Bundy: Oh, there's no question. No question.

President Johnson: I don't want this to be a Democratic campaign manager's . . .

Bundy: Well, that's not something—

President Johnson: . . . brother's thing. But I don't want to say that to Reston.

Bundy: No, no, no, no, no, no. So, when I go back to—

President Johnson: I want this man to be above . . .

Bundy: Yeah.

President Johnson: Above political matters of any kind and not to have been in any wars with Democrats or Republicans.

Bundy: Yeah.

President Johnson: And I want him said—and if I have to tell him, I will; if not, you tell him—that Bobby Kennedy, when the articles were being written that Lodge might come home before the convention when he—I think maybe about Oregon.[22] Whenever—When he was doing so well, Bobby Kennedy wrote me a note.

Bundy: Mm-hmm. Actually, he wrote it later than that.

President Johnson: Well, let's see . . . [*Sound of papers shuffling on the desk.*]

Bundy: It was just last week, I think.

President Johnson: He didn't date it. Yes, he does. Wait a minute. No, that's not dated. "I just wanted to make sure" . . . Well, I don't want to—You see, careful—I don't want to admit that Lodge is coming home at all.

Bundy: No, I know it.

President Johnson: "I just want to make sure that you understood that if you wished me to go to Vietnam in any capacity, I would be glad to do so."

Bundy: Yeah. Yeah. OK.

President Johnson: [*with Bundy acknowledging throughout*] Now, that's the sentence. Now, just take that: "I just wanted to make sure that

---

22. Johnson was referring to the 15 May Oregon primary. Henry Cabot Lodge had unexpectedly won the 10 March New Hampshire primary, which immediately preceded Oregon. His popularity had been at a peak in the intervening period, spurring rumors that he might return to the United States to campaign actively for the nomination. Instead, he remained in Saigon, lost the Oregon primary to New York Governor Nelson Rockefeller, and his nascent campaign collapsed before it had officially begun. Theodore H. White, *The Making of the President 1964* (New York: Atheneum, 1965), pp. 123–43.

you understood that if you wished me to go to Vietnam in any capacity, I'll be glad to do so." And he talks about how important it is. And so forth. Now, that's the only sentence that's important.

Immediately upon receipt of that, the President called him and told him that he appreciated very much his volunteering to help out there in *any* capacity.[23] But under no circumstances did he desire to assign him to . . . relieve him of his present responsibilities.

Bundy: Right. Right.

President Johnson: And just, period.

Bundy: Right.

President Johnson: And . . .

Bundy: OK. I'll deal with it. He'll put some of the others in as his own thoughts or as other people's thoughts, but not yours.

President Johnson: Well, tell him to talk to me. Let me ask him if he's going to mess it up again, it's worse to leave it. I'd rather leave it where he screwed it up this morning.

Bundy: Let me talk to him first, and then [*unclear*]—

President Johnson: Just tell him that I'll be very glad . . . Tell him that I said that if he'll just call me on the phone when he goes to talking about what I'm doing, offering men jobs like that, he can confirm it in one minute. I'll tell him the honest truth and tell him off the record or give it to him. But . . .

Bundy: As of—he did call me yesterday, and I stonewalled because I just didn't—I should probably have checked back with you then. That was my error.

President Johnson: You just please tell him because he's . . . That column does me damage, politically and otherwise. I just don't want him to do it. And this one's going to do more if . . .

Bundy: If it isn't right.

President Johnson: That's right.

Bundy: OK.

President Johnson: Tell him to call me. I'd like to talk to him.

Bundy: Right.

6:46 P.M.: The President went to the Cabinet Room with Walter Jenkins for a meeting with Speaker of the House John McCormack,

---

23. For Johnson's call declining Kennedy's offer to go to Vietnam, see Johnson to Robert Kennedy, 6:11 P.M., 11 June 1964, in this volume.

House Majority Leader Carl Albert, House Appropriations Committee Chairman George Mahon of Texas, Representative John J. Rooney of New York, Representative J. Vaughn Gary of Virginia, and Larry O'Brien.[24]

6:58 P.M.

From James "Scotty" Reston[25]

McGeorge Bundy apparently acted immediately on Johnson's request to tell Scotty Reston to call him, as the columnist phoned in only minutes later. Johnson explained his reaction to Robert Kennedy's offer to go to Vietnam and the context of its rejection so that Reston could write an accurate follow-up to his initial report.[26] More significantly, Johnson asked the columnist for his views on Southeast Asia, and then delivered a defense of his administration's policies.

Johnson left the Cabinet Room to take the call.

President Johnson: Hello?
James "Scotty" Reston: Hello?
President Johnson: Hi, Scotty.
Reston: Am I causing you trouble again?
President Johnson: No. [*Chuckles.*] No, I was just in the Cabinet Room and I had to come out. That's why I was delayed. I'm sorry.
Reston: How are you?
President Johnson: Fine. Fine. I've been out to Cleveland today and had a good meeting, and I'm talking about foreign aid right at the moment. We've got *every* Republican . . .
Reston: [*Unclear.*]

---

24. Both J. Vaughn Gary and John J. Rooney were members of the House Appropriations Committee's Subcommittee on Foreign Operations, which oversaw foreign aid appropriations and was chaired by aid opponent Otto Passman.
25. Tape WH6406.09, Citations #3761 and #3762, Recordings of Telephone Conversations—White House Series, Recordings and Transcripts of Conversations and Meetings, Lyndon B. Johnson Library.
26. James Reston, "Johnson Declines an Offer of Kennedy Aid in Saigon," *New York Times*, 18 June 1964.

President Johnson: Every Republican going against us to try to make a go at this [Otto] Passman to cut the aid bill $500 million.[27]

Reston: Hmm.

President Johnson: And I asked less this year than Eisenhower asked a single one of his eight years. Isn't that responsibility?

Reston: Yeah. Yeah. Yeah, well, they're funny. They've lost their way, these guys. They've got a death wish in that party, I think.

President Johnson: Well, they—this afternoon, every damn one of them want to give the women back their cosmetics and cheap demagoguery on excise taxes. And we just beat them 207 to 185. Voting as a party. Tomorrow, they don't want you to have a debt limit.[28] And it's pure demagoguery. Nothing you can do about it: You've got to have the debt limit.

Reston: Sure.

President Johnson: But every one of them as a man. They say we won't get one Republican vote.

Reston: Oh, my gosh.

President Johnson: You talk about blind opposition.

Reston: Yeah. After all you did to help Eisenhower—

President Johnson: [*with Reston acknowledging*] I just told a group in here that . . . [William] Knowland voted against Eisenhower on an appropriation bill, and I cast the last vote and the deciding vote to report his bill just as he asked it.[29] And I asked less this year for foreign aid than Eisenhower asked *any single year* he was there. Kennedy asked four-nine [$4.9 billion] last year, and I cut it to three-five [$3.5 billion]. A billion-four [$1.4 billion]. And even [Lucius] Clay, Eisenhower's buddy, reduced it to four and a half [$4.5 billion].[30] He said we needed four and

---

27. A determined and—until 1964—effective opponent of foreign aid, Representative Otto Passman of Louisiana chaired the House Appropriations Committee's Subcommittee on Foreign Operations. See George Mahon to Johnson, 1:48 P.M., 15 June 1964, in this volume.

28. For the excise tax and debt limit issues, see Larry O'Brien to Johnson, 6:40 P.M., 10 June 1964; and Johnson to George Smathers, 2:48 P.M., 1 June 1964, in this volume.

29. A member of the family that controlled the *Oakland Tribune*, William Knowland was a Republican senator from California (1945–1958).

30. Johnson was referring to General Lucius Clay, who had served as deputy to General Dwight D. Eisenhower during World War II, and then as military governor of the U.S. zone in postwar Germany. In 1962, President Kennedy had appointed Clay to head the Committee to Strengthen the Security of the Free World, which he charged with reviewing U.S. foreign aid programs. The committee had recommended significant shifts in program emphasis, along with targeted cutbacks and administrative changes. Jacob Viner, George Meany, Fowler Hamilton, Otto Passman, and Paul Hoffman, "The Report of the Clay Committee on Foreign Aid: A Symposium," *Political Science Quarterly*, 78:3 (September 1963): 321–61.

a half. I come along three and a half [$3.5 billion]—a billion under Clay. [*Chuckles.*]

Reston: Yeah. Goofy world.

I just wanted to make sure in this sensitive relationship that I didn't write anything here that was going to cause you trouble, or the Attorney General, or Ambassador [Henry Cabot] Lodge. And I've talked to Mac [Bundy] since . . . in the last ten minutes, and the story . . . he says that the best way to word this is to say first of all that the Attorney General sent you a note saying he would be willing to volunteer to serve in Saigon in any capacity you wanted him to. That when you got that note, you called him up, and you told him that you would not send him there . . .[31]

President Johnson: I told him under no circumstances would I consider the thought for a moment. Period. Just that definite. And what he says about the Attorney General is exactly correct. I don't want you to quote it because it's private correspondence, but he says: "I just wanted to make"—"Dear Mr. President, I just wanted to make sure you understood that if you wish me to go to Vietnam in *any* capacity, I would be glad to do so."

Now, we sent [Dean] Rusk out there, and we'd sent [Robert] McNamara out there, and there's a lot of talk about Lodge might come back from Oregon and all this kind of stuff: He'd be home any day.[32] And half a dozen of them indicated a willingness to do it, and he did. And I never let it get off the ground: The moment I received it, opened it, read it, I picked up the phone and called him. Period. And that's all there was to it. And there's never been given a moment's thought.

Reston: Well, I think that's   I think that's a very perceptive . . . I hadn't thought of the family angle, but it is a . . . it's a goofy—

President Johnson: Well, without the family. If he was single, I wouldn't send him.

Reston: Hmm.

President Johnson: If he . . . and if his name was Brown, I wouldn't. We've got all these problems here with civil rights. We've got—He's been heading this division. There's talk of his running for office for other things.[33] There's a good deal of speculation about our relationship, and they're not ever going to catch me banishing somebody to the isle. [*Chuckles.*]

---

31. See the previous conversation, McGeorge Bundy to Johnson, 6:38 P.M., 17 June 1964, in this chapter.
32. Johnson was referring to Lodge's defeat in the Oregon primary.
33. Johnson was referring to Kennedy's consideration of entering the New York Senate race.

Reston: Well, it would be said that you were sending him to Siberia to get rid of him.

President Johnson: Yeah . . . it wouldn't—I didn't let them say it a second. When I read your column this morning, I just wished, "God, I wished Scotty would call me, because I'll just tell him *all* the truth and he can—what he can publish." And you can publish that he said to me, and . . . that he would be glad to help out in *any* capacity. He didn't say [William] Westmoreland['s] job or Lodge's job, he said *any* capacity. And I said, "I would not consider it for a moment." Period. "Thank you very, very much. I appreciate your offer and your loyalty, but I wouldn't think of it." Period. So I don't want that one to get started.

Reston: No.

President Johnson: And I just—

Reston: I got the impression, however, that lately you have been talking to him more.

President Johnson: I've been talking to him ever since I came here. All the time. I've—There's never been . . . There's never been a month since I've been in Washington I haven't seen more of him than I have of almost any Cabinet officer, and since I've been President, with the exception of Rusk and McNamara, whose duties require more of it.

Reston: Mm-hmm.

President Johnson: There's never been anything to the thing we didn't see each other.

Reston: I think I got it. I'll do a little story and straighten it out.

President Johnson: Thank you, my friend.

Reston: Thank you. Take care of yourself.

President Johnson: What . . . Tell me . . . [*sighs*]. What's your feeling about Vietnam?

Reston: Oh, I'd just depress you if I told you my feeling about Vietnam. I—

President Johnson: No, I want to know it.

Reston: Well, I've always thought, you know, that it's always unwise to assume that other people would stand for things—other great nations would stand for things we wouldn't stand for ourselves. And I just think that if there was a hostile power in Mexico, Communist government, that you wouldn't be able to keep the drunks from flying out of Dallas and Houston and Chicago every Saturday night until we got those bastards the hell out of there.

And I've . . . I hate—the Lord will strike me dead for saying anything in favor of Mr. [Charles] de Gaulle, but I've always believed that, in the long run, his experience, or France's experience, is right: that nothing *big* can be done there over a long period of time without the acquiescence of China.[34] Now, there's no sense in talking about long-range things because we've got a short-range thing, and we can't do anything about it except go on doing what we're doing now. I don't think we got any easy options: We can't get out, and we can't go smashing into China à la Mr. [Barry] Goldwater.

President Johnson: All right. Now, that's exactly the way I look at it. I never discussed it with you, but . . . President Eisenhower said, "Here, I've got this problem on my hand," and whether good or bad or whether he was wise or unwise, after he did, he wrote [Ngo Dinh] Diem a letter and says, "I want to help you help yourself any way you can. And I'll help you economically and militarily and spiritually and any other way I can, but you'll have to help yourself, and we'll do our best to save your freedom. Basically because our national honor is at stake—we've got a treaty—and second, we like to see people free. We love freedom ourselves, and we've helped other people keep theirs. And third, it's very important to the world."

So he writes him that and said, "Our policy will be to do this. Now, not to go in with our own troops, ground troops, or with our own air or not to drop atomic bombs and burn the trees and not to involve China, but we'll help you."

Now, some of them come along and say, "Mr. de Gaulle says you oughtn't to do that, that you ought to have neutralization." We say, "All right. We'll neutralize. We'll get out and come home if you can get anybody to agree to leave their neighbors alone." And Mr. de Gaulle, every day I send somebody back to him and say, "Give me your blueprint." And he said, "Well, we haven't got any yet because . . . We'll . . . we've got to be strong, and you've got to have strength out there, and you've got to get in the shape where they're willing to sit down and talk, and they're not willing to do that. But someday you'll have to do that." Well, we say, "OK. We're willing to do it any day they're ready." But we've seen no indication that the Chinese or the Vietnamese or the North Vietnamese are willing to—the Vietcong—are willing to leave South Vietnam alone.

So, neutralization. I say that to [Mike] Mansfield: "Where's your plan?" None of them have got a blueprint. So, neutralization's out. Some of them almost like Mansfield are ready to pick up and come on home:

---

34. French President Charles de Gaulle had proposed the neutralization of Southeast Asia. France, the former colonial power in the region, had been driven out following a series of military defeats that culminated in the 1954 siege of Dien Bien Phu.

[Frank] Church, [Ernest] Gruening, and [Wayne] Morse.[35] And I say, "Have you ever considered what *that* means?" And so . . . You reject that.

So the only thing you got left is try to make this thing more efficient and more effective and hold as strong as you can, and keep this government as stable as you can, and try to improve it as you can. And that we're doing day and night. And . . .

Reston: It's all you can do.

President Johnson: OK, my friend. Come by and see me.

Reston: I will, sir.

President Johnson: All right.

Reston: Very kind.

President Johnson: Bye.

Reston: Bye.

7:08 P.M.: Unrecorded call to George Reedy.

7:10 P.M.: President Johnson returned to the Cabinet Room.

7:28 P.M.

To David Bell; President Johnson joined by George Mahon[36]

Johnson returned to a meeting with the House Democratic leadership and Democratic members of the Appropriations Committee to discuss the foreign aid bill. From the Cabinet Room, Johnson called Agency for International Development Chairman David Bell to ask him whether any additional cuts in the fiscal 1965 appropriation could be made because of unspent funds left over from the fiscal 1964 budget. Johnson felt pressure to make a small cut in the aid appropriation as a face-saving gesture for Otto Passman. Ultimately, the subcommittee would approve a $200 mil-

---

35. Democratic senators with liberal reputations, Frank Church represented Idaho, Ernest Gruening represented Alaska, and Wayne Morse represented Oregon. Morse and Gruening were the first senators to speak out against the war in Vietnam and both would vote against the Tonkin Gulf resolution in August. See Johnson to Robert McNamara, 10:58 A.M., 27 April 1964, in Guian A. McKee, ed., *The Presidential Recordings, Lyndon B. Johnson: Toward the Great Society, February 1, 1964–May 31, 1964*, vol. 6, *April 14, 1964–May 31, 1964* (New York: Norton, 2007), pp. 234–37; Fredrik Logevall, *Choosing War: The Lost Chance for Peace and the Escalation of War in Vietnam* (Berkeley: University of California Press, 1999), pp. 136–39.

36. Tape WH6406.10, Citation #3763, Recordings of Telephone Conversations—White House Series, Recordings and Transcripts of Conversations and Meetings, Lyndon B. Johnson Library.

lion cut in economic aid, instead of the more draconian $515 million cut proposed by Passman. This would be the smallest cut in the President's prepared foreign aid budget in the history of the program.[37]

President Johnson: . . . [*unclear*].

David Bell: Yes, sir.

President Johnson: I thought that we asked the same amount this year for our foreign aid that they gave us last year.

Bell: When you count the various carryovers and so on in, it's about 100 million [dollars] higher this year, the request, than . . . than—

President Johnson: That include the 125 [million dollars] extra that we asked—[38]

Bell: No, I beg your pardon. No, that was before the 125. You'd have to add the 125 to that.[39]

President Johnson: All right. Now, George Mahon's here with me now. He says you're asking three-seven [$3.7 billion] this year.

George Mahon: [*in the background*] For the program.

Bell: Uh . . .

President Johnson: For the whole program.

Mahon: Including carryover . . .

President Johnson: Including carryover and everything.

Bell: That's right. . . . That's right. And the carryover's—It was three-five [$3.5 billion] in the present year, counting the carryovers and so on.

President Johnson: And it's three-five in the present year?

Bell: That's right.

President Johnson: And 125 [million dollars] extra for Vietnam.

Bell: Well, isn't that—doesn't that include the 125—

President Johnson: Well, it does. Three-five and 125 would be three-six 25 [$3.625 billion]. But he says it's three-seven [$3.7 billion].

Bell: [*with the President acknowledging*] No, no, it . . . What I meant, sir, is that the . . . doesn't the three-seven include the . . . Yeah. The 125.

President Johnson: If we ask three-five and we added to it 125, that's three-six 25.

---

37. *Congressional Quarterly Almanac*, 1964, vol. 20, p. 312.

38. On 18 May, the administration had submitted a $125 million supplemental request to fund additional economic and military aid for South Vietnam. Ibid., p. 296.

39. The final foreign aid appropriation for fiscal 1965 represented a $250 million increase over 1964. Ibid.

Bell: As I said a minute ago, we did ask for about 100 million [dollars] more for next year . . .

President Johnson: Mm-hmm. Well, that's what it'll make it—that'd be 70—[*Mahon speaks inaudibly in the background.*]

Bell: Before Vietnam, sir.

President Johnson: Yeah.

Bell: Before Vietnam.

President Johnson: Yeah.

Bell: So that that makes it 200 million [dollars] in all, counting Vietnam.

Mahon: [*in background*] Plus the carryover funds of 242 million.

President Johnson: [*to Mahon*] Yeah. He says [its] about three-seven. All right. Now, what were you getting ready to say while I got him on?

Mahon: Well—

President Johnson: [*to Mahon*] Therefore . . .

Mahon: I was getting ready to say that I believe that you could live with, without any humiliation, with some sort of reduction in view of the fact that Dave Bell will tell you—

President Johnson: [*to Mahon*] Hang on—

Mahon: —that he now has about $100 million in funds that were not known to be available when he submitted the budget. So you can take 100—

Unidentified: [*in background*] That's carryover from this year.

Mahon: That's the carryover, and—

Unidentified: From this year.

Mahon: —it's $100 million that can't be cut.

Unidentified: And he stated, Mr. President, to the committee that if he had any carryover, that he would come in and ask that it now be reduced by that amount.

President Johnson: They say you stated to committee if you had any carryover you'd ask it be reduced by that amount, and you have 100 million carryover.

Bell: Well, we—

Unidentified: That you hadn't anticipated.

Bell: With the figures we gave—

President Johnson: That you hadn't anticipated. Is that correct?

Bell: No, sir. Not 100 [million dollars] we hadn't anticipated. The figures we gave Frankel . . .[40]

---

40. "Frankel" is spelled phonetically and remains unidentified (the reference does not appear to be to *New York Times* reporter Max Frankel).

President Johnson: [*to people in room*] Said not 100.

[*to Bell*] Go ahead.

Bell: . . . was 102 [million dollars], and of that we *had* anticipated 30, and we had already reduced—

President Johnson: All right. Had 102 and of that you'd anticipated 30, so that leaves you 82.

Bell: That's right. And we are . . .

President Johnson: Seventy-two [million dollars].

Bell: Seventy-two. That's right. Now, just a half hour ago, Mr. President—I don't know whether you want to tell them this. We are proposing to go up and talk to them about it. We agreed that we would propose to put 50 [million dollars] of that into this special—into a loan to Brazil.[41] So that we are expecting, as of right now, to end up with only 22 [million dollars], which represents dribs and drabs in various little appropriation accounts that, you know, are what we anticipate will be left when the books are all balanced as of June 30.

President Johnson: Mm-hmm.

Bell: And that will be the lowest actual carryover of any year that we've ever had.

President Johnson: In the national interest, can you cut this any, and if so, how much?

Bell: Uh . . .

President Johnson: Now, just put it out on the line hard and cold and true. And let's don't pad; let's don't speculate; let's do just what we've always tried to do. And then let's take our position on it and stand on it and let anybody else take whatever position they want to.

Bell: Mm-hmm. Uh . . . well, I expect, Mr. President, that we *will* need the funds we have asked for. I think that it would be . . . There is a range on any loan program in which deferring next spring a loan to India, say, for a power plant from April to July . . . It's a very hard thing to say that that's absolutely essential in the national interest. But the way this program runs, we expect to use *all* of what *you* have asked for, what *we* have recommended to *you*. It is a minimum—

President Johnson: All right . . . OK. Let's just stand on it then. OK.

Bell: Right. OK, sir?

President Johnson: [*to people in room*] He says that—[*Hangs up.*]

---

41. Brazil's government had been overthrown in early April by a right-wing military coup.

7:40 P.M.

To Telephone Operator[42]

Johnson calls the operator and requests her to "tell that boy in the galley to bring me an orange drink." He then asks if others want one, counts the requests, and indicates that they need "six orange drinks in the Cabinet Room."

TIME UNKNOWN

Office Conversation[43]

The recording then captured a segment of the meeting in the Cabinet Room.

President Johnson: Walter, I just might as well not ask you to call him anymore if you can't understand him.

Walter Jenkins: Well, I understood him. [*Someone in room chuckles.*] I understood it wasn't a full commitment. He made that clear. He [*unclear*].

Carl Albert: If you get [William] Natcher [*unclear*].[44]

Unidentified: [*Unclear.*]

President Johnson: Whatever I do, I've got to do tomorrow. I leave at 7:00 the next day for San Francisco.[45]

[*to Valenti*] Jack, that speech is all right. Tell Bill [Moyers] to go on and get it, the mimeograph. I think there ought to be some applause lines in it, and there's not a one. And I think you ought to have some of those little short sentences, four-letter words, saying that every child can go to school. You remember those lines we put in? [*Unclear response by Valenti.*]

---

42. Tape WH6406.10, Citation #3764, Recordings of Telephone Conversations—White House Series, Recordings and Transcripts of Conversations and Meetings, Lyndon B. Johnson Library.
43. Tape WH6406.10, Citation #3765, Recordings of Telephone Conversations—White House Series, Recordings and Transcripts of Conversations and Meetings, Lyndon B. Johnson Library.
44. William Natcher was a Democratic representative from Kentucky and a member of Otto Passman's Subcommittee on Foreign Operations. For his position on foreign aid, see George Mahon to President Johnson, 1:48 P.M., 15 June 1964, in this volume.
45. Johnson would make a political trip to California from 19–21 June.

All right. Put about five of them in there. A roof over every family's . . . A roof over every family.

Unidentified: No child go unfed and [*unclear*] school.

President Johnson: That's right. And then . . . I got 27 applauses in 20 minutes today at the communication workers.[46]

Unidentified: That's good.

President Johnson: Twenty-seven applauses in twenty minutes, I think that's right.

Unidentified: [*Unclear.*]

Unidentified: I've been checking on this fellow [William] Scranton, you know. He spent two years in the House.[47] I bet he's [*unclear*]—

The operator interrupts to report that she cannot locate Congressman Jack Flint from Georgia. The President asks for Congressman Joel Montoya from New Mexico.[48]

President Johnson: No answer at either place.

Unidentified: All I can find out, Mr. President, is the [*unclear*]—

Unidentified: Mr. President, I [*unclear*]—

Unidentified: —[*unclear*] morning and I think [*unclear*].

Albert: [*Unclear.*]

President Johnson: Huh?

Unidentified: He's not here right now.

President Johnson: [*to Moyers*] Bill. Tell him that he doesn't need to go to California unless he wants to.[49] I'm afraid he's overworked. He looks pale to me. Lady Bird gave me a lecture about him this afternoon. He got those bleeding ulcers, and we sure don't want him to drop out: We'll be murdered if he do. So tell him that he . . . If he feels like going, wants to go, all right. Otherwise I want him to take off July the 4th and get some rest, so see that he does.

[*to Valenti*] How many applauses did we get, and how long did we speak today?

Jack Valenti: Twenty-two minutes and twenty-seven applauses.

---

46. "Remarks in Cleveland at the Convention of the Communications Workers of America," 17 June 1964, *Public Papers of the Presidents of the United States: Lyndon B. Johnson, 1963–64* (Washington, DC: GPO, 1965), 1:778–81.

47. William Scranton, the current governor of Pennsylvania and Republican candidate for president, had served as a Republican representative from Pennsylvania in the preceding Congress, 1961–1962.

48. Both congressmen were members of the Subcommittee on Government Operations.

49. Johnson may have been referring to Special Assistant Walter Jenkins, whose overwork had become a concern to many in the White House. Merle Miller, *Lyndon: An Oral Biography* (New York: Ballantine Books, 1980), pp. 513–15.

President Johnson: Twenty-seven in twenty-two minutes?

Valenti: Yes, sir.

President Johnson: How do you know?

Valenti: Mr. President, I counted them. I gave it to Juanita [Roberts] for the archives. I've got it all down.

President Johnson: Marked each one of them?

Valenti: Yes, sir.

President Johnson: Mr. Speaker, that's pretty good: 27 applauses in 22 minutes. That's less than one a minute.

Valenti: [*Unclear*] they came to their feet and applauded for over a minute when he said, "And the President of the United States is with you too." They thumped their feet and applauded for a full minute. [*Unclear background exchange.*]

President Johnson: I sure did wrap my arms around the labor boys, though, the communication workers today.

Unidentified: [*Unclear.*]

Unidentified: [*Unclear.*]

President Johnson: This fellow Joe Beirne is a pretty able fellow, you see.[50]

Unidentified: [*Unclear*] one more [*unclear*].

Unidentified: [*Unclear.*] I can remember back when that was a real [*unclear*] with Joe [*unclear*].

Several unidentified voices are talking in the background.

Unidentified: Mr. President, you didn't hear me. The only thing Scranton did while he was a member of the House [*unclear*]—

The operator interrupts to report on her unsuccessful attempts to reach Montoya. The President replies that he will "just talk to him tomorrow."

President Johnson: Neither one of them are at their office—

Recording ends when phone is hung up.

    8:35 P.M.: President Johnson adjourned the meeting and went out on the White House porch, where he indicated to secretary Vickie McCammon that he would go to the driveway to greet the wife of Speaker John McCormack, who had apparently come to the White House to meet her husband.

---

50. Joseph A. Beirne served as president of the Communications Workers of America. "Remarks in Cleveland at the Convention of the Communications Workers of America," 17 June 1964, *Public Papers, Johnson, 1963–64*, 1:781.

8:50 P.M.: Unrecorded call to Walter Jenkins.

8:56 P.M.: Unrecorded return call from Jenkins.

Time Unknown

To Lady Bird Johnson[51]

Lady Bird Johnson had called the office at approximately 7:50 P.M. to inquire about when the President would be able to return to the Mansion. In his final recorded call of the day, Johnson returned her call and asked about the schedule for dinner. A notation in the White House Daily Diary suggests the call may have been made at 8:58 P.M., a possibility that is supported by the context of the conversation and Lynda Bird Johnson's call to her father at 9:00 P.M. Johnson would not return to the White House Mansion for dinner until 10:15 P.M.

President Johnson: Darling?

Lady Bird Johnson: Yes, dear.

President Johnson: When are you going to be ready to eat?

Lady Bird Johnson: I think we can be ready on short notice. I'll see. How quickly would you like?

President Johnson: I'm in no hurry. I'd say 30, 40 minutes. Walter [Jenkins] has got Jesse [Kellam] on the phone, and I'm going in there and we're going to talk to him, and I'll come over there in 30, 40 minutes.

Lady Bird Johnson: All right. You want to bring anybody with you?

President Johnson: No, I might bring Jack [Valenti], but I'm not sure. I'll call you back if I'm bringing—

Lady Bird Johnson: You don't need to call me for just Jack. I'll say three in 30 minutes.[52]

President Johnson: All right . . . all right.

Lady Bird Johnson: OK.

President Johnson: Maybe 40.

Lady Bird Johnson: OK.

President Johnson: Any other news? How you feeling?

Lady Bird Johnson: I'm feeling fine. I'm sitting in here talking on my

---

51. Tape WH6406.10, Citation #3766, Recordings of Telephone Conversations—White House Series, Recordings and Transcripts of Conversations and Meetings, Lyndon B. Johnson Library.
52. Valenti would not join the Johnsons for dinner.

talking machine and had a wonderful talk with Luci Baines and then—
and Lynda Bird, I got cut off in the middle of a talk with her only to find
out that the one she really wanted to talk with was *you*. So when I was cut
off, I told the operator not to try to reconnect *me*, but to channel it into
your office if she could.

President Johnson: Mm-hmm. OK.

Lady Bird Johnson: So don't be surprised if you hear from her.[53]

President Johnson: How long ago was it?

Lady Bird Johnson: That was not more than 10 minutes ago, and if
you don't want to talk to her right—

President Johnson: Why do they keep cutting you off out there, I
wonder?

Lady Bird Johnson: I don't know.

President Johnson: Did she have any news?

Lady Bird Johnson: No, we were just—We had just been talking a few
minutes, and mostly she was asking *me* questions, and really, I think she
wanted to talk to you more.

President Johnson: OK. Thank you.

Lady Bird Johnson: OK. Bye.

9:05 P.M.: Unrecorded call from Walter Jenkins.

9:15 P.M.: Unrecorded call to Bill Moyers, which lasted until 10:12
P.M.

10:13 P.M.: Unrecorded call to Mrs. Johnson.

10:15 P.M.: President Johnson departed the Oval Office and returned
to the Mansion, where he ate dinner with Mrs. Johnson.

10:28 P.M.: Unrecorded call to Jenkins.

11:27 P.M.: Unrecorded call from Mac Kilduff.

11:30 P.M.: Retired for the evening.

---

53. Lynda Bird Johnson called her father at 9:00 P.M., shortly after this conversation.

Thursday, June 18, 1964

> *Mr. Speaker, I'd rather never get a vote or a bill or anything than let Charlie Halleck tell me when I could meet and when I didn't. I think that's the most blackmail thing I ever heard. . . . I'd tell him to go straight to hell. If he don't believe in civil rights and won't give you a vote, I'd point it up to the world.*
>
> —President Johnson to John McCormack

With a vote pending the next day in the Senate on the civil rights bill, Arizona Senator and leading Republican presidential candidate Barry Goldwater flew to Gettysburg, Pennsylvania, to meet with Dwight Eisenhower at the former President's farm. Goldwater explained to Eisenhower that he would vote against the bill because he viewed its bans on discrimination in employment and fair accommodations as unconstitutional. He then announced his decision to reporters. Although William Scranton, Goldwater's primary rival for the Republican nomination, immediately called on the senator to support the bill, Goldwater's choice established what would become the key political framework of the fall presidential election.[1] Appealing to conservatives nationally and alienated white southern Democrats specifically, Goldwater would adopt a platform of stark opposition to both Johnson and moderates within his own party. The strategy proved spectacularly unsuccessful for Goldwater in November,

---

1. Charles Mohr, "Goldwater Says He'll Vote 'No' on The Rights Measure," *New York Times*, 19 June 1964; Chalmers M. Roberts, "Barry Crosses Political Rubicon," *Washington Post*, 19 June 1964; Rick Perlstein, *Before the Storm: Barry Goldwater and the Unmaking of the American Consensus* (New York: Hill and Wang, 2001).

as he would carry only his home state plus five states in the Deep South. Future Republican candidates, however, would have far more success in appealing to white resentment of racial integration.

Meanwhile, the conflict over protests in St. Augustine heightened when police beat black and white activists with clubs following an incident in which a policeman dove into a swimming pool to arrest protestors who had staged a "swim-in" to integrate the facility. After the arrest of 16 protestors, Martin Luther King—who had witnessed the police beatings—and other civil rights leaders refused to accept a special grand jury's proposal of a 30-day cooling-off period in St. Augustine.[2]

7:30 A.M.: President Johnson woke, ate breakfast in bed, met with Jack Valenti, performed his exercises, and received a blood pressure check from Dr. George Burkley.

9:25 A.M.: Unrecorded call from Walter Jenkins.

9:31 A.M.: Met with McGeorge Bundy.

9:31 A.M.: Unrecorded call to David Bell.

9:55 A.M.: Unrecorded call to Congressman George Mahon.

11:00 A.M.: Arrived in the Oval Office.

11:02 A.M.: Unrecorded call to Bundy.

11:11 A.M.

To Robert McNamara[3]

The President's first recorded call of the day began with a discussion of possible candidates for the position of U.S. ambassador to South Vietnam, as well as the overall U.S. position in Southeast Asia.

President Johnson: Who's his successor?

Robert McNamara: Uh . . .

President Johnson: Who's your candidate?

McNamara: I don't have any comment other than the one I gave you

---

2. "Police Club Negroes in Motel Pool," *Washington Post*, 19 June 1964. Taylor Branch, *Pillar of Fire: America in the King Years 1963–65* (New York: Simon & Schuster, 1998), pp. 354–55.
3. Tape WH6406.10, Citation #3767, Recordings of Telephone Conversations—White House Series, Recordings and Transcripts of Conversations and Meetings, Lyndon B. Johnson Library.

yesterday: that at the moment Max [Taylor] seems the best.[4] I'd like to suggest you defer talking to him until midafternoon or so, Mr. President. I'm just looking over the list again to see if I can't get some better ideas.

President Johnson: [*Pauses.*] Yeah, I'll do that. But has something developed?

McNamara: No, nothing has developed. As a matter of fact, I talked to Max last night. He called me, and he said that he felt perhaps he had given me the impression the day before yesterday that he'd cooled a little on his earlier statement that he'd volunteer for service. And he just wanted to make clear that he was perfectly willing and ready to go if you thought that was desirable.

Nothing else has developed. I think that . . . I don't think Dean Rusk is enthusiastic about Max going out there. And there are the problems associated with a military officer appointed to the post, as you have pointed out, the *New York Times*, [Walter] Lippmann, the [*Washington*] *Post*, et cetera.[5] And I just wanted to give one last hour or two of thought to alternatives.

President Johnson: What we've got to bear in mind is the . . . the number one objective is holding there and not seeing South Vietnam and Thailand, Cambodia, all of them go under. Now, in order to do that, we've got to get the man who will most unite this country.

McNamara: Yeah.

President Johnson: Now, from the standpoint that we look at it, he [Taylor] is less vulnerable than anyone else has suggested, but he is seriously vulnerable from the liberal line that you're talking about.

McNamara: That's right.

President Johnson: You're still going to catch hell from the right-wingers. He's not going to alleviate any of that. And you . . . in addition to that you're going to grab the left-wingers here.

---

4. General Maxwell D. Taylor served as chairman of the Joint Chiefs of Staff and would be the choice to replace Henry Cabot Lodge as ambassador. McNamara had actually last spoken to the President about the issue two days before. Johnson to Robert McNamara, 9:55 A.M., 16 June 1964, in this volume.

5. Walter Lippmann was a nationally syndicated columnist for the *Washington Post* who had criticized administration policy in Southeast Asia and advocated neutralization. During the week of 15 June, his columns had focused on the Republican presidential nomination rather than the ambassadorship, concluding with a charge that former President Dwight Eisenhower had in retirement become a Goldwater-conservative "without the harum-scarum jingoism." Walter Lippmann, "Today and Tomorrow . . . The Republican Struggle," *Washington Post*, 16 June 1964. The *New York Times* and *Washington Post* had been broadly critical of Johnson's foreign policy.

McNamara: Yeah.

President Johnson: That troubles me.

McNamara: Yeah.

President Johnson: But I don't see anybody that will make it less, and I think he'd be more competent. I believe that . . . I thought this morning we might send him as special assistant or even as chairman, Joint Chiefs [of Staff], for a month or two [to] stay in there and plan and organize and work closely with [Nguyen] Khanh, and . . . I believe Khanh's going to be pretty upset when this man goes out and he gets a second-rater he never heard of.[6] And maybe name Alexis Johnson as ambassador and let Max keep his present place, and after six or eight weeks come in for a couple of weeks and then go back until we get through with this thing and planning new defenses and offenses and initiatives and so on and so forth.[7]

I guess that just wouldn't work at all, but we've got to find some way—Taylor can give us the cover that we need with the country and with the Republicans and with the Congress.

McNamara: Yeah.

President Johnson: We need somebody to give us cover with the opinion movers.

McNamara: Yeah.

President Johnson: I don't know how to do that. That worries me. You see Bobby's [Kennedy] instinctive reaction: political job, not a military job. Then a good many of them say, "Well, it's Mac Bundy's—It's the military taking over." And there's been a little feeling like that in the State Department. They've got the biggest bunch of leaks in the country. You know damn well they'll start giving backgrounders immediately about the . . . "The military's won; the Army's taking over."

McNamara: Yeah.

President Johnson: "It's all going to be a military operation. Tom Mann's got another Brazil going."[8] That's the type of stuff that the *New*

---

6. Major General Nguyen Khanh was Prime Minister of South Vietnam.

7. U. Alexis Johnson was deputy under secretary for political affairs. On 1 July, he would be named deputy U.S. ambassador to South Vietnam, serving under Maxwell Taylor.

8. Assistant Secretary of State for Inter-American Affairs Thomas Mann had been widely criticized by liberal and left-wing commentators for reversing some aspects of the Kennedy administration's emphasis on democratization and economic reform in Latin America for a strategy of anti-Communism and privately financed economic development. This perception had only been furthered by tacit and at times overt U.S. support for a recent coup d'état in Brazil carried out by right-wing military officers. David F. Schnitz, *Thank God They're On Our Side: The United States and Right-Wing Dictatorships, 1921–1965* (Chapel Hill: University of North Carolina Press, 1999), pp. 264–82.

Republic and the *Nation* and the *Reporter, New York Times, Washington Post, Louisville Courier, St. Louis Post Dispatch*—that's what they're going to do.

McNamara: That's right. And this worries me a little bit. It may be a price we have to pay to get the right man out there, particularly a man that will buck up Khanh and give the country a feeling of strength in our response. But I'd like to avoid that cost if we could, and that's really what I'm thinking about this morning.

President Johnson: It seems to me the greatest danger we face there now is losing Khanh and being asked to get out.

McNamara: That's right.

President Johnson: Now, the man that could give him the most confidence and the most strength would be Taylor, I believe. I don't believe George Ball, [Roswell] Gilpatric, Mac Bundy, and any of those fellows are going to give him any strength because they're going to catch—we're going to start catching hell the minute we announce them.[9] And the only man I really know that's got . . . that's not regarded as a warmonger, that's got a bunch of stars and got standing is Taylor.

McNamara: Yeah.

President Johnson: He's not too old . . .

McNamara: Well, let me think about it, and I'll call you . . .

President Johnson: All right. Please do.

McNamara: After lunch. Thanks.

11:16 A.M.

To Robert Anderson[10]

Soon after concluding his conversation with McNamara, Johnson called former Treasury Secretary Robert Anderson in New York City. Despite his generally conservative political and economic views and his service in the Eisenhower administration, Anderson was a Texan and an old friend who had emerged as an unofficial adviser to the President. During

---

9. For Johnson's assessment of former Deputy Defense Secretary Roswell Gilpatric as a candidate for the ambassadorship, see McGeorge Bundy to Johnson, 7:56 P.M., 15 June 1964; and Johnson to Robert McNamara, 9:55 A.M., 16 June 1964, in this volume.
10. Tape WH6406.10, Citations #3768, #3769, and #3770, Recordings of Telephone Conversations—White House Series, Recordings and Transcripts of Conversations and Meetings, Lyndon B. Johnson Library.

the 1964 presidential campaign, Anderson would join the National Independent Committee, a group of Republican business leaders who publicly endorsed Lyndon Johnson.[11] In this call, Johnson sought a conservative perspective on the ambassadorship appointment and on the situation in South Vietnam more generally.

President Johnson: Bob, how are you?

Robert Anderson: Fine, Mr. President. How are you?

President Johnson: Good to hear you.

Anderson: [*Unclear.*]

President Johnson: You know any news?

Anderson: Well, the . . . I'm trying my best to keep up with all of the business activities. Encourage everybody I can to . . .

President Johnson: Talk a little louder, Bob. I'm having trouble.

Anderson: I say I'm trying—

President Johnson: Yeah.

Anderson: —to keep up with all the business activities. I'm having meetings with people from time to time to get them to expand their capital expenditures because this is the longest way of stretching out the good period of economics that we have. I'm meeting with a good deal of success in talking to those people. I think that you have the support of 90 percent of the people who have control of the expansion of facilities. I think there are going to be some more announcements made between now and November—very large capital expenditures that are going to be made.

I was in Europe and spent some time with some of the central bankers over there, some of the commercial bankers. I would not be surprised if [*unclear*] because of the depreciation of the lira, the inflation of the franc, and the fear that they may have a Labour government in Great Britain. So all in all I think things are looking pretty good.

President Johnson: Who am I going to run against?

Anderson: My guess is you're going to run against [Barry] Goldwater. [*Pauses.*] I have—

President Johnson: Did you ever get that man to succeed [Henry Cabot] Lodge if he comes home?

Anderson: Yes, the man I suggested is Draper, Bill Draper. Bill

---

11. Theodore H. White, *The Making of the President 1964* (New York: Atheneum, 1965), p. 418.

Draper was a general in the last—in World War II.[12] He was sent by Eisenhower all around the world on assessing the military capabilities of the United States. You may remember that he and [Arthur] Radford, after Radford retired, and two or three others went around.[13] Bill was the chairman of the committee . . . submitted the thing called the Draper report. He has a high regard for you because he's talked to me about you. I think that you could appoint him. He's a man who's got—I don't know whether he ever served as an ambassador or not, but he certainly has got a great public image. He's a Republican. He commutes between United—I mean, New York and California. And I would think that you just couldn't get a better man that would be better received than Bill Draper.

President Johnson: Bob, I don't believe he's well enough known— here or out there. I think you've got to have the biggest name you can get, a fellow following after Lodge who'd been [ambassador to the] United Nations and vice president and senator.[14]

Anderson: Yeah.

President Johnson: And that fellow [Nguyen] Khanh, the greatest problem we got is letting him know that we're in there to stay all the way, and we're not sending him second-raters, and we've got the best . . . the top man in this country. That's what disturbs me.

Anderson: Well, Mr. President, I think Bill is better known than probably you give him credit for because if you go back and look up some of these reports that came out, these things were circulated all over the world. And he was traveling around with Radford, who was regarded as

---

12. Major General William H. Draper served on the War Department's General Staff during World War II, oversaw economic reconstruction in Germany and Japan under the Marshall Plan, served as under secretary of the Army under President Truman, and as U.S. representative to Europe and NATO under President Eisenhower. Both before and after his military and diplomatic service, Draper worked as an investment banker. During the 1950s, he became an advocate of population control and in 1959, headed a commission that made the first public recommendation that family planning programs should be included in U.S. foreign aid policy. "Maj. Gen. W. H. Draper Dies," *Washington Post,* 27 December 1964.
13. Admiral Arthur W. Radford had seen extensive service in the Pacific Theater during World War II, participating in (and in some cases directing) the naval campaigns in the Gilbert Islands, Wake Islands, South China Sea, Iwo Jima, and Okinawa, as well as serving for a period in Washington as chief of naval air operations. During the Korean War, he led the U.S. Pacific Fleet and then served as chairman of the Joint Chiefs of Staff from 1953 to 1957; in the latter position, he unsuccessfully argued that the United States should intervene in support of France in its war in Southeast Asia. "Adm. Arthur Radford, 77, Ex-Joint Chiefs Head," *New York Times,* 18 August 1973.
14. Lodge had been the 1960 Republican nominee for vice president.

a military expert. I've forgotten who else, whether it was Jack McCloy or somebody else, that . . .[15]

President Johnson: What about Jack McCloy?

Anderson: I think Jack, frankly, is just pretty well up in years.

President Johnson: Mm-hmm.

Anderson: Now, I don't know how old he is, but he retired from that bank and I think—three or four years ago—and I think the retirement age is 65.

President Johnson: Mm-hmm.

Anderson: Another man who might do it but whose health is not all together is Gene Black.[16]

President Johnson: Yeah.

Anderson: But Gene, of course, has not had any military background. The thing that I have been puzzling over is to send somebody out there who has had a military background.

President Johnson: What about Max Taylor?

Anderson: To relieve him of his present command and make him an ambassador?

President Johnson: Yeah.

Anderson: [*Pauses.*] Well, I think this could be done. You might even get Arleigh Burke.[17] [*Pauses.*]

President Johnson: He'd frighten them too much, and Taylor probably would because there's too much military. They'd say it's a civilian thing, and—

Anderson: Yeah.

President Johnson: —the military's taking over. We need a military man to deal with Khanh, though—that's our great danger, is another government. And with all this attack coming at home and divisions here, this could be very fatal to us.

Anderson: Well, here's what—here are the elements that I have been putting together: Number one, get a Republican. Number two, get somebody that's well known in the country. Number three, get somebody who is a civilian but who has had military experience, actual military experience.

Now, I've thought about this thing a great deal, and of course I don't

---

15. A New York lawyer and adviser to presidents Kennedy and Johnson, John "Jack" McCloy had served as assistant secretary of war (1940–1945), president of the World Bank (1947–1949), and high commissioner of occupied Germany (1949–1952). He was born in 1895.

16. Eugene R. Black had been World Bank president from 1949 to 1962.

17. Admiral Arleigh Burke had been chief of naval operations during the Eisenhower and Kennedy administrations.

know whether Bill Draper can be had or not. But I do believe that if you check with some of your—

President Johnson: I have, Bob, and I don't get . . . I don't get that kind of a reading on him.

Anderson: I—

President Johnson: First, I don't get many people that really know him.

Anderson: Yeah.

President Johnson: And those that do know him don't feel that he has the standing with the people of the country or would have it necessarily with Khanh. We got to get somebody . . . Now, Khanh is crazy about Lodge, although Lodge is no administrator at all.

Anderson: No, he's not. No, he isn't.

President Johnson: He just screws everything up. But Lodge is going to [in] my judgment get back here and try to get in this fight and try to put over [William] Scranton.

Anderson: Yeah, my guess is that he's going to do that.

President Johnson: And I'm going to have to make up my mind. The best one I've got now is Taylor, and he's not a rigid military man. He's got a . . . He's an objective fellow and a very fair and just fellow. And I can't tell anything about what he . . . Democrat or Republican—I never had any indication one way or the other. He's well accepted on the Hill and with the people and surely with Khanh. And he knows exactly what's happening and what needs to be done.

Anderson: Yeah.

President Johnson: But the *New York Times* and the *Washington Post* and all the left wing . . . The right wing will give us hell for not going in and defoliating and bombing and so forth. The left wing will give us hell for having a military dictatorship.

Anderson: Yeah.

President Johnson: But he's the best one I can see at this point. His wife has some problems that I've heard of [when Taylor was serving] as Joint Chief [of Staff]. Her mother's sick, and she has to be tied down pretty much. She can't go with him, and that's hell to ask a fellow to go out there.

Now, everybody in the Cabinet's volunteered to go. [Douglas] Dillon hasn't. Some of them think Dillon would be good. Bobby Kennedy wrote a note said he wanted to go, and [Dean] Rusk offered to go, and [Robert] McNamara offered to go, and [McGeorge] Bundy offered to go. That's very confidential: I don't want another human to know it but you, but they—

Anderson: I understand.

President Johnson: —over the last three months they've all done it.

Anderson: Yep.

President Johnson: I was kind of hoping Dillon would, but Dillon never . . . They talked to him about it, but he never gave his judgment.

Anderson: Yeah. Well, let me do a little more thinking during the day, and . . .

Now, I don't know how well Rosie O'Donnell is known.[18] You know, Rosie just retired.

President Johnson: Mm-hmm.

Anderson: As an Air Force general.

President Johnson: Yeah. I'd be afraid of that because our people all over the world are awfully frightened by this Air Force and by the [Curtis] LeMay line.[19]

Anderson: Well, I don't blame them.

President Johnson: And we got to watch it here. That's one disadvantage to Taylor going: Taylor's held this group together pretty well.

Anderson: Yeah.

President Johnson: And we've got Nixon and [Nelson] Rockefeller and Goldwater wanting to go in, and go north, and bomb.[20] Eisenhower thinks that we ought to do what we're doing. He says step up the propaganda some more and some minor things, but I don't think we're doing all of that we know how to do. But he's pretty well balanced on it. I'm surprised that these other men would be so far off, but all of them just really want to do anything, and that puts a good deal of pressure on us.

At the same time, I've got the [Wayne] Morses and the [Ernest] Gruenings and the [Frank] Churches and the [Albert] Gores and all that group that want to pull out completely.[21] And the policy that he set up there ten years ago to help these people help themselves is the best one, if we can hold it.

---

18. General Emmett "Rosie" O'Donnell Jr. led the first B-29 bomber raid over Tokyo in November 1944 (the first U.S. raid on the Japanese capital of any kind since the famous Doolittle raid of 1942). He held a variety of posts in the Air Force after the war and eventually commanded the Pacific Air Forces. U.S. Air Force biographies, http://www.af.mil/bios/bio.asp?bioID=6638.

19. Air Force Chief of Staff General Curtis E. LeMay had served as chief of the Strategic Air Command (SAC) and was a virulent cold warrior and advocate of nuclear weapons. He would retire in 1965 and in 1968 would be the running mate of George Wallace.

20. Nelson Rockefeller served as governor of New York and until he withdrew on 15 June, a candidate for the 1964 Republican presidential nomination. Richard Nixon was also an unannounced, dark horse contender for the nomination.

21. All Democratic senators with liberal reputations, Wayne Morse represented Oregon, Ernest Gruening represented Alaska, Frank Church represented Idaho, and Albert Gore represented Tennessee.

Anderson: Why don't you ask Milton Eisenhower to go?

President Johnson: [*Pauses.*] I don't believe he'd go, but that might be a suggestion.[22]

Anderson: Well, I don't know whether he'd go or not, but if he went, you would certainly have a man who's well known, and you'd have the absolute, unquestioned support of Eisenhower back here because he thinks he's the smartest brother he has, thinks he's the smartest member of the family. I don't happen to think so, but *he* thinks so. [*The President chuckles.*] And Milton's got a flair for liking to do these things, and he traveled all over Latin America for Eisenhower. I don't know whether he went to the Middle East or not. But he just might be a fellow you would want to consider. [*Unclear*] Khanh couldn't [*unclear*] object to the quality of the nationally known character that was coming out there. [*Pause.*]

President Johnson: No, that's . . . I don't guess he['s] got much military experience.

Anderson: I don't guess he's got any. But certainly Lodge didn't have very much. He was in a tank over in France, but that doesn't give you very much military strategy. Besides, you can send somebody over there with him that you have confidence in that is a military strategist.

President Johnson: We've got an excellent man there now in . . .

Anderson: [*Unclear.*]

President Johnson: [William] Westmoreland.

Anderson: Yeah. Milton might be an answer to him. [*Pause.*] Or I'll tell you another thing you might do: You might ask one of the other Rockefeller brothers. Ask Larry. David, I don't think would go because he's president of the bank. But Lawrence is certain to go. The other brother [Winthrop Rockefeller] probably wouldn't go, and you probably wouldn't want him because he's running for governorship of Arkansas. Lawrence might be your man to go. [*Pauses.*]

I was trying to think of somebody in the Eisenhower Cabinet that might be asked, but I can't think of anybody that I think that either would be eligible or that would go.

President Johnson: Eisenhower going to support Scranton?

Anderson: My guess is yes. Now, he came up and I had lunch with him . . . about three weeks ago—well, it was right after this Cleveland

---

22. Milton Eisenhower was the president of Johns Hopkins University and the brother of former President Dwight Eisenhower.

thing.[23] And the gist of the conversation was that he thought that at *that* time Goldwater pretty well was so far down the road that it'd be difficult for anybody to catch him, and he wasn't happy about it. But he said, "I guess I have no choice if he's nominated." He'd just support him, but he sure wasn't happy about it.

Now, I just don't believe myself as a tactical man that you can get a fellow who's got as—[*a buzzer sounds*]—much votes as Goldwater and then take them away from him. [You] might take *some*, but I just don't believe you can take enough of them around to make Scranton the candidate.

President Johnson: [*Pauses.*] Who do you think's the easiest one for me to beat?

Anderson: Goldwater.

President Johnson: Mm-hmm.

Anderson: You see, what's going to happen is that Goldwater will take some southern states. I don't know which ones. He won't take Texas, Louisiana, or some of those[24] . . . He'll take some of them just because of his civil rights stand and because, you know, in that part of the country there's a lot of right-wing people. But when you get north of the Mason and Dixon line, people just aren't going to support him.

I've got a lot of friends among the Jewish community. I've been asking the Jewish people what they think, and I just don't find any support at all among the Jewish people. And they're pretty potent in some of these big cities.

President Johnson: Mm-hmm.

Anderson: Which one do *you* think you can beat?

President Johnson: I think Goldwater.

Anderson: And I think my own guess is Scranton's not going to make it. I think you're going to have a lot of Republicans stay home. Most of the women are not going to support Goldwater [*unclear*]. There are more women voters in this country than we thought. I've been talking to these women in Greenwich, and they're 95 percent Republican. I can't find a woman out there who's going to vote for him except one. These women are a powerful influence in this country. [*Pause.*]

---

23. Speaking at the National Governors' Conference in Cleveland on 8 June, former President Eisenhower had called for greater assertiveness by state governments and argued that "there is no need for groveling before any part of the federal government." Earl Mazo, "Eisenhower Backs Power of States," *New York Times*, 9 June 1964; Walter Lippmann, "Today and Tomorrow . . . The Republican Struggle," *Washington Post*, 16 June 1964.

24. Goldwater would carry his home state of Arizona along with Deep South states Alabama, Georgia, Louisiana, Mississippi, and South Carolina.

President Johnson: How are you getting along on Panama?[25]

One minute and thirty-three seconds excised as classified information.

President Johnson: Mm-hmm. [*Pauses.*]

Anderson: But I will try to think during the day, and if I may, I'll call you back. Milton would be a good selection, in my judgment, if you can get him to do it.

President Johnson: Wouldn't the right wing be awful upset? Couldn't do much about it, though, could they?

Anderson: No, they couldn't do anything about it, and besides, Ike is more regarded as more on the right wing than he is on the left wing.

President Johnson: Mm-hmm.

Anderson: And presently if he deviates from the middle of the road, he deviates to the right instead of the left. And I don't think he'd try and upset that. In fact, I'd have to talk to some of the right wingers myself and tell them what fools they'd be if they tried to look at it.

President Johnson: Mm-hmm. [*Pauses.*] Are you concerned much about this "too much military"? In a military operation with a military man?

Anderson: Yes, frankly, I am. I tell you I'm concerned about two things on that vein. One of them is there is a number of people who talk about all the trips that are made out there. Not that they object to making the trips, but that after the trips are made, the status quo comes . . . remains pretty much the same. The trips that are being made out there are just not effective; nothing really comes out of them. I'm sure a lot does come out of it that needs to be made public. But last trip that was made [*unclear*] actually had been on all of them. I would have a little bit of concern that you took a man out of the chairman of the Joint Chiefs of Staff—

President Johnson: Louder, Bob.

Anderson: I say I would have a little concern that you will take somebody out of the Joint Chiefs of Staff and send him there. On the other hand, people might very well say, "This evidences a determination on the part of the President to take his top military man and relieve him of his responsibilities here, and this means damn well that we're there to stay and we're going to win." And it might have just the opposite effect. It might have the effect of giving public confidence rather than something else.

President Johnson: Yes, I think that's the effect it would have. But I think the liberals would gripe at me and say, "It's too much military, and

---

25. In April 1964, Robert Anderson had been appointed by President Johnson as a U.S. special representative to negotiate with Panama on the future of the canal treaty.

it's a civilian post, and the job to be done there is a political job in the hamlets and the provinces, and that this is a military man. We've got a hell of a good military man in Westmoreland, and we oughtn't to be taking chairman of the Joint Chiefs away and putting him out there." I think that's the *New York Times'* line.[26]

Anderson: Well—

President Johnson: Now, what has happened is—we can't say this, and we're not going to say it—but Lodge ain't worth a tinker's damn as an ambassador. He just spends his time talking to the *New York Times.* And he is good with Khanh because Khanh thinks he's a great man in this country. And about every four weeks you have to go out there and say, "Here are the things to be done in these hamlets and these provinces and these raids and these airplanes and these bombs and so forth." And list them. And then you have to go back four weeks later and say, "Why in the hell haven't you done them, and go on and let's do some more of them." You've got to be an administrator in absentia.

Anderson: He has never been good at anything, Mr. President.

President Johnson: Well, that's right—

Anderson: I've known this fellow a long time.

President Johnson: That's right. But that's why we go, and that's why we can't say we have to go on that account.

Anderson: Yeah.

President Johnson: If you've got a foreman at your ranch that ain't worth a damn . . .

Anderson: That's right.

President Johnson: You just have to go every Sunday and tell him what to do next week.

Anderson: That's right.

President Johnson: And then go and check him. And McNamara has just—and Taylor—just been shoving the hell out of him and also been trying to keep this fellow's courage up. Khanh's about to go under. He . . . Everyday—he sleeps in a different house every night. He's scared to death, and they—He's afraid they're after him, and we just don't think we can take another thing. And it does boost their morale to beat hell just to see Taylor and McNamara.

Anderson: Yeah.

---

26. The *New York Times* instead offered a different critique: On the day of Taylor's appointment as ambassador, an editorial focused on the failures of U.S. strategy, as it noted that Taylor was the "chief architect" of U.S. policy in the region and that "his choice comes at a time when his policy has not seemed to be working very well. Under his close supervision it may do better." "Mr. Lodge Heads Home," *New York Times,* 24 June 1964.

President Johnson: And . . . Last—reason I sent them to Honolulu last time and brought Lodge up there is because we had to have a province program and do something out in these areas around Saigon that they're eating away and nibbling.

Anderson: Sure.

President Johnson: But we had given it to Lodge, and Lodge hadn't done anything about it. So we all agreed on it in Honolulu.[27] They came back and recommended it. I immediately approved it, sent it out to Lodge—he was a party to the agreement—and damned if a week later he didn't come back and say he didn't believe he'd put it in effect.

Anderson: Well, I'll be dad-gum.

President Johnson: So that's the kind of administrative problem you've got.

Anderson: Yeah.

President Johnson: Now, I can't say that because they'd say it's politics and I'm jumping on a Republican, and it would hurt the morale of the people out there and just look like a partisan attack. But the truth is, he ain't worth a damn.

Anderson: Well, why don't you give a little thought either to sending Milton out there or asking him if he'll go, and then I'll try to think of one or two more names during the day and call you back.

President Johnson: What would you think of Dillon?

Anderson: [*Pauses.*] Well, who would you put in his place?

President Johnson: Have no idea.

Anderson: You've got a topflight fellow there if he'll take it, and that's [Robert] Rosa.[28]

President Johnson: Yeah. What about Don Cook?[29]

Anderson: If you could send Dillon out there and put Rosa in Dillon's job, I think that'd be all right.

President Johnson: Mm-hmm. . . . What about Don Cook?

Anderson: Don is able, capable. I got the impression talking to him back in the earlier days of your administration that he was going to be

---

27. Leading U.S. foreign policy, diplomatic, and military officials had met on 1–2 June near Honolulu to discuss the situation in Southeast Asia and the future course of U.S. policy there. "Summary Record of a Meeting, Honolulu," 1 June 1964, 8:30 A.M.–12:30 P.M., and "Summary Record of a Meeting, Honolulu," 1 June 1964, 2:15–6:15 P.M., and "Summary Record of Meetings, Honolulu," 2 June 1964, 8:30–11:50 A.M. and 2:15–4 P.M., U.S. Department of State, *Foreign Relations of the United States (FRUS), 1964–1968: Vietnam 1964*, ed. Edward C. Keefer and Charles S. Sampson (Washington, DC: GPO, 1992), 1:412–33.

28. Robert Rosa was under secretary of the Treasury.

29. A longtime friend and adviser to President Johnson, Donald Cook was president of the American Electric Power Company.

reluctant to give up what he has now because he will—it's such a crucial period in his career.

President Johnson: That's right. He doesn't want to do anything, but I was just thinking about whether he'd be a competent secretary of the Treasury. I think he would.

Anderson: Yeah, I would think Don would be competent. Don and I have some differences in judgment as to how the Federal Reserve ought to be run. That doesn't mean that I'm right and he's wrong. I'm more on the side of a greater degree of flexibility and anticipation by the Federal Reserve, I think, than Don is.

President Johnson: Mm-hmm.

Anderson: But that doesn't make any difference . . .

President Johnson: I don't think Dillon wants to go because they've talked to him about it, and he didn't say anything. So I just assumed that if he'd have felt like it was his duty, he'd [have] said so.

Anderson: Yeah.

President Johnson: And I don't believe—I don't see that he's . . . would be any ball of fire anyway.

Anderson: He's never going to be a ball of fire anywhere. [*Pauses.*]

President Johnson: Well, now, we need the best man we got. Do you think [Lucius] Clay's too old?[30] Too rigid?

Anderson: Well, Clay's rigid as hell. And Clay is an egotist. And if he got out there, he'd want to run that thing the way he wanted to run it. That might suit you and it might not suit you. But he's the kind of a fellow that's just as rigid as he could be. And I think he might have some times where he said, "Well, if we can't do this, I'll just throw in the [*unclear*]—"

President Johnson: He did that every Saturday night in Berlin.

Anderson: Yeah. And that would be my worry about . . . That would be my worry about Lucius Clay. Jack McCloy, I think, is . . . might do it, but he's pretty well up in years. However, I wouldn't rule Jack out because Jack just might go do it.

President Johnson: Is he a Democrat or Republican?

Anderson: He's a Republican, nominally.

President Johnson: Mm-hmm.

Anderson: Another man that you might think about is George Cham-

---

30. Beginning in 1947, General Lucius Clay served as commander in chief of U.S. forces in Europe and military governor of the U.S. zone in Germany. He later served as John Kennedy's personal representative in Germany during the period of the Berlin Wall crisis in 1961. At the time of this conversation, Clay was 67 years old.

pion. George is [*a buzzer sounds*] chairman of the board of the Chase Manhattan Bank. He was president after [*unclear*], and then when they elected David Rockefeller, why, they made George Champion president—I mean, chairman. And he is a well-known Republican and a man up towards the 57-, 58-[year-old] period, something like that.

President Johnson: You think about it, and I'll talk to you later.

Anderson: OK, my friend.

President Johnson: Bye.

11:40 A.M.: Unrecorded call to McGeorge Bundy.

11:43 A.M.: The President posed for pictures with Democratic National Committee Deputy Chairman Louie Martin and staff member Clifford Alexander (both of whom were African American), who remained until 12:03.

11:55 A.M.: Greeted Mr. and Mrs. Ewel Stone and their son Hunter; the Stones were relatives of Texas newspaper publisher Walker Stone.

11:45 A.M.

From Luther Hodges[31]

Secretary of Commerce Hodges called the President to discuss the possible appointment of businessman Harold Walker to lead the new Community Relations Service that would be established with the passage of the civil rights bill. Walker had been recommended the day before by *Atlanta Journal-Constitution* publisher Ralph McGill. The CRS would be a part of the Department of Commerce. Although Walker appeared to be the leading candidate at the time of this call, the post would eventually go to former Florida Governor Leroy Collins.

President Johnson: Yes?

Luther Hodges: Hello, Mr. President.

President Johnson: Yes.

Hodges: Good morning, sir.

---

31. Tape WH6406.10, Citation #3772, Recordings of Telephone Conversations—White House Series, Recordings and Transcripts of Conversations and Meetings, Lyndon B. Johnson Library.

President Johnson: How are you?

Hodges: Fine. I gave you a ring last night, but it was a little late. I . . . Your man [Harold] Walker, you picked a good one.[32]

President Johnson: Yeah.

Hodges: [*with the President acknowledging throughout*] I talked with [Ralph] McGill whom you have talked to—didn't realize you had.[33] Then later I called Jim Carmichael, who's a director of Lockheed and who was a law partner of Walker. I also took the occasion, Mr. President, to call the governor, Governor [Carl] Sanders.[34] And they all gave him a very high rating. I've got a memorandum; it will be at your desk in about a half an hour. And you also have a letter there I think from McGill, which covers the same thing.

Now, I'm saying in the closing part of my letter I'm ready to call him up here for both of us to see him, if we can get him here tomorrow sometime. I'm ready to go ahead with it and recommend him to you, and we can use—

Oh, I did get both [David] Lawrence and Buford Ellington to agree to let me use their names, and they would do it if you and I asked them to do it.[35] Now, I didn't push them at all because I . . . Dave wanted to know a little bit more about it, and I mailed him a document today about it. And Buford is just ready to do whatever we—

President Johnson: I tell you what I think we ought to do with Buford. I think we ought to make him go and see each governor and ask the governors to help us get people to observe the law instead of us enforce it.

Hodges: Yeah.

President Johnson: I can't call them together because if I do, I think that [with] the television all of them will start demagoguing, and the folks back home will say they're up here selling them out, and every demagogue at home will say they're doing this and that. And [George] Wallace will try to outdo them all, and then they'll have to protect themselves by saying that they're not any Negro lovers, and it'll just be a big

---

32. Hodges was referring to Harold Walker, the president of the Scripto pencil company and a director of Lockheed, who was under consideration as a possible director of the Community Relations Service. See Ralph McGill to Juanita Roberts, 11:40 A.M., 17 June 1964, in this volume.

33. Ralph McGill was the editor of the *Atlanta Journal-Constitution*. He had spoken the day before to one of the President's secretaries and left information about Harold Walker. See McGill to Roberts, ibid.

34. Carl E. Sanders served as the Democratic governor of Georgia from 1963 to 1967.

35. David L. Lawrence had been mayor of Pittsburgh from 1945 to 1958 and governor of Pennsylvania from 1959 to 1963. Buford Ellington had been governor of Tennessee from 1959 to 1963.

mess.[36] But I believe if Buford just got in an airplane and went around to see each one of them and said to them, "Now, here's what we want you to do. Do it."

Now, I'm going to California tonight or at 7:00 in the morning.[37]

Hodges: Mm-hmm.

President Johnson: Another thing we got to talk to—I talked to Bobby Kennedy about this. He's going to check this fellow and call me back. He hadn't done it. We got to talk to him beforehand because we don't want to get static with all the civil rights groups that this guy's no good.

Hodges: Who is he talking about?

President Johnson: Walker.

Hodges: Oh, is Bob Kennedy going to check Walker?

President Johnson: Yeah.

Hodges: Oh.

President Johnson: I talked to him about it yesterday, told him that I thought Walker would be awfully good man.

Hodges: Yeah.

President Johnson: And I also mentioned Dave Lawrence to him. He—I was just going over a group. He gave me some of his suggestions, and he'd been running the bill, and I don't want to just . . . to ignore him and give him . . . have any of that group say that we just . . .

Hodges: Pay no attention.

President Johnson: . . . planted our own people, and tried to run over and leave them. Now, my opinion is he thinks highly of the governor, and he thinks highly of this Bobby Troutman, and Bobby Troutman negotiated the Lockheed thing and that with this fellow, so he must think well of Walker.[38] And every report I've got on Walker is exceptional, and I believe that'll be *his* report.

Hodges: Yeah.

President Johnson: But I'll check that out.

Hodges: Well, do you want to—Would you check that out—

---

36. George Wallace was the segregationist governor of Alabama and a challenger for the 1964 Democratic presidential nomination.

37. Johnson would depart for California the following morning, leaving the White House at 6:53 A.M.

38. Troutman was a Kennedy appointee who had directed the President's Committee on Equal Employment Opportunity and launched the Plans for Progress program until being replaced in 1962 by Hobart Taylor. See "Conversation with Lyndon B. Johnson," 10:25 A.M., 21 August 1962, in Timothy Naftali, ed., *The Presidential Recordings, John F. Kennedy: The Great Crises*, vol. 1, *July 30–August 1962* (New York: Norton, 2001), pp. 541–44.

President Johnson: Yeah.

Hodges: —you don't want me to do anything about it—

President Johnson: Yeah. If you—

Hodges: —check it out today, or do you want me to—

President Johnson: You want to check it out, or you want me to do it?

Hodges: Well, it'd be better if you did it.

President Johnson: All right. OK.

Hodges: [*with Johnson acknowledging*] You can tell him this: that I have checked everybody, and that I had had other names ahead of it, but that I'm satisfied with him. Then we can decide. You can let me know when you want me to bring this guy up here.

President Johnson: All right.

Hodges: I can do it . . .

President Johnson: Probably Monday.

Hodges: All right. We'll be ready to move as soon as you're ready. And I think we can use, then, Buford and some of the others on this national committee and pick them for specific jobs. Dave Lawrence could do some of the same kind of thing at other parts of the country, you know.

President Johnson: Yeah.

Hodges: They know him very well as a whole.

Well, then shall I await your further—

President Johnson: Yeah. I'll try to call you back during the day.

Hodges: All right.

President Johnson: Bye.

Hodges: Thank you, Mr. President.

11:56 A.M.: Unrecorded call to Walter Jenkins.

12:01 P.M.: Unrecorded call to George Reedy.

12:04 P.M.: Unrecorded call from Jenkins.

12:10 P.M.: Accompanied by Jack Valenti, President Johnson went to the Cabinet Room for a meeting with U.S. ambassadors to Latin America.[39]

---

39. The following ambassadors and officials attended the meeting: Lincoln Gordon, Brazil; Jack H. Vaughn, Panama; W. Tapley Bennett Jr., the Dominican Republic; Aaron S. Brown, Nicaragua; Covey T. Oliver, Colombia; John Bell, Guatemala; Secretary Tom Mann; Ralph Dungan; Robert Adams; Anthony Solomon; and William Rogers.

12:14 P.M.

From McGeorge Bundy[40]

President Johnson: [*to an unidentified person in the office*] . . . thing with the ambassadors from various . . .
The operator interrupts, and the President instructs her to connect Bundy's call.
President Johnson: Pardon me for a minute.
[*over phone*] Yes? Yes? Yes? Hello?
McGeorge Bundy: Mr. President, Bob McNamara is here, and I wondered if we could come up and see you about this after you're through with the ambassadors.
President Johnson: Yeah. Yeah. I just started with them, though, and I've got an hour. I'll try to cut it short and come out whenever you-all come up.
Bundy: Well, we can . . . We'll just be around when you're free.
President Johnson: All right. All right.

12:33 P.M.: Unrecorded call to George Reedy (from the Cabinet Room).

12:35 P.M.

To Robert Kennedy[41]

Johnson next called the Attorney General to get an update on the status of the Justice Department's assessment of Scripto President Harold Walker as head of the Community Relations Service.[42] Kennedy was in Boston at the time of the call.

---

40. Tape WH6406.10, Citation #3774, Recordings of Telephone Conversations—White House Series, Recordings and Transcripts of Conversations and Meetings, Lyndon B. Johnson Library.
41. Tape WH6406.10, Citation #3775, Recordings of Telephone Conversations—White House Series, Recordings and Transcripts of Conversations and Meetings, Lyndon B. Johnson Library.
42. See Luther Hodges to Johnson, 11:45 A.M., 18 June 1964, in this chapter.

President Johnson: Hello?

Robert Kennedy: Hi, Mr. President.

President Johnson: Luther [Hodges] called me on this [Harold] Walker thing. Did you get a chance to check him out any?

Kennedy: Yes, we're in the midst of doing it now.

President Johnson: Mm-hmm.

Kennedy: Burke Marshall's working on it.

President Johnson: All right.

Kennedy: And I haven't had any final report on it, however.

President Johnson: He wants to call him up here as soon as he can. He talked to the governor . . .[43]

Kennedy: Yes.

President Johnson: And to [Jim] Carmichael and to [Ralph] McGill . . .[44]

Kennedy: Yes.

President Johnson: And perhaps one or two others.

Kennedy: And they gave good reports?

President Johnson: Excellent.

Kennedy: Well, now can I—

President Johnson: He was almost ecstatic about it, but I told him just to hold down, I wanted to talk to you and others. He also had talked to [Buford] Ellington, asking him to give some thought to it. He thought we could get him. I don't think he's the one to do it. I think that we ought to use him, and when we can, go in and see some of these governors.

Kennedy: Yes.

President Johnson: The rougher ones.

Kennedy: Yes.

President Johnson: And he also talked to [David] Lawrence. He thinks both of those would be alternatives. I just present that to you because I don't know when we'll be talking again.

Kennedy: Yes. I'll be back this afternoon.

President Johnson: All right.

Kennedy: [*Unclear*] to come by.

President Johnson: I am going to leave at 7[:00] in the morning, and I'll be out of pocket until I get back from California on—I got those meetings tomorrow in San Francisco and the next day in Los Angeles. But I'll

---

43. Johnson was referring to Governor Carl Sanders of Georgia.

44. For these individuals, see Luther Hodges to Johnson, 11:45 A.M., 18 June 1964, in this chapter.

call you when I get back, and if you get in before I get away here today, you give me a ring.

Kennedy: I'll be there at 4:30. Would you want—

President Johnson: That's good, yeah. Give me a ring then.

Kennedy: Now, shall I check and call you back if . . . on our report on him?

President Johnson: Yeah . . . yeah. As soon as you can. Because—

Kennedy: All right.

President Johnson: —it's conceivable that if it was good, and I'm sure it will be, that we might just get him up here tonight.

Kennedy: Yes. I think it'd be well, of course, if he could get your imprimatur and . . . and, you know, had it . . . sort of came from the White House rather than just from any department.

President Johnson: Yeah, I haven't looked at him, but I thought if it checked out all right, we might get him in here and then all of us talk him over. I get good reports on folks a lot of times over the phone, and when you look at them you get a different impression. [*Kennedy acknowledges.*] And I think this is pretty key. I think maybe it'd be good for you to give them your ideas about what he could do, and maybe Luther too, and maybe I could make a contribution. We might just have him in here for [a] night session.

Kennedy: That'd be fine. Well, should I see if I can work that out?

President Johnson: You do that, and . . .

Kennedy: Can I call you back in a few minutes?

President Johnson: Yeah . . . yeah, yeah. Yeah.

Kennedy: OK.

12:50 P.M.

To McGeorge Bundy[45]

Johnson called McGeorge Bundy to update him on his arrival for a meeting that would also include Robert McNamara.

---

45. Tape WH6406.10, Citation #3776, Recordings of Telephone Conversations—White House Series, Recordings and Transcripts of Conversations and Meetings, Lyndon B. Johnson Library.

12:55 P.M.

From Robert Kennedy[46]

Kennedy called with news about the Justice Department's evaluation of the possible selection of Harold Walker as director of the Community Relations Service. Although all reports were good, Kennedy pointed out a number of previously ignored drawbacks about the choice of Walker for the CRS position.

President Johnson: [*to someone in office*] Trying to work all over the world with people everywhere.

[*over phone*] Hello? [*Pauses.*] [*Unclear.*] Hello? Hello?

Kennedy then comes on the line.

Robert Kennedy: Hello?

President Johnson: Yeah.

Kennedy: Oh, Mr. President?

President Johnson: Yeah.

Kennedy: Well, now, he's checked on him [Harold Walker]. Burke [Marshall] has been working this morning on it. The reports are good. We haven't got anything really from the Negro community. And he's not well known.

President Johnson: No. No, he's not.

Kennedy: So, the one point that has been raised and which I think has to be considered is the fact that he is not nationally known. That he is a businessman. That he's a southern businessman, and that the Negroes aren't going to really know much about him. And he's going to be appointed operating out of the Department of Commerce, so that the Negroes are going to be suspect, in our judgment, about him. The credibility of the operation of this Community Relations Service is going to therefore have a more difficult time, particularly at the beginning. And whether we want to start in under those circumstances . . . I think we should give a good deal of thought to.

I think if we . . . if we're going to move in this direction we should make sure that somebody like . . . well, some of the Negro leaders are going to say that they think that this is a good appointment. If they don't, I think that it might be subject to all kinds of problems.

---

46. Tape WH6406.10, Citation #3777, Recordings of Telephone Conversations—White House Series, Recordings and Transcripts of Conversations and Meetings, Lyndon B. Johnson Library.

President Johnson: Is Burke going to check that out with them?

Kennedy: Yeah, he's going to. And we should know this afternoon. Do you want us to come over—

President Johnson: Yeah.

Kennedy: —sometime this afternoon and give you a report.

President Johnson: Yeah . . . yeah. Yeah, yeah, yeah, yeah. I haven't looked at my schedule, but talk to Jack [Valenti], and any moment I've got free. I'll be working late tonight.

Kennedy: All right.

President Johnson: And . . .

Kennedy: Take a short time. Now, he had—Burke had two other suggestions as possibilities. One was the present mayor of Atlanta. [*Beeping noise.*]

President Johnson: Mm-hmm. Yeah, yeah. Yeah, go ahead.

Kennedy: Mayor [Ivan] Allen.[47]

President Johnson: Yeah.

Kennedy: And, you know, who's a great . . . has been very helpful on this whole issue and is also a great booster of yours.

President Johnson: Yeah.

Kennedy: The other is this fellow [L. Richardson] Preyer, who's running for governor of North Carolina, who probably is going to get beaten . . .[48]

President Johnson: Mm-hmm.

Kennedy: . . . who is a district court judge. Resigned to run for governor, and it looks like he's going to get beaten, and the primary there is on the 29th.

President Johnson: I'd be doubtful about taking a defeated man, been repudiated that recently by his people, [*Kennedy acknowledges*] putting him in this spot.

---

47. Ivan Allen had been elected mayor of Atlanta in 1961 after he defeated segregationist Lester Maddox in the Democratic primary with the crucial support of the Atlanta Negro Voters League and the NAACP. A racial moderate and representative of Atlanta's business community, Allen testified in favor of the civil rights bill in 1963. Although he maintained the support of black voters in his successful 1965 reelection campaign, Allen's gradualism on other racial issues eventually led the city's black leadership to push for an African American mayor. Ronald H. Bayor, *Race and the Shaping of Twentieth-Century Atlanta* (Chapel Hill: University of North Carolina Press, 1996), pp. 35–42; "Ivan Allen Jr., 92, Dies; Led Atlanta as Beacon of Change," *New York Times*, 3 July 2003.

48. The grandson of the inventor of Vicks VapoRub and Vicks Cough Drops, L. Richardson Preyer served as a judge on the U.S. District Court for the Middle District of North Carolina from 1961 to 1963 and ran unsuccessfully for the Democratic gubernatorial nomination in 1964. From 1969 to 1981, he would serve as a Democratic member of Congress.

I would give a lot of thought to [George] Taylor, if we don't go South.[49]

Kennedy: Yes.

President Johnson: I have the impression that we all felt we ought to take a southerner if we could for the effect it'd have. But if we didn't, I'd give a lot of thought to George Taylor of Pennsylvania.

Kennedy: Yeah. All right—

President Johnson: [*with Kennedy acknowledging*] Tell him to look into that. If I can see that there's merit in what he says about the [Luther] Hodges's thing and the president's thing and the man from Georgia, and so forth. Unless some of the leaders felt that's what they wanted to do. If they don't, then let's give some serious thought to Taylor.

Kennedy: All right.

President Johnson: Check him out, because he's professional.

Kennedy: Yes.

President Johnson: I don't know whether he'd take it or not. Any indication this fellow would take it? Taylor, do you know?

Kennedy: No, we don't know yet.

President Johnson: We don't either.

Kennedy: No.

President Johnson: OK.

Kennedy: Now, we'll make arrangements with Jack Valenti . . .

President Johnson: Yeah. Yeah.

Kennedy: . . . to come over.

President Johnson: Bye.

Kennedy: Fine.

1:10 P.M.: Unrecorded call to George Reedy (from the Cabinet Room).

1:15 P.M.: President Johnson returned to the office and met with a group that included Democratic National Committee Chairman John Bailey, party official Richard Maguire, New York businessman Jerry Finkelstein, banker Arthur Roth, and financier and philanthropist Louis Stern.

---

49. George W. Taylor was a professor at the University of Pennsylvania's Wharton School of Commerce. In March and April, he had served as a federal mediator during the negotiations that had prevented a railroad strike. Eric Goldman, *The Tragedy of Lyndon Johnson* (New York: Dell, 1968), p. 103.

1:18 P.M.: Off-the-record meeting and exchange of gifts with Archbishop Egidio Vagnozzi.

1:21 P.M.: Unrecorded call to Walter Jenkins.

1:22 P.M.: Escorted Archbishop Vagnozzi to Jenkins's office and returned alone at 1:25 P.M.

1:27 P.M.–2:55 P.M.: Lunch in the Mansion with Secretary of State Dean Rusk, Secretary of Defense Robert McNamara, and National Security Adviser McGeorge Bundy.

2:25 P.M.: Unrecorded call from Lynda Bird in Honolulu.

3:05 P.M.: Unrecorded call to Jack Valenti.

3:10 P.M.: Prepared for nap and left instructions that he be awakened at 5:15.

3:30 P.M.: Unrecorded call to Bill Moyers.

3:34 P.M.: Unrecorded call to Valenti.

3:40 P.M.: Unrecorded call to Speaker John McCormack.

3:47 P.M.: Unrecorded call to Jenkins.

4:00 P.M.: Unrecorded call to Larry O'Brien.

4:16 P.M.: Unrecorded call from Reedy.

4:39 P.M.: Unrecorded call to Valenti.

4:52 P.M.: Returned to the office, where Vicki McCammon informed him of pending calls from O'Brien and Robert Anderson.

4:58 P.M.

From Larry O'Brien[50]

Larry O'Brien called the President with an update on the head count for the bill to increase the federal debt ceiling.[51]

President Johnson: You didn't miss but one.

Larry O'Brien: Well, now you gave me this other one. [*Both chuckle heartily.*] I had that 204, and you gave me this other one—I had a heart attack. I chased [Carl] Albert for 20 minutes, but couldn't catch up with him. The roll call started.

---

50. Tape WH6406.10, Citation #3778, Recordings of Telephone Conversations—White House Series, Recordings and Transcripts of Conversations and Meetings, Lyndon B. Johnson Library.
51. For the debt limit, see Larry O'Brien to Johnson, 6:40 P.M., 10 June 1964; and Johnson to George Smathers, 2:48 P.M., 1 June 1964, in this volume.

President Johnson: Mmm. . . . 203 to 182.

O'Brien: Yeah.

President Johnson: All right.

O'Brien: That's a . . . considerably improved situation over the last time around. I don't have it in front of me, but as I remember, we were able to raise the ceiling by an eight-vote margin the last time.[52]

President Johnson: Mm-hmm.

All right, now can we concentrate and do something [to] clean up our . . . our poverty?

O'Brien: Yup, I'm going to get into additional conversations with that now.

I have a memo, Mr. President, that is just completed here, incidentally, on the . . . our situation on civil rights.[53] Could I just send a messenger down with it?

President Johnson: Yeah.

O'Brien: Right now.

President Johnson: Yeah.

O'Brien: Thank you.

5:00 P.M.

From Robert Anderson[54]

Robert Anderson called the President with another recommendation for Henry Cabot Lodge's replacement, as well as with a number of other policy concerns.

President Johnson: Hi, Bob.

Robert Anderson: Hi, Mr. President.

President Johnson: How are you?

---

52. On 7 November 1963, the House of Representatives had passed an increase in the federal debt ceiling on a 187–179 roll call vote. *Congressional Quarterly Almanac;* 88th Cong., 1st Sess., 1963, vol. 19 (Washington, DC: Congressional Quarterly Service, 1964), p. 569.

53. O'Brien's memorandum outlined how the administration might prevent House Rules Committee Chairman Howard Smith from blocking the civil rights bill in his committee once it returned to the House following Senate passage. Lawrence F. O'Brien, "Memorandum For The President," 18 June 1964, "HU 2 5/25/64–7/16/64" folder, Box 2, White House Central Files: Human Rights, Lyndon B. Johnson Library. For a discussion of the memo and its implications later in the day, see Larry O'Brien to Johnson, 5:07 P.M., 18 June 1964, in this chapter.

54. Tape WH6406.10, Citation #3779, Recordings of Telephone Conversations—White House Series, Recordings and Transcripts of Conversations and Meetings, Lyndon B. Johnson Library.

Anderson: Fine. For what it's worth, I had a talk with Max Rabb.[55] Max Rabb is probably [Henry] Cabot Lodge's closest friend. They were in each other's weddings. Max kind of headed up here, at least part of the time, this effort that was made in Lodge's behalf. He has just been visiting with George, who's his [Lodge's] son.

He said, "I don't know." I just asked him as a matter curiosity. I said, "I'm just curious, keep reading in the paper about whether or not Cabot's coming home." And he said, "Bob, I have had no evidence of it." He said, "George certainly hasn't had any news from his father." Said, "I talked to George not over two days ago, and at *that* time his father hadn't said a word to George about it." And he said, "He hasn't written to me about it." He said, "He's written me several letters and thanked me for what I did in his behalf, and that sort of thing." But then he said, "I can't tell you that he's not coming. But I'm doubtful of it; I doubt that he's going to."

President Johnson: Well, I can tell you very confidentially it sure looks that way to me.

Anderson: Well, just—

President Johnson: That much of it. Now, I've got to be prepared whether he does or he doesn't. But . . .

Anderson: Yeah. I've got one more name for you to consider, and that's Lawton Collins.[56]

President Johnson: The former chief of staff?

Anderson: Yeah.

President Johnson: Yeah, we've talked about that, but they think he's slipped a good deal.

Anderson: Well, I don't know. He was in Pfizer, Pfizer chemical company, and was the vice president over there.

President Johnson: Mm-hmm.

Anderson: And . . .

President Johnson: We have that—I believe if we'd go that route, we'd take [Maxwell] Taylor.

Anderson: I see.

---

55. Maxwell M. Rabb had served as secretary to the Cabinet during the Eisenhower administration and had been active in the unofficial effort to promote Henry Cabot Lodge for the 1964 Republican presidential nomination. Later in 1964, he would join Anderson as a member of the National Independent Committee, the Republican business group that publicly supported Lyndon Johnson over Barry Goldwater. White, *The Making of the President 1964*, p. 418.

56. During World War II, General J. Lawton "Lightning Joe" Collins was a division leader at Guadalcanal and then led the VII Army Corps in the Normandy landings and northern European campaign. He later served as Army chief of staff from 1949 to 1953 (during the Korean War) and as a special envoy to Vietnam from 1954 to 1955. Martin Weil, "Gen. J. Lawton Collins Dies; Wartime VII Corps Chief," *Washington Post*, 13 September 1987.

President Johnson: Now civilians, the best civilians we got are presently [John] McCloy, George Ball . . . and probably [Roswell] Gilpatric.

Anderson: Now, let me tell you the other name that I thought of is this fellow who was . . . His name slips my mind. He was—his family's in the Reynolds tobacco company, and he was there under both Mr. Truman and Eisenhower. And he was the head of—

President Johnson: Gordon Gray?[57]

Anderson: Huh? Gordon Gray.

President Johnson: Mm-hmm . . . mm-hmm.

Anderson: [*with the President acknowledging*] He's certainly well known. He held high positions in both a Democratic and Republican administration. He is a Republican, I think. His wife died, and he married another very charming lady, and I don't suppose Gordon's over his early 50s. And . . . he's a good administrator. Good organizer. And he's one of those fellows that will work day and night.

President Johnson: Say, I talked to [Jack] Vaughn this morning.[58] He was here, and he sure was complimentary of the way you'd handled things. Said you came in with dignity and reserve, but friendliness, and had great respect for you, and he just thought that you were going to handle it wonderfully. He—

Twelve seconds excised as classified information.

President Johnson: He sure was high on you.

Anderson: Well, I'm glad to hear it because I think he's a very able young fellow.

President Johnson: He made a talk to . . . with Ambassador [Lincoln] Gordon from Brazil and some of the other ambassadors here.

Anderson: By the way, I heard a piece of news this afternoon that bothered me a little, and—

President Johnson: Before I forget that, they're going to have some luncheons here from time to time, and I told them to put you on some of these lists.

Anderson: Yeah.

---

57. A native of North Carolina from a family that ran the R. J. Reynolds Tobacco Company, Gordon Gray served as assistant secretary of war (1947–1949) and secretary of the Army (1949–1950) under President Truman; under President Eisenhower, he served as national security adviser (1958–1961); he also served on the Foreign Intelligence Advisory Board. Gray was the president of the University of North Carolina (1950–1955) and publisher of the *Winston-Salem Journal.* Wolfgang Saxon, "Gordon Gray, Presidents' Adviser And Business Executive, Is Dead," *New York Times,* 27 November 1982.

58. Jack Hood Vaughn was the U.S. ambassador to Panama. Robert Anderson was a U.S. special representative to the negotiations with Panama on the future of the canal treaty.

President Johnson: They're various businessmen and various people around town that come to them and come [from] out of town. I don't want you to feel you ever ought to come.

Anderson: Yeah.

President Johnson: If you're going to be here and any of it interests you, like the Prime Minister of Australia, the President of Puerto Rico, the Prime Minister of Turkey, or any of these things, you just look at them and be your own judge. And if I wanted you to come, I'll call you, but . . . as an aid to me. But I wanted you to come if you wanted to.

Anderson: Well, God bless you. I appreciate that.

President Johnson: Fine . . . fine. What was it you heard that was distressing?

Anderson: Ed Warren talked to me a little bit and told me that they were having a meeting in Tom Mann's office tomorrow. And—

President Johnson: Yeah.

Anderson: —it looked like they were—there was every likelihood that the Argentineans were going to take over all the oil companies.[59]

President Johnson: He told—Tom told me today that he thought they would.

Anderson: And, of course, the only thing—I don't suppose there's anything we can do about it.

President Johnson: He's doing everything he can. Said looks like he'd postponed it long—he had about run out of his rope.

Anderson: Yeah. Now, the only other thing I wanted to mention. I don't know your position, and I don't know how important you regard it. There is a bill pending here before the Senate Finance Committee by [Paul] Douglas called that—whatever the name of it is—that if you buy an automobile, you buy it on credit, they've got to tell you in the beginning that—[60]

President Johnson: Yeah, they've got that killed, I think. I think [Hubert] Humphrey and [Everett] Dirksen kind of made a deal, and they think they've got it killed.

Anderson: I . . . The only reason that I was concerned about it is

---

59. On 15 November 1963, Argentinean President Arturo Umberto Illia had announced that his government would annul all oil contracts with foreign countries and nationalize their holdings in the country. In June 1964, the Johnson administration was debating whether to apply the Hickenlooper amendment, which banned U.S. aid to any country that seized U.S. property. For a summary of the current situation, see "Telegram From the Department of State to the Embassy in Argentina," 20 June 1964, *FRUS, 1964–1968: South and Central America; Mexico,* ed. David C. Geyer and David H. Herschler (Washington, DC: GPO, 2004), 31:285–87.

60. Paul Douglas was a Democratic senator from Illinois.

because I think that would set back purchases for a while and with all these—dealers got to learning their arithmetic.

President Johnson: Mm-hmm. I don't know anything about it except Humphrey told me . . .

Anderson: Yeah.

President Johnson: . . . that it was a loosely drawn and questionable bill, and Dirksen is very anxious—killing it, and he was going to kind of play under the cover with him a little bit even though Douglas raised hell.

Anderson: Well, I think even if they—just as long as it doesn't get a push from your house or—

President Johnson: No.

Anderson: —anybody like that, why [*unclear*].

President Johnson: No . . . no. No, no.

Anderson: Mr. President, I'll keep trying to think of names. Gordon Gray may or may not—

President Johnson: Thank you, Bob.

Anderson: —[*unclear*].

President Johnson: Bye.

5:06 P.M.: Unrecorded call to McGeorge Bundy.

5:07 P.M.

From Larry O'Brien[61]

Confident of the imminent passage of the civil rights bill in the Senate, administration officials had turned their attention to how they would obtain House approval of the bill as amended by the Senate (the House had passed the bill on February 10). Earlier in the day, Special Assistant for Congressional Relations Larry O'Brien had sent the President a memorandum outlining a series of political maneuvers through which the bill could be moved out of the House Rules Committee—where the powerful chairman, Howard Smith of Virginia, would have a chance to block or at least delay the bill by denying it a new rule. O'Brien had suggested that if the administration could gain the support of either a few south-

---

61. Tape WH6406.10, Citation #3780, Recordings of Telephone Conversations—White House Series, Recordings and Transcripts of Conversations and Meetings, Lyndon B. Johnson Library.

ern Democrats or Republicans on the Rules Committee, the bill could be taken from Smith's control.

O'Brien touched only briefly on Smith in this call, however, as he and Johnson instead discussed the potential schedule for the amended civil rights bill in the House in conjunction with the economic opportunity (poverty) and Appalachia bills, as well as the Republican national political convention that would take place in San Francisco June 13–16.

President Johnson: Yeah. The Speaker's calling me on 9–1; I thought I better talk to you first, though.

Larry O'Brien: [*chuckling*] All right.

Did you see that memo I sent down on civil rights?[62]

President Johnson: Yeah.

O'Brien: Yeah. I think this is . . . I don't pretend I have all—the answer to this damn civil rights thing, except it would appear to me quite probable that the first shot they would get at accepting the Senate bill might be on suspension on July 6. Now, of course, as the memo indicates, I just overheard a good deal of this, this morning. But Charlie Halleck was bugging them. He called them out of the office a couple of times to talk about getting out of here and, of course, trading off with him that *they* can get out. And each one—I told the Speaker. I said, "Hell, that means out of eight weeks left of the legislative period from now until Labor Day, you take one week and give it to them and one week and give it to the Democrats and that takes two weeks out of eight!" And, you know, the Speaker saying, "Well, it's tough to write a platform and have the experience, and all that." But anyway, you know, we'll have to get into that right away.

But the other thing that I wanted to mention while I thought of it, Mr. President, is as you know [Wilbur] Mills is going to mark up this Social Security package next week.[63] He told me he'd finalize his markup during the week. And I don't know what your schedule is, but I just thought I'd mention to you that if there is a possibility of a little social sit-down with Mills . . . And he mentioned to me that his wife was out to dinner the other

---

62. See O'Brien, "Memorandum For The President," 18 June 1964, "HU 2 5/25/64–7/16/64" folder, Box 2, White House Central Files: Human Rights, Lyndon B. Johnson Library.

63. A Democrat from Arkansas, Wilbur Mills chaired the powerful House Committee on Ways and Means and the Joint Committee on Internal Revenue Taxation. In this position, Mills would exercise great influence over the fate of the administration's Medicare legislation. See Larry O'Brien and Wilbur Mills to Johnson, 3:55 P.M., 11 June 1964; and Wilbur Mills to Johnson, 9:55 A.M., 9 June 1964, in this volume.

night, Polly, so apparently she may be well enough now to have a dinner or something.[64]

President Johnson: [*with O'Brien acknowledging*] I'll look at it. It's the worst week in the world: I leave at daylight in the morning and get up at 5:00 to go to California, and I'm gone through Sunday. Monday I've got the Turkish Prime Minister—

O'Brien: Oh, have you? All right.

President Johnson: —Tuesday the Greekish Prime Minister [*chuckles*] and Wednesday the Australian Prime Minister, but if I can I sure will.

O'Brien: Yeah, well, maybe we'd settle the [*unclear*]—

President Johnson: You check with me when I get back next week.

O'Brien: OK.

President Johnson: Now, what should I tell [John] McCormack? Just . . . What do you think?

O'Brien: Well, he's going to—I think, first of all, you have to point out that there's only eight damn legislative weeks that you can figure on getting any production out of this Congress from now until after Labor Day. And that therefore . . . And that [Mike] Mansfield has already stated that the Senate would be in session the week of July 6, so you're assuming, of course, that the House will do the same. You kind of get started on that. And off that . . . let's see. We're waiting for the final Senate action on this civil rights bill, and we know it's a rather difficult, intricate procedure— handling it in the Rules Committee. And we may find ourselves until July 6 on suspension. And why don't we just hold for . . . overnight on this, sleep on it, not come to any conclusions on procedure until tomorrow morning. The House is going to stay in session tomorrow, so we wouldn't lose a day there in getting the bill over from the Senate, in case they don't finish it today.[65]

And the net result of the whole thing is I think our assumption has to be the assumption I made to him today, and that is: Hell, Mansfield is saying that the Senate is going to be out for the week *of* the Republican convention, and, God, I just assumed right along the House was going to do the same thing. And then—so therefore, if that's what we're going to do and the House is prepared to be in the week of July 6, let's see . . . just what the consensus is among the leadership and Justice and others on the procedure. Should we bull this around with Rules, or . . . ?

---

64. Clarine "Polly" Mills had been ill for several months.
65. As O'Brien anticipated, the Senate would not pass the amended civil rights bill until the next day, 19 June.

And I think [Howard] Smith is trying to tie this into the poverty bill.[66] Christ, he winds up, and he'll still be having hearings on the poverty bill next week, and then he has the damn civil rights bill, and then he has Cliff Davis in the wings with Appalachia.[67] And, Christ, we may have to do some strong-arming.

And, God, if Halleck feels all he has to do is sweat us out on all this stuff and get out of here on July 1 or 2 because the—the next thing he's going to say is, "The federal government . . . the legal holiday [is] July 3." I'm looking at the calendar. That means that Charlie has got it all geared to get it the hell out of here July 2. We won't see these bastards until July 20! And he's going to screw up the whole damn program.

So I think the firm position that: God, we would be just amazed to learn that they were *really* seriously contemplating that House not being around the week of July 6. We start at that point and work backward and see just what kind of a procedure we can come up with on the civil rights bill. I said to the Speaker. He said, "Well," he said, "Charlie will trade off smooth progress on the civil rights bill and cleaning it up for a two-week vacation." And I said, "Well, supposing that for Christ's sakes you put the civil rights bill on suspension? Supposing it comes to that? On July 6, are you suggesting to me that the Republicans will just not come back?" You know, how the hell at this stage, they're just—So . . .

I'm a little bit loose on it, because I figure I'm more concerned at the moment about what the hell we can do with the damn poverty bill. I'm a little bit loose, and I don't think [*a buzzer sounds in the President's office*] the Speaker ought to be giving Halleck a concession tonight. Christ, we can worry about it tomorrow.

President Johnson: OK . . . all right. OK.

O'Brien: OK, Mr.—

---

66. Representative Howard Smith was a Virginia Democrat, chairman of the House Rules Committee, and a powerful opponent of the civil rights bill.

67. Representative Clifford Davis was a Tennessee Democrat and one of the primary congressional supporters of the administration's Appalachian development bill. *Congressional Quarterly Almanac*, 88th Cong., 2nd sess., 1964, vol. 20 (Washington, DC: Congressional Quarterly Service, 1965), pp. 288–91.

5:12 P.M.

From John McCormack and Lew Deschler[68]

Johnson spoke with the Speaker of the House and Lew Deschler, the House parliamentarian, about procedures that might get the Senate-amended civil rights bill through the House without a conference committee— and before any recess that might be required for the Republican National Convention.

Jack Valenti: Ambassador [Matthew] McCloskey.[69] He is . . . possibly has gone back. We've been on—
The tape then cuts to the McCormack conversation.
John McCormack: . . . majority of the committee. Of the Judiciary . . . of the Rules Committee, rather. Rules Committee. And then . . . they've got to bring it up then, at seven legislative days.
President Johnson: Here's the way I understand it: [*seeming to read*] "When the bill comes over there, three members can file a request for a Rules Committee meeting."
McCormack: Yes.
President Johnson: "After seven calendar days, including three legislative days, if he has not convened the committee, eight members may address a request to the clerk who [will] call a meeting on a day named in the request." [with McCormack acknowledging] Presumably the next day.
McCormack: [*to Deschler*] Now, Lew, here's the President.
[*to Johnson*] I'll put Lew on, and he—
[*to Deschler*] You tell the President just what it is, will you?
Lew Deschler: Hi, Mr. President.
President Johnson: Yeah. Hi, Lew.
Deschler: How you doing?
President Johnson: Fine.
Deschler: What's the question now?
President Johnson: [*with Deschler acknowledging*] I'm not . . . I haven't

---

68. Tape WH6406.10, Citations #3781 and #3782, Recordings of Telephone Conversations— White House Series, Recordings and Transcripts of Conversations and Meetings, Lyndon B. Johnson Library.
69. Matthew McCloskey, a major fund-raiser for the Democratic Party, had left his post as ambassador to Ireland on 9 June. He was also implicated in the Bobby Baker scandal over his role in financing the D.C. Stadium. *Congressional Quarterly Almanac,* 1964, vol. 20, p. 944.

got any. He was just telling me something, and he said he's going to put you on. I haven't raised any question. He just called me and said that [Howard] Smith wasn't acting. But I think I know what he was trying to tell me about when the bill comes over there. As I understand it, when it arrives, any three House members can file a request for a Rules Committee meeting, and on the expiration thereafter, seven calendar days, including three legislative ones—

Deschler: Well, now this—

President Johnson: —if he hadn't convened the committee, eight members may address their request to the clerk.

Deschler: Yeah. Well, here's the thing . . . the program on it. The first place, we've got to get the message from the Senate.

President Johnson: Mm-hmm.

Deschler: Second, they've got to make a request to take it from the table and concur.[70]

President Johnson: That's objected to.

Deschler: That will be objected to.

President Johnson: Yeah.

Deschler: [*with the President acknowledging*] Of course, we have to have a quorum here tomorrow, because you can't make the request without a quorum. Somebody raises. Then after that objection is made, I would assume [Emanuel] Celler would introduce a resolution providing for concurrence in the Senate amendment.[71] That would be referred to the Committee on Rules. Then the three members would present the Judge with their request for a "call special meeting of the committee."[72] He's got three days in which to consider that. Of course, he could wait three days, and then set the call of the meeting for the seventh day. So that's where you get your seven days.

Now, if he doesn't take any action within the three days, then a majority of the members of the Rules Committee can file with the clerk . . .

President Johnson: You mean within the seven days?

Deschler: No, after the—

President Johnson: Yeah.

Deschler: After the third day the chairman hasn't done anything.

---

70. Larry O'Brien's memo had outlined this step of the procedure. O'Brien, "Memorandum For The President," 18 June 1964, "HU 2 5/25/64–7/16/64" folder, Box 2, White House Central Files: Human Rights, Lyndon B. Johnson Library.

71. Emanuel Celler was a Democratic representative from New York and chairman of the Committee on the Judiciary.

72. Deschler was referring to Rules Committee Chairman Howard Smith, who was commonly referred to as Judge Smith.

President Johnson: Yeah . . . mm-hmm.

Deschler: So a majority of the members of the committee file with the clerk a request for a "call meeting of the committee" and that could be at *any* time . . . And, of course, you've got—One of the problems right now is you're going to have to get some Republican members in order to get the eight.[73] [*Pauses.*]

President Johnson: Mm-hmm. [*Pause.*]

Deschler: And, of course, the Republicans are—

President Johnson: Well, now, that would—

Deschler: You understand what they're doing: They're saying, "Well, look, if we don't get two weeks off for our convention, why, we're not going to help." That's what [*unclear*] was saying.

President Johnson: Well, I'd just point that up to them because they've been blackmailing all year, and I think they ought to show what a blind opposition they are because we'll have to make that . . . We'll just have to go to the country with it. They're against everything: They're against debt; they're against excise tax; they're against poverty.

Deschler: Well, they—

President Johnson: They're filibustering everything. And I—

Deschler: They won't take that tack, Mr. President. What they'll say is, "Well, wait a minute. We're not going to go for concurring in the Senate [*unclear*]. We think you better send it to conference."

President Johnson: Mm-hmm.

Deschler: See, they can play that one.

President Johnson: That's all right. Let them do—let them take on those Negroes. [*Chuckles.*]

Deschler: Yeah, well, I'm—

President Johnson: Yeah.

Deschler: —I'm trying to point out—

President Johnson: That's what I'd do. I'd just . . . I sure think they oughtn't to give them two weeks off there when we only got eight between now and Labor Day, and we haven't got any of our program through. Unless we just want to admit that we're defeated. Get in bad shape as they're in.

Deschler: Well, that's something you-all are going to have to decide.

President Johnson: Yeah . . . yeah.

Deschler: They're going to scream like hell if they don't have time off for their convention [*unclear*].

---

73. Although the majority Democrats held ten seats on the Rules Committee, five were southern Democrats (including Howard Smith).

President Johnson: All right. OK.

Deschler: Want to talk with the Speaker again?

President Johnson: Yeah. Yeah, I guess. He called me. I'm just listening. He put you on, and I haven't raised any question with him.

McCormack: What?

President Johnson: Yes, Mr. Speaker.

McCormack: Well, there's the problem: the—

President Johnson: Yeah.

McCormack: —you've got to have Republican votes on the signature to get a majority because you can't get . . . hardly expect [James] Trimble to sign a petition, fighting for his life.[74] He's a hell of a fellow, none better. And Carl Elliott, of course, while he was defeated—I don't know what Carl would do.[75] Then, with that you wouldn't have . . . The most we could figure on is probably . . .

[*to Deschler*] Six Democratic votes is it?

[*to Johnson*] Would be the most we could get is six Democratic—

President Johnson: Mr. Speaker, I'd rather never get a vote or a bill or anything than let Charlie Halleck tell me when I could meet and when I didn't. I think that's the most blackmail thing I ever heard.

McCormack: [*Unclear*]—

President Johnson: That's what he's been—they've been telling me for a *month* that he was not going to—he's going to get an extra week for convention or he wasn't going to let civil rights pass. I'd tell him to go straight to hell. If he don't believe in civil rights and won't give you a vote, I'd point it up to the world. Even if we didn't get a vote.

McCormack: Well, he hasn't got any promise from us [*unclear*]—

President Johnson: No, I know it, but I'd . . . If what you want is my opinion, that's what I'd tell him. I think he's just too goddamned big for his britches. And I'd let him hold civil rights if he wants to. Just, by God—

McCormack: Well, he—

President Johnson: —just say that the price he's made is too big for you to pay. That's two damn weeks' vacation.

McCormack: He hasn't got away with anything. He thought it at Christmas. Now [*unclear*]—[76]

---

74. James Trimble was an Arkansas Democrat; rather than "fighting for his life" politically, he would win reelection in 1964 with 54.7 percent of the vote in his district. *Congressional Quarterly Almanac*, 1964, vol. 20, p.1025.

75. Carl Elliott was a Democratic representative from Alabama and an unsuccessful candidate for re-nomination in 1964. See Carl Albert to Johnson, 12:44 P.M., 9 June 1964, in this volume.

76. McCormack may have been referring to Johnson's December 1963 victory on a foreign aid bill despite Halleck's opposition.

President Johnson: No . . . Well, that's my judgment, whatever it's worth.

McCormack: You're proceeding on the theory he got away with things. Well, he—

President Johnson: No, no. I'm not proceeding with a theory. I'm proceeding with the theory that he's trying to blackmail us, and I assume that you want my opinion of it, and I've given it.

McCormack: Well, that's—Well, of course, we want your opinion. I'd always want that.

President Johnson: Well, that's my opinion.

McCormack: [*Unclear*] tried to do before Christmas.

President Johnson: Yeah, I know it. And I know it. That's what he tried to do a month ago, and that's what he's trying to do now. And that's what Dirksen's trying to do. They want to keep us from passing any program, and if we can't pass it, we ought to just admit to the damn people that we ain't got the horsepower. But—

McCormack: Well, I [*unclear*] doing pretty good. We've been doing pretty good. We won—these victories—he was confident he's going to lose . . . he was going to win both of them this week. But a lot of inside work was done that won both those victories. Last year, with President Kennedy, there was three extensions. One was sent back. There was three extensions. Then we had to come back for three months.

President Johnson: I've got a 5:00 meeting. You-all think about it, and I'll have Larry [O'Brien] talk to you, and I'll be back and talk to you about it Monday.

McCormack: All right. Here's Carl [Albert]. Say [*unclear*]—

President Johnson: I'm in sure big a hurry, though. Tell him.

McCormack: [*to Democratic leaders in his office*] Say hello.

Hale Boggs: Hi, Mr. President.

President Johnson: Yeah—Hello, how are you?

Boggs: How are you?

President Johnson: Fine.

Boggs: Fine. Here's Carl.

Carl Albert: Have a nice trip.

President Johnson: Thank you.

Albert: OK, sir. Bye.

5:12 P.M.: Walter Jenkins entered the office and remained until 5:21.

5:22 P.M.

From McGeorge Bundy[77]

Bundy called to report that an unnamed person, possibly a Cabinet member, had indicated that he had no interest in the post of ambassador to South Vietnam. The conversation may have been a follow-up to issues that the President had discussed with Bundy and Robert McNamara at lunch. Although impossible to identify definitively, Bundy may have spoken to Secretary of the Treasury Douglas Dillon, who had been mentioned in an earlier conversation as a possible candidate.[78]

An unclear office conversation precedes the call.
President Johnson: Yes?
Office Secretary: McGeorge Bundy is trying to call you on line 0.
President Johnson: OK. Now, I can't take any more calls. I've got a 5:00 appointment. They're just running me crazy.
Office Secretary: All right, sir.
President Johnson: [*with increasing volume*] Hello? Hello? Hello?
McGeorge Bundy: Hello?
President Johnson: Yes?
Bundy: I saw him.
President Johnson: Yeah.
Bundy: Negative.
President Johnson: Yeah, that's what I thought. What'd he say?
Bundy: Well, he went around. He gave me estimates on the various other people, which I used as a way of starting, and then I said, "Is this the sort of thing that you think—
[*apparently to someone in the office*] Would you?
[*to Johnson*]—"that you think someone in the Cabinet ought to do," and he said, well, no, he didn't really think so, and I said I thought it was the most challenging job the government had, and [he said], "Well, I can see that you would think that, but I've done all this sort of thing." [*The President chuckles.*] And he said—I said, "Of course, Bobby [Kennedy], we had to tie him down, keep him from going." "Well," he said, "Bobby never liked that Justice job, and he wants to be secretary of state, and how's he

77. Tape WH6406.11, Citation #3783, Recordings of Telephone Conversations—White House Series, Recordings and Transcripts of Conversations and Meetings, Lyndon B. Johnson Library.
78. Johnson to Robert Anderson, 11:16 A.M., 18 June 1964, in this chapter.

going to get there?" So my guess is that if you said that if he did it for six months, you would promise to make him secretary of state, he'd probably say yes, but not otherwise. [*Chuckles.*]

President Johnson: Hmm. Well, I wouldn't do that, so . . .

Bundy: I know you wouldn't. [*Chuckles.*]

President Johnson: That's that. Bob Anderson is not interested. I didn't mention it, but I talked to him, got every suggestion and told him what I wanted, and he fit the bill, but he didn't take it. He suggested Gordon Gray as a possibility and Lawton Collins.

Bundy: Well, I almost mentioned Gordon. I think Gordon would be a very good protection. I don't think he'd be a very good ambassador.

President Johnson: Mm-hmm. I never was impressed with him. I like him, but I—

Bundy: [*Unclear*] I think that's correct, Mr. President. He's the nicest man in the world and not the most effective. I never hoped to be greeted into government by a predecessor with more grace and generosity than he did.[79] He's a gentleman, but he's not an operator.

President Johnson: All right. I'm going to run, and we'll . . . I guess our best bet now is [John] McCloy, if he comes tomorrow.

Bundy: Yeah.

President Johnson: Run that one out and any other names that you can muster up, and you be on the telephone with me.

Bundy: I will.

President Johnson: There's . . . Read this report where they're raising hell about the way we reorganize the [National] Security Council, not having a . . .[80]

Bundy: Yeah, this is straight Eisenhower. He feels this personally and strongly. It was an affront to him when we abolished the Operations Coordinating Board, and he's taken my hide off personally about it a couple of times.

---

79. Gordon Gray had held Bundy's position in the Eisenhower administration.

80. Johnson was almost certainly referring to the recently released 1964 Republican campaign platform, which stated that "we will insure that an effective planning and operations staff is restored to the National Security Council." "Foreign and Domestic GOP Planks," *Washington Post*, 13 July 1964. Upon taking office in 1961, Bundy and President Kennedy had drastically reshaped the National Security Council and its staff, increasing its role in foreign policymaking, usurping significant authority from the State Department, and effectively raising the agency to Cabinet level. Bundy's most significant structural changes consisted of the elimination of the NSC's Planning Board and Operations Coordinating Board, both of which had been created under President Eisenhower. Andrew Preston, "The Little State Department: McGeorge Bundy and the National Security Council Staff, 1961–65," *Presidential Studies Quarterly* 31:4 (December 2001): 635–59.

President Johnson: Get us an answer to it.

Bundy: Sure.

President Johnson: OK.

5:25 P.M.: The President received a haircut at the White House barbershop.

6:02 P.M.: Returned to the office, accompanied by McGeorge Bundy.

6:06 P.M.: Justice William O. Douglas arrived in the office for an off-the-record discussion of Johnson's upcoming trip to the West Coast. Douglas departed at 6:19.

6:11 P.M.: Unrecorded call to Walter Jenkins.

6:15 P.M.: Unrecorded call from Jenkins.

6:22 P.M.: Met with Kermit Gordon, who remained in the office until 6:24.

6:27 P.M.–7:02 P.M.: Met with Attorney General Robert F. Kennedy and Burke Marshall.

7:00 P.M.: Received Secretary of the Interior Stewart Udall and his Soviet counterpart, Deputy Chairman of the Council of Ministers of the USSR Ignatiy Trofimovich Novikov. Udall and Novikov remained in the office until 7:20.

7:26 P.M.: Unrecorded call to Jack Valenti.

8:30 P.M.: Met with Bundy.

9:00 P.M.: Mrs. Johnson and Dr. James C. Cain came to the office.

8:58 P.M.

From Robert Kennedy[81]

Since at least April, Attorney General Kennedy had hoped to travel to West Berlin to attend a June 26 commemoration of the first anniversary of his late brother's "ich bin ein Berliner" speech. West Berlin Mayor Willy Brandt had invited Kennedy to attend a ceremony in which West Berlin's main square, where the President had delivered the address, would be renamed John F. Kennedy Platz. President Johnson had initially resisted the idea because of Kennedy's deep involvement with the

---

81. Tape WH6406.11, Citation #3784, Recordings of Telephone Conversations—White House Series, Recordings and Transcripts of Conversations and Meetings, Lyndon B. Johnson Library.

civil rights bill but had eventually relented.[82] Kennedy now inquired about whether he should also make a stop in Poland to speak at an unnamed university.

Johnson also asked Kennedy's opinion about whether Madame Nhu, the controversial wife of Ngo Dinh Nhu, the brother and close adviser of former South Vietnamese President Ngo Dinh Diem, should be admitted to the United States for a speaking tour in support of a new book (or as the President and Attorney General interpreted it in the conversation, to campaign for Barry Goldwater). The Kennedy administration had blamed Madame Nhu for increasing the instability and unreliability of her brother's regime. In the months preceding the controversial November 1963 coup in which both Diem and Nhu were assassinated, Madame Nhu had organized a women's army, had repeatedly denounced the U.S. presence in the country as worse than the Communists, and had led the Diem government's unpopular campaign against the country's Buddhists.[83]

An unclear office conversation precedes the call.
President Johnson: Hello?
Robert Kennedy: Mr. President?
President Johnson: Yeah.
Kennedy: I had thought that the State Department talked with the—I guess they had talked with the White House, but I don't know if it got to you . . .
President Johnson: Who?
Kennedy: The State Department on this trip. I had, you know, was going to Berlin. Then there was some discussion about going to either Krakow or Warsaw for a day and speaking to the university there, but I didn't . . . from what I understand, it hadn't been brought up with you, so

82. See Johnson to Bill Moyers, 6:03 P.M., 23 April 1964, in Guian A. McKee, ed., *The Presidential Recordings, Lyndon B. Johnson: Toward the Great Society, February 1, 1964–May 31, 1964*, vol. 6, *April 14, 1964–May 31, 1964* (New York: Norton, 2007), pp. 191–99; "R. F. Kennedy to Speak at W. Berlin Dedication," *Washington Post*, 20 May 1964; Arthur J. Olsen, "Kennedy Renews Pledge to Berlin; 70,000 See Attorney General Unveil Memorial Plaque," *New York Times*, 27 June 1964.
83. Dorothy McCardle, "Her Buddhist Mother Deplores Mme. Nhu's Acts," *Washington Post*, 24 August 1963. For Nhu's letter objecting to an initial rejection of her visa application, see "Madam Ngo Dinh Nhu to the Honorable Dean Rusk," no date, "Folder 6: Vietnam Memos Vol. XII: 6/14–27/64," Country File: Vietnam, Box 5, National Security File, Lyndon B. Johnson Library.

I didn't want to go or even contemplate going unless you thought it was advisable or helpful or . . .

President Johnson: I don't know anything about it. If you think you ought to, go ahead, but—

Kennedy: Well, I don't—I don't know that I *ought* to. I don't know that it's . . . I don't think it's one of those things. You know, I think it's just—

President Johnson: I wouldn't want to say not to do something, but I don't know anything about the wisdom of it. This is the first I heard of it.

Kennedy: Yes.

President Johnson: But I'd be guided by your judgment.

Kennedy: Well, I think that they . . . No, I don't know whether it's helpful or not, Mr. President. I'd had some conversations with the people at the State Department, and they thought that it might be, but I don't know that it would be, you know, so I don't . . .

President Johnson: You just use your own judgment, and I'll ride with it.

Kennedy: Yes. All right. [*Chuckles.*] OK. Fine.

President Johnson: Madame Nhu wants to come in and do a little campaigning between now and November.

Kennedy: For Barry Goldwater?[84]

President Johnson: Yeah, I guess so. She just wants to raise hell with us, that's what she wants to do. Would you let her in? [Dean] Rusk thinks you ought to, and some of the others think she shouldn't. [*Pauses.*] If [we] get [her] in, I don't know how we get her out. [Henry Cabot] Lodge says don't let her in. Said it'll hurt you in Vietnam, it'll hurt our war effort out there. [*Pauses.*]

Kennedy: Where is she now, in Paris, or something?

President Johnson: Yes. And Fred Dutton's told the Constitutional Party or whatever it is that's having her . . . she's speaking up in Long Island, something that's—they're going to approve the visa.[85]

---

84. The stated purpose of Madame Nhu's visit was a book tour, although the topic of her proposed speech to a conservative group in Flushing, Long Island, was "The Truth of the Viet-Nam Affair." Abba P. Schwartz, "Memorandum For: The Secretary; Subject: Impending application by Madame Nhu for a visitor's visa," 11 June 1964, "Folder 6: Vietnam Memos Vol. XII: 6/14–27/64," Country File: Vietnam, Box 5, National Security File, Lyndon B. Johnson Library.
85. Frederic G. Dutton was assistant secretary of state for congressional relations. For a draft State Department telegram indicating that the application would be approved, subject to White House approval, see Benjamin H. Read to McGeorge Bundy (and attached telegram), 15 June 1964, "Folder 6: Vietnam Memos Vol. XII: 6/14–27/64," Country File: Vietnam, Box 5, National Security File, Lyndon B. Johnson Library.

But it hasn't been approved. Schwartz is willing to turn it down.[86]

Kennedy: What is the reason for turning her down?

President Johnson: Well . . . [*reading, apparently from a memo*] "A person about whom there is reason to believe seeks to enter the United States solely, principally, or incidentally to engage in activities which would be prejudicial to the public interest or endanger the welfare, safety, or security of the United States. The provision of the law has been invoked on previous occasions in cases of exiled leaders whose activities in the United States are such as would impair our relations with friendly governments such as [Fulgencio] Batista of Cuba and members of [Rafael] Trujillo regime [in the Dominican Republic] and so forth.

"Lodge says the granting of a visa A to Madame Nhu to visit the U.S. would have a bad reaction in Vietnam. The memory is particularly vivid of her deplorable letter to Ms. [Jacqueline] Kennedy after the President's assassination.[87] Permitting her to go on another American speaking tour would not be understood or approved. I know the above to be [Nguyen] Khanh's feelings. She would be extremely difficult to handle in the United States, and getting her to leave would be very awkward.

"Conservative Party Club of Flushing reported today that the State Department has cleared the way for another U.S. lecture tour by Madame Nhu. The club extended an invitation to her . . . who is living in Paris, to make the keynote address at a truth rally here July the 7th. Madame Nhu—"

Kennedy: I don't think I'd probably let her in.

President Johnson: That's my instinct. I just said that I didn't think you ought to, but . . .

Kennedy: [*with Johnson acknowledging*] I mean, I think it's not a question of we are concerned about her; we let her in before and she toured the

---

86. Johnson was referring to State Department Bureau of Security and Consular Affairs Administrator Abba P. Schwartz. Although willing to accept a denial of Nhu's visa application, Schwartz had actually recommended that the visa be granted on the grounds that on 14 November 1963 President Kennedy had publicly stated that the United States would allow Madame Nhu to return to the country at her request, as well as "our policy of allowing free discussion of all viewpoints." Schwartz, "Memorandum For: The Secretary; Subject: Impending application by Madame Nhu for a visitor's visa," 11 June 1964; and "Excerpt from President Kennedy's Press Conference," 14 November 1963, "Folder 6: Vietnam Memos Vol. XII: 6/14–27/64," Country File: Vietnam, Box 5, National Security File, Lyndon B. Johnson Library.

87. A few days after the Kennedy assassination, Madame Nhu sent Jacqueline Kennedy a letter in which she compared the U.S. President's assassination to that of her husband Ngo Dinh Nhu and his brother, South Vietnamese President Ngo Dinh Diem, and stated that the First Lady's "ordeal might seem to you even more unbearable because of your habitually well-sheltered life." "Mrs. Nhu Recalls Saigon Coup in a Message to Mrs. Kennedy," *New York Times*, 25 November 1963.

United States.[88] And I think—but I'd do it on the basis that we've recognized another country at the present, another government there. I mean, not that we're concerned about her at all here, but that they figure—feel that it's harmful to the effort. You know, I'd put it off on something else, work that out in some way. But, you know—and I think that makes the more, most sense—not that we're concerned at all about somebody, no matter what they say here. But she's had this trip here, she toured the United States, and I don't know that it's helpful to our common effort in Vietnam. I mean, I think that's what . . . and that she can come in some other time, but she's had her full opportunity here. We've shown quite clearly that we allow freedom of speech.

President Johnson: Thank you. Thank you, much obliged.

Kennedy: OK.

President Johnson: Bye.

9:02 P.M.

From Robert Kennedy[89]

In the midst of the Senate's final round of voting on amendments to the civil rights bill, Majority Whip Hubert Humphrey—the Democratic floor leader for the legislation—had learned that his 19-year-old son Robert had been diagnosed with a malignant tumor in his neck. In this conversation, Attorney General Kennedy informed the President of the younger Humphrey's test results.[90]

An office conversation with McGeorge Bundy precedes the call.

President Johnson: I don't want them to be saying the President's sending him to Warsaw or directing him to go or approving him going.[91] I think that's a matter for him to determine.

---

88. Madame Nhu had been on a speaking tour of the United States at the time of her husband and brother-in-law's assassination. Ibid.

89. Tape WH6406.11, Citation #3785, Recordings of Telephone Conversations—White House Series, Recordings and Transcripts of Conversations and Meetings, Lyndon B. Johnson Library.

90. After surgery to remove the tumor, Robert Humphrey made a full recovery. Robert Mann, *The Walls of Jericho: Lyndon Johnson, Hubert Humphrey, Richard Russell, and the Struggle for Civil Rights* (New York: Harcourt Brace, 1996), pp. 427–28.

91. For this issue, see Johnson's preceding conversation with Kennedy. Robert Kennedy to Johnson, 8:58 P.M., 18 June 1964, in this chapter.

McGeorge Bundy: And then leave it—

President Johnson: I'm not going—I don't want to say at the other time I'm not going to let you go.

Bundy: No, you can't.

The secretary reports that Kennedy is on the line again.

President Johnson: Hello?

Robert Kennedy: Mr. President?

President Johnson: Yes, sir.

Kennedy: [*with the President acknowledging*] I spoke to you today about Hubert Humphrey's son. And I spoke to Jack Valenti, and he said that they'd sent some flowers out. They just got a report that, you know, he had an operation on his throat, and that it was malignant.

President Johnson: [*with concern*] Hmm, hmm, hmm.

Kennedy: And he's 19 years old, and it's . . . evidently, there are a lot of different kinds of malignancy, and this is the . . . they have the best chance of curing it. But it was a negative report, and I thought you'd like to know.

President Johnson: Thank you, Bob, I sure appreciate it.

Kennedy: Bye.

President Johnson: Bye.

9:02 P.M.: The President had drinks in the West Lounge with McGeorge Bundy and Jack Valenti.

9:32 P.M.: Returned to the Mansion for dinner with Bundy, Valenti, Dr. James C. Cain, and Mrs. Johnson.

9:57 P.M.: Returned to the office with Bundy and Valenti and received a short briefing with National Security Council staff member Robert Komer and State Department Chief of Protocol Angier Biddle Duke.

10:01 P.M.: Met with Prime Minister Hayato Ikeda of Japan in the Fish Room to discuss the new transpacific cable.

10:25 P.M.: Returned to the office and read the day's press briefings.

10:29 P.M.: Departed for the Mansion.

12:09 A.M.: Unrecorded call to Walter Jenkins.

Friday, June 19, 1964

Nearly anybody that we have in the South has got some problems. I have them; you have them. It's the biggest handicap both of us have, and I think it's our greatest asset that we live there, but they also—they're the most prejudiced people in the world, these Yankees.

—President Johnson to Luther Hodges

If they'll observe the law, then we won't have to take pistols and enforce it.

—President Johnson to Roy Wilkins

One year to the day after President Kennedy had first submitted the civil rights bill to Congress, the Senate approved the much revised legislation in a 73–27 vote early in the evening of June 19. Commenting on the bill's passage, President Johnson highlighted its moral dimensions, but also noted that the legislation reflected the centrality of respect for the law in the United States—implicitly emphasizing the need for peaceful and nonconfrontational implementation of the desegregation measures required by the bill. He also linked the bill to his wider domestic policy agenda, arguing that it challenged the country "to reach beyond the content of the bill to conquer the barriers of poor education, poverty, and squalid housing, which are an inheritance of past injustice and an impediment to future advance."[1]

---

1. "Statement by the President Following Senate Passage of the Civil Rights Bill," 19 June 1964, *Public Papers of the Presidents of the United States: Lyndon B. Johnson, 1963–64* (Washington, DC: GPO, 1965), 1:787–88.

Twenty-one Democrats (all southerners, along with Robert Byrd from the border state of West Virginia) and six Republicans, including leading Republican presidential candidate Barry Goldwater, voted against the bill. In a speech preceding the vote, Senate Minority Leader Everett Dirksen specifically rebutted Goldwater's charge the previous day that the legislation was unconstitutional. The following day, a *Washington Post* editorial argued that Goldwater's "vote against cloture and his vote against the bill itself express more forcefully than any words his unfitness for leadership. He has demonstrated that he and his party are incompatible."[2] The comment summarized much of mainstream, establishment opinion about Goldwater's stance, at least in the nation's capital.

Reacting to the Senate vote, Martin Luther King Jr. suggested that the federal government should undertake a test of the new legislation in a major southern city immediately after the bill became law. Meanwhile, James Foreman of the Student Nonviolent Coordinating Committee (SNCC) indicated that his organization would proceed as planned with its participation in the Freedom Summer campaign of voter registration drives in Mississippi.[3]

> **5:30 A.M.:** The President woke early in preparation for his flight to California and ate breakfast in bed with Lady Bird Johnson.
>
> **6:15 A.M.:** Completed his daily exercises, got dressed, and went downstairs.
>
> **6:53 A.M.:** Departed by helicopter for Andrews Air Force Base, accompanied by Democratic members of the California congressional delegation.
>
> **7:04 A.M.:** Arrived at Andrews Air Force Base and boarded Air Force One.
>
> **7:10 A.M.:** Air Force One departed for California.
>
> **7:20 A.M.:** Walked around the cabin of Air Force One and shook hands with all passengers.
>
> **8:20 A.M.–11:15 A.M.:** Slept in his private compartment.
>
> **11:15 A.M.:** Woke up and ate a "light lunch."
>
> **11:55 A.M. (EST)/8:55 A.M. (PST):** Air Force One landed at Edwards Air Force Base, where California Governor Edmund "Pat" Brown,

---

2. "Redress of Grievances," *Washington Post*, 20 June 1964; E. W. Kenworthy, "Civil Rights Bill Passed, 73–27; Johnson Urges All to Comply; Dirksen Berates Goldwater," *New York Times*, 20 June 1964.
3. Steven Gerstel, "Negro Leaders Plan Immediate Test of Rights Bill," *Washington Post*, 20 June 1964; Bernard J. Roswig, "St. Augustine Jury Turns Down Dr. King's Plan to End Protests," *Washington Post*, 20 June 1964.

officials from the Air Force base, and large crowds of onlookers greeted the President.

9:00 A.M.: Spoke for five minutes and then went to the fence line to shake hands with members of the crowd.

9:15 A.M.–9:35 A.M.: Traveled by motorcade on an inspection tour of some of the advanced aircraft at Edwards, including the C141A Starlifter plane, the F-5A/B tactical fighter plane, the F-4C Phantom II plane, and the X-15 rocket plane. Accompanied by NASA Director James Webb, Johnson also viewed a NASA Lunar Landing Craft.

9:35 A.M.: Returned by motorcade to Edwards Air Force Base and again left his car to shake hands with people in the crowd.

9:45 A.M.: Boarded Air Force One, joined by Governor Brown. Prior to departure, he accepted a model of the X-15 rocket plane.

9:55 A.M.: Departed Edwards Air Force Base onboard Air Force One.

10:05 A.M.: Ate lunch onboard Air Force One with Governor Brown, California Democratic Senate nominee (and former Kennedy and Johnson press secretary) Pierre Salinger, Democratic National Committee Chairman John Bailey, Jack Valenti, Bill Moyers, George Reedy, and other officials.

10:50 A.M.: Landed at San Francisco International Airport, where San Francisco Mayor Jack Shelley and a number of area congressmen met the President.

10:52 A.M.: Departed by helicopter with other members of the presidential party for Concord, California, located east of San Francisco Bay.

11:07 A.M.: Arrived in Concord.

11:15 A.M.: After introductory remarks by Governor Brown, the President spoke and participated in groundbreaking ceremonies for the Bay Area Rapid Transit System.

11:31 A.M.–11:45 A.M.: Left Concord by helicopter and arrived at the Coast Guard Station, San Francisco International Airport.

11:50 A.M.–12:45 P.M.: Motorcaded from airport to the new San Francisco federal building, with one stop to change cars.

12:50 P.M.: Spoke at the dedication ceremony for the federal building.

1:10 P.M.: Motorcaded to Fairmont Hotel.

1:35 P.M.: Was escorted by the owner and general manager of the hotel to the presidential suite.

1:45 P.M.: Went to the suite's bedroom and changed into his pajamas.

1:50 P.M.: Napped for an unrecorded amount of time before placing his first phone call of the day.

2:15 P.M.

To George Taylor[4]

During an April crisis over an impending strike in the railroad industry, Johnson had called on George W. Taylor, a professor at the University of Pennsylvania's Wharton School of Business, to serve as a federal mediator.[5] Working closely with Secretary of Labor Willard Wirtz and to a lesser extent Johnson himself, Taylor had played a key role in averting a strike. The President had been impressed with Taylor's work and now called him at the New Jersey shore to ask him to serve as the director of the new Community Relations Service that would be created by the Civil Rights Act. The position would eventually go to former Florida Governor Leroy Collins.[6]

President Johnson: I've got some bad news for you.
George Taylor: Got bad news?
President Johnson: Yeah.
Taylor: That's too bad. We're at the [*chuckles*] seashore on vacation.
President Johnson: Are you?
Taylor: [*chuckling*] Yes. [*serious*] But that's all right.
President Johnson: [*with Taylor acknowledging*] Doctor, this civil rights bill sets up a conciliation service. We've got 19 states in the Union that do not have any civil rights laws or any accommodations section. I

---

4. Tape WH6406.11, Citation #3786, Recordings of Telephone Conversations—White House Series, Recordings and Transcripts of Conversations and Meetings, Lyndon B. Johnson Library.
5. A well-known specialist in industrial relations, Taylor had in the past served as an "impartial umpire," brokering labor disputes in the hosiery industry and between General Motors and the United Auto Workers. He had also served as the head of the War Labor Board during World War II. Nelson Lichtenstein, *The Most Dangerous Man in Detroit: Walter Reuther and the Fate of American Labor* (New York: Basic Books, 1995), pp. 146–53.
6. For an earlier discussion of the appointment, including a reference to Taylor as a leading choice "if we don't go South" (in the President's words), see Robert Kennedy to Johnson, 12:55 P.M., 18 June 1964, in this volume. On Taylor's role in the railroad negotiations, see Eric Goldman, *The Tragedy of Lyndon Johnson* (New York: Dell, 1968), p. 103.

want to write to those governors and talk to those governors and go see those governors and have my representatives see them, call in any top men in the United States I can, because we're going to have bloodshed if we don't. It's strongly approaching that now. This bill provides for . . .

Taylor: Has the bill passed, Mr. President?

President Johnson: [*with Taylor acknowledging*] I haven't talked this day, but they had a few hours left, and it's due to pass the Senate today, and then it goes to the House, where it'll be there for several days. I want to have a television appearance and tell the people what I'm going to do.

But there's not a Cabinet place I have or anything else that's as important to me in the next six months as trying to keep down violence and bloodshed and having someone with some experience direct and kind of build this conciliation service, and I've looked all over the United States. I hate to call on you, but I just don't know how I can find anybody that's up to your stature in this job, and everybody recognize—

Taylor: I don't know much about this area, you know.

President Johnson: Sir?

Taylor: I really don't know much about this area.

President Johnson: Well, that may be an asset.

Taylor: Well, it's . . .

President Johnson: I have talked to the various groups and checked it out pretty carefully. Everybody has respect and confidence in you, and I just think that we could—I would call anybody you wanted me to. I'd turn over anybody in the government you wanted. I'd make it the first call because this is just going to be a bloody thing unless we take some leadership and tell these folks what they can do and so forth, and—

Taylor: When are you planning to make your announcement?

President Johnson: Oh, as soon as the bill passes and I sign the bill; probably simultaneously with signing a bill.

Taylor: I really feel so . . . so deficient, you know?

President Johnson: Oh, you don't—you're not deficient at all. You don't . . . You've got a Justice Department that will be yours to command, and you got a Commerce Department that'll help you with business any way you can. You got a Labor Department that'll go in with any of the problems of the workers. And you can take some of the better people that you know or that we can find, put them under you that you can dispatch to different places when problems arise. The main thing is to keep them talking to each other.

Taylor: This is a long process, isn't it?

President Johnson: Well, the test in our judgment is going to be the next few months as to whether both sides accept the proposition that they're going to get decency and fairness and justice.

Taylor: Of course, it's the greatest domestic problem, isn't it?

President Johnson: Yes, it's the most—our whole foreign policy and everything else [could] go to hell over this. Yesterday, in the swimming pool in St. Augustine, they jumped in, and police jumped in with their clothes on, and they started pouring acid in the pool . . .[7]

Taylor: I saw that on television. It was very distressing, wasn't it?

President Johnson: Most of the governors want to do, but they need a little leadership. I'm going to try to give it to them, but . . .

Taylor: Could I talk to my folks at the university and call you?

President Johnson: Yes, sir, but you just tell them this is . . . I've got to have a successor to [Henry Cabot] Lodge, and I've got to have you, and I've got to have—these are the two best men I've got to have for the next six months.

Taylor: May I call you, say, Sunday or so?

President Johnson: Yes, sir. Yes, sir.

Taylor: All right. I'll talk to the president of the university because this is a [unclear].

President Johnson: I'll talk to him too, if you want me to.

Taylor: Well . . . let me talk with him.

President Johnson: You do it.

Taylor: And if that seems desirable, I could tell you so on Sunday. How would that [unclear]—

President Johnson: That's fine. I'll do anything, Doctor. This is just . . . this has got to—if I don't have you, I don't know what I'll do.

Taylor: Well, you know, you're doing wonderful. . . .

President Johnson: Yeah—

Taylor: . . . and everybody ought to pitch in if they can, but as I can tell you on this one, I just feel as though . . . I'm so inexperienced, you know?

President Johnson: No, you've got plenty experience to deal with people, and that's all this is.

Taylor: Well, let me call on Sunday. Where will I call on Sunday?

President Johnson: I'll be back in Washington. You just call the White House and tell them that you're returning my call.

Taylor: Good, very good. Thank you for thinking of me.

---

7. For the events in St. Augustine, see the introduction to 18 June 1964 in this volume.

President Johnson: Just call me collect, though, so you won't be out anything. Just tell the White House that you want a report ready on a call the President's got for you.

Taylor: All right, very good.

President Johnson: And don't say no to me now.

Taylor: Well, I'll do my best, Mr. President.

President Johnson: Thank you.

Taylor: Thank you. Bye.

2:28 P.M.

To Luther Hodges[8]

In his next conversation, Johnson called Secretary of Commerce Hodges, who had favored Atlanta businessman Harold Walker as the director of the new Community Relations Service. Johnson seemed to be searching for alternatives in case George Taylor turned down the job. The conversation included a number of revealing comments from the President about his own identity as a southerner and about his fears of what implementation of the Civil Rights Act might bring.

Luther Hodges: Yes. Yes, Mr. President.

President Johnson: I've been working on this conciliation thing, and I've run into some snags on our boy in Atlanta [Harold Walker].

Hodges: Have you?

President Johnson: They say that we've got to have a man that the Negroes will accept and that they know and that they feel will . . . has had experience and will give them justice because if they don't, the first case he settles, even though they may be in the wrong, if he's not a person of some experience and stature and standing that we'll have a big issue there. And we've got a problem with a southern President, and I got to be mighty careful who I put in that place.

[*with Hodges acknowledging*] I've given a lot of thought, and I've tried to get this fellow [George] Taylor—Dr. George Taylor, who handled the railroad strike for me—who is the best conciliator in the business, but

---

8. Tape WH6406.11, Citation #3787, Recordings of Telephone Conversations—White House Series, Recordings and Transcripts of Conversations and Meetings, Lyndon B. Johnson Library.

he hadn't any experience in the race field.[9] But I believe they'd accept him. I haven't talked to any of them, but from a little of his background . . . but I've talked to him, and he asked to take it up with his university people. And I'd said I'd call you back last night, and I didn't get a chance to do it. I just got in my hotel here in San Francisco . . .

Hodges: I see.

President Johnson: . . . and thought I'd better call you and tell you that he says that he will talk to his university people and get back in touch with us.

Now, if he doesn't do it, there's been . . . the mayor of Atlanta [Ivan Allen] has been suggested. I don't think he would take it, and I don't know whether we could get him confirmed with our southern colleagues or not.

Hodges: Mm-hmm.

President Johnson: You might, if you feel like doing it, you might at least check it with [Herman] Talmadge, see what he thinks about the mayor of Atlanta.[10]

Hodges: All right. That's Mr. Ivan Allen.

President Johnson: Yeah, do you know him?

Hodges: Yes, I know him.

President Johnson: What's your estimate?

Hodges: Well, I don't know him in detail, but my estimate is that he's—be very good at this. I think the only objection, as you intimate, is that some people think he's too liberal.

President Johnson: Yeah.

Hodges: But you're going to almost have to have that kind of person. I had found out the same thing you found out, Mr. President, that the Justice Department people found that the Negroes did not know him.[11] But I don't really think it would make a great deal of difference, but if you feel that we better get . . . be *sure* we get started off on the right track, then I think we can—have to turn otherwise.

President Johnson: I think that if the Negro organizations—and they say they don't know him and that they'd be frightened of him—and the very fact that we announce him as someone that hasn't necessarily been on their side. He's been on the negotiating side on the side of the company.

---

9. See the preceding call, Johnson to George Taylor, 2:15 P.M., 19 June 1964, in this chapter.

10. Herman Talmadge was a Democratic senator from Georgia. For Atlanta Mayor Ivan Allen, see Robert Kennedy to Johnson, 12:55 P.M., 18 June 1964, in this volume.

11. Hodges was likely referring here not to Mayor Allen, but once again to Harold Walker. See Kennedy to Johnson, ibid.

Hodges: Mr. President, what do you think of either Bert Combs or Governor [Leroy] Collins, if you don't get the others?[12]

President Johnson: [*Pauses.*] Uh . . . I . . . I wouldn't be enthusiastic about either, but I . . . both of them are my friends.

Hodges: Yes, I know they are, and both of them have a good image on this kind of thing.

President Johnson: Yeah.

Hodges: I think the latter one would probably have the full confidence of the Negro. He'd have a little problem with one or two people, maybe even George Smathers, for example, because they have a little . . . they have had a little opposition in the past, but I don't think—I don't know that you could get him, probably couldn't because he's making a lot of money.[13]

President Johnson: Yeah, I don't think he'd quit that job. [*Hodges acknowledges.*] The more I think about it, the more I think that our best hope is not necessarily going to the South or to the North, but going to some professional that has made it his business to bring people together all of his life.

Hodges: Mm-hmm.

President Johnson: This boy Ted Kheel is wonderful in New York, but he's a New Yorker, and he looks a little bit too much like a Yale man and a Brooks Brothers type, but he's awfully good if Taylor didn't do it.[14] I think we've got to might near go to some fellow that on merit is experienced in this field and just put him in it, and then we've got to support him with everybody that we can bring into it.

Hodges: Of course, he's been used to dealing with groups across the table. It's a question of whether he can get out in the community to make the right kind of impression such as one of your governors could do, say, such as [Buford] Ellington or Combs or somebody like that.[15]

---

12. Bert T. Combs was the former governor of Kentucky (1959–1963); Leroy T. Collins was the former governor of Florida (1955–1961).

13. George Smathers was a Democratic senator from Florida. As governor of Florida, Collins had a reputation as a racial liberal, integrating the state's public educational facilities and pushing for integration of commercial facilities, such as lunch counters. Since leaving the governor's office, he had served as president of the National Association of Broadcasters. Glenn Fowler, "Ex-Gov. LeRoy Collins Dies at 82; Floridian Led Way in 'New South,'" *New York Times*, 13 March 1991.

14. Theodore W. Kheel was a labor relations specialist from New York who had served alongside George Taylor during the railroad negotiations. Goldman, *The Tragedy of Lyndon Johnson*, p. 103.

15. Buford Ellington had been governor of Tennessee from 1959 to 1963.

President Johnson: I brought up Ellington. Nearly anybody that we have in the South has got some problems. I have them; you have them.[16]

Hodges: Yeah . . . surely.

President Johnson: It's the biggest handicap both of us have, and I think it's our greatest asset that we live there, but they also—they're the most prejudiced people in the world, these Yankees.

Hodges: Yeah. No question.

President Johnson: So . . . I had this . . . the mayor of Raleigh suggested. Is he any good?

Hodges: The mayor of Charlotte, you mean?

President Johnson: Charlotte?

Hodges: Mayor of Charlotte, Stan Brookshire. He's good. He's not as well known as some of the others. He's done a magnificent job in Charlotte. Now of course the mayor of Raleigh, I just said it was Charlotte because that's the one that the Attorney General's crowd has been talking about is the mayor of Charlotte. The mayor of Raleigh has not had the same kind of experience, is not as well known. I know him very well too, Jim Reed.

President Johnson: What is he like?

Hodges: Well, he's just high grade, a former—he's a youngish man, about 45, a wonderful personality, very pleasing, would do an excellent job. He's simply—and he's a local boy. Just do a fine job. He's not as well known as a couple of the others.

President Johnson: Which would be the better one?

Hodges: Well, Brookshire, I think, [has] had more experience in dealing with it and would probably be better received since he's a little better known. The other man's got a better personality, but Brookshire's all right. I think we could get—in fact, I think we could get either one of those if you or I went after them.

President Johnson: Well, we ought to give some thought to those two and the mayor of Atlanta.

Hodges: I'll check out with—

President Johnson: I have a feeling that if we get somebody that's progressive enough to do the job, it'll conflict with Dick Russell or Sam Ervin, and they'll think that we're trying to embarrass them or something, and I don't want to do that.[17]

---

16. Hodges served as governor of North Carolina from 1954 to 1961.

17. Russell and Ervin were Democratic senators from Georgia and North Carolina, respectively, and both had adamantly opposed the civil rights bill.

Hodges: I don't believe they'll go that far, Mr. President, but you could—your judgment would be better than mine on that. I'd be—

President Johnson: No, no—

Hodges: Let me try it out with . . . let me try it out with Herman and see what he thinks.

President Johnson: Ask Herman what he thinks about—tell him we've got to have a conciliator.

Hodges: All right.

President Johnson: And that I told you that I thought he had awful good judgment and I had respect for it and I know he don't have much liking for this [civil rights] bill. And none of us are going to like it before it's over—it's going to be bloody as hell—but we've got to get the best man we can. Tell him I'm trying to get this Dr. Taylor.

Hodges: All right.

President Johnson: And if I don't get him, I'm going to have to get some others, and see what he thinks about the mayor of Atlanta.

Hodges: All right. Can we afford to talk with him without mentioning it to Dick Russell?

President Johnson: I think you talk to Herman, and if Herman would go for Allen, then you could mention it to Dick. If he didn't, if he turned him down, there ain't no use talking to Dick.

Hodges: All right. All right, sir, I'll check into that—

President Johnson: I'd tell him to keep it quiet and just tell him that you know what—he's right there in Atlanta, and see what he thinks about it. Tell him that the mayor of Atlanta and the mayor of Charlotte and the mayor of Raleigh and the mayor of Houston [Louie Welch], a few of these mayors, have had some experience in this field.

Hodges: Yes.

President Johnson: And we'd like to get a southerner, but we . . . if it's one that the people hate, if it's another [Estes] Kefauver deal, we don't want to do that.[18]

Hodges: Yeah. All right, sir. Do you want me to call you back out there [unclear]?

President Johnson: No, no. No, I'll call you as soon as I hear from Taylor and then we'll back it up.

Hodges: All right, thank you.

---

18. In 1956, Senator Estes Kefauver of Tennessee was Adlai Stevenson's vice presidential running mate in the race against Dwight Eisenhower. Eisenhower won a resounding reelection, and he carried five of the eleven former Confederate states, including Tennessee.

President Johnson: I'll be traveling. Good-bye. I'll see you Sunday.
Hodges: Have a good night.
President Johnson: Thank you.

3:30 P.M.

To Bill Moyers[19]

Still in the hotel suite, Johnson called Special Assistant Bill Moyers and requested his presence for a discussion of "our problem."

President Johnson: Bill, what you doing?
Bill Moyers: I'm working on this Irvine statement.[20]
President Johnson: Well, when you get through with it, [*unclear*] some of our problem.
Moyers: I'll come over right now if you're free.
President Johnson: All right.

4:00 P.M.

To Hubert Humphrey[21]

President Johnson next phoned Hubert Humphrey to express his concern about the senator's son Robert, who had just been diagnosed with throat cancer.[22] He also discussed the progress of the civil rights bill, for which he served as floor leader in the Senate. While the two men talked, other U.S. senators made their final statements on the civil rights bill. Seventy-three senators would soon cast votes in favor of the bill, assuring that

---

19. Tape WH6406.11, Citation #3788, Recordings of Telephone Conversations—White House Series, Recordings and Transcripts of Conversations and Meetings, Lyndon B. Johnson Library.
20. On 20 June, President Johnson would speak at the dedication ceremonies for the new University of California campus at Irvine. For the speech, see "Remarks at the Dedication of a New University of California Campus in Irvine," 20 June 1964, *Public Papers, Johnson, 1963–64*, 1:793–95.
21. Tape WH6406.11, Citation #3789, Recordings of Telephone Conversations—White House Series, Recordings and Transcripts of Conversations and Meetings, Lyndon B. Johnson Library.
22. See Robert Kennedy to Johnson, 9:02 P.M., 18 June 1964, in this volume.

Humphrey's greatest political accomplishment would come at a moment of personal pain.

President Johnson: Hubert?

Hubert Humphrey: Hello, Mr. President.

President Johnson: I heard about your distress yesterday, late last night, and I wanted to call you, but I got out before 7[:00] this morning and I thought it would be too early, and I just wanted to tell you I was grieving with you.

Humphrey: Well, bless your heart. Thank you very much. I think it's going to come along. We're a little worried, I must confess, but just one of those things. I just don't know. We were so surprised. He's an awfully healthy young fellow, but they discovered a little malignancy there in one of those lymph nodes. They're just having to take some more tests on him to see what it leads to.

President Johnson: Well, count me in if there is anything in the world we can do.

Humphrey: I know that. Lady Bird called. She was so sweet to do so. I'll—

President Johnson: I asked her to call this morning. I just got in the hotel here in San Francisco.

Humphrey: Well, I know it.

President Johnson: We had a mob out here of 400,000.

Humphrey: I'll bet they did. Oh, I'm glad you're out there. That's good; they need you out there.

President Johnson: Well, will you know a little more in a few days?

Humphrey: Yes, I will. I'm going out home tonight, and I'll be back Monday, and I'll surely let you know then.

President Johnson: Where is he?

Humphrey: He's at Saint Barnabas Hospital in Minneapolis. The . . . his physician is the head of the tumor clinic at the university and a very fine doctor. But we may want to have him checked out a little bit more around. We're just going to wait and see this weekend what these last tests [*unclear*]. They've been doing a bone marrow on him and, oh, lots of tests [*unclear*] . . . testing, what have you. But so far it's localized, as far as we can find, and that's a very heartening sign.

President Johnson: Are you—have you—when are you going to pass your civil rights?

Humphrey: In about 30 minutes.

President Johnson: Uh-huh.

Humphrey: And it's going to go through, about 75 votes or more.

President Johnson: Uh-huh. What's your interpretation of the significance of [Barry] Goldwater's vote?[23]

Humphrey: Oh, I think that he really didn't have anything else to do. It would have looked almost completely phony had he done anything else. He decided to hold his conservative vote.

President Johnson: Will it cost him the nomination?

Humphrey: I think it may. I think it may if he hasn't got it locked up, and I doubt that he's got it really locked up. It's the big money in the East here, you know, Mr. President, to move in as they've done before.

President Johnson: I've seen them do it, like that—'52 when [Robert] Taft had Pennsylvania and Fine arrived strong for Taft and next morning, when steel got through with him, he turned a flip.[24]

Humphrey: That's right, and I think some of that can happen again.

President Johnson: What's the situation with our pay bill?[25]

Humphrey: The pay bill, Olin [Johnston] talked to me about it today.[26] He told me that there was some problems on the Republican side, and I thought that we wouldn't do very much about it until we got this thing out of the way. He's speaking now in terms of floor action. The pay bill, we ought to be ready to take that up here next week.

President Johnson: You sure ought to, because everybody—the

---

23. Goldwater had spoken in opposition to the civil rights bill on 18 June, explaining that although he opposed segregation, he believed the bill represented an unconstitutional intrusion into personal and commercial affairs enacted by a Senate motivated by "emotion and political pressure." On 19 June, he voted against the bill. For a contemporary summary and critique of Goldwater's position, see James Reston, "Deeper Split in G.O.P.," *New York Times*, 19 June 1964.

24. At the 1952 Republican convention in Chicago, with delegates closely split between General Dwight Eisenhower and Ohio Senator Robert Taft, Pennsylvania Governor John Fine controlled a crucial block of more than 30 uncommitted delegates from his state (a majority of the Pennsylvania delegation were loyal to the county chairman and were already pledged to other candidates). Under heavy pressure from his state's powerful and economically important steel industry, Fine eventually swung his votes to Eisenhower, helping to seal the nomination. Drew Pearson, "Eisenhower Went Far for Beginner," *Washington Post*, 11 July 1952; James Patterson, *Mr. Republican: A Biography of Robert A. Taft* (Boston: Houghton Mifflin, 1972), pp. 550–58.

25. For the federal employees pay bill, see Johnston to Carl Albert, 4:44 P.M., 9 June 1964, in this volume.

26. Olin Johnston was a Democratic senator from South Carolina and chaired the Committee on Post Office and Civil Service, which had jurisdiction over the pay bill.

constitution out here [in California], every state employee and local employee is tied to the federal pay wage.

Humphrey: Uh-*huh.*

President Johnson: And it means a lot in this state, and they're all asking me about it. They . . . some of them told us that we had some trouble in that committee. I couldn't conceive, but they said—

Humphrey: Well, there's trouble on the 10,000, that's the problem.[27]

President Johnson: Said that [Mike] Monroney is raising a lot of hell.[28]

Humphrey: Yeah, he is. He's been just acting up something terrific. But I believe we'll track him down on it.

President Johnson: Is Olin saying when he can report it?

Humphrey: He did not tell me that. But I'm sure that he'll have it next week.

By the way, [Allen] Ellender told me that food stamp here . . . he'd send it today.[29] He'd hoped to report it out early next week.

President Johnson: He's already had the hearings, then?

Humphrey: Yes, sir, all complete. The bill will be reported out first part of next week. So, we'll be able to act on it next week.

President Johnson: OK, my friend. Give your boy my love.

Humphrey: I will. I'll tell him you called.

President Johnson: Bye.

Humphrey: Thank you. Bye.

Almost an hour later, Johnson received word of the Senate's passage of the civil rights bill.

---

27. The original version of the federal employees pay bill had included $10,000 congressional, Cabinet, and judicial pay raises, but the resubmitted version of the bill tried to blunt opposition by cutting the raise to $7,500. The Senate restored the $10,000 raise for Cabinet members, a change that was then sustained in conference committee. *Congressional Quarterly Almanac,* 88th Cong., 2nd sess., 1964, vol. 20 (Washington, DC: Congressional Quarterly Service, 1964), pp. 416–23.

28. A Democratic senator from Oklahoma, Mike Monroney would take over chairmanship of the Committee on Post Office and Civil Service in the next Congress.

29. Allen Ellender, Democrat of Louisiana, was chair of the Senate Agriculture and Forestry Committee, which would report the food stamp bill on 29 June. For background to the bill, see *Congressional Quarterly Almanac,* 1964, vol. 20, pp. 110–15.

4:55 P.M.

From Larry O'Brien[30]

One of the architects of the civil rights legislation, Special Assistant for Congressional Relations Larry O'Brien called to tell the President that the Senate had passed the bill in an overwhelming 73–27 vote. Johnson noted this historic triumph in understated fashion and quickly moved on to press O'Brien for updates about the status of other legislation.

During the conversation, Johnson's boyhood friend Otto Crider and his wife entered the office for drinks with the President. In 1924, Johnson and Crider had traveled together to California in search of work. The Criders still lived in Cloverleaf, California.

Larry O'Brien: Yes, Mr. President, 73–27.

President Johnson: Wonderful, wonderful. 73!

O'Brien: Yeah.

President Johnson: Well, [*unclear*] . . . Then the fellow voted, didn't he, [Clair] Engle?[31]

O'Brien: Yeah.

President Johnson: I read a story this morning where they said the Republicans had ordered a straight party vote on foreign aid: 500 million [dollars] . . . cut.

O'Brien: Well, at the moment, we've got Sil Conte still swirling around the place, but he certainly hasn't joined in anything like that.[32]

President Johnson: You ought to see the *New York Times* story.[33] I read

---

30. Tape WH6406.11, Citation #3790, Recordings of Telephone Conversations—White House Series, Recordings and Transcripts of Conversations and Meetings, Lyndon B. Johnson Library.
31. Despite being fatally ill and rendered almost mute by a brain tumor, Clair Engle, Democrat of California, was wheeled into Senate chambers to cast his voice vote, which he did softly. He died a little over a month later, and Johnson's former press secretary, Pierre Salinger, was appointed to serve out the final three months of Engle's term. "Engle Votes in Wheel Chair," *New York Times*, 20 June 1964; "Naming of Salinger to Senate Is Upheld by California Court," *New York Times*, 11 August 1964.
32. Silvio Conte was a Republican representative from Massachusetts and a member of the House Appropriations Committee's Subcommittee on Foreign Operations—which had jurisdiction over the foreign aid appropriations bill. For background on the issue, see George Mahon to Johnson, 1:48 P.M., 15 June 1964, in this volume.
33. The *Times* story reported that House Minority Leader Charles Halleck of Indiana and Republican conference chairman Gerald Ford of Michigan were lobbying Republican members of the Foreign Operations Subcommittee for a party-line vote in favor of subcommittee chairman—and dedicated foreign aid opponent—Otto Passman's proposed $500 million cut in the foreign aid appropriation. Felix Belair Jr., "G.O.P. Will Seek Foreign Aid Cut of $500 Million," *New York Times*, 19 June 1964.

it out here in San Francisco. Front page says that they're going to cut it 500 billion [*sic*]. [Charles] Halleck and Jerry Ford and all the Republican leadership said that they . . . that was their orders.

O'Brien: [*Chuckles slightly.*] Well, Ford, as I told you, is exerting heavy pressure on Conte in the committee, and so is [John] Rhodes, and Halleck has talked to him at length, and he's pressing very hard, and they've talked 500 million to him.[34] But I talked to the Speaker this afternoon at some length on a variety of matters, the mass transit for the most part, but we got into this.

President Johnson: [*to someone in the room*] Come on in, and—tell him.

O'Brien: Hello?

President Johnson: Yeah.

O'Brien: And he's going to talk to [William] Natcher.[35] He called me a little while ago, and he hasn't gotten Natcher yet, but George Mahon was anxious for the Speaker to—[36]

President Johnson: [*to Otto Crider, who has entered the room*] Hello there, big shot!

O'Brien: To talk to Natcher.

President Johnson: [*to O'Brien*] Wait just a minute.

[*to Crider, whose responses are inaudible*] Hello, Otto. Glad to see you. You've got a fancy crew cut there, haven't you?

[*to O'Brien*] Go ahead, Larry.

O'Brien: So, that's . . . is just about where we stand there. Certainly, we haven't firmed up anything very meaningful because Mahon is saying that maybe this thing is—that this may turn out to be a cut in the vicinity of 200 million [dollars].[37]

President Johnson: Well, did he—what did—[what] kind of meeting did he have with his three yesterday?[38]

O'Brien: Well, it wasn't productive. Not certainly in the sense of holding

---

34. John Rhodes was a Republican representative from Arizona and the ranking Republican on the Foreign Operations Subcommittee.

35. William Natcher was a Democratic representative from Kentucky and a member of the Foreign Operations Subcommittee.

36. A Democratic representative from Texas, George Mahon chaired the Committee on Appropriations.

37. As Mahon had predicted, the subcommittee cut the appropriation by $200 million, the smallest cut in the foreign aid program's history and an amount that Otto Passman derided as a token. The outcome was widely interpreted as a significant Johnson victory. *Congressional Quarterly Almanac*, 1964, vol. 20, p.312.

38. Johnson was referring to Democratic members of the Subcommittee on Foreign Operations who would be swing votes between the administration and Passman positions.

to the full amount. [*Johnson acknowledges.*] He said that they haven't gotten any specific figure agreement, or anything like that.

President Johnson: Did he get any of them to say, though, they'd stay with him against [Otto] Passman on the 500 [million dollars]?

O'Brien: Oh, yes! Oh, yes. I honestly, and I will say this: that Sil Conte will never go with them in the committee for 500 [million dollars]. Never. That would be my view. Now, Sil isn't the bravest guy in the world, as I told you the other night, but . . . and I'm sure Sil would fold probably in the vicinity of 200. But . . . God, Conte would just have to show himself to be a total faker in the eyes of some of his press friends that he enjoys chatting with all the time if he ever went at 500. Christ, the *New York Times* would take his skin off.

President Johnson: Well, they looked like they were worked up about it this morning. You look at that story.

O'Brien: I will. How's it going out there?

President Johnson: Oh, we had a half million today.

O'Brien: No kidding.

President Johnson: Yeah, the biggest crowd they ever had, they say.

O'Brien: Gee, that's great.

President Johnson: Anybody. Said bigger than [Douglas] MacArthur when he was here.[39]

O'Brien: My God. Well, that's great.

President Johnson: We had a wonderful day: had three speeches, and I'm just getting ready to go make another one.

O'Brien: Yeah, I knew on your schedule you must be about due to head out again.

President Johnson: You hear anything on the pay bill in the Senate?

O'Brien: No. The only thing I've heard on that in the last day is that Johnston . . . Olin's problem is, he's telling everybody that he meets that this is the worst thing that's ever happened to this country, this civil rights bill. It's awful; it's ruined his state and what have you, and he's very, very bitter about it. And he puts that in the context of, "Oh, Christ,

---

39. In April 1951, during the Korean War, President Truman removed General Douglas MacArthur as commander of U.S. forces in Asia on grounds of insubordination. MacArthur returned to a triumphal welcome in the United States, stopping first in San Francisco where crowds of "several thousand" greeted him at the airport and a massive traffic jam followed his motorcade to the city. MacArthur continued to Washington and addressed a joint session of Congress before proceeding to New York City for a ticker tape parade. Lawrence E. Davies, "M'Arthur Is Hailed by San Francisco; Great Crowds Roar Hero's Greeting; Bradley Opposes Widening Korea War," *New York Times*, 18 April 1951; James T. Patterson, *Grand Expectations: The United States, 1945–1974* (New York: Oxford University Press, 1996), pp. 226–34.

these guys want me to help them on pay and all that sort of thing, and look what they've done to *us*."

President Johnson: Mm-hmm.

O'Brien: But other than that, there hasn't been anything, particularly. The committee has indicated in a first go-around situation, as you know, that they might want to raise the top executive to 35.[40] But, [Mike] Monroney is still acting up totally in the committee, and Olin is, you know, sulking. That's, I think, probably better to describe his situation at the moment.

President Johnson: Mm-hmm. [*Pause.*]

O'Brien: So there really . . . there wasn't a hang of a lot occurred around here today other than our conferences on mass transit and that sort of thing—[41]

President Johnson: How are you on that?

O'Brien: Well, we had a hard head count this afternoon, and it bore out—we had everyone up there at the Speaker's office—it bore out the count we had yesterday. We are at this point with 170 firm Democrats and 30 Republicans. And I would say that 30 Republicans, I'm a little more optimistic that it would be closer to 30 now than to 25.

So we're in striking distance of this, and it's going to be on the floor Wednesday to be voted Thursday. And it'd be a good one to put away if we can do it, and I think we can do it. We've got some work to do, but at least we are in a decent enough shape to move on from here.

President Johnson: Well, 200 will pass it this time of the year, won't it?

O'Brien: Yeah, pretty much so, but there again, we have to worry about our absentees too. [*Johnson acknowledges.*] But I think we have shots at about, oh, 8 or 10. I would think we could pick up from 170 to somewhere in the vicinity [of] 176 to . . . even at the very outside 180, but probably land around 176, [1]78. And I think those Republicans will hold.

The . . . contact was made with the textile people; for example, today, [Robert] Jackson and those people.[42] The Speaker and [Carl] Albert got

---

40. The pay bill raised the existing pay ceiling for the vice president from $35,000 to $43,000 and for Cabinet members from $25,000 to $35,000. *Congressional Quarterly Almanac*, 1964, vol. 20, pp. 416–17.

41. Johnson was referring to the urban mass transportation bill. See Johnson to Larry O'Brien, 7:00 P.M., 12 June 1964, in this volume.

42. O'Brien was referring to the administration's cotton-wheat bill, passed in April, which included a subsidy for the domestic textile industry, and probably to Robert C. Jackson, the executive vice president of the American Textile Manufacturers Institute. *Congressional Quarterly Almanac*, 1964, vol. 20, p. 98; "Textile Manufacturers Pick Head of Trade Group," *New York Times*, 6 April 1964.

on the phone with them and said that it was their turn now to reciprocate here and that they should produce some votes in North Carolina and South Carolina, Alabama and elsewhere, wherever they could. And by God, that . . . the Speaker did very well with them, and so did Albert. Said that they had always said that if cotton worked out that they'd be glad to help on something else, and now we're calling on them for help, so maybe stir up a little bit there.

And we've got these railroads moving again, and we're[43] . . . we got back to Jimmy Van Zandt and suggested that [William] Scranton had—he had sent a letter to each one of the Pennsylvania Republicans urging the vote for this bill—that what that governor should do now is wire his Republican friends in the Congress, if he has any, and put it on the public record that he supports this bill, and let's see now just what he's got going.[44] So we did a few things like that to stir it up.

President Johnson: Mm-hmm. Anything on poverty?

O'Brien: No. No, no new developments on poverty. [*Pauses.*] The thing of it—there's one [*unclear*]—yes, Albert said that there is some indication that [Howard] Smith might conceivably not have any hearings on poverty next week.[45]

President Johnson: Just go ahead and report him?

O'Brien: No. That he's afraid that if he calls the Rules Committee together that they'd probably try to pull the civil rights rule out. And he wants some kind of an agreement on Monday. They talked to him at some length, and they'd all decided to sleep on it and talk about it again Monday morning, and I guess what they're trying to get to is some kind of a deal. Halleck wants a deal, as you know, for that extra week.

President Johnson: They can't afford to go to that Republican convention without this. If they do, they're ruined.

O'Brien: I agree.

President Johnson: So we oughtn't to give an inch.

O'Brien: No, I agree, and I know you're not concerned.

President Johnson: And just tell them that they . . . Just tell them that they can't afford to go. And just tell them [*unclear*]—that would be the best thing [to] happen to us if he'd go.

---

43. O'Brien was probably referring to the administration's successful efforts to avert a strike in the railroad industry and the resulting political obligation of the major railroads to assist with the President's political and legislative priorities—in this case, lobbying Republican congressmen to support the pay bill.

44. Jimmy Van Zandt remains unidentified.

45. Representative Howard Smith of Virginia chaired the House Rules Committee.

O'Brien: I agree. Well, that's just what I said to them today.

President Johnson: What did they say?

O'Brien: Well, they . . . they haven't gotten into any deal with them; they're just sort of playing their cards close.

President Johnson: They know I don't want them to, don't they?

O'Brien: Pardon?

President Johnson: They know I don't want [*unclear*]—

O'Brien: [*with the President acknowledging*] Oh yes, sure they do. Sure they do. They have that clear in their minds. I think frankly that's what's concerning them because I think without that knowledge that you don't want them to, they probably would. [*amused*] I think that's all we've got going for us, [to be] very honest, because all I do is, like a broken record, keep repeating your view.

President Johnson: Now, somebody told me that they had finished hearings on food stamps, so we ought to get that up in the Senate early in the week.[46] You better check that.

O'Brien: Yeah.

President Johnson: Better check [Allen] Ellender and see . . . tell him I'm sure anxious for him to bring it up, and see when he'll bring it up for me.

O'Brien: I will.

President Johnson: And . . . what else have we got in the Senate to come up? Just appropriation bill?

O'Brien: Yeah, well, we've got . . . I'm going to be talking to [Mike] Mansfield in the morning, the first thing, and we're going to go over all this stuff that is on the . . . that the House has completed. You know, there are several items that he can . . . he has the list of all those items that you discussed with him last Tuesday, and he wanted to have an opportunity to go over this whole thing immediately after the civil rights thing was cleared away, so I'll be up there to see him in the morning.

President Johnson: OK.

O'Brien: Good luck. Good trip.

President Johnson: Thank you.

O'Brien: OK, Mr. President.

---

46. See Johnson to Hubert Humphrey, 4:00 P.M., 19 June 1964, in this chapter.

5:20 P.M.

To Roy Wilkins[47]

From the hotel suite, Johnson called NAACP President Roy Wilkins to get his view of potential appointees to the directorship of the new Community Relations Service.

President Johnson: . . . feel pretty good?

Roy Wilkins: Well, I do feel pretty good. I haven't got the official news yet. I've been at a—

President Johnson: 73 to 27.

Wilkins: [*surprised*] 73–27?

President Johnson: Yeah.

Wilkins: Mr. President, that's very good news.

President Johnson: Well, you're a mighty good man. You deserve all the credit, and I sure do salute you, and I'm mighty proud of you.

Wilkins: Mr. President . . .

President Johnson: Our troubles are just beginning. I guess you know that.

Wilkins: Yes, I know. . . . However, out there, we issued a statement, which your press office ought to have by now, from one of the afternoon papers absolutely disassociating and disavowing any involvement out there.[48]

President Johnson: Well, we had—I haven't seen any yet. I've got—

Wilkins: We have . . . I have a wire, if you'll indulge me one minute, a wire from our office in San Francisco said the following statement was issued today: Quote, "NAACP disavows any involvement in demonstration during President Johnson's visit. NAACP is not officially involved in the local area, regional, or national level. In fact, the executive committee of the San Francisco branch voted last night not to participate in any such demonstration, and it is understood that President Nathaniel Burbridge will so inform the public. Mrs. Pittman pointed out that it is against NAACP policies to picket the president and that all branches of

---

47. Tape WH6406.11, Citation #3791, Recordings of Telephone Conversations—White House Series, Recordings and Transcripts of Conversations and Meetings, Lyndon B. Johnson Library.
48. For the civil rights situation in the San Francisco Bay area, see Lawrence E. Davies, "Racial Activity Rife in Bay Area," *New York Times*, 21 June 1964.

the NAACP in the West Coast region were called upon to observe this policy." Period, end of quote. Now, that was given to the San Francisco press this noon, I imagine. I got it about 3:30 out here.

President Johnson: Mm-hmm. I haven't heard anything about it. We had a half a million on the streets. They said the biggest crowd that anybody ever had in the history of San Francisco.

Wilkins: You deserve twice that many.

President Johnson: Just took us two or three hours to get to the hotel, and I just came up and put in a call for you. I want to talk to you about this conciliator.

Wilkins: Yes.

President Johnson: Has anybody talked to you about it?

Wilkins: Nobody talked to me at all. I've been at Ted Kheel's to a party. You know Ted Kheel.

President Johnson: Yeah. Oh, I'm very fond of him.

Wilkins: Good.

President Johnson: [*with Wilkins acknowledging throughout*] I talked to Bobby [Kennedy] yesterday, and we think that a good deal of the success of whether we get this thing going or not is going to depend on getting the right man for conciliator. And we've thought of a lot—first thing we decided was we probably ought to get a southerner that had the confidence of our organizations, and maybe we could bring the two together that way and give us some leadership, and . . . but every time we run into one, why, we run into one that either wouldn't have y'all's confidence or wouldn't have the other side. [*Wilkins chuckles.*]

So we finally—I concluded that maybe we ought to try to get a professional. So I called Doctor Taylor, George W. Taylor, who settled the railroad strike for me. He's a professor up in Pennsylvania. He was the head of the War Labor Board during the war under Roosevelt.

Wilkins: Yeah. I know his name. He has a very good reputation.

President Johnson: [*with Wilkins acknowledging throughout*] Oh, he's a wonderful man. Bobby said he had checked with a good many people and that they all thought that he would be mighty acceptable if we could get him. Now, they don't know him in the South, but he's a fair man and he's got a judicious temperament, and he's kind of like you are: He doesn't shoot—he sees what he's doing before he moves, and he's quiet and humble, modest. I saw him handle these tough railroad boys pretty well, and . . . So I called him, and he said well, he didn't know whether he could do it, whether his university would let him off or not. I'm going to talk to him again Sunday.

I talked to Ralph McGill about a fellow down at Atlanta who's . . . who was the one that desegregated the Lockheed plant [Harold Walker], the first one that we started on, you remember?[49]

Wilkins: Yes, yes, I remember.

President Johnson: [*with Wilkins acknowledging*] He's a young lawyer there, and he's general counsel for that plant. Ralph McGill said he's just— we just couldn't find a better one. I called the governor [Carl Sanders], and the governor thought that he would just be tops, but . . . talked to Bobby about him, and we concluded after discussing it that he wasn't well enough known in the North.[50] Nobody had ever heard of him, and they'd just say, "Well, he's Lockheed employee, and he's from Atlanta, and . . . Although Ralph McGill and Gene Patterson and them thought he would be ideal, we thought we ought to get a name that could recruit some top conciliators to volunteer, and we could bring in people like Ted Kheel and others, then, and so forth.[51]

Now, wished you'd think about it a little bit and call me and give me any suggestions you got.

Wilkins: Mr. President, I like the southern idea. If you could find the man, it would be ideal, but I know that if you and Bobby have explored it, you've come up with people that you feel that the North wouldn't go for . . .

President Johnson: Well, we've got the possibility of the mayor of Atlanta [Ivan Allen]. What do you know about him?

Wilkins: Well, I would instantly give him my approbation. I would instantly do that.

President Johnson: They've also—

Wilkins: Now, the fact that he testified for the bill marks him in northern eyes as setting apart from the general run.[52]

President Johnson: Yeah, yeah.

Wilkins: I like the idea of a southerner on this if you can get the right kind of man because I think it will . . . it will get the confidence of the South; it'll, in a sense, rebuke the North by saying that the southern man is really ready to take the lead on this thing. I think it would make the road a lot easier. I'm not saying that Dr. Taylor isn't a good man. He is.

---

49. Ralph McGill was the editor of the *Atlanta Journal-Constitution*. See Ralph McGill to Juanita Roberts, 11:40 A.M., 17 June 1964, in this volume.

50. Robert Kennedy to Johnson, 12:55 P.M., 18 June 1964, in this volume.

51. Gene Patterson remains unidentified.

52. Atlanta Mayor Ivan Allen had testified in favor of the original Kennedy-proposed civil rights bill on 26 July 1963, shortly after it had been submitted to Congress. Richard L. Lyons, "Atlanta Mayor Backs New Rights Laws," *Washington Post*, 27 July 1963.

And if you can't do any better—I mean, if you can't get a southerner, he's the next best man.

President Johnson: Well—

Wilkins: But I like the idea of a southerner, sir.

President Johnson: Well, that's good. Now, we—there's a fellow, the mayor [Stan Brookshire] of Charlotte's been suggested. Do you know him?

Wilkins: I don't know him, but I can find out about him pretty quickly.

President Johnson: Well, you better look at him. They say he's a good man and he's done a good job with his problem, but . . . Bobby thought he was excellent. I don't know him.

Wilkins: Well, I'll be glad to make some inquiries right away.

President Johnson: You just . . . you just do it, and then you make some others, and let's don't get it out, but you talk to—

Wilkins: I understand.

President Johnson: —anybody you want to among your leaders and then give me any suggestions.

[*with Wilkins acknowledging*] Now, I've urged and just pled with Dr. Taylor to take it. I rather doubt he's going to. He's got to talk to his university, and if he will, then our problem will be solved. Even though he's not from the South, I don't think that they would resent him, because he's handled so much of the work, and I know this:—

Wilkins: Well, he—

President Johnson: —I know he's a good, fair man and he's got lots of savvy on how to bring people together.

Wilkins: Good. Well, this is what we need, of course.

President Johnson: [*with Wilkins acknowledging*] He knows how to handle—he had this old boy from Dallas that was just really kicking over on the railroad strike. He's the head of the trainsmen. He's got a strike going in Texas now, and he's just mean as hell.[53] But Dr. Taylor just took him and wrapped him around his fingers [*Wilkins laughs*] in about three days. And I think he could get in there, and . . .

---

53. Johnson was almost certainly referring to Charles Luna, the president of the Brotherhood of Railway Trainmen and a fellow Texan. Although initially a strong proponent of a strike during the railroad labor negotiations, Luna had eventually emerged, according to historian and Johnson adviser Eric Goldman, as "something of a cheerleader" for the administration's effort to broker a settlement. Eric Goldman, *The Tragedy of Lyndon Johnson* (New York: Dell, 1968), pp. 104–7. For the intensity of Luna's initial pro-strike position, see Willard Wirtz to Johnson, 12:20 P.M., and Johnson to Arthur Goldberg, 12:28 P.M., 9 April 1964, in David Shreve and Robert David Johnson, eds., *The Presidential Recordings, Lyndon B. Johnson: Toward the Great Society, February 1, 1964–May 31, 1964*, vol. 5, *March 9, 1964–April 13, 1964* (New York: Norton, 2007), pp. 862–70.

Wilkins: I'll give a lot of thought to it, Mr. President, and start work on it right away.

President Johnson: Now . . . I'm going to try to get up a little statement when the bill's signed. If you've got any ideas, I'd like to have that.

Wilkins: That's good.

President Johnson: The other thing, I want you-all to come by—and I want to probably come by either one of your cocktail parties, or one of your sessions, or have you-all by the office when you're there—but I want to take some leadership. I'm just afraid of what's going to happen this summer, like I saw yesterday at St. Augustine.

[*with Wilkins acknowledging*] Now, I've talked to that governor [Farris Bryant] two or three times, and our people, Lee White, says that he moved in a hundred people, then he moved in another hundred, and that he was given reasonably good protection there.[54] And I thought the result we got there—maybe I ought to try to call each one of the individual governors. Then I decided that would be too many: there's 19 states that don't have accommodation laws. So I'm going to write them all a letter.

Wilkins: I see.

President Johnson: I'm a little afraid to call them to Washington because I'm afraid the local demagogues will say that they're selling out to Hubert Humphrey and Bobby Kennedy and Lyndon Johnson.

Wilkins: Good. Yes. Yes, yes, you're right about that.

President Johnson: And we get them up there, [George] Wallace and [Paul] Johnson would probably take the lead and start ranting, and the other fellows be afraid not to outdo them.[55]

Wilkins: Yes. . . . That's right; that's right. Well—

President Johnson: So if you think of anything I *can* do. I thought maybe I ought to get one or two men representing me that kind of had their viewpoint, that would carry my message and go around and see these governors and just tell them that "you've got to call meetings now of all your people, and we've got to have observance instead of enforcement."

Wilkins: Yes. Well, I think—

---

54. Johnson was referring to the protection provided to Martin Luther King Jr. in St. Augustine. Farris Bryant was the governor of Florida. Lee C. White served as associate counsel to the President and, as a key adviser on civil rights issues, was monitoring the St. Augustine situation on the ground.
55. George Wallace was the governor of Alabama and Paul Johnson was the governor of Mississippi; both were outspoken opponents of civil rights, and Wallace had challenged Johnson in a number of Democratic presidential primaries.

President Johnson: If they'll observe the law, then we won't have to take pistols and enforce it.

Wilkins: That's right; that's right. Well, the . . . this is the thing—I'll think about that, and I'll do whatever I can to help. I can't . . . nobody can think of as many ideas as Lyndon Johnson. [*The President chuckles.*] I say that, I say that in all honesty.

President Johnson: Well . . .

Wilkins: But I'll do whatever I can.

President Johnson: Well, we've come a long ways in six months. [*Laughs.*]

Wilkins: You've . . . did you happen to see that—you must have seen that cartoon of the big Texas boot [*Johnson laughs again*] and the little fellow looking up there, the Republican, and saying, "I know they grow them big in Texas, but this is ridiculous"? [*Both laugh.*] I've thought about that.

And one other thing, if I may keep you one second.

President Johnson: Sure, I got plenty of time.

Wilkins: That speech of yours in Ann Arbor . . .[56]

President Johnson: Well, thank you.

Wilkins: This . . . I mean I'm supposed to be interested in civil rights, and I am interested in civil rights, and that's my first business, but I'm interested in my country too.

President Johnson: [*softly*] I know that.

Wilkins: And I think that speech in Ann Arbor was simply magnificent.

President Johnson: I want to thank you so much.

Wilkins: It was a magnificent speech.

President Johnson: We got a lot of nice compliments on it.

But you remember when we were talking: We had to get that petition signed to try to get it out of the [*chuckles*] Rules Committee.[57]

---

56. Wilkins was referring to Johnson's 22 May commencement address at the University of Michigan, in which he outlined for the first time the ideals of the Great Society that would form the core of his domestic presidential agenda. "Remarks at the University of Michigan," 22 May 1964, *Public Papers, Johnson, 1963–64,* 1:704–7.

57. In order to get a rule for floor debate of the civil rights bill in the House from Rules Committee Chairman Howard Smith, the administration and House leadership had to threaten to use a discharge petition, a rarely employed measure by which a bill could be brought to the floor without Rules Committee approval if enough members signed the petition. Johnson to Larry O'Brien, 11:50 A.M., 18 January 1964, in Kent B. Germany and Robert David Johnson, eds., *The Presidential Recordings, Lyndon B. Johnson: The Kennedy Assassination and the Transfer of Power, November 1963–January 1964,* vol. 3, *January 1964* (New York: Norton, 2005), p. 618; Robert Mann, *The Walls of Jericho: Lyndon Johnson, Hubert Humphrey, Richard Russell, and the Struggle for Civil Rights* (New York: Harcourt Brace, 1996), pp.388–89.

Wilkins: [*chuckling*] Yes . . . yes.

President Johnson: And we finally had to get 185, and now we've gone the hard way every bit, cloture and everything else, but we've done it.

Wilkins: Yes. . . . It was absolutely magnificent, and of course [Richard] Russell put his finger on two things: [*the President chuckles*] First he said it was Lyndon Johnson, and second he said it was the clergy.[58] [*The President chuckles again.*] And he hasn't been wrong much. [*Both laugh.*]

President Johnson: Well, I just hope that . . . I just hope that we can get through the summer.

You give me your ideas, and I haven't heard from you; pick up that phone and call me once in a while.

Wilkins: Thank you, sir.

President Johnson: Bye.

Wilkins: And keep on the good work.

President Johnson: Thank you.

Wilkins: All right.

President Johnson: You talk to Whitney [Young] about this, will you?[59]

Wilkins: I'll talk to him right away.

President Johnson: And anybody you-all think of down South.

Wilkins: I'm going to be down in Washington tomorrow . . .

President Johnson: All right, well—

Wilkins: Beginning about noon with our preconvention stuff, and then I'll be there all week long.

President Johnson: Well, I'll see you.

Wilkins: I'll be [*unclear*].

President Johnson: I've got the Prime Minister of Turkey and the Prime Minister of Greece and the Prime Minister of Australia all coming this week. I'll get to see you, though.

Wilkins: Very good, sir.

President Johnson: Bye.

Wilkins: Good-bye.

---

58. On 18 June, in his final floor speech before the Senate vote on the civil rights bill, Georgia Senator and Johnson mentor Richard Russell had lashed out at the press for making "emotional appeals" for the bill, at the clergy for engaging in a "philosophy of coercion" comparable to the Spanish Inquisition, and indirectly at the President for using the South as a "whipping boy for the political aggrandizement . . . of any political party." E. W. Kenworthy, "Civil Rights Bill Due to Be Passed By Senate Today," *New York Times*, 19 June 1964.

59. Whitney Young served as executive director of the National Urban League.

6:10 P.M.

To Kathryn Loney[60]

Johnson next placed a call to his first school teacher, who was in the town of Rough and Ready, California.

Kathryn Loney: . . . [*unclear*] is. I know how busy you are. [*Chuckles.*]

President Johnson: Well, they've been running me a little bit. I'm sitting here talking to Otto Crider from Johnson City.

Loney: You what?

President Johnson: I'm sitting here talking to Otto Crider from Johnson City.

Loney: You are? Oh, for heaven's sakes. Does he live there?

President Johnson: No, he lives up near Cloverdale.

Loney: Oh! Well, for heaven's sakes. Well, that's pretty nice; it's kind of like being home. [*Chuckles.*]

President Johnson: Is John Dedrich your brother?

Loney: Yes.

President Johnson: He knows him. He said he saw him not long ago.

Loney: Yes, I was hoping you could see him, Lyndon. That's the one I said looks, they think, looks like *you.*

President Johnson: Yeah.

Loney: Uh-huh.

President Johnson: Well, how are you doing?

Loney: Well, we're doing pretty good, and we were just wondering if we're going to ever go to Texas. Are you going to Texas this summer?

President Johnson: Yes, I expect so, but I don't know when. I expect I'm going to be pretty busy trying to get you Republicans to vote for me.

Loney: Well, I think so too. Well, we're working for you.

President Johnson: Well, you going to get me any Republican votes?

Loney: Yes. Some of them at least.

President Johnson: Otto said the Republicans are just thick as piggies around them.

Loney: I know they are. And they're all through there.

---

60. Tape WH6406.11, Citation #3792, Recordings of Telephone Conversations—White House Series, Recordings and Transcripts of Conversations and Meetings, Lyndon B. Johnson Library.

President Johnson: Well, I hope you're feeling all right.

Loney: Yes, well, we're doing pretty good. We're kind of getting the cattle ready for the mountains.

President Johnson: Well, I got your letter about them. We're doing all we can. The trouble is you just raise too many.[61]

Loney: Well, we don't have very many; that's the trouble. [*Chuckles.*]

President Johnson: No, but I mean everybody did.

Loney: I know it. That's—

President Johnson: They [*unclear*]—the supply's up from 92 million to 106 million.

Loney: Oh, yes, I know it. It's—

President Johnson: But we sent over a first shipload last week to England, and we think we're going to be able to export it, and the price is up about a dollar this week.

Loney: Yes, we got that. We were going to send some to market. How about the dam, do you think there's anything to do with that?

President Johnson: I don't know.

Loney: It's hard to tell.

President Johnson: Yeah, it is.

Loney: Well, this progress is going too fast for us, I guess.

President Johnson: Yeah. Well, I wanted to say hello to you and tell you I love you.

Loney: Well, I sure appreciate it, and this—it means a lot to hear from you. And you have to go back, I noticed from the papers.

President Johnson: Yes, I'll be going early in the morning.

Loney: Oh, boy, I don't see how you stand it, but don't overdo it, Lyndon.

President Johnson: I won't. I'm glad to talk to you.

Loney: And if you ever go to Texas and know it ahead of time, give me a buzz. [*Chuckles.*]

President Johnson: OK.

Loney: Thank you for calling.

President Johnson: Bye.

Loney: Bye.

---

61. Despite administration efforts to cut supply and purchase surplus meat, beef prices remained low in the United States in 1964, and the industry had begun to push for more aggressive price supports and expanded overseas market opportunities. See Johnson to Charles Murphy, 10:40 A.M., 5 May 1964, in Guian A. McKee, ed., *The Presidential Recordings, Lyndon B. Johnson: Toward the Great Society, February 1, 1964–May 31, 1964*, vol. 6, *April 14, 1964–May 31, 1964* (New York: Norton, 2007), pp. 456–59.

6:30 P.M.–6:56 P.M.: The President attended a reception in the Fillmore Hotel's Crown Room and then returned to the presidential suite.

7:02 P.M.: Autographed two copies of Willam S. White's *The Professional* (a recently published laudatory biography of Johnson). With the Criders still in his room, along with secretary Yolanda Boozer, Johnson complained that his eyes were burning, and indicated that he planned to take a nap.

7:03 P.M.

To George Reedy[62]

Instead of napping, Johnson placed a call to Press Secretary George Reedy to discuss a United Press International story that warned of the risk of war posed by current U.S. policy in Southeast Asia. Reedy suggested that the story, which appeared to be based on a briefing given by Secretary of State Rusk, might have certain salutary effects.

George Reedy: There's a UPI story out which says, [*reading*] "The United States is prepared to risk all-out war with Red China to prevent further Communist gains in Southeast Asia. This was understood today to be the position of the Johnson administration, which apparently feels its European allies do not realize the very real danger of a major conflict in the Pacific in Asia. Veteran observers do not discount the possibility of some element of psychological warfare in this stance; however, the grim view being taken by the administration is being underlined by comparisons between the U.S. commitment to defend Berlin at all costs and its pledge to save Laos and South Vietnam."

Now, Brom[ley Smith] says that that story comes from an off-the-record talk that Dean Rusk had today at the Overseas Press Club.[63] Brom called me from home, and he has a copy of the full text down in the Situation Room. He's going down to look at it. I don't think there's anything we can do about it. But I thought that you should know about it in case . . . in case somebody hits you with a question, or something like that.

---

62. Tape WH6406.11, Citation #3793, Recordings of Telephone Conversations—White House Series, Recordings and Transcripts of Conversations and Meetings, Lyndon B. Johnson Library.
63. Bromley Smith served as the executive secretary of the National Security Council.

President Johnson: Hmm.

Reedy: All Brom knows are some notes that were read to him of what Rusk said, and apparently . . . AP [Associated Press]—Brom tells me, I don't have that story yet—AP led by saying that a high administration official expressed dismay that the allies are not helping us more in Southeast Asia. But Brom says he thinks the AP will re-lead after they take a further look at their notes. And I'm trying to get—I'm sending out for a copy of the AP story now. And, as I said, I don't see anything you can do about it at the moment because you sure can't deny something about an unnamed high administration official. But Brom said that from the notes that he has, that Dean Rusk apparently went pretty hard in this background, off-the-record briefing, and that Chal—

President Johnson: Doesn't look like it's much off the record, does it?

Reedy: No, it sure doesn't. Chal[mers] Roberts was there, and apparently Chal has talked to Brom about it and is very excited.[64]

President Johnson: What about?

Reedy: About the hardness of the line and the indications of a war psychology. [*Pauses.*]

President Johnson: Mm-hmm.

Reedy: I'm waiting now for a call from Brom, and . . .

President Johnson: Well, they didn't—I don't see anything that he says that they quote. They're just . . . looks like to me they make it up, most of it.

Reedy: Well, what they're hanging it on, I gather, is that he's comparing this to Berlin. And of course the theory is that we made it quite clear that we were willing to fight in Berlin, go the whole hog, and this gives the impression we're going the whole hog in Southeast Asia. And I'm not even sure that this is bad, but that's another point. [*Johnson acknowledges.*] I think it's probably good maybe, but it . . . I didn't want you popped with somebody asking a question on it and you being completely unaware of what had happened.

President Johnson: Well, what are we going to say?

Reedy: You just—I think you have to say that you don't know what high administration official they're talking about, that you've made the position in Southeast Asia entirely clear, and that you've seen . . . there's been nothing to change your position.

President Johnson: Hmm. OK.

Reedy: OK, sir. I'll stick here until I—

---

64. Chalmers Roberts was a reporter for the *Washington Post*.

President Johnson: All right.

Reedy: —get it straightened out.

7:05 P.M.

With Signal Corps Operator[65]

The recording system captured a conversation with the Criders in Johnson's hotel room as the Signal Corps operator attempted to reach an unidentified individual and Robert McNamara.

President Johnson: He's just reading to me. [*Long pause.*]

Signal Corps Operator: We're still trying to locate him, sir.

President Johnson: Hmm?

Signal Corps Operator: We're still trying to locate him for you. It'll be just a moment. [*Pause.*]

President Johnson: [*to Crider, who is in the room with the President*] Otto, what is the real estate fees out here when you sell a man's house for him or his land, 5 percent?

Otto Crider: Six [*unclear*] percent. [*Unclear*] land, but it's hard to come up with [*unclear*]. It varies. I think it's 5 [*unclear*] percent [*unclear*].

President Johnson: You don't do much selling, though: you're buying and sell it—stuff you own yourself?

Crider: It's hard to say.

President Johnson: How are things, slow now?

Crider: No.

President Johnson: Good time? [*Crider's response is inaudible.*] Well, where do you get your contacts: people from San Francisco come out and want to buy some?

Crider: San Francisco, yes. A lot local. And people are moving. People are coming into California, you know. Tremendous influx of people. [*Unclear*] the other day.

President Johnson: Do you bleed a few of them, really stick it to them?

Signal Corps Operator: Mr. President?

President Johnson: Yeah.

Signal Corps Operator: There's no answer at his residence or his

65. Tape WH6406.11, Citation #3794, Recordings of Telephone Conversations—White House Series, Recordings and Transcripts of Conversations and Meetings, Lyndon B. Johnson Library.

office. We're checking to try and locate him. Can I call you back, sir?

President Johnson: Yeah. Did he leave word at the White House where he can be reached?

Signal Corps Operator: No, sir, they're trying to find out from his secretary where he's at now.

President Johnson: All righty. You find out where he is because I want to know where to reach him and where to reach [Robert] McNamara. See if McNamara's there.

Signal Corps Operator: OK, sir, I'll try to get him for you. [*Pause.*]

President Johnson: What's that? [*Crider's response is inaudible.*] Yeah, but some of these strangers in there, I imagine you bleed them pretty good? [*Responses from both Criders are inaudible.*]

President Johnson: Does he?

Crider: I heard [*unclear*] say so. [*Unclear.*]

President Johnson: I don't know. [*Crider's question is inaudible.*] I'd just buy it outright. [*Crider's response is inaudible.*]

Signal Corps Operator: Operator.

President Johnson: Just let him go. I've got to go, and just let him go.

Signal Corps Operator: Right, sir.

7:10 P.M.: President Johnson took the nap he had mentioned before the call to George Reedy.

7:35 P.M.

From George Reedy[66]

Reedy called back with an update on varying wire service versions of Dean Rusk's anonymous briefing on the danger of war with China.

George Reedy: . . . AP.

President Johnson: What do you mean needled?

Reedy: They made it harder, sound harder than the speech actually is, and the various answers to the questions. What [Dean] Rusk was really saying is that if the Chinese Communists don't wake up to their responsi-

---

66. Tape WH6406.11, Citation #3795, Recordings of Telephone Conversations—White House Series, Recordings and Transcripts of Conversations and Meetings, Lyndon B. Johnson Library.

bilities, it's no telling what the situation might be, that it might even lead to a war in the Pacific, or something like that. And I think the UPI just makes it a little bit tougher, not much, but a little bit tougher than it is.

Now, Brom[ley Smith] also read the AP story to me. I still don't have it. And it's, I think, very much down the middle. It says that a high administration official expressed dismay that the allies are not helping us more in Southeast Asia. Then it goes ahead to say that if this continues, we're going to have to keep on resisting, and there's no telling what the consequences may be, which is just about what Rusk said.

President Johnson: OK. All right. Anything else?

Reedy: No, I don't think anything can be done about it tonight.

President Johnson: All right. OK.

Reedy: OK, sir.

President Johnson: Say, is there anything in our speech that causes them to say that?[67]

Reedy: Not that I can see, not a thing.

President Johnson: Well, there's one line in it somewhere—ask Bill Moyer[s] what it is—where they say that we're willing to fight for freedom anywhere.

Reedy: Well, I don't think that would cause this.

President Johnson: No, but . . . but look at it.

Reedy: Right. I will, sir.

8:08 P.M.

To Whitney Young[68]

Shortly after 8:00 P.M., the President called National Urban League Executive Director Whitney Young to congratulate him on the Senate's passage of the civil rights bill and to solicit his opinion about the director of the Community Relations Service. In addition, Young inquired about a controversy that threatened to undermine an antipoverty research and demonstration program in Harlem that had been a model for the administration's proposed War on Poverty. Founded in 1962 and funded in

---

67. Johnson was referring to his speech that evening at a fund-raising dinner in San Francisco, in which he stated that "we have used that strength not to incite our enemies but to indicate our intention to defend freedom wherever it is necessary." "Remarks in San Francisco at a Democratic Fundraising Dinner," 19 June 1964, *Public Papers, Johnson, 1963–64*, 1:788–93.

68. Tape WH6406.11, Citation #3796, Recordings of Telephone Conversations—White House Series, Recordings and Transcripts of Conversations and Meetings, Lyndon B. Johnson Library.

part by the President's Committee on Juvenile Delinquency under Robert Kennedy, the Harlem Youth Opportunities Unlimited (HARYOU) organization had completed an influential study of the problem of poverty and its causes, particularly among young people, and outlined an ambitious plan to attack poverty in Harlem. Headed by the prominent sociologist Kenneth B. Clark of the City College of New York, HARYOU compared impoverished inner-city areas to colonies in which the pervasive sense of powerlessness and lack of social mobility transfigured the ambitions of the young into pathological behaviors that reinforced poverty. HARYOU's plan proposed to remove barriers to opportunity for inner-city young people by organizing community-directed projects and reorganizing public and private social services—the basic concept at the core of the War on Poverty's Community Action program. HARYOU had also secured $110 million in federal and foundation grants to implement its program.

The influential Harlem Congressman Adam Clayton Powell, however, had succeeded in establishing a parallel antipoverty organization known as Associated Community Teams (ACT), which had also secured a federal grant to establish a trial domestic peace corps and adult Volunteer Service Corps in Harlem. Both HARYOU and ACT effectively functioned as an extension of Powell's political operation. The original intent had been that the two organizations would merge at the implementation stage. Instead, as the merger date approached, a bitter struggle for control had broken out between Clark and Powell, with each proposing his own candidate for the position of executive director of the combined HARYOU-ACT. Earlier in the week, the dispute had been referred to the White House, which declined to support one side or the other. On June 15, Young had joined CORE National Director James Farmer, American Negro Labor Council President A. Philip Randolph, and NAACP President Roy Wilkins in condemning the dispute and warning that it threatened to undermine the War on Poverty program not just in Harlem, but around the United States. Even as he spoke with the President, Young himself was being mentioned as a possible compromise candidate for the position. Within weeks, however, Powell would prevail, and his preferred candidate would be installed as executive director.[69]

---

69. For an overview of the project, OEO, see "The Office of Economic Opportunity During the Administration of President Lyndon B. Johnson; November 1963–January 1969," 1969, "Volume I, Part I; Narrative History" folder, Box 1, Special Files: Administrative Histories, Lyndon B. Johnson Library, pp. 103–15; Allen J. Matusow, *The Unraveling of America: A History of Liberalism In The 1960s* (New York: Harper & Row, 1984), pp. 257–58. For details, see R. W. Apple, "HARYOU and ACT: Merger Problem," *New York Times*, 11 June 1964; "4 Leaders Decry HARYOU-ACT Feud," *New York Times*, 16 June 1964; Paul L. Montgomery, "Harlem Factions Seek Compromise," *New York Times*, 20 June 1964.

President Johnson: Yes.

Whitney Young: Hello?

President Johnson: How are you, Whitney?

Young: Hello. Hi, Mr. President.

President Johnson: You doing all right?

Young: I'm having a rough time. [*Chuckles.*] I've been flying around over New York for two-and-a-half hours. I just got in from out in Michigan, and it's . . . The pace is too much. How are you doing?

President Johnson: Fine. We had a half a million out here in San Francisco today, and they just mobbed us.

Young: Is that right?

President Johnson: Yeah.

Young: You know you ought to feel awfully good, but please take it easy.

President Johnson: Well, I want to con—

Young: I just worry to death about the pace you're taking.

President Johnson: I want to congratulate you. It was a good day for all of us.

Young: Well, I was just delighted about the civil rights bill. I talked to Hobart [Taylor] tonight, though, Mr. President, a few minutes ago.[70]

President Johnson: Yeah.

Young: He was here in New York. And I had asked him about . . . oh, about three weeks ago to let you know that I thought that we ought to get together because we could avoid some things that happened today in the newspapers and will be happening in the next week or so. I don't want to see . . . I know that you're working on the southern governors; you're working on the southern businessmen and all this to comply. And I don't want to see [Martin Luther] King and [James] Farmer and everybody else talking about how they're going to insist on immediate compliance and tests and all this.[71] If you could keep, as you are, the southerners from issuing defiant orders, then we ought to not be talking about—loudly, you know, how are we going to test them.

President Johnson: Yeah.

Young: And I think we need to get together. I think we need to get

---

70. Hobart Taylor, an African American, served as associate counsel to the President and executive vice-chairman of the President's Committee on Equal Employment Opportunity.

71. James Farmer served as national director of the Congress on Racial Equality, a leading civil rights organization.

together about Mississippi.[72] I'm just delighted with the leadership you've chosen on this civil rights bill. You know, just between me and you, since we're on the phone privately . . .

President Johnson: All right. I—

Young: We've got something that we wouldn't have gotten if you hadn't been in there.

President Johnson: Well, I think so. I think we've come a long ways this six months since we started to . . .

Young: It's just *amazing.*

President Johnson: The key to this thing—one thing that's going to be very important to us I think is to get a good conciliator.

Young: Yeah.

President Johnson: Do you know Dr. George Taylor?

Young: No, I don't.

President Johnson: The head of the War Labor Board and the fellow that I had on the railroad strike?

Young: George Taylor?

President Johnson: Yeah, from Pennsylvania. He's a professor in Pennsylvania.

Young: No, I . . .

President Johnson: I wish you'd kind of check into him because I'm giving him pretty serious thought.

Young: George Taylor?

President Johnson: George W. Taylor. T-a-y-l-o-r. He's a professor at the University of Pennsylvania; he was Roosevelt's head of the War Labor Board, and I had him work on this railroad strike [that] hadn't been settled [in] five years, and he and Ted Kheel and I settled it in . . . about six months ago.

Young: Yeah, I know. I know Ted well, you know.

President Johnson: But . . .

Young: Do you know Donald Strauss?[73]

President Johnson: No, I don't.

Young: Well, he's a top-notch mediator in this field too.

President Johnson: Where's he from?

Young: New York.

---

72. Young was referring to the Freedom Summer project already underway in Mississippi, in which college students from around the United States would join local activists in a voter registration campaign. Freedom Summer had already generated significant opposition in the state, an opposition that would soon spark violence.
73. Donald Strauss remains unidentified.

President Johnson: Yeah.

Young: And I think you'd—to have him checked out [*unclear*]. But I'll check on this George Taylor and let you know.

President Johnson: You do that, and we'll talk next week when I get back.

Young: All right. Now, you know, I accepted this arbitration of the HARYOU thing, this [Adam Clayton] Powell, and . . . what's his name?[74] Powell and [J. Raymond] Jones?[75]

President Johnson: Yeah.

Young: The thing up here in New York. I accepted it because the mayor called me yesterday, and he . . . both Powell and Jones and [Kenneth] Clark and all of them had said that they . . . I was the only person that they would accept.

President Johnson: Yeah.

Young: So I accepted it because I thought—he said you wanted me to.

President Johnson: I didn't know anything about it, but I'm for anything you do.

Young: Yeah, well, I've—it's going to take me the next two days. I'm going to spend full time on that because that's important. If we . . . if that program is killed because these people can't get together, it's going to affect what happens in the Harlems all over this country.[76]

President Johnson: It sure will. You do a job on it, and I'll talk to you later in the week.

Young: All right.

President Johnson: Thank you, Whitney.

Young: I'll get busy on it. Thanks a lot.

President Johnson: Bye.

Young: Bye.

---

74. New York City Mayor Robert Wagner had asked Young and Deputy City Administrator Henry Cohen to mediate between the two factions. Montgomery, "Harlem Factions Seek Compromise," *New York Times*, 20 June 1964.

75. Young was probably referring to New York City Councilman J. Raymond Jones, a political opponent of Powell who served on HARYOU's board and was a leading supporter of Kenneth Clark. On 17 June, Powell ally John H. Young of the All-Harlem Leadership Committee had called for Jones's resignation from the board on the grounds that the New York State Investigation Committee had begun an inquiry into his involvement in a number of public housing projects, despite the committee's public denial that Jones was the target of such an investigation. Paul L. Montgomery, "Ex-Powell Aide Bids Jones Quit," *New York Times*, 18 June 1964.

76. Young was quoting language from the joint statement of civil rights leaders decrying the HARYOU-ACT dispute. "4 Leaders Decry HARYOU-ACT Feud," *New York Times*, 16 June 1964.

8:55 P.M.: President Johnson left the Fairmont Hotel to attend a fund-raising dinner at the San Francisco Hilton.

9:07 P.M.: Arrived at the Hilton and proceeded to the Continental Ballroom.

9:10 P.M.–10:45 P.M.: Attended the fund-raising dinner with the theme "Salute to President Johnson." In his remarks at the dinner, Johnson spoke about the legacy of President Kennedy, the passage of the Civil Rights Act, and his vision of the Great Society.[77]

10:52 P.M.: Left the Hilton and returned to the Fairmont Hotel.

10:58 P.M.: Arrived back at the Fairmont and proceeded to the presidential suite.

11:55 P.M.

To Thomas Corriden[78]

Following the Senate's historic vote on the civil rights bill, Massachusetts Senator Ted Kennedy and his aide Edward Moss joined Indiana Senator Birch Bayh and his wife Marvella on a two-engine plane for a flight to the Massachusetts Democratic Convention in Springfield. Approximately 15 miles from Springfield, near Southampton, Massachusetts, the plane crashed in foggy conditions, killing the pilot (who had been a last-minute replacement). Kennedy suffered a broken back, internal injuries, and abrasions. Senator Bayh injured his hip, and Marvella Bayh experienced minor injuries. Moss, however, would die in the hospital as a result of his injuries.[79]

President Johnson had learned of the accident while on his way to the Hilton Hotel prior to his speech. Approximately an hour after returning to the Fairmont Hotel, he placed a call to Dr. Thomas Corriden, the senior surgeon at Cooley-Dickinson Hospital in Northampton, Massachusetts, where the surviving crash victims were being treated.

---

77. "Remarks in San Francisco at a Democratic Fundraising Dinner," 19 June 1964, *Public Papers, Johnson, 1963–64*, 1:788–93.

78. Tape WH6406.11, Citation #3797, Recordings of Telephone Conversations—White House Series, Recordings and Transcripts of Conversations and Meetings, Lyndon B. Johnson Library.

79. "Senator Kennedy Hurt in Air Crash; Bayh Injured, Too," *New York Times*, 20 June 1964; "Edward S. Moss Dead, Aide to Sen. Kennedy," *Washington Post*, 21 June 1964.

President Johnson: Mr. Corriden?

Thomas Corriden: Yes.

President Johnson: How is Teddy [Kennedy]?

Corriden: Well, he's . . . is this the President?

President Johnson: Yes.

Corriden: Well, he's better than he has been. His blood pressure's coming up a bit. We feel a little bit better about him right now than we did earlier in the evening.

President Johnson: Oh, that's wonderful.

Corriden: He's conscious, and . . .

President Johnson: He is conscious?

Corriden: Yes, he is conscious.

President Johnson: Oh, that's wonderful.

Corriden: Yeah. I can hear you a little better now.

President Johnson: Yeah.

Corriden: We're a little happier about him. Still not out of the woods, of course. He very likely has a chest injury, but he was in deep shock there most of the evening, but he's—begin to come out of it now, so we feel a bit better about it.

President Johnson: Oh, well, that's so . . . that's wonderful.

Corriden: The senator and his wife, Senator [Birch] Bayh and his wife [Marvella], are all right.

President Johnson: Were they in the plane with you?

Corriden: Yes, they were in the plane with him, but they're all right. They weren't . . . there were only minor injuries.

President Johnson: Uh-huh. . . . . What happened? Was it bad weather?

Corriden: Bad weather; it was foggy and the pilot was killed, of course.

President Johnson: What kind of a plane was it?

Corriden: I can't hear you, Mr. President.

President Johnson: [*louder*] What kind of a plane was it?

Corriden: I don't know. [*Confers briefly with people in the room.*] It was a two-engine plane, they tell me.

President Johnson: Well, I'll be darned. Well, where'd it happen?

Corriden: It happened over in Southampton, that's just—I'm talking from Northampton now.

President Johnson: Yeah.

Corriden: But it happened over in Southampton; that's about 15 miles from here.

President Johnson: Uh-huh. Well, I was just praying for you. I just heard it when I was making my speech tonight, and . . . I'm in San Francisco, and I just got back to the hotel room, and I wanted to call him and tell him I was thinking of him.

Corriden: Well, I think we're doing all right so far, Mr. President. We've got a couple of specialists here, and we've got a couple coming up from Boston. So I think we're going to do all right.

President Johnson: Anybody else hurt?

Corriden: Well, not seriously—well, the fellow named Moss? Edward Moss, he was hurt quite seriously. They did a brain operation on him. He's critical.

President Johnson: Who is he?

Corriden: Well, I—[*Confers briefly with people in the room.*] He's one of Senator Kennedy's men.

President Johnson: Oh, yeah. Well, that's awful bad. Was Teddy cut up very much?

Corriden: No. No. He's got some injuries to his chest and to his left flank and the possibility he may have some damage to his kidney—left kidney—but neurologically, the . . . Doctor Hann from Springfield says that he looks pretty good as far as he's concerned.

President Johnson: Oh, well, that's wonderful. I just—I'm praying for you, and tell them all that I'm interested, and I'll call you tomorrow.

Corriden: Very good, Mr. President.

President Johnson: Thank you so much.

Corriden: Good night.

After the call to Dr. Corriden, the President went to bed.

Saturday, June 20, 1964

Not any question about him dying, is it?

—President Johnson to Walter Jenkins

Beginning on June 20, cars and buses carrying white and black volunteers for the Council of Federated Organization's Freedom Summer campaign began to arrive at locations around Mississippi. Over the previous week, participants had attended a training session at Western College for Women in Oxford, Ohio, where they received instruction from Mississippi movement veterans. Tensions during the week had at times run high, as instances of naiveté and cultural insensitivity among the mostly white volunteers, drawn primarily from elite northern and western colleges and universities, shocked the more experienced black movement activists. While in Oxford, the Freedom Summer volunteers also met with John Doar of the U.S. Department of Justice, who warned them (despite his own sympathy for their efforts) that the federal government would not be able to offer reliable protection in most areas of Mississippi.[1]

Upon arrival in Mississippi, initial tasks facing the activists included the investigation of a June 16 Ku Klux Klan attack on the Mt. Zion AME

---

1. Others in the administration viewed the Freedom Summer campaign far less favorably. In a recent memorandum to Johnson regarding a request from the parents of the Freedom Summer volunteers for federal protection, Associate Counsel to the President Lee C. White had written that "it is nearly incredible that those people who are voluntarily sticking their head into the lion's mouth would ask for somebody to come down and shoot the lion." Lee C. White, "Memorandum for The President; Subject: Students Registration Program In Mississippi," 17 June 1964, "HU 2/ST 24 1/1/64–7/16/64" folder, Box 26, White House Central Files: Human Rights, Lyndon B. Johnson Library; John Dittmer, *Local People: The Struggle For Civil Rights In Mississippi* (Urbana: University of Illinois Press, 1994), pp. 242–46; Taylor Branch, *Pillar of Fire: America in the King Years 1963–65* (New York: Simon & Schuster, 1998), pp. 351–52.

church outside of Philadelphia, Mississippi, that resulted in the burning of the church and the beating of three church stewards. Mt. Zion had been scheduled to be the site of a Freedom School, designed to bolster the Freedom Summer's voter registration drives with educational programs in history and civics. The church's designation as a Freedom School had been arranged by James Chaney and Michael Schwerner of COFO's Meridian office. Unbeknownst to the Freedom Summer volunteers, the attack on the church presaged an outbreak of murderous violence in Mississippi.[2]

> **7:40 A.M. (PST):** Lyndon Johnson woke up and ate breakfast in the living room of the Fairmont Hotel's presidential suite, overlooking San Francisco Bay.
>
> **7:45 A.M.–8:45 A.M.:** Met with Jack Valenti and Bill Moyers, read newspapers "thoroughly," and received messages from the White House. He then received a rubdown from Chief Mills.[3]

9:15 A.M.

To Walter Jenkins[4]

Still in the hotel suite, Johnson called Walter Jenkins to receive an update on developments in Washington and to discuss issues such as journalists' investigations of Johnson's business holdings, Ted Kennedy's plane crash, a travel scare involving the President's daughter Lynda Johnson, and press coverage of Johnson's California trip.

President Johnson: How you doing?
Walter Jenkins: Fine, sir.
President Johnson: What's happened?
Jenkins: Sir?
President Johnson: What's news?
Jenkins: Well, not a . . . there's really not—it's very quiet here. We're

---

2. Claude Sitton, "Rights Campaigners Off for Mississippi," *New York Times*, 21 June 1964; Branch, *Pillar of Fire*, pp. 352–54.
3. Mills is referred to as "Chief" in the Daily Diary. The term may refer to "chief petty officer," as Mills was a naval officer, probably associated with the White House military staff.
4. Tape WH6406.12, Citation #3798, Recordings of Telephone Conversations—White House Series, Recordings and Transcripts of Conversations and Meetings, Lyndon B. Johnson Library.

about the only ones here, as a matter of fact. There's not much going on. Bill Doherty called me awhile ago to tell me he'd been checking the Senate committee very carefully and they were going to meet again Monday.[5] He said Mike Manatos told him that we wanted to hold to the $10,000 figure, but he says it's very touch-and-go, and he's not sure whether we can or not. The chairman himself has very little heart for it.[6] Most of the members don't either but said that's what they're trying to do.

George Mahon called me last night, said you had tried to reach him and he had been out, and I told him I imagined you just wanted a report on how things were going along, and . . . He's rather discouraged: He thinks that [Silvio] Conte has been firmed up a good deal . . . and . . .[7]

President Johnson: On our side?

Jenkins: Yes, sir. And thinks that probably all of them but [William] Natcher are in pretty good shape, but Natcher's not, and he doesn't think he will be.[8] And he thinks it really is about six and six.

President Johnson: See if you can't talk to Earl and see if we can't do something for him someway or other, to where he won't go along with them in their cut even if he'll moderate ours.[9]

Jenkins: Well, Henry Wilson told me this morning that some—again whether it's Larry [O'Brien] or him—had been in touch with Natcher, and Natcher wants, he thinks, a cut, but perhaps not all of the cut that [Otto] Passman wants.[10]

---

5. Jenkins was referring to the pay bill, which was under the jurisdiction of the Post Office and Civil Service Committee. William C. Doherty was the former president of the National Association of Letter Carriers and still served on the Advisory Board of the Post Office Department. He had resigned in April as the U.S. ambassador to Jamaica. For background on the bill, see Johnson to Carl Albert, 4:44 P.M., 9 June 1964; and Johnson to Hubert Humphrey, 4:00 P.M., 19 June 1964, in this volume.

6. Mike Manatos was a legislative liaison for the administration; Senator Olin Johnston of South Carolina was the chairman of the Post Office and Civil Service Committee.

7. Jenkins was referring to the foreign aid appropriation bill. George Mahon, Democrat of Texas, chaired the House Appropriations Committee. Silvio Conte was a Republican representative from Massachusetts and a member of the Appropriations Committee's Subcommittee on Foreign Operations—which had jurisdiction over the foreign aid appropriation bill. For background on the issue, see George Mahon to Johnson, 1:48 P.M., 15 June 1964, and Larry O'Brien to Johnson, 4:55 P.M., 19 June 1964, in this volume.

8. William Natcher was a Democratic representative from Kentucky and a member of the Subcommittee on Foreign Operations.

9. Earl is spelled phonetically and remains unidentified.

10. Henry Hall Wilson Jr. was an administrative assistant to the President who worked under Larry O'Brien. Otto Passman, Democrat of Louisiana, chaired the Subcommittee on Foreign Operations and for years had used the position to exact significant cuts in foreign aid appropriations.

President Johnson: Well, just see if Earl won't go . . . try to see what our program ought to be.

Jenkins: All right.

President Johnson: We can't take that. We can't take—let Passman win it. Now, we've got to have—come up with a counteroffer someway.

Jenkins: All right. And . . .

President Johnson: Anything with Jesse [Kellam]?

Jenkins: Not a word.

President Johnson: What does Abe [Fortas] say about this?[11]

Jenkins: Abe's in Connecticut. I talked to him just once long distance and told him about it, and really, he didn't have much in the way of suggestions. He said that he had talked with his wife [Carol Agger] and that as far as the general information was concerned, there wasn't much we could do about it. They were entitled to it. As far as the names of the people, why, it probably—probably weren't they—while they weren't entitled to it, why, he couldn't see that it hurt too much that these contributions were small and legitimate. Didn't see how they could make too much out of it.[12]

President Johnson: Anything else? Anything on Ted Kennedy?

Jenkins: Well, I've been getting the tickers right along. I talked to . . . during the middle of the night—I guess George Reedy told you—to the doctor. He's very serious, but he's holding his own, and he's got . . .

President Johnson: Not any question about him dying, is it?

Jenkins: Doctor said he didn't think so, that he felt sure he was going to live, although his pulse was not strong, and he was in and out of shock, and that he had a broken back and very serious injuries.

President Johnson: What does that mean? Do you recover from that?

Jenkins: Yes, sir. Perhaps not completely, but . . .

President Johnson: What caused it, do you know?

Jenkins: Fog, and . . . they were coming in for a landing at this little airport up there near to where they were having this convention, and weather

---

11. Abe Fortas was a powerful Washington attorney, Johnson adviser, and future unsuccessful Supreme Court nominee. His wife, Carol Agger, was a prominent attorney in her own right. Johnson probably was referring here to a matter involving the Johnson family business enterprises.

12. Jenkins was referring to a number of recent journalistic investigations into the activities of the Lyndon and Lady Bird Johnson's philanthropic foundation, part of a wider set of inquiries about the Johnsons' business and financial interests. See George Reedy to Johnson, 12:31 P.M., 9 June 1964; Walter Jenkins to Johnson, 7:35 P.M., 15 June 1964; and Carol Agger and Walter Jenkins, 7:55 P.M., 15 June 1964, in this volume.

was not too good. They don't know for sure, all the same . . . everything about what caused it.

President Johnson: What kind of plane?

Jenkins: I don't know. All the articles refer to it as a small plane. I don't know the brand.[13]

President Johnson: All right.

Jenkins: I'm sure you've seen the ticker item from Lynda [Johnson].[14]

President Johnson: Yeah. Yeah, about taking her off the plane.

Jenkins: Yes, sir. The papers all indicate that you had a tumultuous reception.

President Johnson: Boy, I did, but they all gave me half a million, except the *New York Times* and the *Washington Post*.[15] [*Pause.*]

Jenkins: Um . . .

Four minutes and one second excised under deed of gift restriction.

10:10 A.M.: President Johnson left the Fairmont Hotel in the company of California Governor Edmund "Pat" Brown and his wife, California Democratic Senate nominee Pierre Salinger, and San Francisco businessman and civic leader Cyril Magnin.

10:10 A.M.: Boarded Air Force One at San Francisco International Airport for a flight to El Toro Marine Air Base. Governor and Mrs. Brown, Salinger, and Magnin joined him in the plane's private compartment. During the flight, he read mail that had been delivered overnight from the White House and took a nap.

12:00 P.M.: Arrived at El Toro; after shaking hands with people in the crowd waiting to see him, took a car to a waiting helicopter.

---

13. The plane was a seven-seat Aero Commander owned by Standard International Corporation President Daniel E. Hogan Jr. Jesse Lewis, "Kennedy Plane's Pilot Was Substitute; Owner Flew Ship on Previous Trips," *Washington Post*, 21 June 1964.

14. President Johnson's daughter Lynda had been removed from a Hawaii-to-Los Angeles flight on the evening of 19 June after a passenger threatened to shoot a woman who had refused his affections. Wire reports indicated that Lynda Johnson left on a later Pan Am flight with a precautionary escort of as many as a dozen military planes. "Jets Guard Johnson's Daughter," *Washington Post*, 21 June 1964.

15. The *Washington Post* estimated that 300,000 people lined President Johnson's San Francisco motorcade. The *Times* did not include specific figures on crowd size in coverage of the President's West Coast appearances. Carroll Kilpatrick, "San Franciscans Hear President Gibe at Goldwater 'Dinosaur Ideas,'" *Washington Post*, 20 June 1964; "President Seeks California Votes," *New York Times*, 20 June 1964.

12:05 P.M.: Left the base by helicopter with the presidential party and flew to Irvine, California.

12:10 P.M.: Arrived in Irvine and presided over the dedication of the University of California's new Irvine campus. His remarks at the ceremony followed speeches by Governor Brown and University of California President Clark Kerr.

1:00 P.M.: Boarded the helicopter and departed for the Beverly Hilton Hotel.

1:20 P.M.: Arrived at the Beverly Hilton Hotel, where he was greeted by Conrad Hilton and members of the hotel management, and then proceeded to his suite.

1:45 P.M.

To Dean Rusk[16]

The President's first call from Southern California went to Secretary of State Rusk to discuss the replacement of Henry Cabot Lodge as U.S. ambassador to South Vietnam.

Dean Rusk: . . . [*Unclear*] and I had a long talk with Jack McCloy.[17] And I didn't let him come to a final answer, but I'm writing it up, and I'll have it ready for you when you return. What . . . but he says this is not the time or the place for him, you know, with his circumstances. Did you have a kind of talk with the other fellow?

President Johnson: Yes, and I never got anywhere. I didn't get to the point where I tried to urge him, but I passed it by him a time or two and got no interest.

Rusk: Right. Well, I think other things are pretty well about as you left them. The various problems like Laos, Cyprus, the rest of them, nothing very unusual happened. But I'm still trying like hell to search for the names.

---

16. Tape WH6406.12, Citation #3799, Recordings of Telephone Conversations—White House Series, Recordings and Transcripts of Conversations and Meetings, Lyndon B. Johnson Library.
17. A New York lawyer and adviser to presidents Kennedy and Johnson, John "Jack" McCloy had served as assistant secretary of war (1940–1945), president of the World Bank (1947–1949), and high commissioner of occupied Germany (1949–1952).

President Johnson: Will Max [Taylor] and Alex [Johnson] be the answer?[18]

Rusk: I think it's likely to work out the best; I think it's likely to work out the best. I talked to Jack Goodman just before [*unclear*] Lucius [Clay], but I still think that's probably not the right answer, but . . .[19]

When are you getting back, Mr. President?

President Johnson: Tomorrow, late.

Rusk: I'd like to see you if I may when you get back. [*Unclear*] tell you what Jack said and his comments on who [*unclear*]. [*Pauses.*]

Are you getting any . . . much reaction out there to the vote in the Senate?

President Johnson: No. No, I think it's more or less accepted.

Rusk: All right.

President Johnson: Well, I guess we'll just wait and talk about it when we get back.

Rusk: I [*unclear*]—

President Johnson: I understand that we need to be ready for something Monday. Is that right?

Rusk: No, I think it's—well, I think—

President Johnson: What did you say to the fellow, [*unclear comment by Rusk*] did you tell him to send me his letter?[20]

Rusk: No, I said his problem is possible. We do have his letter. But I didn't, you know, speak [*unclear*].

President Johnson: Did he send the letter to me?

Rusk: Yes, it's a very good letter.

President Johnson: That's fine.

Rusk: But it does not mention the day.

President Johnson: Well, that's good. So then you think we've got a day or two next week?

Rusk: Oh, yes, in fact, I do, but [*unclear*] I think it might be well because I know this is very much on your mind for you [*unclear*].

President Johnson: That'll be good; that'll be good. I'll call you.

Rusk: OK.

---

18. Maxwell Taylor was chairman of the Joint Chiefs of Staff. U. Alexis Johnson was deputy under secretary for political affairs.

19. Before retiring from the Army in 1949, General Lucius Clay served in the Corps of Engineers, was in charge of materiel in World War II, and in 1947 became commander in chief of U.S. forces in Europe and military governor of the U.S. zone in Germany. Jack Goodman remains unidentified.

20. Johnson was almost certainly referring to Henry Cabot Lodge's letter of resignation as U.S. ambassador to South Vietnam.

2:05 P.M.: Ate lunch with secretaries Gerri Whittington and Yolanda Boozer.

2:30 P.M.: Took a nap in the hotel suite after asking Whittington to bring him newspapers from the hotel lobby. The Daily Diary does not list the time that the President awoke, but indicates that he then received a briefing book on the Cyprus crisis and the upcoming visit of Turkish Prime Minister Ismet Inonu from military aide Paul Glynn.

5:50 P.M.: Lynda Bird Johnson, who had just returned from a trip to Hawaii, arrived to see her father.

6:45 P.M.

To Robert Kennedy and Jacqueline Kennedy[21]

Johnson's third and final recorded call of the day went to the Kennedy family retreat in Hyannis Port, Massachusetts, to share his sympathy regarding Senator Edward Kennedy's injuries in the plane crash the previous evening. He spoke to both Robert Kennedy and Jacqueline Kennedy, the widow of the assassinated President.

President Johnson: Bobby? I'm sorry I—

Robert Kennedy: I just wanted to tell you that, you know, that Birch Bayh and his wife are fine and that Ted Kennedy is coming along well.[22]

President Johnson: How's Teddy, Bob?

Kennedy: Well, he's got a lot of broken bones and his back is in bad shape, but he's not paralyzed. And it's going to take . . . they suppose anywhere from six months to a year, but he's going to be fine at the end of it.

President Johnson: Oh, well, thank God, he's safe.

Kennedy: Well, I do thank you for calling for . . .

President Johnson: Looks like you just have more than you can bear, but you're a mighty brave fellow, and you have my sympathy and all your family, and . . .

---

21. Tape WH6406.12, Citation #3800, Recordings of Telephone Conversations—White House Series, Recordings and Transcripts of Conversations and Meetings, Lyndon B. Johnson Library.
22. Indiana Senator Birch Bayh and his wife Marvella had been slightly injured in the plane crash.

Kennedy: Thank you, Mr. President.

President Johnson: Any way in the world I can help, I'm just as close as the phone.

Kennedy: Well, I think [*unclear*].

President Johnson: Well, I appreciate it so much. It's so distressing, and I know you're carrying a heavy load. I wished I could do something to help you. Give your mother my love.

Kennedy: Jackie just wants to say hello to you too.

President Johnson: Thank you, Bobby.

Kennedy: Hold on, Mr. President.

President Johnson: Bye.

Jacqueline Kennedy: Hello? Mr. President?

President Johnson: My dear, it looks like you have more than we can bear, don't you?

Jacqueline Kennedy: Yeah, boy, that was just such a hard day. But you're so nice to call.

President Johnson: Well, I'm thinking of you, and I wished I could do something.

Jacqueline Kennedy: Well, everyone here is very touched that you were. They thank you so much.

President Johnson: I talked to Mr. [Thomas] Corriden last night about 3[:00] or 4:00 [A.M.], and he thought that it was going to take time, but everything's all right—is that it?[23]

Jacqueline Kennedy: Yes, that's it. I think he'll pretty much be in bed and everything, but at least, you know, everything will be all right.

President Johnson: Give Joan [Kennedy] a hug for me.[24]

Jacqueline Kennedy: I will.

President Johnson: Thank you, Jackie.

Jacqueline Kennedy: Thank you, Mr. President.

President Johnson: Bye.

7:15 P.M.: The President left the Hilton with Lynda Bird Johnson and Jack Valenti.

7:37 P.M.: Arrived at the Hollywood Palladium for a fund-raising dinner hosted by the California Democratic State Central Committee.

---

23. Thomas Corriden was the senior surgeon attending Ted Kennedy and the other victims of the plane crash. See Johnson to Thomas Corriden, 11:55 P.M., 19 June 1964, in this volume.
24. Joan Bennett Kennedy was Ted's wife.

9:30 P.M.–9:45 P.M.: Spoke to the dinner guests before leaving the event.

9:50 P.M.: Left the Palladium and proceeded to the Ambassador Hotel for the President's Club Supper Dance.

10:01 P.M.: Arrived at the Ambassador Hotel and proceeded to the Royal Suite for the dance.

10:28 P.M.: Went to the Embassy Room of the hotel for the dinner portion of the event. Lynda Bird Johnson returned to the Beverly Hilton Hotel.

12:30 A.M. (June 21): Stopped after leaving the President's Club event to greet thirteen-year-old Lyle Peskin and his father Leon. Lyle's Bar Mitzvah had originally been scheduled for the Embassy Room that evening, but had been moved to a nearby room to accommodate the President's Club dance. As compensation, the hotel had offered the other room for free, along with a private audience with the President.

12:40 A.M.: Left the Ambassador Hotel accompanied by Governor and Mrs. Brown and Valenti and returned to the Hilton.

1:00 A.M.: Arrived at the Hilton Hotel and returned to his suite. He received a rubdown from Chief Mills and went to bed at 1:20 A.M.

Sunday, June 21, 1964

Certainly, sir, anytime, and you too, you know, we'll be glad to give you a real vacation.

—John Burns to President Johnson

Among the Freedom Summer volunteers who had arrived in Mississippi late on June 20 were James Chaney, Michael Schwerner, and Andrew Goodman. Chaney, an African American from Meridian, Mississippi, and Schwerner, a social worker from New York, had already worked extensively in the Mississippi civil rights movement. Goodman, also from New York and from a family with a tradition of social activism, was a college student volunteer who during the week in Oxford, Ohio, had been personally recruited by Schwerner for the Freedom Summer effort in Meridian. Earlier in the spring, Goodman had joined a march of Queens College students in support of the Congress on Racial Equality's protests during Lyndon Johnson's appearance on the opening day of the New York World's Fair.[1]

On the Sunday morning following their arrival in Meridian, Chaney, Schwerner, and Goodman set out to visit members of the Mt. Zion AME Church, which had been burned by the Ku Klux Klan on June 16 because of its designation as a CORE Freedom School. This affiliation with the

---

1. Chaney had worked with CORE since October 1963, while Schwerner and his wife Rita had worked mostly out of CORE's Meridian office since January 1964. In the months that followed, Chaney and the Schwerners had worked on a number of projects together and had become friends. John Dittmer, *Local People: The Struggle For Civil Rights In Mississippi* (Urbana: University of Illinois Press, 1994), p. 246; Seth Cagin and Philip Dray, *We Are Not Afraid: The Story of Goodman, Schwerner, and Chaney, and the Civil Rights Campaign for Mississippi* (New York: Macmillan, 1988), pp. 28–29, 235–41.

Council of Federated Organizations (COFO) project had been the direct product of Cheney and Schwerner's work with members of the church.[2] In midafternoon, after the three men had visited the church site and met with church members who had been beaten in the attack, Neshoba County Deputy Sheriff (and Klan member) Cecil Ray Price arrested them outside of Philadelphia, Mississippi. Released around 10:30 that night, Chaney, Goodman, and Schwerner attempted to return to Meridian, but the deputy sheriff who had made the initial arrest that afternoon stopped their car again. Instead of returning them to the county jail, however, he offered the civil rights workers to a group of Klan members and sympathizers who drove them to a country road, executed them, and buried their bodies in an isolated dam. COFO staff in Meridian made a number of inquiries with local law enforcement when Chaney, Schwerner, and Goodman did not return late in the afternoon, but were unable to mobilize either an immediate full-scale search or a response from local, state, or federal authorities. The Johnson administration's reluctance to establish a strong federal presence in Mississippi meant that COFO had little immediate access to the FBI.[3]

The murders of Chaney, Schwerner, and Goodman remain the best-known episode of racist violence in Mississippi during the summer of 1964, but in reality formed only one piece of a wider pattern of anti–civil rights violence by the state's white population. A leading historian of the Mississippi freedom struggle observes that "in just the first two weeks of the summer project, in addition to the murder of Mickey Schwerner, James Chaney, and Andrew Goodman in Philadelphia, Mississippi, there were at least seven bombings or fire-bombings of movement-related businesses and four shootings and a larger number of serious beatings. The state was clearly primed for violence."[4]

---

2. COFO was the umbrella organization coordinating civil rights activism in Mississippi. Its constituent organizations included the National Association for the Advancement of Colored People (NAACP), the Congress of Racial Equality (CORE), the Southern Christian Leadership Council (SCLC), and the Student Nonviolent Coordinating Committee (SNCC).

3. Dittmer, *Local People*, pp. 246–49; Taylor Branch, *Pillar of Fire: America in the King Years 1963–65* (New York: Simon & Schuster, 1998), pp. 352–53, 361–65. On 8 June, Attorney General Kennedy had warned the President that "there has unquestionably been . . . an increase in acts of terrorism" in Mississippi, and that "law enforcement officials . . . are widely believed to be linked to extremist anti-Negro activity, or at the very least to tolerate it." He suggested that the FBI implement "new procedures for identification of the individuals who may be or have been involved in acts of terrorism," including law enforcement officers. Robert F. Kennedy, "Memorandum for the President," 8 June 1964, "24 1/1/64–7/16/64, HU 2/ST" folder, Box 26, White House Central Files: Human Rights, Lyndon B. Johnson Library.

4. Charles M. Payne, *I've Got the Light of Freedom: The Organizing Tradition and the Mississippi Freedom Struggle* (Berkeley: University of California Press, 1995), p. 301.

Lyndon Johnson would not learn about the missing civil rights workers until June 22. The events in Mississippi, however, would cast a pall over the passage and signing of the Civil Rights Act, brutally clarifying the distance the nation still had to travel—despite even the most momentous legislation—to secure any real measure of racial justice.

8:00 A.M. (PDT): President Johnson woke, ate breakfast in bed, and met with Bill Moyers, George Reedy, and Mac Kilduff.

8:30 A.M.: After daily exercises, he received a rubdown from Chief Mills and then shaved and dressed.

8:34 A.M.

To John Burns[5]

The President placed only two recorded calls on 21 June, and both went to Hawaii Governor John Burns. Johnson's elder daughter, Lynda, had just returned from a trip to the state. The President thanked the governor for his hospitality towards Lynda and instructed him on how to handle press inquiries regarding an incident at the Honolulu Airport as Lynda prepared to depart on the evening of June 19. The Secret Service had removed Lynda Johnson from a Hawaii-to-Los Angeles flight after a passenger threatened to shoot a woman who had refused his affections. Wire reports indicated that Lynda Johnson left on a later Pan Am flight with a precautionary escort of a dozen military jets. Johnson disputed the press claims about a military escort.[6]

President Johnson: Jack?

John Burns: Yes, sir.

President Johnson: How are you?

Burns: Good morning, Mr. President. Fine, sir.

President Johnson: Well, my girl [Lynda Bird] sure had a good time out there.

Burns: I hope she did. We sure tried to do it and give her the best we could.

---

5. Tape WH6406.12, Citation #3801, Recordings of Telephone Conversations—White House Series, Recordings and Transcripts of Conversations and Meetings, Lyndon B. Johnson Library.
6. "Jets Guard Johnson's Daughter," *Washington Post*, 21 June 1964.

President Johnson: Well, she said that she did. I believe she's worn down, though.

Burns: Yes, sir, she did.

President Johnson: Have you seen this UP [United Press] story filed out of Honolulu about the 14-plane guard escort for her?[7]

Burns: No, sir, I haven't.

President Johnson: [*reading*] "United Press International reported from Honolulu that at least 14 military aircraft were involved in the elaborate, protective measures established for the 2,500–mile jet flight over the Pacific. Efforts to obtain an explanation for the reported air escort of Miss Johnson's commercial plane brought no response from the presidential party here. Upon landing at International Airport, she went quickly to a waiting car, was driven to Beverly Hilton Hotel," and then so on and so forth.

Now, it seems that your Air National Guard had some routine training flights that left about 30 minutes after she took off. They did not know she was aboard the plane. She did not request any escort, and they did not provide any.

Burns: That's right.

President Johnson: But UP has got this story, and it's pretty damaging. It's a banner headline . . . eight columns wide, and I don't know . . . UP is usually pretty irresponsible, but I didn't know they was that irresponsible.

Burns: I never heard of anything that crazy happening because I know planes couldn't escort her from here.

President Johnson: Well, they say there's some National Guard . . . [*to someone in the room*] What are they?

Burns: We've got F-102s.

President Johnson: F-102s.

Burns: That's all we have.

President Johnson: Well, they were the ones that were supposed to be providing it.

Burns: Well, this is not—we don't provide that, so it definitely wasn't done. This is my National Guard operating on full-time duty. But it's my National—the Hawaii National Guard.

President Johnson: What I think you ought to do is talk to your top man there.

[*to someone in room*] Who'd you talk to, Major [*unclear*]? [*The person's response is inaudible.*]

---

7. For the UPI story, see "Miss Johnson Flies Pacific Under Extra Security Guard," *New York Times*, 21 June 1964.

Burns: I've got General Stevenson.

President Johnson: He talked to—

[*to someone in room*] You know who?

Burns: Yes, sir.

President Johnson: He talked to the Pacific Command airpost, some captain. Captain North.

Burns: Captain who?

President Johnson: North. N-o-r-t-h.

Burns: North.

President Johnson: I would think, though, that you ought to talk to the head of your Guard, get him to check and see what did happen.

Burns: Yes, sir.

President Johnson: And then tell the UP that no escort was requested, none was supplied. They had nothing to do with this flight at all. They didn't even know she was aboard the flight, and they've done a great disservice to a innocent little girl.

Burns: Sure have, and to the country and everything else. I'll be very happy to get on that [*unclear*]. No, I haven't seen it at all.

President Johnson: OK, I sure do thank you.

Burns: Well, certainly, sir, anytime, and you too, you know, we'll be glad to give you a real vacation.

President Johnson: Thank you. Thank you, Jack. Good luck to you.

Burns: OK. My best to you, sir.

President Johnson: Bye.

Burns: Bye.

8:50 A.M.

To John Burns[8]

A few minutes later, Johnson called Hawaii's governor again, this time to remind him to preserve the secrecy of the previous call.

President Johnson: Jack? I forgot to tell you, don't let anybody know I called you because that'll make a bigger story.

John Burns: I won't.

---

8. Tape WH6406.12, Citation #3802, Recordings of Telephone Conversations—White House Series, Recordings and Transcripts of Conversations and Meetings, Lyndon B. Johnson Library.

President Johnson: Just tell them that you heard from the Los Angeles paper, find out what it is, and you get your man, the Guard man, to get UP on the phone and tell them that you're planning on having a correction because there's no truth in it. [*Any response by Burns is inaudible.*] OK.

9:07 A.M.: Unrecorded call from George Reedy.

9:50 A.M.: The President greeted hotel bellboys and maids as he left the Hilton Hotel and chatted briefly with the hotel's general manager.

9:52 A.M.: Boarded a helicopter that took him to the airport.

10:02 A.M.: Departed on Air Force One from Los Angeles International Airport, bound for Andrews Air Force Base. Shortly after takeoff, Johnson walked around the cabin and talked with other passengers. He then returned to the private compartment with Pierre Salinger, Democratic National Committee Chairman John Bailey, Bill Moyers, and Lynda Bird.

2:05 P.M. (EDT): Met with Salinger in the private compartment.

3:30 P.M.: Ate lunch with Salinger and Moyers.

5:32 P.M.: Landed at Andrews Air Force Base.

5:36 P.M.: Boarded a helicopter to return to the White House.

5:46 P.M.: The helicopter landed on the South Lawn of the White House, where Lady Bird Johnson, Dean Rusk, and McGeorge Bundy greeted the presidential party.

5:50 P.M.: Met with Rusk and Bundy in the White House Mansion.

7:10 P.M.: Went for a walk with the First Lady on the South Grounds of the White House.

7:20 P.M.: William S. White, an old friend, journalist, and author of a newly published biography of the President, arrived with his wife.

7:25 P.M.: The Whites joined the Johnsons and Bundy in the White House pool.

8:30 P.M.: Jack and Mary Margaret Valenti arrived at the White House and went to the pool.

9:30 P.M.: The Johnsons ate dinner with the Whites, Valentis, and Bundys.

10:28 P.M.: Unrecorded call to Chief Mills.

11:15 P.M.: Retired for the evening.

Monday, June 22, 1964

I have never felt that the SEC ought to be made up of a certain group of people from New York City that are tied in with the investments and all that kind of stuff. I wanted to move it out to the West where the people could have a good, objective, judicious fellow on it.

—President Johnson to Everett Dirksen

Late in the morning of Monday, June 22, Associate Counsel to the President Lee C. White received a phone call from Congress of Racial Equality (CORE) Chairman James Farmer, who informed him that three civil rights workers had failed to return to their office in Meridian, Mississippi, and were presumed missing. Farmer had already contacted the Justice Department's John Doar, and the FBI had become involved in the case. This appeared, however, to be the first notice that the White House had received about the disappearance (and in reality, murder) of James Chaney, Andrew Goodman, and Michael Schwerner. Through White, Farmer appealed to the White House for assistance "in any way possible." As search efforts intensified in Mississippi, White monitored the situation, remaining in contact with Burke Marshall at the Justice Department and speaking again to Farmer late in the afternoon. The next day, White wrote that by 8:00 P.M., "a full scale search was on."[1]

---

1. Lee C. White, "Memorandum To The Files; Subject: Disappearance of Three Participants in Mississippi Project," 23 June 1964, "24 1/1/64–7/16/64, HU 2/ST" folder, Box 26, White House Central Files: Human Rights, Lyndon B. Johnson Library.

It is not clear exactly when White (or others) notified the President about the developing situation in Mississippi, and the President did not mention the crisis in any of his recorded calls until June 23.[2]

9:00 A.M.: Unrecorded call to Secretary of Defense Robert McNamara.

9:03 A.M.: Unrecorded call from labor relations expert George Taylor in Dayton, Ohio.

9:11 A.M.: Unrecorded call from Secretary of State Dean Rusk.

9:24 A.M.: Unrecorded call from Secretary of Commerce Luther Hodges.

10:10 A.M.: President Johnson arrived at the office.

10:15 A.M.: Met with Undersecretary of State George Ball and National Security Council staff member Robert Komer.

10:26 A.M.: Greeted Prime Minister Ismet Inonu of Turkey on the South Grounds of the White House.

A band played the national anthems of the two countries before Johnson and Inonu reviewed the troops assembled for the ceremony and made brief remarks. The two leaders then walked through the Rose Garden.

10:55 A.M.: Met with Inonu in the Oval Office, along with Ball and a number of Turkish officials.

11:46 A.M.: Unrecorded call to Walter Jenkins.

11:48 A.M.: Unrecorded call to Jenkins.

12:00 P.M.: Met with California Assembly speaker Jesse Unruh.

12:07 P.M.: In a Flower Garden ceremony, presented the Distinguished Federal Civilian Service Award to four federal officials, including John Doar of the Justice Department's Civil Rights Division.

12:27 P.M.: Returned to the office.

12:31 P.M.: Unrecorded call to Jack Valenti.

12:32 P.M.–1:50 P.M.: Luncheon for Prime Minister Inonu in the White House Mansion.

12:34 P.M.: Unrecorded call to the White House operator.

2:35 P.M.: Took a nap in the Mansion.

3:36 P.M.: Unrecorded call to the White House Operator looking for

---

2. The first mention of the case in the media came on 23 June. The *New York Times* reporter who filed the story had been threatened by a white mob in Philadelphia, Mississippi. Claude Sitton, "3 In Rights Drive Reported Missing," *New York Times*, 23 June 1964; Taylor Branch, *Pillar of Fire: America in the King Years 1963–65* (New York: Simon & Schuster, 1998), pp. 363–64.

Lady Bird Johnson; the First Lady was away from the White House, hosting a luncheon on the presidential yacht *Sequoia* for the wife of Prime Minister Inonu.

3:45 P.M.: Unrecorded call to White House staff member Ashton Gonella.

3:56 P.M.: Unrecorded call to Jenkins.

4:20 P.M.: Unrecorded call to Jenkins.

4:25 P.M.: Unrecorded call from Jenkins.

4:27 P.M.: Unrecorded call to Attorney General Robert F. Kennedy in Hyannis Port, Massachusetts.

4:34 P.M.: Unrecorded call to Valenti.

4:40 P.M.: Unrecorded call to McGeorge Bundy.

5:00 P.M.: Unrecorded call from Jenkins.

5:09 P.M.: Returned to the office.

5:10 P.M.

From Larry O'Brien[3]

Immediately after Johnson returned to the office, Special Assistant for Congressional Relations Larry O'Brien called with bad news about the progress of the administration's Medicare bill in the House Ways and Means Committee. Representative Wilbur Mills of Arkansas, the powerful committee chairman, had conveyed a message that he did not have the votes to report the bill to the full House and that he preferred to vote out a smaller package that featured only an increase in Social Security cash benefits. The American Medical Association had launched a vigorous lobbying campaign against the bill and Mills himself had long opposed it, at least formally. Supporters, however, believed that his willingness even to debate it in the Ways and Means Committee suggested a possible softening in his position on passing some form of Medicare legislation. In an effort to coax Mills along to a point of political and policy comfort (Mills was adamant that any expansion of the Social Security system be done on a demonstrably sound actuarial basis), the administration had modified its Medicare package in recent weeks, replacing an option for partial coverage of 180 days of hospital care with a provision for 45 days of full hospital coverage, eliminating a provision for limited coverage of nursing

---

3. Tape WH6406.12, Citation #3804, Recordings of Telephone Conversations—White House Series, Recordings and Transcripts of Conversations and Meetings, Lyndon B. Johnson Library.

home care following hospitalization, and increasing the Social Security taxes that would fund the coverage. These efforts had apparently failed to satisfy Mills, whose influence might have swayed enough votes to report the bill out of the committee. Meanwhile, other members had independently developed doubts about the advisability of Medicare in light of the fall campaign. Mills did leave open the possibility that the Senate, where support for Medicare was stronger, might amend the Social Security bill to include the measure and that a compromise might be reached in a conference committee—with himself as a broker credible to both sides.[4]

On June 24, Mills publicly indicated that he could not support the proposed Medicare legislation, and the next day, the Ways and Means Committee approved a 5 percent increase in Social Security benefits funded by gradual increases in the Social Security payroll tax between 1965 and 1971. The benefit increase itself, however, seemed to threaten the actuarial viability of any future Medicare package. In August, Mills would block a Senate attempt to include a Medicare rider on the Social Security bill, forestalling any action in 1964. Nonetheless, he indicated that he might be ready to undertake a new round of Medicare negotiations in 1965—the start of a process of policy development that would eventually lead to the enactment not only of Medicare but also of Medicaid, which became the primary form of health insurance for the nation's poor.[5]

President Johnson: Larry?
Larry O'Brien: Hi, Mr. President.
President Johnson: Yeah.
O'Brien: The Wilbur Mills situation has deteriorated.
President Johnson: Mm-hmm.
O'Brien: I would say at this moment, totally. I had [Anthony] Celebrezze and [Wilbur J.] Cohen over here early this afternoon.[6] Mills killed a couple of hours in the committee this morning, but there

---

4. Arlene J. Large, "Key Tests on Medicare, Other Issues Due This Week as Rights Bill Returns to House," *Wall Street Journal,* 22 June 1964. For background on Medicare, see Wilbur Mills to Johnson, 9:55 A.M., 9 June 1964; and Larry O'Brien and Wilbur Mills to Johnson, 3:55 P.M., 11 June 1964, both in this volume. See also Julian Zelizer, *Taxing America: Wilbur D. Mills, Congress, and the State, 1945–1975* (New York: Cambridge University Press, 1998), pp. 212–54.

5. "Social Security Benefit Lift of 5% Voted by Panel," *Wall Street Journal,* 25 June 1964; Zelizer, *Taxing America,* pp. 226–30.

6. Anthony Celebrezze was secretary of health, education, and welfare. Wilbur J. Cohen was a longtime administrator in the Department of Health, Education, and Welfare and a policy expert whom John Kennedy referred to as "Mr. Social Security." Edward D. Berkowitz, *Mr. Social Security: The Life of Wilbur J. Cohen* (Lawrence: University Press of Kansas, 1995).

was no action. He talked to Cohen following that and feels that he just can't put this thing together, that he's suggesting "why not vote out just a Social Security bill in the morning?" He's going to have the final markup, and with an increase in benefits that he wouldn't ask for any vote on Kerr-Mills and kind of put that over to next year.[7] And that he can either vote Medicare, which we'd lose, or perhaps he could skip that vote entirely, and why didn't we try to do something over on the Senate side with the Social Security bill when it went over there to attach Medicare to it. And at that point, conceivably something could happen in conference, and what have you.

Now, I asked them just what . . . they both felt that short of a conversation again between you and Mills, that there wasn't anything that could happen tomorrow morning except to lose this thing totally, that the best that would happen is that they not take a formal vote. It would require . . . that will require talking to Gene Keogh and others to keep them away from demanding a formal vote because Keogh has been raising hell with Mills on inaction as it is.[8]

The whole thing is at a point where I think there has to be another conversation of some sort. Very frankly, I don't have the handle. I am not . . . I know I'm sort of just dumping a problem in your lap without the answers to it, but I think that perhaps what we ought to do is suggest to Mills, which *I* can do, that perhaps he could postpone tomorrow morning's meeting until Wednesday; that we talk to the leadership further in the morning; that we conceivably even have Mills at the leadership breakfast if you think that's worth a damn, or we arrange for a conversation in the morning with Mills down here that might lead, if Mills—it could be presented to Mills, "Hell, Wilbur, apparently you're out of steam because you feel you don't have the votes and you're talking about [John] Watts and [Albert Sydney] Herlong, and apparently you're right: You don't have them.[9] But what do you think about having the Democratic members of the committee get together in one group and let us, you and I, Wilbur, put the pitch on them to come out of here with some piece of this bill?"

---

7. An option available to Mills was to pass a relatively minor expansion of the Kerr-Mills Act of 1960, which gave states the option of providing federally subsidized health care insurance to the elderly poor. For the Kerr-Mills legislation, see Larry O'Brien and Wilbur Mills to Johnson, 3:55 P.M., 11 June 1964, in this volume.

8. Eugene Keogh was a Democratic representative from New York and a member of the House Ways and Means Committee. He was a strong Medicare supporter.

9. Both Democrats and members of the Ways and Means Committee, John Watts represented Kentucky and Albert Sydney Herlong represented Florida.

Now, we can do that, or just try to avoid a vote in the committee and let them just vote the Social Security aspect of this out and then concentrate our efforts on the Senate side, with Mills feeling that conceivably he could be of help. Now, it's a reverse situation: It isn't so much he would be of help, but he would be in good shape with the AMA [American Medical Association] if he could convince the AMA that something strong was going to come out of conference and therefore he would be the mediator cutting back and helping them to avoid having them have a debacle in conference.

The whole thing, therefore, adds up to a pretty dismal situation as of this moment, and I thought I should, number one, report it to you. I'm sorry that I don't have specific suggestions that would be meaningful at this point in the corrective end of it, but I did want you, if you would, to advise me on just what you think off this . . . that we could possibly do at this point.

President Johnson: I guess the best thing is just to let him go on and vote out Social Security and pass it in the House and see if we can add the other on in the Senate.

O'Brien: Yeah, that may be the answer. If we can avoid an up or down vote on Medicare in that committee, which, you know, will take some . . . we ought to be awfully careful of that: that we don't get caught in a crack where this thing with the White House, you know, just succumbed. I don't know. . . .

But anyway, that's one possibility. I don't know whether it's worthwhile. I suppose there's nothing to be lost, in a way. If I could call him and say, "In view of all this, Wilbur, I don't think your committee should meet in the morning. You ought to wait another day, and . . . "

These labor fellows are on to this, see. [Andrew] Biemiller called and left a message here that, apparently, all hell had broken loose and things had fallen apart in the Ways and Means Committee and just what were we going to do about it, that type of message.[10] I didn't talk to him because I anticipated that's just what the hell he was calling about. He's always helpful that way, you know, just tell you how bad things are—

President Johnson: Mm-hmm.

O'Brien: —without any answers. But I did want to alert you to it. I am inclined at this point to ask Mills if he would consider not having the committee meet in the morning and to try and grab another 24 hours here in the hope that maybe we . . . lightning strikes somewhere. I just

---

10. Andrew Biemiller was the AFL-CIO's liaison to Congress and a former Wisconsin congressman.

don't know where it will strike, and it'd have to be a miracle at this point to pull something off. And then if we can't find anything in 24 hours, try to work out an agreement with them during that period, so that he would ensure that no vote would be taken on this, no formal vote in the committee, and that he would have no formal vote on Kerr-Mills and go with Social Security and we'll try it. Now, I don't know whether it's worth getting into that involvement or whether I should just go straight and say, "Wilbur, how about just skipping the vote in the morning?" I just don't know what 24 hours is going to bring us. I guess it's like everything else: You play for time, I suppose.

President Johnson: Well, I don't either. [*Pauses.*] I don't see much to be gained by the 24 hours. You think, though, if you don't have 24 hours, they'll vote on Medicare in the committee, and you will get beat, and then that'll be against you?

O'Brien: Yeah. . . yeah. Yeah.

President Johnson: Well, can't you ask him if he can keep them from voting, or you have to get your Democrats to do that?

O'Brien: Yeah. . . . Well, I'll have to . . . I think that I could ask him, and he would say, "Well, sure, I'll be willing to cooperate with you, but it'll be up to you to hold off the Cec[il] Kings and the Al Ullmans and the Gene Keoghs and so forth, which we can start working on.[11] But, you know, as I say, what the hell, we may have to do that anyway and just take the chance that people don't misinterpret it and say, "Well, what the hell: These fellows succumb to Mills. In addition to that, they screw around advising ardent supporters of this thing to lay off."

I don't know. It's a little tricky, and I don't want to—I'm not throwing it in your lap. I just want to advise you that, you know, things are in a lousy state at the moment, and I don't have an answer to a damn thing. Celebrezze and Cohen didn't have any answers either. I think maybe the next step is that . . . why don't I start talking to Mills, at least open up conversation. It's a quarter past five tonight, and we have the rest of the night and until 10:00 in the morning before that committee is actually called. He in many occasions in the past has knocked off committee meetings a few minutes before they're scheduled to start, so that—but he has announced in the press that the vote will be taken in the morning on this Medicare.

President Johnson: Mm-hmm. Well, why don't you talk to Keogh or your best friends on the committee and try to avoid a vote if you can, and

---

11. Both Democratic members of the House Ways and Means Committee, Cecil King represented California and Albert Ullman represented Oregon.

if you can't, then ask Wilbur to give you another day so you can tell him what you're trying to do and you—Did he give you any encouragement that you could add it on in the Senate?

O'Brien: Well, no, not particularly. He's just saying, "Well, you must have the votes to add it on in the Senate," and I'm sure that we do. Of course, what the hell . . . Well, we can do it. We've lost—we can't count on [Clair] Engle, and of course Teddy Kennedy will not be voting anymore this year, so that's two votes that you have to worry about.[12]

But I don't see daylight—where Mills is suggesting that he will be helpful in the conference, assuming that you'll tack it on in the Senate and you are at conference, if Mills would say, "Well, hell, in conference I will play ball totally to get a good piece of this thing accepted and run it through the House." That's one thing. But I am afraid what he's getting at is that his role would be that at the point of conference if *we* could convince or become convincing that this thing was in the process of, you know, full settlement in our way, that then Mills moves in on behalf of the AMA, and he's the guy cutting back, and he's a hero with the AMA. And, at the same time, he's indicating, of course, that he's a big help to us.[13]

It's a pretty tricky operation. You know, it's just . . . I don't know, but anyway, why don't I not burden you further at this point and let me get a feel of it with him and just see what in God's name we might come up with during the evening. I just don't know at this point what in the hell we can do. So that's one matter, and just so I can always be giving you [*chuckles*] good news, I might as well give you the other piece of relatively bad news, and that is that [George] Mahon is insisting that you talk to [William] Natcher directly to emphasize to him—[14]

President Johnson: I tried to get him, but his office says he's not there and they don't expect him.

O'Brien: Well, that's the word we got on him, and I thought maybe he was just plain ducking, but—

[*to Wilson, in room*] Henry, on Natcher, is he . . . where the hell is

---

12. Clair Engle, Democrat of California, was fatally ill and rendered almost mute by a brain tumor. He had been wheeled into Senate chambers to cast his voice vote for the foreign aid bill on 19 June, but his participation in any other votes remained uncertain. Engle died a little over a month later.

13. Although the Senate in August did attempt to add the Medicare bill, Mills actually worked to undercut the amendment and killed Medicare for the year. Julian Zelizer, *Taxing America*, pp. 212–54.

14. George Mahon, Democrat of Texas, chaired the House Appropriations Committee. William Natcher was a Democratic representative from Kentucky and a foreign aid swing vote on the Appropriations Committee's Subcommittee on Foreign Operations, which was considering the foreign aid appropriations bill.

he?[15] The Speaker indicated to me he talked to him this morning. Is he in town, is he—

Henry Hall Wilson: He's in town. I called him. He's ducking the call.

O'Brien: Yeah.

[*to the President*] Henry said that he's convinced he's in town. He's not in his office, that he's holed out somewhere.

President Johnson: Mm-hmm.

O'Brien: And this—

President Johnson: They . . . George Mahon wanted me to talk to [Joseph] Montoya and [John] Flynt and the third one I forgot, Natcher.[16]

O'Brien: Hmm . . . Yeah.

President Johnson: So I thought I'd try to. Walter's [Jenkins] already talked to him once. You think you ought to talk to him?

O'Brien: Yeah, well, I think this: that . . . I think the key call is, at this point, is . . .

President Johnson: Natcher?

O'Brien: Natcher.

President Johnson: Well . . .

O'Brien: And hell, if there's some reasonable way to—

President Johnson: Think I should try to get him at home?

O'Brien: Yeah. I wanted to—I would just have the board—I'll tell the board to find Natcher for you.

President Johnson: All right, I've got—OK.

O'Brien: All right.

5:24 P.M.

From McGeorge Bundy[17]

Johnson's next call came from National Security Adviser McGeorge Bundy, who informed the President that Chairman of the Joint Chiefs of Staff General Maxwell Taylor had arrived. In the meeting that followed, Taylor would be offered the position of U.S. ambassador to South Vietnam. He would accept.

---

15. Henry Hall Wilson Jr. was an administrative assistant to the President who worked under Larry O'Brien.

16. Joseph Montoya and John Flynt were Democratic members of the House representing New Mexico and Georgia. Both served on the Foreign Operations Subcommittee.

17. Tape WH6406.12, Citation #3805, Recordings of Telephone Conversations—White House Series, Recordings and Transcripts of Conversations and Meetings, Lyndon B. Johnson Library.

President Johnson: Yeah?

McGeorge Bundy: General [Maxwell] Taylor is in my office when you're ready.

President Johnson: All right, let's see what Jack [Valenti] is—

[*to someone in office*] General Taylor is on right now. [*Unclear, covering the receiver.*]

[*on phone*] He's got something here, thank you.

5:25 P.M.: Unrecorded call to Walter Jenkins.

5:26 P.M.: Unrecorded call to George Reedy.

5:27 P.M.: Officials of the Texas Livestock Association presented the President with a "$2,500 saddle with gold ornaments" and posed for photographs.

5:32 P.M.–5:45 P.M.: Met with General Maxwell Taylor to discuss the ambassadorship to South Vietnam.

5:46 P.M.

To Robert McNamara[18]

Immediately after Taylor's departure, Johnson called Secretary McNamara to discuss the meeting. He commented on the need to assist Taylor with his domestic arrangements and briefly inquired about press reports of movements of U.S. Marine forces near Southeast Asia.

President Johnson: Bob?

Robert McNamara: Yes, Mr. President.

President Johnson: Had a wonderful talk with this good man, and . . . he certainly is a good man.

McNamara: He surely is, Mr. President.

President Johnson: I had intended to call you, and I just—he got in before I realized it was 5:30—to ask you about the Alex Johnson thing, but he seemed to be real enthusiastic about it.[19] He raised it himself.

---

18. Tape WH6406.12, Citation #3806, Recordings of Telephone Conversations—White House Series, Recordings and Transcripts of Conversations and Meetings, Lyndon B. Johnson Library.
19. U. Alexis Johnson was currently the deputy under secretary for political affairs. On 1 July, he would be named deputy ambassador to South Vietnam under Taylor as ambassador.

McNamara: I talked to him about it after I got back. He was very pleased. He and Alex Johnson served together in Japan, 20 or 30 years ago.

President Johnson: He said that he felt a little sad he was leaving his military career and this would end it for him. He has a problem with his family, a little more serious, really, than I had understood, but I'm glad I didn't because it might have deterred me. He said that he doesn't know . . . he got to get them settled, and he's got this nice house and he's got to move out of it. He said he could take a little time, and he wants to go around [and] look, try to find something—

McNamara: I [*unclear*].

President Johnson: Isn't there some way we can tell the new man to stay put for a while—

McNamara: Oh, yes. I talked—

President Johnson: —and not move that woman right quick?

McNamara: That's right. I told Max he could have one week, one month, six months in that house. Not to worry about it—

President Johnson: Well, tell your new man that—what your problem is, and that you will send him off and move him into some other place and let that woman stay there a while.

McNamara: That's right; I fully agree with that.

President Johnson: He's going to want to come back within a year.

McNamara: Yeah.

President Johnson: And if we could just change titles but let him keep the house for a while, I think it'd be a good thing because he's going to be worried with her, you know, and she's going to be upset moving, and you know how those things are.

McNamara: Yeah.

President Johnson: So you look into that for us, and I—

McNamara: I will.

President Johnson: —talked to him about . . . if he had any financial problems and told him we'd work on those, and he said well, he hoped he wouldn't have, but if he did, he'd talk to you about them.

McNamara: Well, he will, and I told—in the sense that I'm sure the compensation will be different; he'll have extra costs—and I told him I'd definitely take care of that one way or another: either out of government funds or out of private foundation funds.

President Johnson: All right. Now, I told him to get any people here that he wanted, and if anybody was hesitant to go or to turn them loose, let me know and I'd call them. I don't know, he . . . we talked about [William] Gaud and [Michael] Forrestal and [William] Sullivan and some of them.[20] And he said he was going to talk to Alex Johnson, and they'd get a list of people that they wanted, but let's sure enough get him the best ones we can.

McNamara: I think we ought to ensure that they take at least two out of that four.

President Johnson: I wished you'd be thinking what I could say at a press conference, and I might have to meet with you and [Dean] Rusk and some of them in the morning. I think I'm going to have to have one pretty soon. They're getting pretty . . . I haven't had one in three weeks now, and they're getting pretty rough over here, and I imagine it'll be a rough one.

I see the Hearst paper's got a banner headline that we're moving a Marine division into the Vietnam area. There's nothing to that, is it?

McNamara: No, no.

President Johnson: Taylor said he didn't know about—wait just a second, let me—[*goes away from line to retrieve paper, then reads*] "Showdown in Asia, We Move up Marine Division, Hong Kong."

McNamara: No.

President Johnson: [*continuing to read*] "A United States airborne Marine division has been moved into Southeast Asian waters in support of a continuing buildup for American air strength in the area."

McNamara: We don't have an airborne Marine division. The Marine divisions, which there are three on active duty, are all seaborne and directly associated with the Navy. We keep units of a Marine division at sea out in that area, and they may be referring to something of that kind.

President Johnson: [*reading quickly*] "A supercarrier *Kitty Hawk*, which carries atomic weapons, [is] cruising the coast and a strong force jet bomber also has been moved south in Japan and Okinawa. These moves are interpreted in both military and diplomatic circles as deterrent, but obviously an instant could precipitate a crisis in which neither side could easily withdraw. It is assumed that on long view America is increasing its armed strength, rallying wider Western support, and adopting a tougher line in general so as to be able to negotiate in a position of greater strength. Right or wrong, it is a hardening conviction . . . North Vietnam . . . because of acute economic problems," so forth.

---

20. William Gaud was a deputy to David Bell, the director of the Agency for International Development. Michael Forrestal was a member of the National Security Council staff. William Sullivan was the secretary of state's special assistant for Vietnamese affairs and head of the interagency Vietnam Coordinating Committee.

"Showdown in Asia," that's the banner, and then under it says we move up [a] Marine division.

McNamara: Well, there's nothing to it, Mr. President.

President Johnson: Well, I hope they read it. [*Chuckles.*]

McNamara: Yeah. [*Chuckles too.*] We—that is one of the moves we can take at some time, [*Johnson acknowledges*] but we haven't made any unusual deployments. We embark and disembark Marine units on these Navy task forces as they move through that area and out again. But this is . . . there's nothing unusual going on at present.

President Johnson: OK, much obliged.

McNamara: Thank you.

> **5:51 P.M.:** Unrecorded call to secretary Marie Fehmer; a White House Daily Diary entry indicates that the President asked Fehmer to "tell [McGeorge] Bundy to come on in. I'm going to be in the bathroom, but come on in anyway."
>
> **5:52 P.M.–6:03 P.M.:** The President met with Bundy; Jack Valenti joined them at 6:00 P.M.
>
> **5:55 P.M.:** Unrecorded call to Fehmer; the Daily Diary notes Johnson's request that Fehmer "find out what time Mrs. Johnson wants me. She says 6:00 . . . Bess says 6:35 . . . I don't want to keep her waiting."

6:05 P.M.

To Everett Dirksen[21]

In their first recorded conversation since the Senate's passage of the civil rights bill, Johnson and the Senate Minority Leader discussed a gathering controversy over the President's recent appointment of former Idaho Congressman Hamer Budge to a Republican seat on the Securities and Exchange Commission (SEC). Budge's appointment had generated significant unhappiness among House and Senate Democrats. In a conversation on June 5, House Majority Leader Carl Albert had described Budge to the President as "about the meanest Republican."[22] Senators William

---

21. Tape WH6406.12, Citation #3807, Recordings of Telephone Conversations—White House Series, Recordings and Transcripts of Conversations and Meetings, Lyndon B. Johnson Library.

22. Johnson to Carl Albert, 1:00 P.M., 5 June 1964, in this volume.

Proxmire of Wisconsin and Paul Douglas of Illinois, both of whom served on the Senate Banking and Currency Committee that had to confirm any appointment to the SEC, had begun to express their discontent on the grounds that while in Congress, Budge had consistently opposed all forms of federal regulation.[23]

President Johnson: [*with Dirksen acknowledging throughout*] . . . general counsel of the Defense Department after [Robert] McNamara looked into him good. He came back and [Charles] Halleck said that he didn't want that because there might be a change of administration, McNamara might not be here, and he wanted something [for] five or six years so that he could work out his retirement and so forth.[24] I've never mentioned that to anybody but you, but that's why he wanted the commission.

I have never felt that the SEC ought to be made up of a certain group of people from New York City that—

Everett Dirksen: I agree with you.

President Johnson: [*with Dirksen acknowledging throughout*]—are tied in with the investments and all that kind of stuff. I wanted to move it out to the West where the people could have a good, objective, judicious fellow on it.

So I put the FBI on him before I ever indicated to Halleck what I would do. They show that he attended the college at Idaho—Caldwell, Idaho—from '28 to June '30; that he attended Stanford University, 1930 to May 1933, had a good record; that he came back in '33, graduated from Stanford and went to June '36, University of Idaho and received an LLB degree. He got his AB from Stanford and his LLB from the University of Idaho. He practiced law and went to the legislature from '39 to '41 and from '49 to '50. He had two terms in the state legislature. In '50, he was elected and came here and served until July 1, '61. Then he was defeated and he became a judge out in the third judicial district of Idaho. So he's been a lieutenant commander in the Navy. He's been two terms in the state legislature, five terms in the Congress, and a judge on the bench. He's married and has a daughter. He was released from the service: He went in, in '42 and stayed until '45. He was honorably discharged; his record is clear.

Frank Church—this is confidential now—was interviewed.[25] He said

---

23. "S.E.C. Nominee to Be Examined," *New York Times*, 22 June 1964.
24. Representative Charles Halleck of Indiana served as the House minority leader.
25. Frank Church had been a Democratic senator from Idaho since 1957.

he's known [Hamer] Budge for many years and they're on opposite sides of the political fence, but that Budge enjoys an *excellent* reputation in the state of Idaho. He's never heard anything of a derogatory nature concerning his character, loyalty, or associates. Then Jordan says about the same thing, Len Jordan.[26]

Now, there was some story that said that I did this to get his vote. I never talked to him in my life, and he hasn't even recommended him to me.

Dirksen: That's right.

President Johnson: So I never talked civil rights to Halleck.

Dirksen: That's right.

President Johnson: [*with Dirksen acknowledging throughout*] Or to you, but they all—these liberals are trying to divide us, you see, and cause this trouble.

Now, Ralph Harding that he defeated, had defeated him: Ralph Harding, United States representative, Democrat, Idaho, interviewed in March, advised he had known Budge since 1960 when he defeated Budge in an election. He advised—although he disagreed with Budge as far as their political beliefs are concerned, he considers Budge a personal friend who is an exceptionally fine man. He stated his integrity, character, reputation, loyalty, position of trust and responsibility. Compton White, Democratic representative from Idaho, was interviewed, and he advised he [was] not personally acquainted with Budge, but knows him by reputation and that he is a high-type, professional man of excellent personal habits.

Then it goes, we had some Republicans: Frank T. Bow, United States representative from Ohio; Earl Smith, justice, Idaho state supreme court. He says that he and other members of the Budge family are *all* reputable citizens. He would recommend him for *any* position of trust and responsibility. Then John Rhodes from Arizona, William Springer from Illinois, Elijah Forrester from Georgia—that's "Tic" Forrester—William Tuck from Virginia, John Williams of Mississippi.[27] And 13 others, and all of them say he's a very solid, able citizen. He has no bad checks, good bar association record, and good passport record, and the Central Intelligence and the FBI have nothing derogatory. Now, that's his FBI [report].

So upon that basis, this SEC came up, and I told Halleck that this man was a judge and he came from Idaho.

---

26. Leonard Jordan had been a Republican senator from Idaho since 1962.

27. All members of the House of Representatives, Rhodes and Springer were Republicans and Forrester, Tuck, and Williams were Democrats.

Four seconds excised under deed of gift restriction.

President Johnson: I would recommend him if he thought it was all right. Then I told you I was going to recommend him. You didn't recommend one way or the other, but you said well, you didn't object, and . . .

Dirksen: That's right.

President Johnson: So I submitted his name. Now, I wanted you to know all that. They're trying to make a big stink out of it, and . . .

Dirksen: Yeah, [Paul] Douglas and [William] Proxmire are the two.[28]

President Johnson: Well . . . I don't know what they're going to— what do they expect the man . . . what's wrong with this man? I can't find out what's wrong with him.

Dirksen: [*amused*] I don't know what they want.

President Johnson: He's a Republican, and he votes conservative. Now, the intent of these laws was to give the other party the kind of a man they wanted, wasn't it?

Dirksen: Yes, sir.

President Johnson: That's what I always interpreted.

Dirksen: Yeah. Well . . .

President Johnson: Will you talk to your people and see that they're there and—

Dirksen: You bet I will.

President Johnson: OK.

Dirksen: OK.

President Johnson: Listen, Everett, what about our pay bill?

Dirksen: The impression—

President Johnson: Somebody told me that [Frank] Carlson and some of our people were getting pretty cool on it.[29]

Dirksen: [*with the President acknowledging*] No. They took out, or will take out, that [Morris K.] Udall escalation clause.[30] I talked to [Elmer] Staats and the Budget Bureau and suggested they get up a new draft on an amendment to fill that hole, to set up a commission to find a permanent solution to this matter. They have three drafts. I turned those over

---

28. Both Democratic senators with liberal reputations, Paul Douglas represented Illinois, and William Proxmire represented Wisconsin and served on the Senate Banking and Currency Committee.

29. Frank Carlson was a Republican senator from Kansas and a member of the Committee on Post Office and Civil Service, which had jurisdiction over the pay bill in the Senate.

30. Morris K. Udall (the brother of Secretary of the Interior Stewart Udall) served as a Democratic representative from Arizona and as a member of the House Committee on Post Office and Civil Service, which had jurisdiction over the pay bill in the House.

to Olin [Johnston] this afternoon.[31] They hope they can get a bill out tomorrow or Wednesday.

President Johnson: OK, all right. You follow that for me.

Dirksen: Sure.

President Johnson: Don't let your boys weaken on it.

Dirksen: I won't.

President Johnson: OK. Now, you know we made a commitment over in the House that we'd report out that 10,000 [dollars]?[32]

Dirksen: Yeah, I know.

President Johnson: So we could get California to go along with us.

Dirksen: That's right.

President Johnson: OK.

Dirksen: Yeah. [*The President starts to hang up.*] Hey?

President Johnson: Yeah?

Dirksen: I've got one or two matters I ought to talk to you about—

President Johnson: Walter [Jenkins] talked to me about a parole thing this morning. Yeah, you want to come down?

Dirksen: Yeah.

President Johnson: I'll call you someday as soon as I get these Turks out of town.[33] You in a hurry?

Dirksen: No hurry.

President Johnson: All right, I'll call you soon as I get the Turks out of town.

Dirksen: OK.

President Johnson: This . . . your friend out in Southeast Asia [Henry Cabot Lodge] may be coming home.

Dirksen: Oh! [*Chuckles.*] Why?

President Johnson: You can imagine.

Dirksen: Why, you know, you told me—you gave me your word he wasn't going to come home.

President Johnson: Well, that's . . .

Dirksen: And I said to you, "Well, who gave a damn?" [*The President*

---

31. Senator Olin Johnston of South Carolina chaired the Senate Committee on Post Office and Civil Service.

32. Johnson was referring to the question of whether the pay bill would include a congressional salary increase of $7,500 or $10,000. The California Democratic House delegation had been particularly adamant in arguing for a $10,000 raise. For this issue, and the pay bill generally, see Johnson to Bernie Sisk, 4:48 P.M., 9 June 1964; and Olin Johnston to Johnson, 3:19 P.M., 11 June 1964, in this volume.

33. Turkish Prime Minister Ismet Inonu was visiting Washington on 22–23 June to discuss the Cyprus situation.

laughs, and Dirksen chuckles too.] You remember that at breakfast?

President Johnson: Mm-hmm; hmm.

Dirksen: OK.

President Johnson: Well, he's . . .

Dirksen: Well, maybe it's too hot out there.

President Johnson: *[Chuckles.]* No. No, I would imagine it has to do with this other thing.

Dirksen: Send him word and say, "It's hot here too."[34]

President Johnson: *[Laughs.]* Don't say a word about it until I know for sure.

Dirksen: OK.

President Johnson: Bye.[35]

6:12 P.M.: Unrecorded call to Walter Jenkins.

6:14 P.M.

To John Sparkman[36]

Johnson called Alabama's Democratic senator to request his support for the appointment of Hamer Budge to the Securities and Exchange Commission (SEC).[37] Senator Sparkman served on the Senate Banking and Currency Committee, which had to confirm Budge for the position.

President Johnson: John?

John Sparkman: Hello?

President Johnson: John?

Sparkman: Hey.

President Johnson: I understand that some of the members of the committee, particularly [William] Proxmire, may raise hell about my nomination of Homer [*sic*] Budge.

---

34. Johnson and Dirksen were jokingly referring to the contest for the Republican presidential nomination between Arizona Senator Barry Goldwater (the presumptive nominee) and the late entry to the race, Pennsylvania Governor William Scranton, who would receive Lodge's support.

35. Despite strenuous opposition, Budge would be confirmed on 27 June. "Budge Wins Nod on SEC Post," *Washington Post*, 27 June 1964.

36. Tape WH6406.12, Citations #3808 and #3809, Recordings of Telephone Conversations—White House Series, Recordings and Transcripts of Conversations and Meetings, Lyndon B. Johnson Library.

37. For this issue, see the preceding conversation between the President and Everett Dirksen.

Sparkman: Yeah . . . yeah.

President Johnson: And I wanted to tell you the background and see if you're in a position to help me if they do.

Homer [*sic*] Budge has served two terms in the Idaho legislature, five terms in the Congress. He's a conservative Republican. He's a great friend of Charlie Halleck's. He was defeated by a boy named Ralph Harding in 1960. He went on the court out there in Idaho and [has] been serving as a judge since '60. I asked [Everett] Dirksen and Halleck, as presidents do under these laws that require the other party to be represented on these commissions, to give me some of their recommendation[s].

Sparkman: Mm-hmm.

President Johnson: I don't like to put certain types of fellows from New York City constantly on the SEC because that's where your Wall Street and that's where your problems [are], so I like to reach out. The last one I appointed was a member of the securities commission from the state of Oklahoma.

This time I wanted to go west, and I decided that I'd look into this fellow Budge when Halleck recommended him. They told me he was one of the abler members of the House and was a strong Halleck man when he was there. I put the FBI after him, and they interviewed the man that he defeated, and he said well, they didn't agree politically but that there was not anything against his character and he was [a] well-qualified man. Showed he went to Idaho college, then went to Leland Stanford University and got an AB degree in California, then got his law degree, LLB, from the University of Idaho and has lived there all of his life. FBI found nothing wrong with him and everything—every man that was interviewed complimented him and said something nice about him.

Sparkman: Mm-hmm.

President Johnson: Now, Proxmire and some of the liberals have decided to raise hell because he's a conservative Republican. I guess if that's true, Eisenhower, when [Sam] Rayburn and I recommended some liberal Democrats that we did from time to time, he shouldn't have put them on, but we did, and I think the intent of the law was to have another viewpoint represented there.[38] Now, I don't believe this man is corrupt or I don't think he's unqualified or I don't think there's any reason for his not being named, and I thought he was a rather good selection—with five terms in Congress and two terms in a legislature and on the bench now—for the SEC.

---

38. A political mentor of Johnson's from Texas, Sam Rayburn had been Speaker of the House from 1940 until his death in November 1961.

Sparkman: I'll tell you what I told some of them that have been . . . some that have talked to me about him. As quick as I heard about it—Charlie Halleck called me and talked with me about it. First thing I did was to go to Everett Dirksen. Everett gave him a complete approval. Then I went to Len Jordan, a Republican from Idaho, and he is very strong for him. I haven't talked to Frank Church, but I asked of Len if Frank joined him in endorsing him, and he said he did. And I told someone—maybe it was Willis Robertson, I'm not sure—I said it seems to me that this is a Republican vacancy and the Republicans have a right not necessarily to name a man, but certainly to have their man considered and construe doubts in his favor.[39] That's the way I rather feel about it.

President Johnson: Well, I just think they're trying to be very vicious and murder a man for no reason because—

Sparkman: Well, of course, you know . . . [*chuckles*] you know I know Bill Proxmire, and you do too.

President Johnson: Yeah. . . . I wished you'd go to that meeting in the morning though, and—

Sparkman: It's not in the morning, it's Wednesday morning.

President Johnson: Well, whenever it is, and—

Sparkman: I'll be there.

President Johnson: And I've read to you from the FBI record and there's not one criticism in this boy's record. I never saw him until he came in this office to be appointed after he'd been recommended, but I had the FBI carefully check him, and even Church and the boy he ran against both said they didn't agree with him politically, but that he was a fine man.

Sparkman: Yeah. I—we've got a meeting tomorrow, but I understand he's not coming up until Wednesday; however, I'm going both days.

President Johnson: Fine. . . . Fine. Well, I will sure appreciate it.

Sparkman: Fine.

President Johnson: Thank you.

Sparkman: Bye.

6:20 P.M.: Unrecorded call to Walter Jenkins.

6:22 P.M.: Secretary Vickie McCammon relayed a message to the President that Lady Bird Johnson would prefer that he came to the East Room at 6:40 to attend the conclusion of an unidentified Shakespeare play.

---

39. Willis Robertson was a Democratic senator from Virginia and the chairman of the Banking and Currency Committee.

6:24 P.M.

To Charles Halleck[40]

After briefing Charlie Halleck on how he should prepare Securities and Exchange Commission nominee Hamer Budge for his confirmation hearing before the Senate Banking and Currency Committee, Johnson engaged the House minority leader in an animated debate over whether the House could recess for the Republican National Convention before acting on the remainder of the President's legislative agenda. In particular, Johnson wanted the House Rules Committee to grant the economic opportunity bill a rule for floor debate. Halleck countered that he had already helped deliver the tax cut and would deliver the amended civil rights bill—for which he believed that the President would gain sole political credit—and demanded that the House recess from the July 4 holiday until after the Republican convention.

In a conversation with the President four days later, Larry O'Brien would report that Halleck "thought maybe you were a little peeved at him because he had a conversation with you the other night and maybe he was a little rough, but he had had a couple of pops and all that, so I don't know what that's all about." Johnson responded, "No, every time I talk to him, he's drinking."[41]

President Johnson: . . . good idea for him to say that he wasn't an applicant, that he understood that the President was looking for somebody outside of New York City. He wanted somebody in the West that had some judicious experience—

Charles Halleck: Let me go back over that. Wanted somebody outside of New York City.

President Johnson: Yeah, for the Securities . . .

Halleck: That's right: Securities and Exchange Commission?

President Johnson: That's right. And he wanted, preferred someone from the West.

---

40. Tape WH6406.12, Citation #3810, Recordings of Telephone Conversations—White House Series, Recordings and Transcripts of Conversations and Meetings, Lyndon B. Johnson Library.
41. Johnson to Larry O'Brien, 11:28 A.M., 26 June 1964, in Kent B. Germany and David C. Carter eds., *The Presidential Recordings, Lyndon B. Johnson: Mississippi Burning and the Passage of the Civil Rights Act, June 1, 1964–July 4, 1964*, vol. 8, *June 23, 1964–July 4, 1964* (New York: Norton, 2011), pp. 207–9.

Halleck: And somebody from the West.

President Johnson: And he wanted someone that had legislative experience.

Halleck: Legislative and judicial experience.

President Johnson: And judicial experience.

Halleck: And a good legal background.

President Johnson: And that he didn't know anything about it until the FBI started investigating it. The FBI made a very thorough check. Now, I've got the FBI report in front of me and it's a perfect report. There's not one critical thing.

Halleck: Yeah, [*unclear*] a goddamn thing. This is a good man, Mr. President.

President Johnson: Now, let me tell you, Frank Church says . . . now write this down. I just—this is confidential, but you can use it. Frank Church says he's known [Hamer] Budge for many years. They're on opposite sides of the fence, but Budge enjoys, quote, "an excellent reputation in the state of Idaho." He has never heard anything of a derogatory nature concerning his character, his loyalty, or his associates.

Halleck: That's right.

President Johnson: Now, [Leonard] Jordan is a Republican senator. I've never talked to him, but he says the same thing. I won't go over it. [Ralph] Harding says—he's one of those sons of bitches that stirred up a lot of this—that he has known Budge [*reading*] "since '60 when he defeated him in an election to the office, that although he disagrees with Budge as far as their political beliefs are concerned, he considers Mr. Budge a personal friend who is an exceptionally fine man. He stated that Mr. Budge's integrity, character, reputation, loyalty, and associates are above question, and he recommended him for a position of trust and responsibility." Now, that's the man that defeated him.

Halleck: Yes.

President Johnson: Compton I. White: He said that he does not know him but by reputation and he is a high-type, professional man of excellent personal habit.

Halleck: Yes.

President Johnson: Then Frank Bow.

Halleck: Just a good man.

President Johnson: [*with Halleck acknowledging throughout*] Then Earl B. Smith, justice; John Rhodes, William Springer, [E. L.] Tic Forrester, William Tuck, John B. Williams, 13 other associates: [*reading*] "all of these advise that he's a loyal American whose character, reputation, associates are above question.[42] Those acquainted with the other members of his family advised they're all reputable persons. He was described as a very capable individual, a very solid citizen. They recommended him for a position of trust and confidence."

Now, I think you can very well say that he doesn't know anything about this back stuff maneuvering they're talking about. First he knows about was . . . the President had this FBI [investigation] made, he wasn't an applicant for anything, he was on the bench doing his job, and the President called him into his office and said that he wanted a man that had legislative experience, had served in the service, and had judicial experience and asked him if he'd accept the job. And that he said well, if the President wanted him to, he'd do it. And that's all his—

Halleck: I'll keep myself clear out of it.

President Johnson: Well, that's what I'd—I'm not going to hesitate . . . that doesn't make a difference. But I think any senators you can talk to, you ought to do it. I've called John Sparkman. He told me he'd already talked to you, but he's going to help us.

Halleck: I called John. You know something, I just called him because he and I are friends.

President Johnson: Yeah, he's a good man and he's your friend, and he's going to help.

Halleck: Yeah.

President Johnson: And I told Walter Jenkins to call some of the rest of them, but that's a pretty liberal committee—[Paul] Douglas and [William] Proxmire—and it's the same group that gave me hell—

Halleck: I [*unclear*] that [Edward] Long of Missouri kind of—[43]

President Johnson: Well, Walter's calling him now and calling Willis Robertson, too. And—

Halleck: Mr. President?

President Johnson: You ought to see that your Republicans are there. I called Dirksen—

Halleck: I'll be—

President Johnson: —and I went over the FBI report with Dirksen and he's strong for him.

---

42. John J. Rhodes was a Republican representative from Arizona; William L. Springer was a Republican representative from Illinois; E. L. "Tic" Forrester was a Democratic representative from Georgia; William M. Tuck was a Democratic representative from Virginia; John B. Williams was a Democratic representative from Mississippi.

43. Edward Long was a Democratic senator from Missouri and a member of the Banking and Currency Committee.

Halleck: He'll be right there.

President Johnson: So let's don't let them hurt the boy. They tried to hurt John Connally, you know, when he was secretary of the Navy, they tried to butcher him up.[44]

Halleck: I understand. . . . They can't do it.

President Johnson: All right.

Halleck: Mr. President?

President Johnson: Yes, sir.

Halleck: Could I just ask you?

President Johnson: Yes, sir.

Halleck: We're going to get your civil rights bill.

President Johnson: Good.

Halleck: So you can sign it on July 4. But let us get away July 2 or 3.

President Johnson: Well, if you get some of those things passed out of there, damn it.

Halleck: We can't—now wait just a minute. I don't know what the heck you're talking about, but you say to me, "Do the poverty bill." You can't get that rule out. You can't possibly do it. Why don't you meet with your people in the morning and give us Republicans a kind of a generous sort of a thing? We got 17 boys on that Resolutions Committee:[45] We've got Mel Laird [of Wisconsin], the chairman; we've got Charlie Goodell in New York—God, he's been in your corner more times than you can shake a stick at—and we got Glen Lipscomb of California's helping him. And I've got to go out there; I got to go out there. Clarence Brown's [of Ohio] got to go out there, Mr. President. Don't barrel these people to keep us here that week.

President Johnson: Well, Charlie, you know when they let us get out: the day before the convention.[46] I don't want to keep you—I'd love for them to all go out, and the only way . . . only thing you got to do is just go on and act on these things you got. Now, you know that you oughtn't to—

----

44. John Connally had served as secretary of the Navy under President Kennedy from 1961 to 1962 before being elected governor of Texas. During his confirmation hearing, he had undergone intensive questioning regarding his prior work as a lobbyist for the oil industry, including inquiries about defense contracts and his own oil company holdings. For details, see Drew Pearson, "Rumblings Against John Connally," *Washington Post*, 16 January 1961; John G. Norris, "10 Pentagon Nominees Win Approval," *Washington Post*, 19 January 1961.

45. Halleck was referring to the Resolutions Committee for the 1964 Republican National Convention. Representative Melvin W. Laird of Wisconsin chaired the committee. Others listed in the following passage were Republican representatives and members of the committee. Cabell Phillips, "Platform Fight Looms for Republicans," *New York Times*, 28 June 1964.

46. Johnson was probably referring to the 1960 Democratic National Convention in Los Angeles.

Halleck: Now, which—which do you mean?

President Johnson: Well, I mean, I don't know. We got 31 proposals at one house or the other.

Halleck: I understand. Now, wait a minute, Mr. President. I appreciate your calling me, and I don't want to detain you because you're a damn sight more important than I am. But let me just tell you this, my friend: We get your civil rights bill passed, and you can't do it without us, understand? You sign that up July 4. Give us the next two weeks off in the House—I'm not talking about the Senate—for our convention. We got 17 guys on that Resolutions Committee. You can't pass anything that next week. I'll guarantee you, you can't.[47]

President Johnson: Well, Charlie, why don't you let us go on—why don't you let us take these things up, let the majority decide it?

Halleck: Well, I'll let you—now, goddamn it, Mr. President, I'll do a few of those things, but you ain't going to curry any favor with me, I might as well be blunt about it, making us stay here when we got 20, 30 guys from the House wanting to go to our convention. What you going to take up the week before our convention?

President Johnson: I'd like to take up every one of these 31 that we need to pass.

Halleck: Hmm. Well, we got four weeks between our convention and yours. If you want to keep the Rules Committee in session, that's OK. I . . . And as far as I'm concerned, I think a lot of these things ought to be voted on, Mr. President. But I'm telling you right now, when you . . . I tell you, I'm going to be a little tough to get along with if you keep us right here . . . And you've got a lot of guys on your side going to be tough to get along with, on the House side.

President Johnson: Well, Charlie, don't you think I ought to try to get my program passed?

Halleck: Yes, you do. But I don't think you can do it—

President Johnson: If you were in my place—if you were in my—

Halleck: [*Unclear*] Now wait a minute.

President Johnson: —place, and you had a House—

Halleck: Wait a minute, Mr. President—

President Johnson: —meets on Tuesday, Wednesday, and Thursday—

Halleck: You're not going to do it . . . you're not going to do it the week after the 4th of July. And ahead of our convention. I don't think you are.

---

47. The Republican National Convention would begin on 13 July in San Francisco.

And I'm . . . I was about to call you, Mr. President—

President Johnson: Well, do it between now and the 4th of July, get these things passed. You oughtn't to hold up my poverty bill. That's a good bill, and there's no reason why you ought to keep a majority from beating it. If you can beat it, go on and beat it, but you oughtn't to hold it up. You ought to give me a fair shake and give me a chance to vote on it. I've got it in my budget—

Halleck: Well, [*unclear*]—

President Johnson: —I've cut my budget a billion under last year.

Halleck: [*curtly*] [*Unclear.*] Wait a minute. Let me talk to you just a minute. You want this civil rights bill through, you wanted the tax bill through, and I helped you do it. And *goddamn* it, did I help you on civil rights?

President Johnson: Yeah, you sure did. You helped Kennedy . . .

Halleck: Well, for Christ's sake—

President Johnson: You agreed with it.

Halleck: —I helped Kennedy and I've helped you.

President Johnson: That's right.

Halleck: Now wait just a minute, my friend.

President Johnson: Then you helped yourself. Course you-all want civil rights as much as we do. I believe it's a nonpartisan bill. I don't think it's a Johnson bill.

Halleck: No, no, no, no, no, you're going to get all the political advantage. We are not going to get a goddamned thing.

President Johnson: No . . . no. No, no.

Halleck: Wait just a minute. Now, we got a lot of things in that bill, but I don't know what in the hell the Senate put in there. Maybe we ought to kind of take a little look at it.

President Johnson: Well, maybe you ought to. I'm not saying that you ought—

Halleck: Now wait a minute, Mr. President. I'm just looking at it hard-boiled. And once in a while I can get hard-boiled.

President Johnson: Well, you wouldn't want to go to your convention without a civil rights bill, would you?

Halleck: You know, as a matter of fact, if you scratch me very deep, Mr. President . . .

President Johnson: I wouldn't scratch you at all because I want to pet you.

Halleck: Wait just a minute. Wait just a minute. [*The President chuckles.*] If I had my way, I'd let you folks be fussing with that goddamned thing before *your* convention instead of ours. But I'm perfectly willing to give you the right to sign that thing on July 4. Now, I think you're taking advantage of a[n] Independence Day thing that ain't right. But that's not for me to say.

President Johnson: I don't know what you're talking about.

Halleck: You want to sign this . . .

President Johnson: I haven't heard anything about that. I haven't . . . I haven't said—

Halleck: . . . civil rights bill on July 4. Well, the papers have been full of it.

President Johnson: No. . . . I haven't said a word about it. Nobody's asked me anything about it.

Halleck: And I'll tell you something: If you sign it that day, I ain't going to be there, because I'm going.

President Johnson: Mm-hmm.

Halleck: I'm going. Mr. President, I wish you . . . what you'd do . . . and God knows I . . . Look, you got a tax bill, you got a civil rights bill, you got a hell of a lot of other things coming along. Don't press us too goddamn hard. I'll do just about anything I can for you.

President Johnson: Well, go on and report my poverty bill. Quit holding it up there in that damn Rules Committee.

Halleck: Now wait just a minute. Let's—we'll get at that—

President Johnson: They've had that all debated. They've debated it, they've delayed, they—

Halleck: All right [*unclear*]. . . . If you try to shove that . . .

President Johnson: I'm not trying to shove. Hell, I've been trying for six months to even get a vote on it.

Halleck: Yes, Mr.—

President Johnson: They held it up over there. I never saw such a spectacle. Every man, they were bitter and mean and vicious and—in the Labor Committee—and then they got it over there, and now they're up testifying in Rules.

Halleck: Well, wait a minute. . . . Now let's just go back over a little bit: You've got a great important thing called the civil rights bill, with a hell of a lot of far-reaching amendments. I'm sorry I'm holding you up this much, but I'm just going to do it. A hell of a lot of amendments. You want me to buy those without any chance in the House to look them over. Well, Mr. President, I guess maybe I'll do it, but, Jesus Christ, don't push me too far. Now, give me a little chance—

President Johnson: I haven't pushed you at all, my friend. I haven't even discussed it with you.

Halleck: [*Unclear.*] No, I understand.

President Johnson: Have I?

Halleck: I understand.

President Johnson: Have—

Halleck: Well, look, no, no.

President Johnson: I haven't even asked it. I haven't discussed it with them.

Halleck: No, no, no. No—

President Johnson: I just let you-all run your own show.

Halleck: —[*unclear*]. Look, Mr. President, let me go back over it.

President Johnson: I was discussing something else. I wasn't talking about legislation.

Halleck: You haven't pushed me. . . . You haven't pushed me.

President Johnson: Hmm?

Halleck: You haven't pushed me.

President Johnson: No, I sure don't want to, Charlie. I want to be . . .

Halleck: Now, wait a minute. I want to pass the civil rights bill, but let me tell you what I want to do: I want to pass—I'm going to help you do it—the civil rights bill as it passed the Senate, understand?

President Johnson: You give me a rule on my poverty bill and let me vote on that, Charlie.

Halleck: Now wait just a minute. I'll give you a rule in due time, but don't press me, and don't—[48]

President Johnson: I'm not pressing you, I'm just . . . I'm not—

Halleck: Goddamn it, Mr. President—

President Johnson: I'm not pressing you any more than you pressing me, my friend. I'm just making a statement. Please . . . I'm telling you about things I'm interested in and you want to, I think, be helpful.

Halleck: All right, in due time, I'll give you a [rule], but if you—

President Johnson: OK.

Halleck: —keep me here, I got to deal.

President Johnson: No, [*unclear*] Charlie, I want to sure enough try to get it acted on in the Senate. They don't want to go into working on the bill and the hearings until we act on it in the House. [*talking over Halleck*] And you could do that: You could let me have that rule tomorrow if you wanted to.

Halleck: Just—could I . . . Look, you're an old Senate hand.

President Johnson: Yeah, an old House hand too.

Halleck: Wait a minute. And you're a House man.

---

48. The House Rules Committee would not grant a rule for the economic opportunity (poverty) bill until 28 July.

President Johnson: An old Halleck man.

Halleck: All right, [*the President laughs*] and you're a Halleck man and I'm a Johnson man. But, Christ—

President Johnson: [*chuckling*] Give me a little rule up there in the morning.

Halleck: Am I glad you called me [*the President laughs*] because, my friend, I just wish I was right there with you.

President Johnson: Well, we'll get together this week.

Halleck: Let me tell you something.

President Johnson: We'll get together this week.

Halleck: Mr. President?

President Johnson: Yeah?

Halleck: Jesus Christ—

President Johnson: I'll call you this week, and we'll—

Halleck: Us guys—Wait a minute. Us guys in the House have carried the hod for you . . .[49]

President Johnson: Well, you call them up and tell them to give me a rule on that poverty bill so I can get it—[*Unclear comment by Halleck.*] I've got it over in the Senate, you see?

Halleck: All right, now wait just a minute. I ain't going to give you any rule on the goddamn poverty bill until I know what the hell we're doing.

President Johnson: Well . . . well, what can I tell you—how can I tell you what we're doing? I'll tell you anything I know. I'll call you any day this week that you're free, and we'll sit down and talk together.

Halleck: OK.

President Johnson: OK.

Halleck: Thank [you].

President Johnson: Bye.

TIME UNKNOWN

Between Ralph McGill and Juanita Roberts[50]

At some point after the Halleck call, *Atlanta Journal-Constitution* publisher Ralph McGill called to dictate a letter to the President suggesting possible strategies for gaining the acquiescence and even support of southern

---

49. A hod was an apparatus used by masons to carry mortar or bricks.
50. Tape WH6406.12, Citation #3811, Recordings of Telephone Conversations—White House Series, Recordings and Transcripts of Conversations and Meetings, Lyndon B. Johnson Library.

governors and businessmen in peaceably implementing the Civil Rights Act.[51] McGill had just begun to discuss his recommendation for the position of director of the Community Relations Service when the recording was cut off.

> *The recording begins with an exchange in which the operator mistakenly connects to Roberts a caller seeking the White House switchboard operator to place a call to Minneapolis for a Mr. Rowe. The McGill call is finally connected to Roberts.*
>
> **Ralph McGill:** Hello?
>
> **Juanita Roberts:** Hello?
>
> **McGill:** Hello?
>
> **Roberts:** Hello. How are you, Mr. McGill?
>
> **McGill:** [*Unclear*], how are you?
>
> **Roberts:** Fine.
>
> **McGill:** I wanted to dictate a little something for the President?
>
> **Roberts:** Yes, sir.
>
> **McGill:** Well . . . "Dear Mr. President."
>
> **Roberts:** All right.
>
> **McGill:** [*dictating*] "With regard to reaching the governors, it seems to me that" . . . no, wait a minute. "With regard to reaching the governors, the only thing I have been able to think of is for you to make a nationally televised talk at the time you sign the bill, or shortly thereafter, directed toward governors, mayors, and local officials in general. I then think a" . . . no, "I also think a personal call to each governor ahead of the signing of the bill, in which you would say that it had been passed and that the federal government certainly does not wish to intervene in any local situation and that the way to avoid the necessity of this is to have local cooperation, to ask for it."

New Paragraph. "My impression this morning by the story out of St. Augustine, which states that the businessmen there have pledged themselves to accept the civil rights legislation when and if it becomes law. If there is some way national attention can be called to this pledge of

---

51. This question was under internal discussion within the administration on this day as well. For a summary of a conversation between Lee C. White, Bill Moyers, Jack Valenti, and Richard Goodwin, see Lee C. White, "Memorandum for The President; Subject: Contact with Governors of Southern States," 22 June 1964, "HU 2 5/25/64–7/16/64" folder, Box 2, White House Central Files: Human Rights, Lyndon B. Johnson Library.

acceptance, there might be an opportunity to create a snowball effect. I have an idea that a number of businessmen in the larger southern cities will accept the law when it is signed and put into effect. It might be, then, a good idea if today or tomorrow, some national attention could be called to this pledge in St. Augustine."

Roberts: Mm-hmm.

McGill: New Paragraph. "With regard to the other matter of Mr. Harold Walker of the Lockheed Company, I began—"[52]

The call is then interrupted by Lee White telephoning to speak with Juanita Roberts. When told that she is on the other line, he replies that he will come and see her shortly.

6:32 P.M.: President Johnson joined Lady Bird Johnson in the White House East Room for a reception marking the 400th anniversary of the birth of William Shakespeare.

7:36 P.M.: Left the White House with Lady Bird Johnson.

7:45 P.M.: Arrived at the Turkish embassy to attend a reception for Turkish Prime Minister İsmet İnönü.

8:20 P.M.: Returned to the White House.

8:47 P.M.: Unrecorded call to Walter Jenkins.

8:53 P.M.: Unrecorded call to Lynda Bird Johnson.

9:10 P.M.: Ate dinner with Lady Bird Johnson.

9:14 P.M.: Unrecorded call to former Kentucky Senator Earle C. Clements.

9:38 P.M.: Unrecorded call to Texas Congressman George Mahon, the chairman of the House Appropriations Committee.

9:45 P.M.: The President retired for the evening.

Over the following weeks, Lyndon Johnson would continue to struggle with many of the same issues that had characterized the first three weeks of June. Along with advancing his ambitious legislative agenda, Johnson's focus would include the crisis over the disappearance of the civil rights workers in Mississippi, and the implications of the Freedom Summer campaign for his own national political convention; the challenges of

---

52. Earlier in the month, McGill had recommended the appointment of Scripto Company President and Lockheed Director Harold Walker as director of the new Community Relations Service created by the Civil Rights Act. See Ralph McGill and Juanita Roberts, 11:40 A.M., 17 June 1964, in this volume.

maneuvering the Senate version of the civil rights bill past the House Rules Committee and planning for the bill's actual implementation; the uncertainties of U.S. military and political engagement in Southeast Asia; and, not least, the prospect of an upcoming presidential campaign against the most conservative Republican candidate in a generation.

Index